STRAT  NT

MW00618258

An Organization Change Approach

Herbert Sherman
Daniel James Rowley
Barry R. Armandi

University Press of America,® Inc.
Lanham · Boulder · New York · Toronto · Oxford

Copyright © 2006 by
University Press of America,® Inc.
4501 Forbes Boulevard
Suite 200
Lanham, Maryland 20706
UPA Acquisitions Department (301) 459-3366

PO Box 317
Oxford
OX2 9RU, UK

Library of Congress Control Number: 2005935689
ISBN 0-7618-3364-1 (paperback : alk. ppr.)

❈ CONTENTS ❈

❧ PREFACE ❧

In the age of knowledge management, learning organizations, volatile markets, and hyper-competition, firms need to become change masters in order to develop and maintain distinctive competencies that will lead to sustainable competitive advantages. The text we have written is an effort on our part to develop an understanding of the basics of the strategic management process, the process in which the firm decides where and how the firm will compete, along with an emphasis on the change processes needed in order increase the firm's competitiveness. This second element is unique in the strategy literature and sets aside this book from the other mainstream texts in the market.

More specifically, this text equates strategy with organization change. In the strategy formulation phase of strategic management, the firm must be prepared to change its strategic direction, if necessary, by first developing a mission, goals, objectives, and strategy as well as tactical strategies. Next an assessment must be made of its external and internal environments to determine the firm's fit. Strategy implementation follows, which is then the enactment and the institutionalization of those changes and involves the active intervention of the firm into its own structures, systems and culture. These interventions (techniques employed by organizational change agents) can take place at differing organizational levels ranging from micro levels of intervention (intrapersonal, interpersonal, dyad-triad), through subsystems (intra-group, inter-group, operating subsystems), to macro interventions (organization-wide, inter-organizational, industry, and national). Lastly, strategy evaluation then continuously assesses the outcomes of the change processes to determine if the firm's goals and objectives were actually met and what further changes and interventions the firm may still need to implement in order to reinforce its competitive advantage.

An aspect of the text that the authors thought was quite important is that the text needed to address the practical and applied realities of putting the developed strategic plan into action. Each chapter therefore begins with a short (2-3 page) case and portion of the content in the chapter is related to the chapter case. Numerous real world examples are interjected throughout each chapter so that students can connect the theory and concepts of strategic management to the practice.   End of chapter exercises strongly emphasize the practical nature of strategic management and prepare students to perform their own analyses of a firm. The experiential exercise at the end of some chapters provide examples of assessment and intervention techniques that not only provide students insight into change processes but also allow for self-reflection and personal development.

Purpose

The purpose of our textbook is to bridge the gap between the theoretical and practical material covered in traditional strategic management textbooks with the theoretical and practical material that one can find in the fields of organizational behavior and development. This begs the question where is the gap and why.

We think that, in general, the current strategic management (SM) textbooks do a fairly good job in describing how strategy is formulated. That is, they provide a very thorough prescriptive or how-to rational approach to how organizations ought to decide what their strategy should be. However, these texts only pay lip service to a normative approach to strategy formulation.   They do not use a stakeholders' approach when actually instructing students on the SM process.

Strategy formulation in these books tends to be cookbook in nature. They include an analysis of the company's mission, goals and objectives; an industry analysis; a SWOT analysis (situation audit); and a financial analysis of the firm. These analyses usually lead the student through a strategic choice matrix (given the results of your analysis and/or the life cycle of the firm, the choice of grand strategies are then developed) and ultimately to a selection of a corporate strategy (and perhaps some operational tactics) for the firm based upon the selected strategy.

We perceive the real gap in these textbooks is that when they go from strategy formulation to strategy implementation, that the material in these texts goes from being prescriptive to merely descriptive -- that is, most texts in the field of strategic management rarely discuss the actual methodologies or techniques associated with creating the internal transformation dictated by the changes associated with the new organizational strategy.

For example, most texts describe the different types of organizational structures associated with certain types of strategies, industry and organizational life cycles. Yet they do not provide guidance or examples of how to realistically change a firm's structure. We believe that this is a serious flaw in the current texts in the field, since students are left assuming that implementation is merely a given (i.e. we'll change the firm's culture) and the details can be left unstated. Ironically, much of the literature in the field has demonstrated that many companies' strategic plans fail from poor implementation.

Our text interjects material related to change management from the field of organization development (OD) into the implementation portion of the text while using the concept of strategy as change as the fundamental underpinnings of SM. Strategy implementation provides a conceptual framework for enacting a strategic plan while OD provides the nuts and bolts methodology of organizational change needed in order to operationalize the implementation at a more personal and individualized level. OD and strategy implementation represent complementary portions of the same phenomenon - the need to plan and enact change that will produce a sustainable competitive advantage for the organization. It is our belief that students need to understand both fields (and how they complement one another) in order to properly understand, predict and then recommend changes that would maximize an organization's performance.

We cover the major topics in the field of strategic management so that our text contains the mainstream material that would be found in any other strategic management textbook. However, our presentation of that material, especially in the area of strategy implementation, is somewhat different and at times quite innovative.

Approach

We have written this textbook so that it could be employed for both undergraduate and graduate business capstone courses. The book is theory based and applications-oriented but the language has been tempered and the text includes numerous diagrams and illustrations so that undergraduates can quickly grasp important concepts.

This book is fairly comprehensive in nature as are most strategy texts in the field. We believe that depth of information will be necessary in order that students will be able to both understand and then apply the theories and techniques described in this text. It is comparable to the "concise" versions of other, more traditional textbooks in the field.

Since the purpose of this book is to bridge the gap between the theory and practice of strategic management and therefore the authors present a balanced approach (concepts and applications). The text includes many examples and critical incidents (mini-cases) in order to provide students substantive illustrations of theory at work. We use an integrating theme throughout – "strategy as change" which is supported by the infusion of organization change literature all the way through the text.

Besides the theme of "strategy as change", a second chapter on strategy implementation has an entirely new focus and orientation. Rather than merely discussing the need to change structure, culture, leadership style, etc., this new chapter goes beyond the theory by presenting students with actual intervention techniques that allow organizations to implement the changes required to properly implement their strategic plan. This "how-to" chapter is quite critical since many students do not understand the difficulties involved in actually implementing corporate strategies. We structured the text in such a fashion, however, that if a faculty member chose not to cover the material in this chapter that the text would still flow smoothly.

Though the content in the implementation section somewhat differs from other texts, this book employs the SWOT model/portfolio analysis favored in the most popular older texts in the field and integrates it with the more modern competitive advantage/resource dependency/value chain/learning organization approaches in the newer accepted texts. This provides the instructor flexibility in teaching methodology.

In terms of future instruction, we believe that this book is a "cutting-edge" textbook with the integration of strategic management and organization development and change. More specifically, both the content related to organizational change and intervention, and the intervention exercises, provide instructors with both content and learning exercises for students to utilize and experience. Coming into contact with these interventions will demonstrate to students how these organization development techniques actually work and allow the students to critique organization change/implementation processes.

Herbert Sherman, Southampton College – Long Island University
Daniel James Rowley, University of Northern Colorado
Barry Armandi, SUNY @ Old Westbury

⁊ INTRODUCTION ⁊

Analysis and the Use of Models and Modeling

There is a very old tale about several blind men who had stumbled across a dead elephant in the forest yet could not agree as to the nature of the creature. The one that was holding the trunk of the elephant believed that the creature was a snake, the one holding the ear believed that it was a large bat, another holding a leg believed that the creature was a water buffalo, while the one holding the tail did not think that it was a creature at all, rather a branch from a tree.

Each man had created an image in his mind about what the creature was and the attributes associated with the creature in question based upon his particular experience with the animal. It is not surprising then that their ensuing discussion about the creature was at first very confusing (as each one described his own experience with the creature in question), and then at times combative (as each individual agreed or disagreed with the description of the others). One or two of them may, at one point in time, have suggested that each examine for himself the other parts of the creature while others may have disagreed as to the number of creatures involved and decided that their position was the right position. They may even have at one point tried to form a composite picture of the creature (or creatures) given the facts that have been presented to them, even if their conclusions were absolutely erroneous.

Regardless of the outcome, these blind men were trying to make sense out of their circumstances, that is they were trying to place "items into frameworks, comprehending, redressing surprise, constructing meaning, interacting in pursuit of mutual understanding, and patterning"[i] This is no different than what managers and employees try to do with organizations and their marketplaces. Workers try to develop a model of the organization,[ii] that is, a description of the nature of reality in the corporation as he or she sees it. In essence each person develops their own system of logic, a system that connects pieces of the institution they are experiencing in unique and subtle ways.[iii] Managers, through their work experiences, have created their own world view. What managers therefore do, whether they are conscious of it or not, is to create a simplified version of reality.

The interesting challenge for managers and employees alike is that they both have a need to share their model of the organization (its internal and external environments). How else can they make rational predictions about the performance of the organization if there is not a common definition of the organization? The manager furthermore must intervene in the organization's operation in order to maximize both its effectiveness (goal attainment) and efficiency (resource allocation) – that is, a manager must make decisions about changing the organization and/or its environment, in part or in whole, given his or her limited knowledge of the organization he or she is running and predict the outcome derived from those decisions.[iv]

The quandary for managers is how to take their own perception of the organization and to put it into a common context (as is the predicament for our blind men describing the parts of the elephant to one another), to reach an agreement as to what the organization actually is. Enter the realm of science. The purpose of scientific inquiry is to establish an agreed upon knowledge-base derived from a combination of inductive (developing theory from observation and incomplete data) and deductive (hypothesis testing) reasoning. Through scientific inquiry, managers can take perceptions of the world, test them, reject those that have little empirical and/or phenomenological support, and then adhere to those that have stood the test of time.

Management scientists also create models of how organizations and humans behave, just like managers, in order to understand, test and predict behavior in the marketplace. The difference lies in the fact that scientists test not only their own models but models of other scientists in order to make them more valid (generalizable) and reliable (consistent). From a strategic perspective, these models can help managers understand the nature of the market and how organizations can or should change in order to maximize the organization's competitive advantage.

Definition of a Model. For the purposes of this text we will define a model as "formalized concepts developed by scientists and applied researchers."[v] Many scientists refer to a model also as a theory, a theory being a system of laws and facts united in order to provide an explanation about an event or phenomenon.[vi] We will use the terms synonymously throughout the text. More importantly, a model provides a very particular perspective on an event or phenomenon.

Case in point. Capitalism is built upon the theory that human behavior is motivated by greed and self-interest while socialism assumes that man, once freed from the need for material possessions, would be motivated by higher order needs. These differing perspectives as to the nature of man lead to differing definitions of equity (for capitalism equal opportunity, for socialism equal wealth), governing systems (for capitalism ensuring a free competitive market, for socialism control of the means of production), and power (for capitalism power is vested in the individual consumer, in socialism power is vested in the state).

Models include assumptions about a particular event or phenomenon, and denote relationships and linkages between concepts within the model's framework. In a more practical sense, models help researchers and managers alike in problem-solving by :

1. defining and limiting the description of the problem
2. developing solutions for various values of the parameters [variables in the models]
3. suggesting modifications and more refined models for similar problems.[vii]

An Example of a Model. Many business students who have taken economics courses are well acquainted with models and modeling. For example, the relationship between demand for a good or service and its impact on the price of the good or service is a common economics model. Students know that the law of demand refers to the fact "that the quantity demanded of any commodity is inversely related to its price, other things being equal."[viii] This relationship can be depicted in a flow chart form, see Figure I-1.

Figure I-1
The Law of Demand

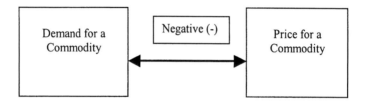

Note that in this model that price and demand act as both independent and dependent variables – they are negatively interdependent. An independent variable, also known as an explanatory variable, is a variable that may cause differences or provide an explanation for another variable. The variable impacted by the independent variable is called the response, outcome or dependent variable.[ix]

You should also note that the law of demand includes limits or conditions to the model. First, the model only works with goods and services that are commodities. Commodities are defined as goods and services that are interchangeable from one company to another, that is there are no perceived differences between competitor products. Specialized products and services, i.e. sports cars, may have fixed prices, regardless of the consumer demand, since profit margins on these types of cars may be higher than the more basic automobile. "The law of demand [only] applies when other things, such as income and the prices of all other goods and services, are held constant."[x]

These other things are called confounding variables in that they affect the dependent variable and are also related to the independent variable. Factors impacting demand and therefore price at a certain demand level include consumer income, tastes and preferences, prices of related goods (substitutes), expectations about the economy, and number of potential buyers. These factors may have both positive and negative impact on demand, that is they may shift the demand curve (the units demanded for a commodity at a certain price level) so that people demand more or less units at a certain price. For example, during high unemployment, all things being equal, consumer demand for a product is lower at a specific price level then during low unemployment. (See Figure I-2 below.)

Figure I-2
The Law of Demand Including Some Determinants of Demand

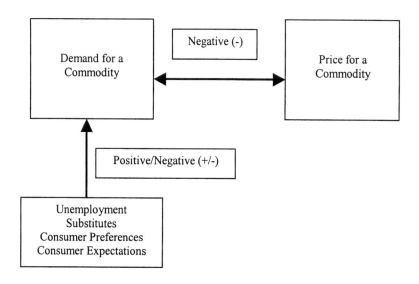

Please note that in this model a change in price impacts the quantity demanded for a commodity while unemployment, substitutes, consumer preferences and expectations impacts overall demand. "Demand refers to a schedule of planned rates of purchase ... quantity demanded is a specific quantity at a specific price."[xi]

Acknowledging the Strengths and Weaknesses of Modeling. What the above exercise highlights is that modeling of concepts, theory building, has some inherent strengths and weaknesses. One apparent strength is that modeling allows an individual to translate descriptions of variables and their relationships to one another through visual representation, to take one's ideas of how a system works and to provide a better framework for mutual understanding. This forces an individual to translate their concepts of how the organization works into constructs (an agreed upon image or idea specifically developed for theory building and/or for general usage).[xii]

A second apparent strength is that modeling allows one to develop and test hypotheses through inductive and deductive reasoning, to ask 'what-if' questions. In the above example one could ask, what would be the impact on demand if unemployment increased yet consumer outlook for the future was increasing as well? One could also ask what other variables besides demand influence price (i.e. supply)? One could use the model to deduce the answers and then perform experiments in order to verify the truthfulness of the model. Models may also be employed as creative, brainstorming mechanisms in that different individuals' perspectives of a situation can be modeled, and then compared and contrasted in order to find new and innovative problem-solving approaches.

Models also have some inherent weaknesses. First, we have to be very clear on our constructs, our variable definitions. Going back to our example of demand and its impact on price you will notice that the definition of demand changes as we move from factors that impact demand to the quantity of demand given a certain price per quantity. To more accurately depict the constructs we would therefore have to reconstruct the model so that determinants of demand impacted overall commodity demand. The interaction between commodity demand and price would then result in a quantity of demand at a particular price, the demand curve. See Figure I-3.

The real problem with theory building or modeling can be described as a tradeoff between accuracy, simplicity, and generalizability.[xiii] For example, theories that are both simple and generalizable tend to be very inaccurate. Our current model describing the relationship between demand and price, has yet to factor in the

Figure I-3
The Law of Demand Including Determinants and Quantity of Demand

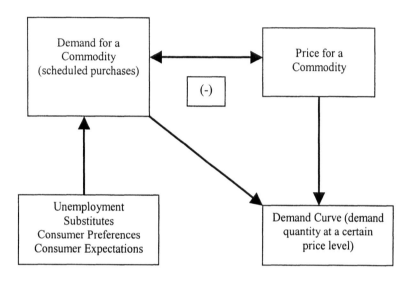

concept of supply, a critical variable impacted by price since higher prices lead to increased supply. There is also an interaction between supply and demand where at the point of price equilibrium; there is neither surplus nor shortage.[xiv]

Models that are accurate and generalizable tend to be very complicated. As we widen our scope of analysis to encompass a broader range of variables, the greater the probability is that we will exclude confounding variables and/or misread the relationships between variables. Back to the example of supply, demand and price. A supply shortage is described as a "situation in which quantity demanded exceeds quantity supplied at a price below the market clearing price" while scarcity is defined as "a situation in which resources available for producing output are insufficient to satisfy all wants."[xv] One must recognize that these two definitions refer to differing economic situations: shortages are priced-based situations that can be altered by raising prices, reducing demand, or increasing supply while scarcity refers to the fact that regardless of the price and the demand, there is not enough supply to meet demand at any price level.

Theories or models that are simple and accurate are rarely generalizable and therefore have very little utility outside of a specific situation. The model that works in one particular situation does not work for another because of the need to keep the number of variables low while clearly describing the situation in question. Case analysis, when disconnected from the theory, is a good example of this model. One only examines the important variables in the specific case and performs a thorough analysis of the problem at hand. Recommendations are driven by case particulars and not necessarily connected to any body of knowledge.[xvi]

Please keep the limitations of models in mind as we describe models of organizations in our next section.

Models/Theories of Organizations

Businesses, and organizations in general, have been explored for thousands of years resulting in numerous preliminary models describing man's relationship first with society, government and then fellow humans (i.e. Plato's *Republic*, Machiavelli's *The Prince*, Thomas Moore's *Utopia*). These models either tried to develop a hypothetical organization where, given new arrangements, the effectiveness of the organization would improve or these models tried to change the nature of man in order to create a more perfect organization (or society).[xvii] In order to better understand strategy and organizational change it is important to understand the major models, or paradigms (a way of thinking), describing human interaction and organization behavior.

Rational Approaches to Management and Human Behavior. The earliest models of business, including the works of Adam Smith,[xviii] asked the question "what is the best way to organize people and to maximize their productivity and efficiency?" Pioneers such as Frederick Taylor, Mary Parker Follet, Henry Fayol and L.

Urwick tried to employ scientific methodology in order to maximize individual job performance and management; one group through job redesign (a bottom-up approach using time and motion studies to change the way people worked); another group through the development of management principles and the use of logic in describing management functions (a top-down approach using reasoning to change the organization as a whole).[xix]

Interestingly, those proponents of scientific management accepted man's greedy nature and developed a reward system that reinforced production (piece rate system) and would motivate those who wanted to earn more to learn the best method of performing a task. Those who focused on management functions assumed that in a logical system that managers and employees would always maximize their efforts. Both approaches however were very prescriptive in nature; managers ought to follow these methods because they have either scientific validity or they have been rationally thought through.

Scott[xx] called these models closed rational systems; they were considered closed systems because they did not take into account the environment's impact on the organization and rational because these models treated the organization as a tool designed to achieve specific organizational goals. These models were fairly simple and generalizable but turned out not to be accurate.

Natural Approaches to Management and Human Behavior. The natural or human relations approach to management and human behavior took what some would call a more phenomenological perspective to management and human behavior – organizations were studied in the field, in their natural state. Researchers such as F.J. Roethlisberger and Elton Mayo found that trying to impose a predetermined work method on managers and employees was not yielding the results they had expected (piece work was not yielding higher worker productivity) and decided to analyze the nature of work groups and the organization as a social system.[xxi] They found that more was going on in the organization than just work and that managers would have to deal with issues of group dynamics, friendship, power (rather than authority), and status. Man was a social animal[xxii] and managers would have to learn to adjust their management models to deal with emotion and irrationality.

W. Richard Scott[xxiii] called these models closed natural models because, like their earlier counterparts, they did not factor in external environmental influences and because the models attempted to describe (rather than dictate) the nature of managerial work as psychosocial phenomena. These models were still fairly simple and generalizable but also turned out not to be accurate.

An Open Systems Approach to Management – Rational Perspective. Beginning in the late 1950's and with the advent of the Russian Sputnik (the first major satellite launched into space), theories and models described management as a system; a set of interconnected parts which, when properly aligned, formed a complex unity where the sum is greater than all of its parts.[xxiv] The beauty of the open systems approach was that it recognized the complexity of management and its interface with the environment; that the organization influenced and was influenced by forces outside of its internal structure. The first systems models to emerge were rational in nature and were based upon general systems concepts including: inputs, transformation processes, outputs, the external environment and a feedback loop. These general terms were then translated into more managerial terms: inputs referred to organizational resources, the transformation process referred to the functions of a manager, outputs dealt with managerial results, the external environment became the marketplace, and the feedback loop described organizational reinvestment and use of slack resources. See Figure I-4.

Notice in this model that the independent variables are resources, the confounding variables are the management functions and their interaction with the marketplace, and the dependent variable is results. Like its closed system counterpart, this model assumes that in order to maximize the organization's results, management must follow a set of principles or guidelines (prescriptive theory). However, these guiding principles must be adjusted for variations and changes in the external environment, leading to a contingency or situational approach to management.

An Open Systems Approaches to Management – Natural Perspective. Early systems theorists who believed in the logic of the business enterprise quickly gave some ground in the 1970's to other theorists who found that an organization's effectiveness had as much to do with its ability to politically maneuver in highly dynamic, ever changing, and complex environments than its ability to meet specific goals beyond survival.

Figure I-4
Management as a Rational Open System

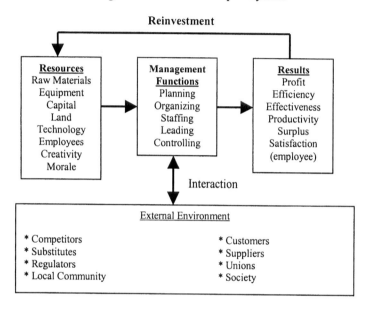

Stakeholders (those who had an interest in the firm) pushed and pulled the organization in that they controlled the resources that the organization needed to survive. This politicized environment also impacted the internal operations of the firm in that those who appeased the more powerful external stakeholders themselves benefited and rose in power. The organization was regarded as a set of subsystems that interacted with each other as well as the subsystems' external environmental counterparts. See Figure I-5.

Figure I-5
Management as a Natural Open System

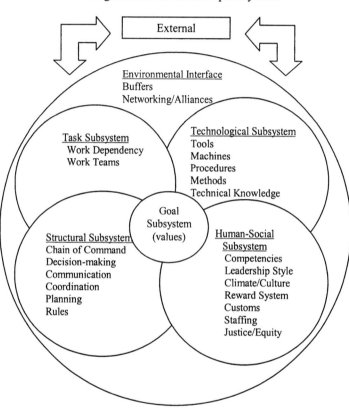

Strategic Management and Change Systems Models

Strategic management as a field of study has, for the most part, has adopted a rational open systems model.[xxvii]   The strategic management and change process flows from strategy formulation (creation of a mission, goals, and strategy given a SWOT analysis), to strategy implementation (changing the organization and/or the marketplace in light of the new strategy), to strategy evaluation (ensuring the strategy has been implemented properly in light of changing organization and market conditions) with feedback loops throughout to ensure interaction between the steps in the process. See Figure I-6.

Figure I-6
The Rational Strategic Management and Change Process

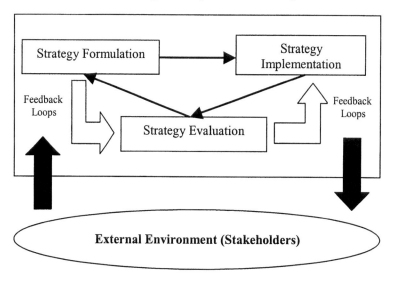

The irony of employing a prescriptive and rational approach to strategic management and change is that it assumes that the change process is deliberate with specific intentions behind the change strategies.[xxviii] However, we know that organizations are constantly in flux, undergoing change from forces from within and without, whether management has planned those changes or not.[xxix] What the rational model of strategic management and change implicitly tries to do is to have managers accept the notion that change is inevitable and therefore it is their responsibility to plan for change.[xxx] The allure then of this model is in its inherent value system; that strategic planning and confronting change is the right thing to do and therefore it ought to be done purposively and logically.

The rational approach of strategic behavior, however, excludes the politics of strategy formulation, that strategy may in fact be unintended and/or the result of a compromise between socio-political actors both within and without the organization. It also may or may not include the possibility that strategies may be imposed on organizations by external forces including government agencies and industry standards.

Strategic Management as a Natural, Open System. Most textbooks in the field of strategic management have paid lip service to Mintzberg's[xxxi] notion of emergent strategy and the implications it has for redefining strategic management as a natural open system, but inevitably fall back upon the rational approach to strategy. Mintzberg's own textbook[xxxii] has attempted to avoid the rational approach by purposely not separating strategy formulation and implementation. "In reality, formulation and implementation are intertwined as complex interactive processes in which politics, values, organizational culture, and management styles determine or constrain particular strategic decisions" (p. xiii). Mintzberg et. al. first examined the concepts of strategy (which amusingly enough has a chapter on strategy formulation), then considered the forces that shape strategy, and finally took into account the context (situations) in which strategy is applied.

Unfortunately there is no one natural model of strategic management and change proposed by Mintzberg et. al. as counterpoint to the rational approach. Instead, they cite an earlier work by Mintzberg and Lambel[xxxiii] that indicated that there are in fact seven different descriptive or natural approaches while listing three prescriptive or rational approaches . In order to get out of this strategic management jungle, Mintzberg and Lambel recommended combining all ten perspectives, a daunting task given their lack of guidance on how one would accomplish such an undertaking.

Getting Beyond the Strategic Management Theory Jungle. It is evident that combining rational and natural approaches to strategic management will provide managers with both a realistic picture of the way in which organizations really do deal with strategy as well as with a methodology and tools for how strategic management may be implemented. Sherman[xxxiv] attempted to explain the differences between some of the varying approaches to strategic management by examining the organizational unit of analysis which researchers and managers employed. He realized that those researchers who focused upon the social-psychological level of analysis in strategy, coined the micro level, looked at individual and group interactions within the organization and the political, social, behavioral and psychological impact of strategy formulation and implementation processes (the natural approach). Strategy therefore emerged from these processes as a resultant, mostly unintended set of actions.

Managers and analysts, on the other hand, who treated the organization as a single entity consisting of subunits or subsystems took a structural or macro perspective to strategy. These researchers and managers assumed that strategies were predominately deliberate actions created and disseminated by top management and therefore they concentrated their analyses on content and outcomes issues (what is the strategy? what were the results of implementing that strategy?). By treating the organization as a living entity (the rational approach - reification), that is concentrating on systems not people, these managers and researchers overlooked the complexities associated with how decisions were reached and what were the human forces driving those decisions.

Last, some managers and researchers saw the organization as a part of a much larger system, whether that system is an organizational life cycle, a market niche, a strategic grouping, or an entire industry. This ecological or industry level of analysis examined the dynamics of a broader system than the organization (i.e. what forces are driving the industry, what forces are driving a nation?)[xxxv] and how the organization impacts or is impacted by the dynamics of that system. Organizations' strategies were therefore determined by market or industry conditions through adaptation (changing to fit the market niche/life cycle/industry) or cooptation (changing the market niche/life cycle/industry to fit the organization).[xxxvi] Here strategy is considered to be externally imposed with little consideration given to the complex nature of the organization and its subsystems (deterministic approach).

The Solution, a Merged Approach. Sherman[xxxvii] noted that a few theorists and practitioners had included more than one level of analysis in their strategic management approach but failed to develop a method that was inclusive of all three levels of analysis. Our answer to the level of analysis problem has been to use the rubric of change management and learning organizations. We have defined strategic management as a set of processes by which organizations and its members consciously or unconsciously try to change the people, the subsystems, the organization, and its marketplace in order to increase organizational performance. This requires that all levels of analysis be considered in order to determine which levels are having a negative effect on performance and therefore where management needs to intervene in the operation of the firm (or its marketplace) in order to change its course of actions. Therefore, we see strategic management as a set of planned changed processes with the understanding that the internal and external forces impacting the organization (at the micro, macro, and ecological levels) may not be completely controllable given the best of plans and intentions. Therefore the results obtained from planned changes, the company's strategy, may not necessarily be the predicted or desired results.

Levels of Organizational Analysis

In order to gain a more thorough understanding of the nuances associated with change processes and strategic management, it is imperative that the levels of analyses be as clearly defined as possible. We have therefore constructed a hierarchy of analysis, going from the most micro to most macro, to indicate where change can occur and where management may need to intervene in order to formulate and implement corporate strategy. See Figure I-7.

Intra-personal. If strategic plans require an employee to change, change cannot occur if the employee does not understand what the change is, is unable to make the change, or is unwilling to change because he or she sees no benefit in changing.[xxxviii] There are numerous factors that impact individual behavior in the workplace including employee motivation, maturity level and attitudes, role expectancy, competency, career aspirations, and learning style… etc. There may also be non-work related negative factors including family-related stress (divorce, death of an immediate family member), alcoholism and drug abuse.

Interpersonal. Many changes impact the way people interact with one another (coworkers, superiors, subordinates, customers, suppliers, etc. …) and more specifically may impact dependency in working relationships (the multiple roles and power of the workers). Conflict may arise in that these modifications lead to too much or too little cooperation or competition, with these conflicts resulting in reduced worker performance.[xxxix]

Figure I-7
Levels of Organizational Analysis

Intra-group. Strategic change may impact the makeup, membership and dynamics of the work group in terms of both its formal and informal structure. Groupthink[xl] or lack of team effort[xli]

may decrease group effectiveness and lead to poor strategy formulation and/or implementation.

Inter-group. Many strategies require coordination between organizational units within the firm in order to accomplish a specific task or function. This may require intervention in how groups interact (conflict management), establishing liaison or linking pin positions within each group, creating cross-functional work teams and/or ad hoc committees, or changing the information flow between the groups.[xlii]

Subsystems. Organizations, as depicted in the natural open systems model, are comprised of different subsystems where certain strategies may require changes in these subsystems. For example, businesses that want to become technological leaders in their field must possess the expertise (staff), the reward systems, and the values (risk-taking and experimentation) that would support this strategy. If these capabilities are not in-house, the organization must choose to alter the subsystems or drop the strategy.

For rational systems analysts, subsystems refer to either the major business functions (finance, operations, marketing, human resource management, and research and development) or the value chain (how value is added through primary and support activities as products and services flow from the supplier to the customer) and the strengths and weaknesses of those functions or activities. Again, new strategies may require changes in those functions or activities.

Subsystem Interfaces. Strategies may also require changes in how subsystems interact with one another. In the last example, not only must there be internal subsystem changes, to implement technological leadership but it may also be necessary to change other subsystems in order to support the original changes. For example, the organizational structure and the task subsystems may need to be modified to allow for greater worker autonomy (support risk-taking behavior and specialists) while simultaneously support a team concept (specialists need to learn to work together in R&D). Subsystems interface in terms of organizational functions and activities deals with how these functions and activities are coordinated, whether through task design, organizational structure, or information technology. Technological leadership, for example, may require employing coordinating mechanisms which increase information processing, reduce bureaucracy, and create more self-governing functions and activities.

Organization/Business Unit. This is the typical level of analysis for most strategists and involves analyzing the organization's mission/vision, goals and objectives, strengths and weaknesses, opportunities and threats, and then developing a strategic plan for the firm. Issues such as competitive advantage, leadership, core competences, organizational learning, culture, and overall performance are examined to determine how the organization can best compete in the marketplace to sustain profitability.

Inter-organizational (Conglomerates/Operating Environment). This level of analysis involves two different types of analyses; analysis dealing with conglomerates, and analysis dealing with business to business transactions. The first type of analysis deals with conglomerates and multinational firms, corporations comprised of separately incorporated business units. These firms need to examine the relative fit of each of their businesses in terms of their overall strategic plan. The typical methodology for exploring the potential synergies between these businesses has been through portfolio analysis, treating each firm within the conglomerate as a strategic business unit (SBU) and determining whether the unit adds or detracts value from the holding company.

The second type of analysis looks at a business's relationship with other organizations in its marketplace; specific competitors, suppliers, customers, and regulators (commonly called a stakeholder analysis). At this level, analysts examine mergers, acquisitions, joint ventures, strategic alliances, licensing and franchise agreements, and network organizations. They also examine the differing interests of each stakeholder group and the impact of the group on the firm's strategy.

Strategy at this level of analysis includes cooperative agreements which reduce competition while concurrently increasing organizational interdependence. These agreements also allow companies to pool their skills and resources.[xliii]

Market Niche/Positioning. A higher order of analysis looks at the positioning of the firm within its overall marketplace both in terms of its competitors[xliv] and its target markets.[xlv] The notion is to create a position within the market (or a series of positions) that is unique in terms of competitors while being attractive to a target market. A firm's strategy must therefore identify the method in which the company creates a competitive niche (through low cost competition or differentiation) and specific target markets (socio-demographics, product features and benefits, price range).

An alternative approach is to "examine the potentially competing firms in a market and then assess their legal, institutional, and structural differences to identify populations of organizations."[xlvi] By looking at these different types of organizations within a market niche, these analysts (called population ecologists) can determine why certain types of organizations within a market segment are more successful than others. The greater the number of a certain type of firm in a market niche (called population density), the more successful that firm type generally is. Strategy at this level of analysis means adapting to changing market conditions by imitating the firm type that is most popular in that niche.

Industry. There are two distinct types of analyses at the industry level of analysis. The first is an analysis of the forces that shape an industry (suppliers, buyers, substitutes, entrance barriers, and industry rivalry). These forces determine the relative profitability of an industry and therefore whether a particular industry is worth competing in.[xlvii] A second approach to industry analysis is to examine the industry life cycle (birth, growth, shake out, maturation, and decline), determine which stage of the industry life cycle the particular industry is in, and then employ the proper strategic approaches given the particular life cycle stage in question. For example, firms that enter an industry during the birth phase can either enter as market pioneers (called first movers), or as market followers (called second movers). Each strategy has strengths and weaknesses and requires a certain set of resources, skills and competencies.

National and Macro Environment. Beyond industry analysis, Porter argued that there were four more macro factors that may provide a competitive advantage or disadvantage for a nation's firms in a particular industry, they are:

1. *Factor conditions.* The nation's position in factors of production, such as skilled labor or infrastructure, necessary to compete in a given industry.
2. *Demand conditions.* The nature of home demand for the industry's product or service.
3. *Related and supporting industries.* The presence or absence in the nation of supplier and related industries that are internationally competitive.
4. *Firm strategy, structure, and rivalry.* The conditions in the nation governing how companies are created, organized, and managed, and the nature of domestic rivalry.[xlviii]

International competition occurs at the industry cluster level (supplier industries, industry rivalry, customer industries) where a culmination of these forces, combined with both chance and government intervention, may impact the competitive factors.

The macro environment, also referred to as the general marketplace, is the broadest level of analysis and examines the political, economic, environmental, social and technological forces that shape non-industry specific market conditions. For example, internet technology has impacted every aspect of business operations (from intra-personal work patterns to national conditions) that every organization, including colleges and universities, need to address the role of e-business in their operation.[xlix]

Levels of Analysis and Change. Given the ten (10) levels of analysis previously discussed, it becomes fairly evident that change processes at the more micro levels of analysis (intra-personal, interpersonal, intra-group) are easier to manage and implement than change at the more macro levels of analysis (industry, national, macro environment). Ironically, most discussions of strategy, i.e. strategic shifts, require more macro, systems wide changes and are therefore much more difficult for the firm to implement and control as compared to changes at the micro level such as increasing employee skills and job redesigning.

Second, the more macro levels of analyses deal with change forces that are more difficult for the firm (or individuals in the firm) to directly affect or buffer against since the more macro in nature these forces become (i.e. industry, national, marketplace) the more difficulty the firm has changing those forces to fit its own circumstances (whether that reaction is co-optation, cooperation, or competition). For example, tobacco companies have been unsuccessful in changing the tide of public opinion in the United States and have finally admitted their culpability in producing cancer causing products after many years of denial and legal battles. While they were engaged in these legal disputes, however, they changed their strategy and diversified and internationalized their business operations (i.e. Phillip Morris now operates Kraft Foods, Phillip Morris International, and Phillip Morris Capital Corporation. On April 25, 2002, the shareholders of Philip Morris Companies Inc. granted the Company's Board of Directors the authority to change the name of the holding company to Altria Group, Inc. in order to downplay its tobacco label).[l]

Systems Dynamics (Levels/Patterns/Timing)

One of the major assumptions of systems theory, whether we're talking about natural or rational systems, is that systems have a tendency towards a state of dynamic homeostasis. Dynamic homeostasis refers to the fact that systems are in constant flux and that there may be changes at different levels of the organization. These change forces push and pull the organization in different directions, causing disequilibria, and lead to a pattern of adaptation based upon those particular change forces acting on the system as a whole or its parts.[li]

Patterns of Change. Systems have a tendency towards stability, that is, the forces acting on an organization have a propensity to try to balance each other out. In terms of strategic management, Mintzberg[lii] referred to this balance as the emergent pattern of strategic behavior of the organization. These behavioral patterns, what some would call patterns of adaptation to the change forces, can take several different forms or shapes.[liii]

When these forces for change do cancel each other out, the result is a pattern of equilibrium – a resultant model of no change, commonly called the static mode. People may leave or join the company over time but the company's culture, structure and strategy may remain relatively the same (therefore the expression the more things change, the more they remain the same). Other patterns of change include growth and decline curves (gradual increases or decreases), bell and u-shaped curves (build ups and collapses and visa versa), s-shaped curves (growth, stabilization, decline, growth), and oscillating curves (connected growth and decay curves). These patterns of change are discussed in more detail in the chapters dealing with organizational and industry life cycles.

Timing and Systems Dynamics. Change is multidimensional in the sense that not only does change have a pattern but that the pattern of change occurs over time. Change may occur over a specific time period and those change time durations may have differing impacts on the organization and its change patterns. Change *in the short run* in an organization (hours to a few months) deals with the cause-and-effect chain at any level of organizational analysis.[liv] Changes in the internal or external environment cause an immediate response from a certain level or levels of the organization, that is a pattern of change begins to emerge in reaction to the initial change event. Short run changes tend to impact lower levels of analysis first at and have the greatest effects at the lower levels. The change incident therefore acts like a pebble in a calm lake where the initial impact sends ripples throughout the organization.

For example, a change in an individual's personal circumstance (marriage, divorce, death in the family) may not only impact the person's immediate job performance (change at the intra-personal level), but may also influence how the person works with others (interpersonal) and how he or she works in groups (intra-group). At a more macro level of analysis, a change in the national economy, like decreased consumer spending, may not only immediately impact national and industry competitiveness but in the longer term may influence an organization's overall strategy, its operations (production and inventory), and its number of personnel.

There may be malingering after affects from the cause-effect change incidents that have more lasting and long term consequences for the organization. *Moderate run changes* (from about six months to two to three years) tend to deal with more middle and upper levels of analysis in that these changes have a more lasting impact on subsystems, systems, and environmental alignments.[lv] Moderate run changes require that we first understand the nature of the subsystems/systems/environment interfaces, that is, we need to know how well these parts of the system/supra-system fit together before the change incident occurred and how the change incident has changed the consistency and congruency of the organization/industry/nation. We need to understand the interaction of these variables in the system, to be exact we need to know how the system works.

Going back to our last example on decreased consumer spending, we know from Figure I-3 (The Law of Demand Including Determinants and Quantity of Demand), that decreased consumer spending may impact the demand for a particular commodity, that is scheduled purchases for that product. If the product is a staple item, the demand may not go down while demand for a luxury item may drop dramatically. In tightly connected systems, we would know what those relationships are and/or they would make sense i.e. lower prices increase the product demand. Loosely coupled interfaces, on the other hand, are less obvious or make little sense (at least at face value), i.e. higher prices increase product demand. Once we have discerned the looseness or tightness of the subsystems/systems/environment interface under consideration, then the real question becomes whether the change incident has altered the systems' alignments or not.

For example, a downturn in the economy may in the moderate run be beneficial for firms that have overreached their ability to meet the demands of the market. These firms may have found that their production capacity (their task system) could not meet the goals of the firm (i.e. growth) given their current technology and reporting structure. These organizations now have the time to realign their subsystems: they can either change their goals subsystem to accommodate the recent change in the economy (and therein better align the goals with the task system) or they can invest in technology and change their structure in order to increase their production capacity while simultaneously trying to rekindle product demand (marketing efforts) and thereby better align theses subsystems with their overall goal.

Interestingly, the above example could have the exact opposite affect on a firm. Firms which are operating at full plant capacity (their task, technology, and goals subsystems are aligned) may have to not only change their task subsystems (short-term cause and effect) but might have to adjust their goals, their culture (dealing with downsizing), and their organization structure given a reduction in product demand. Firms which are already operating inefficiently (operating using only a portion of their plant capacity, or have an excess finished goods inventory) may experience a multiplier effect where their already unaligned systems may become even more disconnected.

Evolutionary changes, changes beyond a three to six year period, are referred to as *long-run changes* and deal with the system's driving forces as well as the relative adaptability of the parts of that system.[lvi] The driving force or forces for a system are those forces that most dramatically impact systems dynamics and are the determinants of most outcomes from that system. In the airline industry, for instance, the huge fixed costs of operation (airplane and fuel oil) act as a driving industry force since the variable costs of operating a plane are minimal once it is fueled, maintained and paid for. Airlines try to fill as many seats on a plane as possible since there are so little costs associated with passenger services. To fill empty seats, many airlines will deeply discount ticket prices, and reduce passenger services (i.e. meals). These actions increased industry rivalry and have lead to price wars.

Driving forces may change over time. At one time government regulations fixed prices and routes in the airline industry thus partially offsetting the impact of fixed costs as a driving force. With no competition and fixed ticket prices, airlines competed for busy hubs (not customers) and kept apace with consumer demands for new airline terminal locations. Profitability was built into the system with the firm with the largest share being the most lucrative.[lvii]

Changes in the factors that affect a system's driving forces (organization/industry/nation) need to be analyzed to determine the extent of the shift of those forces and how they act on the systems' elements. In analyzing those factors, a question that must be addressed is the comparative adaptability or flexibility of the parts of the system – are they pliable enough to accommodate systems changes? Can they flow with the system's driving forces? Going back to the airline example, when the government stopped regulating the industry certain airlines could not adapt to a more competitive environment. Airlines like Braniff, Eastern, Pan Am and even Trump and People's Express (two newcomers who entered the market once it became deregulated) could not withstand the increased rivalry unleashed through government deregulation; they could not resist the new driving forces and could not adapt to a new way of doing business.

The Elephant Revisited: Change and Organizational Competency

Much has been written about learning organizations and organizational competency by such writers as Quinn[lviii] and Senge.[lix] In Chapter 1 we put forth a definition of learning and organizational competency that was strongly grounded in the philosophy and practice of change management, strategy and organizational development.

Organizational learning, from a change perspective, is defined as adaptation to changes in one's internal and external environment, whether those changes are in the short, moderate or long run. Here adaptation refers to actions taken by the organization to either change its internal operations to adjust to the forces of change and/or actions taken by the organization to adjust the forces of change to better fit the organization. The organization's competency is therefore a function of the organization's ability to manipulate its internal systems and subsystems as well as its ability to influence the marketplace (stakeholders and driving forces).

To be considered competent, organizations must first know themselves and their operating domains; they must understand the complexities of the business enterprise. Many dot.com companies failed because they did not understand one of the most basic principles of business, revenues must exceed expenses and therefore you cannot price a product below your cost to obtain and/or produce and distribute it. Ironically, the more these businesses sold they more they lost and eventually they grew themselves into bankruptcy and oblivion.

Decision-makers in the organization must therefore be able to define all of the parts of the system of the organization, using a multilevel approach, and create a model of the organization within its environment. Like the blind men of folklore, top management must divine the nature of the organization from the bits and pieces of information they can garner and consciously try to construct their elephant, understanding that their model will never be perfect but needs to just be good enough in order to make decisions.[ix] In strategic management terms, we need to learn about the organization's situation, determine the nature of the beast.

This text details, from both descriptive and prescriptive points of view, how and what managers learn about their organizations, and how they try to make competent decisions about how best to compete in their marketplaces. The first part of the text concentrates on the formulation of strategy, namely, how managers determine what their firms' competitive advantage is and predict how the changes they propose to make in the organization will bolster their competitive position. The second portion of the text focuses upon strategy implementation, what managers need to change in the organization or its environment to create the advantage. The last portion of the text deals with evaluation and control, an assessment of how well managers really understood their marketplace and the organization and how well they implemented their strategies. This is where managers ask whether they have successfully implemented their change strategies and whether those changes have brought them the expected results. In other words, have they learned enough about themselves and the marketplace in order to formulate and implement successful strategies?

Footnotes

[i] Karl E. Weick (1995). *Sensemaking in Organizations*. Thousand Oaks, Ca.: Sage Publications, p.6.
[ii] Karl E. Weick (1979). *The Social Psychology of Organizing*. 2nd Edition. Reading, Mass.: Addison-Wesley Publishing Company.
[iii] Robert Dubin (1969). *Theory Building*. New York: The Free Press.
[iv] Ibid.
[v] Robert G. Murdick (1969). *Business Research: Concept and Practice*. New York: International Textbook Company, p.10.
[vi] Robert Dubin , *Theory Building*.
[vii] Robert G. Murdick, *Business Research*.
[viii] Roger Leroy Miller (1997). *Economics Today*. 9th Edition. Reading, Mass.: Addison-Wesley Longman, Inc., p. 46.
[ix] Jessica M. Utts and Robert F. Heckard (2002). *Mind on Statistics*. Pacific Grove, Ca.: Duxbury.

[x] Roger Leroy Miller, *Economics Today*.

[xi] Ibid, p. 55.

[xii] C. William Emory (1980). *Business Research Methods*. Revised Edition. Homewood, Ill.: Richard D. Irwin, Inc.

[xiii] Karl E. Weick (1979). *The Social Psychology of Organizing*.

[xiv] Roger Leroy Miller, *Economics Today*.

[xv] Ibid, p. 66.

[xvi] Laurence E. Lynn, Jr. (1999). *Teaching & Learning with Cases: A Guidebook*. New York: Chatham House Publishers.

[xvii] James V. Downton, Jr. and David K. Hart (1971). *Perspectives on Political Philosophy. Volume I: Thucydides Through Machiavelli*. (Eds.) New York: Holt, Rhinehart and Winston, Inc.

[xviii] Adam Smith (1937). *An Inquiry into the Nature and Causes of the Wealth of Nations*. New York: Modern Library. Originally published in 1776.

[xix] Daniel A. Wren (1994). *The Evolution of Management Thought*. 4th Edition. New York: John Wiley & Sons, Inc.

[xx] W. Richard Scott (1981). *Organizations: Rational, Natural, and Open Systems*. Englewood Cliffs, N.J.: Prentice-Hall, Inc.

[xxi] Daniel A. Wren (1994). *The Evolution of Management Thought*. 4th Edition. New York: John Wiley & Sons, Inc.

[xxii] Elliot Aronson (1980). *The Social Animal*. 3rd Edition. San Francisco, Ca.: W.H. Freeman and Company.

[xxiii] W. Richard Scott, *Organizations*.

[xxiv] Richard A. Johnson, Fremont E. Kast, and James E. Rosenzweig (1963). *The Theory and Management of Systems*. New York: McGraw-Hill Book Company, Inc.

[xxv] Karl E. Weick (1979), *The Social Psychology of Organizing*.

[xxvi] John P. Kotter (1978). *Organizational Dynamics: Diagnosis and Intervention*. Reading, Mass.: Addison-Wesley Publishing Company.

[xxvii] Herbert Sherman (1991). "A Typology of Strategic Management: Rational, Natural and Ecological Approaches." *Journal of Management Science and Policy Analysis* (Spring/Summer), Volume 8, Numbers 3 & 4, 331-345.

[xxviii] Henry Mintzberg (1987). "Strategy Concept I: Five P's for Strategy." *California Management Review* (Fall), Volume XXX, Number 1, 11-24.

[xxix] Rosabeth Moss Kanter (1983) *The Change Masters: Innovation for Productivity in the American Corporation*. New York: Simon and Schuster.

[xxx] Warren G. Bennis, Kenneth D. Benne, and Robert Chin (1969) *The Planning of Change*. (Eds.) 2nd Edition. New York: Holt, Rhinehart and Winstron, Inc.

[xxxi] Henry Mintzberg, "Strategy Concept I."

[xxxii] Henry Mintzberg, Joseph Lampel, James Brian Quinn, and Sumantra Ghoshal (2003). *The Strategy Process: Concepts, Contexts, Cases.* 4th Edition. Upper Saddle River, N.J.: Prentice-Hall.
[xxxiii] Henry Mintzberg and Joseph Lampel (1999). "Reflecting on the Strategy Process" *Sloan Management Review*, Volume 40, Number 3, 21-30.
[xxxiv] Herbert Sherman, "A Typology of Strategic Management."
[xxxv] Michael E. Porter (1985). *Competitive Advantage: Creating and Sustaining Superior Performance.* New York: The Free Press. Michael E. Porter (1989). *The Competitive Advantage of Nations.* New York: The Free Press.
[xxxvi] Jeffrey Pfeffer and Gerald R. Salancik (1978). *The External Control of Organizations: A Resource Dependency Model.* New York: Harper and Row.
[xxxvii] Herbert Sherman, "A Typology of Strategic Management."
[xxxviii] Chester I. Barnard (1938). *The Functions of the Executive.* Cambridge, Mass: Harvard University Press.
[xxxix] L. David Brown (1983) *Managing Conflict at Organizational Interfaces.* Reading, Mass.: Addison-Wesley Publishing Company.
[xl] Irving L. Janis (1971). "Groupthink." *Psychology Today Magazine* (November), 43-46, 74-76.
[xli] F. J. Roethlisberger (1955). *Management and Morale.* 11th Edition. Cambridge, Mass.: Harvard University Press.
[xlii] Jay R. Galbraith (1977). *Organization Design.* Reading, Mass.: Addison-Wesley Publishing Company.
[xliii] Jeffrey Pfeffer and Gerald R. Salancik, *The External Control of Organizations.*
[xliv] Michael E. Porter (1985), *Competitive Advantage.*
[xlv] Orville C. Walker, Jr., Harper W. Boyd, Jr., John Mullins, and Jean-Claude Larreche (2003). *Marketing Strategy: A Decision-Focused Approach.* New York: McGraw-Hill Irwin.
[xlvi] Michael T. Hannan and Glenn R. Carroll (1995). "An Introduction to Organizational Ecology" in Glenn R. Carroll and Michael T. Hannan (Eds.) *Organizations in Industry: Strategy, Structure & Selection,* 30.
[xlvii] Michael E. Porter (1985), *Competitive Advantage.*
[xlviii] Michael E. Porter (1989), *The Competitive Advantage of Nations,* 71.
[xlix] Daniel J. Rowley, Herman D. Lujan, and Michael G. Dolence (1998). *Strategic Choices for the Academy: How Demand for Lifelong Learning Will Re-create Higher Education.* San Francisco, Ca.: Jossey-Bass Publishers.
[l] http://www.philipmorris.com/home.asp, October 24, 2002
[li] Kurt Lewin (1951). *Field Theory in Social Science.* New York: Harper.
[lii] Henry Mintzberg, "Strategy Concept I."

[liii] Steven Cavaleri and Krzysztof Obloj (1993). *Management Systems: A Global Perspective.* Belmont, Ca.: Wadsworth Publishing Company.
[liv] John P. Kotter, *Organizational Dynamics.*
[lv] Ibid.
[lvi] Ibid.
[lvii] Michael E. Porter (1980). *Competitive Strategy: Techniques for Analyzing Industries and Competitors.* New York: The Free Press.
[lviii] James B. Quinn (1992). *Intelligent Enterprise.* New York: The Free Press.
[lix] Peter M. Senge (1990). *The Fifth Discipline: The Art and Practice of the Learning Organization.* New York: Doubleday.
[lx] Herbert A. Simon (1976). 3rd Edition. *Administrative Behavior: A Study of Decision-Making Processes in Administrative Organizations.* New York: The Free Press.

☙ Chapter One ❧

The Importance of Strategic Management

1

Chapter Objectives

1. To understand the concepts terminology of strategic management.
2. To develop an appreciation for change and how it impacts any organization's ability to survive, grow, and prosper.
3. To gain an insight of the basic strategic planning and strategic management processes.
4. To create an understanding of how the strategic management makes a difference in the organization's ability to survive and prosper.

Introductory Case: United Airlines Hits Turbulent Times

Monday, December 9, 2002 – Headline - United Airlines files for bankruptcy. Almost one year and 2 months after the tragic events of September 11, 2001, in which two aircraft belonging to United Airlines and two other aircraft belonging to American Airlines were taken over by terrorists and used to attack the World Trade Center in New York City and the Pentagon in Washington, D.C. and potentially another unknown target in the Washington, D.C. area, United succumbed to the burden of heavy debt, reduced passenger load, and losses in the billions of dollars. What happened? How could the second largest airline in the United States as well as one of the biggest airlines in the world have fallen so low so fast? As recently as the year 2000, United was making money. It was growing. It was expanding its service area and looking to become the dominant airline in the world with a bid to acquire US Air.

Then disaster hit. First, the merger with US Air failed to gain governmental support. Many regulators were fearful of the combined airline and what it would do to competition and competitive airfares. Others were concerned about the tremendous debt burden United Airlines would take on in acquiring US Air. Eventually, the merger was called off, but at a cost of $600 Million Dollars to United. The Airlines stock began to plummet. Profits were erased and United started to see its thriving business head into leaner times and lots of red ink.

On the morning of September 11, 2001, a United Airlines 767 passenger jet #175 with 65 aboard left Boston's Logan International Airport at 7:58 am, one moment later an American Airlines 767, flight #11 with 92 people aboard also took off from the same airport. At 8:46 am, the American Airlines flight, now controlled by terrorists of the Al-Qaeda terrorist organization, was crashed into the north tower of the World Trade Center in New York City. At 9:03 am, 17 minutes later, the United flight, again taken over by Al-Qaeda terrorists was crashed into the south tower. By 10:28 am, both towers had collapsed, killing thousands of people. In the meantime, American Airlines flight #77 with 64 people aboard had taken off at 8:10 am from Washington's Dulles Airport. It was taken over and crashed into the Pentagon Building in Washington at 9:45 am, killing another several hundred people. Finally, a second United Airlines aircraft, flight 93 with 45 people aboard had left Newark International Airport at 8:01 am, had also been hijacked and was heading for Washington when passengers aboard the flight overpowered its hijackers and crashed the plane into an empty field in Western Pennsylvania at 10:10 am in order to prevent it from being used against another high-profile target in the nation's capital, perhaps the White House or the Capital Building itself.

The repercussions for the country were gigantic. The apparent isolation of North America, away from all the major trouble spots in the world, was shattered forever. The tranquility of doing business as usual in the greatest country in the world was brought to a swift end. Soon, the United States would declare war against Osama Bin Laden, the Taliban Regime in Afghanistan, and the world-wide Al-Qaeda terrorist network who had (and still has) the capability of causing major destruction anyplace in the world. Americans had been victimized and shocked into a new era.

The same thing was true for business, especially the airline industry. Grounded immediately for five days after the terrorist events, the airlines started to hemorrhage millions of dollars a day as aircraft were not allowed into the air, the only way they can make money. United was especially hard hit and led all the other major U.S. airlines in losing money. When the government did allow airlines to resume operations, millions of passengers stayed away. With all the aircraft in their inventories, the airlines were flying nearly empty planes.

Immediately, the major airline companies cut back their schedules, furloughed a large percentage of their employees and tried to cut costs in whatever manner they could. United curtailed its schedule by 31%[1] and furloughed 20,000 of its employees. Yet, with the huge investment in aircraft (mostly through debt), airport facilities, maintenance facilities, and all the other overhead operations they needed to maintain, they continued to lose millions as much as $5 Million a day in October.

To add to the problem, over the previous couple of years, United had allowed itself to give into union demands and was paying the highest salaries in the industry to employees in every segment of the company. James Godwin, the then-CEO of United, stated in October, 2001 that the airline would most likely have to go through bankruptcy proceedings in 2002. The statement got him fired. His successor, John W. Creighton, tried to quell rumors and fears of employees, stockholders, passengers, and governmental regulators, but things just continued to spiral down for United. Its stock continued to lose value. It couldn't stop the bleeding and continued to lose millions of dollars each month. Passenger traffic did rise, but not to the levels of pre-9/11. In September of 2002, Creighton was fired along with several of the company's top executives and Glenn F. Tilton was hired to try to pull the airline out of its deep descent. He worked with unions to get wage concessions and, with the exception of the machinists' union was able to do so. The company applied for a $1.8 to $2 Billion Dollar governmental loan guarantee, but on December 4, 2002, the guarantee was denied. With huge loan payments due, lack-luster support from its unions (which is interesting in itself, since United is an ESOP, an employee stock option plan company, and its employees own over 51% of the company), and no prospects of governmental help, the airline finally filed for Chapter 11 bankruptcy and hopes to reorganize itself to somehow survive.

United's bankruptcy is one of the ten largest such actions in the United States including the failure of WorldCom and Enron.[2] Further, it was the 11th time a U.S. airline company had filed for bankruptcy since the government deregulated the industry in 1978.[3]

So again, what changed for United? How could an airline doing so well have everything go so bad as quickly as it did for United?

Could, or should, United and the other airlines have foreseen the possibilities of terrorist attacks (especially with the experience of El Al Airlines in Israel fending off terrorists for years and Air France in 1992 nearly having one of its jets at Marseilles Airport in France almost hijacked and, reportedly, used to crash into the Eiffel Tower in Paris)? Why did the airline industry not only take stronger actions to insure higher levels of passenger safety, but to promote higher levels of fiscal safety to structure itself so that it wasn't so heavily dependent upon debt and susceptible to fare wars. Didn't anyone see how bad the situation was? If so, why didn't they do anything about it? Finally, what will happen now? What changes will occur at United in reaction to the bankruptcy? Will other major airlines follow suit and declare Chapter 11, causing investors, stock holders, and creditors billions upon billions of dollars? What is the future of United Airlines and the rest of the airline industry?

The Role of Strategic Planning and Strategic Management

The tragedy of September 11, 2001 was devastating to this nation. It killed thousands of innocent people; devastated their families; disrupted the nation's economy; caused the United States to go to war; and seriously damaged much of the business structure of the country. Without a doubt, much of this could not have been accurately predicted or prepared for. No one could have foretold with any accuracy or credibility what happened or how it would play out.

On the other hand, there were clear signs that trouble was ahead. The threats of Osama bin Laden and others had been known by governments and businesses for years. The airline incidents involving El Al Airlines and Air France demonstrated that such events could occur. Yet, the United States' airline companies (as well as the Federal Government) didn't take these threats seriously and took few effective measures to protect themselves from disaster. H. Igor Ansoff (one of the gurus of the discipline of strategic management) denotes that the environment sends clear signals to firms.[4] The airlines and the government refused to recognize these signals seriously and as a result, disaster occurred.

The field of strategic management is the science of understanding the role of organizations within a set of complex environments and the art of applying this knowledge to the management of the organization to help assure long term success and survival. Strategic management is comprised of a set of activities that assists critical decision-makers to examine the organization's current situation (its strengths and weaknesses) and compare the firm's conditions to the firm's external environment (its opportunities and threats). This strategic analysis allows these decision-makers to develop and implement plans in a well-informed manner as possible in order to achieve a *competitive advantage* over competitors (creating value for customers, and a solid profit return that will help assure survival).[5] To begin, it is important that we define some of the basic terms and processes that are associated with the science and art of strategic management. Therefore, in the next section, we present our definitions of several of these concepts.

Basic Definitions

Environment. The term environment takes on a variety of connotations given the various contexts within which it is used. To many, the environment is the ecosphere—the planet we live on, the air we breathe, the food we eat, and the water we drink. To others, the environment is a behavioral context within which they exist, an environment that may be hostile or supportive or even tranquil. For the purposes of this book, we will define environment in yet a different way and identify it in two different settings.

First, in the study of strategic management, there are two distinct environments of which planners and managers need to be aware: the external environment and the internal environment. The external environment consists of all the forces outside of the organization that have the ability to impact it. Located outside the firm, forces such as the economy, the legal and political entities, societal and demographic forces, technology development, and international activities and events all can impact what an organization does. The environment is then a set of social, political, technological and economic forces that impact an organization and that an organization may try to change. These are pushing and pulling forces that may produce potential opportunities and threats and consequently may cause the firm to react. When the firm reacts effectively, we refer to this as creating a *fit* between the organization and its environment.[6]

For example, the Internet has redefined the marketplace by opening up a new distribution channel for goods and services. Consumers' acceptance of this distribution method, combined with inexpensive access to the Internet, has made e-commerce and e-business a powerful force for "click and mortar firms" to reckon with. Many major retailers (i.e. Best Buy, Barnes and Noble, Toys 'R Us, etc...) have reacted to the Internet explosion by becoming brick and mortar operations, that is, they have both retail stores and Internet sites.

Second, the internal environment consists of all the forces inside the organization that also have the ability to impact the company as well. The state of a company's resources; organizational culture; employees and unions; productivity; and intangible assets such as R&D capabilities, patents, expertise, and aversion to risk all are part of a firm's internal environment and help explain the capabilities and success factors that characterize a single organization.

Strategy. The term strategy comes from the military context, as does some of the other jargon associated with the field. In our interpretation, strategy refers to the central action (or actions) that decision-makers in the firm implement to: 1) help the firm achieve a better fit with its environments; 2) match the firm's resource base with market opportunities; and 3) achieve a competitive advantage by creating value for its customers.[7] Strategy can be both deliberate (planned) and emergent (unplanned).[8] That is, strategy can be developed through a formal planning process or can materialize through unstructured and political processes. Interestingly enough, some companies try to nurture these informal processes as this spurs employee creativity and innovation. 3M, for example, has a policy that allows researchers and managers to work after work hours on their own projects. Post-It was a highly successful product developed in such a fashion.[9]

Most important, the firm's strategy impacts every aspect of the business's operation; from the long-term goals and objectives of the firm, to operational issues such as customer service and hiring practices. Strategy is the core concept which drives the firm. It determines, for example, whether or not the firm should grow by using the resources it generates to support its primary business (moving into a new market, increasing its market share in its current service area, or broadening its product or service lines). This is the corporate level strategy known as *internal growth* and it dictates to decision-makers the types of decisions they need to make on a daily basis to support the organization's overall objective of growing through investing in itself. Another example of a strategy would be *conglomerate diversification*. Here, a parent firm would seek to buy and sell other companies for profit and growth. It has no particular loyalty to any particular product or service. Rather it is only interested in purchasing companies that meet certain portfolio guidelines (such as high profitability, growth potential, earnings capabilities, or success with innovations). For example, Starbucks plans to continue to rapidly expand its retail operations, grow its specialty sales and other operations, and selectively pursue opportunities to leverage the Starbucks brand through the introduction of new products and the development of new distribution channels.[10]

Strategies are long-term in nature. They take time to formulate, additional time to implement, and still more time to measure and evaluate. Companies do not change their overall guiding strategies very often, though they much more often change the policies and procedures they use to play out their strategies, perhaps even on a daily basis. Strategies in fact develop a form of inertia; they continue to be implemented by a firm unless purposely or accidentally altered. To the extent that strategic inertia exists, organizations may find it difficult to adjust to rapid environmental changes that require strategic reorientations.[11]

Can an organization have more than one strategy? The answer is yes. As we discuss the varying types of strategies later on in the book, one will recognize that certain firms can engage in more than one strategy at a time. For example, United Airlines (as part of UAL) has two distinct strategies: (1) the need to create a cost structure that can weather significant economic challenges, and (2) the need to meet and beat competition, including low-cost carriers. These two strategies may lead to disparate actions which include: creating an expanded, integrated suite of travel products that together will enhance and sustain value to their core business customers while offering attractive, competitively priced products to retain price sensitive business and leisure travelers and feed the mainline; maximizing the value and efficiency of UAL's global route network and leverage the power of their worldwide alliances; reducing costs and gain the flexibility needed to compete effectively in a changing market; and ensuring United is an attractive place to work for employees in a way that is real and sustainable through both upswings and downturns in the economy.[12]

Types of Strategies and Organizational Levels. Strategies can deal with the overall direction of the firm (a corporate strategy), the direction of a strategic business unit of the firm in multi-business corporations (for example, Saturn is part of General Motors – a business strategy), and the direction of a major business function of the firm, such as marketing, finance, research and development, operations, and personnel – a functional strategy[13] as demonstrated in Figure 1.1.

Figure 1.1
Levels of Analysis and Strategy

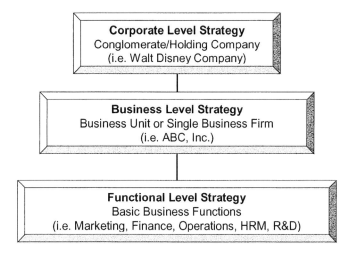

(See Introduction for a detailed discussion of levels of analysis and strategic management.)

Walt Disney and IBM are *conglomerates* or *holding companies* (a company comprised of many other companies); these firms must translate their overall corporate strategy into a specific set of strategies for each of its business units. Business units may have similar or different strategies, i.e. General Motors might try to grow their Saturn Division by increasing the number of Saturn models while GM might grow their Cadillac Division by reducing the price on their luxury vehicles.

These business units, in turn, would have to translate these business level strategies for each of their functional areas. If Saturn is going to increase their product line of cars, they will have to first have to develop a research and development strategy to determine how they are going to determine what models to add to their product line to both meet market demands and fit within Saturn's market segment. For example, do they perform this research in-house or do they subcontract it out? In Cadillac's case, a change in their pricing structure will affect their marketing mix and the firm will have to determine how best to promote, distribute, and price a less expensive luxury vehicle.

Strategic Decisions. Choice is a critical element of strategy (the decision-making processes underlying strategy) and is commonly called strategy formulation. Firms typically make their strategic choices, through serious conscious planning processes, through bureaucratic routinization, through back office politicking, through a series of accidental loosely coupled events, or a combination thereof.[14] This pattern of how firms make strategic decisions will determine whether there is an intended strategy or strategies for the firm (the key decision-makers have made a conscious choice), and whether the intended or unintended strategy(ies) appears to be good enough[15] to create value for customers, and deploy resources to offset weaknesses and take advantage of opportunities, thereby continuing firm profitability (and ultimately survival).[16]

Strategic Planning. Strategic planning is the process that any organization engages in to critically analyze its internal and external environments; formulate a plan of action based on creating the best fit between the firm's resources and environmental opportunities; establish acceptable methods of reducing its own weaknesses and mitigating external threats; identify appropriate tactics for implementing the plan; and then establish methods of measurement that the organization will apply over time to see whether or not the tenets of the strategic plan are leading to the desired results. Strategic planning is then the actions that decision-makers within the firm take to determine what the firm's strategy will be and how resources within the firm will be deployed in order to carry out that strategy.

Unfortunately, strategic planning is often treated as an *event* – a one-time activity that produces an official document called the strategic plan. This is a mistake. Since the planners in the firm must consistently monitor the external environment for changes and adjust their plans (or create new ones) accordingly, strategic planning is only effective when it is viewed as an ongoing *process*. This means that all organizations should have the strategic planning function as a permanent part of their management structure, one that constantly tests the plan itself, analyzes changes in both the internal and external environments, and then takes actions to change the plan itself when necessary.

Strategic planning embodies a certain level of entrepreneurship as suggested by Cornwall and Perlman who stated that, "The entrepreneurial organization is ready, willing, and able to adapt to a changing external environment."[17] Cornwall and Perlman also stated, "Rather than seek to preserve the past, the entrepreneurial organization strives for continuing change in the status quo."[18] What this implies is that effective organizations must constantly be willing to change. Unfortunately, this reality and the implications that go along with it are precisely why many organizations do not do strategic planning – they do not want to change.[19]

Strategic Management. This term refers to all of the planned and unplanned activities associated with formulating, implementing, and then evaluating the strategic plan. We will describe these activities below in more detail (see The Dynamics of Strategic Management).

Tactics. Tactics, another military term, refers to the specific programs, operations, actions, or steps that an organization carries out to accomplish a strategy. For example, a company may have a variety of tactics to implement a corporate, business, or functional strategies –

it could open more international offices or stores; it could choose to expand product lines or services (a store used to sell only TVs and sound equipment, now it carries cell phones and satellite dishes); or it could opt to spend more on advertising to increase market share in its current market. Tactics tend to be much shorter-term in nature, and like a new advertising campaign, might only last a single season. While they can be longer-term in nature as well (developing new outlets or offices internationally would clearly take several years to accomplish) tactics do tend to be very specific, single-focus activities that fulfill the central strategic direction of the organization.[20] Tactics, being short-term, tend to focus on the corporate policies, procedures, rules, and budgets while strategies involve actions related to corporate vision, mission, goals, and the firm's overall competitive approach to the marketplace.

The Nature of Strategy Formulation

Before we can describe the strategic management process, the method in which firms create, implement, and evaluate strategic plans, it is important that we discuss how strategies are formed. We have suggested that there are two ways of developing a strategy: 1) choose a specific strategy to follow, or 2) allow a strategy to evolve over time. This is an important concept as one begins to look at actual companies and how they have developed over time.

Firms that allow strategies to develop over time, unplanned and/or unintended, tend to be reactive to their environments, as we will describe in detail in Chapter 5. Some firms are lucky and end up following strategies that lead them to the ability to create a competitive advantage. This may be due to an environment which nurtures creativity and innovation (as they say, necessity is the mother of invention) and which allows for either incremental or quantum changes in either product develop or process management.[21] Other firms tend to flounder and manifest strategies that really do not lead them to the optimal position they could achieve. On the other hand, if an organization develops a formal plan that successfully analyzes both its own resource base (found in the internal environment) and the best opportunities it can take advantage of (found in the external environment) and can then adopt strategies that maximize the fit between the two, then the firm should be able to create value for its customers and achieve profitability. This type of strategy formulation is intentional and should lead to better outcomes for the organization.[22] Much of the discussion in this text will be related to the importance of developing strategic alternatives intentionally. So then, just how can one determine whether or not an organization follows a strategy that was developed intentionally or unintentionally? The answer lies in the activities of management, the types of decision-making it is involved with and the way it gathers and analyzes the data it uses in making those decisions.

Formulation as Decision-Making. Managers make decisions everyday on a wide variety of issues. What we need to identify, however, is the pattern of decision-making that goes on relative to the strategic issues that the firm faces, such as its growth patterns and its profit strategies. Part of the complexity of an organizational manager's job is that she or he will be faced with a random variety of pressing issues, many of which are day-to-day and which we refer to as *operational*, as well as those issues that can impact longer-term directions and outcomes which we refer to as *strategic.*

It is important that you begin to discern the difference between operational issues and strategic issues; otherwise, it isn't possible to isolate the type of decision-making that is related to strategic issues. Top managers especially make decisions that tend to impact the firm's overall growth and profitability. This is one of the reasons that the study of strategic management focuses on top managers and governing boards.

The specific decisions that create business strategies are those of top managers and governing boards that establish (or reinforce) the overall direction the firm will follow. For example, when an enterprise decides to pursue buying out some of its competition, or merging with a competitor to reduce competition and grow, these are major, fundamental decisions. These types of decisions involve the redeployment of resources which may force the firm to reduce resource usage in one or more segments of its current operations or seek new resources, such as new debt to finance its strategies. These types of actions tend to have serious long-term impact on the firm and also result in a pattern of activity that the company will use again and again in continuing to plan for its future.

Profit concerns are also dealt with at this upper-level of decision-makers. While all managers throughout the firm institute efficiencies and practices that will reduce costs while keeping quality high throughout the company's operations, top-level decision-makers make decisions that impact overall profitability. For example, if a firm wishes to grow rapidly through opening new operations in a broader market area, it may do so by purposefully going further into debt (increasing interest payments which reduce net profitability), or supporting start-ups businesses that don't make immediate profit and have longer break-even points. This conscious decision sacrifices some profits to support growth. Likewise, if profits are squeezed too much, the same decision-makers could decide to reduce the growth rate of the firm to allow the new operations to become profitable before the firm decides to again grow.

Since strategy formulation is an important organizational decision-making process, it is also important to understand that not all decision-making in an organization is rational. Rationality infers following a logical sequence of events aimed at maximizing benefits and minimizing losses.[23] This is important, because a rational decision-making process defines a problem objectively. It involves data gathering and a search for alternative solutions, comparing and evaluating the alternatives, making a choice, implementing the choice, and evaluating the process.[24] There are, however, underlying assumptions to this model that challenges its validity as the only mode of decision-making in a firm. These assumptions include:

1. The decision will be completely rational, that is the appropriate means will be used to achieve the desired ends.
2. There exists a consistent and complete set of values and preferences of the management within the firm that ultimately determine a choice among alternatives.
3. There is complete awareness of all possible choices and the information necessary to select the best choice.
4. There are no limits to the ability of the decision-makers within the firm to determine the best choice (including time, resources, and analytical skills).[25]

Since man is imperfect, it is easy to determine that these assumptions cannot hold true at all times. For example, although as human beings we may attempt to be rational – our rationality is bounded by our limited time, abilities and resources. Our decisions are, at best, good enough to solve the problem, but certainly not the best choice from all alternatives.[26] Second, we simplify the world and tend to take the path of least resistance to decision-making[27] – we are creatures of habit and personal bias. In some cases we may substitute these habits (rules and procedures in organizations) for decision-making or filter situations through our biases. Third, we may employ rules of thumb that simplify the decision-making processes because we cannot handle the complexities associated with the decision.[28]

Besides our limited cognitive abilities, we are also political and social animals guided by emotions, instincts and desires. The basic human needs for security, affiliation, achievement, and power impacts organizational decision-making processes through such factors as conformity (groupthink),[29] individual and coalition domination, and compromise. We use organizational mechanisms such as bureaucracy, mutual dependencies (on resources and information), and power positions (both formal and informal) to reach bargained agreements at best or haphazard and/or disjointed agreements at worst.[30]

Given the social dynamics associated with decision-making, we define strategy formulation as those processes and patterns that employees within the firm enact in order to try to reach a decision in terms of the strategy of that firm. These processes may follow a predetermined pattern that may be a formal, fixed strategic planning process. However, the firm may also have informal and variable social and political processes that exist in lieu of formal strategic planning or operate concurrently with the formal planning processes. A firm's strategy is consequently a composite of deliberate (planned) and emergent (unplanned) strategies, based upon the pattern in which the organization makes strategic decisions.[31]

The Nature of Strategies and Tactics

In the discussions above, we defined strategy as a pattern of activities that seek to allow the firm to achieve high levels of profitability and to establish a good fit with the environment. However, when one goes deeper into the nature of strategies, it is useful to develop an appreciation for why an organization would choose one strategy or set of strategies over another and why it might decide on one particular set of tactics as opposed to others. In later chapters of this book, we will define various sets of strategic choices. These are options that come from the literature and are theoretical in nature. There are some guidelines for choosing one option over another (which will be discussed in Chapters 5 and 6), but we think it is useful for the reader to keep in mind that these strategies are basically concepts; they are not fully defined phenomena.

For example, on our discussion on levels of strategy we discussed conglomerate corporations; multiple businesses operating within a single corporation. Imbedded in the conglomerate corporation is a strategic concept (that of having various businesses owned by a managing corporation), not a prescription-style method of action. There is little specificity about this concept, but it does signify direction, and this is important. It also begins to define a course of action that sets boundaries for focused activities, and this is important as well. Each strategy suggests certain tactics, or domains of tactics, which do not necessarily complement each other. That is why each company must first determine a strategic direction through strategic planning because that direction best matches a particular set of unique tactics.

Going back to the airline industry, Southwest Airlines and American Airlines use the basic overall strategy of *internal growth* (using profits to support growth). Their tactics, however, are dramatically different. Southwest has decided to use a point-to-point flight system; serve smaller airports; use a single model of aircraft; keep operating costs low; strictly maintain a non-union approach; serve the continental United States only; and grow through expansion. American uses a hub-and-spoke system: serves larger airports with hubs at Chicago, Dallas, Los Angeles, San Jose, Miami, and recently St. Louis; has a variety of aircraft in its fleet from a variety of manufacturers; is heavily unionized; has a large international component (including Europe, South America, Central America, Asia, and Australia); and has growth through acquisition of competitor firms (purchase of Pan Am routes in the 1980's and 1990's and more recently the purchase of bankrupt TWA in 2001) and the formation of international alliances. Here, there were two different sets of tactics under the same general strategy. This demonstrates that each organization will select a central strategic direction and may choose that direction which may or may not be a common direction in its industry. However, once the direction is selected, each firm will move within that direction uniquely.

Strategic planning involves a series of choices. The central strategy choice may be easy to discern from an analysis of the external environment, especially the industry environment, and the internal resource base to support one specific direction over another. Choosing tactics to carry out the central strategic choices of the organization is what separates the better strategic managers from the poorer ones. More dramatically, it clearly distinguishes between good strategic managers and those managers of organizations that do not engage in strategic planning at all.

The Dynamics of Strategic Management

Of all the definitions we provided above, the one term that we will concentrate on throughout this book is that of strategic management. Any organization that has good strategic management is one that has a better likelihood of succeeding. Likewise, any organization that does not have good strategic management is much more likely to have problems and perhaps even fail. Since strategic management is a man-made human system, we are interested in the decision-making circumstances of those people in the firm who make the major strategic decisions that will propel the organization in one direction or another. We are interested in who these people are, how they think, what they decide is important, how they transmit their ideas through statements or mission, visions, goals, objectives, and values, and how they interact with each other, fellow employees, and other internal and external *stakeholders* (those who have an interest in the firm). We are also interested in the dynamics of the organization and how the dynamics translate into the firm's strategy and how (and whether) the strategy will become formalized. Then, once the governing bodies of the organization adopt the strategy as a formal plan, we are interested in knowing how the firm will actually put the plan into action, or implement the plan.

Why Strategic Management?

One of the central points of this book and the point of much of our discussion throughout is this: it is better to be involved in strategic management than it is to not be involved. Further, for those organizations that engage in strategic management, it is better to be fully informed and to follow a strong pattern of strategic decision-making than to simply engage in a strategic planning process, treat it as an event, use it for external consumption but continue to operate as usual (such as a business that develops a business plan in order to obtain financing but never utilizes the plan). In a world that is becoming more and more complex and dynamic, the challenge of survival is becoming greater, not less. To survive and prosper, organizations need to not only become involved with strategic management, they need to transform themselves to become strategic organizations and do so from top to bottom.

Change is the Name of the Game in Strategic Management

We are using the phrase, "Strategy as Change," as the central theme of this book. We have chosen this approach because the world in which we live is constantly changing, and it is vital for all organizations (for-profit, not-for-profit, entrepreneurial, and governmental) to produce changes in the marketplace or in the firm that adapts to these changes. Involved with this approach are several major questions: 1) what is changing (the environment and/or the firm); 2) what, then, do we need to change (our strategy, our market, and/or our internal operation); 3) how to change; and 4) when to change. None of this can be done lightly, and much of this cannot be done easily. It takes a concerted effort on the part of managers to develop an understanding of their own organizations and the world in which they conduct their affairs before they should even attempt to confront change. They must have the skills to research, organize data, analyze, and interpret change in order to begin to make organizationally-wide decisions. Throughout this book, we will look at the strategic management as a change process – one in which major decision-makers decide how to use the resources of the firm to take best advantage of the opportunities in their markets while becoming (or remaining) profitable.

The Dynamics of Strategic Action or Change. *Strategic actions* are those which impact the central strategy and direction of the organization and support the central strategy of the firm. In this regard, the actions of United's management aren't strategic at all – the company is purely in survival mode. One could argue that good strategic action 3 or 4 years earlier could have led to changes that would have mitigated the catastrophe of 9/11. Since those did not occur, United made no significant changes in either its customer safety policies or in its financial management. Perhaps United's top managers assumed that it didn't need to change because the economy of the 90's had proven a boon to the airline industry in general (and to United in particular) and they simply didn't want to go through the hassle of change. When bad times came, however, it was too late to make the substantive changes that would have prevented the situation from spiraling out of control as it eventually did. Strategic action implies strategic change. Once an organization determines what are the most conducive opportunities it can take advantage of and what are the most threatening challenges it could well face, then it can begin to move in one direction or another that will benefit it and its stakeholders the most. This is why change is a constant part of effective strategic management

Strategic Change and Implementation. Change hits the operational core of the enterprise in the strategy implementation process. People's jobs may well be affected as the adopted plan means that certain jobs may go and certain other jobs may be created. The new strategic direction could mean exciting opportunities for certain people throughout the organization, but could also mean downsizing or the end of the road for others. Because all organizations are human organizations, the real challenge to strategic managers in implementing their strategic plan is to do so with the human core in mind. This is why we look at several of the principles of organizational development

(OD) as part of the strategic management process. OD helps strategic managers better understand the dynamics of the organization's culture, its human participants, and the forces that either support or challenge change on the most basic level – the level of the individual. (Please see the appendix at the end of this chapter for more information on how OD works within strategic management to facilitate needed strategic change.) We believe that strategic management cannot be effective if it is unable to support and empower the personnel within the firm as a strategic organization. As it turns out, it is almost impossible for top management to simply dictate strategy and have everyone throughout the organization buy in to it. Looking back at the opening case of United, for example, top management could not simply have ordered employees to change to help the company, they had to enter into negotiation and compromise; and even at that, they didn't persuade enough employees to make enough changes to prevent bankruptcy.

The Strategic Management Process

As we indicated in the definition we provided earlier, strategic management is a process in which an organization creates, implements, and evaluates its strategies for best achieving growth and profitability and, therefore, survival. In Figure 1.2, we present a schematic drawing of the strategic management process. Whether a firm is just beginning its strategic planning experience for the first time or is a firm that is already doing strategic planning and is simply entering a new cycle of planning, the process is basically the same. The decision to engage in strategic planning should be the result of a sober evaluation of the current position of the firm. As we will discuss further on, the preparation for strategic planning is almost as important as the planning activities themselves.

Step 1 of the overall process, then, is to look at the firm itself. What is its basic mission? What direction is the firm taking? Is there an internal desire for strategic change? Strategic planners examine the working philosophies and goal-setting activities of the firm. The organization is the sum of its membership, its entrepreneurial beginnings, its ownership, its culture, and its prevailing technology. From this very human core, strategic planners must discern the firm's mission (its purpose and direction); the vision of management for where the organization should go in the future and what it should seek to attain; what is of value to managers and stakeholders alike; and finally, what specific goals and objectives already exist.

Figure 1.2
The Strategic Management Process

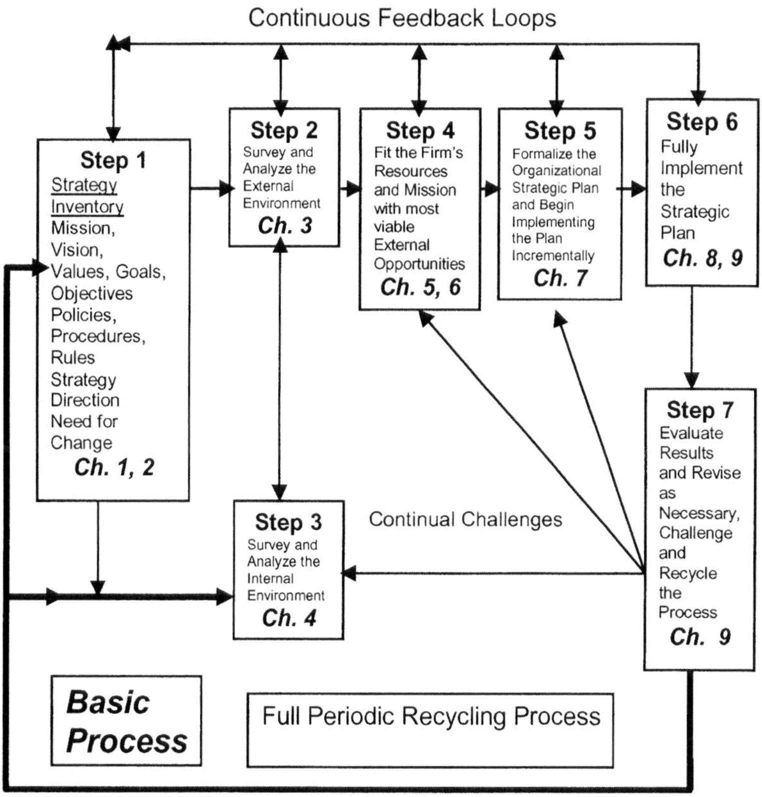

Step 2 continues with an analysis of the firm's external environment. There are two concerns here – what is going on in general all over the world, and what is going on within the firm's primary industry. These two sets of environmental forces will contain opportunities and threats that can impact the firm. Some may be weaker than others, while some will be of paramount importance. While it is impossible to know everything about the environment that can either be positive or negative, effective strategic management is that which is capable of identifying and isolating those external environmental forces that has the most likely ability to impact upon the organization's performance (called key success factors).

Step 3 takes the analysis phase to the next level by creating a full inventory of the organization's resource base and evaluating the firm's internal operations. Understanding how the firm converts its basic resources using its core competencies to create customer value and a competitive advantage is fundamental to understanding how a firm accomplishes its strategies and achieves its goals and objectives.

With all this in mind, in Step 4 the strategic planners can begin to reconcile what they have found from their external and internal environmental analyses with the philosophies of the organization as organizational stakeholders agree to the tenets of the plan and organizational governance has given approval for the plan. The planners then develop corporate and business strategies that create the best fit for the firm with its environment.

Step 5 sees planners move from strategy formulation to strategy implementation. Here is where the planners discuss issues pertaining to organizational learning, leadership, culture, and structure and what changes need to be made in order to align these systems with each other as well as with the marketplace.

In Step 6, managers actually enact the strategy through learning and change processes. Here managers and other staff members utilizing management development techniques aimed at changing individuals, interpersonal interactions, intragroup, intergroup, and interorganizational relations, as well as subsystems' alignments, and the organization as a whole.

Though strategic planners should continually provide feedback as they move from one step to another, and possible go backwards and change something they had determined earlier should the previous assumption prove faulty, Step 7 suggests that once the plan is in place, everything in the plan should be open to scrutiny, assessment and evaluation.   This is part of the idea that strategic planning is a process and not an event.   Just because one step is completed should be no guarantee that it was done correctly or that it cannot be revisited. In an atmosphere of objectively and continually challenging elements of the plan, managers will be able to achieve a firm hold on the strategic management process and thereby better guide the firm through the shadows of future and unknown events.[32]

The Responsibilities of Strategic Managers

The activities of strategic management are in addition to the responsibilities that managers would normally have in conducting the operations of the firm.   These additional responsibilities are outlined in Figure 1.3.

Figure 1.3
The Responsibilities of Strategic Managers

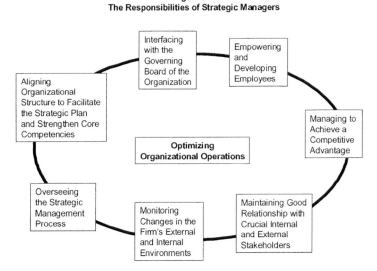

Traditional management theory states that the primary responsibility of management is to assure that the organizations operate in the most humane and efficient manner possible to help assure the optimization of outcomes for the organization's owners, customers, employees, suppliers and other significant stakeholders.[33] None of that goes away with the inclusion of strategic management in the activities of the firm. Further, the decision to engage in strategic management does not imply the addition of additional managerial personnel. Strategic management is an extra set of responsibilities for organizational managers, and it should be this way. There should never be any separation between strategic management and operational management. While some organizational managers will spend more time doing strategic management, such as the firm's CEO and governing board, all operational managers in the organizations need to be a part of the strategic management process, marrying the strategic direction of the organization to the operational activities and day-to-day events for which they were originally hired.

As Figure 1.3 suggests, in addition to effectively managing day-to-day operations, strategic managers must: 1) be involved with all aspects of the strategic management process; 2) align the employees of the organization's structure to conform with the structural requirements of the firm's strategic direction and to maintain core competencies; 3) directly or indirectly assure that the governing board has a clear picture of how the organization is accomplishing its strategic goals and objectives; 4) empower employees and provide them with the training necessary to perform their tasks; 5) be aware of, and inform other strategic decision-makers of changes in the organization's crucial environmental sets with which they interface most often; 6) maintain good relationships between the firm and it external and internal constituencies with whom they come in contact; and 7) keep the objectives and goals of the strategic plan firmly in sight and help the firm achieve them to obtain a competitive advantage. These are crucial responsibilities, and their importance cannot be minimized.

Again, when an organization determines that it wishes to pursue a strategic management approach, things change, responsibilities change, and people change. Over time, operational responsibilities and strategic management responsibilities meld together and the result is a unified approach to management where the long-term strategic direction of the firm is fully integrated into the day-to-day activities of the firm.[34] At this point, the organization should be as strongly positioned to reach its most important goals.

What about Non-Change Strategies?

Throughout the discussion thus far we have indicated that the terms strategy and change go together pretty well. But, is this always true? Are there not instances and organizations that should not and, perhaps, cannot change? Are these firms doomed or can they engage in strategic management and achieve higher levels of achievement as well?

In reality there are some organizations that cannot change or can change very little. Many of these are those found in the public or service sectors, though some can be found in the business sector as well. For example, churches, schools, universities and colleges, governmental agencies, and charitable organizations historically have changed very little over time. Further what changes they experience do not normally come from a posture of engaging in strategic planning as much as shifts in demographics. It is interesting, however, that there is a growing literature base devoted to strategic planning in these very institutions, all of which indicates major benefits from strategic management.[35] Strategic issues such as developing and supporting programming that better matches the populations each entity is serving is an important discussion in all of this literature and demonstrates that developing a strategic attitude can help improve survivability.

What about business firms? Can any of these adopt a no-change strategy? Again, the answer is yes, but with a major caveat. There are only certain industries where change is not common and is not likely to be in the future. Food companies that deal with the basics such as flour, milk, produce, and meat-type products may face little incentive to change. Though profit margins are usually squeezed in such basic commodity companies, volume tends to make up for it and as long as competition doesn't become too stiff, these companies can exist without major change for years. Several utilities also fall into this category, and as monopolies controlled by regulatory power, they not only have little incentive to engage in strategic change, but little ability to do so either.

Interestingly enough, however, this last example is also one in which developing a strategic management mentality early on is a good idea. Across the United States, states are starting to deregulate the utility industry, allowing competition among utility providers. In states such as Texas, utility companies are now free to service customers across traditional boundaries, introducing competition into the generating, transporting, and delivery of energy products. While there has been a great deal of consolidation within the industry, competition is new. This is important because there is no reason to believe that the utility companies will somehow be immune to the impacts of competition that has created so much chaos in the telecommunications industry after the U.S. Government broke up AT&T in the 1980s.

So, then, is the strategy of no change really viable? Again, yes, but it truly is dependent upon the organization's particular situation. If the organization is highly profitable (as compared to the rest of its competitors), is following its mission and achieving its goals, and is considered a market leader, and can foresee little change in its market, then the rational choice is to stay the course. Why fix something that isn't broken? However, many companies must engage in competitive environments, deal with changing products or services, or wish to expand their operations into other environments and industries and do not have the luxury of not changing. Things are changing around them, and if they do not change (and find effective internal methods of creating that change throughout the organization), they will fall behind. It is not certain that these firms will fail if they do not change, but the likelihood of failure has been significantly increased. The bottom line on change vs. no change is that most organizations are going to have to change to continue to have a good fit with their environments, and the best method they can choose to effect those changes is to do so through strategic planning and strategic management. Change may not be inevitable but keeping ahead of change is the real key to business success.

Change, Learning, and Competences: The Foundation of Effective Strategic Management

If change is nearly inevitable, how do organizations prepare for change as part of their strategic management process? The best way to prepare for change is to be adaptable and to overcome resistance to change.[36] Lewin noted over 50 years ago that firms can manage change (what he called unfreezing the organization) through educating employees as to the circumstances surrounding the changes before the organization reacted to those changes[37] – forewarned is forearmed. Consequently firms must become educators and knowledge managers; they must create learning organizations in order to become master managers[38] and thrive on the chaos that change inevitably brings to those caught unaware and off guard.[39]

Organizational learning and knowledge management have become management buzzwords of the 21st century. A quick search of the ABI/Inform Database, from 1999-2002 will yield over 300 articles directly pertaining to these topics. Whether these topics are just another management fad[40] or a very serious issue for academics and practitioners, the underlying principles behind what and how individuals, teams and organizations learn and use knowledge are critical to understand in the context of strategic management since learning and knowledge are the basic tools of change management. This learning and knowledge may be translated into specific individual, team, and organizational competences with a competence being defined as the ability to perform a job or task.[41] We discuss learning, competencies, and knowledge management as it relates to the firm's competitive advantage in Chapter 3.

Individual Competences. At the individual level, that of the employee and/or the manager, the possession of the proper basic skills (reading, writing, mathematics, public speaking, computer literacy, and primary and secondary research), job-related technical skills, human-relations skills (working with others, team management), and conceptual skills (creativity and decision-making) is critical for job performance.[42] Competence at the individual level within a strategic context refers to several skill sets:

1. *strategic planning skills* – the ability to: a) analyze the firm's internal and external environments; b) reconcile the firm's vision, goals and resources with the firm's current situation; c) formulate strategies and tactics that realign the firm's processes and products with market conditions; and d) develop key performance indicators which translate corporate goals and objectives into measurable outcomes.

2. *strategic implementation skills* – the ability to: a) translate business strategies into organization and market change tactics; b) create a strategy-supportive culture (build employee trust) and overcome resistance to change by working with internal and external stakeholders; c) reward (both economically and psychologically) stakeholders who buttress the change process; and d) create flexible systems and processes that allow for changes to the implementation plan.

3. *strategic evaluation skills* – the ability to develop strategic and operational control systems which: a) monitor the progress of strategic planning and implementation processes; b) check the internal and external environments for long-term trends and rapid changes; c) compare actual performance to projected performance; and d) develop information systems that provide appropriate data access and timely feedback.

Team Competences. The ability to form, develop and then alter teams as needed is essential in the strategic management process since much of these processes require group action and decisions. To form a team the firm must have the skills to: identify the team's purpose, establish team goals, create an action plan to achieve those goals, utilize the skills of each member, establish member roles and rules of conduct, and allocate the necessary resources for achieving the team's objectives. Team development skills include employee and team member training in: group decision-making, team work, leadership, effective listening, conflict resolution, negotiation, and running effective team meetings.[43]

Organizational Competences. Authors such as Peter Senge[44] and Chris Argyris[45] have noted that most organizations suffer from what Senge refers to as learning disabilities, that is, the inability to learn from their mistakes and their environment and to see the organization as part of a larger system. Organizational competence is defined for them as systems thinking; the ability to understand the detailed complexities and dynamics of the market and the organization (as described in Appendix B) and the impact of change on those systems. The other competences cited by Senge include personal mastery (know thyself), mental modeling (the ability to develop models of how we see the world), shared vision, and team learning.

Part of organizational learning, and organizational competence, is the ability to break the routine operation of the firm if strategic shifts are required.[46] Rules, routines, policies, and procedures support the operation of the firm by reducing task uncertainty[47] and solving operational problems. As the problems of the firm change, however, these problem-solving methodologies become barriers to change. Business as usual cannot solve new business problems and the organization must unlearn old routines before new ones can be implemented. This is quite difficult to do when routines become ingrained habits; habits which have symbolic values and become part of the customs and culture of the firm.

Organizational learning and planned change then cannot be understood without giving consideration to the principal basis for resistance to change, namely organizational culture.[48] Organizational leadership must create and support a value system that supports change, namely learning cultures and learning leaders. The goal is to create an environment of perpetual learning, a culture that thrives on changes and organizational challenges.

Learning and Organizational Knowledge. In order for firms to become perpetual learners, they must have a system for acquiring, storing, and disseminating knowledge throughout the organization. Organizational knowledge refers to the flow of information within the organization and between the organization and its environment. This flow can occur both formally or informally, through people or technology, and contain implicit (intuitive and unspoken) and/or explicit data. From a strategic perspective, organizational knowledge refers to how organizations learn to do new things and includes not only what the members know but also what they believe.[49]

Now that you understand some of the concepts underlying strategy and strategic management, we can move unto the first step in the strategic management process, strategy formulation and development.

Strategy Formulation and Development: A Preliminary Introduction

Figure 1.2 above identified that the first step in the strategic management process, strategy formulation and development, begins with inventorying the firm's mission, strategic direction, and desire for change. As we suggested earlier, this pre-planning stage is an important part of the entire strategic management process and may well impact the ability of the organization to implement the plan, once it has been formulated. It is this stage where the central purpose for doing strategic planning, and ultimately strategic management, becomes clear to those who will be involved in the formulation process as well as those who will be affected by the resulting strategic plan.

The Potential of Resistance to Planning and Change

Both for-profit and not-for-profit organizations engage in strategic planning, but not always in a productive manner. We feel this is a central concern, particularly for those organizations that fail in developing a meaningful strategic plan or in implementing it. For example, in our work on strategic planning in colleges and universities, it is not uncommon to find that many strategic planning initiatives fail to engender support of faculty and staff. In an environment where campus policy is considered to be the joint responsibility of central administration and campus-wide faculty (often called the principle of shared governance), the initiative to begin strategic planning often comes only from one side, the administrative side. The result is that the members of the faculty see neither the reason nor the need for strategic planning, and often engage in counterproductive behavior that attacks the strategic management process. The larger result is that campuses where these types of conditions exist find themselves unable to either formulate a meaningful strategic plan, let alone implement one.

Business organizations can face the same difficulties, even though they have some advantages in strategic planning. In the business model, planning has historically been accepted as a top-down process, while being enhanced and strengthened by a firm-wide commitment to the process and objective of strategic planning.[50] In not-for-profit organizations, this is far more difficult, and most successful planning processes are the result of unified commitment on the part of both top management and organizational constituents through out the organization.

The end depends upon the beginning.[51] This statement, attributed to St. Benedict, is clearly true for the activities of strategic planning. One of the important reasons that the strategic planning process fails is that top managers fail to communicate properly the true current position of the enterprise to its internal and external stakeholders. And since one of the major implications of strategic planning is planning for change, it is important to understand that most individuals and groups really don't like change, particularly if they don't know why change should occur and/or support the reason for change. Further, resistance to change is not only common, it is normal and should be expected.[52]

Psychologically, most people only support change they understand and believe will benefit them and the organization.[53] They actively resist change that they do not understand or fear may harm them. In strategic planning, where the direction of the process is to solidify or improve the ability of the organization to survive and prosper, the possibility of change could be refocusing, reengineering, reorganization, and even down-sizing. For people throughout the organization that are not told the reason for initiating strategic planning and potentially major structural change, the potential downsides of change may appear to be far greater than any potential upside, and so, they will naturally resist the entire process.

Much of these problems can be mitigated if top organizational managers carefully articulate the current condition and position of the company within its competitive environment. Communication is the key. As in the example of United Airlines at the beginning of this chapter, where the necessities for strategic change are not identified or are poorly expressed, it should not be a surprise when several of the employee unions who were asked to make concessions stubbornly balked, with some even suggesting that it was fine with them if the airline went bankrupt. Rather than creating a mutually agreed upon forum for beginning to make strategic change, United simply reacted to its extremely hostile environment by making unilateral top-down decisions and then sought support from its unions and other stakeholders.

On the other hand, for those institutions that properly articulate the position of the firm to its major stakeholder groups, and are able to gain their support for strategic change, the entire strategic planning climate changes and the potential for more effective and comprehensive strategic plans, as well as the ability of the firms to implement them, increases dramatically.

Overcoming Resistance: Bottom-up and Top-down Planning. We have been discussing strategic planning and the responsibility of strategic planners predominately from a top-down perspective; that the key decision-makers formulate the strategic plan and send it down the organization's chain of command for implementation. However, strategic planning could also involve bottom-up processes as well where committees, task forces, and individual managers or employees pass on their ideas as to how the firm can best compete in its marketplace. This methodology attempts to elicit feedback and commentary from employees who have everyday contact with customers and have hands-on knowledge of the marketplace (a very valuable resource). Secondly, employees who are involved in the strategy formulation process tend to feel more of a part of the firm (stronger commitment and motivation) and are also predisposed to implement the plans they helped to formulate. Numerous management techniques such as Management by Objectives, Total Quality Management, and Self-Managed Work Groups, and Junior Executive Boards have proven the value of employee involvement and input into the planning process.[54] For example, Rowley and Sherman found that faculty become far less adversarial and confrontational when actively involved in academic and strategic planning.[55] The responsibility of managers in the first phase of the strategic management process thus includes obtaining employee input and buy-in.

Moving Forward with the Pre-Planning Process

Once the groundwork is in place, that is, once the need for strategic planning is well articulated and accepted by major organizational constituents, it is time to understand what some of the fundamental underpinnings of the firm are. If gaining organizational-wide support for the plan is a crucial part of the overall process, then it makes sense to understand the firm's preliminary strategic conditions.

This preplanning process is suggested in Figure 1.4. The simple questions that guide this part of the process include:

1. What is our basic mission?
2. How do we currently conduct our business activities?
3. Is our conduct leading to desired results?
4. If we are reaching our desired outcomes, can we be confident that we can continue to achieve desired results if we don't change?
5. If we are not reaching our desired outcomes, what should be changed to improve results?
6. What changes are occurring in our competitive environment that impact our business most directly?
7. Finally, are we in a good position that we are confident will last for the next several years, or do we already know that we must change or face a deteriorating future?

These questions will be revisited throughout the strategic planning process, and it is not our intent to suggest that in this initial phase there will be as much detail as will result from the comprehensive analyses that will occur in substantive steps. Rather, these questions present a strategic exercise in allowing strategic planners to begin to organize their thinking about what the firm is and where it is headed, which is the reason for doing strategic planning.

What is the Firm's Basic Mission? On the surface, this may seem like a silly question. Doesn't everyone in the company know what the company does? Why wouldn't this simply be apparent? In deeper analysis, however, it becomes clear that in many firms, people do not really know what the central purpose is for the existence of the business. This can particularly be true for very large firms that have several different product or service lines. For example, at AT&T today, many different businesses exist where once there was only a single telephone company. From the pioneering days of Alexander Graham Bell, AT&T has first established telephone communication as a local and then nationwide business, and has reoriented and

Figure 1.4
The Strategic Planning Process
Step 1 – Preplanning

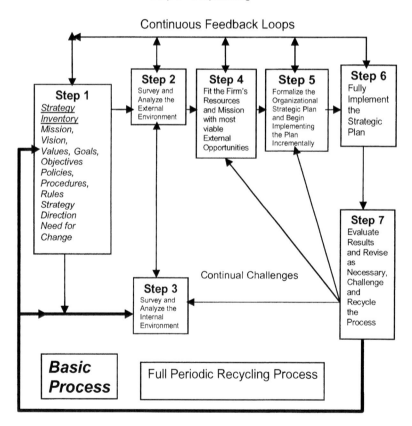

reengineered itself over the years to where it is now not only engaged in telephone communication, but also in a wide variety of other technologies and services as well. So, one might ask, what is the mission of AT&T today? And the answer is not a simple one. Often, insiders and outsiders begin to think that the mission of AT&T is to make money for its top managers and major investors, rather than developing and distributing Information Age communication services to the entire world.[56]

It is this displacement of mission that can create problems in the initial stages of the strategic planning process. Clearly, there are companies who only exist to make money. The infamous revelations over the past few years of Enron and WorldCom are but two of many where top management greed and pursuit of personal wealth have created financial schemes that bilked thousands of investors out of their investments and wrongfully destroyed the retirement funds of their own employees – all for the pursuit of greed.

A clear understanding of a firm's current mission is critical to the strategic planning process as it is to the eventual strategic management environment to which planning should lead. Mission has to do with an understanding of what the firm does to meet the needs of its customers in such a way that it matches or exceeds the activities of its competitors. Mission implies an understanding of a competitive environment and the role each company wishes to pursue in meeting the challenges of that environment in such a way that it can prosper and flourish. A mission is the purpose and direction of the firm and it must be understood by all those closely associated with it. So in the case of AT&T, if top decision-makers and key internal and external constituents truly understand that AT&T strives to provide state-of-the-art communication systems for existing and emerging world-wide needs, then the stage is set for planning to achieve this bold objective through developing a strategic plan. Likewise, if top decision-makers and key internal and external stakeholders at United Airlines understand United's mission as providing safe, convenient, affordable, and enjoyable air travel to business and leisure customers throughout the world, then it becomes easier to restructure the airline during bankruptcy so that it can emerge as a unified, vital, and competitive giant in the airline industry.

What Direction is the Firm Currently Pursuing? While many in a firm may not understand or appreciate the firm's mission, many more do not know or understand the direction it has chosen to take. Again, this tends to be more of an issue for much larger firms than for smaller, more centrally focused firms, but it can exist in both. This results from the nature of work and the work force. A secretary who has been hired to work for an account executive may not understand that he/she is supporting the work of a person who is trying to meet customer needs as efficiently and as effectively as possible; and does not understand that this is important because the company is working hard to serve a particular customer base that it has decided is its best niche for sustaining growth and profitability. The secretary may come to work day-to-day and not feel that what she/he does impacts those larger organizational directions, and when it isn't just one secretary, but a major number of employees who only understand their job as an individual activities and not part of a much more important whole, the impending strategic planning process can again be in peril.

Direction is a choice firms make in determining *how* they will compete within their markets. Strategic firms seek a competitive advantage in their market by identifying specific customers and developing particular products or services that will be most appealing to those customers. Wal-Mart has become a master of providing mega quantities of desired merchandise at low prices to certain middle to lower economic demographic groups. They will not turn Neiman Marcus customers away, but at the same time, they will not stock $25,000 dresses or suits either. Their direction is clear – serve the large majority of middle and lower economic groups by providing wanted merchandise at low prices. This direction has landed Wal-Mart a particular market niche that has proven to be extremely beneficial to them and to their customer base.

United, unlike Wal-Mart, is pursuing several directions simultaneously. United offers nation-wide air transportation using a hub-and-spoke technology (United has 5 major U.S. airports that it uses as hubs and flies out of those hubs to nearby markets; for those people who want to travel beyond the hub, they must first fly to the hub and then make a connection to another destination served by that hub [called a spoke] or fly to another hub airport to perhaps connect yet again to get to a final destination). United also has a separate operation called Shuttle by United which, though temporarily grounded during bankruptcy proceedings, is to be reintroduced to compete directly against Southwest Airlines. These tactics have been developed in order to keep operating expenses low and offer customers competitively priced air transportation.

United also offers international travel in the more traditional point-to-point system, where the airline only provides services from one airport to another without the probability that passengers can connect on the same airline to get to a final destination. Here customers are offered a more convenient, personalized service. United also maintains an air cargo system that competes in a narrow niche of the shipping industry and, despite deteriorating relationships with travel agents due to dramatically reduced fees, United also maintains the Alliance Reservations System (used by approximately 50% of all travel agents in the U.S. and around the world to help travel agents make travel reservations with airlines, hotels, rental car companies, cruise lines, and more).

In this example, it is difficult to see which of the above directions provide the greatest potential for United to achieve a competitive advantage. This very point has come out during the bankruptcy proceedings, and United has been challenged to redefine its direction to one that provides less risk and the potential of a smoother course back to growth and profitability. United will have to change, and should do so only once it has determined what direction makes the most sense for its resource base and competitive niche.

Strategic planning asks the question that demands an answer – should the firm change? Again, it might seem like this is a silly question: if the firm is in trouble, of course it should change; or if the firm is doing alright, there should be no need for change. Yet, change may be imperative in either case.

In terms of firms that already experience problems that threaten their well-being or survival, it should be clear that change of some form is indicated. What makes this discussion much more important, however, is being able to determine what areas of strategic management and/or strategy need to be changed and why. In other words, it is not enough to say, "We're in trouble – we're losing money – we've got to do something about it." It is better to be able to say, "sales in our western branches have declined for 8 quarters now and there is no reason to think they will recover – we need to understand the dynamics of this market and determine whether the decline is part of an industry trend and/or whether the decline is due to our inability to compete in this market." This second statement has strategic overtones and speaks directly to the need for the firm to determine the factors causing the decline and sales, what actions the firm can take, and whether those actions may call for changing the strategic direction of the firm.

Change for change sake makes little sense and may cause far more damage than good. Change is only called for to improve strategic performance. This presents one of the fundamental problems with many strategic planning events – in the very beginning of the process, strategic planners must understand and then articulate the strategic need for change and be able to communicate their conclusions to the rest of the firm's strategic constituencies.

The theme of this book is change, and we believe that most strategic planning and strategic management activities involve change to some degree. This issue is what kind of change is appropriate, and how much change should a firm undergo. As we will discuss throughout much of this book, strategic management continually looks at certain aspects of the internal and external environments to determine the on-going fit between the firm and its environmental sets. Unfortunately, as we described above in our discussion of non-change strategies, the environments of nearly all organizations are in a state of constant flux. As these environments transform over time, the quality of the fit between those environments and the state of the resources of a firm may also change.

Researching the Changing Market. In order for a firm's top managers to determine whether change is needed, information must be gathered about the firm and its marketplace. The quality of their strategic decisions, including the need to change, is often a function of the quality of the data they have gathered to base their decisions on and the depth of the analysis they employ to analyze that data. Igor Ansoff, among others, has written about the importance of data gathering and analysis.[57] For the external environment, for example, he states that it is especially important for decision-makers to understand the trends and driving forces that exist may create change and how they can potentially affect the firm's operations. He goes further and suggests that it is important to detect the weak signals in the environment and begin to monitor them because they may be the beginnings of new trends and changes that the company may wish to embrace early on, or perhaps be in a position to avoid or defend against (assuming that the emergent trend is negative).[58]

Data gathering may be done in a variety of ways. In large firms, research departments develop intelligence systems that constantly gather data on competitors, consumer trends, governmental regulation changes, international competition, financial trends, market trends, emerging technologies, and an additional wide variety of areas that may positively or negatively impact the company operations and future direction. Smaller firms often lack the resources to support such a department, but must gather relevant data nonetheless. Membership in trade associations, subscriptions to trade journals and data bases, net surfing, and customer surveys are just a few of the ways that firms obtain market data.[59]

Gathering the data itself, however, isn't enough. Firms must be able to analyze the data in an objective and sophisticated method and technology has come along way in helping to sort and categorize data to create and store knowledge. Management information systems and tools such as spreadsheets and data mining help in establishing a knowledge management system, but ultimately, a top management needs to make a decision about what the data means and how it could affect the firm. While emerging technology continues to make more and more information available and is now doing a fair job in organizing that data, it is still the responsibility of top decision-makers to determine what to do with it.[60] Again, large firms may employ analysts whose job is to do just this, gather and interpret data. Then, with the data and a reliable analysis in hand, top decision-makers can make an informed decision. For the smaller firm that cannot afford research departments or data analysts, the quality of the decision-making process of upper-level managers is a function of those outside sources of information as well as their ability to employ the data in making the right decision. In either case, it is the responsibility of top-level managers to gather appropriate data, analyze it, and then make decisions that will set the strategic direction of the firm. This is the heart and sole of strategy formulation. Further, this function demands that top-level decision makers have a full understanding of the changing external environment and how these changes create opportunities and threats that challenge its ability to survive.

Some Closing Thoughts on September 11th

Could strategic management have prevented the disaster of September 11th? We cannot definitely say one way or the other; the events that day were highly complex and mostly unexpected. However, if United and American as well as the Federal Aviation Administration and the United States military had used the tenets of strategic management in terms of dealing with potential terrorist attacks (if they had taken note of the previous attacks on passenger airplanes and increased their own security to prevent a repeat of those events) and if they had understood just how vulnerable airplanes were to hijacking in a world becoming more and more dangerous, if they had learned from past events, they *might* have prevented the 9/11 disaster.[61]

This is a lesson from which everyone else can learn. Strategic management provides the opportunity for organizations of all kinds to better understand the world they are a part of, their own abilities to take advantage of opportunities and avoid disaster, but it is a managerial tool that only works when it is fully implemented. Use of jargon, writing strategic plans and then warehousing them, not understanding fully what strategic planning is all about but saying you're doing it anyway, and not being willing to follow through, are not signs of good strategic management. Effective strategic management is what this book is all about. We have tried to combine the best of past practices, and theory with current wisdom on implementation and usage. We believe the result is a treatment of the subject which is informative and useful.

Summary

The study of strategic management is the study of how organizations can develop organizational systems that will help them achieve long term survival by creating a fit between the organization and its external environment. This chapter began by defining both the terms associated with the study of strategic management but a description of many of the basic processes. The discussion made an argument as why strategic management is significantly different from operational management and attempted to describe why firms not only need to adopt strategic management philosophies, but develop strategic mentalities throughout the organization as well. Also discussed was the need to understand that firms follow a pattern of decision-making when creating strategic plans.

The text then discussed the specific processes and methodologies of strategic management and how these activities impact both the strategic direction a firm may follow and how its operations conform to help it achieve its goals and objectives. In this discussion, we also described the conditions that must be present for a firm to engage in a no-change strategy, but pointed out that there are very few companies in very few industries for which these conditions are true – most firms must engage in strategies that involve change and must be able to manage change as effectively as they create their strategic plans in order to achieve overall success.

Since change is such an important issue, as well as an issue that many firms don't deal well with, we introduced knowledge management and organizational development (OD) as concepts that many firms might consider adopting in their attempts to effectively implement change. We specifically discussed the individual, team and organizational competences needed to creating learning organizations and overcome resistance to change. Finally, we presented several issues that firms consider in the pre-strategic planning process stage: the firm's current mission, strategic direction, the need for the firm to change, and the research needed to support the determination to change the firm.

Key Terms and Concepts

After reading this chapter, you should be familiar with the following terms and concepts:
Strategy; tactics; strategic management; strategic planning; strategic decisions; strategic thinking; operational management; corporate level strategies; business level strategies; functional level strategies; environments; strategic change; organizational change; resistance to change; competences; knowledge management; and pre-planning processes.

Web sites

http://www.smsweb.org/ - The Strategic Management Society's official web site. Includes information on conferences and seminars, organizational activities, references, and the *Strategic Management Journal*.

http://aom.pace.edu/bps/;   http://www.aom.pace.edu/odc/   -   The Academy of Management's Division Business Policy and Strategy Division and Division of Organization Development and Change. Includes a newsletter, web boards and conferences, research, teaching and practice resources.

http://www.strategyclub.com/ - The Strategic Management Club On-line.   This user friendly web site for undergraduates and graduates provides strategic planning tools, templates, links, and information that can help you analyze cases and prepare professional-looking reports for class. The SMCO web site is designed to "save you time" in doing case research, preparing matrices, and even job hunting – activities often engaged upon in a business policy class.

http://www.aludosan.net/strategic-mgmt.htm - E-MBA's links to topics and journals related to strategic management.   Includes textbooks, abstracts, and links to the key organizations and journals in the field.

Discussion Questions

1. What are the major differences between strategic management and operational management, and why?
2. Why is strategic planning a process? Why is strategic management a process?
3. Why is pre-planning an important aspect of strategic planning?
4. Is strategic management the purview of upper level managers? Does this add to or detract from the effectiveness of strategic management?
5. What is the relationship between change, learning, organization development, competences and strategic management?

Exercises

1. Looking at the United Airlines case that we referred to throughout this chapter, what are the five most important issues that have strategic implications for the survival of the airline, and why? Prepare a brief report.
2. Can you discern any activities of the management of your college or university that you would classify as strategic? If so, what are they? If not, why do you think the institution is not more concerned with strategic management?
3. What do you think you would find if you did pre-planning for your college or university?
4. List the 10 most important reasons for any organization to engage in strategic management and then prioritize them. Be prepared to defend your choices.
5. Go on the Internet to any firm's annual report. See if you can find any discussion of the firm's mission, strategic direction, and the firm's need to change. Prepare a brief report.

Experiential Exercise

Fast Food Fantasy – Create Your Own Fast Food Restaurant![62]

Learning Objectives
1. To introduce students to the concept of strategy and strategic thinking.
2. To have students practice thinking strategically in terms of their own consumer experiences.
3. To have students compare and contrast strategies of several fast food firms (benchmarking).
4. To have students, based upon their analysis, suggest an ideal model or prototype for a fast food restaurant.

Procedure
1. Split the class up into groups consisting of 4-6 members.
2. Assign one member of the group the role of group spokesperson and your liaison with the group.
3. Have each member in the group complete assignment sheet 1 "Analyzing Fast Food Restaurants" (allow 15 minutes).
4. Have each member quickly discusses his or her analysis (allow 15 minutes).
5. Have the group briefly discuss the members' findings (allow 15 minutes).
6. Have the group complete assignment sheet 2 "Creating Your Own Fast Food Restaurant" (allow 30 minutes).
7. Have each team leader discuss their restaurant (5 minutes each).
8. Summarize findings. Which restaurant was rated highest? Are their any common elements between all of the newly created restaurants? (10 minutes)

Instruction Sheet 1
Analyzing Fast Food Restaurants

Describe how successful each of the firms listed is for each strategic factor listed in the left hand column. Cite examples where necessary. Then rank order each firm on a 1 to 3 scale, 1 being the lowest, 3 being the highest.

Strategic Factor	McDonalds	Burger King	Wendy's
Advertising			
Product Line			
Brand Image			
Average Meal Price			
Distribution Channel			
Customer Value			
Competitive Advantage			
Total Score			

Instruction Sheet 2
Creating Your Own Fast Food Restaurant
Working from Instruction Sheet 1, fill in column two. In column three, quickly describe the firm's characteristics for that strategic factor. In column three, create a name for your fast food restaurant and describe how your firm will match, if not better, the highest rated firm's characteristics.

Strategic Factor	Highest Rated Restaurant	Characteristics	Characteristics
Advertising			
Product Line			
Brand Image			
Average Meal Price			
Distribution Channel			
Customer Value			
Competitive Advantage			

Appendix
Organization Development (OD)

If to achieve higher levels of success, managers need to become perpetual learners and their firms need to become learning organizations that manage knowledge, then what management approaches and tools are available to strategic managers to utilize and transform managers and organizations into institutions of knowledge creation and diffusion? To answer this question, we turn to the practice and methods of organizational development (OD).

Most organizational managers recognize the fallibilities of individuals and groups in organizations and also recognize the importance of an organization being able to achieve its strategic goals. When strategic plans call for changes, an organization must be prepared to manage the change process in a planned fashion.[63]

Managers and strategic planners must recognize that often resistance to change, any change that might substantive affect them, comes from legitimate concerns, beliefs, or circumstances of individual employees and work groups. Much of this type of resistance can result from misinformation, no information, or purposefully jaded information. Knowing the causes of this type of resistance is also the beginning of creating solutions that will correct communications, serve to build consensus and create an environment conducive to learning. Practitioners of OD recognize that resistance may come from forces within an organization's human core such as power seekers, political activities, conflicting goals of organizational stakeholders, distrust, fear of change, or even seemingly irrational destructive motivations.

Because of OD's focus on human development, systems thinking, and research-supported change, it has become one of the most successful bodies of thought that has been able to bridge the gap between organizational strategies (action plans) and tactics (implementation plans). By creating processes and techniques specifically aimed at facilitating change, that is, building trust, OD becomes one of the two major adaptive tactics a firm can employ to create a fit between itself and its environment (the other tactic is changing the marketplace, see Chapter 8). OD is the implementation approach which creates productivity through people (produces respect for the individual), supports worker autonomy and creativity, extols a hands-on philosophy (everyone is expected to contribute), and allows for what Peters and Waterman (authors of *In Search of Excellence)* call a simultaneous loose-tight operation (freedom to perform work in numerous ways while controlling the firm's core values).[64] OD's mission and objective is to help organizations to solve their own problems, to help firms to learn how to learn, to help businesses becoming learning organizations.

What is Organization Development (OD)?

OD is an applied social science for facilitating organizational change by developing adaptability and change processes in both individuals and the organization as driven by shifting, dynamic external environmental forces. OD may be further defined as "a strategy for change that intervenes in the human and social processes of the organization ... themes in action [include] ... interventions into the organization's culture, structure, and processes."[65] There are several underlying premises behind the science of OD that are pertinent to understanding its concepts and techniques.

1. **It is human nature to resist change although change is all around us.** The irony of strategic management is that it asks people to step outside of their comfort zones, in terms of how they think about their organization, how it competes in the market, and how they translate the business's strategy into day-to-day activities. It is expected that certain individuals or groups will resist new strategies both as they are being formulated and put into action due to an innate fear of change.[66]

2. **OD places a high value on people, they are the organization's greatest asset.** When people come to the place where they do their work, they bring their humanness with them. Humanness means that individuals are unique combinations of talents, aspirations, desires, beliefs, histories, and faults. OD seeks to unleash employees' talents in a way that will add to the firm's distinctive competencies and add to the firm's competitive advantage.[67]

3. **OD is a learning process.** OD is "a complex educational strategy intended to change the beliefs, attitudes, values, and structure of organizations so that they can better adapt ... to the dizzying rate of change."[68] OD is based upon the notion that people can and want to learn; that they want to grow as individuals and excel at their jobs. Further, there is a need for all of the members of the organization to become continuous learners and to help create an overall competency of how to better compete in the external environment. OD techniques help people *learn how to learn* so that they can make the changes in themselves and in their organization. The underlying assumption is that once we have learned to learn we will become self-sufficient problem-solvers.

4. **OD is an empowering process.** In order for employees to improve their performance and the performance of their organization, employees must be given the authority to change their work environment. For people to share information and learn about the organization, OD requires collaboration and involvement of all levels of the institution—everyone must be heard and given the opportunity to participate in the change process.[69]

5. **OD is based upon the systems approach.** There is a basic belief that there are varying relationships between a variety of interdependent subsystems that interact with the external environment and the organization creating a tenuous, dynamic balance. Change can occur at many levels of the organization and the causes of change must be determined before change strategies are implemented.[70]

6. **OD analyses and interventions are based upon scientific methodology.** An action-research model which involves data gathering and information analysis drives the OD effort. People will only stop resisting change when they understand why they need to change based upon valid and reliable information. This shifts discussion from debating what the facts are to discussing the facts and working on problem-solving.[71]

7. **The bottom-line for OD, its most basic tenet, is developing and nurturing employee trust, the most fundamental condition for learning organizations.** Organizations cannot change, or even operate effectively, in an environment of distrust. Distrust is the

ruination of any sense of community or team work and it would seem impossible for learning to occur in organizations, in any sense of the word, where employees are suspicious of management and visa versa. Management must work on building employee trust as the cornerstone of their value system.[72]

The OD process. The OD process refers to the methodology in which the organization will perform a self-analysis; to learn about itself. Usually this analysis is assisted by an outside consultant, referred to as *change agents*, (or team of consultants) who possess expertise in both organizational research methodology and organization change techniques.[73] Although described in numerous ways by various authors, the process usually begins with a recognition by the organization that there is a problem with the firm's operation yet the firm can't quite put their finger on what the problem is – sort of an itch that the firm can't scratch.[74] At this point the firm may also scout around for outside assistance (and then need to negotiate with a consultant about their project expectations), or may decide that they have expertise in-house (an *internal change agent*) who can assist in the rest of the phases of the OD process.

The first phase, *diagnosis*, starts with the traditional key performance indicators such as profitability, cash flow, and debt. These gauges are considered symptoms of more deeply rooted problems and the firm needs to collect data about the firm in order to develop a true picture of its current status. There are numerous information gathering techniques, such as interviewing, questionnaires, observations, and secondary data analysis. After this information is analyzed and the real problems are identified, this material needs to be presented to the members of the organization in a feedback session. The second phase, *intervention*, involves the matching of the problems to specific intervention techniques based upon the level of analysis in which the problem occurs and the target group of the intervention. The intervention technique(s) selected must respond to a felt need of the targeted population, involve the targeted population in the planning and implementation of the intervention, and lead to acceptance of the change by the organization's culture. *Evaluation*, the third phase, determines whether the intervention(s) actually solved the problem(s);

it is the feedback loop that allows the firm to continue to diagnosis and intervene if the problem is not solved after the first set of interventions. If the evaluation determines that the problems were solved (the desired changes occurred), the program would be *terminated.*[75]

The content of OD. The content of OD refers to the numerous intervention techniques employed to prepare the firm for change and then assist the firm in implementing those changes. Interestingly enough, these intervention techniques do not normally directly solve the problems identified in the diagnosis phase (what a traditional consultant would do) but educate and train employees in the firm as to how they can identify and solve the problems on their own. Intervention techniques are aimed at increasing the firm's cognitive skills and building an organization that is self-correcting. Which OD technique to employ and with whom to employ it is based upon the focal point of the problem, the symptoms of the problem requiring attention, the type of problem, and kinds of changes sought.[76] We will discuss these techniques in detail in later chapters. Examples of intervention techniques include team building, third party peacemaking, sensitivity training, cultural analysis, and quality circles.[77]

Strategic Management (SM) and Organization Development (OD): An Integration

The field of SM has historically focused on learning about what formulation and implementation strategies would have to be developed to create a competitive advantage. In terms of strategy implementation, the literature in the field usually revolves around changing the 7 S's of the organization—strategy, skills, style, systems, structures, staff, and shared values—but does not describe how the organization is going to institute these change strategies. The field of OD, on the other hand, has focused on intervention techniques that help an organization learn how to implement change with the ultimate goal of increasing the ability of the organization to learn and to become proactive. The differences between these two fields can be explained by examining the type of organizational learning that occurs during strategy formulation and implementation.

Strategy formulation historically has been single-loop learning[78] – it is the transference of information and expertise concerning technical aspects of product, service delivery, and the market. In strategic management nomenclature, organizations develop core competencies either in process management/ innovation or product management/ innovation in order to better compete in the marketplace. We will discuss these strategies in detail in Chapter 5. Breakthroughs in knowledge management and the focus on intellectual capital has redefined strategy formulation to include double-loop learning – becoming expert at learning how to learn and being adaptable enough to change a firm's thinking about itself and its market. Strategy implementation then is the actions that the firm takes in order to enact the firm's knowledge-base and better align the firm with its external environment. In OD language, the organization first defines the problem, intervenes with its current operation in order to produce desired changes, and then institutionalizes those changes.

Strategic management and OD have much in common. They share a systems perspective (see Introduction), seek to increase the organization's sensitivity to the internal and external forces which shape and are partially shaped by the organization[79], include concepts of fit, flexibility, adaptation, and alignment in terms of the organization and its environmental interface, and deal with issues concerning focus or levels of analysis. More specifically, strategy implementation provides a conceptual framework for enacting a strategic plan while OD provides the nuts and bolts methodology of organizational change needed in order to operationalize the implementation at a more human/individual level; OD comprises some of the tactics of strategic management. OD and strategic management represent complimentary portions of the same phenomenon - the need to plan and enact change that will produce a sustainable competitive advantage for the organization. Practitioners utilize both fields in order to properly understand, predict and recommend changes that would maximize an organization's performance. See Figure 1-A.

Figure 1-A
The Integration of Strategic Management and Organization
Development

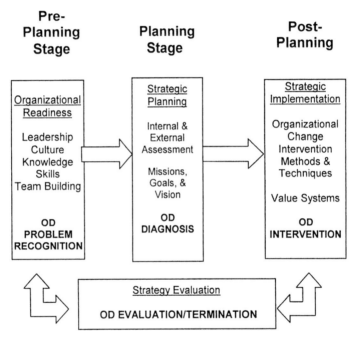

| Pre-
Planning
Stage | Planning
Stage | Post-
Planning |

As you can tell from Figure 1A, OD fosters institutional performance and creates a competitive advantage for the institution by creating a culture prior to strategic planning that supports change, empowers employees and provides them with the tools needed to enact change.   OD is a precursor to strategic management.   Until the organization is ready for change, strategic planning is at best presumptuous and at worst foolish and time consuming.   The skills developed by preparing the organization for change carry through the strategic management process and are critical to successful strategy implementation.   OD is a mechanism for psychologically and technically preparing the institution for strategic planning, and then supporting and reinforcing the change process throughout the strategic management process. This sandwich effect, using OD before and after the planning process, reinforces the cyclical nature of planning and organizational learning.

Up-Date on the United Case

After the bankruptcy filing in 2002, United Airlines has continued to struggle. It has missed several target dates for emerging from bankruptcy by coming up with an acceptable plan for reorganization that will satisfy the courts and its creditors. As of June, 2005, it continues to reorganize and has asked the courts for an extension until early 2006 before presenting its plan.

In the meantime, the airline has made several significant changes, which it hopes will lead it to profitability once again. It has downsized dramatically. Thousands of workers have been furloughed; the company, itself, has restructured; hundreds of flights have been taken off the schedule; service has been discontinued to several domestic and international destinations; ticket offices have been closed; the airline has substituted its larger jet service to many cities by much smaller jets operated by regional carriers under the United Express brand; it has created a new low-cost airline called "Ted" (Ted, being the last part of the word United); and has won major salary concessions from its several groups of unionized employee groups. Most recently, and perhaps most significantly, it has cancelled its obligations under union contract to finance its employees' pension programs.

Clearly, under Tilton, United has tried very hard to cut costs and reorganize to become more efficient. However, many of these changes have come with a significant cost. Employees are generally demoralized and many are either seeking other jobs within the industry or other jobs outside the industry. Passenger service has deteriorated in several markets either due to cancellation of service, down-sizing of service, or service provided by disgruntled employees. Airport authorities (and the cities that own or license them) have had to renegotiate landing rights, landing fees, and gate fees. Some major cities (such as Denver, United's secondary hub airport) has been threatened with United closing its hub at that location (potentially costing thousands of people their jobs, as well as significantly reducing service to the Mile High City). While Tilton remains, many of the top officers and managers at United have been fired or placed in lower-level positions. Quietly, creditors sit on the sidelines, wondering what will happen with the money owed them, and everyone involved with United (customers, employees, managers, creditors, airline partners, competitors, host cities, and many others) are constantly reminded that United could go into dissolution even yet.

Still, United continues to fly, and has actually grown in some markets. For example, it has recently significantly increased its service from the U.S. to Asia, adding several flights to Japan and China. It has even begun service to Ho Chi Mien City (formerly Saigon) in Viet Nam – the only U.S. carrier to now fly to this rapidly growing commercial center. Service to Europe has been virtually unchanged (a few changes have occurred such as dropping Milan, Italy and adding Zurich, Switzerland to the schedule), as has been true of service to Central and South America. This reflects one of the lessons United has learned – the increasing international traffic has proven to be very lucrative, while many domestic routes are money pits. This is particularly interesting when one considered that in the reorganization of United, it went from a multi-divisional structure (which the literature tells us is necessary to operate both a domestic and an international operation) to a functional structure (which the literature tells us is most often best for single-business types of companies). Clearly, United is not following the conventional strategic management theories as it struggles to survive. In terms of its future, we suggest that the jury is still out. Can United overcome its massive problems and survive? Can the airline create a new strategic model that will prove useful to itself and others in the industry, or will its lack of theory-based strategy lead to its ultimate demise? As we say, the jury is still out.

Endnotes

---

[1] United Airlines 10-K405, Filed with the SEC on 2/8/02
[2] "United Files for Bankruptcy,"
http://www.msnbc.com/news/844914.asp?vts=120920020910&cp1=1
[3] ibid.

[4] H. Igor Ansoff (1984). *Implanting Strategic Management.* Englewood Cliffs, N.J.: Prentice-Hall.
[5] Avinash Dixit and Barry Nalebuff (1991). *Thinking Strategically: The Competitive Edge in Business, Politics, and Everyday Life.* New York: W.W. Norton and Company.
[6] Raymond E. Miles and Charles C. Snow (1984). "Fit, Failure and the Hall of Fame" *California Management Review* (Spring) Volume 26, Number 3, 10-28.
[7] Kenneth R. Andrews (1987). *The Concept of Corporate Strategy.* 3rd Edition. Homewood, Ill.: Irwin.
[8] Henry Mintzberg (1985). "Strategy Concept I: Five P's for Strategy" *California Management Review* (Spring) Volume 30, Number 1, 62-73.
[9] Thomas J. Peters and Robert H. Waterman, Jr. (1982). *In Search Of Excellence: Lessons from America's Best-Run Companies.* New York: Harper & Row.
[10] http://www.starbucks.com/aboutus/overview.asp, May 19, 2003.
[11] Michael C. White, Mark Smith, and Tim Barnett (1994). "Strategy Inertia: The Enduring Impact of CEO Specialization and Strategy on Following Strategies" *Journal of Business Research* (September) Volume 31, Issue 1, 11-22.
[12] http://media.corporate-ir.net/media_files/NYS/UAL/reports/10K_03282003.pdf, May 19, 2003, p.2.
[13] Paul J. Stonich (ed.) (1982). *Implementing Strategy: Making Strategy Happen.* Cambridge, Mass.: Ballinger Publishing Company.
[14] Lawrence Smircich and Charles Stubbart (1985). "Strategic Management in an Enacted World" *Academy of Management Review* Volume 10, 724-736.
[15] Herbert A. Simon (1976). *Administrative Behavior: A Study of Decision-Making Processes in Administrative Organization.* 3rd Edition. New York: The Free Press.
[16] Henry Mintzberg, 1985.
[17] Jeffrey R. Cornwall and Baron Perlman (1990). *Organizational Entrepreneurship.* Homewood, Ill: Irwin, p. 180.
[18] Ibid.

[19] John K. Ryans, Jr. and William L. Shanklin (1985). *Strategic Planning: Concepts and Implementation.* New York: Random House.
[20] Lawrence G. Hrebiniak and William F. Joyce (1984). *Implementing Strategy.* New York: Macmillan Publishing Company.
[21] Jones, Gareth R. (2004). *Organizational Theory, Design, and Change: Text and Cases.* 4th Edition. Upper Saddle River, N.J.: Prentice-Hall.
[22] This is not to say that firms with plans are always successful and firms without plans unsuccessful. Much of the literature in the field, however, denotes that firms with plans tend to outperform those without plans. See chapter five's discussion on strategic approaches and generic strategies.
[23] Ronald N. Taylor (1984). *Behavioral Decision Making.* Glenview, Ill.: Scott, Foresman and Company.
[24] E. Frank Harrison (1987). *The Managerial Decision-making Process.* 3rd Edition. Boston, Mass.: Houghton Mifflin Company.
[25] Herbert A. Simon (1976). *Administrative Behavior: A Study of Decision-Making Processes in Administrative Organization.* 3rd Edition. New York: The Free Press.
[26] Ibid.
[27] Kurt Lewin (1951). *Field Theory in Social Science.* New York: Harper and Row.
[28] Robin Hogarth (1980). *Judgment and Choice.* New York: John Wiley and Sons.
[29] Irving L. Janis (1971). "Groupthink" *Psychology Today Magazine* (November), 43-46, 74-76.
[30] Henry Mintzberg (1978). "Patterns of Strategy Formation" *Management Science* 24, 934-948.
[31] Ibid.
[32] Michael Dolence, Daniel J. Rowley, and Herman D. Lujan (1997). *Working Toward Strategic Change: A Step-by-Step Guide to the Planning Process.* San Francisco, Ca.: Jossey-Bass Publishers.
[33] Peter F. Drucker (1954). *The Practice of Management: A Study of the Most Important Function in American Society.* New York: Harper & Row.

[34] Darryl J. Ellis and Peter P. Pekar, Jr. (1980). *Planning Basics for Managers.* New York: Amacom.

[35] Rowley and Sherman, 2001; J..M. Bryson (1995). *Strategic Planning for Public and Nonprofit Organisations.* San Francisco: Jossey-Bass; Paul C. Nutt and Robert W. Backoff (1992). *Strategic Management of Pubic and Third Sector Organizations: A Handbook for Leaders.* San Francisco, Ca.: Jossey-Bass; Peter M. Ginter, Linda M. Swayne, and W. Jack Duncan (1998). *Strategic Management of Health Care Organizations.* 3rd Edition. Oxford, England: Blackwell Publishers Ltd.

[36] Rosabeth M. Kanter (1983). *The Change Masters.* New York: Simon and Schuster.

[37] Kurt Lewin (1951). *"Field Theory in Social Science"* in D. Cartwright (ed.) *Selected Papers.* New York: Harper.

[38] Robert E. Quinn, Sue R. Faerman, Michael P. Thompson, and Michael R. McGrath (2003). *Becoming a Master Manager: A Competency Framework.* 3rd Edition. New York: John Wiley & Sons, Inc.

[39] Tom Peters (1987). *Thriving on Chaos: Handbook for a Management Revolution.* New York: Alfred A. Knopf, Inc.

[40] Robert Birnbaum (2000). *Management Fads in Higher Education: Where They Come From, What They Do, Why They Fail.* San Francisco, Ca.: Jossey-Bass, Inc.

[41] Richard E. Boyatzis (1982). *The Competent Manager: A Model for Effective Performance.* New York: John Wiley & Sons, Inc.

[42] Robert L. Katz (1974). "The Skills of an Effective Administrator" *Harvard Business Review* (Sept./Oct.) Volume 52, Issue. 5, 90-101.

[43] Debra J. Housel (2002). *Team Dynamics.* Cincinnati, Oh.: South-Western Educational Publishing.

[44] Peter M. Senge (1990). *The Fifth Discipline: The Art and Practice of the Learning Organization.* New York: Doubleday.

[45] Chris Argyris (1990). *Overcoming Organizational Defenses: Facilitating Organizational Learning.* Englewood Cliffs: Prentice-Hall.

[46] Bo Hedberg and Sten Jönsson (1989). "Between myth and action" *Scandinavian Journal of Management.* Volume 5, Issue 3, 177-185.

[47] Jay R. Galbraith (2002). *Designing Organizations: An Executive Guide to Strategy, Structure, and Process.* San Francisco: Jossey-Bass.
[48] Edgar H. Schein (1992). *Organizational Culture and Leadership.* San Francisco: Jossey-Bass.
[49] Steven W. Floyd and Bill Wooldridge (2000). *Building Strategy from the Middle: Reconceptualizing Strategy Process.* Thousands Oaks, Ca.: Sage Publications, Inc.
[50] Darryl J. Ellis and Peter P. Pekar, Jr. (1980). *Planning Basics for Managers.* New York: AMACOM.
[51] http://www.cinema-scoping.com/web_pages/emperorsclub.html, Tuesday, May 20, 2003.
[52] Michael I. Harrison (1987). *Diagnosing Organizations: Methods, Models, and Processes.* Newbury Park, Ca.: Sage Publications, Inc.
[53] Chester P. Barnard (1938). *The Functions of the Executive.* Cambridge, Mass.: Harvard University Press.
[54] Thomas S. Batemen and Scott A. Snell (2004). *Management: The New Competitive Landscape.* 6th Edition. McGraw-Hill Irwin.
[55] Daniel J. Rowley and Herbert Sherman (2001). *From Strategy to Change: Implementing the Plan in Higher Education.* San Francisco, Ca.: Jossey-Bass.
[56] http://www.att.com/ar-2002/html/cl1.html, May 27, 2003.
[57] H. Igor Ansoff (1984). *Implanting Strategic Management.* Englewood Cliffs, N.J.: Prentice/Hall International.
[58] ibid
[59] Uma Sekaran (2003). *Research Methods For Business: A Skill Building Approach.* 4th Edition. New York: John Wiley & Sons, Inc.
[60] Henry C. Lucas, Jr. (1999). *Information Technology and the Productivity Paradox: Assessing the Value of Investing in IT.* New York: Oxford University Press.
[61] http://www.cia.gov/terrorism/, May 27, 2003.
[62] Modified from R.J. Lewicki, D.D. Bowen, D.T. Hall, and F.S. Hall (1988). *Experience in Management and Organizational Behavior.* New York: John Wiley and Sons, Inc., 224-227.
[63] Warren G. Bennis, Kenneth D. Benne, and Robert Chin (1969). *The Planning of Change.* 2nd Edition. New York: Holt, Rinehart, and Winston, Inc.

[64] Thomas J. Peters and Robert H. Waterman, Jr. (1982). *In Search of Excellence: Lessons from America's Best-Run Companies.* New York: Harper and Row, Publishers.

[65] Wendell L. French and Cecil H. Bell, Jr. (1995). *Organization Development: Behavioral Science Interventions for Organization Improvement.* 5th Edition. Upper Saddle River, N.J.: Prentice Hall, p. 25.

[66] Newton Margulies and John Wallace (1973). *Organizational Change: Techniques and Applications.* Glenview, Ill.: Scott, Foresman and Company.

[67] Craig R. Hickman and Michael A. Silva (1984). *Creating Excellence: Managing Corporate Culture, Strategy, and Change in the New Age.* New York: NAL Books.

[68] Warren G. Bennis (1969). *Organization Development: Its Nature, Origins, and Prospects.* Reading, Mass.: Addison-Wesley Publishing Company, p.2.

[69] Alvin Toffler (1990). *Power Shift: Knowledge, Wealth, and Violence at the Edge of the 21st Century.* New York: Bantam Books.

[70] Michael Beer (1980). *Organization Change and Development: A Systems View.* Glenview, Ill.: Scott, Foresman and Company.

[71] Michael I. Harrison (1987). *Diagnosing Organizations: Methods, Models and Processes.* Newbury Park: Ca.: Sage Publications.

[72] Daniel J. Rowley and Herbert Sherman (2001). *From Strategy to Change: Implementing the Plan in Higher Education.* San Francisco, Ca.: Jossey-Bass, Inc.

[73] Pierre Mourier and Martin Smith (2001). *Conquering Organizational Change: How to Succeed Where Most Companies Fail.* Atlanta, Ga.: CEP Press.

[74] Alvar Elbing (1978). *Behavioral Decisions in Organizations.* 2nd Edition. Glenview, Ill.: Scott, Foresman and Company.

[75] Michael I. Harrison, 1987.

[76] Stephen R. Michael (1981). "Techniques of Organizational Change: A Summary" in Stephen R. Michael, Fred Luthans, George S. Odiorne, W. Warner Burke and Spencer Hayden (eds.) *Techniques of Organizational Change.* New York: McGraw-Hill Book Company, 331-344.

[77] French and Bell, 1995.

[78] Chris Argyris (1982). *Reasoning, Learning and Action: Individual and Organizational.* San Francisco, Ca.: Jossey-Bass Publishers.

[79] Ibid.

∞ Chapter Two ∞
Mission, Goals and Objectives

Chapter Objectives

1. To develop an appreciation for the importance of organizational mission.
2. To see the relationship between an organizational mission, its vision, its values, and its goals and objectives.
3. To create a connection between strategic goal, operational goals, and underlying goals.
4. To recognize the importance of corporate governance and understand its role in the strategic planning and strategic management process of the firm.

Introductory Case: Enron

Enron was created through the merger in 1986 of InterNorth and Houston Natural Gas, two natural gas companies. Under deregulation, Enron appeared to have found the keys of success in rapidly growing to become one of the nation's largest gas and oil companies as well as showing impressive profits year after year. Under the leadership of CEO Kenneth Lay, Enron soon became a darling of Wall Street and in the 1990s was called one of the country's most admired companies by *Fortune Magazine.*[1]

During the final decade of the 20th Century, Enron continued its impressive growth and reported much higher than average profits in the industry. Its management was touted as both innovative and insightful and many brokerage houses classified Enron as a definite "Buy" for its clients. But in a relatively short period between 2001 and 2002, revelations about how Enron had handled its business activities over the preceding 15 years came to light. Enron had been engaged in very risky financial management practices and had been misreporting its profits and other financial indicators for several years. Overnight, Enron went from being one of the most highly respected and profitable companies to one rated toward the bottom of several Wall Street ranking systems. Soon, the company was forced into one of the largest bankruptcies in history and many of its top decision makers were facing jail time. What went wrong so quickly? Why didn't all the Wall Street analysts see what was happening and provide warning? What happened internally to allow such deception and lead to such a disastrous outcome?

The answers to these questions create some interesting insights, not only into the bad management of Enron, but also into the basic corporate decision-making process itself. As bad as the Enron debacle was, analysis reveals that several other companies could venture into the murky world of factoring and derivatives and potentially misrepresent their performance to shareholders, bondholders, and regulators.

The problems began in 1989, when Enron created a financial management company called GasBank, which eventually became

Enron Capital and Trade Resources (ETC), whose purpose was to hedge risk for natural gas producers and other suppliers. Jeffrey Skilling was hired as CEO of ETC, and he hired Andrew Fastow. ETC provided financial and risk management services for Enron and engaged in a scheme referred to as "asset securitization," which involved selling the rights to sell future cash flows. Future cash flows can be represented as current assets and have the impact of improving profitability. There are quite a few other financial management schemes that Skilling and Fastow adopted to inflate Enron's representation of its financial performance. ETC used asset securitization in Enron's natural gas and oil divisions, thereby reducing Enron's risk rate and cost of financing, while overstating actual profits. As these practices grew and Enron was able to attract more and more investment, it grew into a position where it could begin to buy or trade nearly anything shifting the firm's mission from a natural gas and oil business to a commodities trading firm.

Enron adopted a "mark-to-market" accounting system, which some Wall Street firms use to obtain reference points for valuing securities. Prices, however, are determined by the computer and not the market, which has the effect of over-valuing securities. Along with the swap and securitization practices, the ground was set for financial disaster. Enron needed to maintain a high credit rating in order to successfully swap securities and commodities as a broker between two other traders. It had to keep its debt and ETC allowed Enron an opportunity to continually move debt off its balance sheet. This provided an illusion of liquidity.

As Enron's commodity markets began to mature, it had to deal more with market price rather than computer models and its profits began to sag. Skilling and Fastow created a group called the Friends of Enron and began to funnel money from Enron through their friends who made investments on Enron's behalf with Enron having to only put up 3% of the investment (for many of these investment opportunities, Fastow in particular received gifts from the Friends for providing the opportunities). In investment banking activities, Enron found a way of making loans from investment bankers, but booking the cash as highly profitable sales. Finally, Enron was able to book $1.4 Billion through six different investment houses.[2]

Enron was run by business-schooled trained MBAs instead of by utility executives. They quickly lost sight of their primary business and created a financial empire based on shoddy and highly questionable finance opportunities and reporting practices. Since they were successful, they were also arrogant.[3] In late 2000, credit problems reached a climax and Enron began a series of restructurings which revealed its problems to the world, including the practice of showing promissory notes as owners' equity. Enron tried to merge with Dynegy to help solve many of its problems but the merger died because Enron failed to properly disclose many of its finances (as it had done successfully for the past several years). This time, however the SEC was involved and Standard & Poor's on November 28, 2001 reduced Enron's bonds to junk status, and 4 days later on December 2, 2001, Enron filed for bankruptcy.

One of the sad side issues of the Enron story is that of its accounting firm, Arthur Anderson and Company. Evidence has come to light that several account executives at Anderson not only knew of the shoddy financial businesses practices of Enron, but also covered them up in official reports and filing, and then actively engaged in the shredding of evidence when Enron's major problems began to come to light. An investigation revealed that Anderson was an active accomplice in many of Enron's illegal and unethical acts and Anderson has now gone out of business.

Confirming the Corporate Mission

Step 1 in the strategic planning/management process essentially establishes the mission and goals of the company. As Figure 2.1 suggests, this next stage of the strategic planning process involves the development and confirmation of the firm's mission, vision, values, goals, objectives, and policies.

Figure 2.1
The Strategic Planning Process
Step 1 – Determining the Firm's Mission, Vision, Values, Goals, Objectives, Policies, Procedures, and Rules

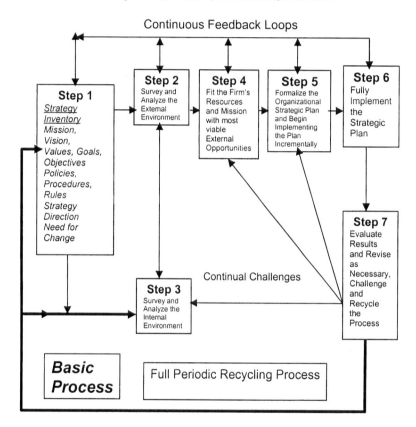

In Chapter 1, we stated that every company has a mission, whether they understand it clearly or not. In that discussion, we stated that it was important that a firm identify its current mission as it began to contemplate the strategic planning process. In this chapter, we go further. It is now time for strategic planners to solidify the mission of the firm (and perhaps revise it based upon a subsequent SWOT analysis). This is important because without a full commitment to a solid mission, the planning process will be significantly flawed.

The Enron case, which we began this chapter with, demonstrates the importance of this point. Why did Enron change its mission from an energy supplier to a financial management firm? Was management aware of the mission shift? If they were aware, why did management feel it could operate under this new mission in secrecy, even in the face of poignant questions from its own stockholders? What were managements' values? What led Enron managers to behave in such unethical and unacceptable manner, and to be arrogant about it? What was the vision of its leaders, and was this vision consistent with stockholders, customers, bondholders, and regulatory agencies? And perhaps more importantly, how can other firms avoid the pitfalls that Enron fell into, operate in a manner that produces profitability without damaging other firms or stakeholders, while maintaining the highest principles of morals and ethics?

We believe that many of the answers to these questions may be founding in the lack of a clear understanding by the top managers of Enron in terms of the company's mission, vision, values, and goals and how its strategic plan delineates the guiding principles of its operations. Well-managed companies that have a solid strategic management process in place are not likely to make this mistake. If a company's management system is based on well-understood directions and values, it is less likely to involve itself in some of the operations or secretive deals that allowed Enron and Arthur Anderson to break the law.

The guiding principle of any organization is embodied in the organization's mission. Simply, **a mission is the *purpose* and *direction* an organization pursues as derived from its vision and values** (and revised based upon the results of a subsequent SWOT analysis). The mission sets the stage for developing goals, objectives, and operational activities that enact the firm's strategic direction (as Figure 2.2 presents).[4] The mission should be well known by all stakeholders and well supported by internal and external stakeholders alike. An organizational mission should be the first and basic definition of what a firm does and what it hopes to achieve through its operations over time.

definition of what a firm does and what it hopes to achieve through its operations over time.

Figure 2.2
Determinants of the Strategic Direction

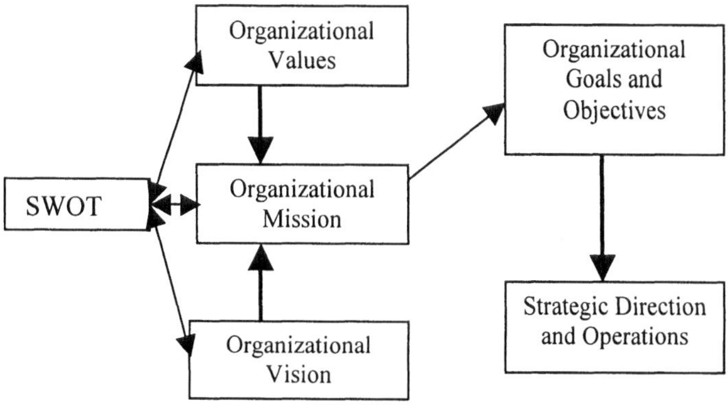

```
                   ┌──────────────┐
                   │Organizational│              ┌──────────────┐
                   │    Values    │              │Organizational│
                   └──────────────┘              │  Goals and   │
                          │                      │  Objectives  │
                          ▼                      └──────────────┘
 ┌────────┐        ┌──────────────┐                     │
 │  SWOT  │◄──────►│Organizational│─────────────►       │
 └────────┘        │   Mission    │                     ▼
                   └──────────────┘              ┌──────────────┐
                          ▲                      │Strategic Direction│
                          │                      │ and Operations │
                   ┌──────────────┐              └──────────────┘
                   │Organizational│
                   │    Vision    │
                   └──────────────┘
```

The Importance of an Organizational Mission

An organizational mission defines the organization. Many times it is obvious, while in other instances it is not. For example, the authors of this book have also done extensive work in the strategic management of colleges and universities and have developed an appreciation for the fact that the central mission of institutions of higher education is essentially the same for all; the development and dissemination of knowledge.[5] Most traditional colleges and universities exist to deliver education to post-secondary school students, do research to discover new knowledge bases, and provide service to its relevant service area. There are today several derivations of the traditional model, such as community colleges, for-profit colleges and universities that do not have the research component, and may only offer an educational component. Even some more traditional colleges and universities have specialized into teaching institutions,

This is important because when one tries to classify a successful college or university, one does not expect to find other activities going on (say investing foundation funds in automobile manufacturing rather than in scholarships and research support) that do not directly contribute to its central purpose and direction. Well-run institutions of higher education use all of their resources to support their central mission: education, research, and service.

In the Enron example, the original mission of the company was to be a natural gas and oil company. Without input from stakeholders (especially shareholders), top management of Enron decided it wanted to become a financial holding company, and did most of its activities behind closed doors. As a result, the public mission (the mission described in its annual statements and 10k reports) of the company and the private mission of the company were dramatically different. Since vision and values support the mission, imagine the confusion throughout the company as the natural gas and oil divisions began to compete with the various financial schemes of the company for resources. It certainly was not clear how becoming a financial management company might fit into the vision of being a power supply company nor how hiding this mission-shift from stockholders would uphold basic core business values such as honesty and integrity. When things got so bad for the company that it had to begin to reveal its actual operations and practices, no wonder so many employees, stockholders, and other stakeholders became so irate.

Organizational Values. The first element constituting an organizational mission is that of values. **Values set the tone for organizational operation** *by defining what is considered right and wrong in the organization*[7] **and what the members of the organization think is important.** For example, faculty at small colleges and universities think that class size is an important college priority allowing more personalized instruction, while faculty at research-oriented institutions put far greater emphasis on support services for research (facilities, equipment, personnel, etc.). Values should emanate from top management since top management should set the general tone that the organization members look to for guidance. Often, however, values emanate from the prevailing culture of the organization; i.e. the way things have been done historically that create a pattern of activity.[8]

The values that organizations members share serve at least three purposes. First, they assist in communicating what the organization values and in shaping employee behavior. Faculty at research institutions may teach two or three courses a year while faculty at small colleges may teach upwards of eight different courses. Values serve as guideposts for managerial decisions and actions. A second purpose of shared values is to build team spirit. When employees embrace stated corporate values, they develop deeper commitment to their work and take responsibility for their actions. Employees are more enthusiastic about doing things they support and believe in. Third, shared values also influence marketing efforts. Corporate behavior is the best indication of what the company values most. This was clearly demonstrated at Enron. Behavior is visible to the public and can foster a positive image if perceived as sincere.[9]

The Disney Company, for example, continues to express many of the values of its founder, Walt Disney, that the company should produce family-oriented entertainment experiences. It was this set of values that helped build the company, and which most of the early employees bought into fully. With the death of Walt, the company tried to follow his value system (the only one they had known, and the one that had brought them the high levels of success that it had experienced over the years).[10]

Disney also demonstrates that values can change over time due to both internal and external pressures. The current Disney Company has a variety of new values, the result of new management, especially that of Michael Eisner, who saw that the company needed to expand its activities into areas that were not necessarily related to pure family values. Touchstone Pictures was created to provide new movie products that would appeal to publics beyond that of families. There was a certain amount of furor as Touchstone produced movies that incorporated adult themes and coarse language, not the types of films a family would want to take its children who were less than 10 years of age. Then, isn't this an example of conflicting values and a serious change of direction for a basically good company?

Values of the firm are highly embedded and are in general the most difficult factor to change in a firm.[11] Disney did not completely cast-off its family values orientation and move into hardcore adult entertainment (X-rated movies, gambling, selling alcohol, etc...) although Disney did expand into new directions in order to survive.[12] Disney fully understood that the values that would support the original Disney Company were different but not antithetical to those that would support Touchstone Pictures. Today, the Disney Movie Division continues to produce films that uphold all of the original values of Walt Disney and the employees who have come after. Touchstone is also clear about its mission and values and has built organizational structures that uniquely support it,[13] including R rated films.[14] The corporate level of the Disney Company has carefully grown its various divisions (which also include theme parks, the ABC Television Network, ESPN, and other entertainment venues), with its own goals, operations, and values. In keeping these entities separate and controlled, the overall operation works by allowing for the broadening of Disney's original values around a core of ideals.

The Elements of an Organizational Vision. Values set the stage; vision begins the play. One of the most important tasks of organizational leadership is to define the organization vision as it sees it and as it intends to play it out.[15] As the nation expects its President to present his vision for the county over the next four years in the Inaugural State of the Union Address, firm stakeholders expect some indication from its corporate and strategic leaders as to what it sees as the central direction the firm should pursue for the next year (or several years). Such pronouncements might be found in the annual report of the corporation for publicly traded companies or it might be found in the company's advertising or other marketing efforts (such as "GE brings good things to life", or "Dupont's better living through chemistry", etc.). For not-for-profit organizations it might appear in the speeches of potential organizational officers as they campaign for office.

What vision includes is what leadership believes are worthy purposes and objectives to aspire to within a given time period and *how the leadership feels the organization can achieve those objectives*. These should be short, inspiring statements that help operational managers to begin to establish the specific objectives and goals they will incorporate in their annual planning scenarios (one very good example being Martin Luther King's "I have a dream" speech).[16] For a government example, John F. Kennedy in 1961 proposed that the United States put a man on the moon by the end of the decade. This set into play congressional committees, specific programming in NASA and its sub-contractors, and, more importantly, the excitement of the American public who were somewhat demoralized by the success in space of our political and ideological competitors in the Soviet Union. Unfortunately, John Kennedy didn't live to see his vision realized, but when Neil Armstrong became the first person to set foot on the surface of the moon in the summer of 1969, the entire world marveled at the dedication and the resolve to succeed that it had taken to achieve such a major governmental goal. In a similar fashion, Microsoft's Bill Gates has called for the development of inexpensive computers, easy access to the Internet, and educational software packages that will allow for all children to become integral parts of the emerging Information Age.[17] This is a broad and noble vision and will impact the activities of Microsoft over the next several years as it develops the technological capability of fulfilling Gates' vision.

These two examples are grand examples of vision. Most organizations look for and depend on far lesser vision scopes to help guide operational planning and operations. For example, in 1985, General Motors (GM) announced that it wanted to produce a whole new class of automobile as its first fully-internally-developed car. This was a sort of revolution for GM in the way it had developed its products, but was seen as a method of helping it recover some of its lost prestige and momentum that had occurred as a result of two major energy crises of the 1970s. In 1990, it rolled out its first new Saturn automobile,[18] the result of major capital investment, research and development, and new operational processes.

The Elements of an Organizational Mission. The two parts of an organizational mission, Purpose and Direction, should be central to all operations. Purpose is the more straightforward of the two. **The Purpose of a firm is why it exists and what it tries to do beyond the basics of its survival and profit motives.**[19] In defining purpose, it is important to ask, "who are our customers?" and "how can we best serve them?" For businesses, their purpose should include the firm's long-term vision and values, their concern for their public image, and their definition of who their key customers and other stakeholders are (who are they responsible for?).[20] Secondly, firms must define, as part of their purpose, their basic activities, products, and operating domain.[21] Businesses need to answer questions such as: who is our customer/market, what is our product(s)/service(s), are we supplying technologically-based services,[22] and how do we accomplish our basic purpose.

Direction is the other factor underlying mission. While purpose is generally evident in most organizations, direction is less well defined. It's analogous to the old question, "What do you want to be when you grow up?" Growing up is the purpose of existence, what one wants to be is far less obvious. **For organizations, Direction can be most easily defined as what they hope to accomplish over the course of their existence.** For example, Hewlett-Packard's mission includes becoming the "leading provider of products, technologies, solutions and services to consumers and business"[23], for Ford it is to turn into "the world's leading consumer company for automotive products and services"[24], and for Coca-Cola it is to maintain being the "world's leading manufacturer, marketer, and distributor of nonalcoholic beverage concentrates and syrups."[25] Having a clear and concise direction as an ingrained part of the firm's purpose is a critical factor for creating organizational excellence.[26]

The Role of Stakeholders (Internal and External). Strategic planning revolves around the needs and wants of its stakeholders. We define the term stakeholders as those groups and/or individuals who have an interest (economic, political, or social) in the organization. Internal stakeholders include employees, managers, executives, and board members while external stakeholders include customers, consumers, competitors, suppliers, creditors, regulatory agencies, unions, politicians, the local community, and society in general.[27] Because of the firm's dependency upon these stakeholders for resources, these stakeholders tend to have a large say in the mission, vision, and values of any organization.

Many authors of several strategic management texts support the notion that strategic planning should begin with the mission of the firm.[28] This is also a notion that is generally supported by many businesses and organizations. For example, though it is now changing, the more recent standards for accreditation by the AACSB (American Assembly of Colleges and Schools of Business) have been based upon a mission-driven application for accreditation.[29]

Several authors of strategic management texts have come to question a purely mission-driven approach.[30]   They believe that mission-driven strategic planning is somewhat flawed because it treats the firm's mission as inflexible and indifferent to the marketplace and the firm's stakeholders. As the tastes, needs, and wants of stakeholder groups change, the organizations that serve them must change as well. This means that the basic components of a firm such as its mission, and vision, need to be responsive to stakeholders. Even values of firms may change over time, as noted in the Enron and Disney examples above. Firms that cannot change their basic mission or vision are stuck finding markets or market segments that fit their original purpose – this limits their strategic opportunities and in the long run, their chances to survive.

When a company making the proverbial buggy whip continues to exist after the need for buggy whips has passed, it could be classified as existing without a consumer-based purpose. The market-driven approach in developing a mission is a practical supplement to firms that possess internally driven missions. This approach allows the firm to adapt to its environment if the firm does not have the ability to change the environment it is in to fit its mission or find a suitable alternative market segment.[31] Adaptation to change is one of the cornerstones of good strategic planning and successful strategic management.

Both external and internal stakeholders impact the specifics of the firm's mission, vision, and values. Simply, an organization cannot do that for which it does not have the adequate resources, drive, competencies, and internal/external market support to perform. Had President Kennedy not known that he had the support in Congress and the American public, the burgeoning resources of a growing economy, and the capabilities in NASA to produce a successful program that would eventually land a man on the moon and bring him back safely, he would never have expressed that as an important goal for the United

States. A small country such as Ecuador could never have pulled off such an accomplishment.

Internal stakeholders, such as employees and managers, must subscribe to the vision and values of top management in order for the firm to properly implement its strategy (which we describe further in Chapter 7) while executives and boards of directors have been empowered by the stockholders to mold a mission that will produce higher than average returns on investment (see corporate governance, below) while maintaining company moral values. Suppliers, customers, unions, the local economy, and society in general also mold the mission, vision, and values of the firm. What is considered proper behavior for conducting business in one country (i.e. providing gifts to hosts) or even one firm may be considered unethical or even illegal in another. This becomes a very large issue as firms broaden the scope of their mission through geographical area (move from a local, to regional, to national, to international, and finally to multinational operation) and will be discussed in more detail in Chapter 10.

Formal Mission Statements

Historically, most strategic planning activities involved the formulation and word-smithing of a particular statement of mission.[32] They were public documents that proclaimed the purpose and direction of the firm in all venues where that was appropriate. One could find statements of mission in annual statements, on company leader-head, on plaques in office lobbies, and in other publicly consumed venues, including the Internet.[33] Formal mission statements are common, but are they necessary?

There are many authors and managers that feel that a formal mission statement is important because it solidifies and legitimizes the true mission of a firm in a very public fashion.[34] Baetz and Bart worked on the issue of developing mission statements with 135 large Canadian organizations. Their results demonstrated that mission statements have been, by and large, used by 86 percent of the firms involved in their study. They reported that the main reasons for having mission statements in large firms were to: guide the strategic planning system; define the organization's scope of business operations/

activities; provide a common purpose/direction transcending individual and department needs; promote a sense of shared expectations among all levels of employees, thereby building a strong corporate culture (i.e. shared value); and finally, guide leadership style.[35] Analoui and Karami in a similar study reported that the majority of respondents (n = 89, 67 percent) considered a written and formal mission statement as an essential factor in increasing firm performance. Only 3 percent of respondents (n = 4) believed that having a mission statement did not play a significant role in developing firm strategies and achieving its objectives.[36]

Mission statements provide a readily identifiable visual statement that lets current and future stakeholders know precisely what the company is all about and where it is going. It provides a connection between the corporate entity, its employees, and its consumers. It provides a course of action that its strategic and operational managers can follow in playing out the long-term and short-term activities of the firm.[37] This course of thinking has been around for several years and as a result, thousands of companies and other organizations (including governmental organizations) proudly publish their mission statements and then stand behind them in many of their public records and pronouncements. Some interesting examples of mission statements are contained in Table 2.1.

Table 2.1
Examples of Company Mission Statements

Ben and Jerry's Ice Cream
"BEN & JERRY'S IS DEDICATED TO the creation & demonstration of a new corporate concept of linked prosperity. Our mission consists of three interrelated parts: Product Mission - To make, distribute & sell the finest quality all natural ice cream & euphoric concoctions with a continued commitment to incorporating wholesome, natural ingredients and promoting business practices that respect the Earth and the Environment; Economic Mission - To operate the Company on a sustainable financial basis of profitable

growth, increasing value for our stakeholders & expanding opportunities for development and career growth for our employees; and Social Mission - To operate the company in a way that actively recognizes the central role that business plays in society by initiating innovative ways to improve the quality of life locally, nationally & internationally."[38]

Sun Computers (Sun uses its vision statement as its mission statement)
VISION: The Network Is The Computer™ - "Sun was founded with one driving vision. A vision of computers that talk to each other no matter who built them. A vision in which technology works for you, not the other way around. While others protected proprietary, stand-alone architectures, we focused on taking companies into the network age, providing systems and software with the scalability and reliability needed to drive the electronic marketplace."[39]

Kodak Camera Company
"With <our> values in mind, we plan to grow more rapidly than our competitors by providing customers with the solutions they need to capture, store, process, output and communicate images— anywhere, anytime. We will derive our competitive advantage by delivering differentiated, cost-effective solutions—including consumables, hardware, software, systems and services—quickly and with flawless quality. All this is thanks to our diverse team of energetic, results-oriented employees with the world-class talent and skills necessary to sustain Kodak as the world leader in imaging."[40]

Enron
Even though Enron is in tremendous difficulties, as we

identified in the opening case, it does have a mission statement. The mission of Enron is: "Enron Energy Services is the leading provider of energy outsourcing products for the commercial and industrial customer markets. Enron is focused on bringing substantial savings to customers by achieving energy cost reductions and realizing economies of scale in service and equipment purchases."[41] They also state that their primary values are respect, integrity, communication, and excellence.

David and David noted that in writing a mission statement, the document should include the following nine components: Customers (the target market), Products/Services (offerings and value provided to customers), Geographic Markets (where the firm seeks customers), Technology (the technology used to produce and market products), Concern for Survival/Growth/ Profits (the firm's concern for financial soundness), Philosophy (the firm's values, ethics, beliefs), Public Image (contributions the firm makes to communities), Employees (the importance of managers and employees), and Distinctive Competence (how the firm is different or better than competitors). Their research indicated that there was an overall lack of completeness in mission statements amongst their sampled firms, a clear indication that business leaders needed to strive to create better mission documents. David and David incidentally rated Ben and Jerry's mission statement quite high while rating banks' statements quite low.[42]

There is an underlying assumption in the prior discussion that firms with poor or no mission statements under-perform firms with strong statements. Analoui and Karami reported on several research studies trying to link the presence and quality of a mission statement with corporate performance and indicated that studies by Pearce and David, and Bart and Baetz denoted that higher performing firms have comparatively more comprehensive mission statements yet other studies by David, Klemm et al., O'Gorman and Doran, and their own, most recent study, demonstrated no correlation between the quality of a mission statement and a firm's performance.[43]

A Trend Away From Mission Statements. Given the mixed research results, it is not surprising that some firms no longer publish mission statements, nor do they use them in their operational activities, either public or non-public.[44] Some of the reasons for this trend is that formal mission statements can suffer from several basic problems: 1) they are poorly written and do not lead to the public reception they are meant to lead to; 2) they change often enough that writing them down tends to be more cumbersome than helpful to the strategic management process; 3) the mission is so basic, that trying to put it into words is completely unnecessary; or 4) the mission statements are merely public relations pieces and have no strategic impact on the firm.

So, what is the overall conclusion? Fortunately, there is seldom a serious downside from either approach. Well-written and well-conceived mission statements can serve a positive value although some have received some very bad press.[45] At the same time, firms that choose not to engage in the activities that lead to the creation (or recreation) of a mission statement do not appear to suffer as a result.

To write a mission statement or not to write a mission statement is most likely an issue of how strategic planners and strategic managers perceive the value of going through the process of writing the statement. If the mission statement writing process engenders trust, allows for stakeholder participation and comment, and results in employees and other stakeholders understanding and supporting the mission of the firm, then the mission statement would have accomplished its real purpose – aligning the firm's purpose with its key stakeholders. In the long-run, writing or not writing a formal mission statement does not significantly impact the basic importance or activities of either strategic planning or strategic management.

Organizational Goals and Objectives

Mission, vision, and values create the framework and conceptual definitions for the organization. The next major issue is that of developing definitions of precisely what the firm should do to fulfill the conceptual set. This is done through the development of goals and objectives. Goals and objectives provide the specific outcomes that the firm knows will demonstrate that it is effectively fulfilling its mission.[46] They also provide definitions that define the operational activities of the organization. In this section, we will look at the role of goals and objectives in the both the strategic planning process as well as an integral part of the strategic management process as well.

Definitions of Goals and Objectives

The terms, "goals" and "objectives" are interpreted differently by different authors. Some suggest that objectives are the larger set, such as "the overall objective of our sales department for the next fiscal year is an increase of 8% over the current year's objectives" while the goals are far more specific in nature, such as "sales in our northeast sales area must increase by $1.2 Billion, sales in our southeast sales area must increase by $984 Million, and sales in our European sales division must increase by $3.3 Billion." Other authors have reversed the order of the terms. In fact, both terms basically describe the same thing, so to reduce confusion throughout this book, we will generally use the term objective, but will use either term as being essentially equivalent.

We define an objective, then, as a specific outcome that results from planned organizational activities and programs and which serves as a benchmark of organizational performance. Objectives enunciate the purposes and mission of the firm and provide milestones for its internal and external evaluation. In order to be useful, organizational objectives need to be measurable, time-specific, attainable, prioritized, acceptable to those who will be asked to achieve them, and related to overall firm performance.[47] Objectives can come in one of two varieties: *quantitative* and *qualitative*[48] and deal with profitability, productivity, competitive position, employee development, employee relations, technological leadership, and public responsibility.[49]

Quantitative objectives. Quantitative objectives are those that are directly measurable and can be expressed numerically. For example, setting a sales goal for a fiscal year of $5,450,000.00 is a quantitative objective. A well-run company will set a wide variety of quantitative objectives for all of its strategic and functional areas of operations. Stakeholders expect this, stockholders expect this, and managers and employees expect this. Not that the same isn't true for qualitative objectives, but quantitative objectives are clear, calculable, and provide direct measurements. They visibly allow firms to express what they hope to achieve in a given time frame and then, following the time frame, allow the firms to provide specific and direct data which allow for immediate comparison between the goal and the accomplishment.

Qualitative objectives. Qualitative objectives are those that measure quality and are difficult to measure directly or give a numerical value to. "We will provide the highest quality of customer service," is an example of a qualitative goal. This outcome of operations should be a high-level objective of any firm, but when it comes to measuring it, problems arise. Looking at the example we provide here, many problems are obvious:

- What is quality?
- Whose definition of quality should we go with?
- How can one know if one is delivering quality?
- How can one measure quality? and
- Will one evaluator's interpretation of quality be different from another evaluator?

As this example demonstrates, quality issues (including behavioral issues) are difficult to measure. Regardless, however, they are clearly important and firms need to develop some method of controlling and measuring them in order to account for all aspects of organizational activities. Many organizations use surrogate measures to convert qualitative objectives into measurable goals. For example, high quality customer service is important to Nordstrom. One surrogate measure that Nordstrom uses is the number of complaints it receives regarding both products and customer service. They can benchmark one year's number with subsequent years' numbers and draw a conclusion as to whether or not complaints (as a percentage of sales) goes up or down – a lower percentage of complaints implies higher quality customer service, where a higher percentage would suggest that quality might be going down. This is not an exact measure of high-level customer service and there may well be other surrogates that are better, but it is still a reasonable measure that provides some basic data that helps support the accomplishment at some level of an important qualitative objective.

Types of Objectives

As we suggested earlier, objectives can be a part of any area of an organization. Still, they should all be related to one another. There are two specific ways of classifying objectives that fit into the strategic management process – structural and time-relations. In this section, we develop these two dimensions of objectives and then show how they are related in combining the strategic and operational dimensions of the firm's objective set.

Figure 2.4
Hierarchy of Objectives

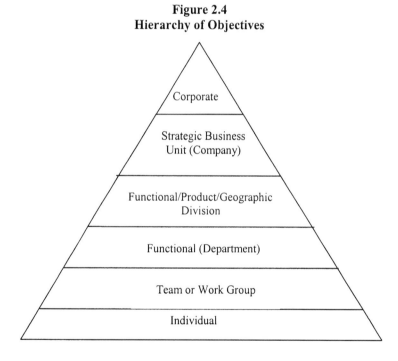

Hierarchy of Objectives. It is clear that the corporation must establish strategic or overall operational goals and objectives for the firm, especially a conglomerate corporation with unrelated businesses.

In order for the firm to reach these strategic objectives, strategic decision-makers must translate these objectives structurally into unit objectives, subunit objectives, functional objectives, team, and individual objectives (see Figure 2.4).[50]   When the hierarchy of organizational objectives is clearly defined, it forms an integrated network of objectives, or means-ends chains. The goals at a low level (means) must be achieved in order to reach the goals at the next level (ends).   And the accomplishment of goals at that level becomes the means to achieve goals at the next level (ends).   In other words, the organization functions as an interdependent system where the outcome of lower level systems becomes the input for higher level systems.

Corporate/Organizational Objectives.   The paramount purpose of a firm's strategic objectives is to help assure its survival. As we indicated in the last chapter, survival is a function of both growth and/or profitability.   Further, it is also important that the firm looks at these as long-term objectives.   Nearly all organizations must maintain long-term trends in both growth and profitability, and the only reasonable way they will be able to accomplish these critical objectives is to have created an effective strategic plan and instituted strategic management that will prudently oversee operations and test them against strategic objectives over time.

As we discussed in the previous chapter, *growth* and *profitability* are crucial outcomes from operations. These two measures are critical since investors will measure the performance of the firm in terms of the annual growth of the company (sales, assets, personnel, location, product line, etc.) and its overall profitability (as compared to prior years and industry averages).   When setting these objectives, the firm must temper the expectations and desires of stockholders and investor for high growth and strong profits with the firm's situation (as determined through the SWOT analysis).   For example, growth and profitability objectives are much easier to establish for a firm in a growth market with strong capabilities than for a firm in a slow or no growth market with little capabilities. Further, in developing and evaluating growth and profitability objectives, strategic decision-makers must use both internal and market driven benchmarks to help them determine the precise value of demonstrated growth and profits from the data they examine before and after budget year cycles.

General economic trends as measured by the Gross Domestic Product (GDP = consumption, investment, and government expenditures plus net exports)[51] and inflation, industry trends, as well as the company's historical trends must be factored into the establishment of corporate objectives.

Ultimately, it is investors who decide whether or not a firm has set and/or is making the level of growth and profits they expected when they purchased the stock. Depending on whether or not stockholders believe the firm can perform at the levels set by the firm over time will generally determine whether investors, buy, hold or sell the security. These decisions lead to the pricing of the stock and may impact the long-term strategic position of the firm (in terms of their ability to raise future capital through new stock offerings).

Competitive advantages may also be expressed as objectives for the firm. Issues such as market share, technological leadership, growth rates compared to the industry and specific competitors, and ability to generate excitement in the market are all objectives that impact a firm's competitive advantage. While none of these issues directly measures an outcome called competitive advantage, they are surrogates that help strategic decision-makers try to guide performance to achieve these characteristics that strongly imply a competitive advantage. More direct measures of competitive advantage may include patents, licenses, and other proprietary technology, operating cost efficiencies, and recognized measures of quality including ISO 9000 and the Malcolm Baldridge National Quality Award.[52] Measuring results, then, helps companies understand whether or not their plans have resulted in the outcomes they expected.

Finally, each firm's strategic health is also related to its overall position in achieving something called organizational effectiveness. Organizational effectiveness is an illusive term,[53] but generally refers to the capability of a firm to satisfy its stakeholders' goals and interests.[54] Regardless, as we have described in the first three chapters of this book, being in a position to satisfy stakeholder demands (customers, suppliers, stockholders, regulators, employees, and managers) is key to achieving an effective fit with a firm's environment. How do strategic decision-makers know when they have achieved overall effectiveness? Unfortunately, as Cameron has pointed out,[55] since there aren't direct measures of effectiveness, firms employ a multitude of surrogate measures. Factors such as increasing sales, low return rates, low complaints, few to no law-suits, low employee and managerial turnover, increasing stock pricing, and higher than average profitability are some of the major outcomes that, together, might be able to imply overall effectiveness. Though, while illusive, this objective is still one that strategic managers need to try to get a firm hold on.

Strategic Business Unit (SBU) Objectives. Multi-business firms, whether they are holding companies, concentrically diversified, horizontally or vertically integrated (see the discussion in Chapter 6 for a more comprehensive description), are corporations that own and operate several firms simultaneously. Individual firms in a portfolio must develop their own set of overall profit, growth, and competitive advantage objectives in order to contribute to the corporation's overall performance. For example, in the 2nd fiscal quarter of 2002 of Phillip Morris Inc. indicated the following performance of its strategic business units (see Table 2.2).

Table 2.2
Phillip Morris 2002 Second Quarter Incomes and Revenues by Strategic Business Unit[56]

Name of Strategic Business Unit	Net Revenues (in millions)	Net Revenue % Change from 2001	Operating Income (in millions)	Net Income % Change from 2001
P.M. USA – tobacco	$4,881	- 4.4%	$1,454	5.1%
P.M. Int'l – tobacco	$7,139	5.8%	$1,428	5.9%
Kraft Foods – N.A.	$5,568	0.4%	$1,444	6.0%
Kraft Foods Int'l	$1,945	-5.1%	$ 316	6.0%
Miller Brewing	$1,422	5.3%	$ 169	0.6%
P.M. Capital Corp.	$ 148	33.3%	$ 104	36.8%

Functional/Product/Geographic Division – each SBU within a holding company may have reporting structures by function, product, geographic area, or by customer (we describe this further in Chapter 6).[57] Customer, product, and geographic managers must convert the SBU's goals and objectives into more specific objectives for their own operational units. For example, Toyota Motors Corporation has 42 major overseas subsidiary corporations and 16 major overseas affiliates.[58] The North American Affiliate, one of the SBU's, is broken down into several companies that handle sales and service, manufacturing, research and development, and design.[59] Each of these divisions (in some cases separate companies) must also develop achievable goals and objectives.

Functional-Operational (Department), Team and Individual Objectives. In the operations of the firm, strategic objectives are broken down into functional areas where specific performance outcomes are important. Here, day-to-day operations occur as people do their individual jobs defined by their job descriptions and/or participate in team projects. From top-level (strategic) managers, mid-level and departmental managers coordinate the work of departments so that the daily work component fits within the strategic context. Yearly sales goals (that flow from the long-term sales expectations of the strategic plan) will be broken down for the sales and production departments to be further broken down all the way to individual employee responsibility areas. Coordinating and controlling these activities *should lead* to the accomplishment of prescribed personal, team, departmental, and overall objectives.[60]

What is the operative role in growth and/or profitability? While strategic planners will set the organizational-level objectives for growth and profits, the manner in which operational personnel and their teams conduct their day-to-day jobs will determine whether or not these organizational-level objectives will actually occur. Here, it's important that all members of a firm feel connected to the overall operation – that departmental employees not only understand that their work is part of the strategic direction of the firm, but that how they perform directly impacts upon the ability of the firm to reach its objectives. If everyone performs at a prescribed level, then the predictability of goal achievement is much greater, helping the firm reach its growth and profitability objectives. On the other hand, if everyone performs above expectation, the overall outcomes for the firm should be higher; just as if everyone performs below expectations, the overall outcomes will probably be lower. In developing an overall team attitude, strategic decision-makers can, then, help assure more positive outcomes than negative ones.

Efficiency, productivity, and effectiveness directly relate to profitability. The keys here are for mid-level and departmental managers to work with their employees to help assure that waste is avoided and motivation is high. Through honest and open communication, through inspiring leadership, and through sharing rewards, efficiency and effectiveness should follow. In those firms where these are problems, however, the firm might well hope to consider some of the issue-resolving techniques we present and elaborate on in Chapters 7 and 8. However team-building occurs, achieving a firm's strategic and operational objectives is dependent upon how well the firm functions as a single team.

Time-Related Objectives. Objectives are further broken down into *long-term, intermediate-term,* and *short-term* objectives. We depict the relationship between time-related and structural objectives in Figure 2.5.

Long-term objectives (the accomplishment of which may occur 5 or more years in the future) will most likely be those which are related to the strategic planning process. These types of objectives reflect crucial long-term accomplishment levels that strategic planners and strategic decision-makers come to believe will help the firm attain a competitive advantage. An example might be Disney's objective of being the world's largest entertainment company. This objective has both quantitative and qualitative components, but also reflects an important strategic objective. Unfortunately, there it little about this objective that might translate into day-to-day activities. Rather, operational employees are much more likely to concentrate on individual tasks and short-term objectives that will result in raises or promotions. Their actual participation in achieving the long-term strategic goal isn't that obvious to them. To the analyst, however, the relationship exists in the activities of strategic planners who not only

Figure 2.5
Time-Related vs. Function-Related Objectives

	Strategic	Operational
Long Term	Extremely Important	Very Low Importance
Intermediate Term	Moderately to Highly Important	Moderately Important
Short Term	Lower Levels of Importance	Extremely Important

define the long-term objectives, but then break them down into intermediate objectives and then into 1-year goals that break down even further to individual employee job expectations.[61]

Intermediate objectives are objectives that they hope the firm will achieve in 3 to 5 years, but which are an important incremental step toward achieving long-term objectives. They are important to the strategic planner because the performance toward achieving them in a 3 to 5 year time frame provides more reliable information as to actual trends than one year data readings tend to provide. For example, events such as September 11, 2001 tended to skew results data for many companies and industries that were hardly typical of normal performance. Decisions of strategic decision-makers regarding longer-term performance based on what may have happened in this one year would not represent actual trend performance. Most firms will recover from 2001, and if decision-makers were to discount this one year and try to draw more reliable outcomes from 3 to 5 year trends, they would most likely make better decisions. For the operational side, intermediate objectives help provide an important connection for employees to see how short-term objectives lead to higher-level organizational trends. This can help provide an important link between individual short-term performance and corporate long-term objectives.

Short-term objectives are extremely important for functional operatives. The traditional reward system of most organizations is related to one-year performance. People are used to one-year orientations in both setting their operational goals and in evaluating their performance. Since this core of a firm's human resource base falls into this category, it is easy to understand why most organizational incumbents have a short-term orientation. For the strategic decision-makers, it is important to have an appreciation for the short-term orientation of most of the firm's employees, but then be certain that short-term operational objectives fit within the firm's strategic intermediate and long-term objective sets. Beyond their relationship to long-term, intermediate, and short-term objective, there are also substantive differences between strategic and operational objective sets.

Management by Objectives (MBO). What we have described above is typical objective setting: senior managers set goals that are broken down into sub-goals for lower level managers to fulfill. Stated in broad terms, senior managers dictate the firm's strategic goals. At each level below the top tier, managers redefine these ambiguous statements into specific operational objectives. During this process of transposing goals into operational objectives, middle and lower level managers impose their biases, and beliefs. The danger here is that goal clarity can change during this process - lower level managers may change the intentions of senior management objectives. Similar to the game "telephone," where one person whispers a phrase into someone's ear until the last person repeats the phrase aloud, the initial and final phrases (objectives) often do not match. MBO takes a very different approach to goal setting. MBO is a system for setting performance objectives jointly be employees and their bosses. They periodically review progress toward goal accomplishment and this serves as the basis for allocating rewards. MBO uses goals to motivate and not just control performance.

Research has demonstrated that when senior management is committed and personally involved in implementing MBO programs, they significantly improve performance.[62]   This finding is not surprising, when one considers that during the MBO process employees have a say in determining what they will accomplish. After all, who knows what a person is capable of doing better than that person? Regardless of which method of goal setting organizations use, objectives are the driver of planning processes. It is imperative that senior managers safeguard the intention of their goals to facilitate middle   and   lower   managements'   effective   translation   and implementation.   Objectives   guide   managerial   activities   such   as budgeting, the development of action plans, staffing and other resource acquisition   decisions. The   organization's   success   then   ultimately depends on the combined outcomes of its interdependent functions and multiplicity of objectives.

Organizational Policies and Procedures

Once objectives have been formulated, the next step is to develop policies, procedures, and oftentimes rules. Policies and procedures abound in all organizations. They are useful to management in that they help in controlling the flow of activities and decisions. But what exactly are these aiding devices?

Policies are broad, general statements that outline the framework within which the objectives must be pursued. They provide boundaries for actions in recurring situations. Policies are not meant to be rigid, since the intent is to provide guidance to managers, but allow them a degree of flexibility. Policies are, therefore, the limits of managerial activities. An example of a simple policy is "Accept all product returns within seven days as long as it is accompanied by a sales receipt." This helps employees in processing returns. It helps to identify what they can and cannot due in every situation. If a person doesn't have a sales slip or returns an item after seven days, the matter must now be referred to a manager. The manager may or may not accept the exception to the policy.

A more detailed policy can be seen from the following example extracted from the City of Anacortes (Washington) nepotism personnel policy:

"Employees' relatives will not be employed by the city under any of the following circumstances:

1. Where on of the parties would have authority (or practical power) to supervise, appoint, remove, or discipline the other;
2. Where one party would be responsible for auditing the work of the other;
3. Where both parties would report to the same immediate supervisor. Every other option, including reassignment within the City workforce, would be considered in good faith before layoff;
4. Where other circumstances might lead to potential conflict among the parties between the interest of one or both parties and the best interests of the City; or
5. Where one of the parties is a department head of the City unless the mayor determines in writing that no potential problem or conflict of interest detrimental to the city exists. If two employees marry, become related or begin sharing living quarters with one another, and in the City's judgment, the potential problems noted above exist or reasonably could exist, only one of the employees will be permitted to stay with the City, unless reasonable accommodations, as determined by the Mayor or his designee, can be made to eliminate the potential problem. The decsion as to which relative may remain with the City must be made by the two employees within thirty (30) calendar days of the date they marry, become related, or begin sharing living quarters with each other. If no decision has been made during this time, the City reserves the right to terminate either employee."[63]

There exists a broad spectrum of reasons for policies. First, policies guide managerial action. Second, they prevent deviations from a predetermined course of action. Third, they permit standardization across all organizational units. Fourth, policies permit closer coordination, without direct interference from upper management. This allows for a greater degree of decentralization and frees top management to focus on more strategic issues. Lastly, they allow a greater amount of empowerment to employees.

Policies are usually contained within manuals for the entire company and perhaps for each department. It is the responsibility of employees to familiarize themselves with policies. Indeed orientation and training programs, as well as on the job training, present employees with polices and subsequent changes. When changes do happen, revisions are sent to all employees to update their manual. This may occur weekly, but usually is performed on a quarterly basis or as needed. More elaborate policies are developed over time, especially after occurrences happen in which no guidance is available.

Policy Types

Besides the simplistic categorization of policies into simple and complex, Filley and House[64] classified policies into three types. First, *Traditional Policies* are those formed from the history and tradition of the organization. Basically over time organizations carry a certain number of guidelines that exist just because they are there. Managers perpetuate this type and pass these policies on to newer managers, ensuring the continuation of the tradition. They have long outlived their usefulness and usually inhibit organizational effectiveness. An examination of an organization's manual will normally turn up a few of this type.

A second type is a *Policy by Fiat*. This category occurs from situations of uniqueness or confusion. When unexpected events happen, managers usually create an instant policy. To maintain order, managers, either individually or as a group, develop policies. Although managers think they are acting correctly, they fail to realize the impact on subordinates. First, most of the time the policy is not written down and thus, may not be implemented by new employees. Second, the policy is usually created by a single department or area and is unknown by other parts of the organization. Coordination and communication subsequently suffers. Third, the policy may be changed at any time by the manager, making it difficult for the subordinate to gauge expectations. Lastly, the more policies of this nature the greater the likelihood of the subordinate becoming a "yes" person and the obvious reduction in subordinate initiative and empowerment.

Rational Policies constitutes the last category. This type is what most people refer to when they use the term "policy." These policies normally emanated from the Board of Directors, top management, or any other governing entity, and permeate the entire organization. They may change as environmental disturbances arise. Such policies have the potential of evolving into traditional policies, unless they are monitored and updated periodically.

Procedures and Rules.   To efficiently achieve objectives, companies use procedures and rules. A *Procedure* is a set of detailed steps to achieve a specific purpose within a certain timeframe. Procedures develop over time as the same situations unfold. These recurring situations call for standardization so all employees are "on the same page". Such procedures are usually referred to as "Standard Operating Procedures" or SOPs. There is little flexibility on the part of the subordinate to deviate from a procedure. An example of a SOP is a statement on how to make a request for a change in benefits. An appropriate form to be completed by the employee usually accompanies SOPs.

A *Rule* delineates precisely what actions are to be taken or not taken in a given situation. Rules allow no flexibility because they are so exact. This precision allows them to substitute for managerial decision-making and permits employees to have a clear understanding as to what must be done. Examples of rules are "Employees must wear identification badges while in the plant" or "no smoking in the building". Breaking of rules is serious and may result in disciplinary actions or poor performance appraisals.[65]

International Impact

On an international basis, it is essential to have a set of standard policies and procedures. All units would follow the same ones, ensuring consistency of action for employees and managers. This would also signal to customers and vendors the unity of the company. It relieves confusion and shows one worldwide image. However, Mendenhall et al. warn of the possible impracticality of a standardized set of policies and procedures.

"…units of the organization may be involved in quite different businesses and may be organized in varied forms. In addition, the contrasting customs and regulations associated with different cultural and national environments often militate against the use of standardized policies and procedures...what may be needed is not tighter controls but different forms of control that are locally acceptable and reflect local laws, customs, and practices. In such a situation appropriate controls may be needed to be developed for each unit of the organization...International managers must become accustomed to managing in this multifaceted environment."[66]

Strategies, Objectives and Policies

Strategic decisions are made within a framework created by organizational policies. Managers consider different courses of action as strategic alternatives. Existing policies indicate the acceptance of one or more courses of action from the alternatives. In other words, policies provide guidance for strategy and behavior.

Let's take an analogy to further show the interrelationships. You need to get to Los Angeles from New York City within a month. You decide to drive your car. After getting a map, you notice there are a number of different routes you can take. Likewise, there are various different stopping points along the way. After some thought, you decide on the route and the cities and towns you want to stop at. You also estimate the amount of time it will take you to reach Los Angeles and how much time you can spend sightseeing along the way.

You begin your trip, noting that some streets, avenues, highways, and freeways are one lane, two lanes or more. Each road has a shoulder. After 500 miles, there is an accident on the road and you must veer off on to the shoulder and around the disabled vehicles. Approximately halfway to Los Angeles, a bridge has been washed out from a violent storm the day before. You consult your map and take some side roads altering your course form a northern route to a southern one. As you move along, you notice there are different speed limits. The highways have sixty-five mile limits, while in the suburbs the roads post a limit of thirty. Within cities and towns it drops further down to twenty. After reaching Los Angeles, you recap the trip in your mind. You have travel thirty-two hundred miles in two weeks. You have seen six different cities and some magnificent scenery along the way. You are satisfied with the trip and glad you chose taking the car rather than the train or plane.

Analyzing this scenario from a strategic perspective, we can see that the objective was to reach Los Angeles within one month. The decision to take the car, the route you would travel, and the stops along the way were all part of your strategy. The procedure you used was to stop in one city after day and spend a day there. The next step was another city, spending a predetermined amount of time there, etc. The policies were the physical limitations of each road, in other words the shoulders. There was some flexibility when you needed to go around the accident. Note that you didn't have to seek permission to do it, you and others knew to use the shoulder and then stay within the lines after passing the disabled vehicles. Also, after you completed your trip the boundaries remained in effect. Policies are the same; they don't disappear after an objective is completed. Likewise, you were obligated to follow certain rules, the speed limits. Breaking the rules, i.e. speeding, would have resulted in some form of punishment, i.e. a fine, imprisonment, or both. Lastly, after an environmental disturbance of which you had no previous knowledge, the washed out bridge, you changed your strategy by going to Plan B, the southern route.

Corporate Governance

Mission, goals and the social responsibility of the firm are ultimately the responsibility of the firm's governing board. An understanding of the basic issues surrounding corporate governance is essential in understanding how corporate strategy is created. Corporate governance is at least partially a study of power, or control of resources. Authority basically belongs to owners, or stockholders. In larger firms, however, owners do not operate the firm (as they do in small businesses) instead they select a Board of Directors, a group that assumes the authority of shareholders/owners. The Board of Directors selects the Chief Executive Officer (CEO) who becomes the single person who represents the Board and stockholders and who is in charge of the operations of the firm. This hierarchy of authority is represented in Figure 2.6.

Figure 2.6
Hierarchy of Corporate Governance

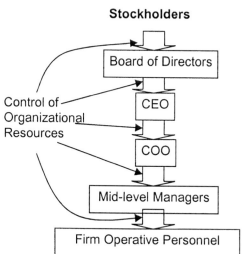

Stockholders

Stockholders – the Core of the Governance Structure

Stockholders take on a variety of shapes and sizes. In very small companies, there may be as few as one stockholder, as one might find in a Limited Liability Corporation.[67] Here, one stockholder is probably the chief operating officer, or at least, the chief decision-maker of the firm with any other stockholders filling in major administrative positions. This is expected, given that this one person (or relatively few people) is taking all the risk in financing the operations – therefore, it is expected that this person (or people) would want to exercise a great amount of control over operations to protect their investment.

As firms grow, it is important for them to raise capital (see Chapter 3, capital formation). One method to accomplish this task is by selling stock to the general public and, although diluting the concentration of ownership, these sales result in the acquisition of major capital resources to support the firm's operation. These new stockholders are not interested in managing the firm but in receiving a return on their investment. Consequently they elect a Board of Directors to represent their interests, who in turn hire a CEO, who in turn hire managers and employees to implement the strategies of the firm. From the stockholders' perspective they are thrice removed (Board, CEO, employees) from the corporation (this is similar to the relationship between voters and non-elected government employees).[68]

From management's perspective, as the number of stockholders increase, the less each individual stockholder has control over the firm to a point where the firms' owners become faceless individuals. Perhaps one of the many reasons that Enron management acted in their own self-interest, and not in the interest of the shareholders, is that ownership of the firm was not personalized by management; since they could not put a face or a name to the millions of stockholders, conceivably it was easy to overlook them.

Stockholder Protection. Then who or what protects stockholders from such unilateral actions of management that are not in the stockholders' best interest? The law states that the firm must protect and nurture stockholder wealth and must act in the best interests of its shareholders.[69] Securities laws enacted by Congress have given the Securities and Exchange Commission authority to protect investors and maintain the integrity of the securities markets.

"The laws and rules that govern the securities industry in the United States derive from a simple and straightforward concept: all investors, whether large institutions or private individuals, should have access to certain basic facts about an investment prior to buying it. To achieve this, the SEC requires public companies to disclose meaningful financial and other information to the public, which provides a common pool of knowledge for all investors to use to judge for themselves if a company's securities are a good investment. Only through the steady flow of timely, comprehensive and accurate information can people make sound investment decisions. The SEC also oversees other key participants in the securities world, including stock exchanges, broker-dealers, investment advisors, mutual funds, and public utility holding companies. Here again, the SEC is concerned primarily with promoting disclosure of important information, enforcing the securities laws, and protecting investors who interact with these various organizations and individuals."[70]

Stock exchanges also have their own set of member regulations with an associated enforcement division. For example, the New York Stock Exchange (NYSE) "is committed to strong and effective regulation of its member firms to protect investors, the health of the financial system, and the integrity of the capital-formation process."[71] The Member Firm Regulation Division conducts ongoing surveillance and annual examinations of the 400 NYSE member firms (some 250 that deal with the public, and 160 floor brokerages, specialist firms and registered traders that do not deal directly with the public) for financial, operational and sales-practice compliance. NYSE staff review and visit member firms and their branch offices to monitor their financial condition, operations and sales practices, and examine their compliance with NYSE trading rules and federal securities laws, such as customer-protection rules, floor-trading requirements, maintenance of required books and records, credit regulation, and anti-money laundering provisions.[72]

Another protection of stockholders has been the use of outside accounting firms to audit publicly traded corporations and attest to the validity of the information reported in financial statements. The Enron case brought to light many problems associated with the relationships between public corporations and their accounting firms and on July 30, 2002, President Bush signed into law the Sarbanes-Oxley Act of 2002. The Act, which applies in general to publicly held companies and their audit firms, dramatically affects the accounting profession and impacts not just the largest accounting firms, but any CPA actively working as an auditor of, or for, a publicly traded company.[73] The Act established a new Public Company Accounting Oversight Board (overseen by the SEC), new roles for audit committees and auditors, criminal penalties and protection for whistle blowers, and new rules and procedures in connection with the financial reporting and auditing process.

Finally, there are also non-for-profit organizations who serve as watchdogs to corporate management. The Conference Board, for example, conducts research, convenes conferences, makes forecasts, assesses trends, publishes information and analysis, and brings executives together to learn from one another about boards' operations in the public's interest.[74] The Board, after the Enron disgrace, formed a 12 member Commission on Public Trust and Private Enterprise to address widespread abuses which led to corporate scandals and declining public trust in companies, their leaders and America's capital markets. The Commission examined compensation, audit, and governance issues facing corporate America and issued best-practices guidelines.[75]

The Board of Directors

Each corporate entity, whether it is a for-profit or not-for-profit firm, must write and file a corporate constitution. In all 50 of the United States, state law requires the creation of a board of directors as well as the appointment of a corporate president and a corporate secretary. Each state has seen the wisdom of creating, in law, certain governing positions with various powers to conduct the business of the corporation in a logical and uniform manner to help assure proper operational performance at the governance level.

The board of directors has the fiduciary responsibility (the responsibility to protect and nurture the assets of shareholders) to represent shareholders, set the strategic direction of the entity, and select appropriate top managers who will oversee the day-to-day operations of the firm. The New York Stock Exchange strongly recommends and NASDAQ requires directors of public companies to receive training on the roles and responsibilities of a board member.[76] Hill noted that these responsibilities include a duty of care, loyalty, and liability[77] while McNamara observed that boards provide input into long range plans, formulated annual objectives, prepared performance reports and monitored goals and objectives, finalized and approved budgets as well as expenditures outside of the budget, and ensure annual audits of the firm's financial condition.[78] According to Korn/Ferry International, Boards typically meet on a quarterly basis (including the annual stockholders' meeting) with meetings usually running between 3-6 hours, and with the CEO spending about 14 hours per week on Board matters[79] - monthly board meetings may be desirable for new corporations.[80]

Boards delegate many of their responsibilities to committees. The committee structure allows the committee members to devote the appropriate amount of time and attention to important issues, and to acquire the specialized knowledge needed for many of the issues and decisions they must make. Committees gather and review information and propose recommendations to the entire board for approval. In order to have access to publicly traded securities markets in the United States, most organizations are required to have, at the very least, an audit committee, a compensation committee and a nominating committee of the governing board. The Securities Exchange Commission (SEC) proxy rules mandate reports from the audit and compensation committees (if either exists).[81] Other committees may be formed that deal with finance, investment, community development, strategic planning, facilities, and personnel.[82]

The level of this responsibility is onerous. Negligence in office is a severe charge for those who accept positions as members of boards of directors and is a charge that cannot be discharged through personal bankruptcy. This may mean that for a failing firm, or one in severe trouble, board members may well face personal lawsuits from shareholders; lawsuits that should they lose may lead to personal financial ruin. This is why it is not uncommon that board members often command and are given large yearly salaries and personal expenses. They assume a great personal risk that most other organizational incumbents do not have to be concerned with, and wish to be compensated accordingly.

Internal vs. External Board Members. Another issue that faces members of the board of directors is that of the balance between *internal* and *external* directors. Internal directors are members of the board who are also regularly employed by the firm (this can include former CEOs and other major corporate officers). The advantage of these people is that they bring an intimate and concrete knowledge of the firm and can help the board make decisions based on actual conditions and facts. The disadvantage of internal directors is that they lack an objective view and may not provide a wider-vision to the strategic decision-making process. External directors are members of the board who bring their expertise to the board, expertise that they have gained from other companies and other industries (including governmental service). The advantage of outside members is that they bring objectivity to the board and an appreciation for business practices other than those of the focal firm. The disadvantage associated with these people is that they do not have the intimate knowledge of the focal firm and might support decisions that do not meet corporate culture or tradition. Achieving a good mix between internal and external directors should be the objective is selecting an optimal set of board members. Korn/Ferry International noted that the typical board had three inside members and eight outside members.[83] This, along with the specific quality of the people (their knowledge and decision-making abilities) is what tends to distinguish a good board from a poor board.

Board independence and the definition of who is an independent board member has become a critical issue in the post-Enron era. Researchers have shown a strong relation between the independence of the board of directors and the likelihood of fraudulent financial reporting. Studies have also found that greater audit committee independence is associated with reduced risk of financial reporting problems and higher-quality financial reporting. Good governance is associated with positive accounting outcomes.[84] In light of this research, and the Enron debacle, the SEC and the NYSE have decided to redefine and narrow the definition of an independent board member. "A director who receives, or whose immediate family member receives, more than $100,000 per year in direct compensation from the listed company (other than director and committee fees and pension or other forms of deferred compensation for prior service not contingent on continued service), is presumed not to be independent until five years after he or she ceases to receive more than $100,000 per year in such compensation."[85] For example, in its 2002 annual report Walt Disney revealed that while CEO Michael Eisner was promoting a good-governance agenda, yet the company maintained undisclosed ties to five directors, including two independents. That brought to 11 the number of directors on the 17-member board with company ties, five of whom it considered insiders.[86]

Interlocking Directorates. Yet another issue that has gained a fair amount of attention over the past several years is that of the ethical issues involved in *interlocking directorates.*[87] Interlocking directorates occur when principles of two firms serve on each others' boards. Interlocking directorates also occur when the principles of a supplier firm or distributing firm serve as directors for their customers/suppliers. Ethically, there may not be problems here, but the appearance of impropriety exists and the potential for unethical behavior exists. Again, such realities exist and, as a result, can create problems with stockholders and regulators. In any situation where a firm allows the possibility for a conflict of interest, the ethics of the situation could well be compromised (in the first example a firm with common principles and directors, the conflict could be under-the-table agreements that reduce free trade; in the second example a firm has board members from supplier firms or distributor firms, the conflict could again be agreements that reduce free trade by creating an advantage in the bargaining process through board participation).

The Chief Executive Office (CEO)

In selecting a CEO, the board gives up operational rights to the firm, but retains the right to hire and fire the CEO and the rights to select the strategic direction of the firm as well as review firm outcomes. The CEO of an organization is the one person who is of the greatest interest to the strategic analyst. This is the person who is selected by the board to provide the strategic direction and define the mission of the organization. This is an extremely important person who, as we described earlier in this chapter, sets the vision of the firm and then takes the responsibility to institute it. With the backing of the board, this person sets the agenda for the firm, both long-term and short-term and oversees the general operations of the organization. In this position, the power of the corporation becomes concentrated in one person and it is this one person that will make decisions as to how those powers should be used.

Dual or Separate Roles?   In most organizations, the CEO can take either one of two positions – as the chairperson of the board, or as the president of the firm. There are no rules here – each board of directors will make its own decision as to which position it wishes to invest the strategic powers of the organization in. Hermanson believes that reform is long overdue in separating the CEO and board chair roles, especially in the wake of Enron. From her perspective, the fundamental problem with combining these two jobs in one person is that the roles simply are incompatible. "How can one person-the CEO-run the company and also run the board, when the board's primary job is to monitor the CEO? It's like having one of the basketball players also serve as the referee. It simply doesn't make sense."[88]   On the other hand, proponents of the dual COB/CEO structure suggest that this duality provides a focal point for the company's management team which in turn provides a potentially clearer organization mission and strategy.[89]

Research on the relationship between dual/separate structures and corporate performance has had mixed results. Tan, Chng, and Tan indicated that CEO duality is beneficial in a turbulent environment,[90] Simpson and Gleason found that a lower probability of financial distress was found in banks when one person was both the CEO and chairman of the board,[91] and Mueller and Barker found that turnaround firms are more likely to have CEOs that are also board chairs.[92] On the other hand, Rechner and Dalton in a longitudinal study found that firms employing independent leadership outperformed dual structures[93] yet their earlier latitudinal study found no performance differences.[94] Sridharan and St. John conducted their own longitudinal study and concluded that that the relationship between CEO duality and firm performance continues to be unresolved. However, they did find that stability in duality status had positive effects on the market's assessment of firm performance (stock price), but that changes in duality status were associated with higher profit margins.[95] Neither structure would then seem to be more correct than the other.

The CEO is the primary strategic decision maker of the firm and maintains the greatest amount and number of contacts with external constituencies (and is externally-oriented). In most cases, however, the CEO will concentrate on these external connections and pass along operational powers to the COO. However, in some cases, the CEO and the COO are the same person, even if the two responsibilities are two different job descriptions.

Chief Operating Officer (COO)

The COO is the person who is responsible for translating the strategic direction of the board of directors and the CEO into operational definitions. One of the major responsibilities of this position is to translate the long-term plans into shorter-term objectives, policies, procedures, rules and budgets. Again, it is not straightforward as to whom this individual might be in terms of title. For those firms where the CEO is the Chairperson of the Board, the President will most likely be the COO. In those firms where the CEO is the President of the firm, the Senior Vice President will most likely be the COO. So while there are no rules relative to title, the position is still one of great importance and whoever is in the position has a significant role in the overall strategic management of the firm. In translating strategic objectives into operation objectives, the COO then details and defines strategic plans so that mid-level and departmental-level managers can further define the plans to the operational level. The powers, or control of resources that the COO delegates, then, are those that allow the operational core to be as effective as possible in using those resources to do the basic work of the organization.

Mid-Level Managers, Departmental Managers, and Organizational Operatives

Finally, resources are delegated down to the level of divisions and departments. The objective of top management is to push as much control over physical resources to departmental managers and departmental employees. This is the area where physical resources will be translated into finished goods or services and the greater the amount of these resources that can be made available to these most basic of operations, the greater the opportunity to transform these resources into finished goods and services with the least amount of waste. Doesn't every firm do this? No, many firms maintain a certain level of capital resources at higher levels. For example, if a given employee in one department reports that he/she needs a new computer, the decision to provide that computer might be that of a senior vice president who will decide that the money to buy a new computer for one employee might be better spent in providing additional education for another employee in another division. Here, the decision and use of resources is centralized. In another example, the same given employee makes a request of a supervisor who oversees resources for her/his department and decides that the request is legitimate and allows the employee to order the computer of his/her choice. Here, the decision and use of resources is decentralized.

Getting adequate resources to all levels of the firm is a major decision-making issue for any organization. Given that decision-making capability is also a major resource available to organizational managers (strategic and operational), the choices they make can significantly impact the ability of the firm to be strategically nimble and agile enough to respond to opportunities and threats from the firm's external environment. Governance will help define and then implement these decisions and how governance is structured will determine its capability of responding in an effective manner.

Summary

This chapter has looked at several importance concepts in strategic planning and strategic management for organizations. It began with a discussion of the importance of a corporate mission, the central purpose and direction of a firm. The mission is developed by top management incorporating their values and vision. Once strategic planners can formalize its mission (perhaps into a formal mission statement), the firm should then set specific goals and objectives, both strategic and operational, which will provide explicit outcomes which match with strategic directions and fulfill its mission. Organizational policies and procedures are devices used to help follow the plan and achieve objectives. Finally, we described the concept of corporate governance and how control of resources flow from stockholders down through the organization to the operational employees of a firm.

Key Terms and Concepts

After reading this chapter, you should be familiar with the following terms and concepts:

Organizational mission: elements of an organizational mission; organizational vision; elements of an organizational vision; organizational values; elements of organizational values; mission statement; elements of a mission statement; goals and objectives; hierarchy of objectives; strategic objectives; operational objectives; policies; procedures; rules; stockholders; boards of directors (BOD); chief executive officer (CEO); BOD/CEO duality; chief operational office (COO); mid-level managers; departmental managers; and operative employees.

Web sites

http://management.about.com/library/howto/ht_stmt.htm - The Business Directory's library. "How to Draft a Mission Statement" provides steps for writing the statement plus helpful tips that will make the job easier. This site also provides access to other management topics including business ethics, corporate governance, strategic planning, and organization development.

http://www.1000ventures.com/business_guide/mgmt_mbo_main.html - 100ventures.com's e-coach site. Has a very thorough discussion on MBO including hotlinks throughout the discussion for further information. Also on this site are links to case studies, venture financing, and managing.

http://www.corpgov.net/ - Corporate Governance's homepage. Corporate Governance serves as a discussion forum and network for shareholders and stakeholders who believe active participation by concerned shareholders in governing corporations will enhance their ability to create wealth. Site provides news, internet links, and a small reference library supported by purchases through Amazon.com.

http://www.ratical.org/corporations/ - Ending Corporate Governance's homepage.   Provides an anti-corporate approach to organizational governance including a short history of how corporations became entities and how corporations have failed to serve their original purpose.

Discussion Questions

1. What is the difference between a mission and a mission statement?
2. Why are organizational strategic objectives important?
3. Why are organizational operational objectives important?
4. Discuss the effectiveness of an organization not using policies and procedures.
5. Discuss the pros and cons of a dual Chair of Board/CEO position.

Exercises

1. Does the firm you are studying have a formal mission statement? If so, is it a good one; how do you know; is it leading to the results it should? If not, can you determine a guiding corporate mission; what is the central purpose and direction of the firm; why do you think the firm has not written these characteristics into a formal statement?
2. List five demonstrable objectives of your firm. Back these up from evidence you can find on the Internet.
3. Cite examples of policies and procedures in your firm. Give an example of a policy and a procedure with which you disagree.
4. Describe the governance structure of your company.   In particular, who is the CEO, who is the COO, and what is the structure of your company's Board of Directors (what is the mix of internal and external directors, and is there any evidence of interlocking directorates)?

Endnotes

[1] For a more detailed description of Enron's history, see Cruver, B. 2002. *Anatomy of Greed: The Unshredded Truth from an Enron Insider.* New York: Carroll & Graf Publishers.

[2] Berger, E. & Fowler, T. 2002. "The fall of Enron: Enron masked loans as sales, report says; Deals inflated bottom line by $1.4 Billion." *The Houston Chronicle*, September 22, 2002, Section A1.

[3] Swartz, J. 2002. "As Enron purged its ranks, dissent was swept away." *The New York Times*. February 4, 2002, Section C1, pg. 54.

[4] Steven Drozdeck and Karl F. Gretz (2002). "Differentiating yourself from the competition" *Personal Financial Planning Monthly* (September) Volume 2, Issue 9, 23-26.

[5] Daniel J. Rowley and Herbert Sherman (2001). *From Strategy to Change: Implementing the Plan in Higher Education.* San Francisco, Ca.: Jossey-Bass, Inc.

[6] Ibid.

[7] Richard C. Chewning (1984). *Business Ethics in a Changing Culture.* Reston, Va.: Reston Publishing Co., Inc.

[8] Joanne Martin (1992). *Cultures in Organizations: Three Perspectives.* New York: Oxford University Press.

[9] Stephen P. Robbins and Mary Coulter (2002). *Management: Activebook Version 1.0.* Upper Saddle River, N.J.: Prentice-Hall, Inc.

[10] Albert J. Milhomme (2002). "EuroDisney/Zero Disney Case" *Journal of the International Academy for Case Studies* Volume 8, Number 5, 45-56.

[11] Mary C. Gentile (1998). "Setting the Right Course: Business Ethics" *Risk Management* (September) Volume 45, Issue 9, 45-64.

[12] We thank the reviewer from the University of Norter Dame for this observation.

[13] Laura M. Holson (2002). "Reviving the Family Film to Reverse a Lackluster Box Office" *New York Times* (June 10) Late Edition (East Coast), C.1.

[14] http://touchstonepictures.go.com/main.html, June 16, 2003.

[15] Warren Bennis (1990). *Why Leaders Can't Lead: The Unconscious Conspiracy Continues.* San Francisco, Ca.: Jossey-Bass Publishers.

[16] http://web66.coled.umn.edu/new/MLK/MLK.html, January 6, 2003.

[17] More specific reference is available on the Microsoft site at http://www.microsoft.com/education/?ID=About .

[18] More information about GM's Saturn Automobile may be found at their website: http://www.gm.com/flash_homepage/

[19] Jenny Weingart (2001). "Unlocking Value Through InternalAudit" *Financial Executive* (March/April) Volume 7, Issue 3, 53-56.

[20] Robert E. Kemper (1989). *Experiencing Strategic Management.* New York: The Dryden Press.

[21] Kiyoshi Yamauchi (2001). "Corporate Communication: A Powerful Tool for Stating Corporate Missions" *Corporate Communications* Volume 6, Issue 3, 131-138.

[22] Anonymous (2002). "Executive Resources" *Internet World* (September) Volume 8, Issue 9, 12-14.

[23] http://www.hp.com/hpinfo/abouthp/, January 6, 2003.

[24] http://www.mycareer.ford.com/OURCOMPANY.ASP?CID=23, January 6, 2003.

[25] http://www2.coca-cola.com/ourcompany/index.html, January 6, 2003.

[26] Craig R. Hickman and Michael A. Silva (1984). *Creating Excellence: Managing Corporate Culture, Strategy, and Change in the New Age.* New York: NAL Books.

[27] Thomas G. Marx (1985). *Business & Society: Economic, Moral, and Political Foundations – Text and Readings.* Englewood Cliffs, N.J.: Prentice-Hall, Inc.

[28] John A. Pearce III and Richard B. Robinson, Jr. (2000). *Strategic Management: Formulation, Implementation, and Control.* 7th Edition. New York: Irwin McGraw-Hill; Arthur A. Thompson, Jr. and A.J. Strickland III (2001). *Strategic Management: Concepts and Cases.* 12th Edition. New York: McGraw-Hill Irwin; Fred R. David (2003). *Strategic Management: Concepts and Cases.* Upper Saddle River, N.J.: Prentice-Hall, Inc.; and Stephen J. Porth (2003). *Strategic Management: A Cross-Functional Approach.* Upper Saddle River, N.J.: Prentice-Hall, Inc.

[29] http://www.aacsb.edu/accreditation/standards.asp, January 6, 2003.

[30] Michael A. Hitt, R. Duane Ireland, and Robert E. Hoskisson (2001). *Strategic Management: Competitiveness and Globalization.* 4th

Edition. Cincinnati, Oh.: South-Western College Publishing; L.J. Bourgeois, III, Irene M. Duhaime, and J.L. Stimpert (2001). *Strategic Management Concise: A Managerial Perspective.* Fort Worth, Tx.: Harcourt, Inc.; and Robert A. Pitts and David Lei (2003). 3rd Edition. Cincinnati, Oh.: South-Western College Publishing.

[31] L.J. Bourgeois, III (1980). "Strategy and Environment: A Conceptual Integration." *Academy of Management Review* (January) Volume 8, Issue 1, 25-39.

[32] Daniel A. Wren (1994). *The Evolution of Management Thought.* 4th Edition. New York: John Wiley & Sons, Inc.

[33] Abe Peck (2002). "The Mission Position" *Folio : The Magazine for Magazine Management* (November) Volume 31, Issue 11, 62-64.

[34] Forest R. David and Fred R. David (2003). "It's Time to Redraft Your Mission Statement" *The Journal of Business Strategy* (January/February) Volume 24, Issue 1, 11-14.

[35] M.C. Baetz and C.K. Bart (1996). "Developing Mission Statements Which Work" *Long Range Planning* Volume 29, Issue 4, 526-33.

[36] Farhad Analou and Azhdar Karami (2002). "CEOs and Development of the Meaningful Mission Statement " *Corporate Governance* Volume 2, Issue 3, 13-20.

[37] Steven Drozdeck and Karl F. Gretz (2002). "Differentiating Yourself from the Competition" *Personal Financial Planning Monthly* (September) Volume 2, Issue 9, 23-26.

[38] Ben and Jerry's mission statement as found on their website, http://www.benjerry.com/our_company/our_mission/

[39] Sun's mission statement as found on their website, http://www.sun.com/aboutsun/coinfo/mission.html

[40] Kodak's mission statement as found on their website, http://www.kodak.com/US/en/corp/careers/why/valuesmission.jhtml

[41] Enron's mission can be found in their 1998 and 2000 annual reports which are available at http://www.enron.com/corp/investors/annuals/

[42] David and David, 2003.

[43] Analou and Karami, 2002.

[44] Anonymous (2001). "Business Trends Down" *New Zealand Management* (August) Volume 48, Issue 7, 9-10.

[45] Craig Smith (2002). "Top employers put vision and values in to get value out" *Marketing* (October 10), 19.

[46] George S. Odiorne (1965). *Management by Objectives: A System of Managerial Leadership.* New York: Pitman Publishing Corporation.

[47] Pearce and Robinson, 2000.

[48] Victor A. Thompson (1963). *Modern Organization..* New York: Alfred A. Knopf.

[49] Pearce and Robinson, 2000.

[50] Andrew J. DuBrin (2003). *Essentials of Management.* 6th Edition. Mason, Oh.: South-Western.

[51] Roger L. Miller (1997). *Economics Today.* 9th Edition. Reading, Mass.: Addison-Wesley Logman, Inc.

[52] Michael E. Porter (1985). *Competitive Advantage: Creating and Sustaining Superior Performance.* New York: The Free Press; James R. Evans and James W. Dean, Jr. (2003). *Total Quality: Management, Organization and Strategy.* 3rd Edition. Mason, Oh.: South-Western.

[53] See discussion in Cameron, Kim S. 1982. *Organizational Effectiveness: A Comparison of Multiple Models.* New York: Academic Press.

[54] Discussions of different definitions are put forth by Cameron, Kim S. 1989. "Critical Questions in Assessing Organizational Effectiveness," *Organizatioal Dynamics.* 9(1), pg.s 66-80; and by Zammuto, R. F. 1984. "A Comparison of Multiple Constituency Models of Organizational Effectiveness," *Academy of Management Review.* 9(4), pg.s 606-616.

[55] Ibid.

[56] Created from http://www.philipmorris.com/docs/investor rel/ 2Q2002_FactSheet.pdf, January 8, 2003.

[57] Richard P. Rumelt (1974). *Strategy, Structure, and Economic Performance.* Boston, Mass.: Harvard University.

[58] http://www.toyota.co.jp/en/ci.html, January 8, 2003.

[59] http://www.toyota.com/about/operations/na-affiliates/index.html, January 8, 2003.

[60] George S. Odiorne, 1965.

[61] For an example, see http://www.treasury.govt.nz/budgetpolicy/ 2000/shortterm.asp, January 8, 2003.

[62] http://www.performancesolutionstech.com/FromMBOtoPM.pdf, January 8, 2003.

[63] http://www.mrsc.org/govdocs/A5nepotism.aspx, December 30, 2004.

[64] Alan Filley and Robert House (1969). *Managerial Process and Organizational Behavior.* Glenview, IL: Scott, Foresman, and Company, p. 161.

[65] Victor Lazzaro (1959). *Systems and Procedures: A Handbook for Business and Industry.* Englewood Cliffs, N.J.: Prentice-Hall, Inc.

[66] Mark Mendenhall, Betty Jane Punnett, and David Ricks(1995). *Global Management.* Cambridge, MA: Blackwell Publishers, pp. 368-369.

[67] Anthony Mancuso (1998). *How to Form Your Own New York Corporation.* 4th Edition. Berkelely, CA.: Nolo Press.

[68] Frederick C. Mosher (1982). *Democracy and the Public Service.* 2nd Edition. Oxford, England: Oxford University Press.

[69] See Chapter 38 Directors, Officers and Shareholders in Henry R. Cheeseman (2001). *Business Law: Ethical, International & E-Commerce Environment.* 4th Edition. Upper Saddle River, N.J.: Prentice-Hall, Inc.

[70] http://www.sec.gov/about/whatwedo.shtml, June 20, 2003.

[71] http://www.nyse.com/regulation/p1020656068597. html?displayPage=%2Fregulation%2F1022221392702.html, June 20, 2003.

[72] http://www.nyse.com/about/p1020656067652.html? displayPage=%2Fabout%2F1022221392718.html, June 20, 2003.

[73] http://www.aicpa.org/info/Sarbanes-Oxley2002.asp, June 20, 2003.

[74] http://www.conference-board.org/aboutus/about.cfm, June 20, 2003.

[75] http://www.conference-oard.org/knowledge/governCommission.cfm, June 20, 2003.

[76] http://www.conference-board.org/knowledge/govInstitute.cfm, June 20, 2003.

[77] http://www.boardmember.com/network/index.pl?section=1100 &article_id=11120&show=article, June 20, 2003.

[78] http://www.boardmember.com/network/index.pl?section =1086&article_id=10351&show=article, June 20, 2003.

[79] http://www.boardmember.com/network/index.pl?section= 1086&article_id=11300&show=article, June 21, 2003.

[80] http://www.boardmember.com/network/index.pl?section =1085&article_id=10526&show=article, June 21, 2003.

[81] http://www.boardmember.com/network/index.pl?section= 1086&article_id=11027&show=article, June 21, 2003.

[82] http://www.boardmember.com/network/index.pl?section= 1086&article_id=10359&show=article, June 21, 2003.

[83] http://www.boardmember.com/network/index.pl?section= 1086&article_id=11299&show=article, June 21, 2003.

[84] Dana R. Hermanson (2003). "Does Corporate Governance Really Matter? What the Research Tells Us" *Internal Auditing* (March/April) Volume 18, Issue 2, 44-45.

[85] http://www.boardmember.com/network/index.pl?section= 1086&article_id=11478&show=article, June 21, 2003.

[86] Louis Lavelle and Edited by Sheridan Prasso (2002). "Disney: More Insiders At the Castle" *Business Week* (December 30) Issue 3814, 14.

[87] Loizos Heracleous and John Murry (2002). "Networks, Interlocking Directors and Strategy: Toward a Theoretical Framework" *Asia Pacific Journal of Management* (June) Volume 18, Issue 2, 137-160

[88] Dana R. Hermanson (2003). "What Else in Corporate Governance Should be Changed? *Internal Auditing* (January/February) Volume 18, Issue 1, 44.

[89] Uma V. Sridharan and Caron H. St. John (1988). "The Effects of Organizational Stability and Leadership Structure on Firm Performance" *Journal of Managerial Issues* (Winter) Volume 10, Issue 4, 469-484.

[90] Ruth Seow Kuan Tan, Pheng Lui Chng, and Tee Ween Tan (2001). "CEO Share Ownership and Firm Value" *Asia Pacific Journal of Management* (July) Volume 18, Issue 3, 355-371.

[91] W. Gary Simpson and Anne E. Gleason (1999) "Board Structure, Ownership, and Financial Distress in Banking Firms" *International Review of Economics & Finance* Volume 8, Issue 3, 281-292.

[92] George C. Mueller and Vincent L. Barker, III (1997). "Upper Echelons and Board Characteristics of Turnaround and Nonturnaround Declining Firms" *Journal of Business Research* (June) Volume 39, Issue 2, 119-134.

[93] Paula L. Rechner and Dan R. Dalton (1991). "CEO Duality and Organizational Performance: A Longitudinal Analysis" *Strategic Management Journal* (February) Volume 12, Issue 2, 155-160.

[94] Paula L. Rechner and Dan R. Dalton (1989). "The Impact Of CEO As Board Chairperson On Corporate Performance: Evidence vs. Rhetoric" *The Academy of Management Executive* (May) Volume 3, Issue 2, 141-143.

[95] Sridharan and St. John, 1988.

✂ Chapter Three ✂
The External Environment

Chapter Objectives

1. To identify the four levels of external environmental forces affecting the firm and describe the potential impact of each on firm performance.
2. To gain an understanding of how these forces affect the strategic decision making of the firm.
3. To conduct an industry analysis based upon Porter's five forces model.

4. To evaluate each level of the external environment and determine potential opportunities and threats for a firm.
5. To understand how changes in the external environment create new opportunities and threats for a firm.

In Chapter 1, we looked at the case of United Airlines, a company deeply impacted by the tragic events and changes brought on by the September 11, 2001 incident, but also a company that had rather recently enjoyed high levels of growth and profitability. While we questioned the amount of strategic planning and emergency management used at United, there is another side of the issue which also contributed to the problems that most major carriers in the airline industry face. This is the issue of external environmental forces that have changed dramatically over the past 15 years and has forever changed the nature of the industry.

Introductory Case: The Changes in the Airline Industry

Deregulation of the airline industry occurred in 1978, over a quarter of a century ago.[1] Prior to deregulation, airlines were treated more as utilities rather than as competitors. With governmental regulation came governmental support - the government often subsidized unprofitable routes prior to 1978 to insure service to smaller communities or strategic destinations. The various airlines in the United States were under the control of the Civil Aeronautics Board (CAB) which established routes and fares. Pressure to deregulate the system to promote competition, improve routes, and keep fares in check grew to the point that the United States Congress passed the Airline Deregulation Act on October 24, 1978 and President Carter signed it into law 4 days later. It took a while for the changes to occur, but airlines were free to choose their own routes and destinations as of December 31, 1981 and could set their own fares as of January 1, 1983. Finally, the CAB ceased to exist on January 1, 1985 and the process of deregulation was complete.

With the exit of CAB, the airlines were free to do as they pleased domestically, although the Department of Transportation continued to regulate international traffic (this continues to be true even today, but the U.S. Government has negotiated a series of Open Sky agreements with several foreign nations that has also dramatically reduced regulation in this area as well). However, with deregulation all that government support was gone and carriers were subject to the same laws of profits and loss as all other companies engaging in competition in the free market.

Business strategies changed dramatically for the U.S. airlines. Not used to dealing in a competitive environment, many expanded rapidly, adding additional destinations, buying new aircraft to accommodate the increase in business that did occur, and engaging in fare wars to woe passengers from one airline company to another. The airlines also abandoned the point-to-point system of routing and largely adopted the hub-and-spoke system (moving from simply serving 2 cities with a single route to servicing a variety of cities through a central hub, an airport where aircraft comes in at approximately the same time, allows transfers, and then spokes out to many new destinations with all aircraft leaving at approximately the same times). Deregulation also allowed the emergence of many new carriers and competition became fierce in a very short amount of time.

Within only a few years, many of the major airlines were in trouble. No airline seemed to have had a good transition strategy that was needed from operating under regulation to being totally deregulated and several carriers found they were unable to make the adjustment. They had not planned their change strategies well and the environment of a deregulated world was proving to be much more difficult to operate in from the environment of a regulated world. The ability of many of the air carriers to find new methods of operations that fit well with the new market for air travel was becoming highly suspect.

Between deregulation and United's bankruptcy petition in 2002, the changes in the industry led to 10 major U.S. airlines declaring bankruptcy. Among the most notable were Pan Am, Braniff, Continental Airlines (twice), TWA, and U.S. Air. The competitive structure further changed as consolidations earmarked the deregulated world of airlines and such long-time giants such as Eastern Airlines no longer operated. Part of the cause for all this turbulence was the basic structure of airline operation, which was fine during regulation but had not changed in order to build new strong foundations that would allow airlines to easily survive in deregulation. Airlines historically have high cash flows, but also are capital and labor intensive, heavily unionized, show low profit margins, are reactive to fluctuations in oil prices, and are seasonal in nature.[2]

To counter increasing competition, airlines have altered their strategic tactics. Frequent flier programs, airline-controlled travel agency reservations systems, code sharing, and strategic alliances were all developed to entice the traveling public (especially the business traveler on whom many of the larger airlines had become dependent upon) to fly one airline versus another. Yet fare wars continue even in today's market and the advent of discount carriers, especially Southwest Airlines and Jet Blue, has proven to be large hurdles the larger carriers have yet been able to successfully compete against.

September 11, 2002 was the proverbial straw that broke the camel's back. Public fear of flying was the most devastating aftermath of the terrorist attack on the World Trade Center in New York.[3] Along with that came an even more substantial blow – the loss of the business traveler due to the post 9/11 United States economic downturn. This was critical because the airlines had not only catered to the business traveler who flew often, but had come to depend on the willingness of the business flyer to pay full fare or even upgraded fares for business or first class seats. Airport security added both costs and sometimes huge inconveniences to flying and many travelers decided to either travel by car or not travel and using convergence communication technologies (the merging of communications capabilities such as television, wireless devices, and the internet as one fully integrated communication system) for virtual meetings.[4]

It is worth noting that during the period since deregulation, only one major airline has been able to grow and produce profits on a steady basis. Southwest Airlines has yet to show a loss (even in the aftermath of September 11th).[5] For over 29 years, many during regulation, Southwest has adopted an independent strategy that has focused on low-fares, point-to-point domestic service, frequent flight schedules, service to smaller less-expensive airports, no alliances, and no ticketing through travel agencies. They have bucked the trend of the major carriers and apparently has found a competitive strategy that works in the deregulated airline industry. Jet Blue has adopted the major tenets of Southwest airlines' strategy and has in three years since its inception achieved nine quarters of profitability, including five consecutive quarters of double-digit operating margins.[6]

So while the external environment has proven extremely hostile to the airline industry as a whole, there are exceptional airlines such as Southwest and Jet Blue. They appear to have been better at understanding the change in their market and the emergent new air travel environment. In the meantime, the rest of the industry is looking for answers, and with bankruptcy after bankruptcy, apparently is unable to find them. They have yet to figure out how to prosper in this altered environment of deregulation.

Defining the External Environment

As we indicated in Chapter 1, an environment is a set of forces that have the ability to impact an organization. We identified two different important sets of organizational environments, external and internal. In this chapter, we discuss the elements of the external environment as suggested in Figure 3.1. These are the trends and driving forces that occur outside of the boundaries of organization's operations. Understanding the dynamics of the external environment is crucial to strategic management because these dynamics represent one of the major forces for change. The interactive forces in the external environment have the ability to either support the operations of the firm or to detract from it; they can create market opportunities or threaten the very existence of the firm.

From the field of marketing, one of their rules of good business is *"never to make a good or provide a service because you want to – rather, discover what the customer wants and then provide the good or service at a price the customer is willing to pay."* What this rule says is that companies cannot make the mistake of providing any goods or services that they feel like – instead, they need to only provide those goods or services that they know have a ready market. Perhaps even more simplistically, this rule states that the customer is in charge, *not the firm.*[7] If this is true, and we believe it is, the lesson is a basic strategic one: firms that produce goods or services because that's

Figure 3.1
The Strategic Planning Process
Step 2 – Analyzing the External Environment

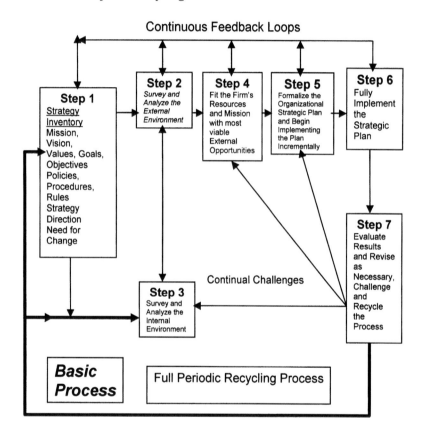

what they've always done, or that's what they really do enjoy doing, or that's what the founder wanted, these are firms that usually end up in trouble. One of the other lessons here is that forces outside the organization are the ones that should at least partially control what the firm should and should not produce.

There are, of course, exceptions to this rule. Many products and services have been developed in a vacuum, without an assessment of consumer needs, which have been highly successful and in fact have changed and revolutionized the way that consumers think about a particular product or service.[8] For example, how many people really thought that they needed to have a computer in their home, or a place to drink a refined coffee, and read their papers in an undisturbed, pampered environment, or even a pet rock? Many innovations, inventions and technological developments have tapped into the unspoken and unknown wants and desires of consumers – they have provided a stimulus that has provided a direction for fulfilling consumers' unexpressed needs and desires.[9] These firms, in essence, create new markets and/or change market dynamics without the benefit of market information with luck and timing playing a key role in the business's success. However, keep in mind that many a dot.com company was started on the wishes and desires of their owners and developers and failed miserably because there was no market or business plan for their product or service.[10]

Firms that do good research by gathering data on consumer needs and wants, market trends, competitor strategies, and industry structures, are the firms that will most likely succeed. Again, there have been exceptions to this rule; firms that plan often may not plan well or may not be able to implement their plans. Organizations such as McDonalds and Coca Cola who have a very strong reputation for product and market testing have on numerous occasions produced products and services that the public could not abide - for example, The McLean, McPizza, Vanilla Coke, and New Coke. Their products or services failed, not due to a lack of information gathered about the market but perhaps through a misinterpretation of the data or poor implementation of the new product strategy.

Firms who conduct research seek a fit between themselves and those specific external forces they are most likely to interact with. This creates the need to develop specific understandings about what those forces are, where they are, what they can do to impact the firm, and what the firm can do to optimize its interactions with them. In studying external environments, organizations are able to discover *opportunities* that they can take advantage of to improve growth and profitability as well as ***threats*** which can limit or prevent them from doing so. Some of these opportunities and threats challenge the ethical practices of companies and will be discussed in more detail in Chapter 11 –Strategy Changes: Ethical and Technological Causes.

In the following sections, we present the external environment from a series of perspectives as shown in Figure 3.2 below.

Figure 3.2
The Elements of the External Environment

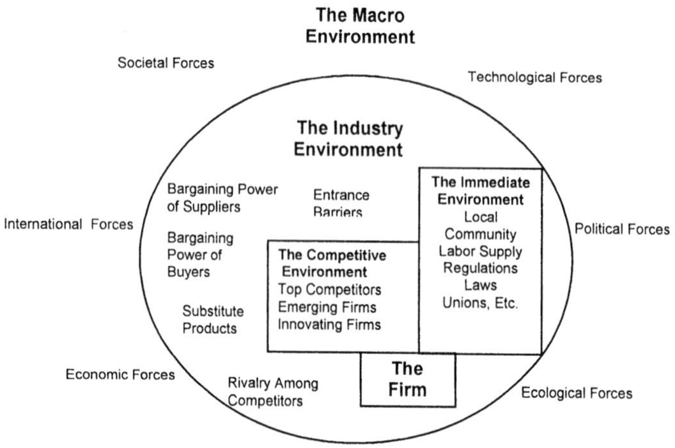

First, we introduce and discuss the Macro Environment, a set of external forces that encompass literally everything that is going on anywhere in the world. Second, we identify the Industry Environment, a set of driving forces that are much more concentrated in the operating arena where a firm does business. Third, we define a subset of the Industry Environment called the Competitive Environment which contains the elements and forces that create the level of rivalry between a given firm and the other firms in the market. Fourth, we identify another type of environment, the Immediate Environment, a set of forces that tend to impact and influence a firm's ability to do business with its other stakeholders, individuals, and groups that have an interest in the firm, besides its competition.

Together, these environments have the potential of overwhelming both the firm, and the learner who is studying that firm's strategic activities. However, the good news is that not everything in the world is necessarily something that all firms need to be concerned with. For example, if it rains heavily today in Beijing, is there an impact on Microsoft? Probably not.

However, if it is raining heavily today in Beijing and the airport is closed, it does impact China Airlines, United Airlines, and Air Canada, three international airlines that provide daily service between Beijing and cities in North America. So while Microsoft probably doesn't need to worry about rain in China as something that can provide either opportunities or threats to its operations, the three airlines do. That is the key to understanding external environments: knowing which environmental elements to be aware of (what is in the organization's *operating domain*); observing any changes in these factors; understanding precisely what the impact of these changes can be on a firm; and being in a position to change the firm if necessary.

The Macro Environment

As we suggested above, the Marco Environment contains literally everything that is going on in the world. Most of these elements, trends, and forces do not necessarily have the potential ability to either help or harm a given organization. However, there are some global trends and forces that do have the ability to positively or negatively impact a business and these are the ones that the strategic managers of a firm must be familiar with, monitor, and be prepared to respond to if the change in the forces become strong enough to affect the firm's operations. To gain a better handle on these forces, it is useful to segment them into common areas so that when a strategic decision-maker begins an analysis of the external environment she/he can start by looking at specific categories and then begin to examine those categories to determine what the precise forces found there have the potential of affecting the organization. It is important to note, however, that these segments are not mutually exclusive and do interact with one another. These segments are: Political Forces, Economic Forces, Ecological Forces, Social Forces, Technological Forces, and International Forces (PEESTI).[11]

Political Forces. Political environmental elements control the government, legal and regulatory activities that help run towns, cities, counties, states, nations and society as a whole. These forces are comprised of stakeholder groups (groups that have an interest in the firm) that include politicians, government agencies, political parties, political action groups, industry associations, community coalitions, chambers of commerce, and lobbyists.[12] They seek control of legal and political power which they then use to define the rules of the marketplace - what is right and what is wrong from their own perspectives and back these new definitions with the force of law, the most important of which is punitive actions.[13] Laws and lawmakers establish boundaries for actions by people and organizations, and define sanctions for those people or organizations who cross those boundaries, especially if these people or organizations damage others. From a business's perspective then, political forces determine the rules of the game through the passage of laws that regulate the marketplace, and enforce those rules through government oversight agencies.

A good legal system offers protection from illegal or unfair practices by competing firms who may influence law-making (through lobbying) or political decisions (again through ethical practices such as lobbying) and can help make regulatory bodies more aware of specific issues and conditions, which could be beneficial to these firm or an entire industry. It is interesting to note that different countries have different laws about doing business and businesses are offered varying sets of protection. For example, Japanese foreign trade policies keep out foreign competition yet those same policies are not tolerated in the United States. Second, collusion among competitors is illegal in the United States, but considered common business practice in Japan.[14]

Besides establishing the rules of the marketplace, politicians and government agencies are also active players in the market. Politicians enact statutes and laws which allow government agencies at the federal, state, county, and local level to: purchase goods and services from businesses, provide goods and services that may compete with the private sector (i.e. college education), and supply goods and services to the private sector (i.e. government-backed loans). Furthermore, the government, through its tax structure, collects and distributes funds in order to carryout the business of government, stimulate the economy, and redistribute wealth to those less fortunate in need of government assistance.[15]

Opportunities and threats that come from this environmental segment are based upon the changing demand for goods and services from the public sector, the changes in the laws that regulate the market, and the changes in the tax structure. These changes are a function of the politicians in office - specifically their party allegiances (and the economic platforms of that party), the politicians' relationships with business sectors and their regulating agencies, and the influence of lobbyists and political actions committees.[16] Changes in administrations could consequently present prospects and/or problems for certain firms since new political administrations may have differing objectives than previous administrations..

For example, under the 1978 Carter Administration, there was a national drive to build alternative energy sources to counter the United States' growing dependence on foreign oil. As a result of this change in national policy, several existing firms and new companies began to explore and hoped to exploit energy sources such as oil shale, solar energy, wind farms, and sea water conversion. Under the following 1980 Reagan Administration, most of the incentives for developing alternative energy sources were removed and the companies that had ventured into alternative sources suddenly were faced with no economic support or direction. The opportunities that were created by the Carter Administration were wiped out by the Reagan Administration, to the detriment of many startup alternative energy firms.

Economic Forces. Economic forces to the casual observer may defy explanation in many instances. Why does the stock market go up or down? It isn't always clear why, but it does alter over time in conjunction with other economic indicators. Consumer buying trends, money supply, unemployment trends, currency exchange rates, interest rates, inflation rates, and as we learned from September 11th, random events can all impact the economy. Since capital comes from the economic sector, individual firms need to have a steady eye on what is going on with the economy because changes there can easily affect both the firm's market and its operations.

Opportunities that come from the economy can be extremely beneficial to a given firm. If the economy is expanding, if people are optimistic and are spending, if companies are hiring and growing, the potential for significant profitability and growth is great. Low interest rates mean that companies can borrow more to expand operations with less of a cost and less dependence on selling stock (and spreading out ownership). If inflation is in check, the firm's strategic planners can more accurately predict future costs and better manage their company's profitability. If the dollar is strong, then it might be a good idea to increase foreign investment where local currencies are weaker. These and many more examples provide many positive opportunities that a company would want to be aware of, especially if the economy was good. We should note that there are also opportunities that arise when the general economy is bad, such as being able to find bargain acquisitions in terms of competitors who are not faring well and are more willing to sell out.

Threats from the economic sector can be devastating to firms, especially those that have not built their financial structures with prudence and soundness. The example in Chapter 1 of United Airlines again demonstrates the case of a company that was not structured well financially and was eventually forced to seek bankruptcy protection because it was starting to run out of money for operations. Beyond terrorist activities, however, all of the economic forces we described as potential opportunities can be potential threats as well. Consumer buying trends, currency exchange rates, interest rates, and inflation rates can all be negatives just as they can be positives. If consumers are concerned about savings or retirement issues, they may stop buying luxuries (or even some essential goods and services) which can hurt producers significantly if they are not prepared for it. Currency exchange rates could push the dollar into a very weak position, making foreign investment much more costly or encouraging foreign-made goods to flood American markets. Interest rates could climb, making debt more costly to service and reducing profitability as a result. Finally, inflation rates could climb unexpectedly making it very difficult to plan for proper purchasing or inventory levels to support future sales.

It is important to remember that it is not only the state of the economy but the shift in the state of the economy and the shift within specific economic sectors that is so critical for businesses to track. For example, while the U.S. gross domestic product grew from a little over 7 trillion to 10 trillion dollars from 1994 to 2001, a growth rate of 42% over an eight year period, the construction industry grew nearly 75% (275 billion in 1994, 480 billion in 2001) yet manufacturing grew at only 17% (1.2 trillion in 1994, 1.4 trillion in 2001).[17] Recent trends in the overall economy have been much poorer than the 1994-2001 average annual GDP growth rate of 5.25%. The GDP growth rate in 2002 was 2.4%, with an estimated GDP growth rate by Morgan Stanley in 2003 of only 2%, increasing to 4.1% in 2004. In terms of industry sectors, Morgan Stanley projects the highest long-term growth rates to be in information technology, the lowest in telecommunication services.[18]

Ecological Forces. The physical environment is a force that for many years was not considered as a key segment of the macro environment. It was taken for granted that resources were self-renewing, or that new technology would provide substitutable, new resources, or even worse, that there was no consideration at all as to how resources were to be replaced. As we discussed in Chapter 1, the field of strategic management uses the term in a more complex manner, but the physical environment is clearly part of the environment strategic managers must be concerned about. When many people talk about the environment, they now refer to the ecosphere.

Why does this change in the way businesses think about the ecosphere? First, there is in general a growing concern in the public for sustainable growth, pollution, depletion of natural resources, husbandry of our planets wildlife, forests, and waters, and reclamation of previously poisoned or devastated lands, are all a part of the world we live in, whether we are individuals or organizations.[19] Like the earlier reference to rain in Beijing, many firms are becoming aware of the elements of the ecosphere because it is now quite clear that disregarding the physical environment can overlook business opportunities as well as potential threats.

Opportunities for businesses have emerged under the rubric of greening businesses. For example, faced with ever-diminishing non-renewable resource supply and political insecurity weltering around the supply still in the ground, British Petroleum (BP) moved into the design and supply of photovoltaic equipment. To date BP has sold solar energy equipment in more than 160 countries and expects to have 20% of the world market share within a few years – a growth market, it should be added.[20] For most businesses, however, greening their business refers to pollution prevention through the 3R's of waste management (reduce, reuse, and recycle) with the objectives of lowering operating costs, producing safer employee working conditions, and reducing the cost of regulatory compliance.[21] Some businesses, however, treat environmental protection as more of a public relations campaign than anything else, though some companies have actively sought to be responsible corporate citizens by championing certain environmental causes and leading the way in restoring or protecting ecological treasures. Many companies make changes in their operations to help preserve or protect rare natural resources (like some utility companies that build wind farms as an alternative source for energy),[22] while others actively restore resources they have used (such as several firms in the lumber industry that replant forests). So while many firms pay lip service to supporting environmental causes, several other firms do find ways of operating to actually improve our ecosphere and build their businesses upon these policies.

Threats from the ecosphere create a much larger discussion. The most critical concerns are business practices involving pollution and resource depletion. For example, many manufacturing firms in the U.S. use a tremendous amount of fossil fuel to operate their businesses. Fossil fuels are, unfortunately, a limited commodity. Some studies suggest that by the year 2060, nearly all of the easily recoverable fossil fuels such as petroleum will have been exhausted.[23] Businesses, along with the American driver and automobile drivers all over the world, are perpetuating a problem that could prove catastrophic within the next few decades. The weather is another potential threat to a surprisingly large number of businesses. Hurricanes, tornadoes, droughts, floods, uncommonly cold winters, or uncommonly hot summers can create havoc for organizations, especially for those in the agricultural sector.

Lee Korins, a survivor of the World Trade Center terrorist attacks has identified that many organizations and businesses do not have adequate disaster plans.[24] While Korins was speaking specifically about the damage that was done to the City of New York and much of the country's financial structure the day the terrorists struck the World Trade Center, his message is for all managers. Anything can happen in the world we live in today, whether that be by man-made-disaster or nature-made-disasters. If firms do not adequately prepare to for the worst, when the worst comes, they may not be able to survive.

Social Forces. Society is often a difficult concept to grasp because it is broad, global and hence complex in nature. It contains such diverse factors as demographics, religion, culture, economic market systems, political movements, cultural activities, poverty and wealth, and mob mentality.[25] Anything that has to do with human beings in a communal setting is social in nature. More importantly, social forces are the result of human behaviors in a communal setting – behaviors that influence other humans to behave in the same or in opposite manners creating the need for responses. This segment is basic to all environmental forces and organizations need to be highly responsive to the portion of society that it serves and works with because through the market, society has the greatest potential to be helpful or harmful to any organization. To coin a phrase, society giveth and society can taketh away.

Opportunities that come from society are limitless. This is, after all, where the markets reside. It is for society that organizations exist in order to provide goods and services; making a certain level of profitability is a strong indicator as to how well the firm has efficiently and effectively met societal needs. Finding just the right niche in society to provide unique goods or services is one of the keys to success for any firm. It does not come, however, all that easily. Organizations need to keep their finger on the pulse of society in order to determine   what the trends are and which way they are going. Because (outside of certain totalitarian governments) no one can dictate to society, organizations must research societal needs and wants and then aspire to satisfy them. As we said in chapter 1, strategic managers must gather data, analyze it, and then formulate strategy that best fits with societal realities if they hope to survive and have a long-term future.

Threats that come from society, unfortunately, are also limitless. Because society is actualized through behaviors of people, the future is relatively unpredictable. What someone wants today, they may not want tomorrow and there is no way of controlling these types of patterns. Societal forces can emerge as political powers and act out parochial political agendas which can be either good or bad for the firm. Again, a commitment to research, monitoring, and analysis can provide a firm with its best defense against negative movements from social forces. By maintaining a vigilant attitude toward shifts in societal preferences or needs, firms can remain a step or two ahead of both positive and negative events that occur in this volatile but most promising of environments. The key is a strategic management mentality.

Again, it is the change in societal forces that businesses must be most cognizant of. According to Gitman and McDaniel, the United States is undergoing a dramatic socio-demographic shift. No longer is the U.S. dominated by a white, western culture. There is a very strong emergence of three ethic minority groups; U.S. Hispanics, Asian Americans, and African Americans.[26] The U.S. Census projects by the year 2050, the percentage of whites in the U.S. will drop from approximately 80% to 75% while blacks will rise from 12 to 15%, Asian from 4 to 9%, and Hispanics from 12 to 24% (persons of Hispanic origin may be of any race).[27] Other minority cultures such as U.S. Middle East, ethnics from the former Soviet Union, and even Native Americans are changing both the employment and consumer landscape.

Lifestyle and work trends have also changed over the last few decades. The changing definition and role of the family as well as the establishment of working women (many of whom serve as head of households with little free time) has changed business products as well as the way businesses sell their products and services. More and more people are starting home-based businesses and telecommunicating (approximately 35% of the U.S. workforce according to Dr. Glen Muske, a home-based and micro business specialist) due to their desire to control more of their life and/or the need to provide care for elderly parents and children.[28]

Technological Forces. Certainly the most rapid and revolutionary changes that businesses have had to confront has been in the area of technology management. During the last half of the 20th Century, the world in general and the United States in particular began to move out of what many have referred to as the Industrial Age and into the Information Age.[29] The primary driver for this fundamental shift in how we do business in the 21st Century is the advancement of information technology, especially in computers and communications. For example, the authors have written this book by e-mailing chapters to each other and the publisher, and obtaining many of our examples and information sources from the World Wide Web. Word processing and Internet communications make it possible for the authors to live 2,000 miles apart, but to communicate with each other and share what we have written instantaneously. Sure, like our predecessors, we also use the phone to communicate, but unlike our predecessors, speed dialing, use of cell phones, and the availability of cheap long distance services make our phone conversations routine and easy instead of the event they were in the past. From an inefficiency standpoint, we talk less, communicate far more, and get a lot more work done!

Where we are today in technological development must be understood as only a point along a never-ending continuum. Every day new technological advances come to the market. Each day we can read about new ideas that are in the developmental stage that give a virtual presence to almost every aspect of our personal and business lives. Firms must understand this too, and even for those who do not create and distribute new technologies, they must understand that this growth of technology will impact them. The severity of that impact can be positive or negative and the firm's ability to predict and plan for the use of technology may well mean the difference between success and failure, and not in the all-too-distant future. The world of technological advancement and control is already here.

Opportunities in the technology segment are only limited by one's imagination. In 1996, a remarkable 33% of GDP growth came from information technology industries alone with internet-based businesses accounting for $330 billion dollars of transactions in 2000.[30]

We live in a world in which the impossible begins to be possible. While we do not predict that technology will take over our very lives and relegate human beings to servitude of robots (the real fear present in many science fiction movies and books such as *Terminator, Metropolis,* and *I, Robot*), technological advances will continue to impact our lives as individuals and will certainly impact all organizations. Technology holds the promise of doing business better, faster, at a high level or responsiveness and quality, and more profitably.

World-wide communication and travel has been dramatically improved through satellites and computerized tracking and usage systems. Industries such as medicine and education are being revolutionized by technological advances that make their services more readily available, of higher quality, and easier to manage. E-business is not only common jargon, it's a burgeoning commercial reality. While marketers have quickly discovered the promise of the Internet and are rapidly building a strong virtual presence for retail concerns around the world, traditional business are discovering the improvement of inventory management (such as JIT, just-in-time inventory systems) which result from computerization.[31] And this list could go on and on. Technology holds tremendous promise for the future.

Threats from technology exist as well. Technology can be used to invade privacy, conduct illegal activities such as the distribution of child pornography, annoy (such as some purveyors of telemarketing), and inappropriately control the activities of others. E-business isn't always what it's supposed to be. Organizations are just as susceptible to abuse from unethical users of new technological services and tools as are individuals. Hackers can gain access to an organization's computer system and steal, alter, or erase important data (even in sensitive government installations). Internet experts can invade a firm's website and alter or destroy it. Internet viruses are common and where successful severely damaging. The glories of technologies appear to come with a whole new era of hazards and all firms who develop a dependence on technology, especially publicly-accessed technology, must have back-ups and security systems to guard against what might happen in this crucially important segment of our 21st century environment.

More importantly, convergence marketing has emerged as a critical area of research in that many consumers exhibit what Wind, Mahajan, and Gunther call hybrid consumer behavior. That is, consumers will use one form of technology for researching a purchase, such as the Internet, yet purchase the product or service through a different medium (i.e. in stores sales, telephone purchase, or through catalog). How consumers combine their on-line and off-line behaviors is vital to how businesses can promote their products and services and facilitate purchases.[32] Secondly, the marketing of high-end technology products and services in terms of business-to-business sales has required the emergence of relationship marketing and the understanding of high-tech consumers.[33]

Those firms who do not bend with the wind of technological change usually are destroyed by it. The annals of history are strewn with a list of dinosaur corporations such as Western Union (telegram), Smith-Corona (typewriters), Western Electric (rotary telephones) and Atari (computer game systems) all of whom were innovators in their time but who could not change fast enough to keep up with new technological products.

International Forces. We include the international segment in this discussion because of the explosive growth of international commerce, travel, and communication. Certainly linked to the global growth of technology, as we identified it above, internationalism is also a growing economic reality with the formation of the European Union (EU), the North American Free Trade Act (NAFTA), and the World Trade Organization (WTO).[34] The fall of communist governments in Europe during the late 1980's and early 1990's removed a serious threat to international cooperation and spurred dramatic investments in Eastern Europe and China (which is still officially a communist state, but one that has chosen to adopt many western business practices and now enjoys the status as one of the world's richest markets). Trade barriers still exist, but they have been dramatically lessened in the past several years making it much easier for American businesses to expand in many other parts of the world, but also making it much easier for foreign businesses to expand into the United States. In the U.S., we can no longer be solely concerned about the domestic market. It is important to now recognize the existence and growing importance of a world market, one that contains many opportunities as well as many threats.

Opportunities in the international segment may be found in the areas of developing third world nations with expanded business into new markets, taking advantage of cheaper labor markets for production (and even some services), increasing the organization's basic knowledge base, and taking advantage of different exchange rates.[35] Perhaps the greatest of these opportunities is that of expanding into new markets. Just as entering the Chinese market holds the promise of rapid expansion to meet the demands of an immensely important new market, labor markets that offer cheaper labor and relaxed regulations help domestic firms compete more aggressively in an intensified world setting. Also, some firms find that there is a natural appeal in many new markets of things that are American and a ready market for U.S. goods and services. This is particularly true with countries such as Russia and Japan. Partnering is another major opportunity for domestic and foreign firms. For example, one of the true strategic successes of United Airlines has proven to be the strategic alliances it has with 13 other airlines around the world in the Star Alliance.[36] Though United is an international airline, its foreign destinations are limited (and will probably become even more limited after the bankruptcy filing), but it can still write tickets and send passengers almost anywhere in the world on a United Airlines ticket because of its code sharing capabilities and transfer agreements within the Star Alliance.

Threats also come with a world-wide economy. When a company chooses to do business in a foreign country, the laws of that country may be different, perhaps even significantly different, from those of the United States. Accounting systems also vary from country to country, allowing for varying degrees of openness (called *opacity*), a critical factor for U.S parent companies and overseas investors.[37] Further, U.S. law says that for U.S. companies, the law of the United States is always paramount. So while collusion may be legal in several countries around the world (including Europe), any U.S. company that engages in collusion is in violation of U.S. law. This presents an uneven playing field in several foreign countries and can be a serious threat to American businesses.[38]

Besides legal threats, political threats, consumer threats, and cultural differences can all prove to be hazardous to U.S. firms doing business in other lands. So while the statement in the previous paragraph indicated that there are some places where American goods and services are sought after, there are other places where American goods and services are reviled. Politicians in France continually berate McDonalds Corporation for the proliferation of its golden arches throughout France and how unseemly fast food is in a society that has traditionally viewed meal times as nearly religious experiences. While we note here that the McDonalds restaurants in France continue to be popular with the French people and growth in France continues to meet McDonald's expectations, the negative political environment is simply a threat the golden arches chain needs to contend with.

In this category, please note that we do not include different languages and cultures as necessarily threats in doing business internationally. Certainly if a firm such as Citibank opened up a new office in Tokyo, staffed it with American employees who didn't speak Japanese, and thought it could be successful, this would be a serious blunder. We don't believe that most firms would make such a fundamental mistake – further, these types of issues tend to be operational and not necessarily strategic in nature.[39] Rather, the types of threats we identify in the international segment of the macro environment would be more strategic in nature (miscalculating a country's political stability, not matching goods or services to specific country needs or wants, or underestimating the strength of foreign competition whether that be in doing business domestically or in a foreign setting). We also feel it important to understand that this is one of those areas of the macro environment with which every firm must become more familiar. It is a rapidly growing and expanding segment that is becoming more pervasive for both domestic companies developing a foreign presence and foreign companies establishing a presence in the United States.

International markets are clearly subject to alterations due to changes in the other environmental factors. For example, the increase of terrorism in the U.S. has changed U.S. international policy under George Bush Jr. who therein has placed American troops in both Afghanistan and Iraq. The presence of U.S. troops in the Persian gulf has provoked highly negative reactions from some of the U.S.'s closest trading partners (i.e. Germany, France) with the war efforts negatively impacting the world's economy.   Preliminary estimates are that terrorism alone has cost $1.7 trillion, with the reconstruction of Afghanistan estimated at $ 20 billion[40] and Iraq at $100 billion.[41]

Industry and Market Structures

Once the macro environment has been analyzed, the firm needs to direct its attention to its environmental domain; its industry and market structure.

The Industry Environment

Every organization belongs to an industry. An industry can be defined as a group of firms that provide similar goods or services. So, in making the decision to begin a business, or to continue to operate a business in a given industry, the firm is subject to the specific characteristics, patterns of acceptable activity, competitors, and other industry forces that impact firm performance. Some industries are better, and more attractive, than others. That is, certain industries have higher net incomes than others as shown in Table 3.1. Some industries contain virtually unlimited opportunities, while others have nearly no new opportunities at all. If one were starting up a business from scratch, a study of the industry in which the new firm were to be a part would help identify up front whether or not it was a good idea to break into one particular industry as opposed to another.

A quick examination of Table 3.1 shows that certain industries (such as electric power generation and other arts and entertainment) have a much higher net income than other industries (such as natural gas distribution and coal mining) and the industry average while certain other industries (for example the combination gas and electric and electric power generation) have a higher percentage of firms with a net income than other industries (such as coal mining and natural gas distribution) and the industry average. This information indicates that not all industries are alike and that certain industries have both greater risk (lower percent with positive net income) and greater rewards

Table 3.1
A Comparative Analysis of Several Industries' Average Net Income (2002)[42]

Corporate Profitability by Industry	Average Net Income as % of Revenue	% of corporations with Net Income
Totals- all active corporations	6.3%	56.9%
ARTS, ENTERTAINMENT, AND RECREATION		
Other arts, entertainment, and recreation	10.0%	44.2%
Amusement, gambling, and recreation industries	6.5%	54.1%
AGRICULTURE, FORESTRY, FISHING & HUNTING		
Agricultural production	5.2%	51.7%
Forestry and logging	3.9%	55.0%
Support activities & fishing, hunting and trapping	4.6%	55.8%
MINING		
Oil & gas extraction	6.7%	55.5%
Coal mining	2.8%	17.3%
Metal ore mining	6.1%	47.3%
Nonmetallic mineral mining & quarrying.	7.1%	45.5%
Support activities for mining	9.3%	47.8%
UTILITIES		
Electric power generation, transmission & distribution	11.4%	64.6%
Natural gas distribution	2.0%	39.8%
Water, sewage & other systems	8.5%	56.5%
Combination gas & electric	9.8%	92.5%

(higher net income) when benchmarked against overall industry averages. Certain industries are consequently more attractive for new and existing businesses than others.

Going back to our opening case, the air transportation industry has a net income of 5.7% with 42.9% of firms showing net income[43] versus the industry average of 6.3% and 56.9% respectively. Clearly the industry has more risk and less reward then industry averages yet these figures do not reveal to us what are the forces that have impacted the industry and yielded such a poor financial performance.

Writer Michael Porter provides us with a generally accepted schema for determining industry attractiveness. He does this by identifying five different forces that characterize various industry elements and then provides us with a way of viewing that industry to determine if it is, in fact, the optimal industry in which a firm can sustain a healthy growth pattern and achieve better than average profits. The stronger these competitive forces are within the industry, the greater the overall competitive nature of the industry will be and thus the lower the profitability of that industry and the attractiveness of that industry.

For example, the professional sports industry generates over $8 billion dollars[44] a year yet team sports such as baseball, basketball, and hockey have predominately unprofitable teams.[45] Several writers have alluded to the fact that costs have risen in the industry spurred by the change to free player agency status (players may pick and choose which team to play for), team expansion, overlapping seasons, the increased number of games, and the over saturation of sports in the media.[46] As a pure business enterprise, sports teams do not seem to be a very attractive investment and investors might be well advised to invest in businesses with stronger industry fundamentals. So what are these major driving forces?

The five major forces that impact industry attractiveness are depicted in Figure 3.3 and include; 1) the bargaining power of suppliers; 2) the bargaining power of buyers; 3) the level and intensity of inter-competitive rivalry; 4) the existence of substitute produces or services; and 5) the threat of new entrants.[47] The strength of these forces may change as the industry evolves over time, for the betterment

of the industry or for its worse, as seen in the introductory airline
industry case.

Figure 3.3
Industry Structure and Competitive Forces

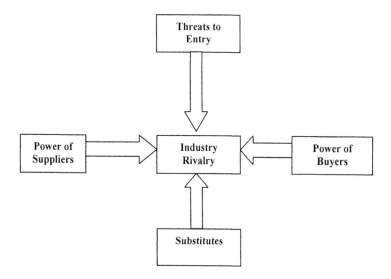

⟨ **The Bargaining Power of Suppliers.** Suppliers constitute
any source in the supply chain that controls a firm's ability to obtain
resources. From obvious suppliers such as vendors of raw materials to
other suppliers not quite so obvious as the labor market, anyone or any
organization that can influence a firm's ability to acquire the input
elements it needs to operate as efficiently as possible is of concern in
determining the attractiveness of a firm's industrial environment. In
certain industries, there are a wide variety of suppliers who compete
with each other for the firm's business. This is obviously good for the
firm who can find the highest quality inputs at the lowest possible
price. Here, the bargaining power of suppliers is low. On the other
hand if there are few suppliers and there is a demand for their goods or

services, then the bargaining power of supplier is high and firms will acquire their inputs at higher cost and potentially of lesser value.

In examining the airline industry, Grimm and Smith suggested that two major concerns for airlines would be the relatively few suppliers of aircraft (now down to only two globally, Boeing and Airbus), and the high degree of unionism.[48]   Both of these characteristics are major threats to airlines who have little control over the cost of new aircraft or how much they both pay and manage labor. Fuel costs are yet another major threat. Opportunities in this area would include many suppliers and an abundance of supplies. For the airline industry these could include a plethora of catering services, and empty gates at airports. In general, however, supplier power is strong in this industry thus reducing its profitability and making it less attractive.

Other industries may have stronger or weaker relations with their suppliers. For example, the pharmaceutical industry's main sources of supplies are mined chemicals, a commodity, while the soft drink industry's products are predominately comprised of water and carbonation. Both of these industries benefit from low, competitive supplier pricing since they purchase in bulk and the raw materials are highly standardized. On the other hand, firms in the ambulance industry must purchase their vehicles from specialized vehicle converters, not the major automobile manufacturers. These converters act as job order shops, that is, they work on a demand basis. They either convert existing vehicle bodies (hearses or vans) or build their own box chaises which are placed onto a cab's frame. The cost of the base vehicle, coupled with the cost of the conversion process, dramatically increases industry operating expenses with lack of supplier inventory leaving little room for price negotiation.[49]

The Bargaining Power of Buyers. When buyers have little choice among firms for the goods or services they need, this creates major opportunities for those firms.   On the other hand, when consumers have a choice, and particularly if they have a wide choice, their bargaining power is great and thereby a threat to the firm. Monopolies and oligopolies can create major opportunities for themselves in dealing with consumers. Utility companies and cartels such as OPEC can dictate to the consumer and the consumer can do little about it. Of course, in the United States, monopolistic behavior is heavily regulated to curb the potential abuse and collusion is illegal for U.S. companies (though even U.S. law cannot curb the negative market effects of foreign cartels such as OPEC whose members do business in the United States).

Again in Grimm and Smith's examination of the airline industry, they pointed out two elements that affect this particular market force – a large customer base and the high degree of purchasing leverage.[50] The large customer base is a clear opportunity for airlines, as is a time when no other airlines are engaged in fare wars (here, airlines often charge higher ticket prices knowing that competitors are likely to match them). These same two elements, however can also be threats. As September 11th demonstrated, when the flying public becomes panicked and stops flying, this is a tremendous threat to the airlines. Likewise, when competitors begin fare wars, other airlines servicing those routes almost always go along and discount their fares as well, thereby reducing their profitability.

More importantly, the internet explosion has allowed consumers to not only shop airline websites and easily compare prices, but bargain and discount websites as well. Most of the airlines in the industry, with the exception of Southwest Airline and Jet Blue, allow discount e-companies such as Priceline.com, Cheaptickets.com, and Orbit.com to serve as intermediary vendors for their seats and must share a percentage of their profits with these brokers.

Other industries have an even weaker hold on the customer than the airline industry. For example, in the health care industry many health care providers are not selected based upon the consumer's perception of who provides the best health care service (doctor, hospital, or surgeon) but by whom the consumer's insurance company or health maintenance organization is willing to reimburse. If the doctor or medical facility is not a member of the consumer's insurance program, then the consumer is not likely to choose that provider since expenses would come out of his or her own pocket. In many states and counties, Medicaid (government provided insurance for the poor and the disabled) has removed freedom of choice completely from the consumer and dictate who the medical provider will be for the Medicaid recipient.[51]

⌐ **The Existence or Potential Threat of Substitute Products or Services.** Most firms in an industry need to be concerned about the potential that their current customer base may become dissatisfied with their industry's products and services. The greater the access customers have to industry substitutes, the more competitive and less attractive the industry. Substitutes usually refer to competing industry products such as data storage devices (hard drives, disks, tapes, CD's, DVD's) or drink containers (glass, aluminum, or plastic) where there is fairly clear separation of industry products and services. Industries like clothing, food, and housing, have minimal substitutes while other industries such as the airline industry have numerous substitutes including driving one's own car, taking the train or boat, or forgoing a trip. In Grimm and Smith's study of the airline industry, they identified other transportation modes especially for short flights and telecom innovations as potential threats.[52] As the airlines have seen, both of these threats have become very real following September 11th. Interestingly enough, in Europe and Japan, the train service is often better than airline service and has been an excellent substitute for a long time. The events of 2001 have only deepened this threat to the European and domestic Japanese airline industries.

Substitutes clearly play a role in technologically driven industries. For example, the changing forms of information storage for personal computers (cassette tapes, floppy discs, hard discs, tape backups, MP3's, CD's and DVD's) has challenged both storage technology firms and personal computer manufacturers to keep up with the changing technologies and has dramatically dropped the costs of the older storage devices. Other industries, such as emergency transportation (ambulance and emergency airlift) and higher education (degree programs) have few acceptable substitutes given the nature of the product or service and thereby allow firms in those industries to increase their prices (unless otherwise regulated) and obtain greater profitability and attractiveness.

Technology, industry evolution, or firm strategy may challenge some of these industry delineations. For example, the soft drink/soda industry, historically defined as carbonated drinks, had been threatened by changes in consumer preferences in the 1990's for such unlikely industry product substitutes as bottled water, iced tea, and other specialty cold drinks. Rather than forcing customers to choose between products in different industries, the major firms in the soft drink industry (Coca Cola and PepsiCo) redefined the industry through product development and acquisitions to encompass these other products. Also, change in technology from analog to digital recording and playback devices for audio, video and computers has integrated the information storage industry through CD's and DVD's. The separation between the computer industry, and audio and video electronics has become smaller and smaller.

    The Threat of New Entrants in the Industry. Dealing with the current competition is hard enough. Being in an industry that allows or invites new competitors makes things just that much harder for firms trying to compete successfully in their chosen industries. As indicated earlier in Table 3.1, some industries have higher profitability and lower risk than others and are attractive enough to encourage new firms to join them; other industries make it easy for new entrants with low barriers to entry (little capital investment and/or industries that encourage high levels of entrepreneurialism); while still others have entry barriers so high that it's very difficult to break in to. The automobile industry, for example, is so extremely capital intensive that it's nearly impossible to start a new car company and compete with the American or Japanese car makers. Often it isn't just an issue of capital – tradition, a loyal customer base, and reputation may be barriers too high to get over. On the other hand, industries like the restaurant industry allow new companies to enter with relative ease. The harder it is for new organizations to enter an industry, the lesser the threats to the industry and the higher the industry attractiveness and profitability. However, the easier it is for new organizations to enter an industry, the greater the threats to current industry incumbents.

    In their study of the airline industry, Grimm and Smith identified three significant forces at work – frequent flier programs, slot restrictions at airports, and ownership of computerized reservation systems[53]. All of these present barriers to new entrants. Frequent flier programs have the express purpose of building loyalty between the airline and its customers. Frequent fliers are going to patronize the same airline if they know they are accruing credits for free flights, upgrades, or other benefits. The opportunity of devising a frequent flier program, then, marries passengers to a particular airline and makes it more difficult for an up-start to gain the same customer loyalty since frequent flier programs are costly to the airline, obligate future resources, and create additional accounting and monitoring systems.

Slot restrictions are a barrier when one airline is able to monopolize the limited slots allotted to each airport for flight landings and takeoff. Likewise, being able to control a reservation system (such as the Alliance Reservation System owned by United and the Apollo Reservation System owned by American) allows an airline to preference its flights when travel agents are selecting flights for clients. United's and American's systems control almost 100% of all U.S. domestic reservations through travel agents – a severe threat to other current airlines as well as new entrants. An opportunity for the other airlines is to counter with web-based airline sites which also make reservations, often at a discounted price (such as Southwest Airlines and Jet Blue).

Changes in entrance barriers usually occur through changes in government policy (increased or decreased industry regulation) or technology. The deregulation of the airline industry in 1978, as stated in the introductory case, reduced entrance barriers by allowing for price competition and competitive routes. Information technology, such as e-mail, streaming audio/video, chat rooms, and search engines has made learning easier and more consumer-friendly and has lead to the emergence of a new breed of colleges and universities – universities without walls.[54]

The Level of Rivalry Among Competitors. Different industries tend to have different traditions for rivalry amongst competitors. The predictors generally tend to be the number of competitors in a market or the volatility of the product or service. For an industry such as the soft drink industry, the rivalry between Coke and Pepsi is legendary. Each company continually tries to outdo the other, spending millions upon millions of advertising dollars to try to convince the soft drink public that their particular products are better than their competition's. This high cost of doing business depresses both Coke's and Pepsi's ability to earn high profits on their primary product and forces both to look at expanding their businesses into other areas to help improve profitability. An important secondary effect of this rivalry, however, is that Coke and PepsiCo have cornered most of the soft drink market by outnumbering the other competitors' products in their market and by outspending the rest of the market in advertising.

Grimm and Smith described several elements of the airline industry that impact industry rivalry.[55]   They cited moderate concentration or airline companies within the market, little product differentiation, information being readily available to both consumers and competitors, and relatively high marginal costs as forces that increase the rivalry in the industry. Retail clothing chains also engage in high levels of rivalry and continuously are challenged by stocking issues as they attempt to provide the public with the height of fashion at the best price. Inventory costs and miscalculations can be disastrous. On the other hand, industries such as those of utilities have little to no rivalry and don't have to worry about advertising or inventories in the same way as the retail industries. Between these examples, however, is a large continuum of other industries where the level of rivalry can vary from high or low.

As we suggested in Figure 3.3, changes in industry rivalry are caused by changes in the other four forces. New substitutes increase the competitive pressure on firms in the industry as a whole by imposing price ceilings.   For example, consumers continued to purchase VCR's over DVD players until the price of the DVD players dropped to a point where consumers felt the higher price was warranted by the perceived greater value of DVD's.   Strong entrance barriers reduce rivalry, as in the case of regulated monopolies such as cable services, while few entrance barriers lead to increased competition and the possibility of price wars, such as in the retail clothing.   Last, supplier and buyer power determine the ability of the industry to buy low and sell high, which in turn affects industry rivalry. When costs are low and customers have little buying power profits are high and there is little need to compete.   On the other hand, when firms are squeezed by both their suppliers and buyers and profits are low, competition ignites. Rivalry will be discussed in more detail throughout the text and in particular the upcoming section on market structures.

Using the Porter Model to Analyze an Industry

Given the importance of understanding the driving forces of an industry and the impact of these forces on the existing firm, it is imperative that a firm's industry be analyzed. We recommend the following steps in analyzing any industry:[56]

1. **Define the industry.** The U.S. Census Bureau's *Standard Industry Classification Manual* can be searched on-line using the Standard Industry Classification (SIC) six digit code at http://www.osha.gov/oshstats/sicser.html. This code, however, was replaced in 1997 and updated in 2002 by The North American Industry Classification System (NAICS). NAICS (http://www.census.gov/epcd/www/naics.html) was developed jointly by the U.S., Canada, and Mexico to provide new comparability in statistics about business activity across North America. A translation table (SIC to NAICS) is available at http://www.census.gov /epcd/www/naicstab.htm.

2. **Obtain information about the industry.** Industry studies may be available from brokerage houses, consulting firms, trade associations, state and local governments, the press, watchdog groups, agency regulators, and trade magazines. Dun and Bradstreet offers a free search service at http://www.zapdata.com/ that allows you to look up a company by SIC code and obtain industry reports. Field data may also have to be gathered from buyer and supplier groups.

3. **Breakdown the industry into its five major forces listing the major factors/groups for each force.** (See Table 3.2) Delete any factors or forces that have little or no impact on the industry at first glance.

Table 3.2
A Sample Breakdown of the Five Forces for the Airline Industry

Buyer Groups	Supplier Groups	Substitutes	Entrance Barriers	Rivalry
Business	Fuel	Train	Frequent Flyer Programs	High Marginal Costs
Vacation	Airplanes	Car	Slot Restrictions	Commodity Product
Resellers	Capital	Bus	Computerized Reservations	Prices Easy to Obtain

4. **Make a judgment as to the relative strength of the force as it affects the industry and then assess the industry as a whole.** There are several differing methodologies that could be employed to perform this type of analysis.   The most orthodox and comprehensive method is to analyze each of the subfactors described by Michael Porter for each force.[57] These subfactors are located in Table 3.3, below.

Sherman and Wilcox© recommended evaluating each factor on a 1-5 scale (1=leads to no competition, 5= leads to intense competition), and, if necessary, weighting each subfactor (using personal judgment).   Each force's score is then calculated by multiplying the score for each subfactor by its weighting factor, summating the product for each subfactor, and then dividing the total score by the number of subfactors. See Table 3.4. A total industry score is obtained by summating each force's score and then dividing by that number by 5 (the number of forces). Weighting could also be applied to each force, if necessary.[58] See Table 3.5.

Although the data derived from this analysis is judgmental in nature, it can be combined with more objective measures (i.e. industry growth rates, industry profitability) for purposes of industry comparisons. Analysts are then able to make judgments as to which industries seem more or less attractive to be in. More importantly,

Table 3.3
Five Forces Subfactors[59]

Buyer Groups	Supplier Groups	Substitutes	Entrance Barriers	Rivalry
# of Customers/ Volume	Concentration of Suppliers	Substitute Attractiveness	Economies of Scale	Equality of Size and Capability
% of Industry Purchases	Substitute Supplies	Switching Costs	Product Differentiation	Product Demand
Product Differentiation	Importance of Industry/ Customer	Differentiation of Substitute	Capital Requirements	Fixed and Storage Costs
Switching Costs	Importance of Supplier Products		Switching Costs	Product Different-iation
Buyer Profitability	Supplier Product Differentiation		Distribution Channels	Economies of Scale
Threat/ Backward Integration	Threat of Forward Integration		Cost Disadvantages	Diversity of Competitors
Industry's Importance			Government Policy	Stake in Success
Buyer Information			Expected Retaliation	Exit Barriers

Table 3.4
Industry Analysis: Supplier Power

Concentration of Suppliers			
Substitute Supplies			
Importance of Industry/Customer			
Importance of Supplier Products			
Supplier Product Differentiation			
Threat of Forward Integration			
	Scale 1-5	100%	Total/6=Score

Table 3.5
Industry Analysis: Master Chart

Force	Assessment	Weighting	Subtotal
Buyers			
Suppliers			
Rivalry			
Entrance			
Barriers			
Substitutes			
	Scale 1-5	100%	Total/5=Industry Competitiveness

Figure 3.4
Industry Competitiveness Trend: Ambulance Industry

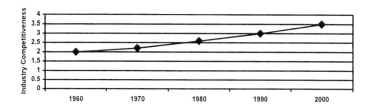

these industry competitiveness rating scores can be taken over a period of time and then plotted to determine whether and how the industry's attractiveness has changed. Forecasts based upon trend analyses can be developed from these industry analyses as demonstrated in Figure 3.4. Note that in this hypothetical analysis of the ambulance industry competitiveness has increased over time making the industry less attractive.

Market Structures

Another approach to studying rivalry in an industry is by examining the particular competitive structure of the market. Those who have studied basic economic theory understand that there are basically four different types of market structures that a firm may be operating in: perfect competition, monopolistic or imperfect competition, oligopoly, and pure monopoly.[60] Market structures partially determine the strategies available to the firm and form a continuum of strategies based upon a firm's ability to compete on low price or product differences as shown in Figure 3.5 below.

Figure 3.5
Market Structures[61]

	Perfect Competition	Monopolistic Competition	Oligopoly	Monopoly
Number of Sellers	Numerous	Many	Few	One
Ability to Set Price	None	Some	Some	Substantial
Product Substitution	None	Substantial	Some	None

Perfect Competition. In *perfect competition*, there are numerous sellers (each firm has a small market share), unrestricted market entry and exit, the products sold by each firm are similar, and buyers and sellers have equally good information. Under these market conditions long-run profitability is minimal since firms are forced to set their prices equal to market conditions, otherwise consumers will purchase competitors' less expensive products. Short-term profitability is achieved by setting the number of units produced to a point which maximizes total profits (the greatest difference between total revenue and total cost).[62] Industries that operate in this fashion, that is sell commodities, include agriculture and coal.

Rivalry under these conditions requires that the firm's strategy focus on adjusting plant size and capacity until profits are maximized both in the short run and in the long run. That is, firms in these markets focus on the efficiency of their operations, not competitor actions nor product innovation, and produce just enough units to satisfy consumer demands for a good at a specific price level. In these market conditions profit is extremely hard to come by since it is only achieved through effective management decision-making, not through the specific actions of any one firm to change market conditions.

Monopolistic Markets. The opposite market condition to perfect competition is a *monopoly*. Although this term beckons images of chicanery, skullduggery, and consumer swindling, the concept of a monopoly is quite simple – a single supplier of goods and services for an entire industry where there are no acceptable substitutes.[63] Monopolistic markets are those markets that have one seller, stiff barriers to entry, significant ability in setting prices, require huge investments of capital, lack economies of scale (the more units you produce the less profit you make), have government restrictions through regulations and tariffs, and involve intellectual property (such as patents).

The reality for firms in monopolistic situations is that they cannot charge just any price they wish for a product. Consumers do not have limitless resources and demand for the product will be directly connected to the demand for the product at certain price levels; the higher the price the lower the demand.[64] Even products that are inelastic in nature (those products that have no substitutes and are considered vital, i.e. milk), will be subject to the laws of demand since these products may have imperfect substitutes (for milk, perhaps soy milk) or consumers will reduce the frequency of their purchases.

Competitive strategy for a monopolistic firm is defined by either a firm's ability to find the production point which maximizes total profits (total revenues – total costs), where price is set by a demand curve or by government regulation. The irony of a monopoly is that some monopolies may be unprofitable – this may occur when the government sets the price so low as to negate profit at any production level or when the cost structure of the industry makes it impossible to obtain a price that would yield a profit (in both cases the demand for the product at every price level is lower than the cost of producing the product). This has occurred to some extent in the health care industry where HMO's (Health Maintenance Organizations) and government reimbursement programs (Medicare, Medicaid) have decreased their payout rates to medical providers to such an extent as to make certain medical services unprofitable.[65]

Due to the perception that consumers can be overcharged in monopolistic markets, firms may try to create a monopoly by banding together to form a *cartel*. This an association of producers who set prices and production quotas, such as OPEC (Organization of Petroleum Exporting Countries) for oil and the ACPC (Association of Coffee Producing Countries) for coffee, and the European Union (EU) for currency. This would seem to make sense in commodity markets (i.e. corn, gold, and coal) since these products would normally be subject to market pressures found in perfect competitive markets. Such practices are, however, illegal for firms operating in the United States.

Interestingly enough, world economies are so intertwined that when OPEC dramatically increased the price of oil in the United States in the early and mid-1970's in an attempt to boost their members' economic situation, the scheme backfired. The increase of the price in oil in the U.S. (including the creation of price-driven oil shortages) negatively impacted the economy of the U.S., the major consumer of OPEC oil. This reduced the value of the dollar relative to other world currencies (which many OPEC oil countries were holding) and decreased the demand for OPEC oil. OPEC was forced to drop their price of oil to a point where in 2003 the average price of a barrel of crude oil (around $25) is quite low compared to the 1970's, accounting for inflation.[66]

Monopolistic (Imperfect) Competition. Most firms find themselves in either imperfect competition or in an oligopoly. *Imperfect competition* is defined as markets where there are numerous sellers of varying size and capacity, there is a lack of price collusion, there is easy market entry, products vary in style and features, sales promotion and advertising are employed to gain consumer attention, firms have some leeway in setting prices, and long-run economic profits are not possible for most firms.   Examples of imperfect competitive markets include clothing, retail appliances, and personal computers.

Because of varied product features and styles between competitors, firms are guided by their own supply-demand curves and set their output to the production point that maximizes profit.   Profits and losses are determined by the firm's ability to charge prices equal to or greater than the average industry cost, especially in those cases where the firm's costs are below those of the industry.   In these markets, consumers are willing to pay higher that what a perfect competitive industry would charge for a product or service due to the variety of optional features available for a product or service type.[67] Product variations raise product prices to a point where the consumers just become indifferent to the extra features – these features must add value in the eyes of the consumers.

An excellent example of how price varies over product features and functions can be observed in the motel/hotel industry. Firms such as Motel 6 and Days Inns offer minimal accommodations and features and basically offer customers a simple, clean place to stay for the night at a lower than average industry cost.   Other hotel chains such as Marriot and Hilton feature numerous amenities (i.e. HBO TV, room service, plush accommodations) which increase room costs above the industry average yet are justifiable in the eyes of the consumers.

Oligopolistic Markets.   In this last type of market, there are a small number of firms in an industry and each firm is pretty well aware of what their competitors will do in terms of product pricing and production; *oligopolistic* competition.   These market structures occur due to huge entrance barriers (i.e. government regulations, economies of scale) and through mergers and acquisitions.   Firms in these markets charge prices that exceed those that would occur in perfect competitive markets since cooperative pricing behavior amongst competitors minimizes the need to compete directly with one another.

Interestingly enough, price changes in these markets tend to be minimal since a raising of prices may lose customers to competitors who may maintain their price and lowering prices will merely produce a price war since competitors will be forced to match lower prices or lose customers. Firms in these industries tend to absorb changes in their cost structure (increase/decrease) and maintain their price since the gain/loss of profitability is minimal and given the fact that shifts in price will have no positive long-term affect on profitability.[68] Oligopolies are alive and well in the United States and include products such as cigarettes, automobiles, movie cinemas, and airlines.

Strategy and the Industry Life Cycle

Another way of looking at the attractiveness of an industry is to be able to see where the industry lies along a life cycle continuum. Figure 3.6 provides a schematic drawing of the basics of industry life cycle theory.[69] There are five different stages in an industry life cycle: introduction, growth (rapid and steady), shakeout, maturity, and decline. Each of these stages in an industry life cycle have a dramatic impact on the firms within it and create its own set of opportunities and threats.

Overview. In general, when a new idea or set of products or services become evident, firms that decide to promote and deliver these products or services create a new industry. For example, when Steven Jobs and Steve Wozniak decided to build a small personal computer, they started an industry. While other major computer companies were aware of the concept (IBM had the technology for a personal computer already developed through the R&D process, but had decided to sit on the idea until they felt the time was right), Jobs and Wozniak were the first to bring their personal computer to market in a meaningful way. They created the personal computer industry.

Introduction. At the beginning, sales are minimal, and costs of production are high yielding a net loss. The diagram in Figure 3.6 traces these two crucial outcome indicators and shows that initially, founding firms, and thereby the industry, have small sales and net losses. However, as sales pick up, losses begin to decline. This stage of industry development normally requires highly entrepreneurial firms who have enough working capital to get past the rough beginning times and slow sales and have the belief that their efforts will eventually be rewarded. This was clearly true of Jobs and Wozniak.

Figure 3.6
Industry Life Cycle

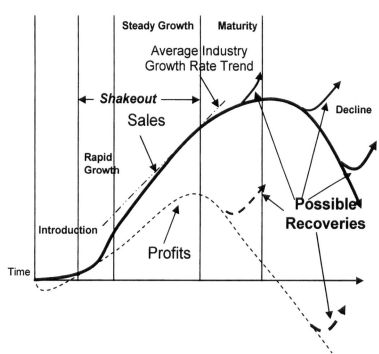

Opportunities in this stage of the industry life cycle are speculative, but for those firms who decide to jump into an emergent market control of the market provides major benefits. Threats stem from the reality that until the market proves itself and reaches takeoff status, the market could also prove to be non-existent. Firms that bet on such a market could lose everything.

Growth. The second major part of the cycle is that of growth. However, there are two distinctive parts of the growth segment – rapid growth and steady growth.[70] *Rapid growth* takes place at a point referred to as takeoff. After a period of developing a market, suddenly the new product or service becomes popular and the firm takes off.

The threats that come with this are that one of two things can happen. The firm may not be able to meet demand and will either one, lose customers due to non-performance, or two, purchase products from competitors or pay additional expenses (such as overtime) to try to meet customer demand. In either case, profits may be squeezed or non-existent and financing major growth could be damaging to the firm's bottom line. However, for those firms that can take advantage of takeoff through strong financial and management structures, the opportunities from rapid growth can include growing profits and the opportunity to eclipse weaker competitors.

Steady growth is where most firms want to be. Steady growth is defined as supporting growth at approximately the same level of growth as the industry or slightly above it as shown in Figure 3.6 (and which can only be defined when steady growth is true for the industry and not necessarily for the firms within it). When a firm is able to achieve steady growth, it is better able to predict future sales trends, plan effectively, and create the financial and marketing structures that will support that growth. Opportunities here include expanding into new markets to sustain steady growth, expanding product or service lines, or perhaps taking over weaker competitors to reduce competition while continuing to grow. Threats include that competitors will find ways of achieving a competitive advantage over the focal firm and causes that firm to begin to lose sales (begin to enter the maturity phase). Management weaknesses in this stage can be costly.

Shakeout – a Bump in the Road to Maturity. Growth in any industry attracts numerous new entrants who want to take advantage of an already developed market that still may have an untapped customer-base and additional revenues. These new competitors may or may not have the resources and capabilities required in order to take advantage of these growth opportunities, however, like sharks they smell blood in the water and cannot help themselves from trying to take a piece of the market. A shakeout occurs when there are so many competitors in the industry that the industry becomes over-saturated with products and services to a point where industry growth (the demand) is slower than industry supply.[71]

This hyper-competition changes the dynamics of the industry. Firms, who because of the inherent growth in the industry normally did not need to heavily compete with rivals firms (there were enough customers for everyone), now find themselves fighting not only for new customers but struggling to maintain their current customer base. Expansion plans are put on hold (i.e. building new plants, developing new products) in order to put revenues into marketing, customer service, and/or price wars in order to build entrance barriers and force out new competitors.

It is inevitable that once the floodgate of competition is opened that some firms, both new and existing, will be washed away. These tend to be firms who lacked a strategic direction or who went into heavy debt in order to support their expansion plans. Going back to the airline industry in the 1970's after deregulation, firms such as People's Express (a new entrant) and Braniff Airlines (an established airline) continued to grow their operations through new routes and the purchasing of new airplanes while the industry was entering a shakeout phase. Braniff in particular continued to pour millions into such extravagances as the 'ultra' look and hired the famous designer Roy Frowick Holston to create an elegant flight attendant uniform. A new color uniform of rich earth tones and luxurious leather seats were also introduced to the aircraft fleet while the company spent $75 million on a new 446,000 square foot world headquarters, "Braniff Place", at Dallas-Forth Worth airport. Given this excessiveness in a tough market, it was inevitable that Braniff would close its doors on May 12, 1982.[72]

Maturity. We define the maturity phase as a time when firms begin to grow at a rate below the historical average of the industry, and do so for a significant period of time. A word of caution here – September 11th led to a general decline in the economy and many firms and many industries experienced lower sales levels. Does this mean that they were in maturity? Obviously not. This is one of the important challenges to the analyst. If the economy experiences a major shock, such as 9/11, firms still must respond to a decline in demand, but cannot confuse the decline in demand with a lack of enthusiasm for their products or services.

That said, maturity does occur when those industries that have reached their peak of attractiveness to their central markets (demand has stabilized) begin to lose business to other industries that have successor or attractive substitute products. Because of the already large investment in capital structures and systems, a decline in the sales growth rate is not always matched with a decline in production expense, resulting in a decline in profits. As long as this process goes unchecked, profits continue to decline and can even become negative. The American automobile industry may well be in the maturity stage. Innovation exists, but the cost of new automobiles, the presence of major international competition, the general improved quality of automobiles all lead to lower sales for the industry in general.

There are both opportunities and threats for firms who find themselves in a mature industry. Threats include the inability to change rapidly enough to parallel declining sales with declining costs and keep the profitability steady; being so focused on the firm's traditional business that it fails to see substantive changes in its own industry structure; and waiting too long to respond. Opportunities include new products or services that come from R&D activities that can reignite industry attractiveness; recognizing trends early and moving assets into businesses in other industries; and finding new economies and efficiencies that allow management to treat the company as a cash cow to repay stockholders and prepare for an industry exit.

Decline.   Not all, but some industries enter the final stage, decline. Decline is defined as a negative sales rate for the industry for a demonstrable period of time. Once more, for 2002, the airline industry experienced a net decline in sales and negative profits but there are other factors including 9/11 that need to be understood before declaring the airline industry in decline.[73]   The passenger rail services in the United States, however, are clearly in decline: losing money, losing consumer support, and being unable to compete with other forms of passenger transportation. Will the industry die? It is a very realistic possibility. Should a new firm enter this industry? Most likely not. What's the prognosis for firms in the industry? It isn't good. This is the threat of decline – death. Any firm that finds itself in a declining industry is in peril of closing its doors.

Industry declines can also occur through changes in technology leading to product and process innovation. The telecommunications industry has experienced a dramatic decline not only due to deregulation but also due to the fact that technology has allowed for numerous inexpensive communications methods outside of the traditional use of the telephone. E-mail, telephony, such as computer-driven phone service, cable phone service, wireless phones, chat rooms, etc... have pitted regional and long-distance phone companies against cable companies, wireless phone companies, and internet access suppliers.[74]

Are there opportunities in declining industries? For competitors outside the industry there may well be. Airlines could provide more convenient and lower priced fares on routes currently served by rail lines and capture the business. While bus services are not in particularly good shape, they have the opportunity for providing service to smaller markets the airlines aren't interested in. For the railroads themselves, there are opportunities as well: they could develop high-speed services that compete with the airlines (such as the Japanese and European railroads have done and continue to do); or they could create a greater presence in commuter areas to relieve commuter congestion.

Possible Recoveries. As Figure 3.6 also indicates, the maturity and decline stages are not necessarily unavoidable, there is the chance for recovery. Opportunities that can result in recovery for the industry occur when firms within the industry develop new product or service lines; open new markets; benefit from a trend shift in consumer preferences; or when substitute products and services prove to be of only temporary interest to consumers. However, as the chart also indicates, it is better for firms within the industry if the recovery occurs earlier rather than later. Losses are harder to overcome the further along an industry slips, and in the later stages of decline, there may be few firms left in the industry to benefit from a turnaround.

Change and the Industry Life Cycle. As we will see in future chapters on business strategy and strategy formation, a firm's strategy is partially dependent upon the stage of their industry's life cycle. For example, it is harder to adopt a business growth strategy when the industry the firm is a part of is in decline. It is paramount that firms not only understand which stage of the life cycle their industry is in but to also discern when there is a shift in the life cycle. Shifts create opportunities and threats for the firm in that there is a potential mismatch between the firm's and its competitors' strategies and the market. Foreseeing these shifts will allow firms early on to consider exit strategies if the industry is forecasted to decline or expansion strategies in case of a rapid growth.

In summary, understanding an industry in terms of where it is within its own life cycle is another way of determining industry attractiveness. While some industries, such as the food industry, tend to defy basic industry life cycle theory, most others help provide strategic decision-makers with valuable knowledge that help them formulate the strategic directions for their companies.

Strategic Groups and Competitive Analysis

The third major environment that organizations must be aware of is the specific area of their industry that contains their most crucial competitors. These are the markets where the focal firm and one or more major competitors go head to head in trying to dominate that market. A strategic group is defined as a set of competitors within an industry with common assets and common strategies.[75] Competitors within strategic groups are very alert to their rivals' activities. Coke is most aware of the competitive activities of Pepsi and vice versa. General Motors is most aware of the competitive activities of Ford and vice versa. It isn't that Coke and Pepsi aren't aware that there are other competitors, including food company store brands; however, these other brands have little impact on their customer base. They also look forward to taking advantage of any missteps their chief competitors make in the same areas.

For instance, when Coke made the mistake of retiring its very popular cola product in favor of a new product, New Coke, a Pepsi-tool-alike, Pepsi took full advantage of the situation and capitalized on its competitor's horrendous mistake.[76] Coke survived, of course, and the rivalry continues, but the incident represents the importance of being fully aware of competitive activities in order to acquire or maintain a competitive advantage.

Competitors in differing strategic groups within an industry use differing capabilities and differing strategies to compete in their marketplace. For example, Coke and Pepsi compete on brand name recognition and offering consumers a broad product line while companies like Adirondack Beverages and Arizona Beverages offer a narrow product line of high quality products, and companies like Royal Crown Cola and Pola Beverages offer low-priced beverages.[77] We will be discussing strategic groups and competition within and between groups in more detail in Chapter 5.

Immediate Environment

The last environmental set we identify here are the forces that exists within the immediate working locale. These forces include the activities that occur in the local community, government regulations that specifically target the firm (or perhaps industry), unions, local labor supply, local costs of living and local standards of living, and other localized phenomena that firms must reconcile in order to conduct their operations as smoothly as possible.[78]

Many firms take local conditions into account when they look at their overall strategic positions. Many purposefully locate in areas where the labor supply is well educated, paid reasonable (or perhaps below market) wages, where local taxes are business-friendly, governmental regulations are low, and community acceptance is high. Over the past several years, states in the eastern part of the United States have lost businesses due to high taxes, highly regulated operating rules, unions, and decaying cities and infrastructures. Many firms in this region have moved south or west where the business climates are far more accommodating and where they can achieve better growth and profitability. More importantly, many such firms have located major installations in the greater global environment to achieve greater levels of growth and profitability.

Smaller businesses are more susceptible changes in the immediate environment than larger firms. These firms may not have the ability or desire to move their operation when local economic conditions change for the worse and are more apt to wait out bad times. Ironically, small businesses in the U.S. represent about 99% of all employers, hire 51% of the private work force, while producing 51% of the private sector output, and include about 22.4 million businesses.[79] These firms may protect themselves from changes in the immediate environment by becoming active members in their community (such as join influential community groups like the local chamber of commerce, the local town's board of trustees, a religious or not-for-profit organization, etc.) and by making their business the community's business.[80]

Summarizing Findings - Opportunities and Threats

Once a strategic decision-maker has completed gathering data from the external environments, the next step is to examine the data for those elements that are clearly desirable opportunities as well as for those elements that are clearly threats to the organization. A list should be developed for each of the four major levels of the external environment, broken down by the specific factors, that describes the specific opportunities and threats. Please note that this analysis has already been detailed for industry attractiveness. See Table 3.6 for an example.

Table 3.6
Macro Environment: Listing Opportunities and Threats

Opportunities
Threats

From this list of each of the factors, a table should be constructed that delineates the four major levels of the external environment (Macro, Immediate, Competitive, and Immediate) and summarizes the findings from the previous factor lists. Each opportunity and threat receives a weighting based on the strategic decision-maker's analysis of the data. The values may shift over time as elements in the external environments themselves go through their constant change process, which again confirms the importance of strategic planning being a process and not an event. At the time of an analysis, however, the categorization of opportunities and threats then provides the strategic planner with some concrete options for developing a solid strategic plan. A value judgment should then be made as to the strength of the opportunities and threats for each of these factors (0= no strength, 10= very strong). See Table 3.7.

Table 3.7

Analyzing the External Environment: Opportunities and Threats

External Environment and Sub Areas	Opportunities Rate Each 0-10	Threats Rate Each 0-10
MACRO ENVIRONMENT ➢ **Political** ➢ **Economic** ➢ **Environmental** ➢ **Social** ➢ **Technological** ➢ **International** **INDUSTRY ENVIRONMENT** ➢ **Industry Competitiveness (from Industry Analysis- Porter)** ➢ **Market Structure** ➢ **Industry Life Cycle** **COMPETITIVE ENVIRONMENT** ➢ **Rivalry** ➢ **Strategic Groups** **IMMEDIATE ENVIRONMENT** ➢ **Local Community** ➢ **Government Regulations** ➢ **Unions** ➢ **Consumers** ➢ **Local Labor Supply** ➢ **Local Economy**	(note: each sub area most likely has several specific opportunities and EACH opportunity should be listed and evaluated here)	(note: each sub area most likely has several specific threats and EACH threat should be listed and evaluated here)
Number of Factors Used in Analysis = N	**Average Weight**	**Average Weight**

     This data could then be placed on a continuum by subtracting the score for threats from the score for opportunities as we suggest in Figure 3.7.

Figure 3.7
A Continuum of Opportunities and Threats

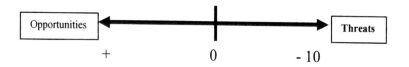

    +   0   - 10

     The next step is to analyze the internal environment, which we take up in Chapter 4.

Summary

     In this chapter, we began with an introductory case on the airline industry as it moves from a regulated to unregulated environment.   A discussion then followed as to the external environments of organizations and why strategic decision-makers must be conscious of the potential opportunities and threats that are found in them. These environments may be classified into four distinct sets: the Macro Environments where everything happens; the Industry Environment where general forces of attractiveness and competitiveness shape acceptable and unacceptable levels of fit between the firm and the industry; the Competitive Environment, a subset of the Industry Environment, but an environment that is created between a focal firm and its most immediate competitors; and finally the Immediate Environment with encompasses the resources, local conditions, and operating realities that characterize the locations where a firm chooses to do business.

     More specifically, the Macro Environment consists of political, environmental, economic, social, technological and international forces which create opportunities and threats for a firm while Industry Environment can be analyzed through an analysis of the five forces driving an industry (power of the buyers and suppliers, substitutes, potential entrants, and rivalry), the market structure (perfect competition, monopoly, imperfect competition, and oligopoly), and the industry life cycle (introduction, growth, shakeout, maturity, and decline). Tables and graphs are provided in order to assist in the external analysis. Finally, we discussed a method of evaluating the data a strategic decision-maker would gather in an external analysis to help determine specifically which are the most important opportunities and which are the most important threats in a firm's external environment.

Key Terms and Concepts

After reading this chapter, you should be familiar with the following terms and concepts: case analysis; strategy formulation; external environments; macro environments; industry environments; competitive environments; immediate environment; five forces model; industry life-cycle; market structures; forecasting; opportunities; and threats.

Web sites

The following websites (besides those in the endnotes) should be of interest:

http://www.businessforecasting.com/ - The Institute for Business Forecasting's official website. The site includes about the organization, seminars and conferences, forecasting discussion groups, books and journal articles, and jobs in forecasting.

http://www.bea.doc.gov/bea/dn2.htm - The U.S. Department of Commerce's Bureau of Economic Accounts Industry Accounts Data. Includes industry data on gross domestic product, input-output data, and capital flow.

http://www.mgmt.utoronto.ca/~baum/v21_toc.html - Volume 21 of *Advances in Strategic Management* focuses on the relationships among

industry life cycles, technological change, and firms' strategic choices
– relationships that are central to the fields of strategy, economics, and
organization theory.

http://www.quickmba.com/strategy/porter.shtml   -   QuickMBA's
detailed description of Michael Porter's Five Forces Model of industry
analysis. This includes the specific factors within each force which
determines the relative impact of that force and the competitiveness of
the industry.

Discussion Questions

1. Describe the four levels of external environmental analysis. Why
    do you think some forces of the four different environmental sets
    have different levels of strength, or power, to impact
    organizations?
2. Describe one change in the Macro Environment (PEESTI) as it
    relates to your college education. In your opinion, how has this
    change impacted the industry?
3. Identify an industry that has gone through at least one whole
    industry life cycle. Describe the various stages and how the firms
    within the industry responded.
4. Briefly analyze the airline industry using the five forces model.
    How attractive is the industry?

Exercises

1. Using the introductory case of the airline industry, characterize the
    major opportunities and the major threats that confront individual
    airlines as a group within the industry.
2. By this time in the course, you should have chosen a case you want
    to study (or perhaps the instructor has assigned a case to you).
    Begin to do an external analysis for the case by examining the four
    major environmental levels described in this chapter. Develop a
    list of opportunities and threats for each (see Table 3.6).

3. Evaluate each environmental level using Table 3.7 indicating a score for each factor's opportunities and threats. Obtain summary scores for opportunities and threats.
4. Graph the score using Figure 3.7.

Experiential Exercise

Grocery Store Dilemma[81]

I.   Objective:
To explore the relative merits of three different approaches to developing cooperative relationships among competing businesses in order to successfully compete against a common external thereat to their individual markets.

II.   Process:

Step 1. The Scenario
The instructor will assign you to one of the three grocery stores that are described in the following "Small Town Scenario." Read the entire "Small Town Scenario" concerning the situation facing your grocery store and two other grocery stores in a small town.

SMALL TOWN SCENARIO
You live and work in a small town with three very competitive, small, locally owned grocery stores facing survival-threatening competition from a large supermarket chain that plans to build a super-supermarket in the center of town. You are part of the ownership group of one of these grocery stores; your group has decided to establish an inter-organizational relationship with one or both of the other stores as a means of reducing uncertainty, yet your organization wants to retain as much of the decision-making autonomy as possible. You hire a consultant who has calculated the relative "payoffs" of alternative courses of Inter-organizational Relations (IOR) actions. Soon, a member of your group will meet with representatives of both of the other stores and then privately with the representative of each of the stores: thus three negotiations in which you will agree to some form of

IOR.   The three stores are as follows: Americana Grocery Store specializes in fresh produce but also sells meat and grocery items; Buddy's Grocery Store specializes in locally butchered meat but also sells produce and grocery items; Corner Grocery Store specializes in gourmet and ethnic specialty grocery items but also sells produce and meat. Note that "specializes" means a long tradition of low prices, high quality, and much variety because of personal relationships outside of the organization and technical knowledge of the owners.

Step 2. The Payoff
Familiarize yourself with the following IOR Payoff Schedule.

A.   If your store is not included in any mutual IOR → 0 points
B.   If your store is included in a mutual dyadic IOR:
                contract   → 15 points
                cooptation   → 12 points
                coalition   → 9 points
C.   If your store is included in a mutual triad IOR:
                contract   → 10 points
                cooptation   → 8 points
                coalition   → 6 points

Step 3. The Decision
When the instructor asks you for your grocery stores' decision, write the following sentence on a piece of paper and fill in the blanks without consulting any other store. "Our store, the _____, hereby agrees to enter into a _____ type of inter-organizational relationship with _____ for the purpose of decreasing competitive uncertainty while maintaining a degree of autonomy.

Questions:

1. How could the rules of the exercise be modified to allow for more trust among the three stores?   Would this have made the IOR negotiation easier?

2. If the rules of the exercise had allowed for more complex forms of IOR to be designed, what might one of those have been?

3. Are you aware of a real situation that is similar to the small town scenario of this exercise? How did that situation work out? What form(s) of IOR were involved?

Appendix
Industry References and Other Secondary Sources

In this Appendix, we have listed a wide variety of information resources that an analyst should find useful in getting complete, up-to-the-last-minute information regarding companies and industries. The first part of the list is primarily data bases that can be found in most college, university, and many public libraries. The second part of the list is primarily data bases that one can access directly on the Internet.

North American Industry Classification System (SIC)	-It is an industry classification system that groups' establishments into industries based on the activities in which they are primarily engaged. -Comprehensive system, which covers the entire field of economic activities. -Should be the *first step* in research -Determining the SIC will allow the researcher to use other sources that are organized by SIC codes -This source provides a detailed description of industry groups and sub sectors to assist the researcher in determining, which SIC code best, classifies their topic.
Almanac of Business and Industrial Financial Ratios	-This source gives performance data for 50 operating and financial factors in 179 fields of business. -Some of the highlights of this source are: -It provides fifty performance indicators -Features IRS Data on 3.7 million U.S. Corporations

-It highlights a decade of operating results for 180 industries.

**Encyclopedia of American Industries**

-It is a major business reference tool that provides detailed comprehensive information on a wide range of industries in every realm of American business.
-Separate Volume for Manufacturing & Service/Non-Manufacturing Industry.
-Text
-Sections Included:
 Industry Snapshots
 Industry Organization & Structure
 Work Force
 Current Conditions
 Industry Leaders
 Industry Background &
  Development
 Further Readings

Encyclopedia of Global Industries	-This is a reference source that chronicles the history, development, and current status of 115 international industries.
	-Text
	-Sample of Topics Included:
	    Amusement Parks
	    Credit & Debit Cards
	    Gambling Facilities
	    Gemstone Mining
	    Shipbuilding
	    Aquaculture
	    Aircraft
	    Train Equipment
	-Sections Included:
	    Industry Snapshot
	    Background & Development
	    Current Conditions
	    Organization & Structure
	    Research & Technology
	    Work Force
	    Industry Leaders
	    Major Countries in the Industry

Finance, Insurance, & Real Estate USA: Industry Analyses, Statistics, and Leading Organizations	-A comprehensive guide to statistics on finance, insurance and real estate industries—covering 36 major sectors and their activities. -Combines diverse federal and private sources of data in a unique, synthesized, analyzed format. -Table/Chart format, no written text -It includes more than 2,600 corporate participants with addresses, names, and sales or asset performance -Provides state data, rankings and maps • Covers local data on over 2,500 counties
Industry Norms and Key Business Ratios (Dun & Bradstreet)	-This reference allows researchers to benchmark a company with its industry peers to evaluate financial performance.

-Contains data necessary to assess
 -The stability of an industry's
financial condition
 -Financial trends & profitability
-General financial statement & ratio data
-Various industries included, such as:
 -Agriculture
 -Mining
 -Construction
 -Manufacturing
 -Retail
 -Financial & Real Estate
 -Services
 -Transportation -Services

Manufacturing USA:
Industry Analyses, Statistics, and Leading Organizations

-This source contains comprehensive information on industrial activity over a span of 19 years and feature reanalyzed statistical data on industry performance and company participation.
-Two large volumes, organized by SIC#s
-Ratio & statistical information
-Highlights of source:
Illustrated with graphics & fully indexed
Industry projections through 2000
Recent input-output data
Improved product detail table
Detailed materials consumption tables
Over a decade of industry history
Approximately 75 companies included for each industry.

Manufacturing Worldwide:
Industry Analyses, Statistics, Products, and Leading Companies and Countries

-This source presents detailed statistical and company information on
 manufacturing activities worldwide.
-Statistical data
-Highlights of this source:
 Detailed coverage of more than 500 products
 Manufacturing industry statistics for 176 countries

                                    Comprehensive ratios & indicators
                              for country comparison
                                 U.S. dollar dominated values for all
                              financial data

__Moody Industry Review__   -This source is a comprehensive statistical
                              reference containing key financial
                              information, operating data and ratios on
                              approximately 3,500 companies.
                              -Information is arranged by industry in 137
                              industry groups to compare companies &
                               industry standards.
                              -Resource highlights:
                                Key financial info on operating data
                                Key business ratios on industry groups
                                Composite stock price movement chart
                                Comparisons of industry groups
                                Industry Ranked by: size, revenue,
                                profitability, net income, stock evaluation,
                                            etc…

__RMA Annual Statement__   -This comprehensive source provides
__Studies__   industry-based data on private &
                              public financial statements.
                              -It offers:
                                      Comparative historical data
                                      Financial statement averages
                                      Current data sorted by sales
                                      Financial ratio data
                              -Financial info, no text

__Service Industries USA:__   -This source is a comprehensive
Industry Analyses, Statistics   presentation of analytical data on the U.S.
and Leading Organizations   service sector.
                              -National & state-level data & statistics
                              - It combines federal statistics from a variety
                              of sources on:
                                      Establishments   Revenues
                                      Employment
                              Ownership
                                      Occupations
                              -Highlights of this source:
                              Lists 2,100 services into 151 industries

Industry Projections
Comprehensive data on occupations/
employment
Pre-calculated ratios that provide quick
insight into each sector
Company contact information

Standard & Poor's Industry   -Thin booklets, alphabetically organized.
Surveys   -Text, minimal financial or statistical
information.
-Sections include:
      Industry buzzwords
      Industry profiles
      Detailed Steps on How to Analyze
your Industry
        List of Industrial References
        List of Related Periodicals
        Comparative Company Analysis of
the Largest Companies of your
        Industry

U.S. Industry Profiles: -This is a key business reference source
The Leading 100   covering 100 significant industries in
    the U.S.
-Text format
-Provides a directory of Additional Sources
for Industry Data
-Listings Include:
      Periodicals
Newsletters
      Associations   Societies
      Statistic Sources   Databases
      General Works
-Hundreds of Graphs & Charts that
Represent:
      Market Share Statistics   List of
Top Companies
        Industry Forecasts   Industry
Trends

Encyclopedia of Emerging
Industries

-This source details the inception, emergence and current status of 118 newly flourishing
    US industries and industry segments.
-Each listing includes:
    Industry Snapshot
Organization & Structure
    Background & Development
Current Conditions
    Industry Leaders
Research & Technology
    Further Readings
-Examples of emerging industries:
    Fertility Medicine
Digital Imaging
    Optical Data Storage
Electronic Notepads

Business Rankings Annual:
List of Companies, Products, Services, and Activities compiled from a Variety of Published Sources

-This source contains lists compiled from a variety of published sources :

Companies	Products
Services	Activities

-These lists rank information from hundreds of:

Periodicals	Surveys
Newspapers	Directories,

etc..
-The lists are grouped by subject and subjects are arranged alphabetically.
-Example:
  Most Admired Corporations
  Top Ten Reasons why People use the Internet
  Best Selling Chocolate Candy
  Top North American Amusement Parks

Wholesale and Retail Trade
USA:
Industry Analyses, Statistics, and Leading Organizations

-A comprehensive guide to economic activity in 133 distribution industries covering wholesale & retail trade
-Provides unique analysis and synthesis of federal statistics
-Includes more than 4,300 leading

companies
-Offers details on local distribution
industries in 370 major metropolitan areas
-Each industry listing includes:
        Sale & Employment Graphs
General Statistics
        Indices of Change
Selected Ratios
        Leading Companies & Contact info
Occupations employed by this SIC code

U.S. Industry & Trade Outlook
-This source is an industry-by-industry
overview of the U.S. economy including
        manufacturing, highly technological,
and service industries.
-Text
-Highlights of this Source:
        650 Easy to Read Tables & Charts
        100s of Industry Reviews

        Industry Analyses & Forecasts
        Graphical Snapshots of Industry &
Trade Trends
        Comprehensive Data from Public &
Private Sectors

Dun's Business Rankings:
Public and Private
Businesses Ranked within
Industry Category and State
-This source ranks over 25,000 of the
nation's leading private & public business
-Allows researcher to find the company
ranked by:
        Size   State
        SIC Code   Sales Volume
        Private/Foreign   Owned designation
        Employee Size
-No text, listed data

Market Share Reporter: An
Annual Compilation of
Reported Market Share Data
on Companies, Products,
and Services
-An annual compilation of reported market
share data on companies, products and
        services.
-The categories of Market Share include:
        Corporate   Institutional
        Brand   Product,
Commodity & Facility

Other, Misc.
-Highlights include:
More than 2,000 entries
Includes both private & public companies
   Graphics
   Comprehensive indexes & source lists

World Market Share Reporter:

- A Compilation of Reported World Market Share Data and Ranking on Companies, Products, and Services
-Highlights if this source include:
   -Over 1,600 entries
   -Covers more than 270 geographic locations
   -Coverage of private & public sector activities
   -Corporate, brand, product, service & commodity market shares
- Bar graphs, pie charts & percentage tables

Encyclopedia of Consumer Brands

-This source provides substantive information on products that have been leaders in their respective brand categories.
-Products are broken down into three categories:
   Durable
   Consumable
   Personal
-The following data is included for each entry:
   Early History   Product Innovations   Marketing
   Data at a Glance   Further Readings   Brand Origin

Major Marketing Campaigns Annual

-This source profiles 100 of the most notable advertising and marketing initiates each year.
-Examples of campaigns include:
  American Express "Do More"
  Delta Airlines, Inc "On Top of the World"

VISA "Its everywhere you want to be"
-Data on campaigns is as follows:
                Company Info
                Overview
        Historical Context   Target Market
            Competition   Marketing
                    Strategy
        Outcome   Further Reading

International Directory of   -This source provides accurate and detailed
Company Histories   information on the development of the
world's largest and most influential
companies.
-Text, No Financial data.
-There are two-dozen volumes of this
source, offering detailed and lengthy insight
into thousands of companies worldwide.
-Search directory of any volume to locate
your company.

Best's Insurance Reports,   -The objective of this source is to provide an
Life-Health   overall opinion of a health or life insurance
company's ability to meet its obligations to
policyholders.
-Text & Financial data
-Ratings are divided into two broad
categories—Secure & Vulnerable.
-The sections included in profiled
companies:
                -Current rating   -
Rating Rationale
                -Five Year Rating History -Key
Financial Indicators
                -Premium & Reserve   -
Profitability Tests
                        Analysis
                -Leverage Tests   -
Capital Trends
                -Liquidity Tests   -
Investment Yields

                                        -Financial Statements   -
                        History
                                        -Officers   -
                        New Business Issued

Best's Insurance Reports,   - The objective of this source is to
Property & Casualty   provide an overall opinion of a
                                         property & casualty insurance
                                         company's ability to meet its
                                         obligations to policyholders.
                                         -Text & Financial data
                                         -Ratings are divided into two broad
                                         categories—Secure & Vulnerable.
                                         -The sections included in profiled
                                         companies:
                                                 -Current rating
                                         - Rating Rationale
                                                 -Five Year Rating History
                                         -Key Financial Indicators
                                                 -Financial Statements
                                         -History
                                                 -Management
                                         -Regulatory
                                                 -Varies w/ each company!

Hoover's Guide to   -This source is packed with useful
Computer Companies   information on over 1,000 top global
                                         companies in the
                                                 computer industry, from
                                         hardware manufacturers and microchip
                                         makers to
                                                 software companies and
                                         system designers.
                                         -The highlights of this source:
                                                 -In-Depth Profiles of 250
                                         computer Industry Companies
                                                 -Capsule Profiles of over
                                         1,000 of public & private Co.s

	-An overview of the computer industry.
	-Sections in Profile include:
	    -Company Overview -Who
	    -Where -What
	    -Key Competitors -10 year stock data
	    -Stock Price History -Fiscal Year-End Ratios
	-Capsule Profile companies included in this source offer contact , quick-facts, one-line
	    summary and the highest ranked executives.

Hoover's Handbook of American Business	-This source profiles 750 major US enterprises, including:
	    -VISA
	-Unites States Postal Service
	    -Kaiser Foundation -USAA
	-Text
	-Sections in Profile include:
	    -Company Overview -Who
	    -Where -What
	    -Key Competitors -10 year stock data
	    -Stock Price History -Fiscal Year-End Ratios
	    Graph
	-95% of the companies profiled are public.

Hoover's Handbook of	-This source profiles 300 of the fastest

Emerging Companies

growing US business enterprises, including:
-Yahoo
 -Papa John's
 -Abercrombie & Fitch
 -E*Trade
-Text
-Each profile features the personalities, event and strategies behind the company' success, as well six years of financial data.
-Sections in Profile include:
>   -Company Overview   -
Who
>   -Where   -
What
>   -Key Competitors   -
How Much
-Also contains List Rankings

Hoover's Handbook of
Private Companies

-This source cover 800 major US non-public business enterprises and provides in-depth
>   profiles on 250 of the biggest
and most influential, including:
>   - Prudential Insurance   -
Levi Strauss
>   -Dominos Pizza   -
Hallmark Cards
-Each profile features the personalities, event and strategies that have made these
>   enterprises key players.
-Sections in Profile include:
>   -Company Overview   -
Who

-Where   -
What
               -Key Competitors   -
How Much
-Capsule Profile companies included in
this source offer contact , quick-facts,
summary,
               key competitors, and the
highest ranked executives.

Hoover's Handbook of   -This source profiles 300 of the largest
World Business   and most interesting enterprises
                          headquartered
               outside of the US. Some of
the companies featured from over 35
countries,
               include:
               -Sony   -
Heineken
               -Toyota   -
Samsung
-Each company profile includes up to
10 years of financial data and features
the people,
               events, products, and
strategies that make these companies
global players.
-Sections in Profile include:
               -Company Overview   -
Who
               -Where   -
What
               -Key Competitors   -
When
               -Stock Price History   -
Fiscal Year-End Ratios Graph
               -10 year stock price data

Moody's Bank & *Finance Manual*	-This source covers the field of finance represented by banks, insurance companies, investment companies, unit investment trusts, real estate companies and miscellaneous financial enterprises. -Financial & Statistical Data -The sections: -Distributions -Record of Unit Holders Value -Financial Statements -Schedule of Securities Owned

Moody's Industrial *Manual*	-Provides data on companies listed on the New York and American Stock Exchange
	-Data on each company listed includes:
	     -Capital Structure
	     - Company History
	     -Complete Financial
	     Statements & Notes
	-Financial data, text, small print

Moody's International *Manual*	-Provides a wide reference source for financial and business information on approximately 11,000 major corporations, sovereigns and their municipalities, and national and supranational institutions in 117 countries.
	-Data on each listing includes:
	     -Country Profile
	     -Currency
	     -Banking
	     -Finance
	     -International transactions

                                    -Map
                                    -Corporate Section
                                    -Minimal text, small print,
                               financial data

Moody's Municipal &   -This source contains comprehensive
Government Manual   data on over 17,000 municipal entities.
                               It includes demographic, geographic,
                               statistical, financial and bond
                               descriptive information
                               -This source contains data on state
                               agencies, municipalities, housing &
                               redevelopment agencies, and
                               guarantors/reporting entities.
                               -Sections vary

Moody's OTC Industrial Manual	-This is a reference source for over-the-counter industrial firms domiciled in the United States and offers broad coverage on over 3,176 unlisted on national stock exchanges.
	-Text & Financial Data
	-Sections in profiled entities include:
	      -History
	      -Business
	      -Properties
	      -Subsidiaries
	      -Officers
	      -Directors
	      -Financial Statements

Moody's Public Utility Manual	-This provides a wide reference source for public utility companies, including broad coverage on over 442:
	  -Electric
	  -Water
	  -Gas utilities
	  -Gas transmission
	  -telephone
	  -Text, Statistics & Financial data
	
	-The sections of profiled companies include:
	  -History
	  -Operating Statistics
	  -Financial Statements
	  -Significant Accounting Principles
	  -Ratios
	  -Long Term Debt
	  -Lease Obligation Bonds
	  -Capital Stock

Moody's Transportation Manual	-This manual covers the transportation industry in one volume with statistical

data in some of the following fields:
-Railroads
-Steamship
-Airlines
-Bus Lines
-Truck Lines
-Oil Pipe Lines
-Bridge Co.
-Automobile
-Truck & Leasing
-Text & Financial Data
-The sections of the items profiled,
include:
  -History
  -Control
  -Business & Properties
  -Regulation
  -Competition
  -Subsidiaries
  -Financial Statements
  -Operation Statistics
  -Comparative Statistics
  -In-Depth Analysis

Plunkett's Health Care
Industry Almanac

-This source provides the latest
statistics and trends in:
            -Medical Industry Growth
-Professions & Careers
            -Technology Advancements
-Health Expenditures
            -Medicaid/Medicare
-Private Insurance
            -Hospital Utilization
-Graphs, text & tables
-Provides great facts and comparisons
in an easy-to-understand format

Plunkett's InfoTech
Industry Almanac

-This source provides the latest
statistics and trends in:
    -The Top Info Tech firms
-Professions & Careers
    -Technology & Research
-Communications/Networking
    -Information Management
-Internet/World Wide Web
    -Global Markets
-Text & summary tables
-Excellent resource for career planning,
marketing, investments & research
-InfoTech defined as any technology
that moves or manages voice, data or
video— whether that movement be via
wireless methods, fiber optics, copper
wire telephony, computer or other
emerging methods.

Value Line Investment
Survey—

-This resource is an investment survey
guide.
-The companies listed include the
following data:
  Ranks (BETA, Safety, etc…)
  Financial Strength Assessment (Price
    Stability & Earning Predictability)
  Financial Statement data
    (approximately 7 to 10 yrs)
  Industry Text summary
  Share tracking Graph (PE Ratio,
    Dividend Yld, Recent Price, etc…)

**INTERNET
RESOURCES:**
SEARCH ENGINES:
AltaVista:

-Unrivaled for handling complex

http://www.altavista.com

search strategies and for providing comprehensive results.
-It has a reputation for retrieving more hits than any other engine, which may be overwhelming for broad searches of common terms.

Hot Bot:

http://www.hotbot.com

-It is the only search engine that allows searches to set defaults for a search session.
-Provides an elaborate menu that helps inexperienced searches do advanced searches.

InfoSeek Ultra:

http://ultra.infoseek.com/

-Uses software technology to find plurals, variant word endings, and similar words.
-Known for its ability to retrieve relevant documents.
-Its no frills interface requires users to learn the command language.

Open Text Index:

http://www.opentext.com

-It is the only index to allow searchers to specify word order. Ex: "race horse" but not
        "horse race".
-Small database, but good choice for searching phrases and search strings.

SUBJECT DIRECTORIES

Lycos A2Z:

http://www.lycos.com

-The directory divides 40,000 popular sites into 16 categories and 800 subcategories.
-This is best suited for casual browsing or for searching topics of popular or current interest.

Galaxy:

http://www.tradewave.com

-Its size and coverage are its strongest features, but development appears to have stalled.

	-Galaxy should be used to supplement search results from other services.
Yahoo!:	-It uses a controlled vocabulary that can greatly enhance search retrieval.
http://www.yahoo.com	-One of the most useful and best-known web directories.
	-Great place to find ready reference sources (weather, directories, etc.), homepages of service, current interest topics, organizations & businesses.
METASEARCH ENGINES	
Metacrawler:	-Meta search engines allow users to search several services simultaneously
http://metacrawler.cs.washington.edu	and view results in one list. -Tend to take longer since additional processing in necessary.
SavySearch:	" "
http://www.cs.colostate.edu/~dreiling/	
smartform.html	
REVIEW/RATING SERVICES	
Argus Clearinghouse:	-Review/Rating services provide numeric ratings and or evaluate
http://www.clearinghouse.net	summaries of selected web resources. -This site selects and evaluates user-contributed subject guides to internet resources. -Does not provide detailed evaluations of WWW sites.
Excite Review Service:	-Concept search feature automatically searches for synonyms of key words.

http://www.excite.com	-Great for casual, light ready. -Descriptions and ratings offer little critical evaluation & no rating a criterion is provided.

WEBSITES:

Britannica Internet Guide: **www.ebig.com**	-65,000 quality websites with written descriptions of each site. -You can browse by topic or use a keyword index to search titles & site descriptions. -14 broad subject areas are broken down into various other subcategories.
Wall Street Research Net: http://www.wsrn.com, or www.cnnfn.com	-Has over 140,000 links to help professional and private investors perform research on actively traded companies & mutual funds. -provides important economic data that moves markets & 15 min delay stock quotes.
Web Finance: http://www.webfinance.net, or www.vfinance.com	-Includes several finance & investment links to various banks & brokerage firms. -Not comprehensive, only includes banks & firms with their own homepage.
Web Investor's Dictionary: http://www.webinvestors.com, or www.euro.net/innovation/ Finance_Base/Fin_encyc.html	-Excellent resource for identifying the real meaning behind the terms & phrases that big investors & stock traders throw around everyday. -Offers glossaries of trading terms.

Stock Master:

http:www.stockmaster.com, or

www.amex.com

-Free site that allows you to search by company name, fund name or ticker symbol.
-Provides stock quotes and analysis.

Argus Clearing House:

www.clearinghouse.net

-Provides a central access point for general topic guides.
-Guides identify, describe and evaluate internet-based information resources.

EDGAR:

http://www.sec.gov, or

www.disclosure.com

-Provides annual reports filed by public companies.
-Provides free links to all filings since 1994.
-Also has proposed and final SEC rulings, ticker symbol look-up & mutual fund reports.

PRARS:

http://www.prars.com

-Its an online ordering service for actual company financial (annual reports, 10ks, etc...)
-This service is free to US addresses.

Hoover's:

http://www.hoovers.com

-Provides information on over 2,600 public and private companies around the world.
-Company information includes; identification info, corporate history, current events affecting the company, competitors, EDGAR filings and link to Co. homepage.

BizWeb:

http://www.bizweb.com

-Indexes over 9,300 companies with a presence in the internet in over 120 industry categories.
-Many links to companies that provide only an online catalogue.

Marketing & Advertising Departments:

-Site provided by the advertising department of the University of Texas, Austin.

http://www.utexas.edu/coc /adv/world	-Packed with links to almost any combination of marketing & advertising sites
Internet Scout: Scout.cs.wisc.edu/scout	-Sponsored by the National Science Foundation to provide info to the education community. -Main services are the Scout Report, Scout Report Signpost & the Scout Toolkit.
DATABASES:	• *Database availability depends on institution • (some passwords required or on campus use)
*Article First	-Index of articles from nearly 12,500 journals in science, technology, medicine, social science, humanities, popular culture and business.
*Biographical Information:	-Politicians, business executive & more.
*Contents First	-Complete table of contents page & holding information for journals in many fields. -1990 to present
*Facts.com	-Excellent starting point for researching current events and issues. -Hyperlinks allow for easy cross-referencing. -1980 to present
*First Search	-Access to over 50 different databases worldwide, including Worldcat (a union catalog of library holdings worldwide).
*Lexis-Nexis Academic	-Access to over 1 billion documents.

UNIVERSE	-Full text usually available. -Includes newspapers, legal documents, magazines, corporate financial data and reference books.
***Periodical Contents Index**	-Contains older (1961-1991) issues or periodicals in the humanities & social sciences.
***ProQuest**	-Frequently offers indexes, abstracts, full text and full images of millions of articles from magazines, journals and newspapers. -Full image articles look a lot like a photocopy .
***Quotations**	-Over 10,000 quotes from the famous and unknown.
***Readers' Guide Abstracts**	-Contains popular periodicals that were published in Canada and the US. -Includes: current events, business, sports, fashion, fine arts, nutrition, consumer affairs, news, health, education and others.
***Roper Public Opinion Polls**	-From Roper Public Opinion Center
Uncover	-Allows free keyword searching of article titles from over 17,000 multidisciplinary journals since 1988. -Also allow you to search for journal titles and check the table of contents for issues.
***ABI/INFORM Global**	-It is a business and management database. -Includes info on: advertising,

marketing, economics, human
resources, finance, computers,
companies, taxation and more.
-Also located in ProQuest

* Accounting Literature   -A comprehensive selection of
accounting information.

*Axicom Biz   -Business white pages listing.

*Business &   -Provides access to resources with a
Management Practices   focus on the practical aspects and
approaches to business management.
-Data from 1995 to present.

*Business Dateline   -Contains citations on regional
business activity & trends.
-Also have major stories on local firms,
their products & executives.
-1985 to present

*Business News   -Business articles from newspapers,
magazines, journals, wires and
transcripts.

*Business Organizations   -A directory of new and established
organizations, agencies & publications
worldwide.

*Compact Disclosure   -Provides 5 years of financial data on
public companies.
-This database is updated quarterly and
also available through Company
Financials in Lexis Nexis.

*Company Financial   -Provides detailed information about
Information   US companies.

*Compare Companies   -Allow you to identify companies
based on a variety of criteria.

*D&B Million Dollar   -Provide information on over 1.2
Database   million leading private & public
businesses.
-Includes: SICs, size criteria

	(employees & annual sales), industry info, and type of ownership, principal executives and biographies.
*EconLit	-Allows subject indexing & abstracts of journals, books, working papers and dissertations. -1969 to present
FreeEdgar	-Offers free access to corporate data, which is filed with the Security and Exchange Commission (SEC).
*Industry & Market News	-Information & news on over 25 industries.
IPO Express	-Covers approximately 2,600 initial public offerings & 1,500 underwriters.
Moody's News Reports	-Provides access to the last four weeks of News Reports for the Moody's manuals. -Subjects includes are: OTC, Public Utility, Transportation, Industrial, International, Bank/Finance, Municipal and Government.
*Standard & Poor's Register of Corporations, Directors & Executives	-Provides information on corporations, directors & executives. -Updated monthly.
*StatUSA	-STAT-USA/Internet is a site for business, economic and trade community. -Provides authoritative information from the federal government.
*Wall Street Journal	-Provides full text articles from 1984 to the present. -Can also be selected under Wall Street Journal in ProQuest.
*Wilson Business	-Provides international (but English)

Abstracts	articles from business magazines. -Topics include: accounting, finance, management and small businesses. -1986 to present.
*Worldscope	-Provides reports on companies worldwide.

Endnotes

---

[1] A general history can be found at http://www.airlines.org/public/publications/display1.asp?nid=962

[2] http://www.airlines.org/public/publications/display1.asp?nid=964

[3] Odell, M., "Jet-Setters Cath the Jitters" FT.com Special Reports/Business Travel, February 14, 2002

[4] Brahm Canzer (2003). *E-Business: Strategic Thinking and Practice.* Boston, Mass.: Houghton-Mifflin Company.

[5] http://www.iflyswa.com/investor_relations/fs_news_releases.html - "Southwest Airlines Reports Fourth Quarter Earnings and 29th Consecutive Year Of Profitability"

[6] http://www.jetblue.com/learnmore/pressDetail.asp?newsId=175, April 29, 2003.

[7] Peter F. Drucker (1954). *The Practice of Management: A Study of the Most Important Function in American Society.* New York: Harper & Row, Publishers.

[8] We thank our reviewer from the University of Notre Dame for pointing this out.

[9] Charles W. Lamb, Jr., Joseph F. Hair, Jr., and Carl McDaniel (2001). *Essentials of Marketing.* 2nd Edition. Cincinnati, Oh.: South-Western College Publishing.

[10] Joel Ready, Shauna Schullo, and Kenneth Zimmerman (2000). *Electronic Marketing: Integrating Electronic Resources into the Marketing Process.* Orlando, Fl.: The Dryden Press.

[11] Robert C. Ford, Barry R. Armandi, and Cherrill P. Heaton (1988). *Organizational Theory: An Integrative Approach.* New York: Harper & Row, Publishers.

[12] Alice M. Rivlin (1971). *Systematic Thinking for Social Action.* Washington, D.C.: The Brookings Institution.

[13] H.L.A. Hart (1961). *The Concept of Law.* Oxford, England: Oxford University Press.

[14] Robert E. Axtell (1994). *The Do's and Taboos of International Trade: A Small Business Primer.* Revised Edition. New York: John Wiley & Sons, Inc.

[15] Robert A. Dahl (1961). *Who Governs? Democracy and Power in an American City.* New Haven, Ct.: Yale University Press.

[16] Harold Siedman and Robert Gilmour (1986). *Politics, Position, and Power: From the Positive to the Regulatory State.* 4th Edition. New York: Oxford University Press.

[17] http://www.bea.doc.gov/bea/dn2/gpoc.htm, April 30, 2003.

[18]

https://www.morganstanleyindividual.com/research/ms/exclusive/1Qch artbook03.pdf, April 30, 2003.

[19] Rogene A. Buchholz (1998). *Principles of Environmental Management: The Greening of Business.* Upper Saddle River, N.J.: Prentice-Hall.

[20] http://www.starvingwriters.org/eThis/Work/April/work5.html, April 30, 2003.

[21] http://www.ei.gov.bc.ca/Publicinfo/publications/smallbuspubs /green.PDF, April 30, 2003.

[22] reference to Xcel Energy's wind farm in Weld County.

[23] http://www.fe.doe.gov/education/, December 23, 2002.

[24] reference the IBAM meetings, 2002 in Denver and interview with Rowley and Clinebell.

[25] Alvin Toffler (1970). *Future Shock.* New York: Bantam Books.

[26] Larry J. Gitman and Carl McDaniel (2000). *The Future of Business.* Cincinnati, Oh.: South-Western College Publishing.

[27] http://www.census.gov/prod/2003pubs/02statab/pop.pdf, April 30, 2003.

[28] http://www.familyhealthlink.com/article2.htm, April 30, 2003.

[29] John Naisbitt (1984). *Megatrends.* New York: Warner Books.

[30] Jakki Mohr (2001). *Marketing of High-Technology Products and Innovations.* Upper Saddle River, N.J.: Prentice-Hall, Inc.

[31] Daniel Amor (2000). *The E-Business (R)Evolution: Living and Working in an Interconnected World.* Upper Saddle River, N.J.: Prentice-Hall PTR.

[32] Yoram (Jerry) Wind, Vijay Mahajan, and Robert E. Gunther (2002). *Convergence Marketing: Strategies for Reaching the New Hybrid Consumer.* Upper Saddle River, N.J.: Prentice-Hall, Inc.

[33] Jakki Mohr, 2001.

[34] Carl A. Rodrigues (2001). *International Management: A Cultural Approach.* 2nd Edition. Cincinnati, Oh.: South-Western College Publishing.

[35] Kathleen M. Eisenhardt (2002). "Has Strategy Changed?" *MIT Sloan Management Review* (Winter), 88-91.

[36] http://www.star-alliance.com/cgi-bin/sa.storefront/307499188/ UserTemplate/17, December 23, 2002.

[37] www.opacity.com, May 5, 2003.

[38] Vern Terpstra and Kenneth David (1985). *The Cultural Environment of International Business.* 2nd Edition. Cincinnati, Oh.: South-Western Publishing Company.

[39] David Ricks, Marilyn Y. C. Fu, and Jeffrey S. Arpan (1974). *International Business Blunders.* Columbus, Oh.: Grid, Inc.

[40] Josh Martin (2002). "Rebuilding Afghanistan: A Multi-Billion $ Plan" *The Middle East Journal,* 5-8.

[41] http://www.worldtradeexecutive.com/irr.html, May 5, 2003.

[42] adopted from http://www.bizstats.com/corpnetincome.htm, May 5, 2003.

[43] Ibid.

[44] Christine Lynn Connolly (2002). "The New York Islanders Hockey Club, Inc." in David W. Cravens, Charles W. Lamb, Jr. and Victoria L. Crittenden (eds.) *Strategic Marketing Management Cases.* 7th Edition. New York: McGraw-Hill Irwin, 146-152.

[45] Sean O'Sullivan (2002) "The Boston Red Sox" in David W. Cravens, Charles W. Lamb, Jr. and Victoria L. Crittenden, 37-53.

[46] Gerald W. Scully (2002) "Sports", http://www.econlib.org/library /Enc/Sports.html, December 23, 2002; Robert D. Tollison (2002) "Sportmetrics", http://www.econlib.org/library/Enc/ Sportometrics.html, December 23, 2002.

[47] Michael Porter (1979). "How Competitive Forces Shape Strategy" *Harvard Business Review* 2, 137-145.

[48] Curtis M. Grimm and Ken G. Smith, K. G. (1997). *Strategy as Action: Industry Rivalry and Coordination.* South-Western College Publishing,

[49] J. Kim De Dee (1991). "Note on the Ambulance Industry" in Herbert Sherman (1991). *The Strategic Management Process: Readings, Cases, and Exercises.* 2nd Edition. Needham Heights, Ma.: Ginn Press.

[50] Grimm and Smith, 1997.

[51] Peter M. Ginter, Linda M. Swayne, and W. Jack Duncan (1995). *Strategic Management of Health Care Organizations.* 3rd Edition. Oxford, England: Blackwell Publishers, Ltd.

[52] Grimm and Smith, 1997.

[53] Grimm and Smith, 1997.

[54] Daniel J. Rowley and Herbert Sherman (2001). *From Strategy to Change: Implementing the Plan in Higher Education.* San Francisco, Ca.: Jossey-Bass.

[55] ibid

[56] see also Appendix B in Michael Porter (1980). *Competitive Strategy: Techniques for Analyzing Industries and Competitors.* New York: The Free Press.

[57] Michael Porter, 1980.

[58] Herbert Sherman and David Wilcox (1989). "Applying the Porter Model: Procedure" in Herbert Sherman, 1991.

[59] Ibid.

[60] Miller, 1997.

[61] Adapted from Miller, 577.

[62] Miller, 513.

[63] Ibid, 534.

[64] For a fuller explanation, see the Appendix to Chapter One.

[65] Peter M. Ginter, Linda M. Swayne, and W. Jack Duncan , 1998.

[66] http://api-ec.api.org/industry/index.cfm?bitmask =00100400000 0000000, May 6, 2003.

[67] Miller, 558-564.

[68] Ibid, 565-577.

[69] Bruce D. Henderson (1984). *The Logic of Business Strategy.* Cambridge, Mass.: Ballinger Publishing Company.

[70] Charles W. Hofer and Dan Schendel (1978). *Strategy Formulation: Analytical Concepts.* St. Paul, Minn.: West Publishing Company.

[71] Theodore Levitt (1982). *The Marketing Imagination.* New York: The Free Press.

[72] http://www.braniffinternational.org/history/historyhome.htm, December 24, 2002.

[73] http://scriptorium.lib.duke.edu/adaccess/rails-history.html, December 24, 2002.

[74] Curt M. White (2001). *Data Communications and Computer Networks: A Business User's Approach.* Cambridge, Mass.: Course Technology.

[75] Sharon M. Oster (1999). *Modern Competitive Analysis.* 3rd Edition. New York: Oxford University Press.

[76] Robert F. Hartley (2001). *Marketing Mistakes and Successes.* 8th Edition. New York: John Wiley & Sons, Inc.

[77] http://www.nsda.com/Brands/, December 24, 2002.

[78] Thomas G. Marx (1985). *Business and Society: Economic, Moral, and Political Foundations.* Englewood Cliffs, N.J.: Prentice-Hall, Inc..

[79] http://www.sba.gov/advo/stats/sbfaq.pdf, December 24, 2002.

[80] Fred L. Fry and Charles R. Stoner (1995). *Strategic Planning for the New and Small Business.* Dover, N.H.: Upstart Publishing Company, Inc.

[81] R.L. Daft (2001). *Organizational Theory and Design.* 6th Edition. Mason, Oh.: South-Western, 222.

∽ Chapter Four ∾
The Internal Environment

Chapter Objectives

1. To understand the characteristics and importance of an organization's resources and then how the firm uses them to achieve a competitive advantage.
2. To understand how firms use their resource base to achieve core competencies and then use those core competencies to match external environmental needs.
3. To understand the value chain and how primary and secondary activities are linked to produce customer value.
4. To understand how the basic functions of the firm lead to organizational strengths and weaknesses.
5. To see how a firm's internal strengths and weakness combine to explain its ability to take advantage of external opportunities and threats.

Introductory Case: The Disney Company

Walt Disney was born into poverty in 1901 and began his career in Chicago, Illinois. Opportunities were limited in Chicago, so in 1917, he moved to Kansas City where he hoped to be successful commercial artist.[1] He became interested in the movies, particularly cartoons and soon partnered with his brother Roy in 1923 and they moved to Hollywood. Together, they opened a studio, produced a series of cartoon shorts called "Alice Comedies" and later a series called "Oswald the Lucky Rabbit." The Disney brothers were successful and in 1925 formed the Disney Brothers Cartoon Studio. Their first major film success occurred in November, 1928, when the Disney Studio released a black-and-white cartoon short called "Steamboat Willie," which debuted Mickey and Minnie Mouse. The cartoon and the cartoon characters became instant successes. But Walt had much bigger ideas. In 1937, he and his brother produced their first full-length animated film, "Snow White," which received instant acclaim and cemented the fortunes of the Disney Studio. *TIME* profiled Disney the week "Snow White and the Seven Dwarfs" was released, calling the film "the most ambitious animated cartoon ever attempted." Hollywood insiders pooh-poohed the idea of a full-length animated movie.[2]

Several other cartoon films were produced and released including "Cinderella," "Bambi," "Alice in Wonderland," and "Fantasia" (though Fantasia's popularity came years after it was produced and released – it was considered too avant garde for its time). Disney also got into the regular film business, producing films suitable for families and children. With the advent of television, Disney decided to enter the television industry with the immensely popular Mickey Mouse Club; and with the advent of color television, Disney's Wonderful World of Color. Walt's dream went further still and he began to work on a theme park idea that resulted first in the creation of Disneyland in Anaheim, California, which opened in 1955, and then the dream to open Disney World and Epcot in Florida (which opened after Walt's death in 1966).

Each venture had proven to be a major success, but when Walt died the company suffered from his loss, unable to find a strong replacement for Walt. His brother Roy headed the company until his own death in 1971.[3]

Disney had proven to be an enigma – his image was one of joviality and mirth, but his management style was far different. "If you contradict him, you're out. Nothing is really funny until it's proclaimed funny."[4] Walt's management style seemed to work when the company was brand new, and his work ethic and standards of quality and excellence provided vision and leadership that the company realized during his lifetime. With his passing, the Disney Company seemed left without vision, vitality, and drive.

The company began to flounder. The taste of American movie-goers had changed from Walt's heyday and smaller and smaller audiences showed up for Disney movies. Epcot opened in 1982 at a tremendous cost for the company, and the successors to Walt and Roy committed to Tokyo Disneyland. Profits were down and for the first time, The Disney Company showed losses. Stockholders were getting nervous and management at Disney didn't seem to be able to turn things around.

Michael Eisner took over in 1984 and brought the company into a new, revitalized era. The new management team wanted to reorient the company to match the wants of the huge teenage and adult communities. They created Touchstone Studios, whose first release, "Splash," started a renaissance for Disney. While still producing children and family oriented movies under the Disney Studio brand, the Touchstone brand began to take off. Its successes were good enough that Eisner and company decided to move into television and soon produced the highly successful series, "The Golden Girls." In the meantime, Disney began to align itself with other Hollywood moguls such as George Lucas and Francis Coppola to create new theme areas in Disneyland and Disney World. Diversifications continued when the Disney Company decided to get into the publishing business with the formation of Hyperion Books, Hyperion Books for Children, and Disney Press. This was followed in 1991 with the purchase of *Discover* magazine and the formation of the Mighty Ducks National Hockey League club in Anaheim, California in 1993.

The rest of the company seemed to have resurrected itself well under the new leadership. Walt Disney Pictures had huge successes with "the Little Mermaid," "Aladdin," and "Beauty and the Beast." The television division continued to score big with "Home Improvements," "The Regis and Kathy Lee Show," and "Empty Nest." Spurred by sales of Disney merchandise in the theme parks (which in 1992 included Euro-Disney, later to become Disneyland Paris), the company had opened a series of Disney Stores and in 1996 had 450 the across the United States.   In 1995, Michael Orvitz joined The Walt Disney Company as president and made arrangements for Disney to purchase 25% of the California Angels Baseball Team.   Disney acquired the balance after the death of owner Gene Autry.   Disney continued to diversify its holdings when in 1996, it acquired Capital/ABC. In this $19 billion transaction, the second-largest in U.S. history, Disney became the country's top television network. [5]   It controlled 10 TV stations, 21 radio stations, seven daily newspapers, and ownership positions in four cable networks.

Currently, Disney is a major leader in the entertainment industry with a projected 25-35 percent growth in earnings in 2003 and continued strong growth in 2004.[6] After a rocky year in 2001, Disney's profits were good in 2002 ($1.2 billion, $.61earnings per share),[7] with Disney having entered into the creation of a fifth theme park in Hong Kong, it's third international venture. Disney is a prime example of how core competencies and valuable resources have provided the company with a competitive edge.   And even with its lapse following the death of Walt Disney and problems with the opening of Euro-Disney, the company has been able to use its vast resources wisely to become one of the largest businesses in the U.S. and one of the premier entertainment companies in the world.

The Nature of the Internal Environment

In the previous chapter, we described many of the elements and forces that comprise the external environment.   Much of this is beyond the control of any organization and most strategic planning regarding the external environment seeks to–describe current market conditions, changes in those conditions over time, and opportunities and threats created by those conditions.   The purpose for conducting these analyses is to determine whether or not the marketplace will allow a given organization to grow and/or produce profit to assure long-term survival. We can often infer that a firm has a good fit with its primary market environment when its growth and/or profitability are at or above the average of those similar firms within its industry.

Yet profit and growth are not merely a product of environmental conditions or changes in those conditions. Managers make decisions about the firm's strategy and its internal operations in light of market changes. Opportunities in and off themselves will not assist a firm unless the firm has or can obtain the capabilities to take advantage of them. By examining the internal environment of a firm, the strategic decision-maker will tell how well the firm is managed in terms of maintaining its fit with the environment and producing the profits and/or growth that will sustain it over the long term as suggested in the following equation:

Long Term Survival = f **(growth, profits)** where long term survival is a function of growth and/or profits.[8]

In this chapter, we look at the 3rd step of the Strategic Planning Process as shown in Figure 4.1. The internal environment is much different from the external environment in that elements and forces that comprise a firm's internal environment are by and large the result of the firm's own activities and ability to accumulate resources. Management has created the firm's internal environment, and, in so doing, is responsible for how the firm processes raw materials and other resources into finished products and services. In the words of Walter Kelly's beloved character, Pogo, "we have met the enemy and he is us!"[9]

Management's ability to acquire needed resources, use them efficiently and effectively in its operations, change its resources base to adopt to changes in its environment, and guide both accumulation and use of resources from a sound strategic plan, often is the difference between a successful company and one that fails. The key to understanding resources is the quality and deployment of those resources. Another key to understanding resources is to be able to

Figure 4.1
The Strategic Management Process
Step 3 – Analyzing the Internal Environment

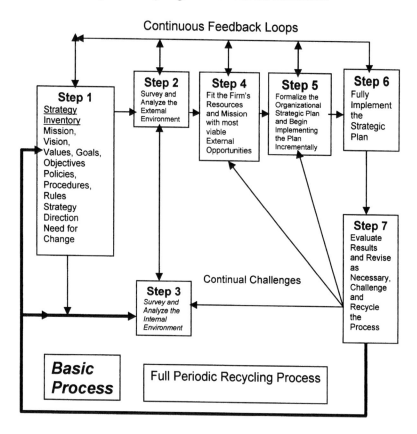

demonstrate that the resources of a firm help it achieve *core and distinctive competencies*, preferably a better set of competencies than its competitors that give the firm an edge in the marketplace. Unless a firm is able to acquire the resources it needs, at the quality level it requires, it may be unable to establish core and distinctive competencies, let alone sustain them.

This is why, then, that the focus of an internal environmental analysis will concentrate on the organization's resource base and how it is used.[10] When strategic decision-makers fully understand the nature of the resource base they are working with, they are then in a much stronger position to go back to their external analysis and begin to match company strengths with market opportunities, and determine how its strengths will help it overcome external threats and whether or not its internal weaknesses will make it vulnerable to market changes.

Establishing a Competitive Edge through Internal Environmental Analysis

Above, we described the need for firms to develop basic and distinctive competencies in order to obtain a competitive advantage in the marketplace. This advantage is obtained by the proper deployment of the firm's resources given customer demands. In this section we will discuss three methods for analyzing how successful the firm has been in developing its distinctive competencies; the resource-base approach, the value chain approach, and the functional approach (see Figure 4.2).

Figure 4.2
The Hierarchy of Internal Analysis

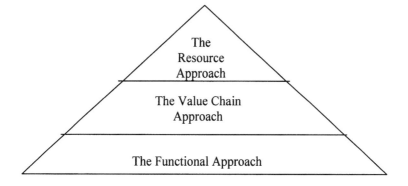

Note that the resource approach is at the top of the hierarchy. This indicates that this approach is the most strategic in nature and compares the overall resources of the firm to those competencies necessary to succeed in the current marketplace (these competencies are called *key success factors*). The value chain approach is more detailed in nature in that it examines the deployment of the firm's resources along the firm's market channel. Each major activity of the firm's operation employs the firm's resources in order to add value to the product and/or service and create a competitive advantage. Lastly, the functional approach refers to analyzing the tactical plans of the firm, that is, how the firm at the operational level enacts the strategic plan. The ability to translate the overall plan into the major functions of a business is essential in order to properly deploy the firm's resources (i.e. how much do we spend on marketing, product development, recruitment, cost of capital, etc…?).

The Resource-Based Approach

In Chapter 1, we described the firm's need for individual, team, and organizational competencies in order to create a learning organization. In this section, we look at how strategically managed firms seek distinctive core competencies and strategic advantages through their resource bases.

As suggested below in Figure 4.3, firms must build upon their resource base to develop efficient operations based on their central mission. Over time, this operation should result in developed employee competences and operational competences where the firm begins to realize efficiencies from operational practices that improve as a result of continual learning. With strategic direction, many of the basic competences should be converted into distinctive core competencies (those operational skills that are superior to similar skills of competitors) which can lead, then, to competitive advantages for the firm. This competitive advantage can be sustained over time through continued knowledge management and organizational development – the creation of a learning and self renewing organization.

The Firm's Resource Base. The nature of a firm's resource base, as shown in Figure 4.3, comes in three varieties: 1) the tangible assets it has captured; 2) the intangible assets it has built; and 3) the competencies it has built over time.[11] Over time, every organization builds a series of resource bases that provide it with the ability to

Figure 4.3
Creating a Sustainable Competitive Advantage
Through Resource Development

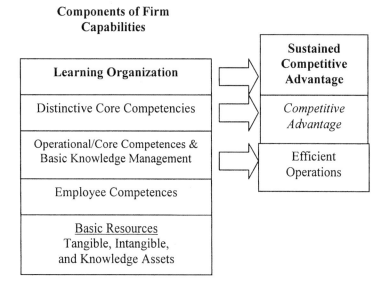

accomplish certain levels of operations and achieve a certain level of outcomes. In this sense, resources have both an empowering as well as a limiting capability.   Resources empower in that they allow organizations to do certain things.   For example, if a clothing manufacturer wants to increase production to meet new orders, it can do so if it is able to accumulate additional resources (material, machinery, personnel, storage capacity, and shipping capacity). However, resources are also limiting because they are often not easily acquired. For example, if our clothing manufacturer needs to get a loan from a bank of $3 million dollars to acquire the resources it needs to fill the order, and the bank says no, the manufacturer will have to turn the new orders down.

Tangible resources are those resources that have capital or material value and are normally thought of as either physical or financial.[12] These include property, buildings, machinery, equipment, labor pool, materials, supplies, bank accounts, investments, patents, etc.. Most of the tangible resource base can be purchased and represents identifiable assets of the firm. (We caution, here, that it is not enough to look at a company's balance sheet to see the extent and nature of tangible assets – the work force, for example, is not valued in an accountant's balance sheet, but having the labor a firm needs to conduct its operations is certainly a very important tangible resource.)

Intangible resources are those resources that are clearly important to the firm, but defy measurement or valuing.[13] These would include a brand name, reputation, expertise level of employees, education level of employees, firm leadership, organizational culture, traditions, etc. These resources defy measuring or have specific monetary values placed on them, which are not indicative of their importance to the organization. Corporate leaders such as Bill Gates of Microsoft, Howard Schultze of Starbucks, and Walt Disney have had a tremendous impact on their firms and are a unique, cherished resource.

Knowledge is a critical resource to highlight (sometimes referred to as intellectual capital) in that it is both a source for producing change as well as a source for managing change.[14] Knowledge has both tangible and intangible features[15] and includes "the expertise and experience of individuals, the routines and processes that define the distinctive way of doing things inside the organization, and the knowledge of customer needs and supplier strengths ..."[16] and historically referred to employee skill, patents, and research. Knowledge can be explicit within the organization, conscious and objective, or tacit (implicit and collective), that is, an individual or the firm is aware or unaware of what he/she/they know(s).[17]

Firms need to leverage their knowledge in order to create and support entrepreneurial ventures (create change in their market) and to create a culture that nurtures organizational renewal, or internal change. Firms also add to their intellectual capital by establishing a social environment that supports creativity and innovation. According to Leonard and Sensiper innovation "is a rhythm of search and selection, exploration and synthesis, cycles of divergence and cycles of convergence"[18] where divergence of skills in a group produces "intellectual conflict ... producing energy that is channeled into new ideas and products"[19] and convergence refers to the coordination, focus and sharing of this new knowledge. Information sharing involves building trust, being open to disclosing and capitalizing on mistakes, and fostering a sense of joint ownership of work products.[20]

Measuring, managing and improving upon intellectual capital has quickly become one of corporate America's top priorities given the macro economic shift to a knowledge economy.[21] High technology firms such as Dow Chemical and General Electric have innumerable patents and have cornered the market of experts in their fields. Dodgson noted that central to Celltech's strategy was a commitment to building a learning organization, both internally and externally, through an active and carefully constructed network of relationships and partnerships.[22] The Conference Board reported in 2000 that over 80% of 200 executives they surveyed had some form of knowledge management effort under way.[23]

The quality of a firm's resource base is one of the key considerations in conducting a strategic internal analysis. Quality may be more important than quantity here, as many firms have discovered. Pan Am was one of the most successful and wealthy of the airlines in the 1960's and 1970's but under deregulation began to lose money. Over the years, their wealth simply prevented bankruptcy at an earlier date as, year after year, Pam Am continued to lose money, often more money in a year than the rest of the industry combined. So while one might argue that early on, Pan Am *should* have had enough resources to turn things around and survive, the quality of its strategic competencies was too low to save the airline.

Barney has suggested that there is a way of looking at resources that will tell strategic decision-makers whether or not their resources are of high or lesser quality and value.[24] He suggested a test, which he referred to as the *VIRO framework* which proposed four different tests of a particular resource in order to determine its true value to the firm. VIRO stands for:

- **Value**: whether or not the resource helps the firm achieve a competitive advantage
- **Imitability**: whether or not the resource is difficult for others to imitate and/or is substitutable[25]
- **Rareness**: whether or not the resource is possessed by competitors, and
- **Organization**: whether or not the firm is able to effectively exploit the resource.

When a strategic decision-maker is able to answer "yes" to all of these characteristics of a given resource, then that person can also conclude that that particular resource is one that should be protected and grown, and one that will help the firm reach its strategic objectives. If, on the other hand, the strategic decision-maker answers "no" to one or more of these characteristics, then another set of decision needs to be made. For example, if the Disney Company were to look at its Disney Studios (the unit that continues to make film features destined for the children's films and family market) and determine that all five characteristics were still true (even in the face of growing competition from domestic and foreign studios), it would conclude that it should continue to support and try to grow the subunit. If, on the other hand, Disney were to look at its Disney Studios and determine that it was no longer particularly rare and had already been imitated successfully by other studios, then it might well want to ask the hard question as to whether or not Disney should close Disney Studios down or try to sell it to a competitor.

For example, Nordstrom's has a reputation of not only selling high fashion and high quality shoes and apparel, but also the reputation of standing behind their merchandise 100% by taking merchandise back without question. This reputation has helped Nordstrom's to become one of the hottest up-scaled retail chains in the country. Other up-scaled retail chains that have not developed the same reputation have difficulty convincing their customers that they are just like Nordstrom's when their customers' prior experiences over the years has been one of poor service.

Competence and *competencies,* according to Jonathan and Ruth Winteron are frequently confused and mistakenly interchanged.[26]

Competences refer to the job-related skills, knowledge, and understandings where the job is defined in terms of tasks, roles and activities. An employee's competence is a function of his or her on-the-job performance as compared to performance standards.[27] Competencies, on-the-other-hand, refer to underlying characteristics of a manager or a firm that lead to superior performance.[28] Competencies refer to generic abilities and resources that develop over time and represent highly developed capabilities of the firm.[29]

As we described in Chapter 1, there is a hierarchy of competences within the organization (individual, team, and organizational). Ultimately, competences can gain an organization a competitive edge if the firm utilizes its competences to create activities that are best matched to consumer needs and wants and are better than those of their competitors; competences then emerge as competencies. On a more basic level, however, competences are the skills and knowledge that a firm develops to make its operational activities work as efficiently and effectively as possible. The number and breadth of competences vary organization by organization and tend to revolve around either product innovation and development or process innovation and development.[30]

Process management skills include not only those skills and knowledge bases needed to run the core operation as efficiently as possible, they also involve the management activities of the firm and how well management is able to coordinate both core operations as well as support operations that reduce waste and improve productivity and profitability. Firms that have strong process management skills have: clearly defined management responsibilities, clearly defined steps in the manufacturing or service process, documented and detailed workflow, established control points and measurements, and control process for handling deviations.[31]

Process management skills are highly interconnected and are systemic in nature. McDonalds has turned fast-food preparation into a science by computerizing much of their cooking operations in some of their restaurants. In plain sight of the customer, a computer-monitored machine dumps frozen fries into a basket that in turn is dunked into hot oil for cooking. Then the machine shakes the fries and dumps them into bins for serving. Robot machines elsewhere prepare drinks.[32]

Product development skills, on the other hand, require such intangible assets as creativity, vision, risk-taking, entrepreneurship, strong product research and development, product engineering, market research, and branding.[33] Referring back to the Disney case at the beginning of this chapter, the company seemed to possess excellent product development skills under its founder Walt Disney, yet lost those skills once he passed away. Disney had to recreate itself, find new magic in its product line in order to serve older children, teenagers, and adults. Then there is the issue of Euro-Disney. Ironically, the failure of Euro-Disney was not due to what some reported as low attendance or acceptance but was attributed to serious operational blunders including insufficient seating capacity in restaurants, poor training of local employees, inadequate ride scheduling, and overestimating customer in-park spending.[34] Product management skills must be added to process management skills if a firm is to succeed.

Operational   (Core)   and   Distinctive   Competencies. *Operational (core) competence*, the third level of the model shown in Figure 4.3 should be common among successfully competing firms. Core competences are a general set of operational methods (technical systems, skills, and managerial systems) that achieve acceptable efficiencies and represents the critical knowledge necessary to compete in the industry the firm is in.[35] For example, Domino's Pizza's core competence is pizza delivery[36] (not the quality of their pizza) while Dunkin Donuts' core is high quality baked goods and coffee.[37]

Core competences, however, are a two-edged sword in that they are tied to the organization's value systems and in that sense may hinder managers from changing the firm's operations. Thus *core rigidities*, the inflexibility of the core, represent past managerial and operational practices and acts as a deterrent to new learning and organizational change.[38] Apple Computers' innovative approach to computer technology and design (their core competences) has simultaneously made Apple one of the leading edge personal computer firms yet has kept them from achieving high profitability – a real irony for the firm that started the personal computer market and reinvented the industry through graphic interfaces.

Distinctive core competencies is the next level. Here, organizations are able to refine especially important competences to a level above that of their competitors - distinctive competencies differentiate a company strategically. This may well become a proprietary competency, something that the firm would guard as a closely held secret, making it valuable, rare, not easily imitated or reproduced, and something that the company can then use to create a competitive advantage. For example, in the introductory case Disney's distinctive competencies included the creation and development of innovative cartoon characters, cinema animation and with Disneyland and Disney World, the ability to take imagination and translate it into tangible entertainment. This formula for success was lost for a short while with the passage of its founders but rekindled under the stewardship of Michael Eisner.

How easy is it to create distinctive competencies? Unfortunately, for most companies distinctive competencies prove very difficult to achieve. It is difficult enough for companies to achieve basic operational competence and compete head-to-head with other like companies with broadly known operational techniques. These techniques improve themselves over time. This is particularly true when improvements come in the form of emerging technologies, which are provided by outside vendors - outside vendors who have an interest in selling to a broader range of business consumers rather than limit their sales to only one firm. These vendors make these new technologies generally available and thus are not the source of creating a distinctive competency for any one firm. Most companies that are able to achieve a distinctive competency develop them in-house, through years of research and experimentation. Like Disney, a firm can't simply go out and buy a vision (their concept of family entertainment) that will provide it with a distinctive competency, it needs to grow its own and that takes both time and patience.

Where a firm has a distinctive competency, such as process or product management is yet another issue. Since distinctive competencies lead to a competitive advantage, various firms in the same industry, assuming the industry is not one of perfect competition, may have differing distinctive competencies. For example, both Wal-Mart and Nordstrom are both retailers yet Wal-Mart's distinctive competencies are focused around cost reduction and broad target marketing (purchasing in bulk, just-in-time inventory, television advertisements) while Nordstrom concentrates on customer service (such as personalized shopping assistants, extra wide aisles, live music, and comfortable seating throughout the store). We will discuss the relationship between competencies and strategies in more detail in Chapter 6 but it is important to note now that there must be a strong connection between the firm's strategy and its distinctive competencies.

Competitive Advantages and the Learning Organization. A *competitive advantage* is defined as the ability to offer products and services that yield a higher profit than competitor firms.[39] This is the goal of every competitive organization. Being in a position to offer goods or services that the consumer feels are superior (due to quality or lower cost) to those of the competition is an accomplishment that provides many important benefits to the firm that is able to do so. Market demand for that firm's goods or services will be higher than for competitive products and the focal firm should be able to optimize both growth and profitability.

Sustaining a competitive advantage would be the second and ultimate goal of a firm. This is often difficult to do because once one firm is able to achieve a competitive advantage, other firms in the industry will begin to target that firm and seek to develop distinctive competencies of their own to eventually overtake the first firm's market position. This means that it isn't enough to simply achieve a competitive advantage, the organization must continue to look beyond current success and envision the next logical step in the development of its goods or services – excellence is a fleeting commodity and difficult to maintain.[40]

Resources, Capabilities and Key Success Factors: Sustaining a Competitive Advantage. In and of itself, when a firm is able to develop a solid resource base and build that base to create distinctive competencies, this still is not enough to ensure the success in any particular market. For example, Apple Computers has always excelled at product creativity and innovation yet only occupies a very small portion of the market it originally created.[41] Firms must also ensure that they also focus the use of their resources to creating a sustainable competitive advantage. They can do this by focusing on the key success factors of the market that they compete in.   These key success factors align the firm's distinctive competencies with emerging market needs.[42]   Firms then interpret what is valuable to customers from market surveys and research into products and services and apply distinctive competencies to try to achieve a competitive advantage.

For example, Southwest Airlines has successfully translated customer desire for low cost, convenient flights into several key success factors that include cost containment, employee commitment, and conservative growth. They have been able to cut operating costs by employing a single aircraft type (a Boeing 737) which reduces training, maintenance and inventory costs, avoiding a central reservation system, offering passengers frugal amenities, and reducing boarding and deplaning time through unassigned seating. They have also maintained a strong 'fun' corporate culture, nurtured by the President Herbert Kelleher's laid-back style, and have only expanded into a few profitable markets, avoiding head to head competition.[43]

On the other hand, other top-notch firms, such as McDonald's have paid a heavy price when they have failed to line up their resources and capabilities with their key success factors.   While expanding internationally in the 1990's at a dizzying rate, McDonald's domestic operation was slumping. Negative relations with franchisees, and menu problems took McDonald's away from the key success factors of the industry: a brief, consistent quality menu; rigorous operational standards; friendly employees; and heavy mass media advertising towards families with children. This has lead to only a 1% increase in same store sales growth versus a 4% increase for competitors Wendy's and Burger King. Only time will tell whether recent purchases of Donatos Pizza (a Midwestern restaurant chain), Boston Market, and Chipotle Mexican Grill will offset the 7% decline in sales experienced in 2000.[44]

Then how does a firm then sustain a competitive advantage? As discussed in Chapter 1, the recent literature in strategic management indicates that truly superior firms maintain their competitive advantage through continuous learning and broadening their distinctive competencies. Zack noted that "business organizations are coming to view knowledge as their most valuable and strategic resource."[45] Obtaining and maintaining unique and valuable resources may not be possible (especially tangible resources) without investment in intellectual resources (besides the traditional investments in research and development). Investment in knowledge assets is necessary in order to "enhance the organization's fundamental ability to compete."[46] In essence, firms cannot continue to take advantage of their unique resources without having managerial systems in place which will allow these firms to learn how to learn to adapt to changes in their environments and deploy their resources wisely.

The Value Chain Approach

The Basic Value Chain. Value chain analysis is another good way of analyzing the internal environment of an organization because it looks at the ability of a firm to add value to its products or services as it converts raw material (or new ideas) into finished goods and delivers them to the customer.

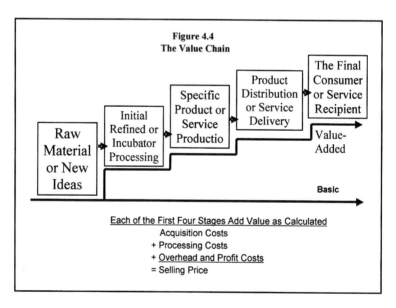

As shown in Figure 4.4 above, all products or services begin at a point where their value is at its lowest level and then goes through a series of operations which refine and package them until they reach the ultimate consumer, where its value should be the highest. The basic value chain has 5 identifiable stages.

Note that this approach works for both products and services. An example of the use of the value chain can be demonstrated through the manufacture and delivery of a piece of home furniture. Stage One consists of the initial recovery of raw materials (such as cutting down trees); Stage Two occurs when the basic raw materials are made useful for manufacturing (cutting logs into planks and then kiln drying the lumber); Stage Three then takes materials ready for the manufacturing processes and produces a final product (a furniture manufacturer buys lumber, cuts and sands it to specifications, assembles furniture, and finally puts on a final finish); in Stage Four, the final goods are sent out to distributors or retail outlets for sale (the furniture manufacturer delivers furniture to a wholesaler or directly to retail furniture stores); and finally in Stage Five, the product is purchased by the consumer (people shop at the furniture store, purchase the furniture, and take it home).[47]

In looking at this example, the value of the wood changed dramatically at each stage. It was at its lowest value in Stage One where its value was calculated initially at the cost of the tree. Then as woodsmen cut down the tree, had it trucked out of the forest to the saw mill, the cost of their labor, cost of their equipment, cost of trucking, and overhead and profit were added to determine the price of the lumber to the saw mill. The saw mill (in Stage Two) purchases the logs at a value higher than the original price of the tree and then adds more value by cutting the logs into planks, and curing the wood through kiln or air drying. The saw mill adds all of these costs to the price of the logs, adds overhead and profits and then makes the kiln-dried lumber available to the furniture manufacturer at a price higher than the price of the logs they purchased. The process continues until the customer buys the furniture, let's say an oak table and pays $2,000 for the table. When one considers that the original value of the oak in the finished table started out at a value of little or nothing, one can see how each step then creates more and more value until the raw oak becomes a beautiful kitchen table.

The internal analysis, here deals with each individual step of the value chain and determines how well each firm does in completing its part of the overall process. In looking at the furniture manufacturer, as an example, several issues come out in determining whether or not the firm performed well.

- One, did it purchase the highest quality lumber at the best available price?
- Two, did it use a proper inventory system to prevent spoilage or loss?
- Three, did it use the best mix of talented labor and efficient machinery to produce the table at the most efficient cost?
- Four, did it keep its overhead and selling costs as efficient as possible?
- And five, did it sell the table to the next recipient of the table at the highest possible price that did not exceed competitors' pricing and reap the maximum profits?

Porter's Value Chain. Value chain analysis has been refined by Michael Porter to include not only the primary activities involved in the development of a product or service (which he defines as inbound logistics, operations, outbound logistics, marketing and sales, and after sales service) but to also include the support activities that assist manufacturing and service delivery. Please note that the Porter model is a generic template and that every industry is different and the value chain may vary. For example, an e-business (internet firm) may have technology and MIS as part of their primary activities.[48]

The support activities are comprised of the firm's infrastructure (general management, planning, accounting, finance, legal affairs and quality control), human resource management (recruitment, selection, orientation, training and development, compensation, and evaluation), technology development (improvement to product or process management – the firm's resources), and procurement (purchasing of raw materials and other supplies required to operate the firm) and support the primary activities by making the value-adding process for each primary activity more efficient and/or more effective.[49] These support activities are linked to the primary activities in a variety of ways. It is important to focus upon these linkages since they may lead to a competitive advantage by producing either greater coordination between the primary activities or by optimizing the use of each primary activity. Value-added is also derived from and the links between each of the primary activities. The purpose of this analysis is not only to maximize those activities that lead to higher customer satisfaction but also to eliminate those activities that add no value from the customer's perspective. For example, Motel 6 and other economy motels minimize the number of amenities placed within the customer's room (such as towels, soap bars, super movie channels like HBO, courtesy bar, coffee makers, and ironing boards) since this reduces cost and is seen as frivolous by the customer as suggested in Figure 4.5.

Figure 4.5
Michael Porter's Value Chain

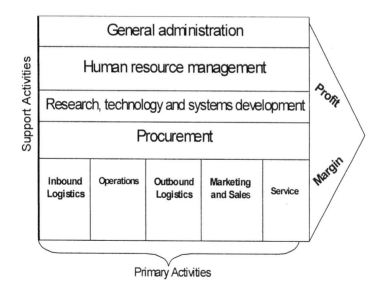

Let's go back to Stage One of the furniture production process. Here the tree is cut down to be converted into logs to be converted eventually into a chair or a table. Procurement can add value to this process by either securing the lowest cost trees or by purchasing the best quality trees, based upon the desires of the targeted consumer. More importantly, procurement might also have looked into other alternative besides tree cutting including purchasing logs and/or wood planks from other firms who may have an oversupply, using recycled press wood, and/or purchase wood futures with the hope of ensuring supply at a stabilized price. Human resource management might add value through training that focuses on both on-the-job safety concerns as well as efficient tree-cutting while top management works with legal affairs to secure future tree supplies from government forests, and new tree-cutting technology is employed to increase wood yields and reduce accidents. This analysis would be repeated for every stage of the value chain including after sales service to ensure that customers' expectations of value have been met if not exceeded.

How important are value chains? The media and communications markets are undergoing a fundamental transformation with information and communication firms such as Time Warner and AT&T pushing into new sectors and altering their value chains in order to integrate and network multimedia service systems.[50] Sony kept innovation alive and boosted sales by capturing more of its value chain through forward integration.[51] Dell's success as a PC retailer came from one simple value chain driven concept, sell computer systems directly to customers.[52] Dial-a-mattress started in business using a similar concept – have customers shop at home by simply dial their toll free number or visiting their website (the firm has since opened retail stores).[53] More importantly, the demise of many e-businesses was due to their inability to develop a coherent value chain.[54]

In analyzing a firm's value chain, Ghosh recommends asking two series of questions – one set is for consolidating the value chain, the other is for creating new values as seen in Table 4.1. The rationale for analyzing the value chain is quite clear in that the firm needs to adjust to changes in its marketplace by altering is value delivery system.

Table 4.1
Evaluating the Firm's Value Chain[55]

Consolidating Value Chains	Creating New Values
1. Can I obtain significant profit margins by consolidating parts of the value chain?	1. Can I offer additional products/services to my existing customer base?
2. Can I create significant value by reducing the number of firms in the value chain?	2. Can I address the needs of a new customer segment by restructuring my value chain?
3. What additional competences and skills do I need to take over other firms' functions in the value chain?	3. Can I use my ability to attract customers to generate new sources of revenue (i.e. advertising, complementary products)?
4. Will I be at a competitive disadvantage if another consolidates the value chain?	4. Will my business be significantly harmed by other companies providing some of the values I do on a partial basis?

The Functional Approach

All organizations develop operations that depend on basic organizational functions and a third approach to analyzing a firm's internal operations is to analyze the business functions that support those operations. Usually referred to as tactical plans, these include:

1. **Financial Function.** The general control of financial operations and indicators
2. **Marketing Function.** The methods used and success of selling the firms goods or services
3. **Technology Function (including R&D).** The state of the firm's technology and how it uses available technology to achieve a competitive advantage
4. **Human Resource Management Function.** The firm's management and development of its human assets, and
5. **General Management and the Production and Operations Management Function.** The ability of the management core to operate the firm. [56]

The Function of Financial Management.   One of the indicators of health (ultimately survival) of a business is that of the state of its finances.   As we indicated at the beginning of this chapter, firm's ability to produce an acceptable profit is a necessary but insufficient condition for survival.[57]   Secondly, as a critical tangible resource, the firm wants to be able to determine whether its financial position in the marketplace can be utilized as a competitive advantage. For example, debt-free firms not only are more profitable due to lack of debt repayment but also have the ability use this position to obtain large funding relative to their asset base with moderately low interest rates and hence take advantage of new market opportunities.   Fortunately, financial health is one of the most readily calculated and available data sources that strategic decision-makers can obtain.   The improvements in accounting technology (whether that be in-house or purchased from accounting firms) have allowed results of operations to be translated through an accounting program and instantaneously allow decision-makers to know where the organization stands financially.

The key concerns for strategic planners, when looking at the financial status of a firm, are the issues of *risk* and *reward*.[58]   We define risk as the *probability* of receiving a specific return on one's investment (the reward); the greater the risk the greater the expected reward or loss.[59]   *Uncertainty*, on the other hand, is the inability to perfectly calculate risk and reward; the greater the uncertainty, the more difficult it is to calculate risk (and determine a firm's relative tolerance for risk) and hence lower risk tolerance.

For example, common stocks from 1926-1983 have had an average rate of return of slightly under 10% while other investments (long-term corporate bonds and U.S. Treasury bills) have a return between 3-4%.   One would then think that investing in the stock market was a given since its return, over the long run, was far greater than these other investments.   However, with that return comes a far greater risk.   The Dow dropped 25% over a three year period from its all time high in 1999, with the average investor losing 20% of his or her asset value.   The average investor in 2002 was highly uncertain as to the future of the stock market.   Investors saw the overall stock market as a bad, risky investment, at least in the short term, since they saw little potential upward market movement and feared much greater downward trends.[60] Businesses must also examine their tolerance for risk given their ability to calculate market trends and determine an acceptable rate of return.

Functional strategies deal with three major topics: capital acquisition, capital allocation, and dividend and working capital.[61] It is self-evident that firms cannot operate without capital and the acquisition of capital is vital not only to a firm's day-to-day operations and its survival but in particular to the firm's long-term, strategic plans. A firm must have access to capital in order maintain its current infrastructure of buildings, equipment, and real estate but may require additional capital if the firm's overall strategic objectives include market expansion and growth.

Capital Formation. There are several ways any organization can raise capital:

1. *Selling Stock.* This method of raising capital through selling ownership has the benefit of not having to be repaid, and no interest is due on these funds. However, when a firm sells stock, it dilutes ownership control and creates a more diverse ownership base which may or may not prove problematic.

2. *Selling Bonds.* Selling bonds or taking out loans has the benefit of not diluting ownership or ownership control. However, interest due on bonds, loans, or class B stock decreases profits by increasing costs. The other side of this issue is that when interest rates are low, this is an attractive way of raising capital, primarily because it does not challenge ownership. When rates are high, however, costs can raise dramatically and reduce the profitability of potential new ventures.

3. *Obtaining Loans.* Banks, financial institutions, and venture capitalists may provide the firm with the needed infusion of capital without the necessity of the firm publicly announcing its need for either short term or long term funds. These institutions will require the firm to pledge collateral (capital assets) against the loan with venture capitalists taking stock and/or stock options.

4. *Profits.* High levels of profitability are extremely desirable for a variety of reasons. One of the most important is that high profits provide additional capitalization without depleting ownership control or introducing the additional cost of debt service. It is

clearly the most desirable way of creating capital for any organization.[62]

Financial experts tell us that well-conceived organizational financial structures are a combination of all four capital bases. Firms need a balanced approach to take maximal advantage of the capital markets, and by exercising flexibility among the markets, take advantage of the various markets as conditions fluctuate. While no financial experts would suggest that profit is not important, they also point out that often profitability alone isn't enough to finance the growth a firm might need to pursue to remain competitive.

Capital Allocation. Capital allocation is the process of prioritizing projects within a firm, and determining the financial hurdles that a project must overcome in order for it to receive financing. One method for determining whether a project should be funded is through the net present value rule. This rule states that "a project should be undertaken if its net present value is positive and should be rejected if its net present value is negative."[63] In order to calculate the net present value of any project, we must first subtract the cost of financing the proposal (called the discount rate) over the time it will take to implement the project. This discount rate could refer to either opportunity costs (the return the firm could receive from putting the funds into a guaranteed investment i.e. a bank certificate of deposit) or borrowing costs (the interest rate, dividend, or bond rate the firm would pay in order to raise the capital). The net present value over one year time period is equal to the present value of future cash flow at the cost of capital minus the initial cash outlay.

The internal rate of return rule is a second method for determining whether or not a project should be funded. This rule states that "a project should be undertaken it its internal rate of return is higher than its cost of capital."[64] The minimum internal rate of return, also known as the hurdle rate, is the discount rate that makes the net present value of a project equal to zero. The internal rate of return is then adjusted for the time value of money (the length of time the project will take).

Yet a third method of making an appropriate decision is to analyze the pay back period (based on the breakeven point) – the time it takes for any project to recoup its initial investment. Most firms employ a two to three year pay back period as their cutoff period; projects above the cutoff period are rejected, those in a shorter time span are funded. Many firms adjust the measure of years using net present value, that is, they discount their cash flow by their cost of capital.[65]

On the other hand, using net present value allows comparisons between projects and internal rate of return does not. The payback method ignores time value of money and all cash flows the moment payback occurs.[66]

Dividends. Stockholders invest in firms for one of two reasons capital appreciation (the value of their stock rises) and two, dividends. The board of directors of a firm will determine the level of dividends based on the consideration that "the amount left over after all acceptable investment opportunities have been undertaken."[67] La Porta et al. posited two reasons for dividend payouts: dividends are the result of effective pressure by shareholders, or corporate officers choose to pay dividends to establish a reputation for decent treatment of shareholders so that firms can raise equity finance in the future.[68] However, there are other factors that need to be considered in the declaration of dividends including: legal, contractual, and internal constraints, growth prospects, and owner and market considerations. The firm must also consider what form the dividend should take besides cash including stock dividends, and whether to split, reverse-split, or repurchase stocks.[69]

The real question is, what message does dividend policies, and changes in those policies, send to both current and potential shareholders? Dividends, according to most financial theorists, contain valuable information about the firm, and act as signals to the market.[70] One would obviously think that increased dividends sends a positive message to the market while decreasing dividends sends the reverse message. According to Said Elfakhani, the dividend signal can confirm good, bad, or indifferent news already conveyed through financial statements. It also can clarify or create greater ambiguity about the firm's financial position. His research revealed that the strength of the market reaction to dividends was determined by whether the dividend confirmed, clarified, or created more uncertainty. Furthermore he found that the market was more concerned with confirming news favorableness than the actual change in the dividend payout.[71]

Working Capital. Usually comprised of cash, inventories, accounts receivables, marketable securities and prepaid expenses, working capital refers to the amount of assets necessary for the day-to-day operations of the firm. Firms can increase or decrease their working capital needs through their credit and collection policies, understanding that more liberal policies may lead to hire sales but greater capital requirements (and greater risk). Firms must also factor into their cash flow projections issues of business seasonality in order to determine both minimum and maximum cash flow needs.[72]

Measures of Financial Performance. There are several measures of financial performance of the firm that we would like to mention at this time, however, the Appendix of this chapter contains these measures and their explanations in detail.

Two financial figures that are of most interest to the strategic decision-maker are *profits* and *sales*.[73] Profits (revenues minus costs), as represented as whole numbers as well as percentages, and give managers a firm understanding of how efficient operations are in producing new capital revenues. This is important because capital that is derived out of profits brings with it no contingent liabilities. Furthermore profits represent excess funds that may be distributed back to stockholders and/or investors without negatively impacting the firm's current operation and may result in further investments in the firm.

Sales represents the potential cash flows (assuming the firm has an excellent record of collections) into a firm and is a critical survival factor; no or low sales means no business. However, sales also measures the firm's effectiveness in determining customer needs, producing goods and services to meet those needs, and then the firm's ability to distribute and market the goods and services. Regardless of how efficient an operation may be, if that operation does not lead to a sale then the firm has ultimately failed.

A third financial performance measure of interest for public corporations is their stock price. Clearly from the shareholders' perspective, increasing stock prices represents one of the two methods in which stockholders obtain a return on their investment. Growth-oriented firms depend upon increasing stock prices to attract and then reward investors, rather than rely on dividend distributions. For potential investors, the stock price, when divided by the company's earnings, known as the price/earnings ratio, indicates the strength and growth potential of the company relative to its competitors as perceived by the marketplace.[74]

Price itself may be an inducement or deterrent to purchasing. Penny stocks, stocks that sell for less than a dollar a share, can be purchased in large quantities by small investors while high priced stocks (such as Berkshire Hathaway, symbol BRK.A , $ 74,000 on May 13, 2003) may limit purchases to mutual funds and wealthy investors. The stock price from the company's perspective represents not only the strength of the company as measured by the marketplace but also the ability of the firm to raise future capital since new issues of stock are sold below the current market price.[75]

Return Ratios. Another major set of financial measures that have strategic implication are ratio analyses. These include liquidity ratios, leverage ratios and profitability ratios. In particular the profitability measures include:

- *ROI.* Return on investment states how well the firm has invested its available capital to achieve a significant return.
- *ROE.* Return on equity tells the analyst how well the firm has used capital raised through the sale of stock to create profitability. And
- *ROA.* Return on assets is a measure that describes how well the firm has used its overall asset base, regardless of source, to produce profits.[76]

All of these return measures give the analyst and strategic decision-maker valuable insights as to how management uses its resources to produce sales and achieve a profit. By looking at all of these measures over time to see if trends are positive or negative, analysts are able to spot favorable or troubling financial trends. They then pass this information along to strategic decision-makers to either determine that current operations produce the desired financial ratio outcomes or that those operations need to be modified to improve financial ratio outcomes.

Ratios provide an invaluable tool for assessing current organizational financial performance, providing comparators for benchmarking, and providing a universally recognized and respected data points for objective analysis. In an analysis of any firm, it is important to not only know what these ratios are, but also how one calculates them, and what they mean. The appendix to this chapter contains several common accounting ratios that businesses use to provide operating information for both strategic decision-making as well as operational decision-making. The appendix also describes how they are calculated and how managers use them to make strategic and/or operational decisions.

Financial Benchmarking. Financial benchmarking is the activity of comparing one organization's performance against a standard and drawing a conclusion.[77] In strategic management, two common benchmarking standards are industry averages and the financial results from a chief competitor in the industry. All of the ratios and measures of financial performance in the appendix of this chapter may be compared to industry standards and top competitors.

For the strategic decision-maker, for example, it is very instructive to be able to say that "our company produced a profit of 7.5%; while the average profits in our industry was 7.2%; but our chief competitor showed a profit of 9.7%." There are a number of issues that come out of a statement like this:

- One, does the 7.2% average return indicate that the focal firm is in an attractive industry?
- Two, does the fact that the focal firm's profit ratio was .3% above the average of the industry good or bad?
- Three, does the fact that our primary competitor's return was 2.2% greater than ours a cause for concern?

The first question tests the industry itself to ascertain whether or not the profitability of the average members of the industry make it an industry worthy of additional investment and exploitation. So, is the figure 7.2% a good figure? It would be if the industry tended to support this level of return on a steady basis over time (extreme conditions such as those created by September 11th not withstanding) and if the industry also supported a healthy growth pattern (as we'll discuss in the next section on marketing management). Of course the bigger response would be whether or not the level of profitability meets the expectation of a focal firm's investors and owners. If they are happy with this return, then the strategic decision-maker could also conclude that further investment in this particular industry was warranted. On the other hand, if the return level is declining over time, owners and investors might become less tolerant of further investments in this one industry and begin to bring pressure on top managers to begin to invest in more profitable industries.

The second question is good news, albeit somewhat tempered. The good news is that the focal firm is not only profitable (which is good news in and of itself), but that its performance is better than the average of the industry. It is performing at a level at least better than 50% of all firms in the industry.

The answer to the third question is the tempered news. The focal firm is obviously not the top performer in the industry, and the firm which the focal firm sees as its chief competitor is doing business and producing a profit that is appreciably better than the focal firm. There are also other firms conducting their operations at a level above it. In other words, there are probably some operational activities the focal firm is involved with that could be reengineered or reorganized that would improve profitability and give the firm a better chance to achieve a competitive advantage. This follows on the earlier discussion of competencies and value chains, and suggests that for the focal firm, one or more of its competencies is not as good as it could be or some primary and support activities are not adding value along the market channel.

The Function of Marketing Management. The purpose of marketing is to inform, educate, and persuade potential customers as to the value of a firm's products and services through what is known as the 4P's of marketing: product, price, placement, and promotion.[78] From a strategic perspective, marketing helps a firm develop a competitive advantage through such activities as product branding and advertising. Marketing management includes the following functions: identifying the firm's target markets, market research to determine what value-added means to customers in terms of product features, functions, and benefits, the creation of a product and service concept, the development of a prototype, product and service testing, product and service promotion, product and service pricing, product and service sales and distribution, and after sales services.[79]

For example, in our introductory case Disney has defined a need (family entertainment) of a particular target market (people of all ages interested in wholesome and creative leisure), carved out a brand name with highly identifiable products and services, requested above average market prices to justify their premium products and services, and has historically had a limited and highly specialized distribution channel for those products and services.

The marketing process is not very dissimilar to the strategic management process in that it involves comparing the organization's mission to market opportunities, selecting a target market and marketing objectives while scanning the environment, selecting a marketing mix (price, placement, product, and promotion), implementing and then evaluating the marketing plan.[80] These plans need to be translated into more specific marketing plans or tactics which provide the firm guidance within the marketing mix.

Product Innovation and Management. There are several questions that a firm must answer concerning the development of a product and the management of its product line. The firm must first determine whether new products or services should be developed or if the current product line can or should be modified in order to meet possible changing consumer needs. The growth matrix, Table 4.2, denotes the differing product tactics available and the associated risk attached to those tactics.[81]

Table 4.2
The Growth Matrix: Product Options and Tactics

	Current Customers	New Customers (higher risk)
Current Product	Product Renewal	Product Retargeting
New Product (higher risk)	Product Innovation	Product Exploration

The second question concerning product management addresses the profitability of the firm's products and product lines and

The second question concerning product management addresses the profitability of the firm's products and product lines and how to create a product mix that maximizes profitability. An ancillary question relates to the actual management of products and product lines (growth products, loss leaders, maintenance, and harvest products) given the strategy of the firm and product manager behavior.[82] Last, the firm must address the image projected from the line of products and services (branding) that the firm has constructed; how do consumers perceive the company given what we sell and how we market our goods? Going back to Disney, how might their shift into more adult oriented entertainment through brand names such as Touchstone Pictures, and Hyperion Books have affected their brand image?

Decisions about product development must be made taking into account several factors including the product life cycle (length of the cycle, stage of cycle product is in, etc.), product turnaround time (what is called speed to market), resources available for development, and the fit of the new product into the firm's overall strategy in order to create a competitive advantage.

Promotion, Publicity, and Advertising. In today's market, there are a plethora of communication channels to try to get the company's message out and attract consumers. With the growth of e-business, the competitive horizon has continued to grow, challenging firms to find messages and delivery tactics that will yield the best possible returns in terms of new and increased sales. Firms need to connect their promotional campaigns to their products and product lines and determine which products or products lines are priorities for the firm. Some of the channels available to firms to advertise today include television, radio, screen media (including theater screens and video tape trailers), print media (newspapers, magazines, and fliers), public display, the internet (banners, websites, and unfortunately SPAM e-mails), and word of mouth.[83]

Choosing the right channel, spending wisely on the right message for that channel, and then following-up as closely as possible, are some of the factors that make one firm's promotional campaign more effective than another's. Marketing is a highly competitive field in itself, but is one of the most important strategic factors that differentiates a competitively successful company from the average firm in the market.

Product and Service Pricing. Firms tie the pricing of their products and services directly to their central strategy as well as the structure of the market in which the firms are competing. If the firms are contending with competitors primarily through low price (either due to the market structure or their competitive advantage in manufacturing and production) then their pricing strategies will be cost-based. In cost-based pricing, firms sets their price by calculating the fixed and variable costs of a product, and then determine a target volume based upon market demand and the desired profit margin. Market-based pricing, on the other hand, may be employed in less-price sensitive markets. Here firms set the price of their product or service to meet customer needs in light of their market position relative to their competitors. Prices are set higher if firms wish to be perceived as having high quality products, lower if they wish their products to be perceived as a bargain. Value-based pricing extends market-based pricing to include buyers' comparisons. The firms' products are compared to others that are reasonably similar in price and performance. Based upon the comparison of product attributes and price, the firms' products are priced above or below the average industry price.[84]

Product Distribution. In distributing its products and services, the firm will take a close look at the marketing channel, understanding how the product normally moves from the producer to the consumer. The firm will consider not only how the channel fits in with its overall strategy but also the risks and rewards associated with narrow and short market channels (few available sellers and few middle men) versus broad and long market channels.[85] Short and narrow channels are easier to control but place the majority of the risk on the producer while longer and broader market channels share risk amongst the channel members but creates a greater dependency of the producer on agents, wholesalers, distributors, and retailers.

Given Walt Disney's need to control product quality and image, Disney for most of its existence had very few market channels (i.e. if you wanted a Disney product, you had to go to Disneyland or Disney World) and only within the last ten years has Disney established alternative market channels for their highly touted movies (now available on DVD in any major retail chain), promotional goods (i.e. Mickey Mouse ears can be purchased through Disney stores and the internet), and entertainment parks (they have expanded their site locations and offered more variety of entertainment milieu's at those sites).

Market Benchmarking. When determining the strength of a firm's marketing, again analysts and strategic decision-makers can use benchmarking to determine how well a focal company is doing. So a top manager at Anheuser-Busch (A-B) might say that, "in 2001 we grew at the rate of 1% over a ten year period; while the industry grew at a rate of 5.02%; and Coors grew at a rate of 3.48%."[86] So, what can we derive out of this type of a statement? Several issues are again suggested:

- One, does the 5% average growth rate indicate that the A-B is in an attractive industry or not?
- Two, is the fact that A-B's growth ratio was 4% below the average of the industry good or bad?
- Three, is the fact that one of A-B's primary competitor's growth rate was 2.5% greater than theirs mean anything?
- Four, what about market share? Does that tell us anything?

The answer to the first question is a "yes," but again with a caveat. It's worrisome that Anheuser-Busch's growth rate is so low, but there does appear to be growth opportunities in the industry which continue to make it a somewhat attractive industry. 5% is acceptable (and is higher then the projected GDP for 2003 and 2004), particularly for more conservatively run organizations. Even though one might be concerned that A-B's growth trend (derived from regression over a ten-year period of time) is very low, it is also true that A-B's profits are good (and for 2001, profits were 13.2%)[87] and dividends are paid on a regular basis (A-B paid out 36% of net earnings to shareholders in 2001), [88] all of which would make shareholders happy. Further, it is important to understand that Anheuser-Busch is not a single-business company which complicates the analysis of their beer division. A-B is involved with theme parks and other entertainment companies (including the St. Louis Cardinals Baseball Club) and has even been involved in the snack business (Eagle brand snacks), all of which are part of the overall growth rate of the company. It is difficult to determine from public records what A-B's growth and profit rates are for their beer production alone, but it is possible that slow growth in A-B's other divisions depressed the company's overall growth rate.

The third question is not necessarily good or bad news for Anheuser-Busch. A-B's closest competitor, Miller Brewing has demonstrated lackluster sales growth over the past several years and Phillip Morris (the company that owns Miller Brewing), has sought to sell it off because of its poor performance. Coors, A-B's 2nd closest competitor is growing faster than A-B, which could be a concern, but we need more information before we can draw conclusions.

The important additional information flows from the fourth question. A-B's market share is huge (nearly 50% of the domestic market in 2001 and up from 45.8% in 1995), [89] while Miller has declined over the same seven year period from 21% to 19.2%. Coors appears to be the more aggressive competitor as its market share over the same period has increased from 10.5% to 11.2%. This information is extremely strong for A-B since their trends seem steady and it is likely that the company will be able to maintain its strong position in the market.

Overall, the marketing analysis of Anheuser-Busch is favorable, but not stellar. Market share figures are particularly encouraging and the company already controls 50% of the market and appears to be increasing that share. The low growth rate for such a large company is understandable and only creates minor concern.

The Function of Technology and Information Management. As we as a society move further into the Information Age, all organizations must keep pace with the growth of technology as a method of improving productivity, marketing, and control. Technology pervades every segment of organizational operations as well as control within the value chain. Connectivity allows monitoring systems to measure performance in a focal firm as well as those the firm relies on in the value chain. Being part of the leading edge of technological capability is probably one of the keys toward any firm achieving a competitive advantage in the 21st Century. [90]

We define the term *technology* as part of a firm's intellectual capital with technology being a combination of equipment (tools and *artifacts*) and the knowledge (*mentifacts*) necessary to use those tools properly in order to accomplish a specific task or function.[91] Recent research indicated that technological leaders were both more profitable and faster growing than their competitors because they could use technology to lower their operating costs and/or offer higher quality products or services.[92] A firm's technological capability is dependent upon several facets of the organization including the existence of a technology champion, adequate levels of technological ability in the executive officers, the organizational design (coordination and responsibility for firm technology), technology transfer mechanisms, and the extent and timing of control systems.[93]

Technology strategy is comprised of six factors: type of technology, desired level of competence, internal/external sourcing, R&D investment, timing of technology introductions, and the organization. In order for these factors to be successfully developed, managers need to understand their technological base, take an international perspective to technology, use technology to add value, integrate business functions through information systems, and focus on rapid response as a competitive advantage.[94]

The process in which a firm manages its technology starts with the firm's inventorying its technological capabilities, that is, what machinery and information is being employed in creating new products and services and/or then manufacturing/ delivering them. This may include such basic technology as telephones and FAX machines but may become as advanced as integrated control systems and e-commerce. In many cases the inventory may yield a gap between worker knowledge and equipment, a sure sign that either the business needs to further train its employees or the firm needs to purchase more updated equipment. Once the inventory is complete and the basic technology gap (if any) is filled, then the firm needs to document how the technology supports either product or process management systems (increase product quality or reduce production costs). Any technology that is superfluous to the product or process is set aside in order to find more effective technologies.[95]

It is somewhat difficult to actually measure technology in a firm, let alone be able to accrue certain organizational performances and outcomes to it. Girifalco suggests that there are four ways in which to measure a firm's technology:

> *technical performance* - the efficiency and effectiveness of the devices

> *the process of technological change* – frequency of innovations, rate of patent disclosures, R&D budgets, and lag time between innovation/invention/production

> *the effects of technology* – corporate sales and profits, productivity, and growth

> *the extent of use of technology* – the number of users in the firm who have adopted the technology (called the diffusion rate).[96]

Like the immediate results of marketing, it isn't immediately clear whether or not the inclusion of a new technological system has materially benefited an organization. Over time, however, technological improvements can make a difference. For example, the only way a Just-in-Time inventory system (JIT) can work is with the assistance of a sophisticated computerized control system. Computerized monitoring tells the inventory manager what products are being sold at what rate and allows her/him to make an informed decision as to when the next shipment of inventory will need to be received in order to match the depletion of the existing inventory. When one considers that most concerns that deal with inventories don't deal with a single commodity, but thousands of different commodities, one can begin to appreciate the role of computerization in successfully implement at a JIT system.

Management information systems (MISs) or computerized information systems (CISs) are crucial tools in helping top decision-makers keep a firm hold on the activities of their organizations as a whole. These systems have matured to the point where managers can monitor not only their own areas of responsibilities but overall organizational operations as well. Further, with the advances in the Internet, managers can log on and be connected from nearly any spot in the world. These are systems that will continue to improve, and the importance to all firms is that they cannot afford to lag behind in the development of their firm's technology base. Today more then ever, lagging behind in technology utilization will have adverse effects on any firm's ability to achieve and maintain a competitive advantage.[97]

The Function of Human Resource Management. All organizations are composed of and managed by people, or human resources. The processes of identifying, hiring and developing employees are extremely important for the firm in establishing effective operations. Increasingly, the belief that "people are our most important asset", is becoming a dominant theme in organizations. Employees are treated as a source of competitive advantage and thus an important component in strategic planning. The functions of human resource management (HRM) include recruitment, selection, orientation, training, career development, union and employee relations, legal compliance, compensation, and performance appraisal. The goal of HRM is to staff the organization with competent, high-performing employees capable of sustaining their performance over the long run.[98]

Human resource planning (HRP) assists in implementing strategy by translating the organization's goals into the terms of the workers needed to achieve them. It has three steps: current assessment, future assessment, and future needs programs. Current issues that impact human resource management include: creating work force diversity, sexual harassment, family concerns, and aids in the workplace. Organization survival is dependent on HRM practices that can positively address these issues and create pools of candidates and populations of employees with superior capabilities.[99]

Earlier in this chapter, we learned that crafting a learning organization is the most fundamental attribute for creating a competitive advantage – a firm with both basic competences and distinctive competencies. HRM needs to ensure that employees have the capabilities to perform their jobs efficiently, and effectively. Whether preparing new employees or responding to job demand changes, decisions have to made regarding when and how provide training. Training can occur either on or off the job. *On the job training* takes place in the employees work unit. A popular method is job rotation and involves lateral transfers where employees get to work at different jobs. They learn many different skills and gain a wider perspective on the organization. Another method has employees learn from a veteran employee. The employee or apprentice understudies with a mentor or coach to learn technical skills. *Off the job training* is usually provided to managers for developing problem solving, technical and interpersonal skills. It involves lectures, videos, and simulation exercises. Vestibule training teaches employees technical skills on the equipment they will use in a simulated work environment and reduces the danger that trainees and others face in hazardous operations. This carefully controlled learning environment allows employees to deal with every conceivable problem without disrupting the actual work process.[100]

Disney is considered one of the benchmark firms for training and development.[101] The Walt Disney World Training Center has not only trained their own employees in quality service, leadership excellence, people management, loyalty, organizational creativity, and value chain management but offers those same services to outside businesses through the Business Institute.[102] Disney also makes this service available to college students through the Walt Disney World College Program. This paid internship experience consists of learning, living and earning components that offers students a multitude of benefits . Six courses, designed by professionals and subject-matter experts from the Disney University and recommended for credit by the American Council on Education, are offered to students as part of their program. Students live in company-sponsored, 24-hour gated apartment communities on Disney's unique campus. Students work in one of four theme parks, more than 20 resorts, three water parks or the dining/entertainment/retail complex interacting with guests from all over the world in a high-volume, fast-paced environment.[103]

General Management and the Function of Production and Operations Management (POM). We begin the discussion of management last, but this in no way indicates the importance of the topic. On the contrary, it is management that makes all the difference in a firm's ability to succeed. Management performs a variety of functions at a variety of levels, yet the basic functions of all managers include planning, organizing, staffing, leading, and controlling.[104]

CEO's and Top Management. Of most interest to the student of strategic management are the activities of a firm's top management core, especially its chief executive office (CEO) and governing board. These are the crucial individuals who make the decisions that determine the strategic direction of the firm. These are the people who feel most personally responsible for the profitability and growth rate of the firm, its return ratios, and performance against competitors. These are the people who must answer to shareholders, regulators, suppliers, and distributors – they have the most public of responsibilities. Beyond these weighty responsibilities, they are also responsible for the activities of their subordinates and the people below them all the way down to the operatives who do the work related to the central mission of the firm.[105]

These individuals are resources of the firm, just as any of the other tangible and intangible resources. We also classify leadership as one of the crucial strategic resources. As such, then, it is reasonable to assume that managers and management systems can also be measured along a continuum of being either effective or ineffective. The economic downturn that occurred after 9/11 exposed many ineffective management systems. Enron and World Com were two or several firms that had allowed managers to misrepresent actual company performance to the point that when these management travesties were made public, the damage was so devastating that the firms needed to declare bankruptcy. In the case of United Airlines, which we have profiled periodically throughout this text, management may not have been criminal, but at least it proved to have been negligent in not developing financial and other management systems that could survive a major economic shock.

However, while there are several examples of managers and management systems that have failed to uphold a strategic direction for their firms, there are many more examples of managers and management systems that have been able to develop a strategic direction that have resulted in their firms achieving a competitive advantage. Bill Gates at Microsoft, Michael Eisner at Disney, and Lee Iacocca at Chrysler are all examples of CEO's who created management systems that helped lead their firms to highly successful competitive positions.

The source of good management is a varied issue. Some companies are able to grow their own. August Busch IV is a successful manager who comes from a successful management tradition, while Bill Gates arose from obscurity as the founder of Microsoft and still leads it successfully. Other successful managers come from outside the firm. Iacocca came to Chrysler from Ford and Eisner came to Disney from Pillsbury. Some top managers are hired by firms because of their reputation as specialists, while others are hired because of their reputation as organizers. Regardless, firms have a choice as to what their top management resource looks like and from the Board of Directors on down, the quality of management that a firm attracts more often than not is the major determination of organizational success or failure.

In the end-of chapter experiential exercise we provide a tool for evaluating the management resource of a firm. It contains both qualitative and quantitative data decision points, and while not a foolproof measuring method to determine effective or ineffective management, it does offer some insights as to what might constitute key managerial competencies.

Operational Issues. Top managers guide the firm and create the operational management systems that will (hopefully) successfully execute the firm's overall strategic plans. Operational management, then, is concerned with the design, operation, and control of transformation processes that convert resources (such as labor and raw materials) into finished goods and services.[106]

Every organizational function is involved somewhat in production and hence every manager in an organization needs to be familiar with operations management to achieve objectives efficiently. Operational planning includes:

1. *capacity planning* - assessing system's capabilities for producing a desired number of output unit for each type of product anticipated during a given time period
2. *facilities location planning* - the design and location of an operation's facility. Is driven by the factors that have the greatest impact on production and distribution (labor skills and costs, energy costs, proximity to customers and suppliers)
3. *process planning* - determining how a product or service will be produced. Requires the evaluation of available production methods and selecting those that will best achieve operating

objectives. Typical considerations include: the level of routine in the technology, degree of automation, levels of efficiency and flexibility, and product or service flow through the operations system

4. *facilities layout planning* - designing a physical arrangement that will best facilitate production efficiency and that will also be appealing to employees and customers. Space needs are assessed in reference to work areas, tools and equipment, storage, maintenance, cafeterias, waiting rooms, parking etc., on the basis of process plans

5. *aggregate planning* - deals with the overall production activities and their associated operating resources for up to one year. Using sales demand forecasts and capacity plans, establishes inventory levels, production rates and estimates the size of the total labor force over the year

6. *master scheduling* - specifies quantity and type of items to be produced, how, when, and where they should be produced, labor force levels and inventory. To make these decisions, master planning requires disaggregation- breaking the aggregate plan down into detailed operational plans for each of the products or services the organization produces. Then, these plans need to be scheduled against one another in the master schedule.

7. *material requirement planning* - after the specific products have been determined, each is analyzed to decide the precise materials and parts that is required for manufacturing. Using a computer, managers analyze product design specifications to pinpoint all needed materials to produce the product. By merging this information with computerized inventory records, management will know the quantities of each material and when it is likely to be depleted. MRP ensures that the right materials are available when needed.[107]

Once the operating system has been designed and implemented, its key elements: costs, purchasing, maintenance, and quality must be monitored. Current topics in operations management include computer integrated manufacturing, ISO 9000, just-in-time inventories, and flexible manufacturing.

Summarizing Findings

As with the external environment, once a strategic decision-maker or analyst has done a thorough investigation of an organization's internal environment along the lines we have suggested in this chapter, it is then desirable to summarize the most salient findings by analyzing the firm's major strategic strengths, and its most important weaknesses.

Strengths and Weaknesses

The inventory one would have created in doing an internal analysis of an organization would potentially contain a large number of items that one could catalog as either strengths or weaknesses. Such a list is not particularly useful in the strategic planning process. Rather, the analyst or strategic decision-maker needs to refine the list to those items that are more significant in nature. For example, one might find that a given firm's inventory turnover ratio is 7:1, where the standard in the firm's industry is 5:1. This is a strength, obviously, but is it a strength that might lead to a competitive advantage? The answer is that it probably isn't. Inventory control and turnover are operational issues that reflect the ability of the firm to perform at a high level on a day-to-day basis. Therefore, this particular strength, while good, is not necessarily strategic in nature. On the other hand, if a firm demonstrates a 10-year sales trend of 3% while its industry demonstrates a growth trend for the same period of 8%, this is the type of weakness that has major long-term strategic implications. This latter statistic should make its way onto the firm's refined lists of strengths and weaknesses

A Strategic Strength. We define a strategic strength as a resource a company has that helps it achieve a core competence and perhaps even a competitive advantage (distinctive competency). Strengths that drive the long-term survivability of the firm are strategic strengths. Resources that accrue out of strong financial performance are clearly strengths. Marketing resources that lead to enhances market positions for the company are also strategic strengths. Strong, mission-driven leadership is another important strategic strength.

A Strategic Weakness. Weaknesses can come in two forms: 1) a resource that a firm might have that it maintains but does not use to achieve a competitive advantage; and 2) the lack of a resource that the firm needs to build core competences and eventually build strategic advantages.   An example of a strategic weakness might be an unprofitable product or service line that a company maintains because it always has had it as a part of its line and has emotional attachments to. At one point United Airlines developed round-the-world service in both directions, west to east and east to west, and was the only airline to do so. This was what United thought was a good tactic to achieve a competitive edge and it hoped to maintain the service for the long term (making it more a strategic decision than an operational one). However, the portions of the world routes between London and New Delhi, India and from New Delhi to Singapore never proved to be popular. It seems like there were fewer people who would get on a plane and simply go around the world than people who got on planes and wanted to go to a singular designation. United maintained the route until other financial troubles started to mount and then it finally axed the service.

Evaluating Strengths and Weaknesses. As was true of our discussion of opportunities and threats in Chapter 3 that derive out of an analysis of the external environment, once a strategic decision-maker has developed a final list of strategic strengths and weaknesses, he/she will need to prioritize them to better understand the true position of the firm. In terms of the three methods of internal analysis discussed above (resource approach, value chain, and functional), we suggest using the following tables to help structure this analysis. See Tables 4.3, 4.4, and 4.5.

The resulting lists should be able to show strategic planners and strategic managers a fairly comprehensive analysis of the firm's capabilities and easily demonstrate what strengths it has that are most likely to allow it to establish distinctive competencies and achieve a competitive advantage. Also, such a list will not only expose strategic weaknesses, but also tell decision-makers the severity of those weaknesses and perhaps even suggest certain areas of operational and strategic performance that should command the attention of the strategic planning activities.

Table 4.3
Analyzing the Firm's Resources, Competences & Competencies

Basic Resources	Core Competences VIRO Framework	Distinctive Competencies	Competitive Advantage
➤ List Tangible Resources ➤ List Intangible Resources ➤ List Employee Competences	Apply VIRO and describe how these resources, assets, and competences lead to competencies and skills in the firm's technical and managerial systems.	Describe how the competencies lead to unique advantages in either product or process management. Explain any other distinctive firm features.	Describe the competitive advantage of the firm –how does it achieve greater profitability than its competitors?
➤ List Needed Resources, Assets, and Competences	List missing core competences and/or impact of core rigidities.	Benchmarking – list distinctive competencies of market leaders.	Does the firm have plans for sustaining its competitive advantage – is the firm a learning organization?

Table 4.4
Value Chain Analysis Matrix – Interrelationships Source and Form of Sharing[108]

	PRODUCTION			MARKET	
	Inbound Logistics	Operations	Outbound Logistics	Marketing & Sales	Service
[1]Production/ Market					
[2]Firm Infrastructure					
Technology Development					
Human Resource Management					
Procurement					

[1]In the production/market boxes, describe the value-added interrelationship at each point along the primary activity value chain.
[2]In the secondary activities boxes, describe the sources of interrelationships and possible forms of sharing with the primary activities.

Table 4.5
Analyzing the Firm's Operational Functions

Functions	Descriptions	Strengths	Weaknesses
➢ Finance ➢ Marketing ➢ Technology ➢ Human Resources ➢ Production/ Operations	Summarize each function.	Identify for each function.	Identify for each function.

Table 4.6 offers a tool for evaluating and prioritizing strengths and weaknesses and is similar to the tool we presented and described in Figure 3.7 in Chapter 3 for evaluating opportunities and threats.

In this method, the analyst would look at each strategic strength and weakness and then classify each factor in terms of its impact on the firm. Note that the analyst makes a qualitative judgment although that judgment is expressed numerically. For example, if an organization was able to produce a net profit of 7% and the industry average was 6% while the firm's opportunity costs were 3%, we would classify profitability as a strength since the firm is outperforming its competitors and earning a profit that exceeds its opportunity costs. When rating profitability as a strength,, one might give it a 3 or a 4, indicating that this strength does not produce a huge competitive advantage. Likewise, experiences of negative growth of -3% (while growth in the industry was +3%) in a given year, would lead to classifying growth as a weakness with a rating of perhaps a 7 or an 8. Again, please note that the ratings are subjective and attempt to indicate the analyst's perceptions of the strength or weakness of each strategic internal factor. The results of this analysis can then be placed on a continuum by subtracting the average score for threats from the average score for opportunities as shown in Figure 4.6.

Table 4.6
Analyzing the Internal Environment: Strengths and Weaknesses

	Strengths Rate Each 0-10	Weaknesses Rate Each 0-10
RESOURCES/CAPABILITIES ➤ **Tangible Resources** *Space* ➤ **Intangible Resources** *Concept* ➤ **Core Competences/Rigidities** ➤ **Unique Advantages/Benchmarking** ➤ **Competitive Advantages/ Sustainability**		

VALUE CHAIN
➤ **Primary Activities**
   o **Production linkages**
   o **Marketing linkages**
➤ **Secondary Activities Linkages**
   o **Inbound Logistics**
   o **Operations**
   o **Outbound Logistics**
   o **Marketing & Sales**
   o **Service**
	(note: each sub area most likely has several specific strengths and EACH strength should be listed and evaluated here)	(note: each sub area most likely has several specific weaknesses and EACH weakness should be listed and evaluated here)

FUNCTIONS ➤ **Finance** ➤ **Marketing** ➤ **Technology** ➤ **Human Resources** ➤ **Production & Operations**		
Number of Factors Used in Analysis = N	Average Score = Total Score/N	Average Score = Total Score/N

Figure 4.6
A Continuum of Strengths and Weaknesses

Combining the External and Internal Analyses – SWOT Analysis

With a completed analysis of strategic strengths and weaknesses that describe the internal environment and a completed analysis of strategic opportunities and threats that knowledgably describe the external environment, we can combine them to obtain an overview of the firm. The result is referred to as a *SWOT Analysis*, or a combined analysis of the firms most important strategic strengths, weaknesses, opportunities, and threats. In general terms, strategic planners would look to couple the most promising opportunities from their external analysis with their best strengths to build core competences, create distinctive competencies, and achieve (or sustain) a competitive advantage. At the same time, planners would be aware of the most salient threats to achieving new strategic goals and see if some or any resources might be able to mitigate those threats. In terms of weaknesses, strategic planners would evaluate whether or not the firm has realistic hopes of reducing them, or perhaps even turning them around and making them strengths.

In order to plot the results of a SWOT analysis, take the results from Figure 3.7 and plot them on the Y-axis of Figure 4.7. Then plot the results from Figure 4.6 on the X-axis. The resulting x-y intercept point graphically depicts the firm's condition (SWOT is sometimes referred to as a situation audit). Results from a SWOT analysis are employed in the selection of possible grand strategies for the firm, as we will discuss in Chapter 7. As a result of this analysis, strategic planners and strategic decision-makers are ready to proceed to reconciling the firms mission, vision, values, goals, and objectives with the outcomes of the SWOT analysis.

Figure 4.7
Graphing a SWOT Analysis

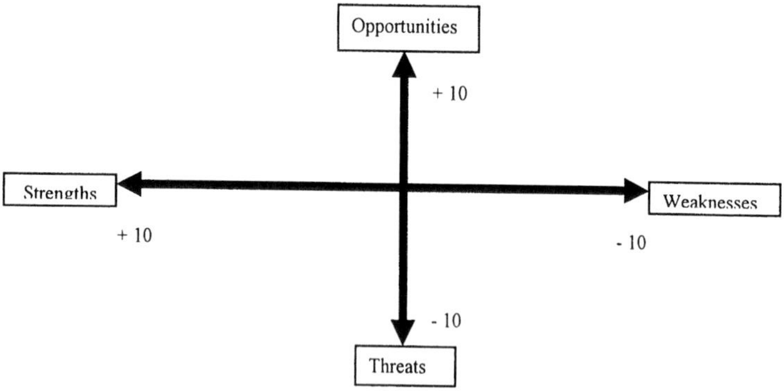

Analyzing the Mission Statement through the SWOT Analysis

Once a firm has done a thorough study of both its external and internal environments as we discussed in Chapters 3 and 4, resulting in a SWOT analysis, it should then compare the results of the SWOT analysis with the mission, vision, and values it has in place and be willing and able to make modifications in its strategy, market position, and/or mission to maximize its opportunities/strengths (O/S) and minimize its threats/weaknesses (T/W). What organizations need to adopt is environmentally-driven strategic planning which will allow these firms to form, reconfigure, or perhaps even reengineer and renew themselves in order to match the specific opportunities and threats that exist in their most crucial environmental sets.[109]

In confirming the mission of the firm, strategic decision-makers must analyze the results of their SWOT analyses as we described in Chapters 3 and 4 to: 1) evaluate how well the results of the analysis match with the present set of organizational mission, vision, values, goals, and objectives. As strategic planners determine the position of the company, as a result of the SWOT analysis, and can establish that there is no substantive challenge to its current mission/goal set, then there is no reason to change the mission. On the other hand, if strategic planners determine that the current mission/goal set is out of sync with the results of the SWOT analysis, then they need to consider changing the mission/goal set if it cannot shift to a market or market segment that better fits its current mission.

As Figure 4.7 demonstrates, a firm would make this choice after determining all of the salient elements of its SWOT analysis and then quantifying the results. After calculating numerical values and weights for its most important strengths, weaknesses, opportunities, and threats (as we describe at the end of Chapter 4), the firm could then position itself on the matrix, as shown in Figure 4.8.

Figure 4.8
SWOT Matrix Compared to Mission, Vision, and Values

As the example suggests, this particular firm is in a quadrant where its mission, vision, values, goals, and objectives have produced a capable firm ready to take advantage of market opportunities – the organization's core mission is aligned with the marketplace. For example, if Microsoft were the company in Figure 4.8, we then conclude that its mission of developing state-of-the-art software and technology systems and becoming an industry leader was a viable one. Microsoft's goals, and objectives, strategic direction and operation would then follow from this basic mission while reaffirming the company's values and vision.[110]   As a further example, assume that Enron would be placed in Quadrant 4 (Q4). The firm would then have to question its own values, vision, and mission, since prior organizational goals and strategies derived from these core factors lead to both illegal actions and poor performance. Enron's mission was misaligned with the market and so needed to reconsider its values and vision.

Summary

This chapter continues the discussion of the importance for strategic decision makers to analyze their environments before proceeding to make specific strategic plans and goals. In this chapter, we identified the various elements of the internal environment that either allow or inhibit a firm from pursuing one strategic direction or another. This is done through analyzing internal aspects of the firm from a resource, a value chain, and a functional approach. In the resource approach, analysts categorize the tangible, intangible, and competency-based resources of a firm and determine which elements are strengths of the firm and which prove to be weaknesses. In the value chain approach, analysts examine how well a given firm performs as part of a market value chain and whether or not linkages within and between the primary and secondary activities add value. In the functional approach, analysts look specifically at the strategic functions of financial management, marketing management, human resource management, management of technology, and production and general and operation management and determine their relative strengths and weaknesses.

All of these areas then lead to developing a greater understanding of how a firm uses its resources to achieve operational competences (or the standard within an industry) as well as distinctive competencies (practices within a firm's operations that are unique to it) and finally the ability to achieve a competitive advantage in the firm's marketplace. When these analyses are complete, strategic planners and analysts summarize their findings of organizational strengths and opportunities, which they then combine with the strategic opportunities and threats (from Chapter 3). The SWOT analysis helps to establish a knowledge base that will guide firm decision-makers in pursuing the next steps of the strategic planning process.

Key Terms and Concepts

After reading this chapter, you should be familiar with the following terms and concepts: Internal environment; resources; resource analysis approach; value chain analysis approach; functional areas of organizations; functional analysis approach; employee competences; operational (core) competences; distinctive core competencies; strategic advantage; sustained competitive advantage; learning organization; strengths; weaknesses; and SWOT analysis.

Web Sites

http://www.netmba.com/strategy/value-chain/ - NetMBA's detailed description of the value chain according to Michael Porter. Includes discussions on connecting cost leadership and differentiation to value chain activities (see Chapter 5 for a full discussion of these generic strategies), the impact of technology, and outsourcing.

http://www.informs.org/ - Home page of the Institute of Operational Research and the Management Sciences. Includes on-line resources, conference and seminar announcements, outside links, bibliographic databases, a section for students, an on-line newsletter, employment opportunities, and scholarships.

http://www.dinkytown.com/business.html - Java Financial Calculators. This company provides java calculators for financial ratios, loans, investments, breakeven analysis, cash flow, working capital, business valuation, debt consolidation, and lease/buy decisions. Just plug your numbers in and the calculators do the rest!

Discussion Questions

1. Why is the resource approach to analyzing the internal environment so important; and how do you define a resource?
2. Why is it so difficult to create and sustain a strategic advantage? Beyond the examples in the book, give a real-world example of a successful company and an unsuccessful company.
3. In Federal Reserve Chairman's Allan Greenspan's speech at the Annual Dinner and Francis Boyer Lecture of The American Enterprise Institute for Public Policy Research, Washington, D.C. in December 5, 1996 he used the term "irrational exuberance" to describe the tenor of the marketplace.[111] Discuss the ramifications of this statement for a firm basing their financial analyses on their stock price.
4. Compare and contrast the three approaches to analyzing the internal environment of the firm. Why are all three approaches needed for a proper analysis?

Exercises

1. Assuming (as in the previous chapter) that you are now studying a particular organization, conduct a functional analysis on that organization picking out the most crucial financial, marketing, human resource management, technological, and management strengths and weaknesses the firm exhibits.
2. Benchmark your findings from Exercise #1 above with comparable figures from the firm's primary industry. Prepare a brief report on your findings.

3. Benchmark your findings from Exercises #1 and #2 above with a firm you consider to be your focal firm's most important competitor. Prepare a brief report on your findings.
4. Combine your lists of strength, weaknesses, opportunities, and threats into a SWOT analysis. Plot the results on the SWOT map and comment (the last figure) on your results. Do you agree with your own analysis? How does your analysis (if it is the same firm) compare to a classmate's?

Appendix
Tools for Conducting a Financial Analysis

In this appendix, we provide you with several financial analysis tools that are commonly used in business to evaluate the financial condition of the firm from a variety of perspectives. These are also very helpful for the person or group that is analyzing a business case in helping them better understand the financial position of the firm they are studying and can suggests areas for sustained performance or improved performance.

Ratio Analysis

Ratio analysis is quite common in business financial statement analysis. Here, we have chosen several of the most commonly used ratios in five categories – profitability, liquidity, activity, leverage, and other common ratios. In each category, we have included the formula for calculating each ratio, how it is commonly expressed (as a percentage, as a decimal, or in the number of days), and a very brief explanation of what the ratio identifies.

Ratio	Formula	Expressed	Explanation
Profitability Ratios			
Net Profit Margin	$\dfrac{\text{Net profits after taxes}}{\text{Net sales}}$	Percentage	Shows after-tax profits generated on net sales
Gross Profit Margin	$\dfrac{\text{Sales - COGS}}{\text{Net sales}}$	Percentage	Shows the total available margin to cover expenses beyond the costs of goods sold, and still result in a profit
Return on Investment (ROI)	$\dfrac{\text{Net profit after taxes}}{\text{Total investment}}$	Percentage	A measurement of management that indicates how well the firm is using all capital investments

			including debt to produce profits
Return on Equity (ROE)	Net profit after taxes ——————— Shareholders' equity	Percentage	A measurement of the rate of return on the book value of Stockholders' investment in the company
Return on Assets (ROA)	Net profit after taxes ——————— Total assets	Percentage	A measurement of management activity - shows the profit generated by on all the assets controlled by management regardless of financing source – the higher the better
Earnings per Share (EPS)	Net profits - Preferred stock dividends ——————— Avg. number of common shares outstanding	Percentage	Demonstrates net profits generated per each share of common stock
Liquidity Ratios	———————		
Current Ratio	Current assets ——————— Current liabilities	Decimal	Shows the ability of the firm to pay its current liabilities with current assets (accounting standard is 2:1 or 2.00)
Quick Ratio (also called Acid Test)	Current assets - inventory ——————— Current liabilities	Decimal	Demonstrates emergency liquidity by the firm's ability to pay current liabilities from current assets minus inventories

Cash Ratio	Cash + cash equivalents ——————— Current liabilities	Decimal	(accounting standard is 1:1 or 1.00) Demonstrates how much of the firm's liabilities can be paid by the firm's available case and near cash equivalents

Activity Ratios ——————————

Inventory Turnover	Net sales ——————— Inventories	Decimal	Measures how many times a year a firm is able to turnover its inventories
Days of Inventory	Inventory ——————— COGS ÷ 365	Decimal	Measures the amount of one day's inventory the firm has on hand at any one time
Net Working Capital	Net sales ——————— Net working capital	Decimal	Measures how well management is using net working capital to generate sales
Asset Turnover	Sales ——————— Total assets	Decimal	Measures the amount of sales generated by each dollar of assets
Fixed Asset Turnover	Sales ——————— Total fixed assets	Decimal	Measures the amount of sales generated by each dollar of fixed assets (capital assets such as building and equipment)
Average Collection Period	Accounts receivable ——————— Sales for year ÷365	Days	Measures the number of days a firm must wait to collect sales revenues after making the sale (implication of credit)

——————————

Accounts Receivable Turnover	Annual credit sales / Accounts receivable	Decimal	Indicates the number of times a firm cycles its accounts receivable a year
Accounts Payable Period	Accounts payable / Purchases for year ÷ 365	Days	Measures the average length of time in days that it takes the firm to pay off its credit obligations
Days of Cash	Cash / Net yearly sales ÷ 365	Days	Given the amount of sales, measures the number of days of cash on hand

Leverage Ratios

Debt to Assets Ratio	Total debt / Total assets	Percentage	Measures the extent to which debt has been used to purchase firm assets
Debt to Equity Ratio	Total debt / Stockholders' equity	Percentage	Measures the amount of debt the firm uses to finance operations as opposed stockholders' equity
Times Interest Earned	Profits before taxes + interest charges / interest charges	Decimal	Identifies the ability of the firm to meet its annual interest costs
Current Liabilities to Equity	Current liabilities / Stockholders' equity	Percentage	Measures the short-term financing that is provided by stockholders
Price/Earnings Ratio	Market price per share / Earnings per share	Decimal	Shows the amount that each stockholder is willing to pay for each dollar of earnings

Other Ratios

Dividend Payout Ratio	Annual dividends per share	Percentage	Measures the percentage of profits

	Annual earnings per share		the firm pays out in the form of dividends
Dividend Yield on	Annual dividends per share	Percentage	Measures the dividend rate of
	Current market		return to common
Common Stock	price per share		shareholders based on the current market price per share

Ratio analyses should be employed as internal longitudinal measures of performance (evaluating the firm's performance in each type of ratio over time) as well as for benchmarking purposes (either against industry averages or against the leading firms in the focus firm's industry). Fraser and Ormistron caution that ratio analyses do have their limitations:[112]

1. Ratios do not provide answers in and of themselves and are not predictive in nature – ratios are indicators of performance but do not necessarily reveal why the firm's operation was successful or not. Furthermore, although financial performance may be forecasted based upon longitudinal data (long term corporate and industry trends), financial ratios in and of themselves do not include the external environmental data (i.e. economic and industry trends) necessary to predict the impact of the environment on firm performance.

2. There is no definitive set of ratios nor is there a uniform definition of all ratios nor a standard for performance for each ratio – some ratios may be very industry and firm specific. For example, in the medical transportation industry a key ratio is the variable personnel costs divided by total revenues. Other ratios may have very different meanings and values. For example, the debt to asset ratio for manufacturing firms may be much higher than service firms since manufacturing is capital-intensive. Secondly, small businesses may also have higher debt to asset ratios since the owners have less capital to invest in their businesses (their invest includes sweat equity) and have relatively less ability to raise investment capital than larger firms who may sell stock publicly or appeal to venture capitalists.

3. There is no rule of thumb when interpreting ratio analyses – ratios need to be analyzed within the context of the particular firm in question, its industry and competitors, and the overall economic environment from which it operates in.

Ratio analyses do interrelate to one another as indicated by the Du Pont system.[113] Here return on investment (net income/assets) is equal to net profit (net income/sales) times total asset turnover (sales/assets) and return on equity (net income/equity) is equal to return on investment (net income/assets) times leverage (assets/equity).

Altman's Bankruptcy Formula (Calculating a Z-Value)[114]

For those companies that appear to be in major financial difficulties, the analyst can use Altman's Bankruptcy Formula by calculating the Z-Value of the firm. The Z-Value is the sum of five different ratios, as calculated below. Scores that are below 1.81 indicate serious financial problems, where scores above 3.0 indicate much more financially healthy company. Companies with scores in between are considered questions marks and could potentially go either way.

Formula is: $Z = 1.2x_1 + 1.4x_2 + 3.3x_3 + 0.6x_4 + 1.0x_5$

Where

x_1 = Working capital ÷ Total assets (Percentage)
x_2 = Retained earning ÷ Total assets (Percentage)
x_3 = Earnings before interest & taxes ÷ Total assets (Percentage)
x_4 = Market value of equity ÷ Total liabilities (Percentage)
x_5 = Sales ÷ Total assets (Number of times turned over)

Example: For United Airlines at the end of 2001, their income statement, balance sheet, and cash flow statements revealed the following.

Total Assets	25,197,000,000.00
Working Capital	9,000,000.00
Retained Earnings	(2,145,000,000.00)
Earning Before Interest & Taxes	(3,771,000,000.00)

Market Value of Equity   97,937,520.00
Total Liabilities   22,066,000,000.00
Sales   16,138,000,000.00

The Z-Value would be calculated as follows:

1.2(9,000,000/25,197,000,000)	=	1.2(0.000357)	0.00043
+ 1.4(-2,145,000,000/25,197,000,000)	=	+ 1.4(-0.085129)	-0.11918
+ 3.3(-3,771,000,000/25,197,000,000)	=	+ 3.3(-0.149661)	-0.49388
+ 0.6(97,937,520/22,066,000,000)	=	+ 0.6(0.004438)	0.00266
+ 1.0(16,138,000,000/25,197,000,000)	=	+ 1.0(0.640473)	0.64047
		=	0.03050

As you can see in this example, United's Z-Value is 0.03, which is well below 1.81 which would indicate financial problems. Since United did declare bankruptcy in 2003, Altman's Bankruptcy Formula appears to have been a good predictor.

Index of Sustainable Growth[115]

The Index of Sustainable Growth is a useful measure that indicates whether or not a firm will be able to continue to growth without having to take on additional debt. Since most firms would prefer to use internally generated funds (profits) to fund growth at their current level, this formula helps decisions-makers better understand whether or not that is possible without having to take on more debt. The interpretation of results is that if $g*$ is lower than the desired growth rate, then the firm will need to seek outside capital funding; if $g*$ is higher than the desired growth rate, then no outside funding is required.

Formula is: $$g* = \frac{[P(1-D)(1+L)]}{[T\_P(1-D)(1+L)]}$$

Where P = (Net profit before taxes/Net sales) × 100
D = (Target dividends/Profit after tax)
L = Total liabilities/Net worth

$$T = (\text{Total assets/Net sales}) \times 100$$

Example: For United Airlines at the end of 2001, their income statement, balance sheet, and cash flow statements revealed the following.

Net Profit Before Tax	(3,357,000,000.00)
Sales	16,138,000,000.00
Dividends	0.00
Retained Earnings	(2,145,000,000.00)
Total Liabilities	22,066,000,000.00
Net Worth	3,033,000,000.00
Total Assets	25,197,000,000.00

The g^* calculations would look as follows:

$P = (-3,357,000,000/16,138,000,000) \times 100 = -20.80$
$D = (0 \times -2,145,000,000) = 0$
$L = (22,066,000,000/3,033,000,000) = 7.275$
$T = (25,197,000,000/16,138,000,000) \times 100 = 1.5613$

$$g^* = \frac{[-20.80\,(1 - 0)(1 + 7.275)]}{[1.5613 - (-20.80)(1 - 0)(1 + 7.275)]} = \frac{[-20.80 \times 8.275]}{[1.5613 + 20.80 \times 8.275]} = -0.99$$

As the calculation indicates, the company is currently experiencing negative growth, which for the time frame 2001-2003 was true. It is not generating any profit, and must use external sources to finance any growth it wishes to pursue.

Endnotes

[1] Schickel, Richard, 2002 "Walt Disney, Ruler of the Magic Kingdom," Time Magazine's 100 Most Important People of the 20th Century, http://www.time.com/time/time100/builder/profile/disney2.html

[2] Time Magazine, Dec. 27, 1937; Vol. XXX No. 26.

[3] "History of the Walt Disney Company," 1998 http://www.angelfire.com/ny/milily98/hist.html

[4] Employee of Walt Disney Productions, Inc., in the 1950s as reported in Schickel, Richard, 2002 "Walt Disney, Ruler of the Magic Kingdom," Time Magazine's 100 Most Important People of the 20th Century, http://www.time.com/time/time100/builder/profile/disney2.html

[5] "History of the Walt Disney Company," 1998 http://www.angelfire.com/ny/milily98/hist.html

[6] http://disney.go.com/corporate/investors/financials/annual/2002/i/lts/lts1.html, May 7, 2003.

[7] http://i.disney.go.com/disneygo/corporate/investors/financials/annual/ 2002/ pdfs/ar_2002.pdf, May 7, 2003.

[8] We are thankful to our reviewer from the University of Notre Dame who noted that firms can survive without growth and may not necessarily want or need to grow.

[9] http://www.halhigdon.com/kelly/, May 7, 2003.

[10] Shelby D. Hunt (2000). *A General Theory of Competition: Resources, Competencies, Productivity and Economic Growth.* Thousand Oaks, Ca.: Sage Publications, Inc.

[11] William E. Rothschild (1976). *Putting It All Together: A Guide to Strategic Thinking.* New York: AMACOM.

[12] Ray H. Garrison and Eric W. Noreen (2000). *Managerial Accounting.* 9th Edition. New York: Irwin McGraw-Hill.

[13] Ibid.

[14] William Burpitt (2003). "Organizational Learning and Knowledge Based Resources: Antecedents to New Entry" *Journal of Behavioral and Applied Management* (Spring) Volume 4, Issue 3, 282-298.

[15] There have been several attempts to create financial measures of intellectual capital. See Tobin's ratio Q (market to book value), VAIP (value added intellectual potential), an Rennie's intellectual-capital accounting as describe by Rudinger Reinhardt, Manfred Bornemann, Peter Pawlowsky, and Ursula Schneider (2001). "Intellectual Capital and Knowledge Management: Perspectives on Measuring Knowledge" in Meinolf Dierkes, Ariane Berthoinantal, John Child, and Ikujiro Nonaka (eds.) (2001). *Handbook of Organizational Learning and Knowledge.* Oxford, UK: Oxford University Press.

[16] Chun Wei Choo and Nick Bontis (eds.) (2002). *The Strategic Management of Intellectual Capital and Organizational Knowledge.* Oxford, UK: Oxford University Press, p. vii.

[17] Donna Marie DeCarolis (2002). "The Role of Social Capital and Organizational Knowledge in Enhancing Entrepreneurial Opportunities in High-Technology Environments" in Choo and Bontis (eds.), 2002.

[18] Dorothy Leonard and Sylvia Sensiper (2002). "The Role of Tacit Knowledge in Group Innovation", in Choo and Bontis (eds.), 2002, 487-8.

[19] Ibid, 489.

[20] Robert F. Dennehy, Sandra Morgan, and Laura Winston (2003). "The Emperor's Challenge: Getting People To Share What They Know" *Journal of Behavioral and Applied Management* (Spring) Volume 4, Issue 3, 188-218.

[21] http://www.cpavision.org/vision/wpaper05b.cfm, May 9, 2003.

[22] M. Dodgson (1991). *The Management of Technological Learning: Lessons from a Biotechnology Company.* Berlin: de Gruyter.

[23] Brian Hackett (2002). "Beyond Knowledge Management: New Ways to Work" in Choo and Bontis (eds.), 2002.

[24] J. B. Barney (1977). *Gaining and Sustaining Competitive Advantage.* Reading, MA: Addison-Wesley. pp. 145-164.

[25] We would like to thank the reviewer from the University of Georgia for the addition of substitutability.

[26] Jonathan Winterton and Ruth Winteron (1999). *Developing Managerial Competence.* New York: Rutledge.

[27] Ibid.

[28] Richard E. Boyatzis (1982). *The Competent Manager: A Model for Effective Performance.* New York: John Wiley & Sons, Inc.

[29] Dave Ulrich and Dale Lake (1990). *Organizational Capability: Competing From the Inside Out.* New York: John Wiley & Sons.

[30] Robert A. Burgelman and Modesto A. Maidique (1988). *Strategic Management of Technology and Innovation.* Homewood, Ill.: Irwin.

[31] Eugene H. Melan (1993). *Process Management: Methods for Improving Products and Service.* New York: McGraw-Hill, Inc.

[32] http://www.corpuschristi.bbb.org/busarch/bus3730.html, May 9, 2003.

[33] Jerry Patrick (1997). *How to Develop New Products.* Lincolnwood, Ill.: NTC Business Books; David A. Aaker (1996). *Building Strong Brands.* New York: The Free Press.

[34] Hartlley, 2003.

[35] C.K. Prahalad and Gary Hamel (1990). "The Core Competence of the Corporation" *Harvard Business Review* (May-June), 79-91.

36

http://www.dominos.com/C1256B420054FF48/vwContentByKey/W256MK9 D221DENNEN, May 13, 2003.

[37] http://www.dunkindonuts.com/about_us/, May 13, 2003.

[38] Dorothy Leonard-Barton (1992). "Core Capabilities and Core Rigidities: A Paradox in Managing New Product Development" *Strategic Management Journal* (Summer) Volume 13, Special Issue, 111-125.

[39] Michael E. Porter (1985). *Competitive Advantage: Creating and Sustaining Superior Performance.* New York: The Free Press.

[40] Craig R. Hickman and Michael A. Silva (1984). *Creating Excellence: Managing Corporate Culture, Strategy, and Change in the New Age.* New York: NAL Books.

[41] http://www.hoovers.com/premium/profile/4/0,2147,12644,00.html, December 24, 2002.

[42] Cornelis A. de Kluyver and John A. Pearce, III (2003). *Strategy: A View from the Top.* Upper Saddle River, N.J.: Prentice-Hall.

[43] Hartley, 2003.

[44] Ibid.

[45] Michael H. Zack (2002). "Developing a Knowledge Strategy" in Choo and Bontis (eds.), 2002, 255.

[46] Ibid, p. 257.

[47] Michael E. Porter, 1985.

[48] We would like to thank the reviewer from the University of Southern Colorado for these suggestions.

[49] Ibid.

[50] Bernd W. Wirtz (2001). "Reconfiguration of Value Chains in Converging Media and Communciations Markets" *Long Range Planning* (August) Volume 38, Issue 4, 489-506.

[51] Allan J. Margrath (1992). "Alternative Strategies to Market Share Battles" *Sales and Marketing Management* (June) Volume 144, Issue 6, 28-29.

[52] http://www.dell.com/us/en/gen/corporate/michael_home.htm, May 13, 2003.

[53] http://www.mattress.com/, May 13, 2003.

[54] Efraim Turban, Jae Lee, David King, and H. Michael Chung (2000). *Electronic Commerce: A Managerial Perspective.* Upper Saddle River, N.J.: Prentice-Hall, Inc.

[55] S. Ghosh (1998). "Making Business Sense of the Internet" *Harvard Business Review* (March/April), 130-132.

[56] William H. Newman, James P. Logan, and W. Harvey Hegarty (1989). *Strategy: A Multi-level, Integrative Approach.* Cincinnati, Oh.: South-Western Publishing Company.

[57] We would like to thank the reviewer from the University of Colorado for this clarification.

[58] William H. Beaver (1998). *Financial Reporting: An Accounting Revolution.* 3rd Edition. Upper Saddle River, N.J.: Prentice-Hall, Inc.

[59] Albert P. Pacelli (1989). *The Speculator's Edge: Strategies for Profit in the Futures Market.* New York: John Wiley & Sons.

[60] http://www.investoradvice.org/research/release%202001-06-25%20%20in cr ease%20in%20risk% 20sensitivity.htm, December 25, 2002.

[61] John A. Pearce, III and Richard B. Robinson, Jr. (2000). *Strategic Management: Formulation, Implementation, and Control.* 7th Edition. New York: Irwin McGraw-Hill.

[62] Dean A. Shepard and Evan J. Douglas (1999). *Attracting Equity Investors: Positioning, Preparing, and Presenting the Business Plan.* Thousand Oaks, Ca.: Sage Publications.

[63] Gabriel Hawawini and Claude Viallet (2002). *Finance for Executives: Managing for Value Creation.* 2nd Edition. Cincinnati, Oh.: South-Western Publishing Company, p. 9.

[64] Ibid, p. 10.

[65] Ibid.

[66] We would like to thank the reviewer from the University of Colorado for this commentary.

[67] Larry J. Gitman (2000). *Principles of Managerial Finance.* 9th Edition. Reading, Mass.: Addison-Wesley Longman, Inc., p. 544.

[68] http://netec.wustl.edu/BibEc/data/Papers/fthharver1839.html, May 13, 2003.

[69] Gitman, 2000.

[70] http://www.studyfinance.com/jfsd/pdffiles/v8n2/elfakhani.pdf, May 13, 2003.

[71] Ibid.

[72] Gitman, 2000.

[73] Hawawini and Viallet, 2002.

[74] Eric Tyson (1997). *Investing For Dummies.* 2nd Edition. New York: IDG Books Worldwide, Inc.

[75] Gitman, 2000.

[76] Diana R. Harrington (1998). *Corporate Financial Analysis In a Global Environment.* 5th Edition. Cincinnati, Oh.: South-Western Publishing Company.

[77] Lyn M. Fraser and Aileen Ormiston (1998). *Understanding Financial Statements.* 5th Edition. Upper Saddle River, N.J.: Prentice-Hall, Inc.

[78] Charles W. Lamb, Jr., Joseph F. Hair, Jr., and Carl McDaniel (2001). *Essentials of Marketing.* 2nd Edition. Cincinnati, Oh.: South-Western Publishing Company.

[79] Ibid.

[80] Ibid.

[81] David A. Aaker (1984). "How to Select a Business Strategy" in Glenn Carroll and David Vogel (eds.) *Strategy and Organization: A West Coast Perspective.* Boston, Mass.: Pitman, 158-166.

[82] Christopher K. Bart (1987). "Implementing Growth and Harvest product Strategies" *California Management Review* (Spring) Volume 24, Number 4, 139-156.

[83] William Wells, John Burnett, and Sandra Moriarty (2000). *Advertising Principles and Practices.* 5th Edition. Upper Saddle River, N.J.: Prentice-Hall , Inc.

[84] Carol H. Anderson and Julian W. Vincze (2000). *Strategic Marketing Management: Meeting the Global Market Challenge.* Boston, Mass.: Houghton Mifflin Company.

[85] David W. Cravens (2000). *Strategic Marketing.* 6th Edition. New York: Irwin McGraw-Hill.

[86] Rates are derived from Yahoo.com – Finance at http://biz.yahoo.com/fin/l/b/bud.html and http://biz.yahoo.com/fin/l/R/RKY.html as well as from Research Insight, 2002, (Standard and Poors, Inc.)

[87] ibid

[88] ibid

[89] calculated with data from Research Insight, 2002, (Standard and Poors, Inc.)

[90] Norma Harrison and Danny Samson (2002). *Technology Management: Text and International Cases.* New York: McGraw-Hill.

[91] Hamid Noori (1990). *Managing the Dynamics of New Technology: Issues in Manufacturing Management.* Englewood Cliffs, N.J.: Prentice-Hall, Inc.

[92] Michael Sadowski and Aron Roth (1999). "Technology Leadership Can Pay Off" *Research Technology Management* (November/December) Volume 42, Number 6, 32-38.

[93] Norma Harrison and Danny Samson, 2002.

[94] Ibid; Pearce and Robinson, 2000.

[95] Mario W. Cardullo (1996). *Introduction of Managing Technology.* Baldock, Hetfordshire, England: Research Studies Press, Ltd.

[96] Louis A. Girifalco (1991). *Dynamics of Technological Change.* New York: Van Nostrand Reinhold.

[97] David B. Yoffie (1994). *Strategic Management Information Technology.* Englewood Cliffs, N.J.: Prentice-Hall, Inc.

[98] Lawrence S. Kleiman (2000). *Human Resource Management: A Managerial Tool for Competitive Advantage.* 2nd Edition. Cincinnati, Oh.: South-Western College Publishing.

[99] Gary Dessler (2003). *Human Resource Management.* 9th Edition. Upper Saddle River, N.J.: Prentice-Hall, Inc.

[100] Kenneth N. Wexley and Gary P. Latham (1981). *Developing and Training Human Resources in Organizations.* Glenview, Ill.: Scott, Foresman and Company.

[101] Thomas J. Peters and Robert H. Waterman, Jr. (1982). *In Search of Excellence: Lessons from America's Best-Run Companies.* New York: Harper & Row, Publishers.

[102] http://disney.go.com/vacations/websites/disneyinstitute/group_programs.html, December 28, 2002.

[103] http://www.wdwcollegeprogram.com/faculty/frameset/frameset_edupartners-ns.html, December 28, 2002.

[104] Andrew J. DuBrin,. (2003) *Essentials of Management.* 6th Edition. Cincinnati, Oh.: South-Western College Publishing.

[105] Albert A. Cannella, Jr. and Kenneth Starkey (2001). "Donald Hambrick and Andrew Pettigrew on Executives and Strategy" *Academy of Management Executive* (August) Volume 15, Number 3, 36-47.

[106] James B. Dilworth (1996). *Operations Management.* 2nd Edition. New York: McGraw-Hill Companies, Inc.

[107] Stephen P. Robbins and Mary Coulter (2002). *Management: Activebook Version 1.0.* Upper Saddle River, N.J.: Prentice-Hall, Inc.

[108] Adopted from Porter, 1985, 338-340.

[109] Gordon L. Lippitt (1969). *Organization Renewal.* New York: Appleton-Century-Crofts.

[110] Anonymous (2002). "Microsoft Priority No. 1: Trust." *Eweek* (April 15) Volume 19, Issue 15, 34.

[111] http://www.federalreserve.gov/boarddocs/speeches/1996/19961205.htm, May 14, 2003.

[112] Lyn M. Fraser and Aileen Ormiston (1998). *Understanding Financial Statements.* 5th Edition. Upper Saddle River, N.J.: Prentice-Hall, Inc.

[113] Ibid.

[114] Adapted from M. S. Fridson, M. S. 1991. *Financial Statement Analysis.* New York: John Wiley & Sons. Pgs. 192-194.

---

[115] Adapted from D. H. Bangs, 1992. *Managing by the Numbers.* Dover, NH: Upstart Publications. Pgs. 106-107.

ℭ Chapter Five ℬ
Business Level Strategies & Market Competition

Chapter Objectives
1. To identify a firms' varying competitive strategies and competitive approaches and how they constitute an overall business strategy.
2. To recognize how marketing positioning impacts the business strategy selection process.

3. To use the strategic matrix as an analytical tool for analyzing a firm's business strategy and suggesting changes to those strategies given the firm's market position.

Introductory Case: Samsung's Out to Be No.1 in Consumer Electronics

In the 1950's and 1960's, when consumer electronic companies like Fischer, Girard, Whaferdale, Scott, Macintosh, SAE and American Research (AR) were the giants of the industry, Asian electronic products from Pioneer, Sanyo and JVC were considered inferior goods[1] that had poor quality and reliability. The late 1970's, early 1980's saw the emergence of Japanese and Korean firms as quality electronics producers, with Sony and Panasonic leading the charge into the US consumer electronics market.

From the early 1970s, Samsung's Electronics Division produced electronic home appliances such as TVs and VCRs, and began to enter the international market.[2] In the last twenty years, Samsung has reinvented itself from a boring copycat into a breathtakingly innovative competitor, with sleek gadgets and breakthrough technology that are winning converts. Since the introduction of monochrome television sets in 1971, Samsung has grown on average 38 percent a year, broadening its product range from simple consumer electronics and home appliances to sophisticated information and communications equipment, computers and peripherals, and semiconductors. Samsung Electronics Co. has grown into the largest manufacturer in Korea, with a sales turnover of $23.9 billion in 1997, and accounts for 32.8% of the total output of the electronics industry.[3] It's a top-three player in a host of products and a top-five patent receiver worldwide. Roger Entner, an analyst at the Boston-based consultant Yankee Group, has stated that "Samsung has done a great job over the past two years ... If you wanted a textbook study on how to enter a relatively closed market like this (the U.S. consumer electronics market), Samsung would be it."[4]

Samsung wants to be not just a global brand, but the global brand, besting mighty Sony by 2005. To do this it must woo U.S. consumers away from their Sony Trinitron TVs, Sony Compact Disk

(MP3) Players, Sony Integrated Stereos and Home Theater Systems. Americans have come to trust Sony as the quality leader in home electronics. How will Samsung do this?

According to Peter Weedfald, VP, North America strategic marketing and new media, for Samsung Electronics America, "Consumers have been voting for the Samsung brand because we have the coolest, newest products at price points in line with their expectations, coupled with superior service, support and follow-up. We design best-of-breed technology, then get it in the hands of consumers through our channel partners before the competition can react. We are in launch mode 365 days per year in all divisions. We are also in customer care mode 365 days a year, globally."[5]

When questioned about Samsung's competitive advantage , Mr. Weedfald replied that "Our greatest asset is our keen product focus. Unlike several of our competitors, we are not in the content provision business, such as creating movies, or PC business applications or Internet sites. And we are also not in the communications pipe business, deliverers of bandwidth such as ISPs or CDMA carriers. We are in the product technology business."[6]

Yet is new technology only what Samsung is all about? For example, In May 2003 Samsung, the world's largest provider of TFT-LCD display panels, announced that it would "advance directly into the 7th-generation, skipping the 6th-generation. The battle over standards in the LCD TV market is also expected to intensify... the introduction of the 7th-generation was to secure an advantage in the competition over standardization, which is predicted to grow even more severe in the days ahead."[7]

However, Samsung provided a further rationale for this new technology. "The 6th-generation is efficient for producing 30" screens, but productivity declines sharply when fabricating 40" models. On the other hand, the 7th-generation size is efficient for both 30" and 40" sizes. ... Samsung predicts a major improvement in LCD price competitiveness in the flat screen display market by adopting the 7th-generation fabrication line. Experience shows that production costs in the TFT-LCD industry fall 20-30% each time a larger screen size is adopted. ... Importantly, the full-fledged market for large screen displays will be formed in 2003, and digital broadcasting is scheduled to start from 2005, fueling rapid market growth. However, price competitiveness is still the most important factor."[8]

Seongjae Yu believes that one must look at Samsung's historical development to under their strategy. "Samsung's competitive advantages represent a culmination of various strategic processes, ... the company's focal point for competitive advantages has shifted over time. During the 1970s, Samsung attempted to win the market by the best pricing strategy, which was feasible only by realizing the lowest costs in the industry. As Samsung became competent in manufacturing, the focal point for building competitive advantages shifted in the 1980s to quality. Continued advancement on the technology ladder enabled Samsung in the 1990s to emphasize technology and innovation as the source of competitive advantage. Although the focus has shifted from cost to quality and then to technology, throughout SEC's history, price has remained the most effective tool to keep the company's competitive edge in the market."[9]

Product innovation and technology, becoming a global brand, superior service, efficiency, price competitiveness – these are the terms used by analysts and Samsung company spokespersons in describing the company's strategies.   How price sensitive can Samsung be while introducing new, cutting edge technology? Are these the strategies needed to topple Sony and Panasonic from the top of the U.S. electronics market?   Should Samsung continue to compete head-to-head with Sony and Panasonic or is there an alternative approach to conquering the U.S. market?

BUSINESS LEVEL STRATEGIES

In the previous chapters we have examined how the external environment (specifically the forces from the macro, industry, strategic group, and immediate environments) and the organization's internal environment (the business's resources, value chain, and functions) act as pushing and pulling forces on the corporation's missions, goals and objectives.   These forces help to shape the role that the organization plays in the marketplace and help determine what would be the best strategy for the firm to follow given market opportunities and threats as well as the firm's strengths and weaknesses (SWOT).

More specifically, changes in the external and internal environments require that the organization recognize that something is different. At this point decision makers must determine the impact of those changes on the organization's key stakeholders; take measures that would prepare the key stakeholders for change (intervene in the current plan and pattern of actions to facilitate change); and then evaluate whether the interventions taken by the firm have effectively dealt with the internal and external changes. How well an organization employs its knowledge (or how it learns) to solve problems brought on by these changes will help it determine, create, and implement its business strategy. The impact of this phenomenon on the strategic management process can be seen in Figure 5.1.

As we discussed in Chapter 1, a firm's strategy determines how it will use its resources, competencies, and market conditions in order to create a competitive advantage. We define a competitive advantage as a company having a distinctive competency that produces a unique position in the market relative to its competitors, which then leads to higher than industry average profits and growth patterns. In the introductory case in this chapter, for example, Samsung decided to no longer produce similar items to its competitors but to take advantage of its in-house skills to produce innovative, cutting-edge products while focusing on the specific target market of the consumer electronic technology product business.

Daewoo, on the other hand, another major Korean producer of electronics, stayed with the old copy cat approach and nearly went into bankruptcy in 1999 due to the failure of their automotive group.[10] This has lead to their electronics group shutting down 8 of its remaining 62 overseas operations. The company reduced their operations in South America and Russia as part of an overall restructuring program. Daewoo Electronics suffered a net loss of 988 billion won ($750 million) in 2000 while sales declined 16.6 percent.[11] Unlike Samsung's Electronics Division, the Media & Electronics Division of Daewoo is providing services in general electronics (Color Televisions, Satellite Video Receivers, DVD Players), computer related products (Personal Computers, Monitors, MP-3 Players) as well as Telecommunication equipment and terminals such as ADSL Modems, Cable Modems, Optical Fibers, Cellular Phones, Faxes, and Internet Phones.[12] Their

Figure 5.1
The Strategic Planning Process
Step 4 – Match the Firm's Resources and Mission with
Business Level Strategic Options

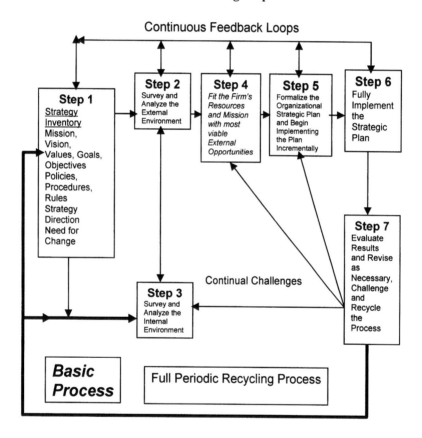

lack of focus on the consumer electronic technology product business placed them in a competitive disadvantage with not only their sister company, Samsung, but with international firms and allowed Japanese consumer electronics firms to increase their sales in Daewoo's backyard, South Korea.[13]

So, what were the differences in strategy between these two companies' consumer electronics divisions who were competing in the same market? Why was one electronics division a success (Samsung) and another a near disaster (Daewoo)?

Strategy, SWOT Analysis, and Market Structures

In Chapters 3 and 4 we examined how to analyze a firm's strengths, weaknesses, opportunities and threats. When one combines the findings from a SWOT analysis of the firm, the results determine the appropriate overall mission of the firm (Chapter 2) and whether the firm should take actions which would either stimulate growth, maintain the status quo, shrink the operation in the short-term, or divest the operation in part or in whole. These four alternatives represent the strategic goals of the firm with the understanding that these goals may change (through the SWOT analysis) given changes in market and organizational conditions.   Optimally strategy acts as a bridge (moderating variable) between the organization's mission and its goals – it is the actions/changes, plans, philosophy and approach that the firm employs in order to realize its mission and fulfill its objectives as indicated in Figure 5.2.

Strategy development plays a pivotal role in assisting firms in reaching their objectives and creating value for the customer. At this point, it is crucial that strategic decision makers understand the various alternatives that are available to them, have a method of choosing the best alternative, and then implement that alternative to maximize performance in reaching objectives.

Strategy, SWOT Analysis, and Change

In Chapter 1 we discussed strategy as an action plan, a plan that might change the organization's market or internal structure in reaction to changes in the marketplace or the need for the organization to change the marketplace. However, it is quite possible that the SWOT analysis may result in no action or change needed by the organization – a maintaining of the status quo. This may occur when countervailing market and/or internal forces for change have cancelled

Figure 5.2
**The Relationship Between Mission, Strategy, Goals and SWOT
Analysis**

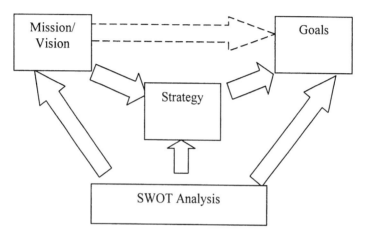

themselves out, that is, new opportunities are balanced by new threats and new strengths balanced by new weaknesses.

Proctor and Gamble (P&G) in the 1960's changed the strategy behind ivory soap from a specialty, more expensive pure and natural soap bar to a simple, basic soap that can be used by the whole family. This change occurred due to the entrance of two competitive products: Dial, the first deodorant soap, and Dove, the first hand lotion soap. Both products challenged Ivory Soap's market leadership as a specialty soap and increased the competitiveness of the market. P&G decided to transform Ivory into a straightforward family soap in order to avoid head-to-head competition and prevent the need to add expensive perfumes or deodorants to the ivory formula. It has been over forty years since that strategic shift and Ivory Soap has continued to maintain its strategy. P&G has been profitable operating Ivory Soap in its current market position and there have been no major competitors to challenge that position and no need to change their strategic direction for the product.

Strategy, Market Structures, and Change

In Chapter 3, we described four basic competitive market structures: perfect competition, imperfect competition, oligopoly, and monopoly. Referring back to Figure 3.3, Market Structures, the market structure limits the practical competitive strategies that a firm may utilize. For example, firms in monopolistic markets need no competitive strategy per se since they do not compete. Their prices are either set by a government agency (if regulated) or set by the consumer's need for the product relative to their ability to pay for the product; consumers will pay a higher price for necessities over luxury items, everything else being equal. On the other hand, firms in perfect competitive markets should not compete on any other product or service feature besides price. Consumers perceive no differences between products in perfect markets (sense no value-added) to justify paying more than what the lowest cost provider charges. Firms who try to compete using any other method will fail unless they somehow can *change* the market's structure and try to undue the customers' perception that their product is a commodity (same as all other products).

A good example of a market that has over the years shifted away from perfect competition is the milk industry. For many years milk was sold as just good old 'plain milk' and was obtained by customers through home delivery, vending machines and through grocery stores. The firms that sold the most milk and had the greatest number of distribution channels (retail, wholesale, delivery, and business to business) obtained the largest market share and became the most profitable. As consumers became more health and choice conscious, the type of milk being sold has varied in fat content (skim, 1%, 2%, whole milk, half and half, cream), lactose and cholesterol content, production procedures (natural milk), milk flavor additives, and non-dairy milks (i.e. soy-based). Since not all firms in the market offer the exact same variety and types of milk, competition in the market was more imperfect.[14]

Firms in imperfect and oligopolistic markets like Samsung and Daewoo have choices as to how to compete. They are not forced by the market structure to compete solely on price and consumers are willing in these markets to pay more for products or services that they identify as having higher value than similar products in that market. This apparent higher value may be due to certain product features or functions, multiple distribution channels, or promotional campaigns (i.e. Samsung's cutting edge products).

Given the fact that different market structures allow for varying forms of competition, firms must make several distinct strategic decisions given the current structure of the market. Firms must decide whether to:

1. Stay and compete in the market they are in - does the firm possess the competencies and resources necessary to implement the available successful strategies given the firm's market structure?
2. Move to a market where the firm's skills and assets can produce a successful strategy - can the firm find a match between its internal strengths and weaknesses and a specific market structure?
3. Change the market structure to better fit the firm's strategy – can the firm change the competitive structure of the industry to take advantage of the firm's distinctive competencies and resources?

In order to answer these three questions, we must describe what are the different approaches that a firm uses to create a match or fit between its strategy and the market, what are the different strategies available to the firm to compete in the market, and how firms can alter their market position and/or their market given their competitive strategy and market approach.

THE CONCEPT OF BUSINESS LEVEL STRATEGIES

When we use the term "business level strategy" we are referring to the fact that no matter what industry the firm is in, no matter what country or region of the world the firm competes in, and even no matter what size or legal form the organization takes, how companies obtain a competitive advantage in the marketplace can be generalized into a universal set of strategies. This universal set of strategies can be divided into two major categories: the firm's overall competitive strategy in the marketplace (how they will obtain a competitive advantage) and their competitive approach to the marketplace (their strategic orientation to the marketplace)[15] as shown in Figure 5.3 below.

Figure 5.3
Business Level Strategies: Competitive Approach and Advantage[16]

"Generic" Competitive Business Level Strategies	
Market Aggressiveness How the Firm Enacts its Method of Competition	**Method of Competition** How the Firm Creates Customer Value
Competitive Approach 1. Prospector 2. Defender 3. Analyzer 4. Reactor	**Competitive Strategy** 1. Low-Cost Leadership 2. Differentiation 3. Focus
5. Adaptor (Flexible)* * A theoretical extension of Miles and Snow supported by research.	4. Blended Strategy (Value for Money/ Best Cost)* * An empirical extension of Michael Porter's work.

Strategic Approaches to the Marketplace (Strategic Behavior)

The first issue that the firm needs to address is their strategic approach to the marketplace; the context or pattern of competition. We define a strategic approach as the organization's overall strategic posture in the marketplace which includes the organization's behavioral and attitudinal perspective and general orientation to competition.[18] Our analysis hence will be focused on the overall tendencies of the firm and not specific actions of functional or product units.

It is vital to understand the firm's pattern of competition, the strategic behavior of the firm, since this behavior is derived from the firm's underlying culture and values and directly impacts the firm's strategic decision-making processes. By examining the firm's approach to the market, we derive insights into the firm's perception of itself and the market - how they would define their own strengths and weaknesses, market opportunities and threats. For example, certain firms may have a bias against change (and may be classified as risk-averse) and see market changes as threats to their operation while other firms not only embrace change but try to bring about market changes (risk-takers). By gaining insight into the firm's strategic approach, we gain insight into just how the firm views and reacts to competition. In the following section we will discuss the differing strategic approaches and how these approaches impact the firm's overall competitive strategy.

     Prospectors.   Prospectors are change masters in that these firms try to change the marketplace by creating new products and services which establish new markets (or market niches) and/or respond rapidly to changing market conditions (including competitive actions).[19] These businesses strongly value being the first mover or pioneer into new markets regardless of possible profitability and also tend to not maintain key competitive positions in all of their markets because they focus their resources on product and service innovation rather than product or service maintenance. Successful prospectors either enter the market in the early stage of the industry life cycle in large scale, or with a high quality product and have a broad product line with heavy promotional expenses. Examples of prospecting firms include Apple Computers, Sony, Bose, EBay, and Amazon.com.

     Advantages. Advantages associated with first movers include:

a.   the ability to define the rules of the game. By creating markets, prospectors set the standards for competition in terms of price, promotion, distribution, product and service quality. Other organizations will have to try to enter the same market at a higher level in order to attract customers. For instance, IBM had to give up their proprietary operating system (DOS) in order to allow other firms to manufacture and sell IBM clones. This allowed IBM and other computer manufacturers to dominate the PC market with their operating system, nearly driving out Apple Computers, the market creator.

b. economies of scale and experience. Prospectors gain market knowledge both in terms of customer service and product improvement and can use this knowledge to either lower costs or further differentiate their products. Bose realized that stereos were becoming eyesores (large speakers, numerous components) and decided to introduce small, high quality wall speakers with a trim-line receiver. This lead to the development of the Acoustic Wave Music System, an integrated stereo including speakers, radio, and CD player which is no larger than a microwave oven.[20]

c. first choice of market position. Prospectors, because they are first to market, not only set the standard for the market or market niche, but also have the luxury of choosing the most opportune strategy or market segment in which to place their products and services. IBM, the first major computer company, has become the leader in the creation, development and manufacture of the industry's most advanced information technologies, including computer systems, software, networking systems, storage devices and microelectronics[21] due to huge name recognition. IBM has been nimble enough to move in and out of overly competitive markets (i.e. personal computers, printers) and has focused much of its operation on the services (what they call "solutions") end of the business which has the greatest profitability.

d. high switching costs to use competitor products. Because prospectors offer a unique product or service, customers will have a difficult time finding substitutes or switching to competitor products or services. Sony was able to maintain a lock on the home video system with their Beta format until Matshushita Electric Corporation allowed their VHS format recorders to be sold under numerous retail electronic brand names (i.e. RCA, Sylvania, and Gold Star) and eventually flooded the market with the VHS format. Sony owners eventually switched to VHS due to lack of availability of Beta-version movies.[22]

   Risks. There are certainly some disadvantages and risks associated with the prospector strategy. The *sustainability* of competitive advantages for prospectors is low due to eventual superior competition and prospectors must abandon markets that they have created. This puts tremendous pressure on the prospector to continually innovate, to develop new markets and/or new products - prospectors are only as good as their last product or service market leader. Companies like Fischer Electronics, Scott, Philips, Harmon Kardon, Kenwood, and Acoustic Research, once leaders in the electronics industry, have all but disappeared due to their inability to produce new products to wow the public like Sony, Samsung, Bose, and Onkyo.

Secondly, prospectors must go through *continual organizational renewal*, become learning organizations that can thrive on chaos.[23] This creates increased stress within the organization and managing human resources through empowerment becomes a critical component of this strategic orientation.

The greatest weakness of a prospector is its "inherent inefficiency". It may "overextend itself in terms of products and markets; ... may be technologically inefficient; ... [and] may underutilize and misuse resources.[24] This reduces the profitability of the firm and would require that the firm charge premium prices for its services. Given the need for higher than average profits, it is interesting to note that some research indicates that a differentiation strategy (competing on product uniqueness) may be more applicable to prospectors since differentiation enables the firm to cater to customers' unfulfilled needs at a higher than average market price as well as assists the firm to identify and capitalize on a broad array of possible market and market segment opportunities.[25] We will discuss differentiation strategies and market segments later in this chapter.

Defenders. As opposed to prospectors, these firms are market leaders that tend to ignore changes in the marketplace that do not directly impact their operation and lag behind in new product development. Rather than change markets, they protect their markets from change by offering higher quality/better service or lower prices to their customers and do so by offering a limited product or service line as compared to the competition. These firms flourish in relatively stable and mature markets and attempt to lock in their positions through operational excellence, product leadership and/or customer intimacy.[26]

Successful defenders focus on either continuous improvement of production and service processes (to create greater operating efficiencies and better service delivery), or continuous improvement of existing products or services (to increase product/service quality). Proctor and Gamble's detergent line (Tide, Downy, Bold and Cheer), longtime products in the clothing detergent market, all have gone through several versions of becoming 'new and improved.' Other defender companies include Coca Cola, McDonalds, Kellogg's, and Del Monte.

Advantages. Advantages associated with market leadership include:

a. a simplified strategy. Defenders, because they have already carved out a position in the market, can fortify their position by merely improving customer satisfaction and repeat business. For example, H.J. Heinz "means a lot of things to a lot of people. In America, it's become almost synonymous with ketchup. In England, 'Beanz Meanz Heinz'."[27] This company has developed strong name and product recognition and has 150 number one and number two brands worldwide.[28]

b. low or limited investment needed for new product/service R&D. Unlike prospectors, defenders have limited expenses associated with new product development. These funds can then be used to improve customer retention (through the measurement of customer satisfaction) service delivery, and product packaging. Heinz has established an easy-squeeze ketchup bottle and has recently introduced an upside-down bottle design that will give the user total control over where the ketchup goes.[29]

c. minimal risk strategies that take advantage of core competences. Defenders, since they continually sell the same product or service to the same customer group, build upon their core competences rather than try to expand those competences.[30] Defenders get more business from their market through market penetration and product/service extension (finding new uses for the product or service). These are particularly low risk strategies in that current and potential customers are already familiar with both the firm and its product/service lines. Arm and Hammer extended the use of their baking soda, which was predominately used in cooking, to cleaning and deodorizing. Their "F.R.E.S.H. Ideas Council" has over 150 uses for their baking soda product including cleaning produce, scrubbing pots, and a clothes freshener.[31]

Risks. The defender strategy is not without its risks. Defenders tend to be *highly resistant to change*. Rapid changes in the marketplace are the greatest threats to a defender organization since the structure of the firm, as well as the people in it, are based upon a stable form of environment. These firms cannot exist in highly volatile markets since they are very good at what they know (how to produce and efficiently manage their product line and meet their current customers' needs), but very poor at what they don't know (how to anticipate customers' future needs or change in customer demands). Secondly, these organizations have a difficult time empowering workers since the tendency in these firms is for *centralized control* where efficiency is valued over creativity. Changes that do occur in the production operation tend to be iterative or *evolutionary* rather than dramatic and revolutionary.[32] Many a defender has paid the price for not foreseeing and dealing with market and industry changes. The big three American car companies (Ford, GM, and Chrysler) for years operated in the defender mode and have paid dearly for their complacency. Ford and GM have lost market share to foreign competitors while Chrysler merged with Daimler-Mercedes Benz.

Analyzers. Analyzers are the middle ground between prospectors and defenders. They maintain a strong position in their key product-market but also try to grow their operation by expanding into related markets. These firms wait for other organizations to create markets that they can enter either through lower cost, or with higher quality; they take a follower approach. They shift the risk of first entry (market creation) to other organizations; learn from their competitors' mistakes, and then leap-frog the opposition.

Analyzers make less frequent and slower market and product changes than their prospector counterparts yet are less steadfast to stability and efficiency than defender organizations. They also try to preserve key product lines and services, however, they cautiously follow a specific set of interesting new developments in their industry. Successful analyzers have superior product technology, quality or customer service or employ larger market entry as compared to prospectors.

Japanese firms in the early 1970's and later Korean firms in the mid-1980's including Samsung employed this approach in several US markets including consumer electronics, automobiles, and clothing. The Japanese firms originally entered US markets with a low-cost strategy, focusing on process innovation and using low cost labor, but later found that better manufacturing processes lead to better made products (especially in electronics and automobiles) which actually shifted their strategy to differentiation.[33]

Advantages. Advantages associated with a follower strategy include:

a. taking advantage of prospector's positioning, product and marketing errors. Analyzers study a prospectors' strategies, learning from their mistakes and then enter the best market(s), with the most suitable product(s) or service(s), and with the most desirable marketing campaign. Wendy's International, first established in 1969, has learned much about the fast-food business and has introduced what they believe the customer really wants; higher quality fast-food than defenders McDonalds or Burger King and including such unique items as baked potatoes, salad bars, and chili. They have been very successful in producing a better fast-food experience by selling better products in a more comfortable eating environment.[34]

b. employing the latest technology. Analyzers can jump over prospectors by using the latest technological advances, as we saw in the Samsung case, to either improve the quality of the product or service or to lower the production costs. This certainly explains the short-term success of many e-businesses since, as new companies with a distinctive competency in e-commerce, they could use this new technology to reach untapped consumers.

c. utilizing superior resources. Many analyzers want to (and may need to) enter the market in a much larger fashion than their prospector counterparts and garner their resources in order to outspend prospector competitors. IBM entered the PC market by making a very large splash in advertising, certainly outspending Apple and any other competitors (Osbourne, Eagle, Atari, and

Radio Shack). IBM also used their existing name recognition, prestige, sales networks, service and distribution channels to quickly get their products to market.

Risks. Although analyzers appear to have the best of both approaches (prospectors and defenders) they also pay a price for adopting this middle-of-the-road approach. The firm must pay close attention to balancing the drive for creativity (how to outdo competitors) with the drive for efficiency (how to consolidate conquered markets), that is, the firm must search for new opportunities while protecting its traditional customer base. The firm suffers from *duality* in many other management arenas including the need for both flexible and inflexible structures, the need for risk-taking and risk-averse cultures, the need for both task-driven and people-driven leadership, and the need for product development and process management skills. Being an analyzer consequently requires that the firm be able manage the inherent, structured conflict created through its twofold nature.

Reactors. Reactors are firms that have no clearly defined or deliberate strategy and lack any real strategic approach to the market – they have in essence chosen not to choose a strategic personality. Their approach and their organizational personality is embryonic at best and perhaps even imposed by the marketplace in that they respond only when forced to by changes in the marketplace. Reactors do not actively compete and are not willing to assume any risk associated with the new development of products or markets. Furthermore, reactors do not have an apparent identity in the marketplace in that they have an inconsistent product-market mix (they neither compete on low-cost, nor product quality).

Being able to survive can be equated to success in reactor organizations. In order to survive, these firms tend to occupy inferior and less profitable markets or niches that have been abandoned by prospectors, defenders, and analyzers; they are the scavengers of the market. Once these markets or market segments become lucrative, prospectors and analyzers will reenter the market with more competitive products and services thereby reducing or even forcing out the reactor organizations. For example, many smaller colleges survived until the 1990's because the micro-segments they occupied, usually based upon geographic region, were of little interest to larger colleges and universities. With the growth of distance learning programs, and specifically internet-based instruction, public, private, and proprietary institutions actively pursed these micro markets. Small colleges who were reactive in nature were not prepared for increased competition and subsequently closed their doors (i.e. Harriman College), sold their campuses to other colleges (Vermont College), or merged/found partners (Albertus Magnus College).

From a more macro perspective, reactor businesses can exist only in less competitive market structures (monopolies and oligopolies) since they lack the desire and ability to compete head-to-head. There is an abundance of research that demonstrates that reactor organizations under-perform rival prospector, defender and analyzer organizations.[35] A detailed description of each Miles and Snow's strategic approaches is provided in the Appendix.

Comments on the Miles and Snow Typology of Strategic Approaches

Much of the more recent literature on competitive approaches suggest that firms have a fairly fixed range of strategic approaches; defenders and prospectors are considered opposites (and unable to emulate the other's approach) while analyzers are "schizoid" (multiple approaches) and reactors have none. That once a strategic approach is created that it has inertia and is self-perpetuating.[36] Analyzers have the most flexibility in their range of market behaviors but, as stated earlier, pay a price in terms of dealing with the tension and conflict created from their duality.

Given this notion of fairly fixed approaches, prospectors would seem to be most profitable entering markets during their introductory phase (see the discussion in Chapter 3 regarding industry life cycles) due to their focus on product and market development, while analyzers would fair the best in growth markets where they can leapfrog market pioneers, and defenders would be most effective in mature markets where they can focus on maintaining their competitive advantage.[37] Evans and Green found that closely-held firms in Chapter

11 bankruptcy who had no clearly defined orientation (no strategies or well-defined marketing plans), reactors, were mostly likely to emerge from Chapter 11.[38] A fit or alignment is created by these firms between their strategic approaches and their industry cycles by seeking industries that best match their strategic business approach.

It is easy to then imagine firms jumping from industry to industry (or market to market) based upon changes in their markets, with the most aggressive firms having to move in and out of markets more quickly than less aggressive firms, especially in those industries with short life cycles. Switching markets or market segments, however, may mean developing new core competences, dealing with new customers, creating a new competitive advantage, and confronting new competitors. The same inertia that would keep a firm from changing its strategic approach may also keep it from changing market segments.[39] Furthermore, recent literature on market leaders (prospectors) noted that firms that stay in the industry they fashioned tend to have a larger market share than followers and late entrants[40] - some firms are very comfortable in their current markets and may rather compete in their current market than switch.

For example, IBM and Apple Computers pose interesting contrasts in both success and staying power in the computer industry. IBM started as the pioneer in the computer industry, being the first to produce many hardware and software innovations in the computer mainframe market. As this market matured, they continued to produce mainframes but allowed other companies, like Apple, to test new markets (i.e. personal computers), and then moved into the "solutions" business (service over production). IBM has continued its growth and success by learning to shift their strategic approach from a prospector, to analyzer, and many times even to defender, in order to account for changing industry and product life cycles. Apple, on the other hand, has maintained their prospector approach, and, although never achieving IBM's success, has stayed in the industry by carving out a niche market.

Approaches are Tendencies. First and foremost, we remind readers that these strategic approaches may be presented as distinctive types of firm personalities; however we view them more as organizational tendencies. "... although no [college or university] *firm* will be a perfect fit with one particular strategic approach, there should be a predominance of characteristics...."[41] Secondly, it is important to note that given the fact that these approaches are tendencies, it should not come as a surprise to find that firms employ a mix of prospector, analyzer, and defender strategies when examining their product strategies (a smaller unit of analysis).[42] Taking this to an even smaller unit of analysis, Bart noted that product managers' behaviors varied with product strategy.[43] These observations are important to note since they indicate that firms have the potential to shift their mix of strategies and that they are not necessarily stuck in one strategic mode.

The Adaptor Firm: An Alternative Strategic Approach. Given the above comments, we pose an alternative approach to Miles and Snow's work; that firms can *change their approach to the market*. Forte et. al. found that in studying organizational adaptation to major environmental shifts, using the Miles and Snow approach, that a fit between environmental contingencies and organizational form related to superior firm performance. The results also provided support for the idea that organizations systematically move toward the higher-performing forms for a given environment.[44] Research also indicated that these adaptive firms will reap the benefits of riding the industry cycle while less flexible firms will have to pay market entry and exit costs in order to accommodate their strategic approach or lose market share and profitability by staying in industries that they are misaligned with.[45] Companies that were in regulated markets that have since been deregulated have certainly suffered for not having flexible strategic approaches.   AT&T, and later the regional bell companies, which appropriately adopted a defender approach, clearly have had difficulty being successfully proactive in their now more competitive markets (being analyzers and prospectors).[46]   Most airlines, as we have described in Chapters 1 and 2, have also not adapted and have minimal profitability.

In terms of the industry life cycle, it is natural for firms to learn about the industry, develop, mature, and to become more stable as the industry evolves.[47] Older firms in fact tend to have higher survival rates than younger firms whose strategic approaches emanate directly from their founders, what Burgelman calls induced strategic behavior.[48] Older firms, especially those firms who have become more complex and are no longer managed by their founders, exhibit autonomous, more flexible strategic behavior (not bound to top management) signifying that "the propensity to change may [actually] increase as organizations grow older …suggesting support for a 'fluidity of aging' hypothesis."[49]

The Two Sides of Strategic Approaches. We are presented with two interesting yet seeming opposing views as to a firm's strategic approach. The firm may pursue its predominate strategic tendency and find a market that matches its character or the firm can change its approach to fit its current market. Ironically, this situation is not too dissimilar to a person looking for a career. An individual can try to match his or her qualifications to a specific career and, if successful, continue in that profession for life. Many college professors for example, the authors included, enjoy their work, earn a good living, have a great life style, and achieve a modicum of success. On the other hand, other faculty may become jaded or discouraged by the politics of their institutions, or have not obtain the level of personal and/or financial success they expected, and decide to obtain new skills and credentials through education and training in order to prepare for a new career.

This analogy may be apropos for strategic approaches as well. Firms can decide to continue to compete in the same manner and logically should do so if their approach leads to firm profitability. Why would a firm change a successful approach to the market? It would not make sense for a firm like Samsung, who seems to succeed as an analyzer, to all of a sudden become a defender UNLESS their market drastically changed.

So when should firms change their strategic approach? Plainly, firms should change their strategic approach when what they are currently doing is not working and when they do not want or cannot find new markets or market segments that would better fit their competitive approach. As we discussed earlier, IBM has morphed from prospector, to analyzer, to defender. Other companies like Ford, Amazon.com, E-Bay, Coca Cola, Proctor and Gamble, Sears, AT&T, Starbucks, and McDonalds have followed similar paths by riding their industry life cycle.

Firms need to be cautious, however, when shifting their strategic approach.[50] A company who has developed a reputation as a product or service innovator (prospectors and analyzers) like Starbucks or Lexus has invested in creating a special brand image. Atari, the first company to make home game systems (the Atari 2600),[51] has managed to survive the death of their own game system by producing innovative games for other home computer systems. *Enter the Matrix*, a game based upon the movie *Matrix 2,* sold over a million copies in its first week of release.[52] On the other hand, when consumers have come to expect new and unique products and services from these companies they show their disappointment when the company merely offers the same old product line. Firms must seriously contemplate adopting a new strategic approach since it may mean disenfranchising some of their current customer base.

After determining the firm's strategic approach it is then important to determine the firm's method of competition – how the firm tries to obtain a competitive advantage.

METHODS OF CREATING COMPETITIVE ADVANTAGE (COMPETITIVE STRATEGY)

Michael Porter has been recognized by both academics and practitioners alike as being the guru of strategy and specifically how firms obtain a competitive advantage in the marketplace.[53] His theory is derived from basic economic theory with coincides with our earlier discussion on types of market structures. According to Porter, firms search for a competitive advantage by selecting a specific method of competition and then choosing how much of the total market they wish to compete in (the breadth of their competition). Firms create a competitive advantage by following one of two strategies: being the low cost producer; or by differentiating themselves from their competitors through specialized products or marketing campaigns; and then competing through either a broad or narrow focus. This results in four possible strategic choices for the firm as denoted in Table 5.1.

Table 5.1
Porter's Approach to Achieving Competitive Advantage

FOCUS	LOW-COST PRODUCER	DIFFERENTIATION
Broad Market Approach	Broad Market Approach – Low Cost Provider	Broad Market Approach - Differentiator
Narrow Market Approach	Narrow Market Approach – Low Cost Provider	Narrow Market Approach – Differentiator

Low-Cost Leadership

In traditional economic theory, those firms who can produce goods and services at a lower rate than their competitors will obtain larger market share (sell more goods and services), obtain a larger cash flow, and eventually continue to lower price to a point where competitors can no longer continue to match price without operating at a loss. We define low cost leaders as organizations that are capable of charging lower prices than their competitors to obtain a similar profit or organizations that can charge similar prices and obtain larger surplus margins.[54]

The Philosophy Behind Low-Cost Strategy. Low-cost producers increase the competitiveness of the industry in the short term, that is, they try to move the market closer to perfect competition, in an attempt to drive out inefficient competitors. This strategy may reduce their profitability in the short-run, that is, their profit per unit sale may be lower than if they charged the average market price, but eventually these actions should lead to firms exiting the industry (or going bankrupt) and creating an oligopolistic market (and, at best, a monopolistic market) where the remaining firms have larger market share. Under these new market conditions, the residual firms may simultaneously raise their prices, thereby recoup their lost short-term profits, and obtain long-term profitability in a fairly friendly competitive environment (remember that price competition in an oligopoly reduces profitability).

Low-cost producers rely on consumers being price-driven and build customer loyalty by offering reliable products and services at competitive prices. These firms compete head-to-head on price because they believe they have a more efficient operation than their competitors, or have access to greater resources, and can win a price war. They compete now, when they believe that market and internal conditions favor them the most, in order to obtain a future market with far less competition and greater profitability for the survivors of a price war.

Skills and Resources of Low-Cost Leaders. Low cost leaders have specific skills and capabilities not shared by their competitors including having a dominant market share, being highly capitalized, and having secured sources of raw materials. Their skills include process management/engineering skills (the ability to innovate ways in which to reduce production and/or operating costs), low-cost distribution and delivery systems, close supervision of labor and/or the technical core, products and services designed for easy distribution, and continued capital investment. From a value-chain perspective, each linkage within primary activities and between primary and secondary activities is focused on cost reduction.

Organizational requirements to support and sustain cost leadership activities must include a structured organization with clearly enumerated responsibilities, frequent reporting, continuous improvement of the operation (including the process of instructional delivery), benchmarking, strict cost control, and incentives based upon specific "targets." Low-cost producers usually stand out in creating an efficient operation which concentrates on expense management. They employ cost-cutting technologies, maximize economies of scale, reduce product frills, and minimize overhead and administrative expenses. Examples of successful low-cost producers include Costco, Home Depot, Best Buy, and Dell.[55]

Risks of Low-Cost Leadership. There are always risks associated with a specific competitive strategy. Organizations pursuing a low-cost strategy in general may find that they have:

1. overestimated their ability to reduce costs and/or survive on lower profits. Some firms, in their desire to drive competitors out of the industry, may accidentally drive themselves out of the industry as well. Firms like K-Mart, Woolworth, and Service Merchandising have gone bankrupt or completely out of business because newer businesses like Wal-Mart and Best Buy have used technology to reduce their operating costs below those of their older rivals.

2. underestimated their competitors' abilities to lower their prices. One of the most difficult tasks for a firm, is the ability to gather data about their competitors' internal operations. It is quite easy for firms to then misjudge their competitors' skills and abilities and make assumptions about their competitors' inability to remain profitable at lower prices. Lowering prices may trigger retaliation from competitors (even lower prices) that may in fact jeopardize the profitability of the firm that started the price war.

3. cost-savings activities that are easily duplicated. Certain cost-cutting measures, for example installation of self-serving electronic cashier devices, may reduce personnel costs for a firm but can be copied by competitors if they can afford to buy or lease the equipment.

4. cost-leadership may become a trap. Consumers may be so driven to look for low prices that their expectations of continued low prices may reduce the product's price elasticity. Firms may find that they cannot pass along extraordinary one time costs, or worse, industry-driven costs to consumers without drastically reducing product demand.[56] This is clearly the case for many airlines which have offered consumers numerous methods of obtaining discounted fares, especially during times of externally driven low demand (i.e. 9/11, Iraq War).

Firms wishing to pursue a low-cost business strategy must analyze their cost structure, decide which activities in their operations produce cost advantages over their competitors, consider the risks associated with cost leadership, and then implement the strategy.

Differentiation

We earlier discussed that in several market structures (monopolistic competition and oligopoly) that firms can opt for an alternative strategy to price competition, that of offering products and/or services that differ substantially from competitors in terms of features and functions. For example, most automobile manufacturers now offer cars with a standard AM/FM CD stereo, but how many offer their cars with an electronic guidance mapping system or infrared night vision and automatic object avoidance braking systems?

Differentiators can achieve a competitive advantage by offering consumers special product attributes at a higher price and that are beyond the basic product function and are considered more valuable by the consumer when compared to competitors' products. These attributes must be judged of critical importance to the customer in order for them to justify paying a higher price for the product or service. In terms of consumer electronics, for example, DVD players all have the same play back quality, however some have additional features (multiple DVD player, MP3 player, playback programming, built-in VHS player/recorder, DVD burner, etc…) that customers are willing to pay extra for.

Organizations may obtain a differentiated strategy by offering higher quality or technologically superior products or services, a broader distribution channel, better customer service, and more widespread promotion. For example, Samsung's moving to 7th generation TFT- LCD display panels and leapfrogging 6th generation technology will allow Samsung to offer larger display screens with a better picture at competitive prices.

The Philosophy Behind Product Differentiation. Rather than competing head-on with other companies who compete as low-cost producers, companies that produce differentiated products or services purposely avoid direct competition. They see greater profit per unit (and less need for high production capacity) by employing a strategy that appeals to a market (or a market segment) with the message "we are not the cheapest, but we are the best" or if not the best then certainly dissimilar from competitors. Apple Computers, for example, has clearly advertised the fact that their computers are unlike the IBM clones both in terms of their computers' unique designs and ease of use while Mercedes-Benz's cars are publicized for their precision, German engineering, and Maytag appliances for their durability, excellent service, and low repair record. All of these firms avoid short-term, direct competition in an attempt to become so unique as to become both indispensable and/or easily recognizable. Products like Scotch Tape, Hellmanns (Best) Mayonnaise, Heinz Ketchup, and Band-Aide bandages have become so strongly identified with the function of their product that their brand name has become part of the language people use for describing the generic product type.

The purpose of a differentiated strategy is to build customer loyalty through an excellent image of the organization and its products and services. This loyalty creates a wall between the organization and its competitors (especially new entrants) and ensures that customers see important product and service distinctions. Customers are also less likely to switch to other, less expensive products if they perceive distinctive quality in the organization's products or services.

Customers may also not switch to other differentiated companies if the way in which the firms in the market differentiate their products or services are different or if switching costs (the cost it takes to move from one product or service to another) are too high. For example, many consumers felt that the Sony Play Station operating system which was CD driven was superior to Nintendo 64's cartridge system since it had additional features that allowed music CD's to be played through the game system and had UBS connections for computer and equipment hookup. Also, the computer home game industry (Sony Play Station, Nintendo Game Boy, Microsoft X-Box, etc...) has always had different companies using differing operating systems so that switching from one manufacturer to another meant purchasing new equipment. Ironically, using operating systems as a means of differentiation has failed in some other industries where at least one firm permitted their operating system to be used by other equipment manufacturers (video players and computer operating systems).

Skills and Resources of Differentiators. Skills and resources that foster differentiation include: product and service engineering skills, exceptional marketing and promotional skills, a reputation for technological leadership or high quality, long industry tradition, a creative flare or strong capability of basic research, a unique combination of skills borrowed from other organizations, and strong cooperation from suppliers and others in the market channel.[57] Apple Computers, for example, has always produced personal computers, laptops, and notebooks that are both creative in design and operation. Apple's iMacs, EMacs, and iBooks have a unique anti-box design and affords the user extreme ease of use and IBM software compatibility.[58]

Organizational requirements to support and sustain differentiated activities include working conditions and benefits that would attract highly skilled labor and/or creative individuals, strong internal coordination between those involved in product and service development and marketing, and relatively subjective measures of performance tied to incentive packages, a history and culture that reinforces staying close to the customer, highly skilled individuals in operations and sales.[59]

Differentiators add value to the product or service by altering one or more activities associated with the value chain (see Chapter 3). This could include, but is not limited to, obtaining specialized raw materials from suppliers (superior stereos for a car – Infinity installs Bose equipment in their vehicles as standard), personalized distribution of the product (Saturn dealers and their employees give a big cheer to Saturn new car owners when they take delivery of their vehicles), and after sales service (Land Rover owners are given driving lessons on how to drive in off-road conditions).

Risks of Product Differentiation. Of course there are risks associated with a differentiation strategy. Organizations pursuing a differentiation strategy may find that:
1. changes in market structure make product differentiation an unprofitable strategy. As markets change from oligopolies to monopolies, and from imperfect competition to perfect competition, product differentiation becomes an unprofitable strategy. In the case of monopolies, it is unnecessary to risk product differentiation since it adds cost to a product that may or may not have justifiable additional value for the customers. This will reduce total demand for the product and thereby reduce profitability at higher production levels. In a similar vein, product

differentiation fails in markets where products are perceived to be interchangeable (commodities). This has clearly occurred in the personal home computer market where consumers are less interested in whether the computer is assembled by Dell, Gateway, or Hewlett-Packard and much more interested in product features, prices and ease of assembly and operation. Customers see little differences in brands and brand-driven advertising results in minimal sales.

2. product differentiation is difficult to maintain given the emergence of imitators. Innovative products and services, unless protected by patents and copyrights, may be easily duplicated by competitors and differentiated companies are constantly searching for new ways to become different from their competitors. Amazon.com has been challenged by such brick and mortar operations as Barnes and Noble and Best Buy who now offer their discounted products over the internet. Many dot.com companies have failed because once their web-based services were emulated, they lost their competitive edge.

3. the cost difference between low-cost competitors and differentiated firms becomes too large to sustain brand loyalty. When the price-gap becomes so large that customers cannot justify paying premium prices, even for higher quality products, firms will be forced to change their differentiation strategies. For example, Mercedes-Benz merged with Chrysler in order to offer a broader line of vehicles that would appeal to the more cost-conscious consumer. Damler-Chrysler has also released a lower class line of Mercedes-Benz cars in order to compete with the price shopping luxury consumer.

4. technological changes that nullify or minimize past investment or learning. For firms who differentiate their products or services through product innovation, or who use technology as part of their distribution channel, new technologies and product development can destroy technologically-driven competitive advantages. Sony had a major setback with the rejection by consumers of the Beta format for videos (due to the introduction of VHS). Yet Sony, as we described above, learned from their mistake and leapfrogged the major player in video games, Nintendo, by introducing the first

CD-driven play system which offered superior graphics and greater versatility.[60]

Firms wishing to pursue a differentiation business strategy must analyze their value chain for advantages over their competitors (through benchmarking) which are perceived vital to their customers, determine if they have the in-house capabilities and skills to deliver value-added products and services desired by their customers, consider the risks associated with differentiation, and then implement the strategy.

Focused Strategy - Narrow Competitive Scope

Porter's third strategy adds a second dimension as to how organizations can compete in terms of low-cost and differentiation; what he calls a focused strategy.[61] We use the term breadth or scope of competition to refer to the relative range of market segments in which an organization chooses to compete in, with the narrower the focus the smaller the market segment that the firm is targeting with its products and services.

Many businesses will pursue some form of a focused or narrow strategy rather than trying to serve an entire market. For example, P. C. Richards is a 42-store home electronics and appliance chain that competes against nationwide retailers such as Best Buy and Circuit City yet serve only the communities of Manhattan, Brooklyn, Queens, Westchester, Long Island, and New Jersey.[62] A focused strategy concentrates on the particular needs of a market segment, usually a segment that is atypical of the normal customer and has specialized requirements and needs. An organization that follows this strategy may service isolated regions, have unique service delivery systems, or modify their product to meet a specific customer group.

The Philosophy Behind Focused Strategies. The rationale behind a focused strategy is relatively simple. By concentrating on a smaller portion of the market the firm reduces the competitive nature of the overall market but increases competition within that particular market segment. The firm knows that it does not have the capabilities of servicing the entire market and wants to carve out a part of the market which best matches the firm's skills and competencies. This allows the firm to concentrate on the needs of that market segment and transforms the firm into a market segment specialist (either low-cost provider or differentiator).

Certain companies have been highly successful using either low-cost or differentiated focused strategies. Starbucks Coffee "is dedicated to sourcing the highest quality coffees available throughout the world"[63] and sells a premium coffee at well above market prices – this is not just another 'cup of Joe.' Furthermore "Starbucks offers a haven where people can relax and enjoy each other's company over a cup of coffee."[64] Coupled with their unique caring for employees, Starbucks has become an international leader in the retailing of branded coffees and has developed a very loyal customer base, although a customer base that represents a small portion of the coffee drinking market.

Hyundai, a Korean automobile manufacturer, started as focused company with a relatively small product line compared to such large players as GM, Ford, and Damler-Chrysler by entering the US market in 1986 by offering its subcompact Excel model at prices well below the industry average. They have slowly broadened their competitive scope by adding other low-cost vehicles to their US product line, introducing the Sonata, a mid-sized sedan, in 1989, the Elantra (a compact sedan) in 1992, the Tiburon sporty coupe in 1997, and the Santa Fe sport utility vehicle and the XG300 full-size sedan in 2000.[65]

Skills and Resources Behind Focused Strategies. Focused firms must be more responsive and more rapid in their response than the broader competitors to target customer needs. This would tend to lend support to the argument that small and/or decentralized companies seem to have a competitive advantage employing focused strategies given their more fluid operations and management structures. Firms using a focused strategy also possess excellent marketing research skills and invite customers to participate in their firm's product and servicing planning.

Risks Associated With Focused Strategies. By having a smaller target market, these organizations can develop an expertise about how to service the peculiarities of their particular customer market. However, focused strategies are not without risk. Risks may include:

1. the focused strategy is imitated. Hyundai's low-cost focused strategy was merely an imitation of Toyota's, Honda's and Nissan's (then Datsun) strategy of the early 1970's. As Hyundai has broadened its competitive scope, other competitors like Kia Motors and Daewoo have already entered this market segment using a similar strategy.

2. new entrants further segment the market. New entrants who do not want to compete head-to-head and will look for narrower market segments to service. For example, Enterprise Rent-A-Car a low-end care rental company, decided not to locate car rental offices at airports to avoid competing with other low-cost competitors like Budget, Dollar and Alamo for airport-rentals, the largest market segment. They opted to go after the replacement car market (insurance and repair rentals) and obtained 78% market share of this market segment as of 1996.[66]

3. The target segment becomes structurally unattractive because demand has dwindled and the market segment has disappeared. Seagate Technologies was founded specifically to build 5.25" hard disc drives for the PC. They have had to expand their product line to other formats for disc drives, magnetic discs and read-write heads, and Storage Area Networks (SAN) since the demand for 5.25" disk drives is minimal in 21st century PC's and alternative storage devices have emerged to replace them.[67]

4. Broad competitors overwhelm the market by reducing the differences between the segments and therein increase their competitive position. Going back to our example of Hyundai, the subcompact and compact car market segments have been flooded not only by focused firms like Kia, Subaru and Volkswagan, but also by broader competitors from Japan (Nissan, Toyota, Honda),the US (Ford, GM), and Europe (Damler-Chrysler).

Broad versus narrow: a matter of degree. Implied in Porter's work, , is the fact that the terms "broad" and "narrow" are general terms. A market may be divided into numerous market segments (through demographic, geographic and behavioral descriptors) and even micro-segments and hence a firm's breadth of competition within a market may vary.[68] Just as firms can chose to compete in many markets, firms may also choose to compete in the entire market, choose several market segments, or choose to compete in just one micro-segment. The ability to pick and choose competitive segments allows the firm greater precision in targeting a specific type of consumer.

An Example of Applying Porter's Four Generic Business Strategies. The appeal of Porter's work is that it is both simple and generalizable. For example, it would be very easy to apply Porter's model to the restaurant industry as depicted in Table 5.2. As you can tell

Table 5.2
Using Porter's Approach to Achieving Competitive Advantage in the Restaurant Industry

FOCUS	LOW-COST PRODUCER	DIFFERENTIATION
Broad Market Approach	Fast Food Franchises	Upscaled Franchises and Restaurant Chains
Narrow Market Approach	Regional and Local Franchises and Local Restaurants	Local Restaurants

by looking at Table 5.2, the industry is divided into two major market segments; one segment including large fast food chains (i.e. T.G.I.F's, McDonalds), the second including regional chains and local restaurants. Note that the largest number of competitors would be in the "local restaurant" market segment yet they would undoubtedly comprise the smallest share of the restaurant market as compared to the other three market segments.

A quick glance at this table will, however, yield some very unsatisfying results. Within the low-cost fast food franchises, for example, include such restaurants as McDonalds, Burger King, Wendy's, and Sonic. However, there are notable differences between these firms' products and services and therefore may not been seen by the customer as equal choices.

Our point is that, theories that are simple and generalizable, like the Porter model, tend to be inaccurate. (See the Introduction for a fuller discussion on this topic.) The Porter model does provide a good overall explanation as to how firms compete in the market yet does not account for the competitive intricacies of those markets and market segments. Firms may differentiate in many different ways (and may create varying strategies within the broad category of differentiation) or as low cost producers may have slight dissimilarities between products. We will explore this issue further later in the chapter in the sections on intraniche and interniche competition.

Beyond Porter's Four Competitive Strategies - Blended Strategy

Porter noted that organizations that are thriving have an overall competitive business strategy of cost leadership, differentiation, cost focus, or differentiated focus. There is a preponderance of research from the 1980's and early 1990's that demonstrates that most organizations that do not have a clear strategic position in the marketplace or those organizations that are simultaneously pursuing low-cost and differentiation (what is called "being stuck in the middle") will be less successful than their competitors.[69] Recent literature has emerged that challenges the stuck in the middle strategy as a weak strategy[70] and that a single generic strategy is not always the best choice. Many times customers demand a mix of satisfactions, and a mixed strategy is required to satisfy them. This mix may include quality, reliability, style, novelty, convenience, service, and price,[71] (such as in the case of companies like Wal-Mart, Home Depot, Southwest Airlines, and Jet Blue) and should be consistent and mutually reinforcing.[72] Samsung, with its concentration on both product innovation (differentiation) and operating expenses (low-cost), would seem to be following a blended strategy.

The concept of blended strategies (also known as value for money[73] and best cost approach[74]) integrates the three generic strategies of cost leadership, product differentiation, and focus. A blended strategy targets both existing consumer norms, but also creates new norms. It actively focuses on low price and differentiation for a certain target market, which in itself serves to differentiate the product or firm further.[75] What seems quite clear from examining successful firms that employ a blended strategy is that these firms have decided to attack a market segment; to adopt a relatively narrow focus. Jet Blue and Southwest service only certain airports and regions of the country, Wal-Mart and Home Depot offer predominately lower end products and services, McDonalds and Burger King have limited menus (as compared to diners) and mass produced food (rather than focus on the culinary arts), Marks and Spencer, PLC and Nordstrom offer similarly priced clothing as other up-scaled stores (i.e. Lord & Taylor and Sachs Fifth Avenue) yet are renowned for superlative service, etc.... All of theses firms have become expert in understanding the customer base in their market niche and also recognizing that they cannot be all things to all consumers in the overall market.

The Philosophy Behind Blending Strategies. Firms achieve competitive advantage through this one-two-three competitive punch by building a huge barrier between themselves and their competitors, usually through either flexible manufacturing systems, networking arrangements, or total quality management systems. These firms can integrate cost leadership and differentiation by offering certain consumers some features of product differentiation (but not as much as their competitors), and low prices (but not necessarily as low as the lowest provider in the market place).[76] This strategy also provides firms with an added benefit of being able to withstand market changes. The firm has the core competencies needed to adopt either a low-cost or differentiation strategy in order to realign their strategy with their market, as needed.

Some firms pursue a blended strategy as an attempt to dissuade potential competitors from entering their markets thereby locking in their competitive position in the marketplace. Enterprise Rent-A-Car in 1996 obtained a 78% share of the replacement car rental market (a segment of the car rental industry which rents cars to those individuals who needed a loaner car) by not only offering low rentals prices but also by offering superior service (they will pick up customers and bring them to their office) and accessible, inner city locations. This strategy has kept many of the large airport-based firms such as Avis,

Hertz, Budget, Dollar, National, Thrifty and Alamo out of this part of the market since these firms would have to have to incur high entrance costs (find new locations) to enter the smallest market segment of the industry (27%).[77]

Certain firms are very successful at using this strategy. Wal-Mart's superstores offer a huge variety of items which never run out (even during the Christmas rush according to their television advertisements) at reasonably low prices; Neiman-Marcus uses a differentiation focus strategy but will buy its merchandise for the best price possible (thereby selling below the competitors in their market niche); and Southwest Airlines is structured as a focused low-cost leader, but differentiates itself through creative advertising, single source web access, and equivalent to competitor customer frequent flyer programs.

Paradoxically, small town grocery stores, pharmacies, and hardware stores have also adopted the blended strategy in order to combat large retailers like Wal-Mart and Home Depot and other superstores who first adopted this approach.[78] In order to sell their products at competitive prices these small business owners will either forgo short-term profits or form cooperative buying networks in an attempt to match these superstores' purchasing powers. Their differentiation and focus occur through true, personalized service to their local community and long-term knowledge of the customer and his/her needs.

Flexible Structures and Systems are the Key to the Blended Agency. For firms to succeed at this strategy, they must simultaneously maintain the structures, systems and processes needed to succeed at being a low-cost producer as well as a differentiator. Low-cost producers have an efficient value chain and control cost drivers while differentiators add unique value from the customer's perspective along the value chain.[79] Firms adopting a blended strategy must have very accurate customer information to determine where to add value to what would essentially be a low-cost value chain or where to cut-cost in a value-chain with high added values.

Fast-food restaurants such as McDonalds and Burger King, who follow a blended strategy, have developed highly efficient food preparation procedures that reduce customer waiting time while maintaining high quality standards at below restaurant prices. Both firms conduct extensive market research to determine what is value in the eyes of the customer. For example, McDonalds has conducted over six years of research to determine if co-branding McDonalds with major gasoline brands would create value for their consumers. McDonalds found that customers believed that this arrangement would provide greater restaurant access, more ease of use, was fast/efficient, and a time saver.[80]

Risk Associated with Blended Strategies - the Perils of Being in the Middle. Many writers and practitioners agree with Michael Porter that simultaneously following both a low-cost and differentiation strategy will lead to ruination since the risks associated with all three strategies are inherent in a blended strategy and in a sense multiplied.   These firms are impacted by changes in their market segment that affect both low-cost producers and differentiators alike and must consequently become change masters in order to keep a good fit between their strategy, structure and the environment.   Secondly, very few firms possess the competencies, skills, and resources required to pursue this integration strategy. Many of these firms inevitably end up failing at either low cost production or differentiation within the market niche and end up accidentally pursuing only one strategy while incurring the unnecessary expenses of the other strategy as well (and therein lowering profitability).

Clearly a corporation who pursues a blended strategy must weigh the substantially higher risks against the expected rewards and determine if the risk/reward ratio is acceptable. Target Corporation, a general merchandise retailer, has its principal strategy as providing exceptional value to American consumers through multiple retail formats ranging from upscale discount and moderate-priced stores, to full-scale department stores (retail divisions include Target, Marshall Field's and Mervyn's).[81]   This places Target's stores clearly in the middle segment of the retail clothing market between discount retailers like K-Mart and high fashion stores such as Sachs Fifth Avenue. According to Barron's online, Target's blended strategy may not be working and should expect slower growth and profitability in 2003. Barron's reported that Target's credit-card losses were high and rising, while the company's retail operations may be stuck between low-priced Wal-Mart and up-scaled Kohl's.[82]

Samsung, however, is not experiencing similar problems as Target. As Samsung expands internationally to become a global brand, its profitability has been low yet stable (2% in 1999, 6% in 2000, and 4% in 2001)[83] and somewhat higher than Sony (2.8% in 1999, 1.7% in 2000, and .2% in 2001).[84] "Sony's sales volume still dwarfs Samsung's, but Sony's profitability is far lower. During the first quarter of 2003, Samsung Electronics earned $942 million in net profit on $8 billion in sales. By comparison, Sony earned a similar amount, $963 million for the full fiscal year ended March 31, but that was on $62.3 billion in sales. Sony announced a profit on sales of 1.5 percent for the fiscal year, compared with 17.5 percent for Samsung last year."[85]

Choices for Creating a Competitive Advantage

We can now examine a firm's strategic options for creating a competitive advantage, as depicted in Figure 5.4. Please note that rather than using the general terms broad versus narrow, we have actually inserted the levels of market segmentation. We have also added the blended strategy as the strategy between differentiation and low cost. This results in a three by five matrix of choices for the firm – the firm can choose from one of three competitive advantages (differentiation, low-cost, blended) as well as from one of five scopes of competitive breadth. Even this fifteen choice matrix could be elaborated upon to include more variations in terms of the number of market segments and micro-segments the firm may choose to operate in.

Going back to Table 5.2, we can now apply this broader methodology to competitive advantages to restaurants. See Table 5.3 below. (Please note that this chart is hypothetical and is for illustrative purposes only.) When examining Table 5.3 you will notice several poignant features.

An examination of the above table reveals some interesting information. Micro-segment restaurants may have very different foci regardless of their strategy yet as restaurants broaden their focus they become much more similar in terms of their overall menu offerings.

Figure 5.4
Business Level Strategic Choices for a Competitive Advantage

Entire Market	Multiple Market Segments	Single Market Segment	Multiple Micro-segments	Micro-segment
DIFFERENTIATION				
BLENDED				
LOW-COST				

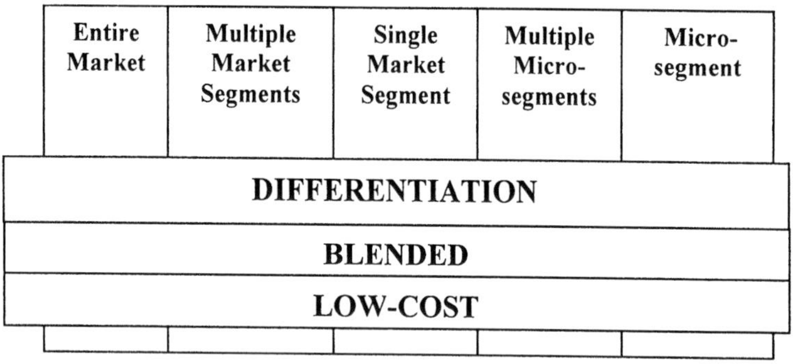

Table 5.3
Hypothetical Examples of Restaurants' Competitive Advantages

Focus   Broad---Narrow

Strategies	Entire Market Compre-hensive	Multiple Segments Regional	Single Segment Specialty	Multiple Micro-segments Small Chain	Single Micro-segment Local Restaurant
Differentiation	Hilton Hotel Restaurants	Emerils	Olive Garden	Ben's Kosher Deli	Peter Lugers Steak House (N.Y.)
Blended	McDonalds	Nathans	Arthur Treacher's Fish and Chips	The Egg and I (Greeley, Co.)	The Salt Lick (Texas)
Low Cost	Sonic	A & W	Taco Bell	White Castle	Tick Tock Diner (N.J.)

We will explore this topic of competition and market segments in the next section.

The Strategy Matrix: Integrating Porter's Modified Generic Strategy with Miles and Snow's Strategic Approaches to the Marketplace

As we discussed earlier, Miles and Snow have described the types of approaches to the marketplace in a manner that could best be characterized as a range of aggressive behaviors (with prospectors being the most aggressive and reactors being the least aggressive) while, Michael Porter has described actual methods of competition. Combining the methods of competitive advantage with the strategic approaches of the firm (including adaptor and blended strategies), the result demonstrates a three-dimensional matrix describing all possible generic strategies.[86] The results from this matrix is a plethora of strategic options for the firm to follow (five strategic approaches, times three competitive advantages, times five market scopes of competitive breadth); seventy-five strategic choices in all as seen in Figure 5.5.

Please note that although the reactor strategic approach is included in this model firms only fall into this category of options when they have either not explicitly chosen an approach or if an approach has not emerged over time. We argue that the strategic options associated with the reactor approach are dysfunctional in nature and should not be considered part of a firm's strategic selection (and therein reducing the actual strategic choices to sixty).[87] We also believe that the blended approach should be employed with great care since the risks associated with competing on both low cost and quality are quite high even though the firm may concentrate on a market segment or niche.

Given this rather complicated matrix, how are firms to choose a generic competitive strategy? It is apparent that before firms choose which strategy (approach and advantage), they need to factor in the competitive density of their market, their competitive position, and their propensity for competition.

Business Competitive Strategy Selection

A firm, either new or existing, chooses its business competitive advantage by examining its core and distinctive competences, value chains, and functional strengths and weaknesses.

Figure 5.5
The Business Level Strategy Matrix:
Combining Competitive Advantage with Strategic Approach

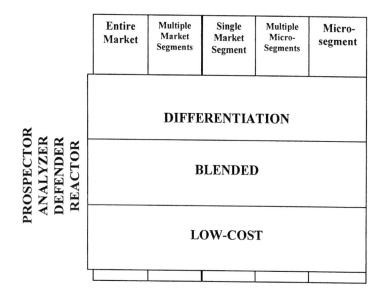

Firms must also match their distinctive skills to their market, that is, find a market where their advantage leads to long term profitability. Firms also need to understand the impact of their competitive advantages, as well as their strategic approach to the market, on market conditions, specifically their market position. See Figure 5.6 below.

We suggest that before the firm selects a competitive strategy, that it needs to chart or map its market position (existing firms) as well as other firms in its market domain.   Understanding a firm's competitive position (or potential position for new firms) requires examining competition within a firm's market sector as well as between sectors.   Table 5.4 represents such a mapping. (Please note this table is incomplete and only for illustrative purposes only.)

Figure 5.6
Factors Affecting the Selection of A Competitive Strategy

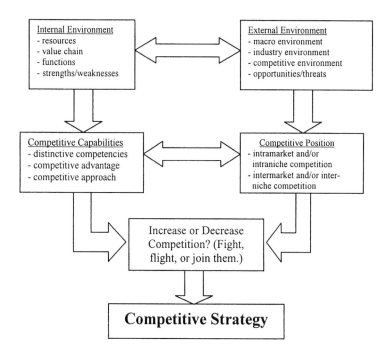

Examining Table 5.4 below you will note that competitive mapping involves listing the markets segments by size (columns - comprehensive to single micro-segment), listing the three possible competitive strategies (rows), placing the firm and its competitors within their respective competitive niches, and then denoting the firms' competitive approaches (in italics).

Intrasegment and Intraniche Competition. As we described in Chapter 3, the level of competition in an industry sector is negatively correlated with the level of profitability or density of firms in that sector. The competitiveness of an industry increases when firms

Table 5.4
Competitive Strategies of Restaurants: A Hypothetical Analysis

Strategies	Market Comprehensive	Multiple Segments Regional	Single Segment Specialty	Multiple Micro-segments Small Chain	Single Micro-segment Local Restaurant
Differentiation	Hilton Hotel Restaurants *Defender* Marriot Hotel Restaurants *Analyzers* Sheraton Hotel Restaurants *Defender*	Emerils *Adapter* Wolfgang Puck *Prospector*	Olive Garden *Defender* Uno's *Analyzer*	Ben's Kosher Deli *Prospector* The Golden Pear *Defender* Marie Callendars *Adapter*	Peter Lugers Steak House (N.Y.) *Defender* Ben Benson (N.Y.) *Analyzer* Carnegie Deli (N.Y.) *Defender*
Blended	McDonalds *Defender* Burger King *Analyzer* Wendy's *Prospector*	Nathans *Reactor* Boston Market *Reactor*	Arthur Treacher's Fish and Chips *Reactor* Carvel *Defender* Red Lobster *Analyzer*	The Egg and I (Greeley, Co.) *Prospector* Meson Ole *Analyzer*	The Salt Lick (Texas) *Defender* Doh Jungs (N.Y.) *Analyzer*
Low Cost	Sonic *Prospector* Checkers *Analyzer*	A & W *Analyzer* Dairy Queen *Prospector*	Taco Bell *Analyzer* Subway *Prospector*	White Castle *Defender* Rubio's Tacos *Prospector*	Tick Tock Diner (N.J.) *Defender* Royal Pizza Parlor (N.Y.) *Reactor*

have similar strategies within a market or market segment since there is a limited number of customers per market. More companies mean potentially lower market share per firm[88] and decreasing profits. Note in the previous Table 5.4 that certain market divisions are highly populated while others are not. In another example, Samsung competes in a market segment of the home electronics market which has several competitors, although Samsung's blended strategy and analytical approach does separate it from other broad market competitors such as Sony (differentiated, prospector) and Technics (low-cost, analyzer).

Interniche and Intermarket Competition. Another form of competition that affects businesses in a particular market or niche is indirect competition. Firms in differing market segments or niches compete with other firms that are relative close to their type of business while simultaneously do not compete with their more distant peers. In Table 5.4, "multiple market segments" restaurants compete with the adjacent "market" and "single segment" divisions. In the same vein, although Hyundai does not produce luxury vehicles like Lexus and Mercedes, they did produce in 2002 a full-size car that can include many, though not all of the features found in the more luxurious car models. Hard economic times (as those experienced in the U.S. in 2002 and 2003) may shift some luxury car buyers into producing lower class vehicles, although it might not shift them into the compact and subcompact line vehicles.[89] The relative rate of competition between niches or markets is a function of the success of that particular market or market segment.

Increasing or Decreasing Rivalry Within and/or Between Market Sectors. The rationale for a corporation choosing a strategy which would increase or decrease rivalry in a market segment is based upon the firm's strategic personality, its internal environment (resources, value chains, distinctive competencies), perception of its position (or potential position) in the market segment, its vulnerability to external market conditions (political, economic, social, and technological forces) and its analysis of opportunities for growth in that sector. Firms have the option to fight in their current market, take flight to new markets, or create competitor interdependencies (join them). Specifically, a firm can:

1. Become more aggressive or passive in terms of its strategic approach in its current market or shift markets. (Predominately adaptors; increase or decrease competition.)

2. Become a lower-cost producer, and/or a greater differentiator than its competitors within a market or market segment. (Increase competition - fight.)

3. Switch to another market niche. (Decrease competition in current niche - flight; increase or decrease competition in new niche – fight/join them.)
4. Increase competitor resource dependency. (Decrease competition – join them.)

These options are not necessarily mutually exclusive. Adaptors, who are the most flexible in terms of their strategic approach, can opt to fight it out in their current market (act like a defender), move into young markets (act like analyzers) and/or move into new markets (act like prospectors). Firms with more fixed strategic approaches have less leeway but may have broad distinctive competencies that allow them to modify their competitive advantage and either increase competition in their current market and/or shift markets.

Increasing competition. Firms employing business strategies that increase the competitiveness of the market usually institute price wars by positioning themselves price-wise at or below the lowest-cost producer. These firms see their loss of profitability as short-term due to increased competition but assume that they will experience a long-term gain by capturing larger market share. Differentiators compete through increased quality and service, that is, they position their company above (in terms of added features and services) the leading differentiator. Both of these types of companies perceive themselves as being in better competitive positions than their peers (i.e. greater resources, higher production efficiencies, stronger marketing, etc...) and increase competition in order to eliminate fringe competitors and gain market share. Defenders, and to a much lesser extent analyzers, would rather fight with competitors than exit the market and tend to respond to rivalry through direct opposition. Microsoft, for example, can and does compete head-on with software competitors given their market share, access to resources, and brand name.

Avoiding competition. Firms that avoid competition see themselves as unable to survive confrontation with their rivals and may seek to inhabit less populated portions of the market. Firms in severe competitive niches may opt to try to reposition themselves into less competitive market segments. They do not possess the resources or competencies to directly compete, and/or a competitive drive, and are willing to serve other market segments (sometimes less profitable ones). This requires long-term planning, an understanding of the other market niches, and a commitment to at least partially shifting the mission of the firm.

Differentiators reduce competition by offering dissimilar products and services (create new market niches) while low-cost competitors can seek to service less desirable customers (those who purchase in small quantities or have bad credit ratings).   Sony Corporation, for example, shifted from being a leading manufacturer of audio, video, communications, and information technology products for the consumer and professional markets to one of the most comprehensive entertainment companies in the world. Sony's principal U.S. businesses include Sony Electronics Inc., Sony Pictures Entertainment, Sony Music Entertainment Inc., and Sony Computer Entertainment America Inc..[90] Prospectors, by definition, create new markets or market segments and avoid competition while reactors end up dwelling in lesser competitive market positions purely out of an instinct for survival. Analyzers look for less dense markets by modifying products and services of prospectors in newly created markets.

Most small businesses, unless they possess a unique market advantage such as proprietary technology, may inhabit less dense markets due purely to their size. They may opt to compete in a market segment or even a micro-segment through a blended strategy because there is little competition in that segment and they have gone into segments where their competitors cannot follow. An example of this type of small business may be a local diner or restaurant. They compete against franchised/chain establishments by providing similarly or even lower priced food with some differences that attracts customers (i.e. table service, greater menu variety and choice, friendly surroundings, etc...).[91] They may obtain a lower profit than their chain competitors but have carved out a distinctive position in the market that may not be challengeable.

Reducing competition through resource dependency (no change in business strategy). Besides avoiding direct competition by exiting the market niche, firms may opt to reduce the competitive nature of the market or market niche by increasing competitors' dependency on their firm for specific resources or skills. The more competitors need the resources provided by the firm, the less likely competitors will engage in combative behavior and try to drive the firm out of business. [92] Firms produce interdependency with their competitors through *cooperation* and *cooptation*. Competitors often collaborate or team together in pursuit of business opportunities including federal procurements,[93] new product and market developments, and R&D and have also entered into cost-sharing arrangements for product manufacturing, employee training, and product delivery. Competitors have similar problems because they operate in similar markets and feel that partnering with one another allows them to share market risks and rewards. Cooperative strategies include mergers, joint ventures, associations, coalitions, and cartels and will be discussed in more detail in Chapter 6.

Cooptation refers to actions taken by firms to bring influential external stakeholders into the firm's operation – to make them a part of the firm. Key stakeholders are appointed to vital decision-making or policy making committees (i.e. boards of directors or trustees, advisory boards, think tanks, etc...) with the idea that once they become insiders they will work for the benefit of the firm and reduce rivalry in the market . This explains why members of boards of directors include representatives from major suppliers, customers and competitors, labor unions, politicians, and local community groups. For example, General Electric's Board of Directors in 2001 included representatives from Fiat SpA (automotive and industrial products), Kraft Foods, Kimberly-Clark (consumer and paper products), Avon Products (cosmetics), Sun Microsystems, Inc. (network computing solutions), and National Broadcasting Company.[94]

A variation of straight cooptation is called the 2-step cooptation approach. This method involves trying to co-opt a third party who has direct power and authority over the second party that the first party wishes to be co-opted.[95] Competitors can try to control one another through third parties including customers, suppliers, creditors, government agencies, and local community groups.

An Example Using Table 5.4. Let us assume that we are the owners of the Golden Pear, a differentiated restaurant (multiple micro-segments) with a defender approach. Let's assume that sales are down and have been shrinking for nearly a decade, due predominately to decreasing differentiation. Previously there we very few restaurants in its operating region that offered high quality coffee and organically-based food but as of late many new competitors with similar products have entered this market nationwide. Specifically, several Sheraton Hotels have also started to offer super premium coffees and featured locally-grown organic menu items. What are Golden Pear's options?

1. *Increase competition through greater differentiation.* Remembering that the Golden Pear has a defender strategy, if the Golden Pear had the resources, they could broaden their menu offerings to include more organic meals as well as more beverage offerings that would parallel their high quality coffee (i.e. espresso, cappuccino, herbal and natural teas, etc...).

2. *Decrease competition through cooperation.* If the Golden pear lacked the resources to compete, they could work with the Sheraton Hotels to make sure that both of their menus would remain distinctive (reach an agreement not to compete through menu offerings). This may reduce their revenues (lost sales due to customer preference for certain menu items not offered at their establishment) but would provide them a buffer from other competitors and the Sheraton since the Sheraton would have an indirect stake in the Golden Pear's success.

3. *Switch to another market niche.* This is quite difficult for defenders. Golden Pear could increase their focus and become more of a coffee house operation, however, this may dramatically decrease revenues do to lost meal sales. They could also try to enlarge their operating domain (move into more regions and become a larger specialty restaurant) but this also would require an influx or resources and would meet with competition from other differentiators in that market niche. A second option, would be to adopt a more blended strategy, that is, increase their operating efficiencies so that they could lower costs and/or offer a line of non-organic meals. This market shift might still produce a competitive response from those restaurants already in that market segment.

4. *Change competitive approach.* Very hard for a defender to do. However, if resources are not available and the Golden Pear cannot

decrease competition enough through cooperation, or would incur more problems by trying to switch markets, then the Golden Pear would be forced to change its spots so to speak and become more aggressive in terms of continuously introducing new menus items, advertising, and running other promotional programs. This change in approach (probably to an analyzer which is less radical than a prospector) will require a strong implementation program.

What ever choice is selected by the strategic planners of the Golden Pear, it should be an informed through a SWOT analysis of the institution. In our the next chapter we will examine corporate level strategies, strategies that are employed by multiple-business firms.

Summary

Strategy plays a pivotal role in assisting firms in reaching their objectives and an understanding of a firm's strategic alternatives is paramount for students and business practitioners. Market structures form a continuum of practical strategies based upon a firm's ability to compete on low price or product differences. As the market structure shifts from perfect competition to monopolistic, the need to compete as a low-cost producer decreases; competing by product differentiation occurs in imperfect and oligopolistic markets.

A firm's competitive strategy is composed of its competitive advantage (low-cost producer, differentiation, and blended) over a broad or narrow market span (the entire market, market segment(s), or micro-segment(s)) and its competitive approach (prospector, defender, analyzer, reactor, and adaptor). Combining the varying advantages and approaches produces a strategy matrix, a set of choices the firm may utilize to compete. Each choice has associated advantages and risks and should be considered within the context of the firm's intramarket (or market segment) and intermarket (or market segment) competition.

Firms will position themselves in their market or market segments based upon their determination as to their ability to compete in those markets and the level of rivalry within those markets. Firms which believe that they can outlast their opponents in head-to-head competition will adopt strategies that increase rivalry. Those who do not will look to either reposition themselves within the market or market niche by changing their strategy, move to less competitive markets or market segments, or try to reduce competition within their current market through cooperation and cooptation.

Key Terms and Concepts

After reading this chapter, you should be familiar with the following terms and concepts:

Competitive strategy, competitive advantage, competitive approach, low-cost producer, differentiation, focus, blended strategy, prospector, defender, analyzer, reactor, adaptor, the strategy matrix, market positioning, cooperation, and cooptation.

Web sites

The following websites (besides those in the endnotes) should be of interest:

http://www.mngt.waikato.ac.nz/depts/sml/journal/special/harfield. htm - Strategic Management and Michael Porter: a postmodern reading. By Toby Harfield. A challenge to Porter's approach to strategy as well as an interview with Michael Porter.

http://www.isc.hbs.edu/index.html - Harvard's Institute for Strategy and Competitiveness (lead by Michael Porter). Site includes many of Porter's publish works as well works the works of other leading scholars.

http://www.quickmba.com/strategy/generic.shtml - QuickMBA's quick overview to Porter's Generic Strategies. Site provides a very good overview to strategic management.

Discussion Questions
1. Describe the concept of competitive positioning in the context of the strategy matrix. Should firms seek markets or market segments

that best fit their strategy or should firms change their strategy in order to move into the most profitable markets (or market segments)?

2. Assuming a firm was not flexible enough to be an adaptor, what strategic approach do you believe would provide the firm the highest profitability? Why? Which approach would provide the firm with the greatest longevity? Why?

3. Blended strategy is a relatively new concept as a method of competitive advantage. In what situations do you believe a should firm implement this strategy? Why? Do you think that this strategy makes sense as a long term strategy for a firm? Why or Why not?

4. What factors influence a firm's decision to either compete in its current market or market segment, move into a new market, or try to reduce competition in its current market? Which strategic approaches would tend to lead firms to either fight, switch markets, or seek cooperative agreements?

Exercises

Part 1

1. Using the strategy matrix, Figure 5.5, describe the strategy of Samsung (the introductory case) and create a Table similar to Table 5.4. If needed, collect additional information from Samsung's website or other secondary sources to support your analysis.

2. Perform the same task as exercise number one working from any company's website and other secondary sources.

Part 2

1. Given your selected company in Part 1, perform a competitor analysis using the concepts of intra and intermarket competition. Do you think that the company is properly positioned in its market or market segment? Why or why not? If not, what market or market segment should it move to?

2. In developing your own case analysis, describe the business-level strategies of your company, of your company's competition, and how well these strategies fit your firm's ability to compete successfully within its primary industry.

Appendix
The Miles and Snow Strategic Variables

In order to determine the firm's approach to the marketplace, planners must determine its characteristics relative to the four strategic types the discussed in Chapter Five. Miles and Snow have constructed a list of variables that denote characteristics by strategic type and are listed below.[96]

The material below should be employed as a checklist to determine what is the overall strategic orientation of a firm. Please observe that although no firm will be a perfect fit with one particular strategic approach, that there should be a predominance of characteristics that border defender-analyzer or prospector-analyzer. Organizations that find that they have a combination of defender-prospector characteristics (and perhaps some analyzer characteristics as well) should be characterized as reactor organizations.

Variables Discerning Strategic Orientation to the Marketplace by Strategic Type[97]

Defenders

Domain Establishment and Surveillance
➤ program-market domain is narrow and stable
➤ aggressively maintains prominence in domain
➤ ignores developments outside of its domain
Growth
➤ penetrates deeper into current markets
➤ occurs cautiously and incrementally
Control
➤ centralized, using vertical information systems
Coordination & Conflict Resolution
➤ uncomplicated and inexpensive forms of coordination (i.e. standard procedures)
➤ conflicts between units handled through normal chain of command
Operational Problems and Solutions
➤ updates technology to maintain efficiency, continuous improvement

➢ establishes core processes (vertical integration) to achieve efficiency

Dominant Coalition and Management Succession
➢ financial and operational experts wield considerable power
➢ coalition has longevity and has been promoted from functional areas

Planning
➢ intensive, oriented toward problem solving, undertaken prior to taking action
➢ planning leads to action which is then evaluated

Structure
➢ functional organizational structure
➢ extensive division of labor and high degree of task formalization

Performance Appraisal and Maintenance
➢ compares present performance with previous time periods

Prospectors

Domain Establishment and Surveillance
➢ domain is broad and in a continuous state of development
➢ has the capacity to monitor a wide range of environmental conditions, trends and events
➢ creators of change in their markets

Growth
➢ primarily through location of new markets and development of new programs

Control
➢ results-oriented, horizontal feedback loops

Coordination & Conflict Resolution
➢ complex and expensive forms of coordination (i.e. project coordinators)
➢ conflict by units handled through project coordinators via confrontation

Operational Problems and Solutions
➢ technology and resources are devoted to the development of new programs

> technology and assets are rooted in people, not routines or mechanical operations

Dominant Coalition and Management Succession
> power centers around marketing and new program development
> coalition is large, more diverse, and transitory
> promotion both from outside and within the organization

Planning
> broad, oriented toward problem finding, contingent upon feedback from experimental action
> evaluation leads to action which is then formed into a plan

Structure
> product organizational structure
> little division of labor and low degree of task formalization

Performance Appraisal and Maintenance
> compares past and present performance with similar organizations.

Analyzers

Domain Establishment and Surveillance
> domain is a mixture of products and markets, some of which are stable, others changing
> extensive marketing surveillance mechanisms
> avid follower of change

Growth
> through program and market development

Control
> manage fundamentally different control systems (centralized for functional units, decentralized for program units)

Coordination & Conflict Resolution
> both simple and complex forms of coordination which operate independently
> conflict is predictable and handled through project coordinators who arbitrate between production personnel (instructors) and applied researchers (program developers)

Operational Problems and Solutions
> "dual" technological core with stable and flexible components welded together by an influential applied research group

➢ a moderate degree of technological efficiency
Dominant Coalition and Management Succession
➢ centers around the functions of marketing, applied research, and production
Planning
➢ both intensive and comprehensive
➢ evaluation leads first to planning and then to action
Structure
➢ a matrix structure – functional and program divisions operate independently
➢ functional divisions are highly formalized while product divisions have low task formalization
Performance Appraisal and Maintenance
  twin appraisal system: stable units use efficiency measures, program units compare performance against revisions

Endnote

[1] John Larkin (2002). "Samsung Tries to Snatch Sony's Crown" *Far Eastern Economic Review* Volume 165, Issue 40, 36-42.

[2] http://www.samsung.com/about/history/history01.html, Nov. 21, 2002.

[3] Seongjae Yu (1998/9). "The Growth Pattern of Samsung Electronics: A Strategy   Perspective" *International Studies of Management & Organization* (Winter) Volume 28, Issue 4, 57-72.

[4] John Larkin, 36.

[5] Joseph Palenchar (2002). "Higher Profile for Samsung Garners Results: This Week in Consumer Electronics" *TWICE* Volume 17, Issue 4, 46.

[6] Ibid.

[7] http://www.samsung.com/PressCenter/PressRelease/DigitalMediaNews/DigitalMediaNews_20030527_0000005904.htm, June 2, 2003.

[8] Ibid.

[9] Seongjae Yu, 1998/9, p. 67.

[10] Henny Sender (2000). "Daewoo Debt Revamping Gains, But a Resolution Looks Elusive" *Wall Street Journal* (May 4) Eastern Edition, A21.

[11] Don Kirk (2001). "Daewoo Closing Units" *New York Times* (March 8) Late Edition (East Coast), W.1.

[12] http://www.daewoo.com/business/media_english.html, November 21, 2002.

[13] Masayoshi Kanabayashi (2000). "With Opening of South Korean Markets Japanese-Electronics Makers Jump In" *Wall Street Journal* (November 27) Eastern Edition, C.15C.

[14] http://dairyoutlook.aers.psu.edu/reports/Pub2002/FutDairyUS.pdf, June 2, 2003.

[15] Rowley and Sherman, 2001.

[16] Porter, 1980; Miles and Snow, 1978.

[17] Henry Mintzberg, 1985; Miles and Snow, 1978.

[18] Henry Mintzberg, 1985; Miles and Snow, 1978.

[19] Rosabeth Moss Kanter (1983). *The Change Masters: Innovation for Productivity in the American Corporation.* New York: Simon and Schuster.

[20] http://www.bose.com/car/jp_awms/, November 30, 2002.

[21] http://www.ibm.com/ibm/us/, November 30, 2002.

[22] Richard T. Pascale and Anthony G. Athos (1981). *The Art of Japanese Management: Applications for American Executives.* New York: Simon and Schuster.

[23] Tom Peters (1987). *Thriving on Chaos: Handbook for a Management Revolution.* New York: Alfred A. Knopf, Inc.

[24] Miles and Snow, p. 67.

[25] Rajaram Veliyath and Elizabeth Fitzgerald (2000). "Firm Capabilities, Business Strategies, Customer Preferences, and Hypercompetitive Arenas: The Sustainability of Competitive Advantages with Implications for Firm Performance" *Competitiveness Review* Volume 10, Issue 1, 56-82.

[26] Michael Treacy and Fred Wierema (1995). *The Discipline of Market Leaders.* Reading, Mass.: Addison-Wesley Publishing.

[27] http://www.heinz.com/jsp/world.jsp#1, November 30, 2002.

[28] http://www.heinz.com/jsp/investor.jsp, November 30, 2002.

[29] http://www.heinz.com/jsp/world.jsp#1, November 30, 2002.

[30] Peters and Waterman, 1982.

[31] http://www.armhammer.com/FrontPorch/fs.asp, November 30, 2002.

[32] Miles and Snow, 47-48.

[33] James R. Evans and James W. Dean, Jr. (2003). *Total Quality: Management, Organization and Strategy.* 3rd Edition. Mason, OH.: South-Western.

[34] http://www.wendys.com/w-1-0.shtml, December 2, 2002.

[35] John A. Parnell, Donald L. Lester, and Michael L. Menefee (2000). "Strategy as a Response to Organizational Uncertainty: An Alternative Perspective on the Strategy-Performance Relationship" *Management Decision* Volume 38, Issue 8, 520-537.

[36] Glenn R. Carroll and Michael T. Hannan (eds.) (1995). *Organizations in Industry: Strategy, Structure & Selection.* New York: Oxford University Press.

[37] Roy B. Johnson (1997). "The Dynamics of Business Strategy: The Miles and Snow Typology and the Organizational Life Cycle" *International Journal of Management* (June) Volume 14, Issue 2, 222-228.

[38] Jocelyn D. Evans and Corliss L. Green (2000). "Marketing Strategy, Constituent Influence, and Resource Allocation: An Application of the Miles and Snow Typology to Closely Held Firms in Chapter 11 Bankruptcy" *Journal of Business Research* (November) Volume 50, Issue 2, 225-231.

[39] Robert A. Burgelman (1990). "Strategy-Making and Organizational Ecology: A Conceptual Integration" in Jitendra V. Singh (ed.) *Organizational Evolution: New Directions.* Thousand Oaks, Ca.: Sage Publications, 164-181.

[40] George S. Day (1997). *Analysis for Strategic Market Decisions (West Series on Strategic Market Management).* New York: Thompson Learning.

[41] Rowley and Sherman, 2001, p. 326.

[42] We would like to thank the reviewer from James Madison University for this observation.

[43] Christopher K. Bart (1987). "Implementing Harvest and Growth Product Strategies" *California Management Review* (Summer) Volume 29, Issue 4, 139-156.

[44] Monique Forte, James J. Hoffman, Bruce T. Lamont, and Erich N. Brockmann (2000). "Organizational Form and Environment: An Analysis of Between-Form and Within-Form Responses to Environmental Change" *Strategic Management Journal* (July) Volume 21, Issue 7, 753-773.

[45] Roy B. Johnson, 1997.

[46] William P. Barnett (1995). "Telephone Companies" in Glenn R. Carroll and Michael T. Hannan (eds.), 1995.

[47] Howard E.Aldrich (1999). *Organizations Evolving.* Thousand Oaks, Ca.: Sage Publications.

[48] Robert A. Burgelman, 1990.

[49] Robert A. Burgelman, 1990, p. 170.

[50] We would like to thank the reviewer from the University of Notre Dame for this suggestion.

[51] http://www.atarihq.com/aghmain.shtml, June 6, 2003.

[52] Anonymous (2003). "Atari Sells a Million Copies of 'Matrix' Game in a Week" *New York Times* (May 24) Late Edition, C.4.

[53] Jay B. Barney (2002). "Strategic Management: From Informed Conversation to Academic Discipline" *Academy of Management Executive* Volume 16, Number 2, 53-57.

[54] Porter, 1980; 1985.

[55] Donald L. Laurie (2002). "Productivity Challenge: Gaining Through Innovation" *Financial Executive* (Oct.) Volume 18, Issue 7, 30-35.

[56] John A. Pearce, III and Richard B. Robinson, Jr. (2000). *Formulation, Implementation and Control of Competitive Strategy.* New York: Irwin McGraw-Hill.

[57] Porter, 1985.

[58] http://store.apple.com/1-800-MY-APPLE/WebObjects/AppleStore?siteID= Mb3fnlCi9cU-2qvuNCXi97TTNGX7AKXqAg, December 13, 2002.

[59] Pearce and Robinson, 2000.

[60] Ibid.

[61] Porter, 1980; 1985.

[62] http://www.pcrichard.com/CGI-BIN/LANSAWEB?WEBEVENT+ L0682E2 448185B7D674D2B35+PCR+ENG, June 3, 2003.

[63] Mary Williams (2001). *Starbucks Coffee Fiscal 2001 Annual Report*, 17.

[64] Howard Schultz and Orin C. Smith (2001). *Starbucks Coffee Fiscal 2001 Annual Report*, 14.

[65] http://www.hyundaiusa.com/, November 27, 2002.

[66] Lew Brown, Joseph M. Bryan, Gary Armstrong, and Philip Kotler (1997). "Enterprise Rent-A-Car: Selling the Dream." In David W. Cravens, Charles W. Lamb, Jr. and Victoria L. Crittenden (2002). *Strategic Marketing Management Cases.* 7th Edition. New York: McGraw-Hill Irwin.

[67] http://www.seagate.com/newsinfo/about/profile/index.html, November 27, 2002.

[68] Orville C. Walker, Jr., Harper W. Boyd, Jr., John Mullins, and Jean-Claude Larreche (2003). *Marketing Strategy: A Decision-Focused Approach.* 4th Edition. New York: McGraw-Hill Irwin.

[69] Rowley and Sherman, 2001.

[70] Bill Merrilees (2001). "Do Traditional Strategic Concepts Apply in the E-Marketing Context? *Journal of Business Strategies* (Fall) Volume 18, Issue 2, 177-190; Steven Davidson (2001). "Seizing your Competitive Advantage" *Community Banker* (August) Volume 10, Issue 8, 32-34; Pradeep Gopalakrishna and Ram Subramanian (2001). "Revisiting the Pure versus Hybrid Dilemma: Porter's Generic Strategies in a Developing Economy" *Journal of Global Marketing* Volume 15, Issue 2, 51-79; Svatopluk Hlavacka, Ljuba Bacharova, Viera Rusnakova, and Robert Wagner (2001). "Performance Implications of Porter's Generic Strategies in Slovak Hospitals" *Journal of Management in Medicine* Volume 15, Issue 1, 44-66; Kamalesh Kumar, Ram Subramanian, and Charles Yauger (1997). "Pure versus Hybrid: Performance Implications of Porter's Generic Strategies" *Health Care Management Review* Volume 22, Issue 4, 47-60.

[71] Danny Miller (1992). "The Generic Strategy Trap" *The Journal of Business Strategy*, (January/February), 37–41.

[72] We would like to thank the reviewer from James Madison University for this observation.

[73] Christos Pitelis and Stuart Taylor (1996). "From Generic Strategies to Value for Money in Hypercompetitive Environments" *Journal of General Management* (Summer) Volume 21, Issue 4, 45-63.

[74] We would like to thank the reviewer from the University of Notre Dame for this observation.

[75] Christos Pitelis and Stuart Taylor, 1996.

[76] Michael A. Hitt, R. Duane Ireland, and Robert E. Hoskisson (2001). *Strategic Management: Competitiveness and Globalization*. Cincinnati, Oh.: South-Western College Publishing.

[77] Len Brown, Joseph M. Bryan, Gary Armstrong, and Philip Kotler (1997). "Enterprise Rent-A-Car: Selling the Dream" in David W. Cravens, Charles W. Lamb, Jr., and Victoria L. Crittenden (2002). *Strategic Marketing Management Cases.* 7th Edition. New York: McGraw-Hill Irwin, 15-27.

[78] http://www.lawmall.com/rpa/chap4.html, November 29, 2002.

[79] Michael Porter, 1985.

[80] http://www.mcdonalds.com/countries/usa/corporate/alliances/concepts/research/index.html, December 13, 2002.

[81] http://target.com/common/page.jhtml?content=targetcorp_tc_index, December 16, 2002.

[82] http://online.wsj.com/public/barrons/this_week, December 13, 2002.

[83] calculated from http://www.samsung.com/PressCenter/images/Press%20Kit.pdf, June 3, 2003.

[84] calculated from http://www.sony.net/SonyInfo/IR/financial/ar/2002/file/e_ar2002_086.pdf, June 3, 2003.

[85] James Brooke (2003). "As Profit Falls, Samsung Turns More Aggressive" *New York Times* (April 26) Late Edition (East Coast), C.4.

[86] This type of matrix has been proposed before in the literature; see Rowley and Sherman, 2001; Walker et. al, 2003.

[87] We will like to thank the reviewer from the University of Notre Dame for this observation.

[88] Howard E. Aldrich (1979). *Organizations and Environments.* Englewood Cliffs, N.J.: Prentice-Hall, Inc.

[89] Hummer introduced the H3 in Spring 2005, a smaller version than the H2, in order to enter the smaller SUV market. http://www.hummer.com/, January 12, 2005.

[90] http://www.sony.com/SCA/index.shtml, December 5, 2002.

[91] Peter Rainsford and David H. Bangs, Jr. (1992). *The Restaurant Planning Guide: Starting and Managing a Successful Restaurant.* Dover, N.H.: Upstart Publishing Company, Inc.

[92] Jeffrey Pfeffer and Gerald R. Salancik (1978). *The External Control of Organizations: A Resource Dependency Perspective.* New York, Harper and Row.

[93]   http://library.lp.findlaw.com/scripts/getfile.pl?FILE=firms/wrf/wrf000001 &TITLE= Subject&TOPIC=contracts_general_2, December 16, 2002.

[94] GE Annual Report 2001, p. 36.

[95] Alison M. Konrad (1994). "Two-step cooptation: Pulling the strings that pull the strings" *The Academy of Management Executive* (February) Volume 8, Issue 1, 81-82.

[96] Notice that the "reactor" strategy was not included for two reasons: administration has failed to communicate a specific strategic approach, or reactor organizations have both inconsistent and unstable patterns and therefore present a "mix" of characteristics of defenders, prospectors and analyzers.

[97] Adopted from Daniel J. Rowley and Herbert Sherman (2001). *From Strategy to Change: Implementing the Plan in Higher Education.* San Francisco, Ca.: Jossey-Bass Inc.

≪ Chapter Six ≫
Corporate Level Strategies

Chapter Objectives

1. To develop an understanding as to the variety of corporate level available to an organization that promote profitability and growth at or above the level of the industry.
2. To establish an appreciation for the risk factors associated with particular corporate level strategies.
3. To create a knowledge of the factors that cause a firm to decide to either use its resources to support its major business or begin to move into other businesses both within or outside its industry.
4. To recognize the values of a variety of cooperative strategies.

5. To understand the importance of short-term corrective
   strategies.

Introductory Case: General Motors – Over a Century of Growth

The name itself, General Motors, denotes that this has always
been a company of purchases, consolidations, and mergers. Of the
major companies that came together to form General Motors, perhaps
the most important one was created by Ransom E. Olds, who created
the Olds Motor Vehicle Company in 1897.   He built his first
automobile assembly plant in Detroit in 1899. Meanwhile, the Cadillac
Motor Company was organized in 1902 by Henry M. Leland. Buick
Motor Company was founded by David Dunbar Buick in 1903.   The
Oakland Motor Car Company (predecessor to the Pontiac Motor Car
Company) was founded in 1907 in Pontiac, Michigan. The founder of
General Motors was Billy Durant, who took control of the Buick Motor
Company in 1904 and organized General Motors (GM) on September
16, 1908. Olds joined GM later in 1908 and GM purchased Cadillac in
1909. GM purchased a ½ interest in the Oakland Motor Car Company
in 1909 and took full control of the company, changing its name to the
Pontiac Motor Division in 1932. AC Spark Plug joins GM. Known as
Champion Ignition Company in 1909, the name is was changed to AC
Spark Plug Company in 1922 and made a division in 1933. Also in
1909, GM acquired the Rapid Motor Vehicle Company of Pontiac,
Michigan, the predecessor of GMC Truck, and Reliance Motor Truck
Co. of Owosso, Michigan.   GM didn't get its way all the time,
however, and in 1909 bankers turned down GM's loan request to
purchase the Ford Motor Company.

All these acquisitions put a strain on General Motors and the
company was near financial collapse in 1910 until bankers interceded
and loaned the company enough money to survive – as long as Billy
Durant was ousted. James J. Storrow became the 2nd president of GM
and under his leadership GM became much more involved in research
and development to make their line of cars top market sellers. In 1911,
the Chevrolet Motor Company of Michigan was organized in Detroit.
On November 16, 1915, at the annual stockholders meeting of GM,
Pierre S. du Pont was elected chairman, but Billy Durant, having held

on to all his stock, and having acquired even more in the interim since his departure from GM, was back in a position of power. In 1916, Durant created the United Motors Corp., a combination of parts and accessories manufacturers that included Hyatt Roller Bearing, led by Alfred P. Sloan, and Dayton Engineering Laboratories, led by Charles F. Kettering. Sloan was named president of United Motors. Later in the year, Durant announced that Chevrolet had won 54.5 percent of GM's outstanding shares and then he took over the GM presidency once again. General Motors was incorporated in the State of Delaware on October 13, 1916 and purchased the remaining assets of Chevrolet the following year. Alfred P. Sloan became president of GM in 1923 and headed the company as president and then chairman until 1956.

Over the years, GM has continued to grow through both investing in their several businesses and by acquiring other businesses. These include the Fisher Body Company and the Frigidaire Corporation in 1919, Opel AG of Germany in 1929 (of which the German Government took over temporary control between 1940 and 1945 – GM completely rebuilt the plant in Germany in 1951), and the Electro Motive Company of Cleveland in 1930. GM opened assembly plants all over Europe in 1924 and organized the General Exchange Insurance Corporation in 1925, which became the General Motors Acceptance Corporation (GMAC). During the 1920s, GM opened plants in South America, Asia, Australia, and New Zealand.

Its first major divestiture was that of Frigidaire which it sold to White Consolidated Industries in 1979. In 1983, GM and Toyota Motor Corporation agreed to form a joint venture which gave GM more opportunities for manufacturing and selling in Japan and Toyota the same rights in the U.S.. In 1987, Greyhound Corporation announced its purchase of GM's transit bus business. In 1988, GM acquired the Hughes Aircraft Company, regarded as one of the leading defense electronics firms in the world. It remained independently managed but soon became GM Hughes Electronics Corporation (GMHE). In 1990, its first fully internally created company, Saturn, produced its first car.

After two decades of recessions, energy crises, and a European and Japanese invasion into the U.S. auto maker, GM found itself in several major financial binds, which led to a major reorganization during the early 1990's. In 1999, GM spun off its Delphi Automotive

Systems as a separate, independent publicly held corporation. But in the same year, GMAC acquired BNY Financial Corporation, an asset-based commercial lending and factoring business from the Bank of New York. In the year 2000, GM increased its equity in Saab to 100 percent. Finally, in a surprise announcement in 2001, GM announced that it was going to phase out the Oldsmobile Division, its founding company's legacy at the end of the 2002 model line.

Today, however, GM is still the giant of all automobile industry and shows no signs of slowing down its growth[1]. Its growth through purchasing other firms, growing its own businesses, consolidating other firm's assets, as well as its pattern of diversifying into other industries makes the company a fascinating study, especially in the field of strategic management.

Corporate Level Strategies

In the last chapter, we described the types of strategic choices that a business would make as it seeks the best avenue to achieve a competitive advantage. Every business needs to adopt a generic, business-level strategy to guide how the business will compete in the market, but what about those firms that contain more than one business? How do these firms decide the overall strategy of the firm relative to those business units? Secondly, how does any firm, multi-business or single unit, translate the firm's goals and objectives into a strategic direction?

Corporate level strategy is quite different from business level strategy since corporate level strategy deals primary with the strategic direction or goal of the firm (also called its grand strategy[2]) while business level strategies deal with how the firm will compete in the marketplace. The firm may follow one of four major strategic directions or goals: growth, maintenance, harvest, or corrective/turnaround.

The choice of a corporate level strategy will set the company in a direction that should lead to higher than average profits and/or increased owners' equity. After going through the evaluation of its external and internal environment, and having reconciled these with the firm's mission, values, goals, and objectives, it is time to adopt a

Figure 6.1
The Strategic Planning Process
Step 4 – Match the Firm's Resources and Mission with
Corporate Level Strategic Options

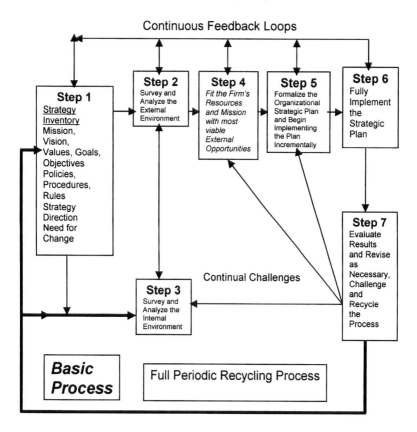

corporate level strategy for the organization as a whole and move toward implementing it. The two major concerns in working with corporate level strategies is to 1) understand what each one of them entails, and 2) which ones are appropriate in which sorts of situations. It is important to understand that strategic decision-makers do not choose one strategic path over the others for no particular reason. Decision-makers choose one strategy (or perhaps two or three strategies) because it meets a variety of criteria and is based upon the firm's SWOT analysis.

We have categorized these corporate level strategies based upon the firm's overall objective of growth, maintenance, harvest or corrective action, as shown in Table 6.1. Please note that we list the corporate level strategies by most preferred within categories. Also keep in mind that certain corporate level strategies fall into several categories and that these categories are not mutually exclusive. For example, more preferred strategies under "maintenance" (i.e. related diversification) would be less preferred under growth conditions.

Second, we have correlated each of the corporate strategic directions of growth, maintenance, harvest, or corrective/turnaround with the results of the SWOT analysis that was performed at the end of Chapter 4, Figure 4.7. Note that growth objectives are recommended when firms' strengths outweigh weaknesses and opportunities outweigh threats; maintenance objectives are recommended when strengths outweigh weaknesses but threats outweigh opportunities; harvest objectives when weaknesses outweigh strengths yet opportunities outweigh threats; and corrective when weaknesses outweigh strengths and threats outweigh opportunities. The choices of corporate level strategies are consequently matched to the SWOT analysis from Chapter 4 and may necessitate a change in these firms' strategic direction. This choice also delimits the overall corporate level strategy choices recommended to firms. We will be referring back to this table throughout this chapter.

Growth Strategies

The largest number of strategies and perhaps the most important are referred to as growth strategies. The main purpose of each of these strategies is to provide the overall organization with optimal growth opportunities over the long-term. What this means is that strategic decision-makers choose a particular line of activity and then look for specific opportunities in their external environments. When the firm takes advantage of one of these opportunities on a on-going basis, the

Table 6.1
Corporate Level Strategy Selection Matrix[3]

	STRENGTHS	WEAKNESSES
OPPORTUNITIES	**GROWTH**	**HARVEST**
	Concentrated Growth Horizontal Integration Vertical Integration Related Diversification	Rethink Concentrated Growth Horizontal Integration Divestiture* Liquidation*
THREATS	**MAINTENANCE**	**CORRECTIVE**
	Related Diversification Conglomerate Diversification Cooperative Strategies	Turnaround/Retrenchment Related Diversification Conglomerate Diversification Divestiture/Liquidation*

* Divestiture/Liquidation are not necessarily high risk strategies but are least preferred.

firm will grow within its industry at a level, hopefully, that is above the average growth rate of other firms in the industry. This is the way most well-managed firms are able to gain market share and strength within their various industries.

As we have stated earlier, firms produce a competitive advantage through the deployment of resources that produce value for the customer by developing distinctive competencies as low-cost producers, differentiators, or through a blended strategy. One of the strategic questions for businesses following a growth objective is, then, whether and how to invest capital resources - specifically should they invest in their primary business and/or invest in other businesses related or unrelated to their current business. Some sort of growth scenario *should* be the most logical answer.

The other strategic concern is that of risk-taking. A predominate number of organizations are fairly risk-averse, especially public corporations, since they have been entrusted with stockholder and bondholder funds; they have interest payments and perhaps dividend payments to make and they cannot afford to upset and/or disappoint these important stakeholders. The greater the amount of risk that a firm takes on; the less likely it is to endure major challenges to its survival. As we described in Chapter 1, United Airlines may well have created the seeds of its own disaster when they took on a very heavy level of debt while their business was doing well in the late 1990's. They engaged in union contracts that provided the unionized-employees of United with the highest wages in the industry, expanded their domestic and foreign routes rapidly, and dropped to low levels of on-time performance and baggage handling. With 9/11, they received such a shock to their system, the weaknesses they had already taken on prevented them from dealing with the terrorist act without suddenly finding themselves in a terrible financial position. The weaknesses were substantive enough that all other attempts to recover didn't make much difference and the airline finally filed for bankruptcy reorganization.

Most companies want to avoid as much risk as they can while obtaining a reasonable profit for their stockholders. Excessive risk is unwarranted even if this risk has the potential for higher profits. In Table 6.1, each of the strategic options is presented in a particular order; the options at the top of each list are the least risky, while the items toward the bottom on each list are the most risky. This is important information to the strategic decision-maker in advising her/his organization because the firm *should* adopt the least risky, most preferred option, provided that that option is available to them.[4] Each company should choose a growth strategy (or perhaps more than one growth strategy) in light of its SWOT analysis based on a variety of factors – including level of desired risk, the industry conditions that support various levels of growth, and the importance of the firm to stay within its primary industry (versus moving into related or unrelated industries).

Concentration on Internal Growth

Concentration strategies, as the very name implies, suggests that a firm should invest its new resources in itself and grow their current operation.[5] Companies do not have to engage in mergers, acquisitions or joint ventures in order to achieve growth in sales, although these alternative strategies have become very popular in the last half century. Instead, internal expansion allows a company to alter their product/market evolution curves by developing new products for established markets, establishing internal teams to develop innovations, and finding new markets for existing products.[6]

Interestingly enough, in most cases firms do exactly that. Except for those firms that follow a related or conglomerate (unrelated) diversification strategy (which we describe later in this chapter), nearly every firm will take its newly available resources and invest in its primary business. There are other benefits: 1) management can very easily centrally control its own operation (its core competences) which allows management to more easily move the firm in one direction or another; 2) the firm needs only concentrate on one single business or single industry strategy and remain highly focused on that strategy; 3) management need only concentrate on the shifts in the external environment that impact a single industry; and 4) no new competences or distinctive competencies need to be developed. All of this reduces task complexity,[7] which reduces risk, which makes it easier to manage the single-business or single industry firm.[8]

For a company like Wendy's Restaurants, new resources from profits (or possibly from new borrowing or issuing new stock) will be used to build more restaurants within their current target market, move into new markets, or modify/enhance their current product line and services. As a later entrant in the fast-food industry to Burger King and McDonalds, it has lots of room for growth and actively looks to exploit opportunities that will allow it to be a bigger player in its current markets.

Risk and internal growth. Concentration on internal growth is the least risky investment any firm can make. This is usually true because all a company is doing is extending it current competency base further into its current market and product line or into new markets that are extremely promising. They can consequently perfect their position as the low cost provider, the differentiator, or the value for money competitor. The firm is not introducing more risk by expanding into additional businesses that operate differently from its core business, and also not using different business-level strategies[9] (not varying the strategies of their strategic business units i.e. Toyota products are always high quality whether sold by Toyota or sold through Lexus).

Instead, the firm is simply doing what it already knows how to do, just more of it.

However, when there are large differences existing between the actual cash values of companies and the value of their common stock, many corporate growth strategies will switch from internal growth to mergers and acquisitions. Other factors that tend to induce companies to acquire other companies include the risks associated with internal development, legal considerations, timing and the maximization of income or wealth to stockholders. The decision to merge/acquire or develop internally in order to grow a firm is basically one of the analysis of alternative investments and strategic fit. This analysis should include the evaluation of profits, cash flow, risks, and capital position with the primary objective of maximizing the return on stockholder interests while creating a coherent strategy for the firm.[10] Mergers and acquisitions will be discussed in more detail later in the chapter.

Internal growth and financial performance. There are few studies which focus purely on internal growth as a general strategy and performance, yet most are positive. Hughes et al. recently studied the U.S. banking industry and found that an increase in firm assets by internal growth was associated with better performance at most banks.[11]   Odagiro and Hase noted that in their study of 243 mergers and acquisitions (M&A) in Japan that the post M&A firms underperformed pre M&A firms in both profitability and growth rates. Japanese management preferred internal growth to mergers and acquisitions due to: the workers identifying their own interests with those of the firm, growth is valuable to Japanese firms for utilizing and enriching human resources and for creating promotion opportunities, labor practices are in many ways firm specific, and the executives of Japanese firms are internally promoted and are less constrained by the stock market's evaluation.[12] An analysis of the largest 250 firms in the top 25 industries in the United States, as reported by Pearce and Harvey, demonstrated that those firms with the most focus on internal growth strategies had the best financial performance.[13] Lee and Yang however found that exporting firms with a market diversification strategy perform significantly better in terms of export level and export sales growth, compared to other groups with a market concentration or a concentric diversification strategy.[14]   Financial performance of other strategies will be discussed throughout this chapter.

The two primary ways of growing through concentration are increased market penetration, development and expansion; and extended product use and product development.[15]

Market Development (Penetration and Expansion).   As indicated above, market development can occur in two way: 1) by expanding one's presence in one' current market; or 2) by developing new markets that hold demonstrated promise for the firms goods or services.   Of the several alternatives for growing a firm, internally developed growth strategies, according to Gautschi and Werner, are often overlooked. The loss of this entrepreneurial outlook in many established industrial firms has resulted from risk aversion, a short-term focus, the bureaucratic decision-making process, and the company's reward system. Although many established firms have discouraged internal entrepreneurial activities, the effort can be successful with proper coordination, cooperation, and a significant commitment from top management.[16]

Market Penetration.   The purpose of market penetration is to convert nonusers in the firm's current market segment into consumers. The firm must deduce through market research why nonusers have not purchased their product or service and then address these consumer groups' objections.[17]   Tactics that execute this strategy include: enhancing the products value by altering its features, functions, and benefits, altering the product design so as to bundle it as part of an integrated delivery system, and promotional efforts addressing the later two changes.[18]

An example of a successful although legally questionable penetration strategy was demonstrated by Microsoft when they integrated their internet Explorer software with their Windows operating system. They gave away this feature (which a customer had to pay for if they were to employ Netscape's browser) in order to entice customers to utilize their underemployed browser and steal market share from Netscape.

Market Expansion.   Firms search for untapped and underdeveloped market segments through geographic expansion (local/state/regional/national/international/multinational – see Chapter

7) and shifting market positions (at the micro and segment level). For a differentiator, this may mean producing private label or in-house brands for a large retailer or distributor. For example, Nissan Motors' first minivan, the Quest, was repackaged for Ford Motor Company as the Villager. Clearly this trend has pervaded the auto industry - GM has taken many of its specific makes and models and spread them over its operating Divisions. A Chevrolet Nova became the Pontiac Phoenix; the Chevrolet Camaro, the Pontiac Firebird; the Chevrolet Caprice, the Oldsmobile Delta 88, etc...

Ironically, one of the greatest international marketing expansion blunders of all time was perpetrated by GM due to a linguistic anomaly. GM's hot selling car, the Nova, was a very reliable compact vehicle that performed well and was popular with U.S. young adults and starting families given its sporty look, low price, and comfortable size. Without realizing it, GM had exported a car to Argentina and to the Spanish speaking world where its name in Spanish translated into 'no go' (No va). The firm quickly changed the name of the car to Chevy or Chevy Special.[19]

Choosing a Market Growth Approach. Which one would an organization choose? The answer is that of market structure and market acceptance. If a market is fairly saturated, and the firm had no apparent competitive advantage, then it would make more sense to begin to move into new markets, hopefully adjacent markets, where it would be fairly easy to begin to expand one's business. If, on the other hand, a market is still fairly open, does not have a large concentration of firms similar to the focal firm, then it would be easiest to simply try to expand into one's current market. GM, for example, has expanded into marine and industrial engines,[20] and military trucks yet has sold its defense unit in London, Ontario, to General Dynamics Corp. for $1 billion.[21]

Unfortunately, the final decision between market penetration and market expansion isn't quite this simple. Market acceptance is another issue that will factor into the strategic decision-making process. Some products or services seem to reach a level of acceptance within a market, a saturation point so to speak, where even though it may seem like there is still lots of room for growth, consumers in that market are not making additional purchases. McDonalds has faced this dilemma in many of its markets where a variety of different fast food chains exist, but eating habits appear to have changed. Issues such as health concerns, proliferation of the fast-food culture, and increasing societal scrutiny on the impacts of fast-food businesses on local economies and the general quality-of-life may all play together to suggest that expansion in the current market isn't the best idea. For example, McDonalds' operations in France have come under a tremendous amount of criticism by certain members of the French government because they feel the proliferation of the golden arches, particularly into smaller, quaint, and stereotypically "French" villages, is an offense to French culture. Ironically, McDonalds Corp.'s French subsidiary is booming. The French have been opening a new McDs every six days, and the typical French customer spends $9 per visit, as opposed to only $4 in the U.S..[22]

Product Development/Extended Use. Product development is the other option for extending one's business through concentration. This type of internal growth involves an organization expanding its basic product or service line, but doing so within its current business setting. Calatone and Cooper analyzed 195 firms who introduced new products and services and found that 72% of the products were successfully received when the new product overlapped the firms' existing products, markets, technical expertise and production competences. Unrelated products within firms' expertise had a 36% success rate while unrelated copycat products outside the firms' experiences had only a 14% success rate.[23]

Firms can use this tactic when there is a need to increase the range of uses of a product or service or to increase the frequency of that usage. To increase repetitive use, firms need to repackage or bundle products, encourage larger volume purchases, and use recurring advertising. Firms develop product line extensions, promote new product and service uses, and encourage new uses through sales promotions and discounting.[24] For example, Ivory Soap increased its sales of bar soap by producing personalized sized bars (one for each member of the family) that could be bundled and sold in large quantities at a discount; Arm and Hammer sold the public on the innumerable ways in which baking soda could be used as a cleaning and deodorizing agent.

Looking further at McDonalds, when it decided to add "Happy Meals" to its basic menu, it was using the strategy of product development to add additional products to appeal to a broader segment of its basic market – in this case, to appeal more to children and their parents by offering a product that they designed specifically for kids (including a toy) and one that makes it easier for parents to place orders for their children. McDonalds often sends up a trial balloon, that is, before it adds an item to its permanent menu, it tries out a possible new product within a specific geographical market. It will test-market the new product first, and if the results are encouraging, it may offer it system-wide, but for a limited time only. After the trial period, McDonalds analysts will look at the numbers. Did the product's sale performance meet expectations? Were sales of the product consistent system-wide? What were the level of recurring sales (was there an initial burst of interest, followed by sustained sales or a dramatic drop off after customers tried the product)? Did the new product add to general sales or substitute for sales of more traditional products? And, were the profit margins for the product consistent with projections? The answers to these questions will lead to the decision as to whether or not the new product did perform above expectations and increase overall sales and whether it would need to do to be added to the general menu.

The fast food industry is constantly testing new products to try to keep ahead of the competition and maintain a strategic advantage, but almost all businesses do the same thing. Buick Motor Division and Honda Inc. each improve their current models and consistently add new features or even new models to try to expand their market presence. Microsoft and Intel continuously improve their current products and seek to add new products to their lines to extend their presence in the growing technology market and gain new customers. Entertainment companies continually attempt to develop new attractions or new ways of doing old things so that they can maintain or expand their audience base. Even industries where new products are not particularly the norm, such as utility companies, will introduce new products or services that will expand their sales bases (telephone companies expanding into cellular services; electricity companies offering their consumers the opportunity to purchase electricity generated with wind power,[25] or water companies producing a non-potable water source for use in watering lawns and gardens). Whenever there is the opportunity to grow by adding products or services that do not increase the cost of production but increase the appeal of the business to a broader segment of the current market, businesses are well advised to pursue these opportunities.

Growth Through Diversification

When growth through concentration reaches a point where it becomes too costly, especially when the market becomes saturated with high competitive pressure and profitability begins to fall significantly (mature or declining markets), it is advisable to look at other growth options. Under these conditions, continuing to invest a firm's resource base in its primary business, where growth is hard to sustain and profits are declining, makes less sense than beginning to invest in other business interests. The decision to diversify has a higher level of risk, generally speaking, than concentration strategies and needs to be made based on additional analyses. The range of diversification strategies is quite large: one can diversify by degree (such as move into a related micro or market segment); one can diversify into businesses related to the primary business; or one can diversify into businesses that are unrelated to the primary business. In terms of financial performance of a diversified firm, the theory is the more unrelated the diversification strategy, the poorer the profitability of the firm. This would make sense from a financial viewpoint since the lower the risk, the lower the expected financial return.

Synergy: Is It the Key to Diversification? In the 1960s, a corporation's growth strategy centered around diversification through merger and acquisition of companies unlike its primary operation. Unrelated diversification was supposed to be a hedge against a downturn in the economy, but the parent companies were unfamiliar with how to run these acquired companies, and many of them ended up in failure. Corporations in the 1970s looked for growth opportunities within the firm itself. If external help was needed, companies that could be bought and that would complement the parent to provide synergistic, related growth were sought. Here a company would develop new products that have synergies with existing products but were not usually meant to be sold in the company's current markets.[26]

Synergy is the realization of economies of scale and economies of scope in manufacturing, marketing. raw materials, research and development, and engineering through consolidation of business units. Synergy also exists if the activities and operations of the different business units are complementary. Diversification into related businesses is to enhance the market strength and profitability of the consolidated corporation that would then improve its long-term competitive position, deterring market into the industry, and allowing the company to exercise some monopoly power in the purchase of raw materials and the sale of its products through the use of predatory pricing. A diversification strategy based on the synergistic motive dictates that a company should avoid diversifying into unrelated business units since there are no operating synergies to be gained by such a move.[27]

Research on diversification strategies and synergy, however, has been quite mixed; some research noted greater benefits accrued when synergies between businesses existed yet other studies indicated that single-businesses outperformed their diversified competitors.[28] Early research by Thomas found that for diversification to work, it must involve synergies, such as financial or operating economies. Paradoxically, although operations economies were most publicized in diversifications, financial synergies were more common.[29] With diversification, firms became burdened with a bureaucratic superstructure occupied by a number of executives overseeing individual operations. Palich et al. denoted that synergy seemed to work for only domestic firms[30] while Porter concluded that industry attractiveness was a key factor in determining the success of any diversification strategy, regardless of synergies.[31]

Risk and Diversification. There are two types of risks associated with diversification: the increased risk (and administrative costs) associated with managing a new business venture (barriers to entry)[32] and the decreased risk associated with spreading the firm's assets over several markets and industries.[33]

Managerial Risk. Risk in diversification is a function of how far the control function of central management will be stretched by attempting to manage and control the cluster of businesses that make up the overall portfolio of the corporate entity. If the similarity of businesses within the portfolio is high, then it is easier to establish common performance measures and control activities, which reduces overall risk. On the other hand, if the differences between businesses within the portfolio are great and require more and more unique measurement and control activities, then the level of risk (and affiliated administrative costs) increases. For example, when companies with no retail experience, like AT&T and IBM, first opened their stores there tended to be large diseconomies of scale and long learning curves – they needed to learn about a whole new link in their value chain. There are two types of risks associated with diversification: the increased risk (and administrative costs) associated with managing a new business venture (barriers to entry)[34] and the decreased risk associated with spreading the firm's assets over several markets and industries.[35] However, retail companies who move into related market segments may experience economies of scale and have short learning curves. Wal-Mart found it very easy to move into the large wholesale club market by opening up Sam's Club.[36]

Another major contributor to increased risk is the need to decentralize the management power structure. This is true, especially when the combination of businesses within a single firm may contain a variety of different business-level strategic approaches. Corporate top-level management will not be geared to oversee a variety of strategy approaches, and is best advised to transfer the decision-making control down to the business top-level managers to uniquely manage their businesses as effectively as possible. However, whenever a firm decentralizes strategic decision-making authority, it weakens its own ability to coordinate rapid responses to new opportunities or avoid emerging threats across diversified businesses.[37]

Yet this issue of risk and management is not that straight forward. Decentralization does not necessarily lead to greater levels of risk. Firms with diversified business holdings (usually called strategic business units or SBU's) can respond more rapidly as a compartmentalized unit to changes in the market since they do not have to refer vital decisions up to corporate headquarters.[38] SBU's decrease managerial risk because they allow for greater unit flexibility and allow the individual units to organize themselves around their particular customer segments.[39] Firms must possess "simultaneous loose-tight properties"[40] in order for a diversification strategy to work effectively - they must be rigidly controlled from the top while allowing for autonomy, innovation, and entrepreneurship at the SBU level (for example, Microsoft's decentralized structure and operating philosophy coupled with a clear mission, centralized strategy, and strong culture). It is apparent then that from a managerial standpoint the firm must weigh the risks associated with losing some control against the benefits derived from close customer contact.

Financial Risk. Similar to the managerial risks and benefits, the financial risks associated with diversification are also double-edged. The real financial risk associated with any new business venture, especially in an industry or market the firm has no familiarity or real expertise in, is that the firm is less familiar with the nuances associated with the industry and the new business. The firm consequently may be unable to construct valid and reliable financial projections.[41] Without accurate projections, the firm is beyond risk-taking where risk/reward tradeoffs can be calculated, the firm is operating under uncertainty and might be considered gambling.[42] On the other hand, the basic underlying principle behind diversification is to 'not put all of your eggs in one basket.' The firm invests in varying businesses and industries in order to blunt the effects of one particular business or industry taking a downturn – risk is reduced by minimizing the loss the firm may take from any one business venture.[43]

Risk, Diversification, and Performance. Lubatkin observed that although theory suggested that diversification may improve the performance of the firm, that empirical studies have not totally supported that hypothesis.[44] So why diversify? Lauenstein noted that although a number of rationalizations for diversification have been promoted, the major force underlying diversification efforts is the desire by top managers to protect and enhance their personal compensation packages. Effective corporate governance and management are the hidden reasons underlying the success of diversification strategies.[45]

This raises a rather interesting question about diversification and risk. Should the firm take on the responsibility of creating a portfolio of companies in order to reduce stockholder risk while maximizing reward or would it be more efficient for the stockholder to manage his or her own risk through a personalized stock portfolio?[46] This certainly must be a question asked and answered by the stockholder. The rise in the 1990's of mutual funds, and managed asset accounts indicated that stockholders, in general, would rather pay for a professional to manage their investments for them then make these choices on their own. Even though most mutual funds in 2000-2002 lost as much (and some even more than) as the Dow Jones 30 or the Standard and Poor's 500, investors are still counting on the fund and account managers to maximize the funds' performance. The same could be said for investors in diversified firms, they too are looking for the firm's management to maximize corporate profitability.

Rumelt found that firms which diversified but restricted their range of activities to some central skill or competence demonstrated superior performance based on return-on-equity (ROE) while firms whose strategies fell into the active conglomerate, related-linked and single business groups exhibited moderate ROE performance, and firms in the unrelated diversification strategy showed lower overall ROE.[47] This research has been weakly reaffirmed by Lubatkin and Rogers.[48] In fact, unrelated diversification "over the last three decades, [the conglomerate] has been chastised, ridiculed and declared dead. Many conglomerates have been broken apart or merged into other companies because their formulas for success stopped working and they suffered a crisis of confidence among investors. Huge companies such as ITT Corp. and Teledyne Inc., which once were stellar players on Wall Street and employed tens of thousands of workers, no longer exist."[49]

So why use a diversification strategy with inherently more risk and less reward? Here, the response is that firms do so because they have to. If all companies are naturally risk-averse, the reason they take on additional risk is because they must in order to maintain their competitive advantage. In the opening case, we described the history of General Motors (GM) as a history of continual product development (concentration strategies) and purchases of other companies both alike and not alike. Why did GM go this route? They followed the strategies of concentration, horizontal integration (purchasing competitors), related diversification (purchasing businesses in complementary industries), and conglomerate diversification (purchasing businesses in unrelated industries) because in order to maintain their competitive position over time, they needed to diversify to overcome competitors in their primary industry – automobiles. If Olds had remained GM's only business, it is unlikely it could ever have battled the competition that was growing as the automobile industry established itself and began to grow. It took major companies with major resource bases to compete with the growing giants, such as Ford Motor Company and, later, the Chrysler Motor Company. Billy Durant seems to have sensed this and began to consolidate five motor companies into one large powerful entity, General Motors. Over time, and even though GM continually spent millions to improve its product lines, Durant and later Alfred Sloan decided to add complementary companies to its basic automobile companies with companies that built auto bodies (Fisher), maintenance products (Delco), and the like to not only provide a large presence for the automobile industry itself, but the products it and its customers depended upon to sustain the company. Later, in going into unrelated industries, especially with the purchase of Hughes Aircraft Company, GM tried to balance its portfolio – it attempted to marry a societal staple, automobiles, with a company that could help lead it more directly into the Information Age. Hughes's Aerospace and Electronic Division helped GM launch On-Star and Direct-TV, two major players in the new economy, while GM's automotive divisions remain dominant in the U.S. market but locked in intense and costly domestic and foreign competition.

GM is an extremely large company that has come to its present position through a variety of strategies. Could it have stayed in the automobile industry and achieved the same level of growth and power? Probably not. If one looks at the history of Ford Motor Company and Chrysler Motors, two different competitors of GM that have relied more on concentration rather than on diversification, it is clear that both companies have not fared as well. Ford diversified later but has only been able to maintain a #2 position, and still doesn't compete as strongly as it otherwise might have been able to do had it emulated its arch-rival, GM. Chrysler was holding a poor #3 position in the U.S. market and losing its market share to foreign competitors, especially Toyota and Honda. It finally merged with the Mercedes-

Benz Motor Company of Germany to become Daimler-Chrysler, and has essentially ceased to exist.

Related or Unrelated, that is the Question. The decision as to whether or not expand into related or unrelated businesses is an important consideration. Though further levels of diversification brings higher risk, as the GM example suggests, in order to survive and sustain a competitive advantage, many companies have little choice but to expand beyond their primary business. Again, as Table 6.1 suggests, related diversification is less risky than unrelated diversification. However, if the central business is in an industry that is increasingly unattractive, it makes more sense to move into unrelated industries, especially industries where the focal firm can use at least some of its core competencies to help acquired businesses to achieve (or maintain) a competitive advantage.[50] For example, Anheuser-Busch moved from the beer industry into the entertainment industry and used its advertising department to improve the image and growth of Busch Gardens theme parks.

Research on this choice provides some assistance. Besides the earlier cited Rumelt study, Nesbitt and King conducted a comprehensive, computer-based analysis of the performance and returns to shareholders of approximately 1,800 diversified companies over a 10-year period. Their research indicated that related and unrelated diversified companies showed similar performance patterns. They suggested that implementation of the strategy, rather than the strategy itself, may be the primary ingredient for corporate success or failure.[51] Wade and Gravil found that amongst information technology firms related subsidiaries out-performed unrelated subsidiaries on a number of dimensions including: performance, survival, and employee productivity growth. Their study also suggested that related diversification in knowledge-based industries, such as IT, plays a more important factor in firm success than in primary or secondary industries. Gillan et al.'s analysis of Sear's related diversification strategy revealed that anticipated synergies did not materialize, and Sears' retail performance deteriorated. Coincident with pressure from institutional investor activists in 1992, Sears announced the divestiture of financial services and a refocusing on retail operations.[52]

Diversification, a Matter of Degree. The other issue is just how far from the core business should a firm diversify? Although Rumelt categorized diversification into four types (single business, dominant business, related-diversified and unrelated-diversified), in actual measurement, there are no standards that identify the degree to which differing firms diversify.[53] Some will do so to a lesser degree, while others will do so to a large degree. United Airlines in October, 2000 established UAL New Ventures (e-network) creating a side company that only accounts for less than 1% of its operations.[54] This is clearly a low level of diversification. Why did United engage in developing this new company, especially when things were not doing so well in its main business? It did so because of two reasons: 1) it has been especially successful in developing the technological aspects of its airline business, and 2) it saw the opportunity to sell its services to other companies who might want to take advantage of the services United has developed.

For classification purposes, and because it does impact the firm's riskiness, it is useful to classify a firm's engagement in diversification in three levels:

1. Low levels – 5% to 20% invested in non-primary business ventures
2. Moderate levels – 20% to 50% invested in non-primary business ventures, and
3. High levels – more than 50% invested in non-primary business ventures.[55]

These various levels reflect two realities: 1) the higher levels of risk are associated with higher diversified operations, monitoring, and control measures; and 2) a lessening of corporate-level managerial commitment to individual businesses within its business holdings. Low levels of diversification would keep the main business first and forefront. Here, the major growth efforts would continue to be found in the major business, with some resources diverted to the minor businesses. In moderately diversified companies, the major investment of resources continues to be on the primary business, but there is a growing level of competition that goes on among smaller siblings for resource allocation (in this case, the company might employ asset allocations based on some of the portfolio techniques described in this text). In those companies with high levels of diversification, more business-like accounting and financial standards tend to apply and better performers can count on receiving new resources, while poorer performers might not only receive fewer new resources, but may be candidates for sale or shut-down.

This last point explains why GM might actually phase out its Olds Motor Division, regardless of its traditional positioning as the first of the many GM companies. Over time, and after the acquisition of dozens of other businesses, GM managers evaluated each division more on financial and growth performance rather than traditional ties. So is GM's decision to phase out Olds Motor Division a good one? Based on tradition, no, it isn't. However, based on performance as a portion of GM's overall corporate health, yes, it is. This is one of the major lessons of strategic management – it is more important for the firm to survive and prosper as an entity than it is for the firm to perpetuate business practices that no longer meet marketing requirements. Of course it is unfortunate, and might even appear to some degree unfeeling, but it is important to understand that GM needs to attain and maintain an overall position of competitiveness that will allow it to maintain its dominant position in the U.S. market and grow in the international environment.   This way, shareholders will not suffer, employees of other divisions will not be threatened, and the dynamic areas of the company will not be impaired as they seek to grow and prosper.

In the next several sections, we describe the various strategic choices that firms have in terms of coming to an optimal choice as to which diversification strategy it will employ.   These choices are presented in terms of two characteristics: 1) its relative level of risk; and 2) the conditions that exist that make it a reasonable strategic choice.

Horizontal Integration. When a firm is in a profitable and growing industry or market segment, and wishes to enlarge its customer base, it will look to acquire other firms in that industry or market segment. Here diversification, and risk, is quite low – the firm stays in the same industry with similar customers and products and merely has to learn the specifics of a particular company's operation.[56]   The primary objective of horizontal integration is to reduce competition, with a secondary objective to support growth. There is important value in any firm attaining a stronger competitive position within its own industry. Greater market share brings greater control, and greater control has the added advantage of reducing competitive risk. However, one of the major side effects of horizontal integration is the additional acquisition of debt and large amounts of debt greatly add to the financial risk associated with this corporate level strategy. Whether one company engages in a *friendly take-over* or, worse, a *hostile take-over* of another company, it usually does so by going deeply into debt to purchase the necessary share base so as to take control of the competitor.

Hostile takeovers. Some companies decide to reduce competition by buying their competition whether their competition likes it or not. Called a hostile take-over, this is when one company makes a public statement that it is willing to purchase the stock of a rival firm, often for a greater amount than the current market price, and seeks to take over the rival regardless of the rival's willingness to be bought. Sometime, as a counter-action, the rival or another more acceptable company to the target company (referred to as an Angel Company or White Knight) will make a counter offer for the stock at a higher price. Again, this offer is usually backed up by financed capital, and, if the target company is able to fend off the tender offer of its competitor, it may end up with significantly increased debt, which can bring on problems of its own.

Employee buyouts, such as those implemented by Algoma Steel and Spruce Falls Power and Paper, are another viable measure to save companies from corporate raiders. Three factors are necessary for an employee takeover to succeed - adequate financing, adequate management expertise, and good relations between management and labor. Just as in any entrepreneurial situation, employee takeovers involve a degree of risk. Having a comprehensive business plan to obtain financing and adequate cash flow to meet projected costs, as well as providing employee-owners with sufficient autonomy, should help minimize those risks.[57] Pugh et al. found that a few measures of firm financial performance do improve significantly with employee buyouts, but this appears to be largely a short-term effect.[58]

However, if the initiating company is successful, it can take over its competitor and combine its operations with its own. It will have decreased competition, but will have introduced two new problems: 1) the need to support and then reduce the new debt; and 2) the need to integrate a hostile work force into its existing labor force. KPMG found that companies which had good communication channels with employees, met cultural differences between the 2 sets of staff head on, used top personnel as mentors, and demonstrated tolerance towards newly-acquired employees had a 100% success rate in hostile takeovers.[59]

Friendly takeovers. There are times when one company will see that its own long-term is tenuous. It may have a very poor resource base and little ability to keep itself competitive. Before things get too bleak, it may offer itself to a competitor as a way of surviving, even though that survival may translate into fewer jobs and a lost culture and organizational identity. If the price is right, and the acquiring company sees real benefits in not only reducing competition, but in utilizing its own particular core competencies to transform the assets of a weak competitor into positive assets, it will agree to a friendly take-over. Normally, an increase of debt for the acquiring company is still involved in that it will need to purchase the assets of the company from its shareholders. However, the increased risk of a hostile workforce will be reduced, and most friendly takeovers tend to work out fairly well. Among other factors, friendly takeovers take more time than hostile takeovers, and both companies have the opportunity to work out potential problems, where in a hostile takeover, the results may become ingrained into the operations and culture of the surviving company for years and create additional operation management headaches that simply aren't there in friendlier take-over environments.[60] It is interesting to note, however, that in a recent study Rajand and Forsyth found that when they examined the performance of both bidders and targets involved in hostile takeovers in the UK and compared them to friendly takeovers of similar size that in the longer term hostile bidders perform relatively well in the post-acquisition period whereas friendly bidder shareholders suffered significantly large losses.[61]

Combined acquisition. In taking over a competitor, the company doing the takeover has a couple of choices. It can either decide to leave the basic company as an independent company, simply a subsidiary of the parent company, or to merge it completely into the acquiring company's structure. The most common is the combined acquisition. Since the major point of the acquisition was to eliminate competition, it makes little sense to allow the identity of the former competitor to remain in the competitive mix. This has been very clear in the pattern of the various acquisitions that have occurred in the banking industry in the United States.[62]   As individual banking companies have acquired competitors (either in current markets where they are competitors or in adjacent markets, where acquisition allows expansion into new markets) the acquiring company has almost always changed the name of the surviving company to that of the acquiring company.

Autonomous Acquisition. However, there are examples when the acquired company maintains its original identification. This is usually the case when the local brand recognition is greater than that of the acquiring firm. The May Company of St. Louis has acquired a variety of other retail department store companies over the years, but has by and large left the firm with its already well established name. For example, the Lord and Taylor brand is associated with a variety of stores across the country, but is still a division of the May Company. In some markets, like in Colorado, Lord and Taylor stores coexist in major area malls with another chain of stores called Foley's. Both Lord and Taylor and Foley's are divisions of the May Company.[63]

Why have two competing firms in the same market? There are two reasons: 1) both brand names have developed their own particular customer bases that demonstrate significant loyalty to one particular brand name over the other; and 2) consumers see a significant enough difference between the two companies that the May Company can effectively double its competitive position in the Colorado market by maintaining two different brand names. A third possible consideration is that at some point in the future, the May Company may decide to sell off (or even spin-off) one of the divisions, and by maintaining it as an independent brand name, it could more easily do so.

Risk associated with horizontal integration.   Risk in horizontal integration accrues from several of the issues we have identified in this discussion. Hostile takeovers introduce expected risk as management must try to reconcile, and assuage angry employees of acquired firms. Even in friendly takeovers, different cultures of the two firms must be reconciled (differing management styles, differing retirement funds, differing union agreements, etc.). Mergers have the same problems, but in addition, mergers introduce the need to eliminate and/or streamline duplicate of structures and multiple management and support systems.

Further, the market impact of acquisitions and mergers is never one-for-one. For example, when American Airlines took over Trans World Airlines in a bankruptcy sale, the resulting market share was not additive (American Airlines 9.6% plus TWA 5.3% to equal 14.9% of the market). Actual combined marketing share in 2001 was only 10.9%.[64]   While the intention of reducing competition is the first priority of horizontal integration, its results may be somewhat disappointing.

Horizontal integration (acquisitions) and financial performance.   Horizontal integration tends to lead to increased corporate performance. Heron and Lie recently conducted a study of operating performance for a large sample of firms that carried out acquisitions between 1985 and 1997. Subsequent to acquisitions, acquirers exhibited superior performance relative to their industry and experienced performed significantly higher than the control firms with similar pre-takeover operating performance.[65] Brown and Rosa found that in their study of firms on the Australian Stock Exchange that acquiring firms were typically firms that had performed exceptionally well in the market's estimation. Their relative performance around a seven-month before/after buy period indicated that, on average, the inter-corporate investments they make to build on their performance increase the market value of their shareholders' equity.[66]   Yet Cherin and Hergert's earlier review of the literature on acquisitions cited several works where shareholders of firms making acquisitions received little to no financial benefit.[67]

Dickerson et al. demonstrated, however, that the negative net impact on profitability of investment in acquisitions was derived from externally, rather than internally, financed acquisitions[68] while Child et al. found that performance improvement was found to be associated with the introduction of changes to management practice rather than with contextual factors such as acquirer nationality, size, date of acquisition, profitability of subsidiary at acquisition or sector.[69] Parrino and Harris in a study of 197 US takeovers from the 1980s, found that the most important determinant of superior post-merger operating performance is whether the target company's management was replaced or retained. When the target CEO was replaced, the post-takeover firm's annual cash flow returns outpaced industry standards by 2% to 3%. In contrast, when target top management remained, operating returns did not exceed industry averages. However, for those takeovers that are followed by significant investment, management replacement did not make a significant difference in post-acquisition performance.[70]

Merger. Mergers are another form of horizontal integration, but we hold it out from the other strategies because its theoretical application is different from the other strategies (see Mergers under Cooperative Strategies below). In a true merger, two competitors decide to unite to form a third company, but a union in which one company does not take over the other. The union does not involve one company purchasing the other, rather both companies come together and create a third base of stock (the stock of the two companies is reissued to stockholders, based on an equity-based formula that takes into account the value of the stock and the book values of the two companies and, through a mutually-agreed upon formula, issue stock in the new country to the stockholders of the previous two independent companies).[71]

Some companies call their friendly-acquisitions mergers, when they are not. United Airlines called its combining with USAir a merger. In fact, it was not. The contractual agreement was that United Airlines was agreeing to purchase USAir. When the "merger" didn't happen, United was obligated to pay USAir over $50 Million as a penalty for not being able to take over the airline.[72] Further, one of the reasons the merger didn't happen was that regulatory agencies were extremely worried about the amount of debt that United would incur in purchasing the stock of USAir held by USAir stockholders. .... sounds like an acquisition.

Vertical Integration. Vertical integration encompasses the activities of taking control of companies that are in the direct value chain of which the focal firm is a member.[73] The rationale behind this strategy is to support the core business by lowering the power of suppliers and/or buyers; those forces that most directly increase competition and lower profitability within an industry (see Chapter 5). Benefits associated with vertical integration include cost reductions due to: avoiding market costs by eliminating the distortion in input costs caused by imperfect competition in the upstream market; reducing transaction costs; decreasing uncertainty or asymmetric information, resulting in a more efficient use of inputs; and by protecting proprietary technology. Vertical integration can also increase profits through higher prices by creating barriers to entry, allowing price discrimination, and reducing service and advertising costs.[74]

An example might be a clothing manufacturer taking control of its cloth suppliers (*backward integration*). It could also be by the same clothing company deciding to open retail outlets of its own or purchasing existing retail outlets (*forward integration*). This is one of the lesser risky options because the companies that the focal company acquires are still within the main industry of the focal company. It is more risky than concentration because this option introduces the firm to at least a second type of business. For example, if Anheuser-Busch (AB) purchases farms that produce the grains it needs to produce beer (backward integration), it may be familiar with what grains it uses on a day-to-day business (low level of risk in working with a new product line), but is now also in the farming business (higher risk) because farming is significantly different from brewing beer, involves entirely different technologies, different management systems, and different organizational systems to be effective.

Backward Integration. When a company decides to purchase its suppliers, it should do so because its sources of supply are threatened, there is no market supplier for its raw materials, or it can achieve a competitive advantage (lower cost, greater differentiation) by bringing their supplier(s) in-house.[75] In the example of Anheuser-Busch, farming is not an endangered industry, and rather than take on the risk of running a second business that is foreign to how AB runs its breweries, it can simply contract with a variety of farmers to produce the grains it needs – especially since there are thousands of farmers, many of whom might be extremely pleased to have supplier contracts with a company as large as A-B.

On the other hand, the wine industry has grown dramatically over the past 50 years, particularly in California, where the best grape-growing regions are within 100 miles of the San Francisco area. The Napa Valley and Senoma Valley regions produce most of the grapes that wineries want and need to produce their high quality wines. The point is that there is only so much acreage that produces high quality grapes and unless a given winery controls a portion of that acreage, it can easily loose a competitive advantage. Here, backward integration makes sense, and wineries in this region often compete to purchase grape-growing farms to insure their own source of supply.

Forward Integration. When a company decides to purchase its distributor or other business activity that occurs between itself and its ultimate consumer, it is engaging in the strategy of forward integration. However, as it is true for backward integration, it should do so when it feels that there is a major threat that will make its smooth delivery of goods or services to the ultimate consumer more difficult or that it can achieve a competitive advantage.[76] When a company like Gateway Computers sees an opportunity to achieve a competitive advantage over competitors by not only getting rid of distributors, but by opening its own stores and encouraging the final customer to do business with it through the Internet, it is engaging in forward integration. While many micro computer companies may depend on retail office supply outlets to purchase and resell their products, Gateway has decided that it can increase its own margins by opening outlets and also by working directly with customers through its own website. Here customers can design their own computers with the specific features they want, and even choose to have them delivered to their homes by choosing one of a variety of options for delivery.

Risks Associated with Vertical Integration. The usefulness of vertical integration strategies has become suspect since it has been demonstrated that vertical integration raises costs due to: mobility and exit barriers which may increase strategic inflexibilities that trap firms into keeping obsolescent technologies and strategies; managerial inefficiencies that may develop because vertical integration creates complex problems of control and coordination among highly interdependent activities; underutilized capacity may increase costs in some stages of production because throughput is unbalanced if technological factors force firms to build plants of differing scales at adjacent stages of production; and vertical integration may force firms to forgo purchasing at low prices in the open market.

Vertical Integration and Financial Performance. Early research by Rumelt demonstrated that vertically integrated firms were the poorest performers of diversified types while D'Aveni and Ilinitch found that vertically integrated firms had a higher risk of bankruptcy than nonintegrated firms. Other researchers have called for the disintegration of vertically integrated firms.[77] Yet in more recent research D'Aveni and Ravenscraft found that vertical integration resulted in economies of scale even after industry effects and economies of scope and scale were controlled for. Vertically integrated lines of business economized on general and administrative, other selling, advertising, and R&D expenditures but had higher production costs and thus lead to only marginally better profitability than nonintegrated lines of business in the same industry. Secondly, the higher production costs were linked to backward vertical integration, suggesting insulation from market pressures and lack of incentive to manufacture the lowest cost inputs. Forward vertical integration was associated with lower transaction-related costs. Thus, evidence of both efficiency effects and bureaucratic costs emerged, with the benefits of vertical integration slightly outweighing its costs.[78]

A better understanding of the relationship between vertical integration and economic performance may be made by considering the role of managerial capabilities in directing integration. A lack of understanding of non-core businesses and the managerial approach necessary for managing integrated activities may contribute to poor integration outcomes. The magnitude of these knowledge deficiencies will be dependent on how far the company moves from its strategic core and on whether corporate managers can abate these deficiencies through knowledge acquisition.[79] It is important to remember that either backward or forward integration introduce new trades to the basic business of the firm, and thereby increase operating complexity. Complexity increases risk. However, if strategic decision-makers can see that these strategies will secure a firm's position in the value chain and/or improve overall growth and profitability trends, then they are well advised to do so.

Related (Concentric) Diversification. A riskier venture than internal growth or vertical integration, concentric diversification occurs when a firm purchases or forms companies that are related to that of its primary business but not directly part of its market channel. There is no particular interest in supporting the primary business (although there may be some possible bundling of products and services), and this type of strategy seeks to broaden a firm's investment into a related industry segment. Synergy is derived from shared activities along the value chain such as resource acquisition or shared processing technologies.[80]

Fast food franchisees, for example, have jumped on the related diversification bandwagon and it is not uncommon to have multiple franchises offering different types of food at one location (i.e. Taco Bell, Baskin and Robbins, Dunkin Donuts, and Subway), with that location possibly being a gas station owned by the franchisee (another related business). Going back to the GM case, GM provides in-house financing for car buyers and replacement parts for their vehicles. Even advertising can be shared - Westin Hotels and Hertz Rent-a-Car are owned by the same company and have entered into an agreement in which both advertise the services of the other; this example of synergy is called cross-advertising.[81] Examples of concentric diversified firms include PepsiCo (beverages and snack foods), Priceline.com (air travel, hotels, car rentals), former Phillip Morris (food products, formerly cigarettes, and alcoholic beverages), and Nike (athletic shoes, apparel and sports equipment).

Core competences and distinctive competencies. The most unique feature associated with related diversification strategies is that these strategies are based upon a specific set of core competences and distinctive competencies of the firm. These firms take their brand name and image (i.e. Toyota, Nissan, and Honda's basic vehicles with high quality) and transfer it to another related business unit (Lexus, Infinity, and Acura's luxury vehicles). GM, however, has paid a heavy price for having a plethora of companies offering products and services that are not derived from their apparent set of core and distinctive competencies – understanding U.S. consumers.[82] Although GM's Cadillac's, Corvettes, and Camaro's have caught the public's desire for

luxury and sportiness, the rest of their product line has been fairly
lackluster including such vehicles as the Geo Prism, the Chevy Impala,
the Pontiac Phoenix, the Buick Skylark, the Opel Cadette, and the Delta
88 Oldsmobile.[83]

Risks   associated   with   related   diversification.
Concentrically diversified companies operate at a relatively moderate
risk level. This is true because decentralization and differences in
business-level strategies among the firms within the portfolio will lead
to higher levels of uncertainty and risk. However, since parts of the
value chain and core competences are shared by each firm, a certain
degree of centralized decision-making, and control, exists at the
corporate level. Again, there are sound strategic reasons for companies
becoming concentrically diversified, but it is important to understand
that for these companies to be successful, they are heavily dependent
upon good knowledgeable managers to oversee their highly complex
structures. Here, strategic managers must develop complex control
systems so they can not only see the outcomes of overall operations,
but also discern the operations of the various companies within its
portfolio and be in a position to make changes expeditiously.

Related Diversification and Financial Performance. As
discussed earlier in the sections describing risk, diversification, and
performance and related versus unrelated diversification, research on
concentrically diversified firms demonstrates that related diversified
firms outperformed performed unrelated but did not necessarily
outperform other growth strategies. Healy et al. examined the acquiring
companies' cash flow performance in the 50 largest US industrial
takeovers from 1979 to mid-1984. The results showed that the acquirers
did not generate any additional cash flows beyond those required to
recover the premium paid. However, while the takeovers were break-
even investments on average, the profitability of the individual
transactions varied widely. There were 2 distinct types of takeovers:
friendly transactions that typically involved stock payment for firms in
overlapping businesses (called strategic takeovers), and hostile
transactions that involved cash payments for firms in unrelated
businesses (called financial takeovers). Strategic takeovers generated
substantial gains for acquirers.[84]

Maintenance Strategies

Strong firms in growth industries have the best of both worlds – excellent market opportunities and the skills and capabilities to take advantage of them. Sound companies in slow growth markets do not have the same luxury. There are several challenges that a firm faces in this type of market including:

1. *failure to anticipate the slowing market trend.* The firm may have excess capacity and higher marginal costs, as well as overestimated future sales. This is dangerous in a period where the firm may have to cut prices and heavily promote products since these actions will result in decreased cash flow.

2. *failure to have a clear competitive advantage.* The firm that has ridden the industry growth curve may have been pulled along so to speak without a clear strategy. When the market slows down, this business will find itself not only stuck in the middle (have no strategy) but also left out in the cold since it will lose market share as competition increases (due to the limited number of customers).

3. *failure to see that an early market advantage means little in a slow growth market.* The firm that had an early lead in a market or industry may sit on its laurels even when the market slows down. If customers perceive little difference in product quality and/or price within the market, being first in the market has modest competitive value. The 'Big Three' U.S. automobile manufacturers (GM, Ford, and Chrysler) may have been the first in the U.S. market but they have given up tremendous market share to foreign competitors.

4. *failure to protect market share in the face of short-run profit gains.* When the market slows and the firm has reducing cash flow, top management may be tempted to cut training, R&D, and perhaps even marketing in an attempt to maintain historic profit margins. In the longer run, the firm will be come less competitive and lose market share in a market where it is very expensive to recoup customers.[85]

Maintenance strategies are thus those strategies that firms employee when they have a strong market position in a slow growth or mature market.[86] The main objective of maintenance strategies is to protect and nurture the corporation's market share. Internal maintenance tactics include those similarly described in the internal growth strategies (increased market penetration, market expansion, and extended use) but here the goal is to improve current customer satisfaction and loyalty while encouraging and simplifying repeat business.

Second, in a slow growth market the organization is looking to cut costs whether it subscribes to a low-cost leader, differentiator, or blended competitive strategy.[87]   Any cost savings that does not subtract from the value of the product or service can then be employed as a buffer against increased competition and projected slower growth. These funds may also be employed to diversify the firm's operation. If the business's current market is slow there may be other markets (related or unrelated) that the firm could invest in that are on the rise.

Conglomerates and Holding Companies (including Concentric Diversification)

As shown in Table 6.1, related diversification strategies are recommended for firms in sluggish markets and have been already discussed under growth strategies. This is a less risky strategy since the new products and services brought into the firm's operation may have some connection to its current line of goods and services and are based upon the firm's core competences. For example, McDonalds noticed that Burger King's market share in the U.S. was increasing from 1993-1999 from 17.9% to 21.9%, a 22% increase overall.[88]   Rather than compete head on with Burger King in this slow growth market, it turned its attention to international markets. In doing so, McDonalds experienced its first percent income loss in 1998, although its total sales grew nearly seven percent that same year. Realizing that they needed to again become competitive in the U.S., they took over restaurants of weaker competitors in different market niches (Roy Rogers, Danatos Pizza, and Boston Market). McDonalds remained in the restaurant business, but broadened their market domain into several market segments.[89]

Risks Associated with Conglomerates.   If concentrically diversified businesses are highly complex and risky, conglomerates are even more so. The major difference between concentrically diversified firms and conglomerates is that conglomerates own other companies simply based on their ability to produce growth or high levels or profitability, and there need be no relationship between these firms. There are usually no shared core competences along the value chain so even the possibility of synergy is removed. Each company within the conglomerate portfolio is completely responsible for attaining growth objectives or profit objections without any assistance from other assets within the holding company's portfolio.[90]

These conditions add additional levels of complexity, the need to decentralize strategic decision-making power almost completely (except for the holding company's ability to buy or sell the firms within its portfolio), and is in theory the most risky form of organization. However, the potential of portfolio management can bring a variety of benefits to the holding company: 1) the holding company can operate a relatively simple operation, essentially employing portfolio experts and analysts who provide strategic decision-makers with the data they need to manage the portfolio; 2) the holding company can sell companies within its portfolio that do not meet expectations; 3) the holding company can buy companies that become available that meet its investment and return criteria; and 4) the holding can pick and choose the companies and industries its analysts believe hold the greatest promise for both growth and profitability.[91]

As attractive as these benefits are, there are also several downsides to a holding company's financial health. As we discussed earlier, the financial performance of unrelated diversified firms has historically been lower than related diversified firms. By choosing this option, strategic planners are selecting a strategy with lower returns and risk. Secondly, just because the holding company *can* sell off a company it no longer wants to own or maintain, there is no guarantee that it *will be able* to do so. The conglomerate could be stuck with a poor-performing firm within the portfolio and may have to face hard decisions about how to deal with it. It might try to intercede in the management of the poor performer and attempt a turn-around; it might decide to discount the price for the firm and try to sell it to a bargain-hunter; or it may decide to liquidate it. In any event, when a company within a holding company's portfolio turns sour, it can be very costly to the conglomerate.

Third, while a conglomerate may purchase other companies that are available, there is no guarantee that it will be able to purchase firms that precisely meet its expectations. Good firms are not generally available for sale, and while the holding company can always engage in a hostile takeover tactic to acquire a target firm, the expense of doing so may lessen the target firm's attractiveness. Companies that are available for purchase may well be available because they are problematic and are either looking to be taken over to have a fresh infusion of cash to solve problems, or may even be owned by a conglomerate trying to offload it. True bargains are hard to find, especially when one considers that there are other conglomerates in the market that are also looking for new takeover targets.

Fourth, even though a conglomerate can pick and choose the companies and industries it wants to be associated with (with a caveat for the above conditions), there is no guarantee that either the company or the industry will remain attractive. Conditions change, as we pointed out in Chapter 3, and opportunities and threats change quickly, making one track of acquisitions seem sound on one day and not so sound on another. Unfortunately, no one is particularly good at predicting the future, and as a result, strategic decision-makers make the best decisions they can about the future based on the information that is available to them today. For example, no one accurately predicted the events of 9/11, let alone predict what companies and industries would be impacted. Imagine the predicament of a conglomerate company that might have purchased a promising firm who just happened to have its world headquarters in one of the two towers of the World Trade Center. The destruction of the buildings was complete and records were completely destroyed. For the new corporate buyer, much if not all of the investment might now be gone (except for that which might be recovered from insurance companies), and there was no way of predicting that anything like this could happen. This is a dramatic example, but conditions change in a whole variety of ways and the unpredictability of any company or any industry is one of the things that adds to the risk factors of conglomerates.

Portfolio analysis is a technique that looks at the assets a firm may have within its portfolio and provides a method and rationale for how the holding company decides whether to invest in a firm, hold it, or sell it. How a corporation treats its various holdings is a function of a variety of forces and not universal. For companies that are slightly diversified, it is likely that other than the primary business, the other companies that it owns could be proprietary (a necessary part of their overall business strategy) i.e. part of a vertical integration strategy. In these instances, the corporate entity will not likely look at the various businesses it owns from a purely financial perspective, that is, that each unit must be profitable in and of itself (no loss leaders). Instead, it will look at these companies from a strategic standpoint and value the ownership of these companies based upon their importance in supporting its primary business and helping it achieve a strategic advantage. Portfolio analysis doesn't make sense for these types of situations.

Cooperative Strategies

A cooperative strategy differs from the above strategies in that two or more firms agree to work together in order to increase their individual abilities to expand their goods or services, or perhaps even engage in new types of goods or services.[92] The relationships themselves can be either short-term or long-term (there are no rules here), but several conditions must be in place in order for these strategies to work. One, the cooperative relationship must lead to demonstrable positive outcomes for all partners. While not all partnerships are equal in terms of investment or participation, it is still important that no one partner take a disproportionate gain or loss out of the relationship. Two, a high level of trust must exist among partners for cooperative arrangements to succeed. Deception or incomplete sharing of information can seriously jeopardize the activities of the partnership, but can lead to lawsuits as well. Three, the term of the partnership needs to be fully defined prior to its onset. Each partner needs to not only understand, but also agree to the time it is willing to commit to the partnership so that it can factor into its overall strategic plan the amount of resources it will contribute to the partnership as well as to the level of that resource commitment.[93]

There are four potential sources of inter-organizational competitive advantage from cooperative relationships: investment in relation-specific assets, knowledge-sharing routines, complementary scarce resources/capabilities, and effective governance.[94] Relationship-specific assets refer to unique assets dealing with site location (locating plants close to one another), physical assets (transaction-specific capital investments such as customized machinery, tools, dies, and so on that tailor processes to particular partners), and human resources (knowledge gained through longstanding relationships with stakeholders) while knowledge-sharing routines refer to inter-organizational learning and the transfer of technology and innovation between partners. Complimentary scarce resources refers to distinctive resources of alliance partners where neither firm in the partnership can purchase the relevant resources in a secondary market particularly specialized expertise and intangible assets, such as reputation.[95] Lastly, effective governance refers to management through either contract arrangements or self-governance; in the case of self-governance there may be formal safeguards such as financial investments or informal safeguards such as goodwill or firm reputation.[96]

Cooperative Strategies and Financial Performance. Do cooperative strategies positively impact corporate performance? The research to date yields mixed results. Gleason et al. found that commercial banks, investment services firms, and insurance companies experienced significant returns of 0.66% on average higher than their competitors when they announced their participation in a joint venture or strategic alliance. These higher returns were significantly positive across the four modes of cooperative activities: domestic, international, horizontal, and diversifying.[97] Golden and Dollinger denoted that small firms who shared resources with competitors, suppliers, trade associations, and the community provided a better outcome than direct competitive strategies. They suggested that small firms with well-defined strategic postures could gain from collaborative relationships with their most critical finding being that most small firms do use cooperative strategies.[98] Yeheskel et al., on the other hand, indicated that medical technology firms in Israel that have undertaken alliances marginally unperformed those that have not, suggesting that the benefits of alliances were outweighed by their drawbacks[99] while Kanter noted that although firms like General Electric had more than 100 formal alliances, that 70% of joint ventures and strategic alliances fell short of partner expectations or were disbanded.[100] Other related studies will be cited by the specific type of cooperative strategy: *joint ventures, strategic alliances,* and *mergers*.

Joint Ventures. In a joint venture, two or more firms create an additional company to produce a good or service that neither firm produces in its primary service area. A joint venture make sense for many such firms because it allows them to share the risk in the new product or service development, or perhaps to share the risk in moving into a new market altogether. By combining some of each company's core competences and distinctive competencies, even newer core competences may be developed and the potential for new competitive advantages can also accrue to the partners.[101]

Successful ventures have five key characteristics: *task-overlap* between the parent companies and the joint venture (producing economies of scale), *strong partners* (i.e. joint venture firms' size, financial attributes, ownership [private, public, government], and previous joint venture experience), *mutual dependence* (joint venture ownership and decision-making [equal versus majority/minority], trust, and interaction), *organizational cultural similarities* (similar life cycles, size, and structure), and *positive country-specific factors* (low political risk, friendly investment climate, skilled labor, high level of economic development, etc...).[102]

For example, Luo studied 293 international joint ventures and demonstrated that previous cooperation bolstered contractual adaptability, which in turn nurtured current cooperation between partners. Contract completeness and cooperation drive led to higher joint venture and parent performance.[103] Pearce and Hatfield examined the relationship between the acquirers of a joint venture's (JV's) resources and the JV's performance in achieving its partners' goals. The analysis showed that JV's receiving a variety of resources from both partners outperformed JVs where JV management was responsible for securing its own resources, and outperformed JVs receiving resources primarily from a dominant partner.[104] Pothukuchi et al. noted that based on data from a survey of executives from joint ventures between Indian partners and partners from other countries, it was found that the presumed negative effect from culture distance on international joint venture performance originated more from differences in organizational culture than from differences in national culture.[105]

Many joint ventures have been used to help companies break into new markets. For example, General Motors has engaged in a variety of strategic alliances with Japanese and Korean motor companies as a means of opening up the two Asian markets, since governmental policies of both Japan and South Korea have effectively cut down on foreign companies' ability to enter their markets. Likewise, these joint ventures also allowed certain Japanese and Koreans firms to enter U.S. markets more easily by having the U.S. firms offer their venture partners' products under their brand name (when GM brought back the Chevy Nova the vehicle was made by Toyota; Ford has used several partners to increase their product line - the Probe [Mazda] and the Villager [Nissan]).

Risks Associated with Joint Ventures. There are also some drawbacks to joint ventures. One, by sharing risk, none of the partners will be able to realize the full benefits of the new venture, they will have to be shared. Two, the relative strengths of each partner at the beginning of a joint venture could change over time perhaps reducing the ability of individual partners to perform well in the joint venture, hence damaging the partnership and the new venture itself. Three, while joint ventures should involve open and honest relations and communications, they don't always work out as such. Joint venture firms can end up missing opportunities, produce unintended outcomes, and be encumbered with lawsuits. Risk in this situation is defined by the amount of uncertainty that results from the joint venture. Since joint ventures tend to be carefully crafted through legal contacts, the amount of uncertainty can be minimized, though never eliminated.

Joint ventures and financial performance. Reuer reported that empirical research on the parent firm valuation based upon joint venture formation has produced rather mixed findings. Several studies report that firms generally obtain a higher return when announcing the formation of an international joint venture or IJV.[106] For example, Merchant found that announcements of IJV formation increased the average capital market value of firms, with the two-day announcement period increasing the returns for these firms by 0.30%.[107]   Other research found average valuations that were negative or insignificant. Parent firms tended to have higher returns when the venture involved capital market diversification, when the parent firm had less international experience and when the venture was formed during a period of a strong home country currency. Returns tended to be worse in the presence of agency hazards arising from dispersed parent firm ownership, high levels of free cash flow, or an inappropriate capital structure.[108]

Strategic Alliances.   A strategic alliance is cooperative agreement among two or more companies which go beyond basic company-to-company interactions but fall short of mergers or joint ventures.[109]   A strategic alliance might involve contracting with suppliers for the long-term to help suppliers secure a market for its goods and the consuming firm with a sure source of supply.   For example, Cisco Systems has strategic alliances with several technology-related suppliers (Microsoft, Motorola, IBM, Sun, and Sony) to provide joint solutions and/or technologies to meet Cisco's customers' needs.[110]   The advantage of a relationship like this over vertical integration is that, while members of a common value chain get the benefits of supply and guaranteed purchasing, each company remains independent and the relationship can be terminated under the terms of the contract.   This reduces risk since, in this specific case, Cisco has not had to take an equity position in the other firms.   At the same time, none of the firms will have the opportunity to reduce their operating costs (which does occur in vertical integration when the successor firm can cut the costs of duplicate functions and management structures).

Another common use of strategic alliances is to extend markets, especially globally, without major additional investment.   The Star Alliance, of which United Airlines is a major partner, has done precisely this within the airline industry.   Currently, there are 14 members of the Star Alliance, including strong partners such as Germany's Lufthansa, Denmark's SAS, Japan's Al Nippon Airlines, Singapore's highly touted Singapore Airlines, and 9 other smaller international partners.[111]   United is the only U.S. based airline in the alliance because of U.S. law and regulations, but through creating an international alliance, United has been able to essentially become an all-global airline without actually creating the costly infrastructure it would have needed to build to fly to all the destinations to which its strategic partners fly. A passenger boarding at a United airport in the U.S. can travel anywhere in the world United's partners fly to as if the entire flight was on United. The ticket shows all United Airlines flights, baggage would only be checked once, and the passenger would only need to deal with one airline (United) to handle changes or problems. Code sharing is also a revenue stream, which can potentially increase profitability.

There are four keys to successful strategic alliances: proper strategy, aligned structures, clear governance rules, and effective monitoring by all parties involved.[112] In terms of strategy, the alliance must fit both with the firm's strategic approach as well as the firm's competitive strategy. It must add to the firm's distinctive competencies, increase value along the firm's value chain, and/or strengthen the firm's business functions. The alliance should also produce additional opportunities in the marketplace and/or reduce threats. Aligned structures not only refer to the legal structure of the alliance or the terms of alliance operating agreements but also refer to aligning the operations of each firm in the alliance so as to reduce task uncertainty and ambiguity. For example, GM's alliance partners have adopted CAD/CAM (computer-aided design/computer-aided manufacturing) software utilized by GM, which will allow for Web-based visualization and collaboration in the design and manufacturing stages of car production.[113]

Strategic alliances should be governed by a clear, fair, and flexible set of rules (as embodied in the operating agreement) and should address four main areas: partner contributions and distributions, control, allocation of risks and rewards, and alliance termination strategies. Lastly, controls should be clearly spelled out and cover admission of new partners or the sale of additional securities, appointment of board members, officers, managers, or outside professionals, compensation of the management of the alliance, terms of transactions with partners and/or their affiliates, and conditions under which the terms of the alliance agreement may be modified and the mechanics for doing so.[114]

Risks Associated with Strategic Alliances. Alliances are fraught with risks, and almost half fail.[115] This risk can be categorized as either relationship risks or performance risks. Relational risk is defined as the probability and consequences of not having satisfactory cooperation and occurs because of the potential for opportunistic behavior on the part of both firms, such as shirking, cheating, distorting information, appropriating resources, and so on. Conflicts arise because firms have their own individual interests that are not necessarily compatible with those of their partners. Furthermore, partner firms may also have hidden agendas in the alliance that may subsequently create serious problems in cooperative interactions.[116] For example, a long-term risk to a business is when alliance partners gain access to and actively use its core knowledge in a competitive challenge.[117] Firms need to clearly delineate to employees what can and cannot be share with alliance partners.

Performance risk is present in all strategies, including strategic alliances, and includes intensified rivalry, new entrants, demand fluctuations, changing government policies, a lack of competence of the partner firms, and luck.[118] Alliance partners may not equally share the performance risk associated with the alliance. This type of risk is normally mitigated through the use of warranty disclaimers, contractual limitations on liability, and exclusion of consequential, special, and incidental damages.[119]

Strategic Alliances and Financial Performance. Research findings on the relationship between engagement in alliances and superior performance are contradictory. Several studies reported general support for the positive significant association between strategic alliances and performance while others reported the existence of mediating and moderating factors governing this relationship, and yet other studies indicated negative or no association between engagement in strategic alliances and firm performance.[120]

The more recent research seems to yield slightly more positive results. Dyer et al. conducted an in-depth study of 200 corporations and their 1,572 alliances and found that a company's stock price jumped roughly 1% with each announcement of a new alliance, which translated into an increase in market value of $54 million per alliance.[121] Tehrani observed that both U.S. and European high technology firms that indicated a higher degree of engagement in strategic alliances outperformed other firms across different segments of high-tech industries. Hence, engagement in strategic alliances seemed to enhance the performance of firms independent of the type of competitive strategies employed, operating environment, and the type of industry. Therefore, a prerequisite to superior performance appears be the extent to which the firms enter into different types of collaborations with other firms.[122] Zollo et al. found that based on their sample of 145 biotechnology alliances, that only partner-specific interaction had a positive impact on alliance performance, and that this effect is stronger in the absence of equity-based governance mechanisms.[123] However, Rowley et al. found in the steel and semiconductor industries that strategic alliances that are highly interconnected with strong ties negatively impact firm performance. This network configuration was especially suboptimal for firms in the semiconductor industry.[124] Rothaermel studied 889 strategic alliances between pharmaceutical companies and new biotechnology firms and found that these alliances were positively associated with the pharmaceutical companies' own new product development which in turn lead was positively associated with firm performance. At the industry-level, it was shown that the pharmaceutical firms preferred alliances that leveraged complementary assets (exploitation alliances) over alliances that focused on building new technological competencies (exploration alliances).[125]

Mergers. Though we dealt with mergers as a strategy of horizontal integration, it also has a component that involves a cooperative strategy as well. Two competitors might find that their unique functional operations are inadequate to meet growing market demands. However, if they were to combine, they would increase their offerings in the market and be in a position to significantly improve their marketing position and market share. In such an environment, over the past several years, some interesting partners have merged to form more competitive firms. This has been particularly true in the finance industry. With deregulation, banks have merged with insurance companies, and stock brokerage houses forming new entities that offer the services of all of the merged organizations.[126]

This type of activity can be considered a cooperative strategy because none of the firms had the resources to create the additional services on their own, especially at the level that was needed to complement the size of the primary firm. It makes more sense to a large bank to merge with a large brokerage house than for the bank to try to create the presence of a large brokerage house within its central business.

Risks Associated with Mergers. Mergers are the most risky of cooperative activities mainly because they are permanent. Both companies' missions, goals, objectives, strategy, culture and identity are amalgamated, with the greatest risk being the incompatibility between each firm's core values and practices. If the surviving firm discovers that it was a mistake to combine the two predecessor companies, it's a little too late and the division of the merged firm may be so costly that it can't be done. Consequently, both managements must perform the necessary due diligence prior to the merger. The purpose of the due diligence exercise is to determine that the information about the "other" company is correct, accurate, and properly disclosed. The due diligence process involves: the identification phase (information gathering and risk identification including an analysis of all loss runs, identification of pending and prior litigation, and reviewing insurance policies and environmental issues); summarizing the data collected and analyzing the exposures compared to existing insurance; performing visits to new locations, consolidation of insurance programs; and addressing administrative issues.[127]

However, when the merger works and the surviving firm fits the market better, then the other risks of merger (having to dispose of duplicate functions and management structures) pale in comparison with the benefits. For example, Amihud et al. found that in cross-border bank mergers, risk neither increased nor decreased after the merger. In particular, on average, neither total risk nor systematic risk rose relative to banks in their own home banking market.[128]

Mergers and Financial Performance. Does merging firms increase a firm's financial performance? The research is also mixed on this topic. Gugler et al. in a recent landmark study analyzed the effects of mergers around the world from 1988-2003. The performances of mergers were examined by comparing the profitability and sales of the merging firms with control groups of non-merging firms. The results indicated that merged firms on average had significant increases in profits, but reduced sales. Interestingly, these patterns were similar across countries, between domestic and cross-border mergers, and between manufacturing and the service sectors. Conglomerate mergers decreased sales more than horizontal mergers.[129] Yet Henry of Business Week reported that 17 out of the 21 mergers in the spring of 1998 were a bust for investors who owned their shares. If CEOs had kept their checkbooks under lock and key and simply matched the stock market performance of their industry peers, shareholders would have been better off. Similar patterns appeared across the 302 major mergers from July 1, 1995, to Aug. 31, 2001.[130] Marshall concurred noting that 75% of US mergers completed in the past few years have failed to deliver on their performance promises due to poor pricing, clashing cultures, poor due diligence, or weak integration.[131] Akhigbe et al. found that both partners of a merger (as well as their rivals) benefited from the merger announcement but that the shareholders of targeted firms (those being solicited to merge) earned significant positive higher returns than shareholders of acquiring firms (those that proposed the merger).[132]

Harvest and Corrective/Turnaround Strategies

Thus far, we have only discussed long-term growth and maintenance strategies. These strategies provide important strategic direction and, underneath, form the basis upon which a company creates its operational structures. However, company structures sometimes run into problems, strategic problems that force strategic managers to reevaluate the firm's central strategy and possibly take corrective actions that will then allow the firm to realign itself with its environments.

The problems we refer to here are separate from operational problems. Strategic problems come from a firm losing its fit with its most crucial environment or environments; when it slows its growth rate to a level below the average of the industry (or worse, realizes negative growth); or when its profitability drops below the average of the industry or becomes negative. These types of problems are life-threatening and require centralized strategic action. Correctional strategies are also short-term strategies. It would be the hope of any firm's top management, its governing board, and shareholders that strategic managers solve its strategic problems quickly and efficiently, thereby allowing the firm to eventually resume its growth strategies. It is these types of problems we address here.

Turnaround and Reorganization: Profit Strategies, Restructuring, and Rethinking Strategy

Weak firms in high growth industries face a real conundrum since they are in a successful market or industry but incapable of taking advantage of the inherent growth in that industry. They are like fisherman who see a school of teaming fish in a lake but do not have proper nets or fishing equipment in which to catch the fish with. These firms seem unable to align their competencies with the key success factors in the industry and consequently merely survive due to the inherent growth in the industry – there is room for these firms to flounder around as long as the industry continues to expand. In these situations the firms that possess a culture of organizational learning have the luxury of merely reformulating their strategic approach to the market, that is, realign their distinctive competencies with those portions of the marketplace that best fits their skills and abilities.[133] For example, in a smaller firm that has been involved with rapid expansion at the expense of profitability and internal development, it may decide to slow down growth, allow consolidation, and build its profits and/or reinvest in its human and capital assets. This is referred to as a **profit strategy**, where the central strategy of concentrated growth is interrupted, but only for a short period of time.[134] Within one to two years, if a proper correction is in place, the firm should be able to resume a more aggressive growth pattern and fulfill its central corporate level strategy.

Restructuring implies much more substantive problems for the firm. Here, the problems a firm experiences result from the reality that its current structure is preventing it from operating in an efficient manner or has caused it to veer into a perilous direction. It is the structure that needs to change, perhaps all the way down to redefining what functions the firm engages in and how it engages in them, and a willingness to change them. Managers may be reassigned or lose their jobs. Entire departments, product lines, or market segments may be eliminated. In restructuring, the firm does whatever it takes to surgically remove parts of itself that are dysfunctional and reorient the remaining elements of the firm to reinvigorate or redefine its operational competencies, reestablish core competencies, and return to a position where it can challenge its competition and create a competitive advantage.[135] Restructuring can be bloody, and no individual or function is immune to reorganization. The central strategic management of the firm, however, must be deeply involved in the restructuring process to assure that the result puts the firm back on a solid strategic path. This makes restructuring more difficult to achieve perhaps, but is necessary for the longer-term health of the organization. The objective here would again to go through this painful process as quickly as possible; certainly a one-shot coordinated action would be always preferable to a longer-term contracted action.

Rethinking Strategy may be necessary when it becomes obvious that the central corporate level strategy isn't working. As industries change, as markets fluctuate, and as consumer tastes change, entire industries that at one time were considered as highly attractive may become unattractive.[136] For example, the fast food industry that has burgeoned in the last 40 years was at one time a panacea for companies that wanted to take advantage of the rapid growth and popularity of American consumers; fast food meant quick growth and high profits. Two things have happened, however, that have made the industry less attractive: 1) there has been a plethora of companies that have joined the industry shrinking growth opportunities for industry incumbents; and 2) a growing concern for the downside of fast food – high fat, high sugar, and digestive issues of eating food too quickly. Being less attractive today than it was just 20 years ago, some of the major players (McDonalds, Burger King, Taco Bell, and Kentucky Fried Chicken) have altered their central strategies. McDonalds now owns a series of other food chains; Burger King is owned by Grand

Metropolitan, a major conglomerate company; and Taco Bell is in a common holding company that includes Pizza Hut and Kentucky Fried Chicken.

Divestiture: Harvest, Retrenchment, Divestiture, and Liquidation

Firms may find that they not only do not possess the right skills and abilities to compete in their current markets, but worse, that their current markets are slow growth, no growth or are in decline. This is a double barrel of bad news for the firms in question and requires quite drastic action in order to alleviate the situation. Firms must drastically reshape themselves or risk going out of business. Depending on the specific problems a firm faces and the severity of those problems, firms might choose from a variety of divestiture strategies.

Table 6.1 suggests that firms in this situation are highly recommended to employ the turnaround strategies suggested in the prior section or opt for concentric or conglomerate diversification. They also may resort to harvest/retrenchment strategies.

A **Harvest Strategy** would apply to a firm that has a portfolio of assets that are attractive to other firms. The firm in trouble might try to sell these companies at a premium price, perhaps even at a price that above market pricing in order to generate a larger than anticipated cash inflow to help it solve other problems. For companies that do not own other companies, they might have a department that is especially attractive to other companies and it might be able to sell off that division (then follow that up with a contractual arrangement which allows the sell or to continue to use the services of the jettisoned division). In either event, the objective is to take a valuable (but hopefully not critical) asset and turn it into serious cash.[137]

Thietart and Vivas in their study of 569 declining operations using the Profit Impact of Marketing Strategy (PIMS) database, indicated that the pursuit of a harvest strategy for declining businesses must be based on the nature of the decline and the firm's level of competitive strengths, since investment reduction will detrimentally affect market share, while improving cash flow. For firms facing a favorable declining environment, that is, their industry was quite stability, there was little technological change, and/or low exit barriers, or having high competitive strengths, niche and leadership strategies rather than harvest strategies lead to high cash flow performance. However, for firms facing unfavorable declining environments, or with low competitive strengths, harvest strategies were more successful.[138]

Retrenchment occurs when a company decides that it can help itself by decreasing the size of the company.[139] There are two tactics that it might use in retrenching, *downsizing* and *downscoping*. Either will decrease the size of the firm and, hopefully allow it to consolidate its remaining assets to achieve profitability.

Downsizing is the activity of retrenching by reducing the size of the company. Here, the firm will cut work forces, reduce its market presence, and/or close operations all in an attempt to reduce costs. In its bankruptcy plan, United Airlines is seeking to retrench by cutting upwards of 40% of its flights, furlough 20% to 40% of its workforce, reduce its international presence, and possibly reduce its number of domestic hubs. All of this is designed to save $2 to $3 billion a year and begin to show some profitability. Once again, this is a short-term strategy in that United hopes that its first decision will lead to the expected results – they do not want to make all of these cuts and then determine it wasn't enough and go through a second round of cutting. Doing so could not only cost it customer confidence, but employee loyalty as well. These outcomes could prove to be the death knell for the company.

Downscoping is the other option in retrenchment. Here, the firm makes a decision to cut the number of functions it is involved with. The goal is to reduce complexity of operations, improve basic business efficiency, and return to profitability. Companies that have engaged in diversification strategies might use the short-term strategy of downscoping to better focus on their primary business. For example, if a brewery had made a decision to purchase farms to supply it with the grains it needs to brew its beer. In an effort to retrench, it might decide to get out of the farming business and put the farms up for sale, hoping to not only generate some cash from the sales (assuming that it didn't use heavy financing to purchase the farms and ends up selling them at a loss), but to simplify its overall operations as well.

Muller and Smith see retrenchment as a problem confronting many public and private organizations, but it may also be a time for creating opportunities and for capitalizing on innovation. They suggest several strategies that can turn retrenchment into an opportunities including: a market-centered strategy, which includes such tactics as subcontracting and seeking revenue diversification; a bureaucratic strategy; which includes such tactics as centralizing decision making and undertaking special studies; a legal strategy, including such tactics as court actions and seeking liberal interpretations of law; and a co-production strategy, which includes such tactics as community activism and coordinating advisory groups.[140]

De Dee and Vorhies, in summarizing the research on declining markets, found critical differences among the lowest, average, and best performers. The firms that either remained profitable or quickly returned to profitability did so only through effective retrenchment strategies. Well-managed companies typically outperformed competitors through disciplined control over the economics of the business, intensive development of appropriate product/ market niches, and a leadership style that sustained entrepreneurial drive and commitment among their managers. Firms engaged in systematic retrenchment during declining environmental conditions enjoyed significant performance benefits over competitors while smaller firms have been less successful in executing turnarounds. Their own research with small businesses indicated that small firms in declining markets did benefit from downsizing and other cost cutting measures but that an overemphasis on cost cutting was counterproductive and cut into market share and sales.[141]

Divestiture is the activity of selling off company assets to generate cash. A firm may sell of part of its operation or other assets it has that can generate new sources of cash. These are usually desperation measures in which a firm risks selling off core competencies (and as a result, its competitive advantage) in order to realize a cash infusion to help it deal with other major financial problems. Most single unit organizations do not recover from a period of divestiture, they are usually so far in the hole that divestiture only buys time, not recovery.

Many firms following a divestiture strategy, like United Airlines, declare bankruptcy. Chapter 11 of the Bankruptcy Code provides a framework for business reorganization (Chapter 11 may also be used for liquidation). In contrast, Chapter 7 solely involves liquidation. Upon the filing of a voluntary Chapter 11 petition, a reorganization case is commenced. Contemporaneously with the commencement of the case, the debtor (the entity filing the voluntary petition) becomes a debtor-in-possession. The filing of a bankruptcy petition creates a bankruptcy estate which includes all legal and equitable interests of the debtor in property as of the commencement of the case. The debtor-in-possession continues to control and possess property of the estate and is authorized to manage and operate its business unless and until otherwise ordered by the Bankruptcy Court. The primary goals of Chapter 11 are rehabilitation of the debtor, equality of treatment of creditors holding claims of the same priority, and maximization of the value of the bankruptcy estate.[142]

Recent literature has indicated that firms with multiple strategic business units, holding companies, which regularly divest businesses (even good, healthy ones) ensure that the remaining units reach their potential and that the overall company grows stronger. It is shown that an active divestiture strategy is essential to a corporation's long-term health and profitability. In particular, companies that actively manage their businesses through acquisitions and divestitures create substantially more shareholder value than those that passively hold on to their businesses. [143] Cherin and Hergert, in reviewing the literature on divestitures and corporate performance, found that stock prices increased when a firm announced the selling off of company assets for strategic reasons while they declined if the firm was selling off unwanted assets. Their own research reinforced the notion that voluntary dumping of corporate assets is viewed favorably by the market.[144]

Liquidation is the ultimate failure of strategic management. In liquidation, the firm sells its remaining assets and discontinues its operation. There are never winners in liquidation. The companies are already so heavily leveraged that creditors can only gain a certain percentage of what the firm owes them, and stockholders usually receive nothing. Employees lose their jobs and may also lose retirement funds. While lawyers tend to make out fairly well, many don't recover enough in fees to pay their expenses for the defense of the failed company. Nobody wins here. For example, the Amtrak Reform Council concluded in November of 2001 that the federal passenger rail services is not capable of delivering the improvements needed despite requiring $25 billion in subsidies during its 30 years of service. Now, Amtrak itself must develop a liquidation strategy while being sued for $200 million by Bombardier Inc., the builder of Amtrak's Acela trains.[145]

Chapter 7 provides a formal, judicial procedure for the orderly liquidation of the assets of the debtor and the ultimate payment of creditors in the order of priority set forth in the Bankruptcy Code. Under Chapter 7, an independent bankruptcy trustee is appointed to conduct the liquidation and is charged with the responsibility of marshalling the debtor's assets, liquidating them, and ultimately distributing the net proceeds to creditors. The trustee is armed with powers that include the ability to avoid and recover preferential and fraudulent transfers made by the debtor and the trustee may assert claims and initiate actions on behalf of the bankruptcy estate.[146]

Sullivan et al. noted that several studies have demonstrated that stockholders and bondholders of liquidating firms gain around the announcement of a liquidation. Their own research confirmed these findings, adding that shareholders gained more when the liquidating firm had been a poor performer, presumably because assets were removed from the control of ineffective management.[147] Kim and Schatzberg analyzed successful liquidations from the NYSE and AMEX from 1963 to 1982 and found that the announcement of liquidation reduced the risk of liquidating shares, the shareholders received substantial gains from successful liquidations, and that the assets of the liquidating firm had been underutilized before liquidation and that voluntary liquidations lead to higher valued reallocations of corporate resources.[148] Akhigbe and Madura found that rival firms in the same industry as firms that went Chapter 7 had lower values indicating that firm liquidation acted as a market signal of adverse industry conditions.[149]

Using the Corporate Level Strategy Matrix for Strategy Selection

In Chapters 3 and 4, we introduced four different scales which analysts and strategic decision-makers might use to evaluate the relative importance of the opportunities, threats, strength, and weaknesses they have determine apply to their firm. In this chapter, we have introduced a number of corporate level strategies that organizations can choose from among in determining their optimal strategic and operating path for the foreseeable future. In Figure 6.2, we combine the corporate strategy matrix (Table 6.1) with the graphical depiction of a SWOT analysis (Figure 4.7) to develop an integrated tool that provides suggestions as to which corporate level strategies a firm might choose, based on the summary scores of a SWOT analysis.

Figure 6.2
SWOT Matrix and Corporate Level Strategies

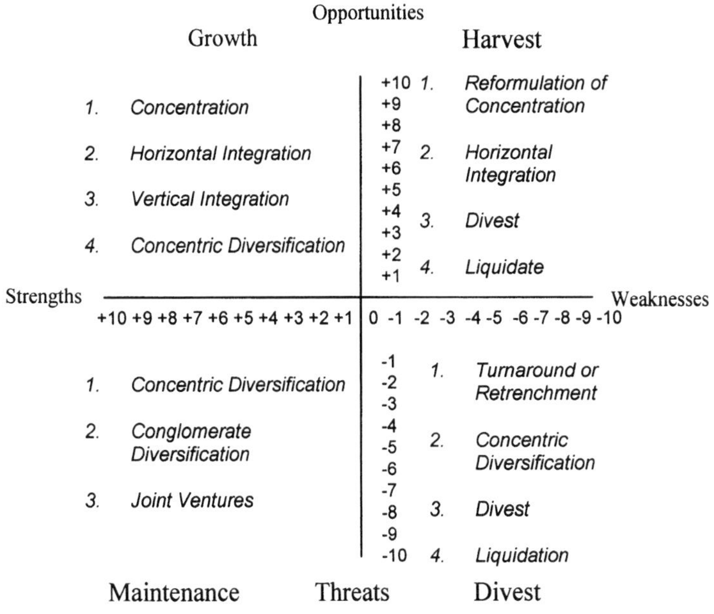

In order to place a firm on the graph (Table 6.1/Figure 6.2), we need to go back to the our SWOT analysis from Chapter 4. Let's assume that a SWOT analysis yielded a score of 2.5 for Strengths/Weaknesses (the x-axis score) and 3.85 for Opportunities/Threats (the y-axis score). This score would indicate that the firm's overall strategic direction should be growth and that the corporate level strategies that the firm should select should include concentration, horizontal integration, vertical integration and related (concentric) diversification as one can see in Figure 6.3 below.

Figure 6.3
Strategy Choice using the SWOT and Grand Strategies Matrix

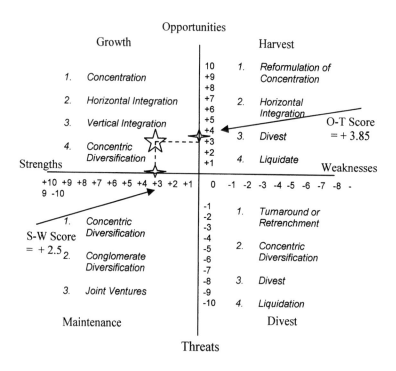

Summary

In this chapter, we stated that corporate level strategy deals primary with the strategic direction or goal of the firm while business level strategies deal with how the firm will compete in the marketplace. The firm may follow one of four major strategic directions or goals: growth, maintenance, harvest, or corrective/turnaround. Growth strategies from investing only in firm's core business (concentration strategies) to investing in related products and services (concentric diversification) and include market and product development, horizontal and vertical integration. Diversification strategies are discussed in terms of their synergy with the core business, the degree of diversification, associated risks, and financial performance. Beyond these growth strategies, in maintenance situations, firms can form conglomerates (a series of unrelated businesses) and also engage in a series of cooperative strategies, which take advantage of new product and market opportunities, and share the risk with another company or set of other companies. In the harvest mode, firms rethink their overall strategy and/or purchase firms that have the core competencies that they lack while simultaneously raising capital minimal through reinvestments and/or partial liquidation. Finally, when organizations get themselves into financial difficulties, they can engage in a variety of corrective strategies that, depending upon the severity of the strategic problem, can range from brief minor corrective strategies to severe reorganization options and even full liquidation.

Key Terms and Concepts

After reading this chapter, you should be familiar with the following terms and concepts:
 Corporate level strategies; growth strategies; concentration; internal growth; market development; product development; diversification strategies; vertical integration; forward integration; backward integration; horizontal integration; hostile takeovers; friendly takeovers; combined acquisitions; concentric diversification; synergy; conglomerate diversification; cooperative strategies; joint ventures; strategic alliances; mergers; maintenance strategies; corrective

strategies; reorganization; profit strategies; restructuring; rethinking strategy: divestiture; harvest; retrenchment; and liquidation.

Web Sites

http://www.att.com/history/history4.html - A brief history of one of the most famous divestitures in business history – AT&T and the baby bells. Also available at this site is the complete history of AT&T as well as current news about the company and employment opportunities.

http://home.earthlink.net/~fpearce/Jointventure.html - The Joint Venture Home Page for Small and Mid-Sized Businesses. Provides a list of small businesses looking for partners, a description of how to develop a joint venture proposal, and a list of successful small business joint ventures.

http://www.mergercentral.com/ - Merger Central , Inc.'s home page. Provides up-to-date information of mergers and acquisitions around the United States. Features of the site include a press kit, the M&A forum, the MergerWeek newsletter, job listings, and an events calendar. Additional benefits require membership (fee-based).

Discussion Questions

1. What are the primary factors that would lead a firm to opt for a concentration strategy exclusive of all other growth options?
2. What are the primary factors that would lead a firm to opt for one or more diversification strategies?
3. How would a strategic decision maker know which type of corrective strategy was appropriate given the problems she/he might be present?
4. What are the primary reasons a firm might engage in a joint venture rather than form a strategic alliance? Give an example.

Endnote

[1] More information about GM may be found at their website: http://www.gm.com/flash_homepage/

[2] Richard D. Teach and Robert G. Schwartz (2000). "Methodology to study firms' strategies and performance over time" *Journal of Marketing Theory and Practice* (Summer) Volume 8, Issue 3, 32-40.

[3] Based upon John A. Pearce II and Richard B. Robinson, Jr. (2000). "Model of Grand Strategy Clusters" *Strategic Management: Formulation, Implementation, and Control.* 7th Edition. New York: Irwin McGraw-Hill, p. 317.

[4] Andrew Bayer (2002). "Pimlico, Laurel Are on Magna's Shopping List" *The Washington Post* (July 12), D01.

[5] Kathryn R. Harrigan (1985). *Strategic Flexibility: A Management Guide for Changing Times.* Lexington, Mass.: Lexington Books.

[6] Jeffrey S. Harrison (1987). "Alternatives to Merger -- Joint Ventures and Other Strategies" *Long Range Planning* (December) Volume 20, Issue 6, 78-83.

[7] Jay R. Galbraith (1977). *Organization Design.* Reading, Mass.: Addison-Wesley Publishing Company.

[8] Arnoldo C. Hax and Nicolas S. Majluf (1984). "The use of the Growth-Share Matrix in Strategic Planning" in Arnoldo Hax (ed.) *Readings in Strategic Management.* Cambridge, Mass.: Ballinger Publishing Company.

[9] Michael Allen (1990). "The New Calculus of Growth" *Chief Executive* (January/February) Issue 55, 30-34.

[10] James W. Bradley and Donald H. Korn (1979). "Bargains in Valuation Disparities: Corporate Acquirer Versus Passive Investor" S*loan Management Review* (Winter) Volume 20, Issue 2, 51.

[11] Joseph P. Hughes, William W. Lang, Loretta J. Mester, Choon-Geol Moon, and Michael S. Pagano (2003). "Do Bankers Sacrifice Value to Build Empires? Managerial Incentives, Industry Consolidation, and Financial Performance" *Journal of Banking & Finance* (March) Volume 27, Issue 3, 417-447.

[12] Hiroyuki Odagiri and Tatsuo Hase (1989). "Are Mergers and Acquisitions Going to Be Popular in Japan Too?" *International Journal of Industrial Organization* Volume 7, Issue 1, 49-72.

[13] John A. Pearce II and James W. Harvey (1990). "Concentrated Growth Strategies" *Academy of Management Executive* (February) Volume 4, Issue 1, 61-68.

[14] Chong S. Lee and Yoo S. Yang (1990). "Impact of Export Market Expansion Strategy on Export Performance" *International Marketing Review* Volume 7, Issue 4, 41-51.

[15] Orville C. Walker, Jr., Harper W. Boyd, Jr., John Mullins, and Jean-Claude Larreche (2003). *Marketing Strategy: A Decision-Focused Approach.* 4th Edition. New York: McGraw- Hill Irwin.

[16] Charles L. Gautschi and Michael E. Werner (1983). "Planning and Organizing for Internal Growth Ventures" *Managerial Planning* (November/December) Volume 32, Issue 3, 21-26.

[17] Ronald Alsop and Bill Abrams (eds.) (1986). *The Wall Street Journal on Marketing.* New York: Dow Jones & Company, Inc.

[18] Orville C. Walker, Jr., Harper W. Boyd, Jr., John Mullins, and Jean-Claude Larreche, 2003.

[19] http://people.smu.edu/acambre/nova/history.html, December 30, 2002; David Ricks, Marilyn Y. C. Fu, and Jeffrey S. Arpan (1974). *International Business Blunders.* Columbus, Oh.: Grid, Inc.

[20] http://www.gm.com/company/corp_info/history/?section=BeyondAuto&layer =SpecialTrans&action=open&page=head, June 23, 2003.

[21] Robert Sherefkin (2003). "Big 3 no Longer are Major Players in U.S. Defense" *Automotive News* (March 31) Volume 77, Issue 6031, 40.

[22] Al Lewis (2003). "McD's Golden Arches Fall" *Denver Post* (January 19) Final Edition, K.01.

[23] Roger Calatone and Roger G. Cooper (1981). "New Product Scenarios: Prospects for Success" *Journal of Marketing* (Spring) Issue 45, 48-60.

[24] Arpan, 1974.

[25] Xcel Energy Company of Colorado offers this as a service for its Northern Colorado customers who are willing to pay a slight additional charge to use energy produced by this non-polluting energy source.

[26] William L. Shanklin (1979) "Strategic Business Planning: Yesterday, Today, and Tomorrow" *Business Horizons* (October) Volume 22, Issue 5, 7.

[27] Michael A. Brost and Brian H. Kleiner (1995). "New Developments in Corporate Diversification Strategies" *Management Research News* Volume 18, Issue 3-5, 24-33.

[28] Tim Morris (1987). "Management Update: Strategy and Organisation" *Journal of General Management* (Winter) Volume 13, Issue 2, 90-96.

[29] Howard Thomas (1983). "Risk Analysis and the Formulation of Acquisition Diversification Strategies" *Long Range Planning* (April) Volume 16, Issue 2, 28.

[30] Leslie E. Palich, Gary R. Carini, and Samuel L. Seaman (2000). "The Impact of Internationalization on the Diversification-Performance Relationship: A Replication and Extension of Prior Research" *Journal of Business Research* (April) Volume 48, Issue 1, 43-54.

[31] Michael E. Porter (1985). *Competitive Advantage: Creating and Sustaining Superior Performance.* New York: The Free Press.

[32] Anne Marie Knott (2001). *Venture Design.* New York: Entity Press.

[33] Charles W. Smithson (1998). *Managing Financial Risk: A Guide to Derivative Products, Financial Engineering, and Value Maximization.* New York: McGraw-Hill.

[34] Anne Marie Knott (2001). *Venture Design.* New York: Entity Press.

[35] Charles W. Smithson (1998). *Managing Financial Risk: A Guide to Derivative Products, Financial Engineering, and Value Maximization.* New York: McGraw-Hill.

[36] Patrick Dunne and Robert F. Lusch (1999). *Retailing.* 3rd Edition. Fort Worth, Tx.: The Dryden Press.

[37] Pearce and Robinson, 2000.

[38] Jay Galbraith (1973). *Designing Complex Organizations.* Readings, Mass.: Addison-Wesley Publishing Company.

[39] Jay R. Galbraith (2002). *Designing Organizations: An Executive Guide to Strategy, Structure, and Process.* New and Revised. San Francisco, Ca.: Jossey-Bass & Sons, Inc.

[40] Peters and Waterman, p. 318.

[41] William D. Bygrave (1994). *The Portable MBA in Entrepreneurship.* New York: John Wiley & Sons, Inc.

[42] Lisa H. Newton, and Maureen M. Ford (2000). *Taking Sides: Clashing Views on Controversial Issues in Business Ethics and Society.* 6th Edition. Guilford, CT: Duskin/ McGraw-Hill.

[43] Emmett J. Vaughan and Therese M. Vaughan (1999). *Fundamentals of Risk and Insurance Management.* 8th Edition. New York: John Wiley & Sons, Inc.

[44] Michael Lubatkin (1983). "Mergers and the Performance of the Acquiring Firm" *Academy of Management. The Academy of Management Review* (April) Volume 8, Issue 2, 218-225.

[45] Milton C. Lauenstein (1985). "Diversification -- The Hidden Explanation of Success" *Sloan Management Review* (Fall) Volume 27, Issue 1, 49-55.

[46] Mark A. Fox and Robert T. Hamilton (1994). "Ownership and Diversification: Agency Theory or Stewardship Theory" *The Journal of Management Studies* (January) Volume 31, Issue 1, 69-81.

[47] Richard P. Rumelt (1974). *Strategy, Structure, and Performance.* Boston, Mass.: Harvard Business School Press.

[48] Michael Lubatkin and Ronald C. Rogers (1989). "Diversification, Systematic Risk, And Shareholder Return: A Capital Market Extension of Rumlet's 1974 Study", *Academy of Management Journal,* (June) Volume 32, Issue 2, 454-465.

[49] James F. Peltz (2002). "Conglomerates Still Cast a Giant Shadow; The multifaceted, Multinational Business Model Continues to Confound Critics and Attract Investors." *The Los Angeles Times* (May 5), C1.

[50] Robert M. Grant (2002). *Contemporary Strategy Analysis.* 4th Edition. Oxford, England: Blackwell Publishers, Ltd.

[51] Stephen L. Nesbitt and Randall R. King (1989). "Business Diversification: Has It Taken a Bad Rap?" *Mergers and Acquisitions* (November/December) Volume 24, Issue 3, 24-27.

[52] Stuart L. Gillan, John W. Kensinger, and John D. Martin (2000). "Value Creation and Corporate Diversification: The Case of Sears, Roebuck & Co." *Journal of Financial Economics* (January) Volume 55, Issue 1, 103-137.

[53] Several studies have attempted to develop measurements for firm diversification. See Rakesh B. Sambharya (2000). "Assessing the Construct Validity of Strategic and SIC-Based Measures of Corporate Diversification" *British Journal of Management* (June) Volume 11, Issue 2, 163-173; Alok Srivastava, Satish Nargundkar, and Ronald F. Green (1994). "An Empirical Evaluation of the Equivalence of Categorical and Continuous Measures of Diversity" *Journal of Business Research* (February) Volume 29, Issue 2, 145-149; Michael Lubatkin, Hemant Merchant, and Narasimhan Srinivasan (1993). "Construct Validity of Some Unweighted Product-Count Diversification Measures" *Strategic Management Journal* (September) Volume 14, Issue. 6, 433-449; Robert E. Hoskisson, Michael A. Hitt, Richard A. Johnson, and Douglas D. Moesel (1993). "Construct Validity of an Objective (Entropy) Categorical Measure of Diversification Strategy" *Strategic Management Journal* (March) Volume 14, Issue. 3, 215-235; Sayan Chatterjee and James D. Blocher (1992). "Measurement of Firm Diversification: Is it Robust?"*Academy of Management Journal* (October) Volume 35, Issue 4, 874-888.

[54] From the 10-K for 2001, files in June, 2002 with the Securities and Exchange Commission.

[55] Adapted from the findings from Rumelt, R. P. 1974. *Strategy, Structure and Economic Performance.* Boston: The Harvard Business School.

[56] Andrew J. Sherman (1998). *Mergers and Acquisitions from A to Z: Strategic and Practical Guidance for Small- and Middle-Market Buyers and Sellers.* New York: AMACOM.

[57] Jeff Buckstein (1998). "Taking on the Takeover" *CGA Magazine* (February) Volume 32, Issue 2, 10-16.

[58] William N. Pugh, Sharon L. Oswald, and John S. Jahera Jr. (2000). "The Effect of ESOP Adoptions on Corporate Performance: Are There Really Performance Changes? *Managerial and Decision Economics* (July-August) Volume 21, Issue 5, 167-180.

[59] Nancy Hubbard (2002). "Merger or Murder?" *Financial World* (July), pgs. 22-26.

[60] Wilbur M. Yegge (1996). *A Basic Guide for Buying and Selling a Company.* New York: John Wiley & Sons, Inc.

[61] Mahendra Rajand and Michael Forsyth (2002). "Hostile Bidders, Long-Term Performance, and Restructuring Methods: Evidence from the UK" *American Business Review* (January) Volume 20, Issue 1, 71-81.

[62] John Reosti (2002). "MAF of Chicago Has Deal to Acquire a Local Rival" *American Banker* Volume 167, Issue 241, 8.

[63] Chern Yek Kwok (2001). "May Completes Purchase of 13 Former Montgomery Ward Stores" *St. Louis Post – Dispatch* (April 13), C8.

[64] Based on data from Research Insight, December, 2002, proprietary software from Standard & Poor's Inc.

[65] Randall Heron and Erik Lie (2002). "Operating Performance and the Method of Payment in Takeovers" *Journal of Financial and Quantitative Analysis* (March) Volume 37, Issue 1, 137-155.

[66] Philip Brown; Raymond da Silva Rosa (1998). "Research Method and the Long-Run Performance of Acquiring Firms" *Australian Journal of Management* (June)Volume 23, Issue 1, 23-38.

[67] Antony Cherin and Michael Hergert (1989). "Acquisition And Divestiture Strategy: The Stockholders' Perception" The Mid - Atlantic Journal of Business (May) Volume 25, Issue 7, 13-24.

[68] Andrew P. Dickerson, Heather D. Gibson, and Euclid Tsakalotos (2000). "Internal vs. External Financing of Acquisitions: Do Managers Squander Retained Profits?" *Oxford Bulletin of Economics and Statistics* (July) Volume 62, Issue 3, 417-431.

[69] John Child, Robert Pitkethly, and David Faulkner (1999). "Changes in Management Practice and the Post-Acquisition Performance Achieved by Direct Investors in the UK" *British Journal of Management* (September) Volume 10, Issue 3, 185-198.

[70] James D. Parrino and Robert S. Harris (1999). "Takeovers, Management Replacement, and Post-Acquisition Operating Performance: Some Evidence from the 1980s" *The Bank of America Journal of Applied Corporate Finance* (Winter) Volume 11, Issue 4, 88-97.

[71] Paul Magnusson (2002). "Tom Ridge's Megamerger: Advice from Corporate America" *Business Week* (December 23) Volume 3813, 41.

[72] O'Donnell, J. 2001. "United, US Airways Call off Merger." http://www.usatoday.com/money/biztravel/2001-07-27-justice-department.htm July 27, 2001.

[73] Michel E. Porter (1985). *Competitive Advantage: Creating and Sustaining Superior Performance.* New York: The Free Press.

[74] Gareth R. Jones and Charles W.L. Hill (1988). "A Transactional Cost Analysis of Strategy-Structure Choice" *Strategic Management Journal* Issue 9, 159-172.

[75] Sean Milmo (2000). "Key Objective" *Chemical Market Reporter* (October 2) Volume 258, Issue 14, 32-33.

[76] Tom Peters (1994). "Forward March" *Incentive* (July) Volume 168, Issue 7, 14.

[77] Richard D'Aveni and David J. Ravenscraft (1994). "Economies of Integration Versus Bureaucracy Costs: Does Vertical Integration Improve Performance?" *Academy of Management Journal* (October) Volume 37, Issue 5, 1167-1206.

[78] Ibid.

[79] Joseph Peyrefitte, Peggy A. Golden, and Jeff Brice, Jr. (2002). "Vertical Integration and Economic Performance: A Managerial Capability Framework" *Management Decision* Volume 40, Issue 3, 217-226.

[80] We would like to thank the reviewers from the University of Southern Colorado, James Madison University, and the University of Notre Dame for their comments.

[81] William Wells, John Burnett, and Sandra Moriarty (2000). *Advertising: Principles and Practices.* 5th Edition. Upper Saddle River, N.J.: Prentice-Hall, Inc.

[82] Gary Hamel and C.K. Prahalad (1994). *Competing for the Future.* Boston, Mass.: Harvard Business School Press.

[83] Ironically, GM has discontinued the Camaro product line as of 2003.

[84] Paul M. Healy, Krishna G. Palepu, and Richard S. Ruback (1997). "Which Takeovers are Profitable? Strategic or Financial" *Sloan Management Review* (Summer) Volume 38, Issue 4, 45-57.

[85] Orville C. Walker, Jr., Harper W. Boyd, Jr., John Mullins, and Jean-Claude Larreche, 2003.

[86] P. Rajan Varadarajan and Manjit S Yadav (2002). "Marketing Strategy and the Internet: An Organizing Framework" *Academy of Marketing Science* (Fall) Volume 30, Issue 4, 296-312.

[87] James B. Edwards (2001). "Kaizen: The leading edge in cost management strategy" *The Journal of Corporate Accounting & Finance* (March/April) Volume 12, Issue 3, 1-4.

[88] Robert F. Hartley (2001). *Marketing Mistakes and Successes.* 8th Edition. New York: John Wiley & Sons, Inc.

[89] Ibid.

[90] Michael Knie-Andersen (2002). "Banks: Advisers or Sellers of Mortgage Loans?" *Journal of Financial Services Marketing* (August) Volume 7, Issue 1, 15-24.

[91] Danny Miller (1986). "Configurations of Strategy and Structure: Towards a Synthesis" *Strategic Management Journal* (May/June) Volume 7, Issue 3, 233-250.

[92] Ian Wilkinson and Louise Young (2002). "On Cooperating: Firms, Relations and Networks" *Journal of Business Research* (February) Volume 55, Issue 2, 123-132.

[93] David Faulkner and Mark deRond (eds.) (2000). *Cooperative Strategy: Economic, Business, and Organizational Issues.* New York: Oxford University Press.

[94] Jeffrey H. Dyer; Harbir Singh (1998). "The Relational View: Cooperative Strategy and Sources of Interorganizational Competitive Advantage" *The Academy of Management Review* (October)Volume 23, Issue 4, 660-679.

[95] C. Oliver (1997). "Sustainable Competitive Advantage: Combining Institutional and Resource-Based Views" *Strategic Management Journal* Volume 18, 697-714.

[96] Dyer and Singh, 1998.

[97] Kimberly C. Gleanson, Ike Mathur, and Roy A. Wiggins, III (2003). "Evidence of Value Creation in the Financial Services Industries Through the Use of Joint Ventures and Strategic Alliances" *The Financial Review* (May) Volume 38, Issue 2, 213-234.

[98] Peggy A. Golden and Marc Dollinger (1993). "Cooperative Alliances and Competitive Strategies in Small Manufacturing Firms" *Entrepreneurship Theory and Practice* (Summer) Volume 17, Issue 4, 43-56.

[99] Orly Yeheske, Oded Shenkar, Avi Fiegenbaum, Ezra Cohen, and Iris Geffen (2001). "Cooperative Wealth Creation: Strategic Alliances in Israeli Medical-Technology Ventures" *The Academy of Management Executive* (February) Volume 15, Issue 1, 16-25.

[100] Rosabeth M. Kanter (1990). "When Giants Learn Cooperative Strategies" *Planning* Review (January/February) Volume 18, Issue 1, 15-21.

[101] John W. Stewart (2002). "Want to Stay in the Home Loan Game? Consider Joint Ventures" *US Banker* (December) Volume 112, Issue 12, 62.

[102] Hemant Merchant (2003). "Joint Venture Characteristics and Shareholder Value Creation: The Pervasive Role of Partner Nationality" *Management International Review* (First Quarter) Volume 43, Issue 1, 21-40.

[103] Yadong Luo (2002). "Contract, Cooperation, and Performance in International Joint Ventures" *Strategic Management Journal* (October) Volume 23, Issue 10, 903-919.

[104] John A. Pearce II and Louise Hatfield (2002) "Performance Effects of Alternative Joint Venture Resource Responsibility Structures" *Journal of Business Venturing* (July) Volume 17, Issue 4, 343-364.

[105] Vijay Pothukuchi, Fariborz Damanpour, Jaepil Choi, Chao C. Chen, and Seung Ho Park (2002). "National and Organizational Culture Differences and International Joint Venture Performance" *Journal of International Business Studies* (Second Quarter) Volume 33, Issue 2, 243-265.

[106] Jeffrey J. Reuer (2000). "Parent Firm Performance Across International Joint Venture Life-Cycle Stages" *Journal of International Business Studies* (First Quarter) Volume 31, Issue 1, 1-20.

[107] Hemant Merchant (2002). "Shareholder Value Creation via International Joint Ventures: Some Additional Explanations" *Management International Review* (First Quarter) Volume 42, Issue 1, 49-69.

[108] Reuer, 2000.

[109] Arthur A. Thompson, r. and A.J. Strickland III (2003). *Strategic Management: Concepts and Cases.* 13th Edition. New York: McGraw-Hill Irwin.

[110] http://www.cisco.com/en/US/partners/pr67/part_strat_alliance_category.html, June 25, 2003.

[111] http://www.ual.com/page/article/0,1360,1258,00.html?navSource=RelatedLinks, June 25, 2003.

[112] Thomas Pietras and Christian Stormer (2001). "Making Strategic Alliances Work" *Business and Economic Review* (July-September) Volume 47, Issue 4, 9-12.

[113] http://waw.wardsauto.com/ar/auto_gm_partners_adopting/index.htm, June 26, 2003.

[114] Pietras and Stormer, 2001.

[115] Jeffrey H. Dyer, Prashant Kale, and Harbir Singh (2001). "How to Make Strategic Alliances Work" *MIT Sloan Management Review* (Summer) Volume 42, Issue 4, 37-43.

[116] T.K. Das and Bing-Sheng Teng (2001). "Trust, Control, and Risk in Strategic Alliances: An Integrated Framework" *Organization Studies* Volume 22, Issue 2, 251-283.

[117] Patricia Norman (2001). "Are Your Secrets Safe? Knowledge Protection in Strategic Alliances" *Business Horizons* (November/December) Volume 44, Issue 6, 51-60.

[118] Das and Teng, 2001.

[119] Pietras and Stormer, 2001.

[120] Minoo Tehrani (2003). "Competitive Strategies, Strategic Alliances, and Performance in International High-Tech Industries: A Cross-Cultural Study"

Journal of American Academy of Business (March) Volume 2, Issue 2, 610-617.

[121] Dyer, Kale, and Singh, 2001.

[122] Tehrani, 2003.

[123] Maurizio Zollo, Jeffrey J. Reuer, and Harbir Singh (2002). "Interorganizational Routines and Performance in Strategic Alliances" *Organization Science* (November/December) Volume 13, Issue 6, 701-713.

[124] Tim Rowley, Dean Behrens, and David Krackhardt (2000). "Redundant Governance Structures: An Analysis of Structural and Relational Embeddedness in the Steel and Semiconductor Industries" *Strategic Management Journal* (March) Volume 21, Issue 3, 369-386.

[125] Frank T. Rothaermel (2001). "Complementary Assets, Strategic Alliances, and the Incumbent's Advantage: An Empirical Study of Industry and Firm Effects in the Biopharmaceutical Industry" *Research Policy* (October) Volume 30, Issue 8, 1235-1251.

[126] Tara J. Shawyer (2002). "Determinants of Bank Merger Premiums" *Bank Accounting & Finance* (October) Volume 15, Issue 6, 26-29.

[127] Steven B. Steinberg (2002). "Due Diligence for Mergers and Acquisitions" *Rough Notes* (December) Volume 145, Issue 12, 14-16.

[128] Yakov Amihud, Gayle L. DeLong, and Anthony Saunders (2002) "The Effects of Cross-Border Bank Mergers on Bank Risk and Value" *Journal of International Money and Finance* (November) Volume 21, Issue 6, 857-877.

[129] Klaus Gugler, Dennis C. Mueller, R. Burcin Yurtoglu, and Christine Zulehner (2003). "The Effects of Mergers: An International Comparison" *International Journal of Industrial Organization* (May) Volume 21, Issue 5, 625-653.

[130] David Henry (2002). "Mergers: Why Most Big Deals Don't Pay Off" *Business Week* (October 14) Issue 3803, 60-70.

[131] Jeffrey Marshall (2001). "Are Mergers Paying Off?" *Financial Executive* (March/April) Volume 17, Issue 2, 26-33.

[132] Aigbe Akhigbe, Stephen F. Borde, and Ann Marie Whyte (2000). "The Source of Gains to Targets and Their Industry Rivals: Evidence Based on Terminated Merger Proposals" *Financial Management* (Winter) Volume 29, Issue 4, 101-118.

[133] Karen Kahler Holiday (2000). "Tough enough to take a few punches" *ABA Banking Journal* (December) Volume 92, Issue 12, 41-46.

[134] Donald C. Hambrick (1983). "High Profit Strategies in Mature Capital Goods Industries: A Contingency Approach" *Academy of Management Journal* (December) Volume 26, Issue 4, 687-708.

[135] Marc Jones (2002). "Globalization and Organizational Restructuring: A Strategic Perspective" *Thunderbird International Business Review* (May/June) Volume 44, Issue 3, 325-351.

[136] Ray Suutari (2000/2001). "Rethinking strategy" *CMA Management* (December/January) Volume 74, Issue 10, 10-15.

[137] Jeffrey A. Timmons (1995). "A Harvest Mind-Set" *Success* (October) Volume 42, Issue 8, 41.

[138] R.A. Thietart and Reyes Vivas (1983-1984). "Success Strategies for Declining Activities" *International Studies of Management & Organization* (Winter) Volume 13, Issue 4, 77-92.

[139] J. Kim DeDee and Douglas W Vorhies (1998). "Retrenchment Activities of Small Firms During Economic Downturn: An Empirical Investigation" *Journal of Small Business Management* (July) Volume 36, Issue 3, 46-61.

[140] Helen J. Muller and Howard L. Smith (1985). "Retrenchment Strategies and Tactics for Healthcare Executives" *Hospital & Health Services Administration* (May/June) Volume 30, Issue 3, 31-43.

[141] J. Kim De Dee and Douglas W. Vorhies (1998). "Retrenchment Activities of Small Firms During Economic Downturn: An Empirical Investigation" *Journal of Small Business Management* (July) Volume 36, Issue 3, 46-61.

[142] David S. Kupetz (2003). "The Fundamentals of Business Bankruptcy (Reorganization and Liquidation)" *Business Credit* (May) Volume 105, Issue 5, 38-44, 46.

[143] Lee Dranikoff, Tim Koller, and Antoon Schneider (2002). "Divestiture: Strategy's Missing Link" *Harvard Business Review* (May) Volume 80, Issue 5, 74-83.

[144] Cherin and Hergert, 1989.

[145] Jeff Taylor (2002). "Train Wreck" *Reason* (February) Volume 33, Issue 9, 11-12.

[146] Kupetz, 2003.

[147] Michael J. Sullivan, Claire E. Crutchlev, and Dana J. Johnson (1997). "Motivation for Voluntary Corporate Liquidations: Distress, Agency Conflicts, and Shareholder Gain" *Quarterly Journal of Business and Economics* (Spring) Volume 36, Issue 2, 3-18.

[148] E. Han Kim and John D. Schatzberg (1987). "Voluntary Corporate Liquidations" *Journal of Financial Economics* (December) Volume 19, Issue 2, 311-328.

[149] Aigbe Akhigbe and Jeff Madura (1996). "Intra-Industry Effects of Voluntary Corporate Liquidations" *Journal of Business Finance & Accounting* (September) Volume 23, Issue 7, 915-929.

❧ Chapter Seven ❧
Strategy Implementation:
An Organization Change Approach

Chapter Objectives

1. To develop an understanding of strategy implementation as a change process that aligns the organization within and without the organizational learning.
2. To establish an appreciation of the ways in which firms can successfully and unsuccessfully implement a strategic plan.

3. To recognize and be familiar with the differing levels of strategy implementation
4. To acknowledge the importance of striving for perfect fit between the firm, strategy, and the organization.

Introductory Case: Where has Chrysler Gone? The Daimler Chrysler Merger

Lee Iacocca was the miracle man of Chrysler. Leaving Ford in 1978, President Iacocca first secured federal loan guarantees of $1.5 billion dollars and made Chrysler profitable by 1983 with the introduction of the K car. By 1988 another miracle was needed and of course Lee delivered. After acquiring American Motors Corporation (AMC) in 1987 (primarily for its Jeep brand), Lee staked the company and his reputation on four major products: the minivan, Jeep Grand Cherokee, the LH sedans, and the Ram full-size pickup trucks.[1] When Iococca left the company at the end of 1992, the company was heading back into the black. From 1993-1997 (before the merger with Daimler), the firm posted an average 5% net profit (ahead of its U.S. rivals GM and Ford) and had increased sales revenues by approximately 25%.

Then came the merger. By the year 1998, Chrysler had started to hemorrhage money. It went through $5 billion dollars in cash and lost $1.8 billion dollars in the second half of 2000 while the value of DaimlerChrysler stock dropped from $ 84 billion in 1998 to $39 billion at the end of 2000. Chrysler, now a unit of DaimlerChrysler, struggled mightily since the 1998 merger of Daimler-Benz and Chrysler, though it showed a bit of life in 2002. Granted, it would be premature to use the word revival. Chrysler lost $1.9 billion in 2001 but it did eke out a profit in the first quarter of 2002 and said it would break even by the end of the year. In April of 2002 its sales stopped falling, and it halted its market-share free fall.[2]

But what had happened? Was the merger to blame? What was it that changed that took a seemingly-well-run company, and created so many problems? As problems became apparent, Daimler Chrysler fired Robert Eaton (Lee Iacocca's successor) along with nine other major executives. It then brought in Dieter Zetche, who felt that

Chrysler had carried considerable baggage and needed reorganization. Zetsche brought in his own management team to replace the fired top level executives. He then proceeded to lead a turnaround based on drastic cuts in purchasing costs and a renewed focus on quality improvement. Chrysler pushed ahead with new products such as the redesigned Dodge Ram pickup and Jeep Liberty SUV that had already been in the works. These tactics seemed to have been quite successful since after an adjusted operating loss of 148 million euros in the second quarter of 2001. As a result, Chrysler made a profit of 788 million euros in the second quarter in 2002.[3]

The 1999 merger of Chrysler Corporation and Daimler Benz involved the creation of a truly global corporation by combining two organizations of roughly the same size and in the same industry, but with two very diverse cultures. Chrysler, grounded in market driven American entrepreneurship and forged in the near bankruptcy of the 1980s, emphasized innovation and flexibility, within a highly focused business strategy. Daimler Benz, characterized by structured, hierarchical management, and German engineering excellence, emphasized luxury markets within a highly diversified corporate structure.[4]

This lead to a major culture clash, one that could have been avoided with strategic implementation plans including cultural intervention, with slow assimilation of Chrysler and Daimler values across business units. What could have been strength through synergy (the merging of the best of the two cultures), became forced German efficiency. "The merged company's actions were tied to an onslaught of cultural misunderstandings, intercultural stereotyping, and misguided attempts to maintain intercultural correctness within and outside the organization. This created a xenophobic discourse blaming either side for financial problems."[5]

But from Chrysler's old guard's perspective, however, the real problem was that they had been sold out – Chrysler was no more. Daimler had created a myth about equal partners, and used their public relations department to sell it to the American public. With the marriage myth, the promotion of the idea of two equal partners, Daimler lead reporters and stock holders down the cultural differences scenario stated above and forget to get into the details of the deal itself.[6] Kirk Kerkorian, the largest shareholder of the old Chrysler, has a suit pending against DaimlerChrysler, contending that it misrepresented the combination as a "merger of equals"[7] when it really was a takeover. Lee A. Iacocca, the former Chrysler chairman, complained in the press about the company's failure to bring him back as a consultant.[8] Some employees still have not accepted the merger and have posted their grievances and suggestions on a Web site called chryslertakeover.com. One of the topics on the site was the hope that Lee Iacocca would regain leadership of the company:[9]

"After the expiration of a "gag" order, Lee Iacocca has indicated his desire to return Chrysler to profitability. "I'd give my right arm to do it...Chrysler was my life. I really feel bad where it is today." [Detroit news, 3/17/02] Employees can change the direction of this company. Chrysler *could* be split-off from Daimler with a combination of major shareholders, employee ownership (similar to most airlines) and new stock offering (IPO). We've already got a REAL turnaround expert on our side who'll take the job. Many of our German friends would also like to see the end of this "merger", and its disastrous effect on Daimler stock; they'd also love to show Schrempp the door."[10]

On February 4, 2003 DaimlerChrysler announced preliminary key figures for the Group's performance in the 2002 financial year including an operating profit of EUR 6.9 billion after an adjusted operating loss of EUR 1.3 billion in 2001. Despite difficult market conditions, DaimlerChrysler's operating profit was thus more than four times as high as in the prior year. The Board of Management proposed to the Supervisory Board to distribute a dividend of EUR 1.50 per share for 2002 (2001: EUR 1.00), a 50% increase.[11] (Please note that as of February 10, 2003 that the chryslertakeover.com site had announced that it would be closing shortly.)

Strategy Implementation

Over the past seven chapters we have explored the strategy formulation process (Steps 1-4 of the Planning Process): surveying the internal and external environment, reconciling the firm's mission, values, goals and objectives with the realities of the firm and its marketplace, and matching the firm's resources and mission with the most viability market opportunities (See Figure 7.1 below).

The formulation of a good strategic plan is a formidable and challenging task since its fundamental duty is to create value for the customer. Value-creation, whether it take the form of low-cost, differentiation, or value-for money, is achieved primarily via strategy formulation through the marketing processes of the firm. A firm's product/services, pricing, promotion, product distribution creates a marketing mix, which determines the firm's relative position in the market re: its competitors and consumers' perceptions (called market-driven strategy).[12] Capabilities associated with strategy formulation therefore include market sensing, customer linking, channel bonding, technology monitoring, and new product/service/strategy development; activities associated with entrepreneurial characteristics of the firm.[13]

Yet finding opportunities, reaching out to stakeholders, and developing strategic plans is not enough to ensure that a firm can capitalize on those opportunities, work with stakeholders, and put the plan into action – make the vision a reality. Firms must also possess the managerial and organizational competencies that support customer order fulfillment, product pricing, purchasing, financial management and cost control, technology development, manufacturing/ transformation processes, human resources management, and health and safety systems (just to name a few) that facilitate the implementation of the strategic plan.[14]

Here is where we can dip into the entrepreneurship literature to help us better understand strategy implementation. Most entrepreneurs who are excellent at formulating winning plans fail to grow their businesses into large firms because demand for their products and services outstrip their firms' support systems. They think big but act small because they do not invest in the infrastructures that support growth (people, skills, technology, culture, operating systems) and cannot transition from an entrepreneurial to a professionally managed firm.[15] They not only must talk-the-talk, they must also walk-the-walk and in short lack the executive skills obligatory to manage a large, complex firm. More specifically, although entrepreneurs are

Figure 7.1
The Strategic Planning Process
Step 5 – Implementation: Human Change Considerations

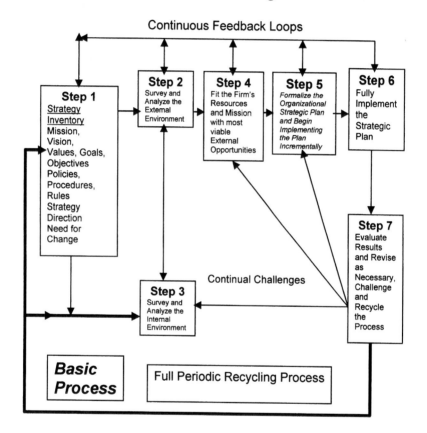

excellent at dealing with and confronting changes in the marketplace, they tend to be weak at seeing and seeking value within their own organization, and also may have a difficult time with issues of employee trust, teaching, and personal integrity.[16]

   This last issue brings us back to the Daimler Chrysler case. The strategy behind the merger seemed a sound one; combine U.S.

entrepreneurship with German engineering and obtain fun cars that performed well. The companies possessed complimentary product lines (Chrysler's lower cost cars including Jeep, trucks and the very popular minivans with Mercedes Benz's luxury quality vehicles) and occupied different market segments. One large company could achieve economies of scale and purchasing power that the two smaller firms could not. So why did it take this merger so long (four to five years) to make a profit after the merger took place?

The problem in this case dealt with how Daimler Chrysler implemented the new strategy. First, Daimler's marriage to Chrysler was clearly a takeover and employees and stockholders resented being lied to. More specifically, Chrysler's management and culture was of no value to Daimler and therefore both were jettisoned when the new company was formed. Top management's unilateral actions led to high levels of employee resistance and therefore slowed down the change process (in structure, strategy, and operations). The Chrysler Division alone lost over $4 billion in the first two years after the merger leaving many observers wondering if the company would survive as a single entity. Only in the later half of 2002, and later in early 2003 has the Chrysler Division turned the corner and demonstrated profitability.

What is Strategy Implementation?

We define strategy implementation as those actions taken by a firm to put their strategic plans into place by either changing their mission, changing their environment, or changing their resources, capabilities and internal operations. The key term in the definition of strategy implementation is change -- can the firm *make the necessary changes* in order to move it into a better market position? Yin, Heald and Vogel suggest that strategy implementation is dependent upon two factors: the inherent validity or strength of the plan developed to position the business (do our decisions make sense in light of the available information?) and the ability to produce the changes the plan requires (can we change ourselves or our market as required by the plan?).[17]

Successful and Unsuccessful Implementation.[18] Under the above definition of strategy implementation there are two types of successful implementation plans and two unsuccessful implementation plans as suggested in Table 7-1.

Table 7-1
Successful and Unsuccessful Implementation Plans

	Required Changes Made	Required Changes Not Made
Valid Plan	Type 1 Success	Type 1 Failure
Invalid Plan	*Type 2 Failure*	*Type 2 Success*

Success Type 1 and Failure Type 1 are easy to understand. The firm develops a justifiable strategic plan and either can or cannot make the necessary changes within the organization or in the marketplace to enact the plan. If changes are made, they result in the better positioning of the firm, a more sustainable competitive advantage, and higher profitability. If the changes are not made, then the firm's competitive position would at best remain stable or perhaps deteriorate over time.

We can easily apply these definitions to the Daimler Chrysler case. Daimler's strategy was to broaden the competitive scope of the firm by merging with Chrysler. Each entity brought to the merged organization differing target markets and differing expertise. The underlying premise is that the merged firm would have a broader set of capabilities derived through synergy and therefore be able to better serve the larger target market of Daimler Chrysler. The implementation failed in the short run since Daimler bungled the preparation of Chrysler's employees for the merger, therefore causing massive losses in Chrysler's operation. In the long run, however, the implementation of the merger strategy seems to have been successful given the firm's profitability in early 2003.

Type 2 Successes and Failures are quite different from Type 1s. A Type 2 Failure refers to businesses having the change processes in place so as to institute an illogical plan. That is, the firm develops a very poor plan but makes the necessary changes in the environment or within the firm to implement the plan. A great example of a Type 2 Failure was when Coca Cola decided to change the taste of its leading product, Coke in 1984. Coke was losing market share to Pepsi Cola from the late 70s and into the early 80s and Coca Cola had conducted market research that showed that soft cola drinkers preferred the taste of Pepsi over Coke. They developed a new coke flavor which taste tested more favorably than either Pepsi or Coke and proceeded to advertise "New Coke" and dump the old Coke line.

The public's reaction to Coca Cola's move was immediate and strong. Major protests arose around the country - Coca Cola was tinkering with an American icon and received over 5000 letters a day objecting to the change. On July 11, 1985, Coca Cola bowed to public pressure and brought back its original formula as Coke Classic.[19] So where did Coke's thinking go wrong? Coca Cola assumed that Coke drinkers were loyal because they equated 'better taste' with sales; taste (a product feature) sold soft drinks. Coca Cola failed to understand the value of their own advertising in making the Coke brand part of American tradition and more importantly did not market test how the public would react to a change in Coke's taste. In this example, Coca Cola had a horrific plan that they properly executed.

Type 2 Successes are quite fascinating in that success occurs when the firm develops an invalid plan and fails to implement it. We are sure that many businesses may have had Type 2 Successes but these are not the types of successes that businesses are bound to report, or to even be reported in many publications, since these firms would be admitting to a double failure. The real question with a Type 2 Success is how did the organization manage not to implement the invalid plan? This question brings us back to the heart of implementation - what are the conditions under which change will or will not be implemented?

Implementation as a Change/Intervention Process

The DaimlerChrysler case helps us define the first definition of strategy implementation, that of *facilitating and supporting the change process*. As we suggested in Chapter 1, it is human nature to resist change and any strategy that proposes a change to the operating systems of the firm will then encounter change barriers. For example, it should have been expected that workers at Chrysler would have opposed the changes in top management and would be resentful if anyone criticizing their way of doing things. But is resistance always to be expected?

Resistance to Change. At the *individual level*, employee resistance to change can be explained through the psychological and work forces acting on an employee. At the *psychological level*, an individual is comprised of a value system; a set of individual values (basic convictions of right and wrong) which tend to be both stable and enduring over time. These values are translated into attitudes (evaluative statements or judgments) that are comprised of cognitive (opinion or belief), affective (emotions/feelings), and behavioral (a bias towards acting a certain way) components.[20] Several researchers in the field (i.e. Elbing, Koolhaas, Festinger) have noted that individuals tend towards consistency between their values, attitudes and behaviors and will seek equilibrium when encountering information that challenges that balance.[21]

For example, a person who has always believed in honesty being the best policy (value), and who hates politicians because he or she thinks that they have to lie and cheat (attitude), and therefore doesn't vote (behavior), may have their belief system challenged if a highly regarded close friend runs for political office. This will create cognitive dissonance for the individual and he or she may seek equilibrium through the use of defense mechanisms (aggression, withdrawal, fixation, compromise, and denial), which oppose change or actually change his or her attitude and behaviors.[22] The person may then change his or her belief (that not all politicians are bad), change behaviors (go and vote for his or her friend running for office) or may take a defensive position and go as far as withdrawing his or her friendship in order to protect his or her belief system.

A second component to consider is the relationship between the employee and his or her job. Much of the work of employees falls into the category of routine behavior in that there is a prescribed methodology for performing a task in a certain manner.[23]   The routinization of work life creates a comfort zone for the employee, that is, the job becomes a habit and is intertwined with other customary behaviors. Even in the cases of non-routine and specialized labor, the work becomes an ingrained part of an employee's persona to a point where the employee may treat a change in working conditions as a threat to his or her self-identity.[24]

At the *group or social level*, the group also has values, attitudes, beliefs and behaviors and is comprised of cultures and subcultures. Resistance to change is derived from conformity to group norms and values; informal pressures and sanctions imposed on the individual to fit into the organization's social order.[25] Any change that is proposed that is contrary to the group's norms will be rejected by its members although at the individual level each member may see the change as valuable.

The *organization's systems and subsystems* are also factors that may hinder change. Organizations are subject to what analysts call inertia,[26] that is, firms will continue to operate in a similar manner (follow the same plan) unless they encounter forces that derail or challenge these processes. Lewin developed the field of force field analysis in order to model the organizational forces that push for and against change and noted that organizations (as well as people) will take the path of least resistance (the path between the pushing and pulling forces) in reacting to these countervailing forces.[27] See Figure 7.2 below.

Overcoming Resistance through Intervention. The ability of the firm to enact change at the individual level (overcome his or her resistance) is based upon the flexibility or maturity level of that individual (called employee readiness) coupled with the appropriate influences and rewards associated with the employee changing behavior.[28] Barnard noted that for an employee to change, that he or she must understand the nature of the change requested, be mentally and physically able to comply with that change, and believe that the change is in his or her own best interest and in the interest of the firm.[29]

Figure 7.2
Internal and External Forces for Change and
the Path of Least Resistance

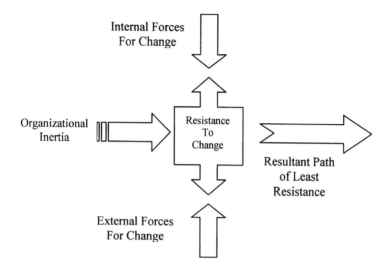

The organization must also deal with the employee's tendency to act out of habit (routine behaviors protected with affiliated attitudes and values) and conforming to group norms while also addressing the firm's tendency to follow old methods and utilize current systems (inertia) in solving new problems.

Hence, to overcome resistance to change, the firm must intervene in the day-to-day activities of employees, groups and the organization as a whole in an appropriate manner to reduce resistance to proposed changes and the newly formulated strategies. Such interventions are "sets of structured activities in which selected organizational units (target groups or individuals) ... with the goals of organizational improvement and individual development."[30] Intervention techniques can include coaching and counseling, skills development, work redesign, structural and cultural changes, and sensitivity training. We will describe these further in detail in the next chapter.

However, one can make the decision to intervene into organizational activities without preparing the firm for change (see Figure 1.3 The Integration of Strategic Management and Organization Development). As we discussed in Chapter 1, the firm must actively take steps to prepare the organization for change prior to both the formulation and implementation of a strategic plan. The first step, unfreezing, requires that the firm determine the competencies, values, motivations, and attitudes of its employees and determine their readiness for change.[31] If the employees are not ready for change, then the firm must invest time, energy and resources to provide a safety net for employees who may feel uneasy about the change, or worse cannot change. This readiness must include the employees' understanding of the need for the firm to change its strategy and how it currently does business. This understanding requires that the firm be open and honest with employees about the current state of the organization's situation (this usually includes financial data and the general state of the industry), sharing as much information as possible, and enlisting employees as active participants in the change.

The second step of overcoming resistance to change involves first performing a SWOT analysis and then the sharing of the findings and as much support data as possible. This also includes showing how the proposed changes developed from the SWOT analysis impact the firm, and that theses changes are both desirable and possible. The purpose then of the intervention techniques is to help *move* the firm from its current path to a new course of action and to allow employees to become part of the change process (be part of the solution and not the problem) as demonstrated in Figure 7.3 below.

Emphasis in the moving process is on empowering employees and sharing with them the new strategy and the allied vision of the firm. The final step, *refreezing*, requires asking whether the changes made by the firm occurred and did the expected results from those changes also take place. We will present and discuss the assessment and evaluation of the strategic plan in Chapter 9 and includes a determination as to whether the firm's performance has changed as per set goals and objectives.

Figure 7.3
Organization Interventions: Resistance and Forces for Change

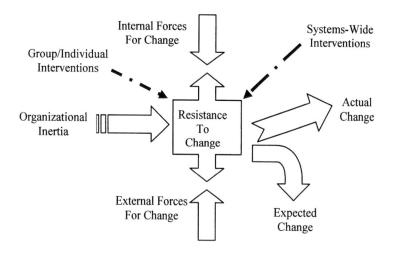

Implementation as a Learning Process

The fundamental underpinnings to overcoming resistance and creating change is that in order for employees, groups, and systems to change, the firm must provide employees with adequate information to persuade them that change is warranted and required. The nature of any intervention is educational in nature, that is, managers need to create a learning environment by employing what is called an action research approach to strategic implementation and therein teach employees problem-solving skills.[32]

As we suggested in Chapter 1, strategy implementation is double-loop learning. It is defined as organizations becoming expert at learning how to learn by developing and nurturing a community of learners. This viewpoint has two common elements: education as a social and socializing function as well as a shift in emphasis from telling to learning thereby changing the manager's role from autocrat to coach and fellow learner. Firms need to create an egalitarian community of learners, where the employees and management share information, expertise and resources in order to solve common problems.[33] Yet this begs the question as to what is the nature of learning.

Learning and Motivation. Central to the learning process is the motivation that drives the employee to learn. Considered a general motivator (unlearned but psychologically-based), curiosity and the drive for competency is considered a core component of human existence.[34] Employees' desires to learn may be driven by a combination of intrinsic motivators (personal satisfaction derived from achievement and self-recognition) and/or extrinsic motivators (learning leads to better performance which in turns leads to higher pay and bonuses).

Regardless of the particular motivator at work, for employees to want to learn they have to have an unmet desire or a specific need that they then translate into a certain set of actions or drives and directed them towards a goal which will satisfy that specific need. These drives are modified by the employee's expectation of reaching the desired goal (by learning this will I achieve my objective?), the desirability of that goal, and the consequences or rewards associated with obtaining that goal (what do I get if I learn this?).[35] This may be disheartening for employers who send employees to off-site training and educational programs without ensuring that some form of reward is in place for these actions, whether the rewards are intrinsic or extrinsic. Learning will not occur unless there is a clear connection for the employee between effort (working hard), performance (demonstrated learning) and outcomes (rewards).[36]

Employee needs. Needs are unique to each learner. However, they can be categorized by the type of need that drives them. The most basic theory of human motivation which most business students are familiar with, Maslow's Hierarchy of Needs Theory,[37] seems to be an appropriate vehicle for providing a general description for the differing types of needs of the learner.

In our discussion here of strategy implementation, we present Maslow's theory in a slightly modified fashion in that we see motivation as not necessarily a hierarchy (higher level needs versus lower level needs), where individuals must satisfy lower level needs in order to become motivated by higher level needs. Research evidence contradicts the hierarchical nature of human needs in that it indicates that multiple needs can exist simultaneously and that these needs may turn into motivational drives (actions taken to reduce a need) as stirred by situational factors.[38] Rather, we envision needs as forming a series of concentric circles where the more external rings represent those needs that are satisfied through external stimuli or resources (i.e. bonuses, promotions) and the more internal rings represent those needs satisfied through personal growth and development. This approach to human needs fuses the concept of locus of control with needs theory, that is, that as individuals begin to view their lives from being controlled by externalities (forces they cannot control) to being controlled by themselves (internal locus), they are then moving from what Maslow would call lower level needs to higher level needs.[39]

Planning, Learning and Organizational Competency. Strategic plans, and the firm, must provide for an environment where employees (based upon their individualized needs) can satisfy their needs and become responsible for their own self-development and learning. Various employees have diverse needs and differing loci of control and implementation plans must be flexible enough to accommodate those differences and employees' ability to manage their own learning processes. Managers need to act as guides to assist employees become better learners and become more proactive in the learning process.

A firm's vision and mission needs to clearly indicate the role that employee development and employee needs play in the formulation and implementation of the firm's strategy. This includes addressing issues of employee empowerment, a focus on employee development and growth, and the sharing of information and ideas. Learning must consequently occur at the more macro, organizational level. As Wick and Leon point out, the learning organization must have a leader with vision, a detailed, measurable strategic plan, rapid sharing of information, inventiveness, and the ability to take action.[40]

Building a learning organization is also about acquiring knowledge from the external environment and bringing it into the organization to be used to adapt and make changes. This results in a circular process whereby information is constantly fed into organizational processes. The successful firm constantly has its organizational ear to the ground. Only by developing learning organizations that use the knowledge they acquire can organizations continue to adapt and respond to their changing environment.[41]

Learning has been taken so seriously in the business sector that the Corporate University idea as an important strategic development platform has taken a firm hold with more than 1,600 corporate universities.[42] For many companies, the move to a CU model is a direct reflection of the escalating intellectual challenge that they face not only in scientific innovation and technological development but in their overall business. Some CUs are much more radical in their approach, involving the introduction of more diverse dynamic management programs and explicit intellectual cultures across broad areas of their organization.[43]

Implementation As an Internal Alignment and External Adaptation Process

The concept of organizational adaptation is based upon the fundamental tenets of systems theory and human evolution; firms (top management), like people, strive to survive by altering parts of the organization so as to better mesh with the marketplace.[44] The central theme in most of the literature on strategy implementation until recently focused less on organizational change, intervention, or learning and far more on organizational adaptation and fit within the marketplace. The premise, which has been supported by research, is that the better the fit the better the organization's performance.[45]

The Micro Level. Adaptation occurs at differing levels of organizational analysis. At the micro or individual level, adaptation refers to the ability of employees to align their personal belief systems, attitudes and behaviors with the culture of the firm. Adaptation also refers to employees' capabilities to perform their jobs effectively. Culture and task performance are viewed as intervening factors between the employee and the external environment with the leadership of the firm charged with the function of creating a culture and placing or training employees that can best service the needs of the market.

The Macro Level. The majority of the literature on adaptation or fit seems to deal with more macro issues of how well subsystems or the organization as a whole fits with the marketplace. Here the focus is on the relationship between the firm (including its subsystems), the firm's strategy, and the external environment where the firm's performance is a function of how well these factors are aligned.

Performance = Function (external environment : strategy : internal alignment)

Maximum Performance = (external environment = strategy = internal alignment)[46]

The firm adapts to its situation either by changing the external environment, changing its strategy, or changing its internal alignment, or in some combination.

The macro level can be further broken down into two separate levels of analysis: one dealing with *group and inter-group dynamics*, the other dealing with structured *organizational subsystems* (such as structure, culture, mission, etc.). As we suggested earlier, individuals need to align themselves with the norms and values of the group in order to facilitate change. Groups must also align their internal processes (values, structure, leadership, interactions, tasks, sentiments) with the firm's goals and objectives.[47]

Team cohesiveness or internal social alignment is not necessarily a strong attribute and a compulsory condition for implementing change since groups are quite susceptible to the phenomenon known as "groupthink."[48] Groupthink refers to situations where cohesive groups act superior, exclusive and feel invulnerable. The group shuts off divergent opinion through social and political pressure and ignores information and requests from outsiders, it purposefully misaligns itself with other groups and the organization. Groupthink can become a major impediment to strategy implementation if the group decides that a plan is not in the best interest of the group or its individual members.

The term *inter-group changes* refers to the alignment of reporting relations between various operating units within the firm.

Implementing strategic plans at the inter-team level is dependent upon the ability of differing organizational units to adapt to one another. Brown suggested that in many cases, there is structural conflict due to task interdependence that requires the acclimatization of each group to the other group's differing cultures, missions and values. For example, many sales departments do not work well with finance, production, and engineering departments since sales people are driven by a strong need for self-esteem and affiliation and tend to be both outgoing and charismatic while accountants, engineers, and production supervisors are driven more by achievement and tend to be more sedate and contemplative.[49]

Brown also noted that, like cohesiveness, it is the level of conflict between these groups that will determine whether the outcomes of these interactions are productive or not. Too much conflict will result in poor decision-making and deterioration of future relations while too little conflict will result in either no decisions being made (or made by default) or decisions made on little information. Appropriate levels of conflict can lead to bargaining and problem solving.[50]

Organizational subsystems are a set of tightly and/or loosely connected components that comprise the inner workings of the organization. They include the organization's hierarchical structure, strategy, task/technology and reward systems, shared values and culture, skills and distinctive competencies, leadership style, and staff (human resources), as suggested in Figure 7-4 below. Some of these subsystems may be tightly connected while others are loosely coupled and misaligned. Tightly connected subsystems reinforce the organization's operation and maintain a dynamic equilibrium while loosely connected subsystems produce organizational dissonance and disconnects. Here, implementation is a function of relative fit of the pieces in the subsystem. Notice that the center or nucleus of the firm's subsystems is its core shared values. The effectiveness of a firm is dependent upon the relative alignment between the subsystems with the core values of the business.

For example, a firm which possesses core values of risk-taking and innovation (such as Chrysler Corporation) but hires top level staff with predominately risk-averse backgrounds (Daimler's efficiency orientation) will find that these executives will either adapt more

Figure 7-4
Well Aligned Subsystems: The 7 S Framework[51]

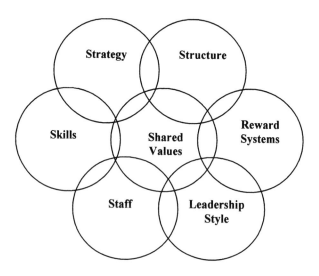

entrepreneurial values (tighten the linkage through employee acclimatization and assimilation), try to change the firm's value system (tighten linkage through a shift in the mission and vision of the firm), or leave the firm (linkage remain loose). The point here is that subsystems need to be linked in such a fashion so that a cause and effect chain develops based upon the relative strength of the linkages in the subsystems. This cause and effect phenomenon is critical in understanding strategy implementation and alignment at the subsystem level in the short run (i.e. why Daimler Chrysler's merger was unsuccessful for the first few years).

However, it is possible that subsystems are so loosely coupled or completely disconnected so that a change in one subsystem has little or no impact on the other; adaptation does not occur. If Daimler Chrysler's shift in values from being proactive and entrepreneurial to being more efficiency-driven in no way affected the employee compensation and reward system at the Chrysler Division, then employees (especially the sales staff) were still being rewarded for pushing product rather than making a better and more cost effective automobile. In Kerr's words, Daimler Chrysler would be "rewarding A while hoping for B" and therefore not properly implementing the firm's strategic plan.[52]

Alignment of the firm's subsystems is also important for understanding the dynamics of the implementation of a strategic plan as a moderate run, perhaps six months to approximately three years. It is a mistake to expect that all subsystems would be perfectly aligned and that perfectly aligned systems would remain so. Internal misalignments are normally cause by either changes in the external environment (political, social, economic, technological, and competitive position) that impact subsystems or internal changes meant to implement strategy and/or realign subsystems.

Clearly in Chrysler's situation, numerous subsystems (leadership style, shared values, staffing, strategy, and skills) were impacted by the change in the firm's ownership structure and Chrysler's shrinking competitive position. Fortunately, most misalignments will realign themselves through the path of least resistance. Again, going back to the Chrysler case, it took several years for Chrysler to turn around its profitability as well as for the employees to accept the new ownership arrangements. Deliberate realignments (what we have called interventions) require planning, resources, time and energy on the part of the top management and arguably could have made implementation of the merger more successful more quickly.

Strategy implementation and change in the long run (three years or more) is impacted by which of the subsystems acts as the driving force for the organization and the relative flexibility of each of the subsystems. A driving force is defined as the subsystem or subsystems that steer a firm and in many cases may be its core values. In the Chrysler case, the driving forces were the merger strategy and its change in structure.

The second factor determining the ability to adjust to market changes in the long run is the comparative flexibility of each of the subsystems. Chrysler's core values (arguably a strength under the leadership of Lee Iaocca) were entrenched and inflexible and it was quite predictable that many employees would resist change in those values as reflected by Chrysler's top leaders. Daimler's intervention, so-to-speak, was to clean house of top management and bring in their own executives who possessed Daimler's core values. This approach met great opposition resulting in the lag time between the actual physical merger and the change in corporate values.

The Ecological/Environmental Level. A third perspective of implementation as adaptation is best represented by the notion of collective fit where the firm has no choice but to implement strategies that are imposed by the marketplace, or at least their industry or market segment.[53] Firms must adapt, perhaps through benchmarking, the best practices of the most successful competitors in their industry or strategic business grouping because to do otherwise would be inefficient and foolish. Following the leaders of the herd is the only safe recourse for survival and profitability.

A less extreme interpretation of this approach identifies stakeholders in the marketplace who control certain resources that the firm requires in order to properly operate and a dependency exists between the firm and these stakeholders.[54] The strategy formulation process addresses these stakeholders through SWOT and industry analyses and may implementing strategies that alter the firm's reliance by creating greater interdependencies between the business and its key stakeholders. For example, the firm might absorb or form joint ventures with competitors, and create strategic alliances and network organizations. This version of adaptation at the ecological level requires that the affected internal and external stakeholders be included in the implementation process; that their interests be co-opted by assuming key roles in the firm's change. This usually involves the development of roles, structures and mechanisms needed to coordinate the efforts of multiple organizations and the differing players who represent those organizations' interests.

Synthesis: The Strategy Implementation Process

Given these varying definitions of strategy implementation, one is left asking whether strategy implementation is worth trying to define beyond making strategy happen.[55] Yet, from our perspective, we see the emergence from the literature on implementation theory a model that is not overly dissimilar to the unfreezing, moving, refreezing change model proposed by Kurt Lewin and refined by Edgar Schein.[56]

Strategy as Fit. We believe that the goal of strategy implementation is the execution of a strategic plan that produces a better fit between the firm, its internal processes, and its external environment. *Adaptation* or *fit* is then the goal of any strategic plan (assuming that a better fit produces greater organizational effectiveness and therein higher profits) with the understanding that the actions that the firm takes in implementing the strategic plan should better align the firm's internal systems with its market. Fit is achieved by:

1. Matching the basic structure and management processes to the selected strategy.
2. Simplifying the operations (because of the fit) leading to pervasive comprehension that strengthens and maintains fit.
3. Simplicity - minimizes the need for coordinating mechanisms therefore freeing up resources (employee time, communication, and equipment).[57]

Early fit is the discovery and articulation of a new organization form that like IBM, Hewlett-Packard, General Motors, and Carnegie Steel were able to sustain their competitive advantage because they adopted new organizational structures (functional, divisional, matrix, dynamic network) that best fit their related industry. Fit changes over time. All organizations may fall *out of fit* given changing market conditions, strategic shifts, or internal reorganization. For instance, when Volkswagen discontinued the Beetle line of cars, they accidentally misaligned their strategy with their marketplace. Barnes and Noble developed a web site for ordering their products and services (a new structure) to be more aligned with consumer demands for on-line ordering. (Amazon.com achieved an *early fit*).

How does the firm then strive for the goal of perfect fit?[58] What is then the strategy implementation process? Fit can be achieved by the firm's leadership:

1. *learning* about the organization's situation

2. preparing the firm for *change* by sharing this information and *educating* employees and key stakeholders
3. *empowering* employees and key stakeholders thereby *overcoming resistance* by developing strategic plans with employee and key stakeholder input
4. using the strategic plan to *intervene* in the firm's current operation and *change* its direction (if needed)
5. *educating* and *empowering* employees to *change* themselves, their groups, subsystems, the organization as a whole, and their relationships with key stakeholders
6. providing *feedback* to employees, groups, and stakeholders as to the progress being made in executing the plan.

The success of implementing a firm's strategy is embedded in how well the firm first formulates the strategic plan as well as how the firm monitors and reacts to the plan as it unfolds over time (which we will develop in Chapter 9). The strategic management process then, although depicted as a linear, rational, step-wise model, has many overlapping functions and activities. Several authors, most prominently Henry Mintzberg, have noted that "the assumption in other texts is that strategy is formulated and then implemented ... in reality, formulation and implementation are intertwined as complex interactive processes...".[59]
It could then in fact be argued that, like the subsystems in a firm, strategy formulation, implementation and control processes are far more organic in nature and are coupled (either loosely or tightly) within the firm. The more aligned and tightly coupled these processes are, the more successful firms will be in having an effective strategic management process. We have depicted in Figure 7.4A below the implementation process as bridging strategy formulation and control. Note that certain functions of the implementation process (learning, empowerment, overcoming resistance) must occur during strategy formulation, that the empowerment and evaluation and feedback, although considered part of the control phase of strategy, is critical to ensure proper strategy implementation.

Figure 7.4A
The Strategy Implementation Process

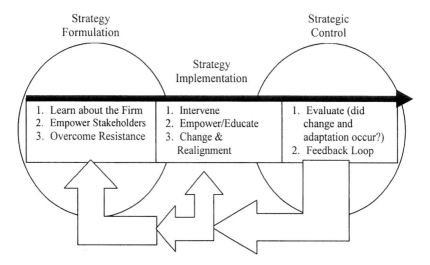

Key Implementation Elements

When top management intervenes within a firm there are usually several organizational elements that the firm changes in order to align its internal processes and adapt to the environment. Besides strategy, which we have discussed at length in the seven previous chapters, firms usually modify their structure, culture, and leadership in order to create a fit with the marketplace. This prior comment in no way reduces the importance of the organization's competencies (skills), its human resources (staff), and its compensation system (reward systems).

In Chapter 1 we explained the importance of developing a learning organization as a crucial component of strategic management. The learning organization is necessary for the organization to develop distinctive competencies and to share and process vital information. The firm must also pay particular attention to its human resource management practices to ensure: that there is enough staff to meet strategic objectives, that the staff has the required skills and abilities for performing current and future jobs, that the staff is properly compensated and that the compensation system reinforces desired behaviors, and that information is available to assess and evaluate employee performance. The human resource department can support the strategic management process through environmental scanning and competitive intelligence, assessing the feasibility of the plan, and providing the firm with lead time for dealing with labor shortages and surpluses through the use of temporary and contingent employees.[60] The HRM function is explained in Chapter 4 within the discussion of the Functional Analysis of the firm.

Organizational Structure

Organizational structure is the formal framework by which job tasks are divided, grouped, and coordinated. The activities of organizational design are seen in the developing or changing the structure by manipulating six key elements: work specialization, departmentalization, chain of command, span of control, centralization and decentralization, and formalization.[61] The managerial challenge is to design an organizational structure that facilitates effective and efficient work as employees strive to achieve organizational goals in light of the strategy of the firm.[62] Structural differences among organizations arise from differences in four contingency variables: strategy, size, technology and uncertainty with the combination of these contingencies resulting in one of two generic organization designs - mechanistic or organic.[63]

Mechanistic organizations are rigid, integrated, and tightly controlled. These efficiency machines create standardization through work specialization, have extensive departmentalization that creates the need for multiple layers of management with high formalization and narrow spans of control. Communication is mostly downward with little opportunity for participation in decision-making by low-level employees. Organic organizations are adaptive, differentiated, and flexible. While jobs are not standardized, there is division of labor. Employees, usually working in teams are empowered to handle diverse job-related problems. They require little direct supervision, minimizing the degree of formalization. Which generic design an organization adopts depends on the following contingency variables.[64]

Size. While larger organizations tend to have more hierarchical structures, the relationship is not linear. Once an organization reaches a certain size, 2000 employees for instance, adding more workers will not drastically impact the structure. However, if the firm has 200 employees and adds 500, then design changes would be necessary.[65]

Technology. Every organizational system uses some kind of technology to process its inputs into outputs. Woodward's work with manufacturing firms suggests that there is no one, best structure. In general, the more routine the technology, the more standardized the structure. However, whether manufacturing involves unit production (small batches of product such as tailor-made suits), mass production (large batch manufacturing such as automobiles) or process production (continuous process producers such as oil refineries), the most successful organizations achieve fit between technology and structure.[66]

Environmental Uncertainty. Uncertainty defines the relative stability or predictability of the environment as it relates to the organization's ability to predict current and future events in the marketplace. The scarcer the resources and the more dynamic and complex the environment, the uncertainty is higher, and the greater the need to have adaptable organizational design. In stable environments with available resources, mechanistic designs are most effective.[67]

Traditional Organizational Structures (Mechanistic). These structures represent the early forms of organization and are mostly associated with agrarian and industrial economies since they tend to create departments around formalized division of labor. Power and authority tend to be centralized in these organizations through a formal chain of command and a narrow span of control

Simple Structure. Entrepreneurial, small business, and agrarian firms usually adopt simple structures that are relatively 'flat' with an informal arrangement of employees. These have a wide span of control, and centralization of decision-making authority - the owner. Employees tend to be generalists and perform many of the tasks required in the firm's operation. Its strength is in its flexibility, low expense, and accountability. Its weakness is its inability to remain effective as the organization grows. Decision-making can come to a standstill when a person has sole authority. It is also risky in that everything depends on that single individual. If anything happens to the entrepreneur or owner, the decision-making center and all information is lost. See Figure 7.5.

Figure 7.5
Simple Structure (Retail Store)

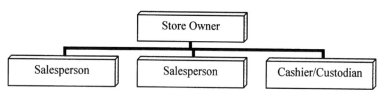

As organizations grow, they need to add employees to meet the requirements of conducting business. As the number of employees increases, the structure tends to become more specialized, formalized, departmentalized, or increasingly, bureaucratic.[68]   These mechanistic style designs can take on one of two forms:

Functional structures group similar or related occupational specialties together. Economy is achieved through specialization with the firm capitalizing on its internal distinctive competencies. However, the organization risks losing sight of its overall interests as different departments pursue their own goals and accountability is solely at the top. Information flows up the chain of command while decisions flow top-down.   Coordination between departments however is quite difficult and Bennis argued that since these structures have generalists managing specialists that their competitive advantages get lost in higher levels of administration.[69]   Note that if the CEO were to leave the firm, or be fired by the Board of Directors, that there is no logical replacement for the CEO since no other manager in the firm has a broad-based, multifunctional perspective. Under each Vice-President would be more specialized departments. For example, reporting to the V.P. of Marketing could be department heads for market research, product development, advertising and promotion, sales, and distribution. See Figure 7.6.

Figure 7.6
Departmentation by Function

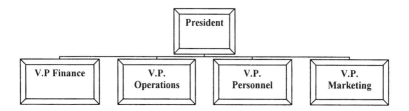

Divisional structures (also known as departmentalization by product, geography or product line) are made up of semi-autonomous units. Division managers create and implement strategic plans. However, a central headquarters typically acts as an overseer to coordinate and control the activities and provide support services between divisions. Divisional structures focus on results. A weakness, however, is the tendency to duplicate activities among divisions as well as for Divisions to offer competing products and services. For instance, General Motors has many divisions such as Chevrolet, Pontiac, Buick, Oldsmobile, Saturn, Hummer, and Cadillac. Each has its own design teams, advertising campaigns, human resource functions, and product lines. While design sets these automobiles apart and contributes to the products' success, human resource functions are not as differentiated. Furthermore, each Division may produce and sell vehicles that may or may not compete with other Division's of GM. For example, Buick, Oldsmobile, and Cadillac sell luxury vehicles; GMC, Chevrolet and Hummer sell trucks/SUV's; and Chevrolet, Pontiac, and Saturn sell small to mid-sized vehicles.

Reporting to the product, geographic or divisional managers would be the department heads in charge of the key functional aspects of the firm (personnel, operations, finance and marketing) who act in a similar manner to their counterparts in other Divisions. See Figure 7.7.

Figure 7.7
Departmentation by Product

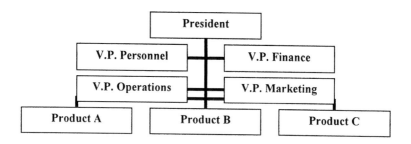

Contemporary Organizational Design (Organic). Bureaucracies are mechanistic designs that function most effectively in stable environments. Their cumbersome design makes it difficult for them to be responsive in dynamic environments where speed and flexibility often determine market performance. Current business forecasts indicate increasing trends in uncertainty resulting from globalization, hyper-competition, and resource scarcity. Thus, managers are redesigning their organizations to be more organic and capable of changing quickly as the environment demands.

Matrix structures. Matrix structures capture the advantages of bureaucracies while eliminating their disadvantages by assigning specialists from functional departments to work on one or more projects led by a project manager. By interlacing elements of function and product departmentalization, greater project coordination and flexibility are achieved. The exclusive feature of this structure is that employees in this structure have two bosses - their functional manager and their project or product manager. The major drawback to this structure is that it institutionalizes conflict. The two-boss manager is in the middle of a potential power struggle between the functional and product bosses.[70] See Figure 7.8.

Figure 7.8
Matrix Structure

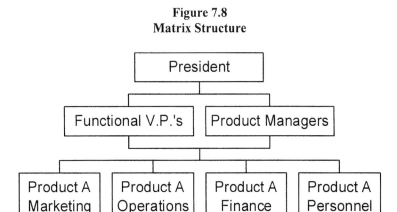

Note that, as compared to the departmentalization by product, product managers are elevated to the same level as functional vice-presidents, however, in return for their higher status they must share authority over their subordinates with these vice-presidents.

Team-based structures and Strategic Business Units. This organizational design breaks the entire organization down into work teams and/or separate firms that perform all of the basic functions of the organization within their organizational unit. Normally called cross-functional work teams or self-contained units, the strengths of these groups lie in their ability to immediately react to the demands of the marketplace without having to refer key organizational decisions up a hierarchical chain. By allowing those closest to the problem to make critical decisions, the organization takes advantage of employee skills and expertise in a quick and reliable fashion. The downside to this structure is the greater need for information processing systems that allow for intra and inter-team planning and communications.[71] Strategic business units (SBU's) in particular make it easy to manage the firm from a portfolio perspective where one can add or delete businesses from the conglomerate since there is little shared operations and/or expertise between units. Each unit can be separately structured to meet the needs of the market. See Figure 7.9

Figure 7.9
A Conglomerate Structure: The Altria Group, Inc.

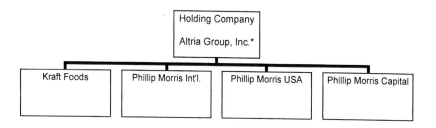

Boundaryless organizations. Also known as network organizations, virtual corporations, or learning organizations, this design breaks the mold of traditional organizational design by assembling a set of loosely coupled organizations that possess complementary distinctive competencies. These organizations are assembled and reassembled to maximize the organization's ability to create as well as adapt to changing competitive conditions. The pooling of economic, technological, and human resources produces a synergy among network members and allows them to better compete in markets requiring expertise beyond each member's separate skill capacity.

Cross-functional teams within the organization are therefore replaced by a network broker organization that brings together specialist organizations that act as product designers, producers, marketing/ distributors, and suppliers. Members are deleted from and added to the network as needed, providing the network the flexibility needed to compete in volatile markets. Individual members also have the freedom to pursue interests outside of the network while remaining a member.[72] See Figure 7.10.

Growth: Evolution and Revolution of Organizational Structures. An alternative approach to situational structuring (the environment and the strategy should determine the structure) is that approach posited by those who believe that organizations follow a clear pattern, a life cycle, in their expansion and development. The stage of

Figure 7.10
Network Organizations

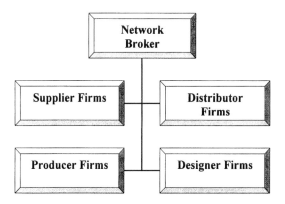

a firm's growth is therefore the key contingency variable in determining its structure. Greiner noted that organizations have evolutionary and revolutionary growth spurts (or cycles) based upon the age of the organization, its size, its evolutionary stage and the growth rate of the industry and therefore a firm's structure evolves over time. Greiner developed a five phase model of organizational growth where evolutionary periods are characterized by a dominant management style and revolutionary periods denoted by a dominant management problem or crisis. The crisis points are directly related to the prior management style with the solution strategy being the next managerial style (organizational phase) followed by a new structure. Again, fit is attained through this model by firms adapting an organizational structure that best matches their growth phase.[73]

Phase 1, *creativity*, signifies the birth of an organization with the focus on creating both a product and a market. The leadership of the company is focused upon technological and/or entrepreneurial ventures and perceives that their main task is making and selling of new products and services. A *leadership crisis* arises as the company grows in that the informal style of leadership is not capable of properly directing the new employees.   A more formalized approach that emphasizes operating efficiency and financial controls is needed in order for the organization to survive its first growth spurt.

In phase 2, *direction*, a functional organizational structure replaces the more simple reporting arrangement with the key functional area managers (marketing, manufacturing, R&D, etc.) taking over responsibility and providing expert direction.   Simultaneously, more formalized managerial systems are introduced (rules, policies, procedures) with incentives and work standards adopted by the company.   A crisis of *autonomy* develops in that, as the company grows and the organization becomes more complex, lower level workers find that they lack the authority to make on-the-spot decisions although they have the expertise and knowledge in which to make an informed judgment.   The centralized system developed in phase 2 cannot respond quickly enough to market demands and the organization stalls without another revolution.

Delegation earmarks phase 3 and denotes a more decentralized organizational structure (departmentalization by geography, division, or by product).   Lower level managers are given greater responsibility and reward systems are developed to stimulate decision-making.   These managers are able to respond more rapidly to market changes and therefore can develop new products which are more aligned with customer needs.   As the company grows, however, higher level managers feel the company slipping away and find that regional/ product managers fail to see the big picture in terms of company operations.

Phase 4, brought upon by a *control crisis* by top management, is distinguished by greater top management *coordination* through formalized control systems.   Decentralized units are merged into product groups and treated as profit centers in terms of allotting funds and human resources.   Staff personnel are hired at the corporate level and manage technical functions including data processing and information systems.   Day-to-day operations continue to be directed by field managers who must justify their actions to corporate staff managers.   The propagation of these control systems, coupled with the increasing tension between corporate staff and field managers, leads to a *red tape crisis*. The organization has become overly complex and cumbersome where following procedures and rules becomes more important than problem solving.

Collaboration, phase 5, focuses on increasing interpersonal communications and team building. Cross-functional teams are created to solve problems while formal systems are simplified in order to allow for quicker response time. Real-time information is coupled with intensive training and development so that managers have the skills and the information support systems in which to test new management procedures. Greiner hypothesizes that the next crisis would be *psychological saturation* where the intensity of team work and innovation negatively impacts employees mentally and physically.

Although not foreseen by Greiner, *networking* and *outsourcing* seems to be the next phase of an organization's evolution where organizations no longer keep all of the organization's functions in-house. Network organizations are a set of loosely coupled organizations that possess complimentary distinctive competencies. It is hypothesized by the authors that the network structure would eventually lead to an *identity* crisis. The organization's mission and culture, the distinctive features of the organization, seem to take on secondary importance as the organization tries to accommodate new network members or assimilate into new network relationships. The organization becomes so embroiled in numerous network members' structures and cultures that the boundaries of the organization seem to disappear.

The following organizational phase would involve a *redefinition* of the organization to include a more externally based, stakeholder-driven approach through co-optation.[74] Organizations seek to assimilate suppliers, consumers, competitors, regulators, labor unions, etc. so as to control resources (and therein costs) and/or develop in-house distinctive competencies.

Organizational Structure and Fit. Galbraith and Kazanjian have proposed several guidelines for creating fit between strategy, structure and environment that seems to fit in well with the organizational life cycle approach.

    a) Single-business and dominant-business companies should adopt a functional organizational structure especially in stable markets. This structure emphasizes specialization and operating efficiencies while centralizing control and decision-making.

b) Related diversified organizations, especially in stable environments, should employ a multidivisional form. Interrelated businesses should be grouped to take advantage of operational and competency synergy. Corporate control should be minimized where synergy exists and where diversity across business units is high.

c) Unrelated diversified businesses, whether in stable or unstable environments, should utilize a holding company (conglomerate) structure. Functions such as finance, accounting, planning, legal, etc. should be controlled at the corporate level where the staff acts to allocate capital and control corporate performance re: acquisitions and divestitures. Operational decisions are decentralized within the business unit.

We would add the following:

d) Small and entrepreneurial firms should adopt a simple organizational structure, especially in unstable markets. This structure emphasizes great flexibility, an all-hands philosophy, and minimizes indirect and overhead costs.

e) Large firms in unstable markets should adopt networking structures. This will allow them to gain competencies and shed expenses quickly and focus on the development of their own core competencies while seeking superior partners and subcontractors.

Organizational Leadership

Leadership is a fundamental attribute of any learning organization and leadership is paramount in strategy implementation. Organizations are increasing their reliance on employee involvement because their strategy's success depends on the firm's ability to harness employee skills and knowledge in executing strategic plans. In order to remain competitive leaders must nurture employees and encourage their initiative. This proactive climate requires more than just traditional managers - it requires leaders who can help develop employees and instill a sense of commitment and engagement.[75] Early research in the field examined leadership traits and behaviors and tried to identify significant leadership characteristics. These theories failed as it became apparent that appropriate leader types are moderated by situational constraints. Contingency theories of leadership dominate the current thinking on transactional (one-to-one) leadership.[76]

Contingency Leadership. The first comprehensive contingency model proposed that effective group performance depends on the match between the leader's style of interacting with subordinates and the degree to which the situation allowed the leader to control and influence. Building on the findings from behavioral approaches, Fielder suggested that leadership styles were either relationship or task oriented. Fiedler suggested three contingency variables for defining situations: *Leader-member relations* - the degree of confidence, trust and respect subordinates have for their leader; *Task structure* - the degree of formalization and standard operating procedure in job assignments; and *Position power* - the leader's influence over power-based activities such as hiring, firing, discipline, promotions, and salary increases. Each leadership situation resulting from these contingency variables could be classified as very favorable, favorable, and unfavorable for the leader. Task-oriented leaders tended to perform better in situations that were favorable or unfavorable. Relationship-oriented leaders performed better in moderately favorable situations. Because leadership behavior is fixed, according to Fiedler, effectiveness could only be improved by restructuring tasks or changing the amount of power the leader had over organizational factors such as salary, promotions, and disciplinary action.[77]

Similar to Greiner for organizational structure, Rodrigues treated organizational life cycles as the key contingency variable in determining the appropriate style of leadership and believed that leadership styles would change in periods denoted by a dominant management problem or crisis.[78] The first, stage, problem-solving, is distinguished by a looming crisis or issue surrounding the firm. Here an innovative leader emerges who can solve the problem by clarifying goals and objectives of the firm and obtaining agreement from employees on those goals. Once the firm has a clear mission, leadership must overcome the second crisis which is employee task ambiguity and uncertainty. A second type of leader, an implementer, arises who can direct and support employees as they adjust to the changes the firm is making in addressing the original crisis. When the firm has stabilized and employees have obtained the competencies and confidence necessary to no longer need close supervision, leadership must address the third challenge or crisis which is employee disenfranchisement and alienation. At this point, leadership needs to shift to a more coaching/counseling approach, a pacifier style of leadership, which empowers employees and provides opportunities for self-development and growth.

Transformational Leadership. Transactional leaders, such as those identified previously in contingency theories, guide followers in the direction of established goals by clarifying role and task requirements. *Charismatic and transformational* leadership theory suggests that followers make attributions of heroic or extraordinary leadership abilities when they observe certain behaviors. Charismatic leaders have certain traits and characteristics including self-confidence, vision, ability to articulate the vision, strong convictions about the vision, behavior that is out of the ordinary and environmental sensitivity.[79] Research has demonstrated that charismatic leadership correlates significantly with follower performance and satisfaction.[80] People working for charismatic leaders are motivated to exert extra effort and, because they like their leader, express greater satisfaction. Research also demonstrate that people can be trained to display more charismatic traits such as maintaining eye contact, having a relaxed posture and animating facial expressions.

Visionary and Transformational Leadership. Visionary leadership goes beyond charismatic leadership by its ability to create and articulate a realistic, credible, and attractive vision for the future of the organization that improves upon the present situation. This vision energizes followers to engage all of their skills, knowledge, and abilities to make it happen. A vision taps people's emotions, has clear imagery, and is the "glue" that holds organizational members together. Visionary firms have been found to outperform comparison companies six-fold on standard financial criteria, and their stocks outperformed the general market by fifteen times.[81]

The key properties of a vision are inspirational, and value-centered. The visionary leader can articulate the vision and direct employees in innovative ways to meet the challenges of the future. Once the vision is articulated, visionary leaders display three qualities: ability to explain the vision to others, ability to express the vision verbally and through behavior, and the ability to extend or apply the vision to different leadership contexts. Bill Gates has been called a visionary leader and has articulated a very clear vision: "A computer on every desktop and in every home."[82] To fulfill this vision, Microsoft provides employees with the resources and goals necessary to challenge their creativity by developing user-friendly practical software.

Transformational leaders pay attention to the concerns and developmental needs of followers, help them look at old problems in new ways, and are able to excite and inspire followers to achieve goals. The transformational leader has charisma but differs from the charismatic leader in that he or she encourages subordinates to question established views including those of the leader. Overall research evidence indicated that transformational leadership, when compared to transactional leadership, is more strongly correlated with lower turnover rates, higher productivity, and higher employee satisfaction. Superiors view transformational leaders as being more competent, higher performers and more promotable.[83]

Leadership and Fit. Transactional leadership, or those processes discussed in contingency theories, create fit by matching leader-member behaviors to situations. This will maximize worker on-the-job performance by providing workers the type of support or leadership style they need. The charismatic, visionary, and transformational leaders, on the other hand, inspire or excite individuals to perform based on their belief in the person, his or her viewpoint, and/or vision for the future. These types of leaders create and sustain competitive advantage by inspiring employees to commit to the firm's vision and mission; they create a fit between the employees and the mission of the firm through empowerment and education.

Some guidelines concerning leadership are as follows:
1. Task-oriented leaders (implementers) are need in situations with relatively high task uncertainty (very unfavorable

situations) or when the work is highly routine (very favorable situations).

2. Human relations leaders (pacifiers) are needed in somewhat favorable situations where the work changes and employees have the expertise to perform their jobs and can manage task uncertainty with little or no assistance.

3. Transformation and charismatic leaders (innovators) are needed in times of crisis or strategic change. May also be needed for obtaining employee commitment when morale is waning.

Organizational Culture

Organization culture is the system of values, rules, symbols, taboos and rituals that evolve over time. It is the common perception shared by members that identifies how thing get done in the organization. Culture drives expected behaviors internal to the organization as well and those engaged when interacting with its surrounding environment. Understanding an organization's culture helps an employee learn the ropes and discover whether their personality is a good fit. The greater the acceptance of key values and norms, the stronger the culture. *Strong cultures* are associated with employee commitment and organizational performance. The strength of culture is determined by the size of the firm, how long it has been around, intensity and turnover rate.[84]

Culture is transmitted through stories, heroes, villains, rituals, material symbols and language. *Stories* retell significant events in an organization's history. They provide keys to what types of behaviors are expected and respected. Stories anchor the present in the past, explain current practices and identify what the organization values. Going back to the Chrysler case, the stories about Lee Iaccoca saving Chrysler on innumerable occasions made him out to be a hero while many Chrysler employees would have cast Dieter Zetsche, the Daimler executive who took over the Chrysler Division, as the villain.

Rituals and ceremonies are repetitive activities that identify and reinforce an organization's key values and denote important actions and events. For most firms, retirement evokes separation rituals while new employees become assimilated through welcoming ceremonies (usually called orientation programs). Both use *material symbols*; artifacts that convey who and what is important, how people are expected to work together, and the degree of egalitarianism. Office layout, for example, whether people work in offices or cubicles, the style of furnishings (metal or wood), executive dining rooms, are all indicators of the organization's character. Over time, organizations develop unique terms to describe their business and operations. These slang expressions can indicate entire sentences of thought with a single word. This specific *language* acts as a common denominator that unites members of a given culture. Each organization, industry and generation of employee creates their communication linguistic.

In addition to the transmission methods mentioned above, organizations communicate culture through their structure and reward systems. Organizations that value teamwork are likely to have: flatter structures, physical space and computer software that is conducive to team work, reward systems based on team goal achievement and managers who operate as facilitators and coaches. Organizations that value individual achievement have competitive environments with individual bonus systems and clear indicators of individual achievement such as gold cufflinks for reaching one million dollars in net sales. Organizations that value authority will be bureaucratically structured, with formal rules and regulations ranging from communicating with superiors to filing equipment requests through central processing.[85]

Creating Fit between People and Organizational Culture. When people join an organization, they are socialized, or taught the procedures and nuances of culture through formal training programs, interactions with mentors and coworkers, and by just being on the job. Within a few months, an employee can determine whether they fit in with the organization's culture.

The idea of fit suggests that people and organizations have personalities. When both achieve a fit, employees begin to feel comfortable with the organization's norms, value system and expectations of behavior. When fit is not achieved, employees may experience conflicts with expectations, disregard codes of conduct, or will not thrive under the work and reward systems. When fit is achieved, people tend to be more satisfied with and committed to their organizations and when fit is not achieved, people become dissatisfied, have sub-optimum performance, may leave the organization, or in the extreme case, engage in sabotage. Huse and Cummings noted that "a lack of fit between culture and the necessary organizational changes can result in the failure to get them implemented effectively."[86]

Changing Culture. When an organization's culture no longer supports its mission, and/or when the environment calls for a change in mission, the culture has to change. Considering that culture is made up of relatively stable and permanent characteristics, it is by nature resistant to change. In other words, the stronger the culture, the greater the resistance. Even in the face of significant environmental movement, an entrenched culture will impede organization response. Cultural change is most likely to take place when a dramatic crisis creates a shock that undermines the status quo and calls into question the relevance of the existing culture; top leadership changes and brings with it a new set of key values (as in the Chrysler case); the organization is young and small, having a less entrenched culture; and the culture itself is weak, where members don't agree on key values.[87]

Given these circumstances, how can managers unfreeze or change culture, especially when it is entrenched in history? Rarely can one single action serve as a catalyst for the emergence of a new culture. However, a combination of assessment, creating urgency, new leadership, new vision and stories, reorganization, and revamping human resource management can create vital momentum.

Culture and Fit. Organizational cultures are either integrated, differentiated, or fragmented.[88] An integrated or homogenous culture "is characterized by consistency, organization-wide consensus, and clarity" (p.61) and this culture reacts to change as a whole as one unit. Differentiated cultures, on the other hand, have conflict and usually have subcultures broken down into those groups in power (the haves, the dominant coalition) and those outside the power structure (the haves not, the minority coalitions). These cultures are inconsistent, have ambiguity in the minority subcultures yet the subcultures have internal consensus. The firm reacts inconsistently to change, with some subcultures embracing it while other parts will resist it, based upon the source of the change. Fragmented cultures are prominent for their heterogeneity, ambiguity and plurality of disconnected subcultures. It is not clear in this structure, which subculture runs the firm (power is diffused) and there is certainly not a stable organizational consensus. In this type of culture differences of subcultures are not only tolerated but considered the norm and subcultures will emerge to address organizational crisis when needed.

Some guidelines can also be provided in terms of what type of cultures would be effective in which types of markets.

1. In stable markets effective cultures should be integrated and homogenous so as to maximize productivity. Everyone understands the firm's mission, subscribes to it, and is committed to enacting leadership's vision.

2. Unstable and growth markets require that the firm have a fragmented culture where differing subcultures become empowered based upon environmental changes and shifts.

3. Differentiated cultures tend to be dysfunctional in nature, but may serve a purpose when drastic culture shifts are required because of crisis situations. The Chrysler case presents an excellent example of how Daimler differentiated the Chrysler culture by supplanting the old creative heroes (Lee Iacocca and other top managers) and empowering efficiency-driven managers.

Perfect Fit: Matching Strategy, Structure, Culture, and Leadership

We now are ready to try to match environmental, strategic, and organizational subsystems in order to determine whether the firm has properly implemented its strategy. Given our previous discussions on different markets, organizational strategies and strategic approaches (Chapters 3 and 5), we propose the following general guidelines (Table 7.1) for proper strategy implementation and creating fit. Notice that, like the corporate level strategies matrix described in Chapter 6, that, except for market structure, the content of each category is not necessary represented by only one option or choice. For example, mixed competitive markets allow for all types of strategies and therefore all types of structures, cultures, and leadership styles. Again, except for monopolies, most market structures allow for variations of firm composition and configurations. Only by examining specific strategic groups within an industry can we discern which combination of competitive strategies, structures, leadership styles, and cultures will lead to the highest levels of performance and therefore produce the best fit between the environment, the firm, and its strategy.[89]

Table 7.1
Strategic Fit: Markets, Strategy, Structure, Leadership and Culture

Market Structure	Competitive Advantage(s)	Structure[+]	Leadership Style	Culture
Perfect Competition	Low-Cost Blended*	Divisional SBU	Task-Oriented Transform-ational	Integrated
Monopolistic Competition	Low-Cost Differentiation Blended*	Simple Functional Division^ Team-Based Network	Task Oriented People Oriented Transform-ational	Integrated Fragmented Differentiated
Oligopoly	Differentiation	Division^ Matrix Network	People Oriented Transform-ational	Integrated Fragmented Differentiated
Monopoly	Market Efficiency[#]	Functional	Task Oriented	Integrated

Government regulated or protected market segment.
*Blended Strategy (Best Cost/Value for Money).
[+] The Strategic Business Units/Conglomerate structure is a multi-market structure and therefore applies to all markets. Each unit may have a different structure.
^ Divisional types include departmentalization by geography and product.

An alternative approach to creating fit would be to examine organizational fit along its life cycle, as in Table 7.2.

Table 7.2
Firm Life Cycle and Fit: Strategy Orientation, Structure, Leadership, and Culture

Stage	Strategy	Structure	Leadership	Culture
Birth	Prospector	Simple	Innovator Transform-ational	Integrated
Growth	Analyzer	Divisional Matrix	Implementer People and Task-Oriented	Integrated
Shakeout	Adapter	Team-Based Network	Task-Oriented Transform-ational	Fragmented
Maturity	Defender	Divisional SBU	Pacifier People-Oriented	Integrated
Decline	Reactor	Functional	Laissez-Faire	Differentiated

Now it is easier to discern which strategic orientation, structure, leadership and culture best fits the firm. Ironically, firms in the decline stage are dysfunctional in nature and have strategies, structures, leadership styles, and cultures that reduce performance. It is usually suggested that firms in this stage follow a birth, or in this case rebirth approach. Use of this model assumes that the researcher can discern where the firm is in its life cycle and that the firm's life cycle will follow typical organizational growth patterns (which it may or may not).

Summary

Strategy implementation are those actions taken by a firm to put their strategic plans into place by either changing their mission, changing their environment, or changing their resources, capabilities and internal operations. The key term in the definition of strategy implementation is change -- can the firm make the necessary changes in order to move it into a better market position? Firms successfully implement their strategy by developing good plans that they enact or by failing to execute faulty plans.

We examined strategy implementation from several perspectives: implementation as a change/intervention process, implementation as a learning process, and implementation as an internal alignment and external adaptation process. We concluded that a synthesized approach to implementation was necessary which described the goal of strategy implementation as the execution of a strategic plan that produces a better fit between the firm, its internal processes, and its external environment. Fit can be achieved by the firm's leadership learning about the organization's situation, preparing the firm for change by sharing this information and educating employees and key stakeholders, empowering employees and key stakeholders overcoming resistance by developing strategic plans with employee and key stakeholder input, using the strategic plan to intervene in the firm's current operation and change its direction (if needed), educating and empowering employees to change themselves, their groups, subsystems, the organization as a whole, and providing feedback to employees, groups, and stakeholders as to the progress being made in executing the plan.

We then went on to examine various organizational structures (simple, functional, division, team-based, and network), the stages of structural change and development (creativity, direction, delegation, coordination, collaboration, and networking/ subcontracting), leadership styles (contingency, charismatic, transformational), and organizational cultures (integrated, differentiated, and fragmented) with the purpose of creating a set of guidelines that align market structures with generic strategies, firm structures, leadership styles, and cultures. A similar guide was prepared based upon the organizational life cycle model.

Key Terms and Concepts

Type 1 and 2 successes and failures; resistance to change; organizational inertia; path of least resistance; employee needs; group and intra-group dynamics; the 7 S model of strategy implementation; imposed strategy; loosely coupled; early fit; tight fit; perfect fit; departmentalization by size, function, division, matrix, and team-based; strategic business unit; network organization; innovator; implementer; pacifier; transactional leadership; visionary and transformational leadership; charismatic leadership; rituals; heroes/villains; customs; ceremonies; socialization; integration; differentiation (culture); and fragmentation.

Web Sites

http://www.cio.com/research/crm/strategy.html - CIO's (Chief Information Officer) Customer Relations Management Center: Strategy and Implementation. Has numerous articles from CIO magazine, the CIO store, CIO conferences, Analysis and Opinions, Resources, Career Placement, Research Centers, CIO services, and related sites.

http://www.human-resources.org/Employee_choices.htm - Human Resources Learning Center's Tutorial on "Change Management and Employee Resistance." Also provides access to newsletters, articles, conferences and events, associations, a bookstore, library, mailing lists, reference sites, software, training and certification, and policy and employment law.

http://www.orgdesign.com/ - The commercial site of Mackenzie and Company Inc. creators of the 7 S model provides excellent information on organizational design methodology and process, an organizational design diagnostic survey, an organizational audit and analysis procedure, and a sample organizational design survey. The site also provides information on management fads, predictions, articles, books, and funny stories.

http://www.organizational-culture.com/ - The Organizational Culture website of Management Strategies, Inc. Allows users to receive free weekly tips, and access to seminars, consultants, downloads, books, articles, training products, CD's, and reports.

http://www.ccl.org/index.shtml - The mission of the Center for Creative Leadership is to advance the understanding, practice and development of leadership for the benefit of society worldwide. The site includes access to a newsletter, programs, products, research, a bookstore, and guidebooks.

Discussion Questions

1. Do you agree with Kurt Lewin that employees and organizations take the path of least resistance? Why or why not? Provide examples to support your position.
2. Why is strategy implementation such a complicated topic? What factors add to its complexity? Is there a way to simplify it?
3. Discuss the impact of leadership, structure, and culture on strategy implementation. Which of these three factors do you believe is the most important? Why?
4. Discuss the Daimler Chrysler merger from an implementation perspective. How was the merger implemented? Was this a success or failure? How would you have implemented the merger?
5. Perfect fit, like organizational excellence, is a metaphor for describing the ideal strategic implementation process. What other metaphors might apply to strategy implementation? Why? Does your metaphor(s) address issues not covered in this chapter? If so, what are they?

Exercises

1. What has historically been your firm's tract record with implementing new programs and strategies and making changes? What seemed to have facilitated or blocked change?
2. Using Table 7.1 Strategic Fit, determine the relative fit of your firm. This requires determining the firm's market structure, competitive advantage, organizational structure, leadership style, and culture. Provide support for each of these analyses and where the fits and misfits are occurring. Also explain the process you used to arrive at this decision and what recommendations you would make to create a more perfect fit.

3. Repeat the exercise using Table 7.2 Firm Life Cycle and Fit. This requires a further determination as to the firm's position in the organizational life cycle, and its strategic orientation. Compare and contrast your answers. If they were different, what were those differences and how might you account for them?
4. Given your proposed changes that would create a more perfect fit, what resistance to these changes would you predict? How might you overcome this resistance?

Experiential Exercise

Organizational Diagnosis of the College Setting[90]

Learning Objective:
To diagnose and making recommendations concerning the fit between the environment of a college and the internal structure of that college.

Process:
Step 1. Complete Questionnaire
When assigned by the instructor, answer the questions in Parts I, II, and III about the organization you work for or your college.

Part I   Environmental Uncertainty (EU)

	To little or no extent	To a slight extent	To a mod-erate extent	To a consid-erable extent	*To a very great extent*
To what extent....					
does the government frequently develop requirements, regulations, and policies that directly affect your organization?	☐	☐	☐	☐	☐

do frequent technological changes or advances make current products or ,operations obsolete, requiring major changes?	☐	☐	☐	☐	☐
is there intense competition among organizations in your field?	☐	☐	☐	☐	☐
do different clients of your organization require individualized attention?	☐	☐	☐	☐	☐
does the environment in which your organization operate change unpredictably?	☐	☐	☐	☐	☐
Add the checks in each column:					
Multiply as indicated:	x 1	x 2	x 3	x 4	*x 5*
Add: EU = =	+	+	+	+	+

Part II   Structural Complexity (SC)

	To little or no extent	To a slight extent	To a mod- erate extent	To a consid- erable extent	*To a very great extent*
To what extent …					
do different groups or units operate on very different time lines (e.g., long-range	☐	☐	☐	☐	☐

versus short-term)?					
do different groups or units in this organization have quite different task goals (as opposed to many groups doing the same or similar things)?	☐	☐	☐	☐	☐
do groups or units in this organization differ in terms of their emphasis or concern for people versus concern for getting the job done?	☐	☐	☐	☐	☐
do groups or units differ in how formal things are (e.g., emphasis on adherence to rules, regulations, and policies, following the chain of command, etc., vs. few formal rules, much informal contact, etc.)?	☐	☐	☐	☐	☐
Add the checks in each column:					
Multiply as indicated:	x 1	x 2	x 3	x 4	*x 5*
Add: **SC** = =	+	+	+	+	+

Part III   Structural Formalization (SF)

	To little or no extent	To a slight extent	To a moderate extent	To a considerable extent	*To a very great extent*
To what extent…					
are rules and policies an important basis for inter-unit coordination?	□	□	□	□	□
are formal plans a major basis for inter-unit coordination?	□	□	□	□	□
are formal liaisons (individuals or teams) a significant basis for inter-unit coordination?	□	□	□	□	□
are regular meetings and problem-solving sessions for mutual adjustment an important basis for inter-unit coordination?	□	□	□	□	□
is there a great deal of formal effort devoted to inter-unit coordination?	□	□	□	□	□
Add the checks in each column:					
Multiply as indicated:	x 1	x 2	x 3	x 4	*x 5*
Add: SF = =	+	+	+	+	+

Step 2. Compute Summary Score
PART I: Environmental Uncertainty (EU) = _____
PART II: Structural Complexity   (SC) = _____
PART III: Structural Formalization   (SF) = _____

Step 3. Place Summary Score on "Fit" Chart
Using the scale below, write in your score in the appropriate box in following Summary Table. (HIGH = 20-25; MODERATE = 11-19; LOW = 5-10) Fit is achieved when all three scores fall within the same factor rating.

"Fit" Summary Table

Factors	High	Moderate	Low
Environmental Uncertainty			
Structural Complexity			
Structural Formalization			

1.   How many class members have organizations with EU-SC-SF "fit"?
2.   What were the most common types of "misfit"? Why?
3.   How would you go about reducing the SC score? Is it either to change the SC score than it is to change the SF score? Why or why not?
4.   What suggestions do you have for creating a fit in the organization you analyzed if one is not present?

Endnotes

---

[1] Robert F. Hartley (2003). *Management Mistakes and Successes.* 7th Edition. New York: John Wiley & Sons.
[2] Danny Hakim (2002). "Chrysler Is Trying to Leave Its Baggage Behind" *New York Times* (May 12) Late Edition, Business Section, 3.4.

[3] Scott Miller and Joseph B. White (2002). "Leading the News -- A Global Journal Report: Daimler Chrysler Net Rises 52%; Auto Maker Lifts Forecast for Year" *Wall Street Journal* (July 19) Eastern Edition, A3.

[4] Jane E. Fitzgibbon and Matthew W. Seeger (2002) "Audiences and Metaphors of Globalization in the DaimlerChryslerAG Merge" (Spring) Volume 53, Issue 1, 40-55.

[5] Elfriede Fursich (2002). "Nation, Capitalism, Myth: Covering News of Economic Globalization" *Journalism and Mass Communication Quarterly* (Summer) Volume 79, Issue 2, 353.

[6] Ibid, 353-373.

[7] Robert F. Hartley, 2003.

[8] Danny Hakim, 2002.

[9] Susan Carney (2002). "Dissident Few Long For Iacocca" *Detroit News* (April 26), A.7.

[10] http://www.chryslertakeover.com, February 10, 2003.

[11] http://www.Allpar.com, February 10, 2003.

[12] David W. Cravens (2000). *Strategic Marketing.* 6th Edition. New York: Irwin McGraw-Hill.

[13] George S. Day (1994). "The Capabilities of Market-Driven Organizations" *Journal of Marketing* (October), 37-52.

[14] Ibid.

[15] Richard L. Osborne (1994). "Second Phase Entrepreneurship: Breaking Through the Growth Wall" in Robert W. Price (ed.) (2001). *Entrepreneurship 01/02.* 3rd Edition. Guilford, Ct.: Duskin/McGraw-Hill, 161-166; Michael J. Roberts (1999). "Managing Growth" in Price, 2001, 158-160.

[16] Kim Clark (1999). "The Effective Executive" in Price, 2001, 62-4.

[17] Robert K. Yin, Karen A. Heald, and Mary E. Vogel (1977). *Tinkering with the System.* Lexington, Mass.: Lexington Books.

[18] Adopted from Daniel J. Rowley and Herbert Sherman (2001). *From Strategy to Change" Implementing the Plan in Higher Education.* San Francisco, Ca.: Jossey-Bass, Inc.

[19] Robert F. Hartley (2001). *Marketing Mistakes and Successes.* 8th Edition. New York: John Wiley & Sons, Inc.

[20] Stephen P. Robbins (2003). *Organizational Behavior.* 10th Edition. Upper Saddle River, N.J.: Prentice Hall.

[21] Alvar Elbing (1978). *Behavioral Decisions in Organizations.* 2nd Edition. Glenview, Ill.: Scott, Foresman and Company; Jan Koolhaas (1982). *Organizational Dissonance and Change.* New York: John Wiley & Sons Ltd.; Leon Festinger (1957). *A Theory of Cognitive Dissonance.* Stanford, Ca.: Standford University Press.

[22] Fred Luthans (1998). *Organizational Behavior.* 8th Edition. New York: Irwin McGraw-Hill.

[23] Herbert A. Simon (1976). *Administrative Behavior: A Study of Decision-Making processes in Administrative Organization.* 3rd Edition. New York: The Free Press.

[24] Special Task Force to the Secretary of Health, Education, and Welfare (1975). *Work in America.* Boston, Mass.: MIT Press.

[25] N. Linda Jewell and H. Joseph Reitz (1981). *Group Effectiveness in Organizations.* Glenview, Ill: Scott, Foresman and Company.

[26] Gregory G. Dess, Joseph C. Picken, and Douglas W. Lyon (1999). "Transformational Leadership" *Human Resource Management International Digest* (May), 8-10.

[27] Kurt Lewin (1951). "Field Theory in Social Science" in Daniel Cartwright (ed.) *Selected Papers.* New York: Harper.

[28] Paul Hersey and Kenneth H. Blanchard (1993). *Management of Organizational Behavior: Utilizing Human Resources.* 6th Edition. Englewood Cliffs, N.J.: Prentice-Hall, Inc.

[29] Chester P. Barnard (1938). *The Functions of the Executive.* Cambridge, Mass.: Harvard University Press.

[30] Wendell L. French and Cecil H. Bell, Jr. (1999). *Organization Development: Behavioral Science Interventions for Organization Improvement.* 6th Edition. Upper Saddle River, N.J.: Prentice-Hall, Inc.

[31] Edgar H. Schein (1987). *Process Consultation: Lessons for Managers and Consultants.* Volume 2. Reading, Mass.: Addison-Wesley Publishing Company.

[32] Adrian McLean, David Sims, Iain Mangham and David Tuffield (1982). *Organization Development in Transition: Evidence of an Evolving Profession.* New York: John Wiley & Sons Ltd.

[33] Russell L. Ackoff (1994). The Democratic Corporation: A Radical Perspective for Recreating Corporate America and Rediscovering Success. New York: Oxford University Press.

[34] Calhoun W. Wick and Lu Stanton Leon (1993). *The Learning Edge: How Smart Managers and Smart Companies Stay Ahead.*

[35] Victor H. Vroom (1964). *Work and Motivation.* New York: John Wiley.

[36] Richard M. Steers, Lyman W. Porter, and Gregory A. Bigley (1996). *Motivation and Leadership at Work.* 6th Edition. New York: McGraw-Hill Companies, Inc.

[37] Abraham H. Maslow (1943) "A Theory of Human Motivation." *Psychological Review* (July), 370-396.

[38] Steers, Porter, and Bigley, 1996.

[39] James B. Rotter (1990). "Internal versus External Control of Reinforcement: A Case Study of a Variable." *American Psychologist* Volume 45, 489-493.

[40] Wick and Leon, 1993.

[41] Patricia M. Buhler (2002). "Building the Learning Organization for the 21st Century: A Necessary Challenge" *Supervision* (December) Volume 63, Issue 12, 20-22.

[42] Anonymous (2002). "The Growth of the Corporate University" *Training Strategies for Tomorrow* (November/December) Volume 16, Issue 6, 16-18.

[43] Daniel J. Rowley has addressed the issue of lifelong learning and the corporation in Daniel J. Rowley, Herman D. Lujan, and Michael G. Dolence (1998). *Strategic Choices for the Academy: How Demand for Lifelong Learning Will Re-Create Higher Education.* San Francisco, Ca.: Joseey-Bass Publishers.

[44] Jitendra V. Singh (ed.) (1990). *Organizational Evolution: New Directions.* Newbury Park, Ca.: Sage Publications.

[45] This discussion has been adopted and modified from Herbert Sherman (1991). "A Typology of Strategic Management: Rational, Natural, and Ecological Approaches" *Journal of Management Science and Policy Analysis* (Spring/Summer) Volume 8, Issue 3-4, 331-345.

[46] Jay R. Galbraith and Robert K. Kazanjian (1986). *Strategy Implementation: Structure, Systems and Process.* 2nd Edition. St. Paul, Minn.: West Publishing Company; Raymond E. Miles and Charles C. Snow (1984). "Fit, Failure, and the Hall of Fame" *California Management Review* (Fall) Volume 26, Issue 3, 10-28.

[47] Jac A. M. Vennix (1996). *Group Model Building: Facilitating Team Learning Using System Dynamics.* New York: John Wiley & Sons Ltd.

[48] Irving L. Janis (1972). *Victims of Group Think.* Boston, Mass.: Houghton Mifflin.

[49] Gilbert A. Churchill, Jr., Neil M. Ford, and Orville C. Walker, Jr. (1993). *Sales Force Management.* 4th Edition. Homewood, Ill.: Irwin.

[50] L. David Brown (1983). *Managing Conflict at Organizational Interfaces.* Reading, Mass.: Addison-Wesley Publishing Company.

[51] William D. Hitt (1995). "The Learning Organization: Some Reflections on Organizational Renewal" *Leadership & Organization Development Journal* Volume 16, Issue 8, 17-26.

[52] Steven Kerr (1975). "On the Folly of Rewarding A While Hoping for B" *Academy of Management Journal* Volume 18, 769-783.

[53] Sherman, 1991.

[54] Jeffrey Pfeffer and Gerald R. Salancik (1978). *The External Control of Organizations: A Resource Dependency Perspective.* New York: Harper & Row.

[55] Paul J. Stonich (ed.) (1982). *Implementing Strategy: Making Strategy Happen.* Cambridge, Mass.: Ballinger Publishing Company.

[56] Lewin, 1951; Schein, 1987.

[57] Raymond E. Miles and Charles C. Snow (1984). "Fit, Failure, and the Hall of Fame" *California Management Review* (Spring) Volume 26, Issue 3, 10-28.

[58] Miles and Snow, 1984.

[59] Henry Mintzberg, Joseph Lampel, James Brian Quinn, and Sumantra Ghoshal (2003). *The Strategy Process: Concepts, Contexts, Cases.* 4th Edition. Upper Saddle River, N.J.: Prentice-Hall.

[60] Charles R. Greer (2001). *Strategic Human Resource Management: A General Managerial Approach.* 2nd Edition. Upper Saddle River, N.J.: Prentice-Hall, Inc.

[61] Robbins, 2003.

[62] Jay R. Galbraith (2001). Designing Organizations: An Executive Guide to Strategy, Structure, and Process. 2nd Edition. New York: Wiley Publishers.

[63] Paul R. Lawrence and Jay W. Lorsch (1969). *Developing Organizations: Diagnosis and Action.* Reading, MA: Addison-Wesley Publishing Company.

[64] Henry Mintzberg (1979). *The Structuring of Organizations.* Englewood Cliffs, N.J.: Prentice-Hall, Inc.

[65] Peter M. Blau and Marshall W. Meyer (1987). *Bureaucracy in Modern Society.* 3rd Edition. New York: Random House.

[66] Joan Woodward (1965). *Industrial Organization: Theory and Practice.* London, England: Oxford University Press; Hamid Noori (1990). *Managing the Dynamics of New Technology: Issues in Manufacturing Management.* Englewood Cliffs, NJ: Prentice-Hall.

[67] Galbraith, 2001.

[68] Amitai Etzioni (1964). *Modern Organizations.* Englewood Cliffs, NJ: Prentice-Hall.

[69] Warren Bennis (1966). *Beyond Bureaucracy.* New York: McGraw-Hill Book Company.

[70] Stanley M. Davis and Paul R. Lawrence (1977). *Matrix.* Reading, Mass.: Addison-Wesley Publishing Company.

[71] Jay Galbraith (1973). *Designing Complex Organizations.* Reading, Mass.: Addison-Wesley Publishing Company; Debra J. Housel (2002). *Team Dynamics.* Cincinnati, Oh.: South-Western.

[72] Raymond E. Miles and Charles C. Snow (1986). "Organizations: New Concepts for New Forms" *California Management Review* (Fall) Volume 28, Issue 1, 11-24.

[73] Larry E. Greiner (1972). "Evolution and Revolution as Organizations Grow" *Harvard Business Review*, (July/August) Vol. 50, Issue 4, 37-46.

[74] Pfeffer and Salancik, 1978.

[75] Dave Ulrich and Dale Lake (1990). *Organizational Capability: Competing From the Inside Out.* New York: John Wiley and Sons.

[76] John B. Miner (1980). *Theories of Organizational Behavior.* Hinsdale, Ill.: The Dryden Press.

[77] Micahel Z. Hackman and Craig E. Johnson (1996). *Leadership: A Communication Perspective.* 2nd Edition. Prospects Heights, Ill.: Waveland Press, Inc.

[78] Carl A. Rodrigues (1985). "Adapting the Innovator, the Implementor, and the Pacifier Leadership Styles to Changing Environmental Demands: A Conceptual Model" in Edward D. Bewayo et al. (eds.) *Management Process and Organizational Behavior: Selected Readings.* Lexington, Mass.: Ginn Custom Publishing.

[79] Jay A. Conger and Rabindra N. Kanungo (1998). *Charismatic Leadership in Organizations.* Thousand Oaks, CA: Sage Publications.

[80] Gary Yukl (1994). *Leadership in Organizations.* 3rd Edition. Englewood Cliffs, NJ: Prentice-Hall.

[81] Richard L. Hughes, Robert C. Ginnett, and Gordon J. Curphy (1999). *Leadership: Enhancing the Lessons of Experience.* 3rd Edition. New York: Irwin McGraw-Hill.

[82] http://www.microsoft.com/presspass/ofnote/08-12pc20.asp, February 19, 2003.

[83] John J. Hater and Bernard M. Bass (1988). "Supervisors' Evaluations of Subordinates' Perceptions of Transformational and Transactional Leadership," *Journal of Applied Psychology* (November) 698-704.

[84] Joanne Martin (1992). *Cultures in Organizations: Three Perspectives.* New York: Oxford University Press.

[85] Steven J. Ott, (1989). *The Organizational Cultural Perspective.* Pacific Grove, CA.: Brooks/Cole Publishing Company.

[86] Edgar F. Huse and Thomas G. Cummings (1985). *Organization Development and Change.* 3rd Edition. St. Paul, Minn.: West Publishing Company p. 353.

[87] Margaret B.W. Graham and Alec T. Shuldiner (2001). *Corning and the Craft of Innovation.* Oxford, England: Oxford University Press.

[88] Martin, 1992.

[89] David A. Levinthal (1994). " Surviving Schumpeterian Environments: An Evolutionary Perspective" in Joel A. C. Baum and Jitendra V. Singh (eds.) *Evolutionary Dynamics of Organizations.* Oxford, England: Oxford University Press.

[90] R. R. McGrath (1985). "Environmental Influences" in *Exercises in Management Fundamentals.* Reston, Va.: Reston Publishing Company, Inc., 187-190.

ᘒ Chapter Eight ᘓ
Implementation Techniques/Interventions

Chapter Objectives

1. For students to understand the purpose of organizational interventions and the action research model as a mode of implementing strategy.
2. To introduce students to the numerous intervention techniques that organizations can employ to educate employees and facilitate change (strategy implementation).
3. For students to participate in an intervention exercise.
4. To have students develop intervention strategies through case method and field research.

Introductory Case: Southwest Airlines is Flying High in Disastrous Times

"2001 marks Southwest Airlines' 30th Anniversary. For 30 years now, we have had one mission: low fares. In that respect, this year was no different. But as we all know, 2001 was a year like no other, in both our Company's and our country's history. .... The National Tragedy struck our collective hearts, minds, and lives in [the] third quarter. In [the] fourth quarter, our nation and our Company began the difficult process of healing together. Nothing will keep us from moving ahead. Freedom, and the Freedom to Fly, will most certainly endure.

Southwest was well poised, financially, to withstand the potentially devastating hammer blow of September 11. Why? Because for several decades our leadership philosophy has been: we manage in good times so that our Company, and our People, can be job secure and prosper through bad times. This philosophy served our People and our Company well during the holocaustic economic catastrophe that afflicted the airline industry from 1990 – 94, when the industry, as a totality, lost a cumulative $13 billion and furloughed approximately 120,000 of its employees, while, during that same 1990 – 94 period, Southwest remained 100 percent job secure and produced profits and Profit sharing for our Employees and Shareholders. Once again, after September 11, our philosophy of managing in good times so as to do well in bad times proved a marvelous prophylactic for our Employees and our Shareholders. ....

On September 11, our Company had the financial wherewithal to withstand and overcome the dire economic emergency with which it, and our nation, were threatened. But what about our Southwest People, as a whole? How would they respond in an atmosphere of incredulity, fear, sadness, uncertainty, and grave economic jeopardy for themselves and their Company?

Here is how they responded: '*Are you guys ready? Okay. LET'S ROLL.*' While still grieving over the events and losses of September 11, our People returned to work with tears in their eyes but resolve in their hearts. They speedily reassembled our airline, after it had been shut down, and got it flowing smoothly again. In a national and Company emergency, they put aside petty complaints and miniscule concerns and both learned, and endured, the multitude of complicated new security measures and procedures mandated by our federal government. And despite the stress and strain of the post September 11 airline industry environment, they smiled, and cared, for their internal and external Customers, while providing superb Customer Service in their usual spirited, joyful, open, warm-hearted, and humanitarian way."[1]

While airlines like United were experiencing monumental loses from the September 11th tragedy, Southwest experienced only a 1.7% loss in operating revenue and a decrease in their net profit margin of slightly over 2%. How did this firm manage to still make over half a billion dollars in 2001, with a 9.2% profit margin and a EPS of $.63 while other airlines were scrambling to avoid bankruptcy?

According to Robert Hartley, Southwest's ingredients for success started with their focus on cost containment. For example, in 1991 Southwest's operating costs per passenger seat mile were 15% lower than American West, 32% lower than United, and 39% lower than US Air.[2] Cost cutting measures were also obtained through streamlining their operations and customer services. For example, Southwest on the ground turnaround time for a plane is four to six times as fast as the industry average. This is achieved through unassigned seating (first come, first seat selection) and quick boarding/deplaning procedures. Furthermore, Southwest's no frills approach (no food, just snacks and drinks), reusable seat tickets, and lack of affiliation with centralized reservation systems (like travelocity.com and priceline.com) have supported their low-cost operation.

Secondly, Hartley indicated that although Southwest is a unionized shop, Southwest has developed a very strong working relationship with the union that has allowed for very flexible working hours and working conditions. More importantly, the firm is committed to their employees and making Southwest a fun place to work and to engender a high morale.[3] Employees are encouraged to joke with each other and the customers. One of the authors is a committed Southwest customer because of Southwest's lack of employee downsizing during hard times and the fact that Southwest employees seem to enjoy dealing with passengers.

Last, Hartley believed that Southwest has avoided "the temptation to expand vigorously."[4] This conservative approach to growth has put Southwest in a very strong financial position. They had over a billion dollars in cash on hand on September 11, 2001, had a debt-to-equity ratio of less than 50%, added over a billion dollars to cash assets that year, and at the end of the 2001 fiscal year were sitting on 2.2 billion of cash and cash equivalent assets.[5]

Yet there is more, far more, to Southwest Airlines than just good business practices; there's Herb Kelleher, the co-founder and Chair of Southwest. When Kelleher and his partner, San Antonio businessman Rollin King, launched the nation's first low-cost airline in 1971, they had no money for advertising. So they sought attention by becoming known as a fun, outrageous company. Southwest's first flight attendants wore orange hot pants and go-go boots and Kelleher, by then CEO, painted airplanes to look like Shamu, the killer whale at Sea World.[6] Kelleher, now 71, is the charismatic, zany force who created the culture, the business model and the financial discipline that has set Southwest apart during its 31-year history.[7]

What's Herb's secret? Most sales organizations are not built for the kind of antics that go on at a place like Southwest Airlines, where former CEO Herb Kelleher gave employees permission to act as silly as they want, as long as customers continue to be satisfied with their service. Herb's own marketing stunts and tireless cheerleading have earned him living-legend status at Southwest. Kelleher has one of the best highlight reels of any top executive, from sketching out his idea for a new airlines route network on a cocktail napkin in 1966, to staging an arm-wrestling match with another company's CEO for the rights to an ad slogan.[8]

An example of such humor was when Kelleher, was asked after 9/11 to serve on a security task force for the FAA. Upon returning from one meeting, he told the Southwest executives that dump searches were being planned, meaning that the content of some passengers' bags would be dumped out for a complete search. Kelleher, mischievous as ever, looked over to Donna Conover, Executive Vice President - Customer Service, and said, "Don't worry, Donna, I bought new underwear." She replied: "Oh, really? I wasn't quite sure you wore underwear."[9]

"Leaders like this typically can use the emotion of the moment to talk to employees and touch them-but it's always strategic thinking, because the emotions are tied to the corporate direction. Executives can build these skills, but they are traits that you need to develop through coaching. You have to realize where your strengths and confidence lie, and also not forget that there are many people and things behind [Kelleher] that made him successful."[10]

Yet Herb stepped down as CEO in the early summer of 2001 and was replaced by James F. Parker. Parker has been described as "an unassuming San Antonio native with undergrad and law degrees from the University of Texas at Austin"[11] and publicly stated that Kelleher is irreplaceable. "And there lies the challenge for Southwest. As it grows and its leadership changes, sustaining its trademark culture may become more difficult. The big question now that Herb is moving into the background, is whether that culture can continue into the future."[12]

Strategy Implementation: Interventions

In Chapter 7 we described strategy implementation as the execution of a strategic plan that produces a better fit between the firm, its internal processes, and its external environment. We further concluded that fit could be achieved by the firm's leadership learning about the organization's situation, preparing the firm for change by sharing this information and educating employees and key stakeholders, empowering employees and key stakeholders, and using the strategic plan to intervene in the firm's current operation and change its direction (if needed). It is the firm's intervention in its own operation and its marketplace that fully implements its strategic plan (see Figure 8.1, below) by moving the firm from its current situation (its relative internal and external fit) to the new position proposed in its strategic plan.

Figure 8.1
The Strategic Planning Process
Step 6 – Implementation: Organizational Tactics

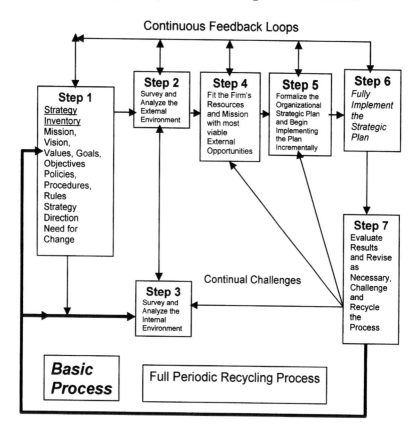

Intervention techniques address the age old issue of "how do we get there from here?" by providing managers specific tools for developing employee competencies and skills, as well as assisting employees to learn how to learn, and changing the firm's processes, systems, and structures.   Intervention techniques are the change mechanisms, the technology of change management and organizational learning, and must be employed carefully, precisely, and with diligence.

Interventions techniques are not only appropriate for implementing strategic plans (creating both revolutionary and evolutionary change) but also can be utilized as continuous improvement and continuous learning instruments. As discussed in Chapter 1 Appendix under the topic of organization development, firms must be prepared for change prior to strategic planning by creating a system and a culture of personal and organizational improvement and growth. This can only be accomplished through the development of human resource maintenance systems and life-long learners; training and development programs that reinforce prior learning and afford employees the opportunity to develop not only a career path but a knowledge path to support career paths.[13]

More importantly, withdrawal or discontinuation of intervention techniques (as part of an organization development or strategic plan) has very negative consequences for the firm in that employees revert back to less productive behavior. Miners et al. found that employees who were exposed to aggressive and widespread intervention techniques increased their productivity and performance. Once this support was withdrawn (although in the cases they studied, non-purposively), employee performance reverted back to lower levels.[14] These findings are strongly correlated to basic learning theory and operant conditioning; new learning will become extinct (decrease over time) if not supported through some schedule of reinforcement.[15]

Going back to the Southwest Airlines case then, the question asked at the end of the case, whether the culture of the firm will continue without Herb Kelleher, is a very apropos question. What conscious actions will top management be taking to ensure that the fun and zany culture that Herb started will continue without his immediate presence? How will Southwest continue to nurture this culture? What intervention techniques will they employ to reinforce this strong culture and make sure that Herb remains an icon and a hero?

An article in the Houston Chronicle has hinted at a possible shift in culture and strategy and reaction from employees. "Southwest Airlines flight attendants delivered a Valentine's Day volley at the carrier's main airport Friday with a protest saying management has lost its loving feeling in asking them to work longer hours. 'We are out here today because our company has suggested that our flight attendants should be working a longer duty day, with shorter rest periods and no breaks,' said Thom McDaniel, president of the Transport Workers Union Local 556, which represents 7,500 attendants at the airline."[16] These actions by Southwest seem to run counter to Herb Kelleher's idea of having fun and put the firm at odds with their employees and their union. Was top management cognizant of the impact of their actions? How did they prepare their workers for this change? Does this bode well for Southwest Airlines?

Effective Intervention Depends on a Good Diagnosis. There are usually several different ways of approaching the analysis and possible action interventions. Some criteria for intervention selection involve: determining the 'root' cause, ascertaining a time frame for problem solving, financial resources, identifying client support, change agent skill, and energy level or the amount of commitment and enthusiasm for a change effort. Interventions can be chosen from two dimensions-the unit of focus (from individual to total organization) and the location of the intervention (internal systems or external environment). Generally, an intervention at the individual level is more time and resource consuming than an intervention in larger aspects of the total system.[17]

Review: Levels of Strategy Implementation and Organization Intervention. As discussed in Chapter 7, strategy implementation occurs at three general levels of analysis within the organization; micro, macro and environmental. Furthermore, we noted in Appendix B that levels of organizational analysis can be broken down into smaller units of analysis which include intra-personal, interpersonal, intra-group, inter-group, subsystems, subsystems interfaces, business/ organization unit, inter-organizational, market niche, industry, industry clusters, and national. Consequently we will be introducing intervention techniques by their level of implementation/ analysis. This will make it easier for students to select the right intervention technique for the right level of analysis.

Risks Associated with Organization Interventions. Meglino and Mobley advised that since organizations and employees differ greatly, organization development interventions involve three risks: risk in diagnosis, risk in prescription, and risk in treatment.[18] The risk in diagnosis refers to the development of possible erroneous conclusions (specifically problem definitions) based upon an analysis of the firm, whether employing SWOT or other organizational investigation techniques. Business research is an inexact science given time and resource constraints, availability of data, limits of design strategies, and the need to interpret data hence the possibility of drawing flawed deductions certainly exists.[19]

Prescription, selecting an intervention based upon the diagnosis, may also go awry in that even if the analysis of the organization is correct an inappropriate intervention technique may be employed. Going back to the Southwest Airline case, for example, if Southwest concludes that the firm needs to reinforce its playful culture, restructuring the organization's hierarchy may not necessary have the same impact as leadership training (specifically of James Parker, new CEO) and/or cultural reinforcement. Firms need to employ the right remedy for the right illness. Lastly, there is a risk in the actual treatment, the execution of the intervention. Improper handling of change techniques, especially failure of the external consultant to have the client assume responsibility for the intervention's process and outcome, leads to poorer results.[20]

For risk to be minimized, according to Meglino and Mobley, the selection of an organization development intervention should be a 5-part process: consideration of different intervention approaches, examination of the impact on a specific unit of the organization, encouragement of inputs from various levels, cooperation between management and the unit levels during implementation, and feedback so that problems can be corrected

Change and Change Agents. Assuming that we can pinpoint the level of analysis (or levels of analyses) for which the organization needs to intervene and make changes and minimize the inherent risks in change management, the question becomes very practical in nature "Who determines what intervention techniques to use and who actually executes the intervention techniques?[21] If intervention techniques are a method for inducing change, then arguably anyone who champions change could be classified as a change agent. Recent literature in the field describes varying types of agents of change including professors, professional researchers, managers, women executives, journalists, management consultants, pay, chief information officers, and 'the office.'[22]

However, this could not be farther from the truth if one examines this issue in the context of the last question. The 'who' part of the question begets three independent but related questions:

1. Who has the power and authority to make decisions regarding the use of intervention techniques?
2. Who has the expertise to determine which techniques should be used to induce what types (s) of change(s)?
3. Who has the expertise and/or experience to perform an organizational intervention?

The answer to the first question seems rather self-evident. Top management has the power and authority (through their agency relationship with the Board) to make a decision about the use of intervention techniques. Driving, guiding and supporting change is the most important job of the CEO or top manager of any organization.[23] Yet rarely does top management have the knowledge, background and skills necessary to determine which techniques to employ and/or the know-how to carry out an intervention and so they must turn to an organizational development or change management specialist. Buchanan, Claydon, and Doyle noted that there was a widespread lack of change management expertise in top management, with external consultants used to fill this skills gap. They also indicated that most organizations do not understand the role of the change agent with many managers believing that the critical skills for these agents include well-developed negotiating, persuading and influencing skills; skills that are actually antithetical to the neutrality required in the position.[24]

The traditional notion of a change agent is that of the singular, top management mandated change agent - usually an internal or external consultant or project manager employed as a professional or expert in managing change.[25] These consultants are generalists in their organizational perspective and specialists in the process of organizational diagnosis and intervention. They have been trained in the use of the action research model (the underlying research model for the field of organizational development), and are expert in using change techniques and technologies.

They foster change by acting as integrators between the top management and targeted populations and between functional areas. An effective change agent is perceived as a disinterested or neutral party to the change process and has little to no power position in terms of those impacted by the change; they occupy marginal roles to the targeted groups.[26] Credibility is another factor. Change agents must be deemed as expert in their fields and have a positive history with the organization. The best change agents are flexible, customizing their approaches to meet changing business conditions. They are persistent and keep their eyes on their mission and objectives.[27]

Competencies of a Change Agent. Eubanks, Marshall, and O'Driscoll surveyed OD practitioners and clients to determine what were the key skills of change agents. They found that (in order of importance) implementing the intervention techniques, using data, managing group processes, contracting, interpersonal skills, and client relations were the six competencies most cited. These skills were then categorized as people skills (group process and interpersonal), data skills, and delivery skills (contracting, implementing, and client relations) and involved the associated behaviors of gaining management support, collaboration, personal preparation, adapting to change, establishing rapport, facilitating group process, demonstrating professionalism, using clients' language, resolve client issues, establishing contracts, collecting data, and follow-up.[28] An earlier study by Carey and Varney yielded similar results. They found that members of the OD Division of the American Society for Training and Development felt that change agents needed to possess interpersonal skills, be perceptive, deal with resistance, use small group intervention skills, do team building, facilitate meetings, train employees, be succinct, specific, and clear, plan, do goal-setting, and be able to see different perspectives.[29]

External Change Agents. Many organizations realize that very few of their in-house personnel have the expertise and the credibility to effectively serve as change agents. External change agents, OD consultants, serve a very useful purpose in that they provide a world view, serve as sounding boards and counselors, provide conceptual stimulation, new ideas and images, tend to be charismatic, and usually energize the change process.

Organizations that use external change agents have the task of educating the change agent as to the organizational processes, functions, and interdependencies (single loop learning) -- it is through this education that the external change agent starts the diagnostic process. The fear is that the external consultant will get drawn into organizational politics and in the long run lose objectivity.

Yet external change agents have their limitations. Robert Metzger observed that most established consulting firms failed to focus upon the right issues when requested to perform strategic interventions, or, if they did, they did not have the change agents required to provide the leadership and technical expertise to help client organization.[30] Many consultants have a limited scope of change techniques, or worse are selling one particular change management product (i.e. TQM, ISO 9000) and may not be able to provide the firm with the support needed to properly conduct an intervention. Jerome Franklin cautioned that the firm needed to select change agents very carefully and look for those agents who had excellent assessment prescriptive skills, not those pre-trained in organization development (OD) or a specific OD technique.[31]

Second, in a change effort, both the external change agent and the client system bring along their own values, goals, needs, skills, and abilities. Ethical dilemmas frequently occur when these factors conflict with one another. This may result in role conflict and role ambiguity between the change agent and the client system which may lead to misrepresentation and collusion, misuse of information, manipulation and coercion, value and goal conflicts, and technical ineptitude.[32]

Third, and perhaps the most important, because the external change agent is not part of the firm, he or she may be perceived as an outsider; a hired gun by top management who at best is well-meaning but owned by management and at worst part of a malevolent plot to take advantage of lower level employees. Regardless of interpretation, by being outside the system (which is needed for objectivity and expertise) the external change agent must immediately win the trust of the workforce in order to minimize resistance to change and properly execute their planned interventions.

Internal Change Agents. Usually coming from personnel offices, training departments, or management service departments (although they may be an assistant or an assistant to a major officer of the organization), internal change agents bring with them a wealth of knowledge about the organization and the biases attached to being members of the organization. An internal consultant's role is to enable change. He or she is a continual learner, teacher of concepts and skills, and problem-solving coach. As enablers of change, internal consultants assist the change process and know when to hand off the ball. In the role of learner, an internal consultant is sensitive to people's needs and values. He or she understands that a learning organization requires a cadre of learning individuals. Internal consultants should view their expectations and relationships as opportunities for insight.[33]

Internal consultants bring a tactical eye to the organization in that they garner information about organizational coalitions and serve as an intelligence gathering mechanism for top management. Secondly, internals can cultivate new ideas and new attitudes by disseminating the proper information to the correct parties. They also serve as trainers by developing and running management training and development programs.

Many organization members, unfortunately, usually see internal consultants as tainted commodities. Internal change agents may be the most honest and sincere people, yet they all have organizational bosses they report to. Those involved with the intervention usually assume that the change agent's boss will eventually learn all and will keep these change agents at arm's length.

The Team Approach. Several authors in the field have noted that the most successful method for inducing change has been to develop a change agent team consisting of both internal and external change agents.[34] This combination allows for the objectivity and expertise required for the development of employee trust in terms of data analysis and confidentiality as well as lays the groundwork for institutionalizing the change process by having in-house personnel learn intervention techniques. Furthermore, the internal change agents provide not only a linkage to the organization for the external agents, they also serve as the first teachers of those agents in terms of the processes and culture of the organization.

Second, as firms are embracing the concept of a continuous learning organization, there is a movement away from using sage consultants and top-down approaches to organizational interventions and a movement towards the development of change novices (upper and middle level managers) into change experts.[35] An increasing number of organizations are experiencing high velocity discontinuous change and to facilitate their adaptation and transformation, many firms are introducing more empowering structures and cultures. This has led them to disperse change agency to a more diverse group of individuals with implications for the way change agents are managed in the future.

This shift to decentralized change management systems, where the learner truly becomes the change agent, will require more systematic support for change management, with respect to better definition and understanding of the role(s) and of the processes through which internal change agents are selected, developed and rewarded. This will include the need for increasing sensitivity to the political issues in change, which become more intense with the complexity and scope of change, but where views on the conduct of the change agent in this domain are divided.[36]

Intervention Techniques: The Process. Before we can delve into the differing intervention techniques available to a firm, we must first discuss the process in which any intervention technique is applied.

Phase One (Pre-intervention) - Convergence of Interest and Intervention Team Building.[37] This phase requires the gathering of interested individuals by top-level management who are convinced that there is a need to both gather information about the organization and take action based upon these findings (this person assumes the role of internal change agent); a proactive team approach.[38] According to Beer and Eisenstat, the pre-intervention phase should develop a partnership among all relevant stakeholders. It is only through mutual influence that the delicate adjustments in roles and responsibilities needed to enact a new strategy can take place between key stakeholders. In effect, members of the organization must "self-design" their organization through their own interventions.[39]

It is important to understand, however, that the individuals who are assembled may have very different interests and agendas, and they all recognize the need to work together in order to meet their separate objectives. Top management hence must foster an environment that supports the development needs of their intervention management team by committing to change interventions, identifying areas of change and associated interventions, coach the team through the intervention, and sustain the changes induced by the intervention.[40]

Whether this group should be formalized or not is an interesting question and open to differences in corporate culture and customs. Regardless of the formalization of the team, the formation of the team needs to account for existing structural and social processes that have been historically empowered with the planning function. For example, if the planning team includes members from all of the major operating Divisions of the firm then it would be appropriate to offer each Division representation on the intervention team.

In creating an intervention team, it seems reasonable that this group be fashioned as openly and as voluntary as possible. Membership of this group should be purely based upon the individual's willingness to contribute to the change process. This should not be just another committee that an individual goes to because he or she is assigned by their unit, but a meeting where the individual perceives that their own self-interest and the interests of the firm can be served. Openness will help assure equal access and involvement of any interested parties.

Phase Two - Establishing a Charter. This phase usually entails locating a consultant with expertise in the field (an external change agent) to assist the group with the intervention as well as the formalizing the intervention team. Team members should include volunteers from the original group as well as volunteers who have the authority to initiate interventions and/or the obligation to respond to it. Once membership is established, the team defines team goals that are related to the intervention effort and that are feasible and justifiable. The last step in the process is formalizing the contract with the consultant based upon the established goals of the team.

Phase Three – Formalizing. The intervention team secures legitimization and sponsorship for its efforts from influential individuals and groups as well as meets resistance to their efforts. These groups and individuals include: those whose approval endorse, formally and politically, the group's actions, those who control the resources necessary to move the project forward, those who remain neutral to the program, and those who actively oppose the program. The primary purpose of this phase is achieved by broadening the circle of people involved in the intervention effort to both internal and external stakeholders while more clearly defining the charter of the effort in the context of received feedback.   The team is seeking permission from the organization to proceed while acknowledging the rights of all of its stakeholders to have a voice in the process.

Phase Four – Intervention Identification and Selection. This phase needs to be systematic in nature and must include the concerns of the widest possible group of stakeholders.   It must also be directed toward significant problems highlighted in the strategic plan with a rationale developed for utilizing specific interventions (what change will this intervention facilitate? what problem(s) will it resolve?). The team, with the assistance of the consultant, creates a list of the problems and develops a general plan of action. This plan describes the intervention process, how the change(s) will occur, the actual intervention techniques that will be utilized to bring about the desired results, and the evaluation methodology to determine whether those results were achieved.[41]

Part of this plan should include a description of the action hypotheses, the how and why the intervention should work. Given problem A, we intend to use intervention technique C, in order to bring about result F. The need to spell out the logic behind the plan is critical to the success of the implementation of the intervention effort -- employees will not follow a plan that they cannot understand and do not think will work.

Phase Five – Reporting. Sharing, not telling or selling, is the next phase of the intervention and is undoubtedly the most decisive. It is at this point that the team comes back to organization to seek their final input before the implementation is put into action. The team must be prepared to describe the logic behind the interventions, deal with obstructionists in a polite but firm manner, and modify the interventions to accommodate viable suggestions and requests. Again, the team must go out of its way to include all of the stakeholders in this process to avoid the perception of underhandedness or exclusion.

Phases Six and Seven – Acting and Evaluating. The final two phases, the action step and evaluation, involves executing the various interventions. This should provide immediate feedback to the intervention team and the firm on the success of the interventions as well as the changes required to implement the strategic plan . Team members should distribute progress reports and hold open meetings to get reaction from both the participants in the intervention and the impacted stakeholder groups. Once the intervention has been completed, the team should conduct a final evaluation of the process in an open forum with firm. The team should then create a final report to be distributed throughout the firm and include balanced commentary from the open meeting.

The final evaluation should address the question of whether the firm achieved its goals in terms of solving its identified problems and any additional actions required to meet any unmet goals. Furthermore, since the intervention process is a fairly arduous one, the institution should also decide whether the previous effort created real value for the firm and whether or not a continued effort would be warranted or desired.

Intervention Techniques: A General Model

Not every intervention technique can deal with every organizational problem consequently it is incumbent upon us to try to provide the reader a guideline in determining when to apply which intervention technique. We have decided to categorize intervention techniques by level of analysis, more specifically, the target group in which the intervention is aimed to impact and change. Levels of analysis - individual, group, intergroup, organizational - are frequently used as diagnostic and intervention frameworks by organization development (OD) practitioners. Typically, levels of analysis catalog organizational dynamics and interventions, which an OD practitioner might use to understand organizational processes and construct interventions.[42] This is consistent with research in the field as well.[43] See Table 8.1 below.

Table 8.1
Organization Interventions by Level of Analysis[44]

Level of Analysis	Intervention Techniques
Transorganizational/Environmental	Stakeholder Analysis, Cooptation, Cooperation, Bridging, and Buffering.
Organizational/Systems Wide	Empowerment, Organizational Mirror, Confrontation Meeting, Stream Analysis, Survey Feedback, Appreciative Inquiry, MBO, TQM, Visioning, Reengineering, and Parallel Learning Structures.
Intergroup/Subsystems Interface	Intergroup Team-Building, Partnering, Organizational Mirror, Lateral Relations, and Cross-Functional Work Teams.
Team/Group/Subsystem	Team Building, Role Analysis Technique, Responsibility Charting, Force-Field Analysis, Quality Circles, Self-Managed Work Teams, Cultural Analysis, Leadership Systems 4, Grid Training, and Restructuring.
Small Group (Dyad/Triad/Interpersonal)	Transactional Analysis, Process Consultation, Third Party Peacemaking, Role Negotiation Technique, Gestalt OD.
Individual (Intra-Personal)	Sensitivity Training, Life and Career Planning, Coaching and Counseling, Education and Skill Training, Work Redesign, Cognitive Mapping, and Behavior Modeling.

Please note that we have not listed these intervention techniques in any particular order within each level of analysis since we do not believe that there are better or worse techniques within each level. Instead, each technique has been developed to address certain specific needs for change and/or improvement within the organization and can be subcategorized by the type of change expected: attitudinal, social, behavioral, technical, and structural.[45] We will now describe one or two of these techniques for each level of analysis. Some of the techniques not described in this section are described in the appendix to this chapter.

Individual (Intra-personal) Interventions. Interventions at the individual level deal with overcoming resistance to change (attitudinal), personal development (educational), developing team players (social), and increasing job performance (behavioral and technical).

Sensitivity Training. One of the oldest techniques for attitudinal change and overcoming resistance is sensitivity training (also known as encounter groups or T-groups). Sensitivity training began in the 1940s and 1950s with experimental studies of groups carried out by psychologist Kurt Lewin at the National Training Laboratories in Maine. Although the groups (called training or T-groups) were originally intended only to provide research data, their members requested a more active role in the project. The researchers agreed, and T-group experiments also became learning experiences for their subjects. The techniques employed by Lewin and his colleagues, collectively known as sensitivity training, were widely adopted for use in a variety of settings. Initially, they were used to train individuals in business, industry, the military, the ministry, education, and other professions. In the 1960s and 1970s, sensitivity training was adopted by the human potential movement, which introduced the "encounter group." Although encounter groups apply the basic T-group techniques, they emphasize personal growth, stressing such factors as self-expression and intense emotional experience.[46]

Considered a management fad of the 1960's,[47] this technique has made a rebirth in the 1990's in the areas of diversity training and international relations.[48] This technique focuses upon the desire to develop the skill of sensitivity in participants in the belief that greater sensitivity to oneself and others would lead to greater understanding and acceptance of individual differences and changing times.[49]

More specifically, the goals of this technique include:

A. increased understanding, insight and self-awareness about the way participants see themselves and others and others perceive them.

B. increased understand and sensitivity to others' thoughts and feelings through the reading of verbal and nonverbal communication.
C. better understand of interpersonal and intra-group interactions.
D. increased diagnostic skills about personal, interpersonal and group interactions.
E. transferring this learning into action so that participants can apply this new learning on-the-job and increase their effectiveness.[50]

Yet how is this to be accomplished? First, the underlying premise is that self-insight and awareness of others must be derived from an experiential learning approach in a group setting. One cannot get in touch with one's own feelings through a lecture or seeing a film; one must be placed in a setting where feelings may be expressed to others, as well as expressed by others to oneself. In this setting group members are used as objective mirrors to provide each participant feedback on their behavior and attitudes.

In order to facilitate an individual's ability to get in touch with one's emotion and create a safe, risk-free environment, the training is usually conducted outside of the business and amongst strangers. This creates a learning laboratory of sorts since participants are separated from their organizations and coworkers in a controlled environment. Variations of group composition include peer groups (workers from the same industry), cousin labs (workers from the same company), and family labs (workers in the same work group); these are considered viable alternatives by some change agents since the ability to transfer learning from these T-groups back to the firm is somewhat correlated to openness and climate of the firm.[51]

Encounter groups generally consist of between 12 and 20 people and a facilitator who meet in an intensive weekend session or in a number of sessions over a period of weeks or months. The group members work on reducing defensiveness and achieving a maximum of openness and honesty. Initially, participants tend to resist expressing their feelings fully, but eventually become more open in discussing both their lives outside the group and the interactions within the group itself. Gradually, a climate of trust develops among the group members, and they increasingly abandon the defenses and facades habitually used in dealing with other people.

The trainer or group leader is the key to learning process in that the trainer's role is to serve as a resource for the group and is to facilitate self-reflection and interaction amongst the members. The process of learning is driven by the passive mode of the facilitator, that is, the facilitator becomes just another member of the group and has no special status or control of the sessions. The trainer's job is assisting members of the group to reflect on individual and group processes and not to lead the session.

The first session of the T-group is started by the trainer who, after briefly introducing him or herself and the role of the trainer, lapses into silence. Individuals in the group are challenged through the trainer's absence as leader to develop an agenda for the group as well as to fill the leadership void. This may cause some real confusion for task-oriented individuals who will find the lack of purpose and leadership upsetting. In many cases, these individuals will try to take over the leadership of the group which may be resisted by the other group members (but not the trainer) and lead to confrontation and arguments.

As the individuals continue to struggle with the purpose of the group and members' roles, the trainer will comment and ask questions concerning participants' feelings and behaviors, and the affect that participant behaviors have on others. Some participants will 'get it' so to speak; understand that the purpose of the intervention is self-discovery through others' feedback while others may withdraw from the process since they see little value in self-examination. The trainer must at all times underscore the supportive, open, and compassionate nature of the intervention and ensure the mental safety of participants.

The effectiveness of T-groups and other forms of sensitivity training have been debated in the literature at length.[52] Openness techniques, such as T-groups, which involve people talking candidly about themselves as they relate and interact with others, has experienced limited success due to the technique gaining a reputation for producing negative results by psychologically hurting individuals or damaging work relationships. Although the increased self-awareness resulting from sensitivity training is presumed to change a person's behavior in daily life, studies of encounter-group participants have raised doubts as to whether their training experiences actually effect long-lasting behavioral changes.

Even when group participants have had a good experience, the participants sometimes had difficulty applying what they have learned to their work, possibly because the intensive group culture and conventional work culture tended toward opposite poles with regard to openness. In addition, the usefulness of encounter groups is limited to psychologically healthy individuals, as the intense and honest nature of the group discussions may prove harmful to persons with emotional disorders. Despite this failure, there is much participants can learn about how openness can, and cannot, operate in organizations.[53]

Cognitive Mapping.[54] Cognition describes the mental models, or belief systems, that people use to interpret, frame, simplify, and make sense of otherwise complex problems. Many writers refer to these mental models variously, as cognitive maps, scripts, schema, and frames of reference. They are built from past experiences and comprise internally represented concepts and relationships among concepts that an individual can then use to interpret new events.

Cognitive mapping is a set of techniques for studying and recording people's perceptions about their environment. These perceptions are recorded graphically in the form of a mental map that shows concepts and relationships between concepts. Cognitive mapping, as an intervention technique, has both strategic and developmental value. From a strategic standpoint, cognitive maps allow planners and administrators to determine from their stakeholders which variables and causal beliefs about those variables are critical to the implementation of the repositioning of the firm and what are the perceived barriers to change. Once the variables and casual relationships are determined, maps are created, and planners can test out their logic and ascertain the viability of their plans. Cognitive mapping has consequently been proposed as a means for managing the creative side of strategic thinking and problem-solving process. Through cognitive mapping, the planners' explanatory and predictive beliefs about a problem and its solutions are graphically modeled so that members of a planning group are better able to understand one another's positions and underlying assumptions. Therefore, members can draw upon their own and others' personal wisdom in creatively developing the firm's strategy.[55]

From a developmental perspective, mapping allows employees of the firm to share their worldview of both the internal and external environment. Furthermore, these maps set the foundation for discussions about the institution and provide a forum for understanding and agreement as to how the world appears to be from varying stakeholders' perspectives. One can gain tremendous value through this sharing process. Individuals receive acknowledgement for their perceptions, acceptance of the fact that different people see the institution differently, and more importantly, can visually see the commonality amongst differing groups and individuals.[56]

Among researchers interested in organizations and management, some of those who use cognitive mapping share a common objective - to improve organizational action. Some intervene directly at the level of the organization while others prefer to achieve this indirectly, by working at the individual level. Those who work at the individual level rely on the emancipating properties of a cognitive map, which facilitates reflection. The cognitive map and its construction are characterized by the notions of natural logic, schematization, representation, knowledge, and schema.[57]

Cognitive maps contain two basic elements, concepts and causal beliefs. Concepts are variables that define some aspect or characteristic of the system under analysis while causal beliefs describe the relationships that link concepts within maps. When a cognitive map is drawn, concept variables are usually represented by points and the causal relationships by arrows connecting the cause variable to the effect variable. Causal relationships may be assigned a direction and value. Values indicate the strength of the relationship and are sometimes used to quantify the maps. Plus signs are used to indicate a positive association between variables (an increase/decrease in x causes an increase/decrease in y) and a minus sign a negative association (an increase/ decrease in x causes a decrease/increase in y). A completed map provides a graphical representation of the structure of the system as perceived by an employee that includes the variables within the domain as well as the relationships between them that influence system processes and outcomes.[58] See Figure 8.2 for an example of cognitive mapping in strategy formulation.

Figure 8.2
Cognitive Mapping of the Perceived Success of Southwest Airlines

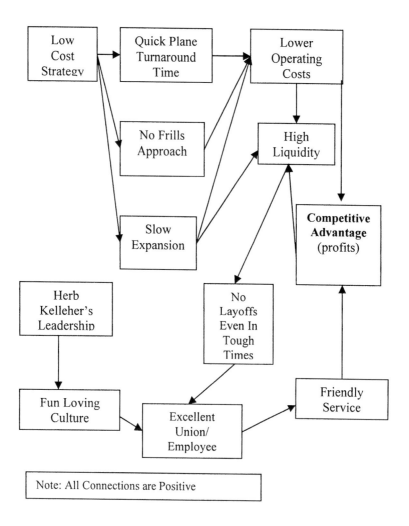

Notice that in Figure 8.2 the authors believe that the variable 'low cost strategy' gives rise to quick plane turnaround, a no frills approach, and slow expansion which leads to lower operating costs and therein high liquidity and a competitive advantage. Further the authors believe that Herb Kelleher's leadership style produces a fun loving culture which leads to excellent union/employees relations hence friendly service, and finally a competitive advantage. We believe that the firm's high liquidity is caused by the firm's slow expansion plans, its low cost operation, and its profitability. This liquidity allows Southwest to have full employment during harsh economic times which also leads to excellent union/employee relations.

Note that cognitive maps are an individual's perception of a situation and, since the map is based upon subjective observation, there is no right way to construct the map. Secondly, part of the exercise in using cognitive maps would not only have the individual explore his or her own perceptions of a situation but also to compare and contrast the cognitive map with others. Thinking about the similarities and differences would lead to self-discovery as well as knowledge of others.

Once the firm has developed an agreed upon composite map, the firm can then answer the question posited earlier about what happens when Herb Kelleher is no longer running Southwest Airlines. Using the authors' cognitive map as an example, without Herb to support the friendly environment perhaps Southwest no longer becomes a fun place to work and employees and the union become less cooperative. Yet what seemed to drive the distress of employees was not that Southwest seemed to become more strict in terms of accepted behaviors but that Southwest was imposing longer working hours and less break time. This suggests that Herb Kelleher's leadership went beyond just shaping culture but had a direct effect on the working conditions of employees (a variable not in the model) which affects employee relations. If this were a strategy session, we would then adjust the cognitive map to include these variables and relationships. This exercise could be repeated in numerous ways as an employee intervention – imagine asking a disgruntled employee of the Chrysler Division to map the DaimlerChrysler merger and then compare his or her map to perhaps the map of a Daimler manager involved in the merger.

Paul (1994) provided an excellent example of a form of cognitive mapping. At an executive training session, Tinkertoy building blocks were used to teach about leadership and decision making in groups. The executives were asked to work in groups to create a model that represented what their organizations looked like. Although hesitant at first, at least some of the executives left with the realization that participation and reflection are initial components of learning and that model building is an effective way to train people in participation. The exercise with Tinkertoy blocks used the idea that a learner can build a symbol to reflect his perspective on an environment. Mapping through the use of the Tinkertoy exercise can be helpful in organizations undergoing change. Having employees at all levels do some cognitive mapping can be a first step in gaining everyone's commitment to participate in a change effort.[59]

Cognitive sculpting is a new technique for helping managers to talk through and develop their view of difficult and complex issues, which are given expression by arranging a collection of objects, some of them symbolically rich, in an arrangement or sculpture. At the same time, the managers describe and develop the meanings being given to, and the relationships between, the objects in question. The technique is in the tradition of elicitation techniques, such as cognitive mapping, in that it encourages a person or a group to dialogue with a physical representation of their ideas. Meanings are not merely described but sometimes actively constructed or negotiated. Theoretically, the technique draws on recent work in cognitive psychology and linguistics on metaphors. It has been argued that, even better than 2-dimensional techniques, cognitive sculpting offers the requisite variety to capture and communicate the richness and metaphoric complexity of managers' views of their world.[60]

Interpersonal and Small Group Interventions. Although many of the techniques described for individual interventions involve group learning and group processes (i.e. T-groups and behavior modeling) and may be used for increasing individuals' skills in interpersonal and group communications (T-groups), their focus is on individual learning and improvement.   The following intervention techniques attempt to change the attitudinal, social, behavioral, and technical aspects of employee interactions at the dyad-triad level of analysis.

Transactional Analysis (TA).[61]   TA is an especially helpful tool for a supervisor's tool bag in that it provides an explanation of the roles we assume in our interpersonal communications and relationships, and identifies the types of relationships that work and those that do not. The field of transactional analysis has been around for about 50 years. Its aim is to show how people interact based on the roles and perceptions they have regarding themselves and others.   The parent-child-adult model (PCA) is an excellent way of viewing personal interactions. It views the roles people assume in communicating with each other, and as the model demonstrates, it suggests that some of the transactions that occur when people assume one of the roles are more functional than others. There are three main roles here, the role of the parent, the role of the adult, and the role of the child. The figure also suggests certain relationships and their effectiveness.

Role of the Parent.   The parent is a strong role in TA.   It comes from the role all of us have experienced as children growing up. Our parents (or those who raised us) employed a system of formal and informal controls that allowed them to direct our actions, thinking patterns, cognitive development, and attitudes. These were care-giving people who nurtured us, protected us, corrected us, and sometimes punished us. The parent can show emotion, both anger, as well as joy and pride. Paternalism is a term often used to describe a good parent. In the workplace, the parental role is alive and well.   Since management is responsible for the organization, controls resources, and is responsible for the activities of subordinates, it is understandable that they might rely on their own parental experience as a model for how to get things done. Paternalism is accepted and sometimes even expected.[62]

Role of the Child.   The child is also a very powerful role. As a child, everyone has had the experience of not knowing what to do, depending on others, being nurtured, learning, being corrected, and being punished. Another one of the most important things that children do is play. As people mature into adulthood, these lessons learned and these tendencies, or predispositions, to act in certain ways continues as a strong influence.

In the workplace, it is easy to allude to the role of the child as the one many subordinates are in – either by choice or by circumstance. Often, the traditions of the organization speak to first-line employees as children – management makes all the plans, management makes all the decisions, management controls all the resources, and management has all the power. In this type of a setting (very similar once again to that which we find in colleges and universities), employees survive when they accept the child role and initiate little initiative or confrontational behaviors. The other circumstance is the choice to be a child – refusing to take the initiative, needing to be led, afraid of responsibility, often very emotional, and just doing the job.

The Role of the Adult. The role of the adult is extremely important in organizations, but the weakest of the three described in TA. The most striking qualities of the behaviors of the adult are that they are objective, honest, and fair. The adult tries to recognize what is true and to act accordingly. On the downside, the adult tries to act without allowing emotions influence decisions or actions.

Inter-role Activities. The roles in and of themselves are interesting to note. However, one needs to view these from a superior-subordinate, interactive perspective, or role set. That is, both superiors and their subordinates enact these roles simultaneously and thereby create a paired set of roles. Some of these paired sets are very functional (these are relationships that can work), some are very dysfunctional (people in these relationships experience a great amount of friction between them), while some can be either functional or dysfunctional depending upon the circumstances. These role sets are represented in Figure 8.3.

Complimentary Transactions. As the model suggests, there are three functional relationships or role sets: 1) one person behaving as a child in the presence of someone who behaves as a parent; 2) one person behaving as a parent in a relationship where the other person behaves as a child; and 3) one person behaves as an adult in a relationship where the other person also behaves as an adult. The parent-child behaviors are understandable and come directly from the

Figure 8.3
The Transactional Analysis Relationships Model

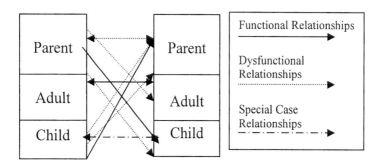

parental-child experiences of growing up. Though familiar, and while they are functional, these relationships are not optimal for the organization and are considered unhealthy to the organization in the long run. For example, the child does not engage in innovation, creativity, or perhaps even honesty, so the organization does not get the full benefits of their skills and competencies. Also, the parent has to spend so much time directing and leading, that other activities go undone or are done less well.

The adult-adult relationship is different. Not only is it functional, it promotes the full use of the human resources in both the subordinate and the supervisor. The relationship is objective, honest, open, and innovative. These are major positives for both the people in the relationship as well as the organization. Everyone wins (a "win-win" relationship).

Crossed Transactions. The model shows a variety of circumstances where the mix of the relationship results in dysfunctional operations and outcomes. When both participants behave as parents, there is obvious friction because neither party recognizes the authority of the other. When one participant behaves as a parent and the other as an adult, there is friction because both participants need a different type of response in their relationship that they are not getting. Here, because of the strength of the parent role, the normal situation is that the adult becomes the child in order to achieve some level of harmony (though resentment could be present). Similarly, when one participant behaves as an adult and the other as a child, friction again comes as a result of neither participant receiving the responses they prefer in their relationships. Often, the extreme power of the child is usually effective in forcing the adult into a parental position.

A Special Crossed Transaction: Child-Child.   The model identifies one final relationship that can be either functional or dysfunctional, based on the circumstances. The child-child relationship is functional, when it is all right to play, and such circumstances exist. Time away from the office, parties, clearly social occasions, and being able to see the humor in a difficult situation are all made more enjoyable when the participants can be more child-like in their behaviors. Child-child relationships can be disastrous when important work needs to be done.   When no one in the relationship takes responsibility, uses initiative, or exercises honesty, results are never good.

Ulterior Transaction.   Here the employee is communicating using one ego state while intending another. For example, the manager asks for the employee's input yet has already made up his or her mind about the situation prior to consultation. By hiding his or her ego state from the other individual, communication is blocked creating an environment of distrust.[63]

Strokes.   These transactions produced what Berne called strokes, the units of interpersonal recognition, which help individuals survive and thrive. Complimentary transactions tend to lead to positive strokes, crossed and ulterior transactions to negative strokes. Understanding how people give and receive positive and negative strokes and changing unhealthy patterns of stroking are powerful aspects transactional analysis.

The TA intervention is based on an examination of interpersonal encounters to determine which of the three ego states - parent, adult, child - are involved. Used correctly, TA can help a manager motivate employees, increase productivity, and improve interpersonal relations. TA comprises four basic parts: structural analysis (having the participants describe the ego states that occur during a specific transaction), transactional analysis (participants describe the types of transactions that occur), game analysis (understanding the underlying motives behind the role playing) and script analysis (analyzing dysfunctional behaviors which have become routine because of previous positive and negative strokes associated with the behavior).[64] Identifying and breaking up psychological games, which can result in injury, mental illness, or even death, is one of the most productive uses of TA. The most common organizational use of TA, however, is as a means for avoiding communication breakdown.[65]

TA has fallen out of favor as an intervention technique in the last decade since it has been criticized as simplistic, superficial, therapy (not training), and ineffective. Hay noted that there are many misconceptions about TA including that the adult state is the only proper state of communication. She postulated that many trainers have abused the TA system and have failed to point out that the purpose of TA is not only bettering interpersonal communications but self-discovery and self-acceptance.[66]

Process Consultation (PC). According to the father of PC, Edgar H. Schein, "PC is a set of activities on the part of the consultant which help the client perceive, understand, and act upon process events which occur in the client's environment."[67] PC consequently helps the client learn how to learn about him or herself and his or her interaction with others. Schein indicated that there are six types of clients in the process consulting: contact clients (the individual(s) who first contact the consultant with a request, question or issue); intermediate clients (the individuals or groups who or which get involved in various interviews, meetings, and other activities as the project evolves); primary clients (the individual(s) who ultimately own the problem or issue being worked on; they are typically also the ones who pay the consulting bills or whose budget covers the consultation project); unwitting clients (members of the organization or client system above, below and laterally related to the primary clients who will be affected by interventions but who are not aware that they will be impacted); indirect clients (members of the organization who are aware that they will be affected by the interventions but who are unknown to the consultant and who may feel either positive or negative about these effects); and ultimate clients (the community, the total organization, an occupational group, or any other group that the consultant cares about and whose welfare must be considered in any intervention that the consultant makes).[68]

So what makes PC different from any other typical organization intervention managed by an external change agent? Schein noted that PC is much more of a clinical approach to organization intervention in that it starts, not with the typical diagnosis phase of gathering data about the organization, but instead with the needs of the client. The client drives the process and involves the researcher in the client's issues rather than the researcher involving the client in the issues the researcher thinks is driving the firm. The word clinical is deliberately used by Schein in order to highlight that some perceived problem of the client is involved and that the consultant takes on the obligations that are associated with being a helper rather than a problem-solver. The interests and the welfare of the client must be protected at all times, and all of the consultant's actions, whether diagnostic or not, are de facto interventions and must be evaluated as possible interventions before they are undertaken.[69]

In process consultation, the consultant becomes deeply involved in the client's system and assists the client in learning about that system whether the system is an individual person, a small group, or the entire firm. The client is actively involved and responsible for the process with the PC consultant providing a strong supportive presence through high client contact. The primary tasks for the consultant are to gather valid information, and to make it possible for the client to make free and informed choices and to help the client become committed to the choices that have been made.[70] PC, however, is highly dependent on group involvement and participation by members of the client system in the diagnostic and problem-solving states. The client and the consultant must discuss the assumptions that they have in order to develop the appropriate psychological contract and role expectations each has of the other. The consultant must start where the client is in terms of readiness for a particular consulting approach rather than forcing a prescribed intervention.[71]

According to Lind, the PC consulting experience consists of: an impulse or idea coming from within the client or sense impressions from the surrounding world, intensified and increased awareness of the client of a problem, a mobilization of energy for change by the client, client change actions, interpersonal and group contact with the consultant, the culmination of the merger of energy and action, resolution or closure, and withdrawal of awareness. These principles and processes apply to individuals, as well as to groups of people. The consultant's function then is to intervene so that conditions for learning are created.[72]

Schein denoted that the consultant must understand that only the client ultimately knows what he or she can do, will do, and wants to do, hence the strategic goal of process consultation must be to develop a process that will build the consultant and client into a team that will own all the interventions. Further, that it is the job of the consultant to educate the client through the early interventions on the potential consequences of later interventions and that everything the consultant does, from the earliest responses to the client's initial inquiries, is an intervention. The consultant must be highly aware of the consequences of different diagnostic interventions.[73]

Even though process consultation has been widely practiced there is only a modest amount of research on the technique. None of the available studies have produced concrete evidence of a favorable impact of process consultation on client groups. Research findings on the effects of efforts to promote group development are somewhat vague. It is important that interventions relate to the criteria of job performance and that their consequences be assessed by those criteria rather than measured against some psychologically ideal state. Most small group and personal interventions appear to be isolated from task performance. The humanistic values of the small group tradition need to be blended with the real complexities of today's organizational life.[74]

Team/Group/Subsystem Interventions. Team and group interventions focus on the social, behavioral, technical, and structural aspects of the group's performance while subsystems interventions deal directly with the system in question (i.e. organization redesign for changes in firm's structure; leadership training in addressing the issue of leadership style, and cultural analysis to examine the firm's underlying social system).

Team Building. The way work is being performed is changing, with middle management being reduced or eliminated by organizations that are flattening their structures through new business process methodologies. Many of these changes are being caused by restructuring, mergers and acquisitions, global competition and changing work trends. Teams are becoming more of the norm in this new workplace and teams are seen as one way of leveraging organizational strengths to offset new competitive challenges. Furthermore, teams are beginning to change the way workers work and organizations are beginning to realize that a 'we' culture may better suit business needs than the traditional 'I' culture.

Group dynamics has been an area of intense study in management since the 1940's and has re-emerged as one of the keys to developing a successful firm. In the 21st century team building, whether it be called developing self-managed work teams or cross-functional work teams, has been one of the hottest, and most applied intervention techniques. Research has shown that team building takes time and effort to produce systematic, lasting results.[75] Team building is one of a few techniques that meta-analyses of intervention studies proved has a positive impact on employee attitude and satisfaction.[76] Teams create more visionary and creative results than one person usually ever can. Building a team is defined as equipping the people of the organization with the necessary information, skills, and competencies to leverage their collective think power. Building a team produces tangible end-results. People are able to identify strategies for addressing issues and opportunities in addition to having realized solutions during the intervention.[77]

Team building is not as easy as it sounds. The team building process often is flawed right from the start since managers may try to form and implement teams without a plan and an understanding of group dynamics. They may initiate team building based upon intuition instead of common sense yet team building requires logic and creativity. Employees must have the opportunity to get used to the idea of teams. For management to demand team building is a mistake since employees who are not used to working with one another or who are used to working independently will resist a mandate to form teams. Potential team members need to know there is something in it for them since if they suspect teams are being built to reduce the workforce or to make them do more work with no reward, they will sabotage the process. There are several guidelines for team building, including start talking about teams early, select team membership for success, go slow to go fast, and create a common goal from the start.[78] Tippet and Peters's research of over one hundred teams indicated that despite positive indications on some of the key team-building elements, overall companies were generally doing a poor job of team building. Weaknesses included lack of effective rewards, inadequate individual and team performance feedback mechanisms, lack of project management skills, and inadequate individual and team goal setting. In a number of cases, management was taking advantage of the downsizing environment and uncertainty by treating employees as disposable assets, knowing they feared for their jobs.[79]

For team building to work, management must put themselves at as much risk as other employees in the team building process, that is, management must be prepared to share the workload related to team building while relinquishing some decision-making power to the team. To lead a successful team, team leaders need to stop acting authoritatively, engage and facilitate people, deal with group dominators, share their vision, and commit themselves to the process.[80] A team leader should concentrate on getting results by creating a high-expectations climate where team members accomplish what they are expected to accomplish. Leaders should coach team members to set high standards to achieve meaningful results. A supervisor can become a more effective team member by helping the team define the results it wants to achieve, praising team members liberally for what they achieve, training the team to do the job, and keeping communication lines open.[81] Some of the most common mistakes made by management in team building are not allowing the team to define its own mission, having someone else do the team's planning, not ascribing due dates to tasks, and not training.[82]

Team building begins with the concepts that the people on the team are all part of the team, are all individuals, all want to succeed to varying degrees, and all have different skills. By encouraging team members to plan together, they are bonded by an agreed upon and common purpose, one in which they can all participate. Teamwork requires commitment and effort, a willingness to accept the uniqueness of others, and an appreciation of diversity. The most successful teams are clear about their goals and how each person contributes to achieving them.[83] Team building is a process in which participants and facilitators experience increasing levels of trust, openness, and willingness to explore core issues that affect excellent team functioning.[84]

The need for team building usually starts with the manager of a work unit noticing a lowering of productivity and/or morale. More specifically, the manager might have observed a reduction of unit output, an increase in the number of complaints and grievances, increased conflict and hostility amongst unit members, unclear roles and task ambiguity, incomplete assignments, apathy and a lack of innovation, ineffective group meetings, hostility towards the manager, increased costs, and customer complaints.[85]   In order to implement team building, firms often turn to outside facilitators, armed with team-building and development skills, to help teams become more viable and productive organizational entities. Team-building facilitators (internal or external) structure their interventions to fulfill three broad goals: they want team members to appreciate and understand the complexity and dynamics of the team-building process; they want members to identify needs and build greater proficiency in the approaches and skills necessary to help the team develop; and they want to create a forum for discourse - a safe and open environment in which team members can ask tough questions and share deep concerns that have been plaguing them and their team's movements.[86]

There are differing models of team building including the goal-setting model (getting the team to establish goals, assign activities, and evaluate its progress, i.e. MBO), the interpersonal model (working on team member communication and interaction, i.e. transactional analysis), the role model (developing an understanding of each member's tasks and responsibilities, i.e. role analysis technique), and leadership model (developing an appropriate team leadership style, i.e. grid training).[87]   Regardless of the model that may be employed, all team building starts with pre-preparation where team members learn about the purpose and process of team building, and, more importantly, given a chance to air their questions and concerns. This will allow the facilitator (external consultant or manager) of the team building intervention to also observe some of the group dynamics of the team and determine the relative readiness of the team to participate in this change technique.[88]   The start-up phase begins the job of creating a climate where people feel comfortable to work and usually involves some sort of ice breaking exercise (i.e. administering a short survey about participants' feelings about the team building intervention, an experiential exercise where the team is asked to describe itself as an object or animal or to draw or construct something that represents the group, or a mock work session where the team is asked to work on a real problem while being observed by the facilitator).   Before the exercise begins, the facilitator may encourage participants to develop systems of rules or "contracts" that regulate the purpose of the relationship and define acceptable behavior in order to create an environment in which team members can exchange the correct type of information.   A task contract deals with the goals and strategy of the team and a personal contract deals with the dynamics within the group. The personal contract should establish safe areas wherein team members feel free to be open and share personal information affecting the group's effectiveness. The creation of safe areas provides the group with a mechanism for dealing with such destructive elements as personal anger and group conflict. Contract packages need to be openly discussed and understood by all participants. As the group develops and matures, contracts require regular review to determine if they continue to meet the group's needs.[89]

        At the end of the exercise the group is asked to discuss the data gathered at this first meeting (whether it be survey data or facilitator and participant observations) and to diagnose the findings. The facilitator starts the diagnosis by asking team members what questions do they think need to be asked about the team and the exercise and helps participants form the questions to be asked. Questions are asked such as: what are the team's strengths and weaknesses; what are their opportunities growth and threats to team development; how can the team use its strengths to overcome its weaknesses and take advantage of opportunities; what technical, human relations, and conceptual skills do group members need to better team performance; is there a critical task or problem that the teams needs to tackle now, etc...

Once the questions have been asked, the facilitator tries to clarify and categorize them into different themes or topics (task accomplishment, interpersonal relations, group process [i.e communication and roles], and team culture). Once the questions have been sorted, the team is asked to prioritize the questions and determine which questions they want to tackle first. The group then develops assignments for team members that usually involve data gathering so that they can answer, as a team, the questions they have posed, and sets deadlines and future meeting dates. These future meetings become working sessions for the team who may ask the facilitator to assist the team by providing specific training services (i.e. case analyses to sharpen problem solving, role playing to enhance interpersonal skills, active listening exercises to clarify communications, etc...). The team is also being asked to assess their progress in addressing the questions they originally posed and to determine what additional resources and support they need in order to become a high performance team. As the team improves, the role of the facilitator will be reduced to a point where, at least in theory, the group is self-monitoring and self-developing and no longer requires assistance, except for occasional consultation.

Intergroup/Subsystems Interface Interventions. These interventions address social, behavioral, and structural dimensions of intergroup behavior and subsystem interface with the intergroup techniques being similar to group and interpersonal interventions. For example, intergroup team building is similar in intent and method to team building except that the separate teams work independently to analyze the problems and then come together as one group to share their findings in order to develop joint questions and create joint problem-solving task forces. An organizational mirror is similar to third party peace making except that in this case the third party is a mutually agreeable team or work group who interacts with the other two teams that are having difficulties.[90]

Lateral Relations.[91] When two or more groups need to coordinate their operations and the firm does not want to permanently change its formal structure in order to create formal reporting lines of authority and communications, the firm may intervene in its own information processing by developing an alternative human information network (a secondary structure) that creates a bridge or interface between these groups. The role of the facilitator or change agent in this intervention is to describe the differing lateral relation options available to the firm, determine what skills or competencies would be required by those involved in the intervention, provide training where needed, and assisting in the evaluation of the intervention. Galbraith notes that there are seven options, see Figure 8.4.[92]

Direct contact, allowing two members from different organization units or teams to contact one another who share a problem without permission from both their superiors (bypassing the normal chain of command), is the most efficient, simplest and least formal intervention. In order to foster interdepartmental or interteam contact, many firms employ job rotation and job transfers between operating units. This breaks down the impersonality of inter-unit contacts by having former team members with prior familiarity feel contact one another.

Liaison roles make direct contact (which is informal in nature and unplanned) a little more formal by designating a particular person on each team to act as the contact person for the group. Any information that needs to be passed from one team to another flows through the two liaisons, who may be asked to serve as ad-hoc members on the other team's meetings and planning sessions. When problems arise in the organization when more than just two or three different teams or work units are involved, the firm may establish a task force, a temporary committee or one may arise informally. Task forces allow input and representation from each of the work units through a designated or emergent representative and simultaneously provide each team feedback through its spokesperson.

If the problems are of a more permanent basis, teams are formally created to address these problems. (See the prior discussion on team building in terms of how to create effective teams.) Teams may vary in purpose and composition. For example, cross-functional teams include a member from each impacted work unit and usually involves several business functions (i.e. marketing, finance, operations, information systems). Self-managed work teams are teams that operate without a designated manager or leader while junior executive boards and quality circles are parallel structures to the board of directors and

Figure 8.4
Types of Lateral Interventions

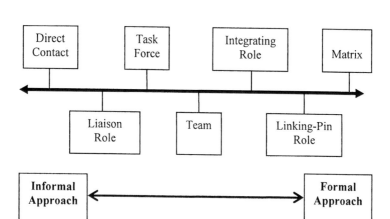

represent the interests of middle-level and lower-level managers and employees. Teams may be formed for the purpose of merely disseminating and sharing information, or making recommendations to a superior, or empowered to actually make decisions.

Integrating, linking, and matrix lateral relations are used as intervention strategies when the firm has highly differentiated operating work units (i.e. specialized units that produce parts of a unique good and service for niche markets), which need to be coordinated in order to create a particular good or service. Each unit must maintain its independence and uniqueness while simultaneously integrating its operation with the other units. Cross-functional teams may be ineffective in these cases since specialization within the cross-functional team would be lower when compared to a unit purely devoted to each of the functions the team performs. Integrating roles are managerial positions established by the firm to assist those individuals and work units in task completion. These individuals do not supervise the work in question but act as general managers for a particular work process (i.e. product or project manager) although they have no formal authority over the workers in question. Integrators hence are staff personnel -- they may chair task forces or teams but must coordinate work efforts through their organizational contacts, the development of trust amongst the different work units in question, their expertise on work processes, and their role as an information center.

The firm may find that information and expert power may be inadequate to properly coordinate the work in question. The work may cut across such a disparate set of business functions and specializations that developing an expertise in all of these areas by one individual may be difficult, if not impossible, thus minimizing the ability of the integrator to influence work processes without formal organizational authority. The firm may then opt to increase the formal authority of the integrator and create a linking manager, an individual that now may have some supervisory capacity of the task of the differing work units. This is accomplished by the firm providing the linking manager at least partial decision-making authority over certain portions of the work process, earlier entrance and influence into the decision-making process surrounding the work, and at least partial control of the budget. Finally, if the firm is not satisfied with the linking manager's ability to integrate work across work units, the firm may opt to completely formalize the linking relationship by creating a matrix structure. Here the matrix manager is given complete authority over the work processes across all of the work units and concurrently reports to all of the managers who are responsible for the operating units involved in the work process (see Chapter 6 for a description of matrix structures).

Organizational/Systems Wide Interventions. These comprehensive techniques impact all of the organization's subsystems and work groups and deal with core organizational issues. Each technique takes a differing approach to total organizational change (i.e. the confrontation meeting has the entire management of a firm meet for one day to analyze the firm and develop action plans,[93] MBO develops a systematic methodology for coordinating goal-setting through negotiations,[94] and TQM creates a management system which focuses on creating total customer service and satisfaction[95]) yet each technique shares in common the need for the firm to master change and therein transform the entire organization.[96]

Empowerment.[97] Empowerment is one of the pinnacle values of strategic management in that it provides the means in which highly competent employees can make decisions without consultation. Empowered employees are motivated employees. They excel at their job and profession. Decisions made by lower level, highly specialized employees, provide for a rapid response to on-the-job problems and/or clients and consequently creates a competitive advantage for the firm.[98] Silver observed that in many workplaces, empowerment is regarded as a fad that had its 15 minutes of fame and has joined the ranks of other so-called management fads including zero-based budgeting, re-engineering, total quality management, and customer focus. Empowerment, however, is different. Unlike other fads, he believes that the desire of all employees to be empowered will only grow over time, and organizations that do not take this concept seriously are ultimately at risk.[99]

Empowerment is an enabling and ennobling process where employees learn how to overcome their feelings of powerlessness and gain power and then invest their power in others. Empowerment interventions focus on the personal characteristics of employees (their task-relevant knowledge, personal attraction, effort, and behavioral fit with the institution's values) and their position characteristics (access to information, impact on work flow, discretion in position, job visibility, and job alignment with organizational priorities). Empowering employees makes them feel that they are important and significant to the organization that their work is both challenging and exciting, that they are part of the firm, and that learning and job competency really matters. Empowerment is the first step in creating a learning, self-renewing organization.[100]

In order to empower employees, Yukl has suggested that managers express confidence in the employees' ability to get the job done, foster employee initiative and responsibility, reward and encourage employees in both personal and visible ways, involve employees in the assignment of work, build on success, and provide a collaborative work environment.[101] Macleod observed that in order for employees to feel empowered, they first need training in self-empowerment. Such programs often make a profound difference in people's lives and careers and allow them to take charge of their lives instead of allowing circumstance to control them. These programs differ in theory, technique, and terminology, but all generally share an emphasis on experimental learning. Learning by experience seems more effective in helping self-empowerment than does learning based on lectures and reading. Employees can be sent to existing, fully structured programs, or instructors can be brought into the company. Existing programs, however, tend to be inflexible in form, content, and schedule. In this training employees will, perhaps, examine their innermost desires; if those desires include a productive career, their value to their employer is enhanced. A company that provides such training may lose a few employees, but those who remain may be so much more effective that the company may gain more than it loses.[102]

Gering indicated that an empowered company pays a great deal of attention to setting up an empowerment framework. This framework includes communicating the company strategy to all managers, setting well defined goals and targets, establishing a clear link between performance and reward, instilling a culture of feedback, developing an organizational awareness of individual strengths and weaknesses, setting authority limits individually, installing a mentoring process, deliberately structure team based activity, encouraging junior and middle managers to make decisions, and managing by walkabout.[103] Lawson saw the four keys to successful empowerment as involving employees in the decision-making process, including employees in the planning process, offering praise freely, and providing continual training and support.[104]

French and Bell suggested starting the empowerment intervention by requesting that participants from their own experience describe their personal best leadership situation. They have the employees reflect on the feelings and behaviors that accompanied these situations and asked the employees and their administrators what both can do to create similar conditions.[105] This coincides with current research which has pointed to trust and leader-member relations as the key mediating variables impacting employee empowerment; the greater the trust and stronger the leader-member relations, the more the employee felt empowered.[106]

Whetten and Cameron described the empowerment intervention as including a skill pre-assessment survey, a series of readings on power and influence, a skill analysis case, skill practice exercises, skill application activities, and skill evaluation.[107] Eylon and Herman developed an in-basket exercise, which introduced the participant to either empowering or disempowering situations. Through survey feedback, dyad, small group and discussions, the group eventually is lead to develop an empowerment plan for the in-basket scenarios and the organization as a whole.[108] Mainiero and Tromley created a series of vignettes (fifteen in all), which required the participants to choose from a series of alternatives in terms of how they would handle each situation. These answers would be scored, with the each vignette answer falling into one of six empowerment styles; assertion, ingratiation, alternatives, coalitions, coercion and acquiescence. A style profile would be generated which would indicate the participants' primary strategy style as well as how this style changed from vignette to vignette.[109] Regardless of methodology, increasing employee participation in the operation of the firm will increase organization performance and employee job satisfaction.

Transorganizational/Environmental   Interventions. Organizations have traditionally sought internal solutions to performance decline and to change their internal operations to fit environmental changes. However, in many situations, a trans-organizational systems (TS) response to organizational decline may be more effective by bringing mutually threatened organizations together to fight for survival since the decline may be part of a market or industry trend. For example, many local stores will band together to contest the introduction of a large chain store such as Wal-Mart or Home Depot since they perceive these chains as direct threats that will destabilize current market dynamics. TS responses will be favorably considered by organizations that face environmental turbulence, perceive interdependence with other organizations, lack options for exiting the market, have strong commitments to social responsibility, and experience a mandate from higher and or external authorities to form external linkages. When decline is a result of shrinkage of the total market for an industry's goods or services, similar organizations, experiencing shared fates and environmental turbulence, will form TS collaborations. An organization facing declining market share will tend to form TS linkages with dissimilar organizations, which experience a shared fate at the community level and have strong social commitment.[110]

The concept of transorganization intervention (TI) is fairly new concept from an organization change perspective in that it attempts to, to paraphrase Ackoff, take a step outside the organization as a system and examine the larger system in which the organization is a part of.[111] Organizations using TI attempt to either adapt to changing markets or try to protect themselves from market changes by changing the nature and structure of competition within those markets. Preston and DuToit observed that large system changes such as changes within nations (i.e. South Africa, Russia) resemble those involved in traditional organizational change, but, because of the complexity of large systems, the interrelation and interaction between the subsystems require careful analysis. There also needs to be a clear understanding of the main actors and probable major intervening factors that can decide both the inputs and outputs in the intervention.[112]

The notion, as developed by Cummings, looks at business alliances, network organizations, consortia, and joint ventures in order to determine who are potential member organizations, then convene possible members, and finally organize the transorganizational system (TS).[113] TI involves multiple, simultaneous interventions aimed at both the TS and its constituent organizations. TI is concerned with creating and modifying networks of TS participants who have a stake in particular outcomes and depend on the network for the accomplishment of their goals. The environment or context within which interactions take place has three attributes: interactions are governed by a negotiation process in which network participants collectively define their organizing or problem issues; domains are created as stakeholders identify their special interests in these issues; and exchanges link participants together in interdependent relations. Negotiating contexts are dynamic and changing and vary as new problems become salient and old issues recede.[114]

Ironically, much of what we have described in this textbook under strategy formulation falls under the transorganizational rubric, that is, firms examining their remote, industry, and competitive environments through industry and SWOT analyses in order to determine their best position and appropriate strategy orientation in their market(s) relative to their stakeholders. Through environmental, industry, and value-chain analyses, firms can determine which environment linkages are too loose or misaligned and what actions they need to take in order to tighten those linkages. Here is where transorganization interventions become management strategy in that we have turned our analyses from within the organization to without.

Many of these interventions we have already described in Chapters 6 under the topic of cooperative strategies (joint ventures, strategic alliances, mergers, and network organizations) and growth or market bridging strategies (vertical and horizontal integration, relating and unrelated diversification, and acquisitions). These structural TI's reorganize the market/industry or the firm in order to decrease the competitiveness of the market/industry by: reducing the number of competitors in the market or market niche, sharing the risk amongst conglomerate or TS members, creating market and industry buffers for the conglomerate or current TS members, and establishing entrance barriers for non-members/competitors.

Buffering. [115] Buffering interventions create walls around the organization that, rather than adapt to market and or industry changes, allow the organization to survive (at least in the short run) in its maladaptive form. More specifically, certain buffers allow the firm's operation to continue by insuring supplies (resources/inputs) and guaranteeing customers (outputs are being purchased). The firm will specifically intervene in the industry or marketplace to ensure inputs by having liquid assets or easy access to capital, stockpiling inventory, using multiple suppliers, locking suppliers into long-term contracts, becoming their own supplier (backward integration), investing heavily in equipment maintenance and repair, and cross-training employees. [116] On the output side, the organization may itself sign long-term contracts with purchasers, sell products to distributors and wholesalers (rather directly to consumers), and become its own customer (forward integration). Note that in both the input or output approaches, the firm in many cases is intervening in its relationships with other organizations in its value chain.

These buffering interventions, however, tend to be defensive in nature by protecting the firm's inputs and outputs but not protecting the market or industry that the firm competes in. Pfeffer and Salancik noted that firms needed to become political actors in their marketplace in order to protect their interests.[117] Business's interaction with government has been well documented by such authors as C. Wright Mills and Harold Seidman; Mills hypothesized the existence of a power elite where businesses colluded with government and the military to protect the status quo while Seidman believed that a similar triumvirate existed between elected officials, businesses, and government regulators.[118]

Regardless of the exact nature of the interaction between government and business, firms do intervene in the political system through direct lobbying, campaign contributions, and indirectly through trade associations in order to influence politicians and government regulators to institute laws that would protect their economic interests and provide benefits to industry members. From the industry's standpoint, these benefits include direct cash subsidies and tax incentives, special tax deductions, entrance barriers (i.e. tariffs), legislation that negatively impacts substitute products or services, regulating prices, and purchasing of industry services. Specific firms in an industry would share these benefits but may also receive specifically earmarked benefits based upon either a set of government program participation criteria (i.e. small business, female and minority-owned businesses) or special government set aside programs.[119]

Use the Appropriate Intervention to Produce the Desired Changes

Derived from systems theory, one of the overriding principles in management is the concept of equifinality, that a manager may use one of several different approaches in order to reach a desired goal or objective; there is no one best way to manage. This certainly holds true in strategic planning where, based upon a SWOT analysis, a firm may chose from one of several corporate level strategies from the corporate level strategy matrix in which to execute the firm's mission and objectives.

However, as discussed in Chapter 6, certain corporate level strategies are not appropriate for firms given the results of a SWOT analysis. One would not select a growth strategy such as market penetration when the results of a SWOT analysis indicate a very weak company in a no growth or declining market. The point we are making is that although there are several alternatives for a firm to follow in choosing a corporate level strategy, there are in fact better and worse choices to make given one's analysis of the firm's situation as well as the knowledge we currently possess about which strategies work under what business conditions. Certain choices consequently lack face validity and will lead to Type 1 failures (as described in Chapter 7).

The same can also be assumed about strategy implementation and the use of intervention techniques to execute strategic change. If the firm decides that it needs to create a more flexible organization, then certain intervention techniques may be reasonable to employ (i.e. empowerment, lateral relations, and visioning) while others may not (i.e. third party peacemaking, buffering, and organizational mirror). In order to determine which intervention techniques are appropriate to use, we suggest asking the following questions:

1. At what level or levels of the organization does the required change(s) in strategy impact? What is the primary target of the change (market, systems-wide, team, etc...)?
2. Given the level or levels in question, what types of change(s) is(are) required? Are the changes attitudinal, social, behavioral, technical, and/or structural, or a combination thereof?
3. What activities seem necessary given the needed changes? Are they diagnostic, team-building, intergroup, education and training, structural, process management, leadership development, conflict resolution, life and career planning, goal-setting, coaching/counseling, and transformational (systems-wide)?
4. Which techniques are acceptable to the participants in the change process?

Since many of the intervention techniques have multiple targets (systems-wide change may require interventions that impact group and individual behavior), may have several change objectives (i.e. transactional analysis impacts attitudes, behavior, and social interaction), and may involve several change activities (most include a diagnostic step in the intervention), the expectation is that there may be several intervention techniques for the firm to chose from that may meet the change needs of the firm. As we suggested earlier in this chapter, an external change agent (consultant) would be quite useful in this selection process as long as the firm understood the biases and limitations of using an outside consultant.

Summary

Intervention techniques provide managers specific tools for developing employee competencies and skills, as well as assisting employees to learn how to learn, and changing the firm's processes, systems, and structures. Interventions techniques are not only appropriate for implementing strategic plans (creating both revolutionary and evolutionary change) but also can be utilized as continuous improvement and continuous learning instruments. There are three risks associated with performing an organizational intervention: risk in diagnosis, risk in prescription, and risk in treatment. In order to reduce these risks, change interventions require the assistance of a team of external and internal change agents. External change agents are trained facilitators who have the expertise and objectivity to assist the organization to learn how to learn while internal change agents understand the organization and how it operates. Both have their inherent limitations (external change agents need to quickly learn about the firm, internal change agents are subjective and may be perceived as biased).

The intervention process has been structured to educate members as to the need for change, involve them in the change process, and then evaluate the success of the intervention to elicit the desired changes. Steps in the process include convergence of interest and intervention team building, establishing a charter, formalizing the process, intervention identification and selection, reporting, acting and evaluating. Intervention techniques are categorized by level of analysis (intrapersonal, dyad/triad/small group, intragroup/subsystem, intergroup/subsystem links, organizational, and trans-organizational) with each technique addressing certain specific needs for change and/or improvement within the organization (attitudinal, social, behavioral, technical, and structural).

Several intervention techniques are described (at least one for each level) including sensitivity training (increasing self-awareness and awareness of others), cognitive mapping (understanding how one sees the organization), transactional analysis (understanding one's role interaction with others), process consultation (a client-driven approach for understanding client interactions), team building (harnessing group dynamics), lateral relations (creating an alternative communication network), empowerment (providing employees psychological ownership of the firm), and buffering (strengthening the firm's value chain and competitive advantage through supplier, customer, and political agreements). There is no best way to select an intervention technique but selection should be guided by the organizational level of the change (target group), the change required (attitudinal, social, behavioral, technical, and/or structural), activities needed for change (i.e. conflict resolution), and the acceptability of the intervention technique to the participants.

Key Terms and Concepts

Interventions; risks associated with interventions; internal and external change agents; facilitator; diagnosis; intervention process; levels of analysis; sensitivity training and T-groups; cognitive mapping; causal and moderating variables; self-awareness; transactional analysis; child, parent and adult roles; complimentary, crossed and ulterior transactions; strokes; process consultation; clinical approach; team building; cross-functional and self-managed teams; lateral relations; direct contact, liaison roles, task forces, managerial linking pins, integrators, and matrix managers; empowerment; transorganizational interventions, buffering; and equifinality.

Web Sites

http://www.ntl.org/ - The National Training Laboratories Institute's website, the home of T-training. Provides information about NTL,

Public Training programs, Graduate and Certificate programs, partners and resources, as well as membership in NTL including e-mail updates.

http://www.itaa-net.org/ta/ - The home of The International Transactional Analysis Association. Offers visitors information about TA (and in numerous applications), a calendar of organizational events, training programs, resources, a library, membership information and e-mail news. The library is a particularly good resource for abstracts and links to articles.

http://www.trainings.org/ - Home page of the Student Empowerment Training Project. This not-for-profit organization was started to provide training, materials, and technical assistance to student governments all over the country in order to make theses governments operate more effectively. The site includes training programs, an on-line manual, a newsletter, and internet links to student governments around the coutry.

http://web.nmsu.edu/~dboje/TDgameboard.html - The TransOrg Development Game, developed by David M. Boje, Editor of the Journal of Organizational Change Management, offers a rather humorous approach to understanding the sixteen approaches to transorganizational change and provides a learning lab of network consultation approaches to multi-organizational change methodologies.

Discussion Questions

1. Discuss the role and use of interventions in strategy implementation. Why can't the firm "just do it", put the strategy into action?
2. Change agents seem to be the key to organizational change and executing organizational interventions. Describe the types of agents and their roles in the change process.
3. Do you agree or disagree that sensitivity training (T-groups) and transactional analysis seemed to have dropped out of favor with change consultants because these techniques do not transfer well to

job environments? Discuss your position and provide support for
it.
4. What changes are needed at Southwest Airlines and what
    interventions do you recommend for producing those changes?
5. Going back to the Daimler Chrysler case in Chapter 7, what
    changes were needed to make the merger a success and what
    interventions do you recommend for producing those changes?

Exercises

1. Going back to the firm that you have been analyzing, what, if any,
    interventions have been tried at the firm to date? Describe those
    interventions and your perception of the success or failure of these
    techniques to produce change.
2. Going back to Chapter 7, exercise questions 2 and 3, discuss what
    intervention techniques would be needed to help the organization
    create a more perfect fit in terms of the market's structure (Table
    7.1) or the industry's life cycle (Table 7.2).
3. Going back to Chapter 7, exercise question 4, which intervention
    techniques might be helpful for overcoming resistance to change?
4. What other interventions might be needed in the firm given the
    firm's strategic plan and the strategic direction that you believe the
    firm needs to follow. Are there skills and competencies that need
    to be developed, systems readjusted, etc...?

Experiential Exercise

Are Your ready to Change?[120]

Learning Objectives:
1. For students to experience an intra-individual intervention exercise
    that is utilized to assess an individual's readiness for change.
2. For students to see how strategic change may require overcoming
    individual, group, and organizational resistance to change.
3. For students to assess their own change competency, and the
    change competency of their in-class group (if they are in one), and
    their class.

Procedure:
1. Complete the following questionnaire utilizing a 1-7 scale where 1 means completely disagree; 4 means neither agree nor disagree; and 7 completely agree.

_____ 1. I believe that an expert who doesn't come up with a definitive answer probably doesn't know too much.

_____ 2. I think it would be fun to live in a foreign country for a period of time.

_____ 3. The sooner we all agree on some common values and ideals, the better.

_____ 4. A good teacher is one who makes you wonder about your way of looking at things.

_____ 5. I enjoy parties where I know most of the people more than ones where all or most of the people are strangers.

_____ 6. Supervisors who hand out vague assignments give me a chance to show initiative and originality.

_____ 7. People who lead even, regular lives – in which few surprises or unexpected events arise – really have a lot to be grateful for.

_____ 8. Many of our most important decisions are actually based on insufficient information.

_____ 9. There is really no such thing as a problem that can't be solved.

_____ 10. People who fit their lives to a schedule probably miss most of the joy of living.

_____ 11. A good job is one in which what is to be done and how it is to be done are always clear.

_____ 12. It is more fun to tackle a complicated problem that to solve a simple one.

_____ 13. In the long run, it is possible to get more done by tackling small, simple problems than large and complicated ones.

_____ 14. Often the most interesting and stimulating people are those who don't mind being different or original.

_____ 15. What we are used to is always preferable to what is unfamiliar.

_____ 16. People who insist on a "yes" or "no" answer just don't know how complicated things really are.

2. To get your total score, first sum your responses to the *odd*-numbered items and write your score here _____. Second add 64 points to that score and create the first subtotal and record that here _____. Third, sum your responses to the *even*-numbered items and write your score here _____. Then subtract that number from the subtotal for the odd-numbered items (second blank) to determine your overall score; _____.

3. Your score should be somewhere between 16 and 112. The lower overall score, the more willing you may be to deal with uncertainty and ambiguity that typically go with change. Research data show that the range of scores for a group is usually between 20 and 80, with a mean of 45.

4. Most capstone courses have students working in groups or on teams. If a group or team structure exists, each group should calculate their average, low and high score. If there are no groups, skip to procedure 5.

5. The instructor should then calculate the average, low and high score for the class and then share this information with the class.

Questions

1. Discuss the importance of change readiness. When during the strategy implementation process should an instrument like the change readiness questionnaire be utilized?

2. How did your score compared to the norms listed above? What do you think that your score indicates in terms of your change readiness?

3. If in a group setting, find out the high, the low and the average score for the group. How did your score compare to your group members' scores? Does this information assist you in understanding your change readiness?

4. How did your group's scores compare with the norms listed above? What do you think the similarities and/or differences in scores indicate in terms of the change readiness of your group?

5. How did the class score compare with your group's and your own scores? Additional learning derived from these comparisons?

6. How did the class scores compare with the norms listed above? What do you think the similarities and/or differences in scores indicate in terms of the change readiness of your class?

Appendix
Description of Other Intervention Techniques

Life and Career Planning

Knowing oneself and others not only allows individuals to better handle change in the work environment it also puts oneself in touch with personal wants and desires. This allows individuals to then reflect on their personal goals and career, looking at the factors that influenced the path that they have so far followed including the role of circumstance and chance. Life and career planning intervenes in an individual's career path by trying to have the individual first learn about him or herself and then systematically develop a plan for reaching their personal and career goals and objectives.[121]

A career is a sequence of positions occupied by a person during his or her lifetime. As recently as fifteen years ago, career development programs were a means for organizations to attract and retain highly talented people. The focus was to provide the information, assessment and training that employees would need to navigate their career within a firm. Current trends in downsizing, de-layering and reengineering have made this version of career development obsolete. The new career concept, a boundaryless career, indicates that individuals and not organizations are responsible for their career development through-out their working lives. The challenge is to choose a career and manage its path without the benefit of pre-existing norms and rules. The marketplace, not the organization dictates the necessary development of skills, knowledge abilities. A good career choice is apparent when an individual develops a positive self concept, does work that he or she thinks is important, and leads a desired lifestyle.[122]

The management of an individual's own career is a big subject and is acutely personal. The task of advising people in general terms about their career in an objective way is very difficult. There is no such thing as the perfect career and careers do not tend to progress at a consistently rapid speed, even amongst the supremely talented. Careers more usually tend to grow in fits and starts, molding themselves to opportunity, domestic issues and circumstances beyond the individual's control.   Whether a person is actively looking for a job or not, reviewing available options as well as the resume is very important. Being ever-ready for an internal promotion, chance invitation or business opportunity, means that the person is more likely to be able to react quickly when the time comes, hence avoiding the risk of opportunities going to waste.[123]

From the firm's perspective, career planning and development attempts to align the needs, goals and aspirations of the firm's individual employees with the mission, goals, and objectives of the firm.   Career planning is making sure that the organization will have the right people with the right skills at the right time. This requires examining strategic plans that may include demand for future skills or the need to reduce the labor force (downsizing).   Andrew Mayo indicated that organizations needed to determine their own level of involvement in employee career planning and development before establishing complex bureaucracies, committees, and computerized succession plans. He suggested that a balance to be struck between those careers being centrally managed by the firm and those being allowed to develop solely through the ambition of the individual. He also recommended that a systematic methodology for creating and managing career planning include assessing the needs of the organization, analyzing the organizational culture, analyzing the organization's structure and its opportunities, reviewing and revising those processes that involve the individual, working out how to hold, manage, and use human resource management data, and reviewing and revising the opportunities for learning through experience.[124]

Career planning usually involves four major steps. The first step, individual assessment, requires that individuals perform a self-evaluation in terms of his or her life goals and career objectives, their abilities, competencies, skills and his or her desire. This may include the employee taking aptitude and skills tests as well as consulting self-help books such as *What Color Is Your Parachute.*[125] The second step entails the organization developing career paths within the firm, that is, that the organization has a structured progression of jobs (as well as related training) that individuals should follow in order to successfully grow within the firm. The third step involves connecting the firm's performance appraisal system to career planning so that the individual is given proper feedback on his or her job performance and promotability. The last step in the process is career counseling. Here the counselor has an open and honest discussion with the employees as to his or her goals and offers advice as to what the individual needs to do in order to pursue his or her goals. This may include coping with early, mid-passage, and late career problems through career counseling programs.[126]

Recent research in the field of career development indicated that personality factors have an influence on career variables while there are many gender differences both in the United States and internationally that impact career paths. Regarding ethnic minority clients, researchers have noted the importance of helping clients process their experience of navigating two cultures while helping them with career-related concerns. Furthermore, the interaction between gender and race should be considered in providing career counseling to clients and mentoring tended to have a positive impact on all employees. In terms of the impact of career counseling on career paths and participants, research indicated that many clients enter career counseling with high levels of psychological distress, and career counseling does reduce many clients' distress levels. Also, clients are generally satisfied with the career counseling they have received. Furthermore, career counseling tended to be helpful to individuals with various psychopathologies. On a more negative note, there were ethnic differences in terms of probability of using career services.[127]

Coaching/Mentoring/Counseling

Coaching is the most often employed on-the-job training technique with the goal of coaching being to motivate behavioral change in employees.[128] Wexley and Latham observed that coaching was a periodic review of employee performance by supervisors and occurred so as to: inform subordinates as to their superiors' evaluation of their job performance, allow employees and supervisors to work together to increase employee effectiveness, increase cooperation and collaboration between superior and subordinate, and provide a structure for creating short and long-term employee career goals.[129]

Blanchard and Thacker indicated that coaching is a five-step process. Step one involves the manager understanding the employee's job (the knowledge, skills, and abilities), the goals of the job, and the resources that the employees has to accomplish his or her tasks. The supervisor should also become well acquainted with the employee's performance history and his or her current level of functioning on-the-job. Once the supervisor has the proper understanding of the employee's behavior, the supervisor then schedules a meeting with the employee to review this information and to set mutually agreeable performance objectives. Part of this meeting may also include discussions for the need for on-the-job assistance (either from a coworker or from the supervisor), personal counseling, career planning, and/or additional off-the-job training and education and/or raising performance standards in order to accommodate more competitive markets.

Step three is creation of a mutually agreed upon plan and/or schedule for achieving the performance objectives. This should be a formally signed, written document that goes into the employee's personnel folder and is tied to the employee's compensation and career progression. Step four obliges the coach to now demonstrate to the employee how to achieve the specifically agreed upon objectives. This may include demonstrating how a particular task of function is to be done, observing the employee and providing feedback on-the-job, and having more formally structured debriefing sessions. Step five is an assessment of the process – has the employee increased his or her performance and if not, what additional assistance may be necessary.

A second form of coaching, called business or executive coaching, has been developed in order to meet the developmental needs of top management. Today's top professional is motivated to excel and to differentiate him or herself from the competition. Executive coaching is a powerful tool that can be used to rapidly introduce new skills into a company's leadership ranks. For both high-potential executives and those newly entrusted with high-level leadership, one-on-one executive coaching can meet developmental, not remedial, needs.[130]

Personal coaches to top executives tend to be external to the firm and are hired on a one-to-one basis. A coaching relationship is a partnership that assists in developing skills by defining directions and the development of obtainable goals in a professional or personal life. The coaching process can be called a guided inquiry into ways that can improve personal and professional lives. Coaching is designed to help in achieving skills such as: learning to actively use past experiences to improve abilities, determining what goals and values are important, and developing specific action plans for reaching goals. Coach referrals can also be received from programs that train coaches or coaching associations.[131]

The aim of business coaching then is to have top managers develop their strengths and natural skills, and put them to use where they can be most effective. It is a process with four basic steps: 1. Establish a goal that is realistic and achievable. 2. Identify what the obstacles are to achieving it. 3. Check what personal and company resources are available for use. 4. Work out a plan that achieves the goal. Tell-tale signs mentioned by many executives who have benefited from coaching include feeling blocked, as if there were obstacles at every turn, and needing to hear a friendly voice - one that is supportive. Getting it right, though, requires willing participants, a robust measurement system, careful feedback, a feedback-based action plan, and strong follow-up.[132]

Mentoring is a specific form of coaching and describes the relationship between a senior level and a junior level employee where the senior level employee is not necessarily the employee's direct supervisor. Mentoring focuses more on learning *The Ropes to Skip and the Ropes to Know*[133], that is, learning about the political and social systems within an organization and/or profession and tends to be an informal, rather than formal intervention technique.   Goldsmith strongly recommended that the firm develop a company mentoring program and formalize this process. He suggested that the program consist of first, deciding if the program is right the company, starting small, asking for feedback about what managers want and what they care about, getting buy-in from the management team, obtaining mentor training for the executive team, creating a culture by being open about current mentor relationships, building trust with those participating and listening to their experiences and ideas, celebrating small victories and showcasing successful mentor relationships.[134]

Research on mentoring has indicated that employees in informal mentorships reported receiving slightly more career-related support from their mentors and higher salaries than those in formal mentorships. Clear differences in outcomes were found between mentored individuals verus nonmentored individuals in terms of organizational socialization, satisfaction, and salary. Results supported a modest relationship between the mentorship functions and the job outcomes.[135]

Counseling is the continuous process of monitoring employee performance and behavior and identifying and addressing problems by determining and implementing courses of action through one-to-one communication with affected employees. The primary purpose of counseling is to address problems at an early stage to minimize their impact or prevent them from growing, and occasionally to provide more generalized guidance and assistance in the absence of specific difficulties.[136] Counseling applies to performance issues that relate more to an employee's attitudinal and behavioral problems than to deficiencies in skills, knowledge, or abilities. Dysfunctional performance behaviors, such as insubordination, lack of respect for authority, not accepting advice, being late for work or leaving early, substance abuse, chronic absenteeism, abusive behavior toward other employees or supervisors, and low energy levels, are often symptoms of the problem employee or marginal performer.

Minter and Thomas noted that in order for an employee to need counseling, the following conditions must apply: the employees performance is consistently below acceptable standards, the employee exhibits emotional and/or behavioral problems that impact his or her own work performance as well as the performance of others, is continuously breaking company policy and regulations, is unable to self-manage, has no previous history of management/supervisor intervention or requires one final attempt at intervention given extenuating circumstances.

They suggested that the supervisor take the following actions in the counseling process: determine if the employee is worth the effort in saving, seek advice from the human resource management department and management; document all facts surrounding the current problem especially as they impact key performance indicators of the employee; have a private confrontation meeting where the employee is appraised of the problem as well as the expected changes in behavior and/or results expected and consequences for continued problems; determine if there is a need for additional training, psychological services, and closer supervision; and conduct a final feedback session to ensure that performance indicators show signs of improvement. Positive feedback should be provided along the entire process.[137]   McConnell recommended that effective counseling is always specific, consistent in application (between with an employee and between employees), be knowledgeable, avoid exciting defensive behavior, timely (quickly after the offense), involves actively listen to employees, using positive feedback, created action plans when needed, and following up with the employee.[138]

Sometimes the problems that the employee is facing is too complicated for the supervisor or even the human resources management department to handle, such as substance abuse or psychological depression. In these cases, referral to an Employee Assistance Program (EAP) is the norm, unless of course the firm is not affiliated with one. According to Petersen, however, these once gatekeepers to mental healthcare and substance abuse treatment programs, EAPs have steadily taken on more counseling roles. This evolution has not been limited to administrative roles, but has occurred in program philosophy and structure as well. Mode of operation is one area in which EAPs are changing their focus. While they once maintained an open door for employees seeking help, they now are as likely to seek out potentially problematic situations before circumstances require expensive interventions. The risk-management approach benefits a company by allowing it to avoid the disruption that occurs when an employee leaves the job, temporarily or for an extended period, due to personal problems.[139]

Education and Skill Training

Managers need to ensure that employees have the capabilities to perform their jobs efficiently, and effectively. Whether preparing new employees or responding to job demand changes, decisions have to made regarding when and how to provide training and education. As described earlier in this text, there are three types of employee skills that can be modified by training.

1. Basic and technical skills include reading, writing, computation and job-specific competencies. The current job market also requires proficiency in computer skills.

2. Interpersonal skills need development because employees are members of work units and need to interact effectively with each other as well as their bosses.

3. Problem solving skills or conceptual skills are particularly important in non-routine jobs. Training includes exercises to sharpen logic, reasoning, creativity and the ability to identify problems.

Teachout and Hall noted that training interventions begin with an assessment of the current skills of the employees and then determining the gaps between their current skills, knowledge and abilities (SKA's) and their current jobs.[140] The assessment should also include task analysis, that is, the comparison of job specifications and job descriptions to task identity; the particular behaviors that are involved in performing a job. Last, it also entails a more broadly-based analysis of the organization as a whole (perhaps as part of a SWOT analysis) which would attempt to ascertain overall job satisfaction, satisfaction with the work itself, satisfaction with co-workers, satisfaction with compensation and advancement, overall attitude towards leadership and supervision, evaluation of communication, attitudes toward company policies, individual's link to his or her job, and relative importance of various job aspects.[141] The result of these analyses should lead to a definition of what each employee needs to learn in terms of his or her specific job, and the current methodologies (if any) provided by the organization to meet those training needs.

Assuming that there may be some gaps in the current training program, the new program must be designed by developing concepts and describing what participants should be able to do after training, listing possible viable training activities to deal with the stated concepts, selecting appropriate training methods, deciding on the sequence of the training program, putting together the training program agenda, and preparing the remaining materials such as an instructor's guide, handouts, outlines for briefings, role-play instructions, and visual aids. Several times during the design process, provisions need to be made to check back on prior steps to be certain that the overall objectives of the proposed program are being satisfied.[142] The design process has been elaborated in recent years to now include: constructing criterion measures and evaluative instruments, writing concise training objectives, choosing delivery systems (in-house, consultant, off-site, educational institution), selecting and sequencing the training content including training strategies and media, and developing and validating training materials. Further specificity includes determining equipment requirements, selecting and training instructors, producing needed training documents, and calculating the costs and benefits of the training program.[143]

Training can occur either on or off the job. On-the-job training takes place in the employee's work unit. A popular method is job rotation that involves lateral transfers where employees get to work at different jobs. They learn many different skills and gain a wider perspective on the organization. A particular on-the-job training technique is Vestibule training. This teaches employees technical skills on the equipment they will use in a simulated work environment. This carefully controlled learning environment allows employees to deal with every conceivable problem without disrupting the actual work process.[144] Off-the-job training is usually provided to managers and employees for developing problem solving, technical and interpersonal skills. It involves lectures, videos, case analyses, role plays, discussions and simulation exercises. Off the job training may be provided by the firm either through its human resource management department or through its own corporate university,[145] through for profit or not-for-profit training organizations and institutes (i.e. Disney Institute, National Training Laboratory), through professional conferences and seminars (i.e. the American Management Association), and through colleges and universities. Many of these services are offered as on-line instruction.

Corporations have several choices when using postsecondary institutions as a venue for employee training. They can contract for specific educational services (either at their own site or at the college's campus), send their employees to non-credited continuing education courses, or have their employees enroll in certificate or degree-bearing programs. Porter and McKibbin conducted a three-year study of undergraduate and graduate business curriculums in the United States. In criticizing business curriculums, they noted that there was too much emphasis on quantitative techniques, insufficient attention to managing people and communication skills, lack of focus on the external business environment, and lack of attention to the international dimensions of business. They proposed the following skills be accentuated: integration across business functional areas (i.e. finance, marketing, management, etc.), communication skills entrepreneurship/creativity, international orientation, and business ethics.[146]

Porter and McKibbin, by challenging management education, indirectly raise the key issue for any training program, is what the learner valuable to begin with and can the learner transfer what he or she has learned in a training session to their work environment? The first part of the question requires that the firm pay particular attention to the development of their own curriculum (if training in-house) or the curriculum of the provider. This requires defining a core curriculum (the basic competencies needed for a task or discipline), change driven curricula (developing courses required to offset obsolescence), course maintenance and replacement (updating and/or substituting courses), and opportunity conversion (altering a course or curriculum due to changes in training technology i.e. on-line instruction).[147]

The second part of the question requires that the firm address the ability of the individual to learn and then apply new learning on the job. This requires that the firm ascertain the individual's trainability or readiness to learn, providing a training environment conducive to learning, and providing desired rewards for learning. Transfer of learning to the job can be maximized by: increasing the similarity between the training situation and the work situation, providing as much practice as possible with the task being taught, providing for a variety of examples and cases when teaching concepts and skills, identifying important features of a job, ensuring that general principles are understood before specifics are broached, designing the training content to make it easy for trainees to see its applicability, and using questions and questioning to guide the trainee's attention.[148] As one would expect then on-the-job training tends to have better transferability that off-the-job training.

Research has indicated that the use of training techniques vary somewhat in relationship to organizational size. Gorb noted that techniques are vastly different for small firms, as opposed to those used for larger companies. Although there has been slow and steady growth in aids designed to help small businesses, few small firms have in-house specialists and must turn to outside agencies for help.[149] Digman found that similar techniques are used by organizations in medium and large firms, however, the typical, smaller organizations rely less on internal promotions, offer less frequent and intensive supervisory training and more formal middle and executive-level training programs, and utilize university-sponsored training programs less than do the larger, well-managed organizations. However, it still remains to be shown if the difference in focus on the different types of training makes any significant contribution to the success of well-managed organizations.[150]

Work Redesign

An alternative intervention to education and training is job redesign. This intervention technique is utilized if the employee cannot be coached or retrained in order to increase job performance; if you can't change the employ, modify the job. The first step in work redesign is conducting a job analysis to define tasks and the behaviors necessary to perform them. This helps determine whether there is a fit between who currently works for the firm and what it needs for its work to be performed successfully. Information for job analysis is collected through direct (viewed) or indirect (taped) employee observation, employee interviews, (either individually or in groups), structured questionnaires, technical conference and expert identification of job characteristics, and employee log of daily activities. Job analysis provides the information for job descriptions (a written description of job content), work environment and conditions of employment, and job specifications (knowledge, skills and abilities needed to do the job effectively).[151]

The Job Characteristics Model (JCM) provides a framework for analyzing and designing jobs. A job can be defined according to five core dimensions:

1. Skill variety, the degree to which a job demands a variety of activities so that an employee can use a number of different skills and talents

2. Task identity, the degree to which a job requires completion of a whole identifiable piece of work

3. Task significance, the degree to which a job has a substantial impact on the lives or work of other people

4. Autonomy, the degree to which a job provides substantial freedom, independence, and discretion to an individual in scheduling and conducting work

5. Feedback, the degree to which carrying out the work required by a job results in direct and clear information about performance effectiveness.[152]

JCM model suggests that these dimensions and their interrelationships impact productivity, motivation and job satisfaction. Skill variety, task identity and task significance combine to create meaningful work. Autonomy provides the employee with a sense of responsibility and feedback provides knowledge regarding effectiveness.

The motivation process indicates that intrinsic (internal) rewards are obtained when an employee learns (feedback) that he or she has performed well (autonomy) on a task he or she cares about (experiences meaningfulness). The links between the job dimensions and outcomes are moderated by a person's growth need strength. The higher the growth need strength, the more appropriate JCM.[153]

Jobs can be scored for motivating potential (MPS); if jobs score high, the model predicts that motivation, performance and satisfaction will be positively affected. To increase a job's MPS, managers can enlarge jobs to increase skill variety and task identity, create natural work units to facilitate employee ownership and sense of meaningfulness, establish direct relationships between workers and their clients to increase skill variety, autonomy and feedback, enrich jobs to increase employee responsibility and control, and provide feedback as employees engage in their jobs, instead of on an occasional basis.[154]

Managers can deliberately engage in job redesign to incorporate the demands of changing environments, the organization's technology, skills and abilities, and individual preferences. When jobs are redesigned with these intentions, employees are motivated to be productive. Managers can choose to enlarge or enrich jobs.

Job enlargement is the horizontal expansion of jobs, increasing job scope - including different tasks required to complete a job. For instance: A supermarket employee working in the bakery can have his or her job enlarged from packing finished goods to include placing them on shelves, and designing displays. While addressing the lack of diversity in work, enlargement sometimes leaves employees feeling as if they now perform more components of boring jobs.

Job enrichment seeks to increase job depth by vertically expanding the work to include planning and evaluative functions. Employees are empowered to assume some supervisory tasks, increasing their independence and responsibility. For instance: the supermarket employee working in the bakery can determine the number of hard rolls to bake, in addition to packaging and displaying them, can monitor sales reports to prepare ingredient orders and adjust next day baking requirements. To improve performance the supervisor needs to provide feedback on quality and accuracy. Although enrichment can improve the quality of output, research demonstrated mixed results regarding its effectiveness.[155]

The preponderance of the most recent literature on work redesign interestingly enough deals with redesigning the work of nurses and other healthcare employees in order to accommodate older workers,[156] and increase service efficiency while maintaining the quality of care delivered, and patient-focused design. The effect of organizational redesign on employees healthcare workers has been mixed, with some investigators reporting no change in job satisfaction and employee autonomy, and others reporting improvements in satisfaction, staff autonomy, job security, and work group relationships. Yet others have reported serious to moderate levels of psychological distress and job dissatisfaction.[157]

Some researchers, outside of the field of healthcare, have called for a more participative style of work redesign in an effort to empower employees and reduce job stress. This new approach enables organizations to redesign themselves fast and cost effectively through the involvement of the people whose work is changing. The core requirements for motivating people to do excellent work include: adequate elbowroom room for decision making, opportunity to learn continually on the job, an optimum level of variety, mutual support and respect, meaningfulness, and a desirable future.[158]

Behavior Modeling

Behavior modeling is a simple and old style teaching technique - just show the learners exactly what one wants them to do, and then let them practice doing it. Behavior modeling is a practical, cost-effective, reliable way to change behavior. The method involves identifying the behaviors required for a particular skill, watching someone demonstrate those behaviors, practicing them, and receiving feedback on performance. The concept behind the behavior modeling technique is to teach generic skills within the context of specific situations. It is important not to teach skills that are not wanted, needed, or used. Typical programs comprise several modules spaced one or two weeks apart so trainers can try out skills on the job. Generic skills follow a progression through three levels: mechanics (the physical actions), dynamics (the connection between the actions), and synthesis (combines knowledge with skills). The trainer's performance can make the difference in these programs. The trainer's most crucial skill is the ability to ask good questions and teach trainees how to ask good questions.[159]

According to May and Kahnweiler, behavior modeling is currently the primary training design for delivery of supervisory interpersonal skills training in business today with the practice component the crux of behavior modeling training.[160] The current behavior modeling training design presents five critical components to ensure effective learning: content overview (the facilitator identifies the skills to be learned and presents factual content about the topic), positive model demonstration or video (learners see the skills demonstrated, generally on video), <u>skill practice</u> (learners practice using and applying the skills in a one-on-one exercise), <u>feedback</u> (participants receive feedback on how well they used the skills), and <u>application on the job</u> (learners discuss how they will apply the skills in the workplace).[161]

Behavior modeling is especially useful for skill training that involves both knowledge that specifies a correct or organizationally preferred mode of execution and doing that benefits appreciably from practice. The modeling display on film or tape is a critical part of the program and must be well designed so trainees can identify with it. There are four major factors which must be decided when designing the modeling display: creating the right balance between identification and credibility in the display while avoiding distractions, whether the performance anticipated should be perfect or coping, whether the content should be real or neutral, and whether the examples presented should be negative or positive. Good behavior modeling requires advance identification of desirable, manipulable, and selectively reinforceable behavior, and the skills that it will try to reach must be outlined in a set of learning points.[162]

Research evidence indicated that videotape modeling demonstrations are as effective as live demonstrations. There are hazards, however, to making video models, and in order to avoid them, the following is recommended: scripted models, professional actors and actresses, professional directors, and a broadcast-quality studio. These practices will make it easier to control the variables required for pure, focused video models.[163]

Research also demonstrated that alternating use of mental and physical practice tends to produce better results than either used alone. Rehearsing new behavior makes it more resistant to breakdown and aids long-term retention.[164] Behavior modeling though is not without its critics. Russell, Wexley, and Hunter noted that in their study behavior modeling prompted an increase in learning and favorable reactions, but did not produce change in on-the-job behavior or improved performance while Parry and Reich observed that user concerns include the simplicity of the models, a lack of theory, boring classes, no use of wrong examples, and weak training transfer. They further criticize role-playing enactments (when used as part of behavior modeling) since they impinge on the reality of the workplace; one player is supposed to act as if they know what is going on so that the other can practice applying key learning points.[165]

Robinson and Gaines suggested that the firm determine whether behavior modeling is appropriate. The decision-making process starts when a possible training need is identified. The seven decisions are as follows: Does the performance deficiency pertain to a lack of skill or knowledge or is it due to other factors? Is the deficiency one of skill or one of knowledge? Can the trainers identify behaviors needed to overcome the skills deficiency? Can a positive credible model be demonstrated? Can each learner practice the skill? Will the new skills be reinforced? Is it cost beneficial?[166]

Behavior modeling in the 21st century faces some new challenges including: increased technological, managerial, and organizational sophistication that requires more complex and different skills; workers in flattened or reengineered organizations have less time for traditional classroom training; fewer professional trainers are available to conduct classroom instruction; self-study programs on CD-ROM, on-line instruction, and other multimedia formats are increasingly popular. There is a plethora of well-produced multimedia programs, real-life simulations, and multiple decision-making opportunities available to develop an individual's interpersonal skills and the confidence to integrate and use them. Computer simulations are also far more realistic and can also provide an understanding of when and how to use specific skills.[167]

Endnotes

[1] Excerpted from the 2001 Annual Report, 1-3; http://www.southwest. com/investor_relations/swaar01.pdf, February 21, 2003.

[2] Robert F. Hartley (2003). *Management Mistakes and Successes.* 7th Edition. New York: John Wiley & Sons.

[3] Ibid.

[4] Ibid, p. 242.

[5] Southwest 2001 Annual Report.

[6] Julie Bennett (2002). "Nothing but Blue Skies ; Employees Help Southwest Avoid Turbulence" *Chicago Tribune* (November 10, Chicagoland Final Edition), 5.5.

[7] James F. Peltz (2002). "Southwest Still Soaring as Other Airlines Stall; Rivals and Analysts are Watching Closely to See in Which Markets the Carrier Will Land Next" *Los Angeles Times* (October 6, Home Edition), C.1.

[8] Adam Bryant (2001-2). "Who's Next: James Parker, CEO, Southwest Airlines" *Newsweek* (December 31 – January 7) Volume 139, Issue 1, 184-185.

[9] Dale Dauten (2001). "Good Laugh Great for Companies" *Chicago Tribune* (November 18, Chicagoland Final Edition), 7.

[10] Erin Strout (2002). "Crafty or Crazy" *Sales and Marketing Management* (April) Volume 154, Issue 4, 28-33.

[11] Bryant, 2002, 185.

[12] Bennett, 2002, 5.5.

[13] Victoria A. Shivy, Susan D. Phillips, and Laura M. Koehly (1996). "Knowledge Organization as a Factor in Career Intervention Outcome: A Multidimensional Scaling Analysis" *Journal of Counseling Psychology* (April) Volume 43, Issue 2, 178-189.

[14] Ian A Miners, Michael L. Moore, Joseph E. Champoux, and Joseph J. Martocchio (1994). "Organization Development Impacts Interrupted: A Multiyear Time-Serial Study of Absence and Other Time Uses" *Group & Organization Management* (September) Volume 19, Issues 3, 363-395.

[15] Harold J. Leavitt and Homa Bahrami (1988). *Managerial Psychology: Managing Behavior in Organizations.* 5th Edition. Chicago, Ill.: The University of Chicago Press.

[16] Anonymous (2003). "Business briefs / Houston & Texas" *Houston Chronicle* (February 15, Three Star Edition), p. 2.

[17] William G. Dyer (1981). "Selecting an Intervention for Organization Change" *Training and Development Journal* (April) Volume 35, Issue 4, 62-68.

[18] Bruce M. Meglino and William H. Mobley (1977). "Minimizing Risk in Organization Development Interventions" *Personnel* (November-December) Volume 54, Issue 6, 23.

[19] William G. Zikmund (2003). *Business Research Methods.* 7th Edition. Mason, Oh.: South-Western.

[20] W. Warner Burke, Lawrence P. Clark, and Cheryl Koopman (1984). "Improve Your OD Project's Chances for Success" *Training and Development Journal* (September) Volume 38, Issue 8, 62-66.

[21] A version of this discussion appears in Daniel J. Rowley and Herbert Sherman (2001). *From Strategy to Change: Implementing the Plan in Higher Education.* San Francisco, Ca.: John Wiley & Sons, Inc.

[22] Frank L Matthews (2003). "Professors: Higher Education's Change Agents" *Black Issues in Higher Education* (January 2) Volume 19, Issue 23, 4; William

D. Coplin (2002). "The Professional Researcher as Change Agent in the Government-Performance Movement" *Public Administration Review* (November/December) Volume 62, Issue. 6, 699-712; Adrian Furnham (2002). "Managers as Change Agents" *Journal of Change Management* (August) Volume 3, Issue 1; 21-30; Myrtle P. Bell (2002). "Discrimination, Harassment, and the Glass Ceiling: Women Executives as Change Agents" *Journal of Business Ethics* (April)Volume 37, Issue 1, 65-77; Miriam Shuchman (2002). "Journalists as Change Agents in Medicine and Health Care" *JAMA* (February 13) Volume 287, Issue 6, 776; Irvine Lapsley (2001). "Transforming the Public Sector: Management Consultants as Agents of Change" *European Accounting Review* Volume 10, Issues. 3; 523; Edward E. Lawler, III (2000). "Pay Can be a Change Agent" *Compensation & Benefits Management* (Summer)Volume 16, Issue 3; 23-27; Thomas Hoffman (1999). "CIOs Tackle Role of Change Agent" *Computerworld* (March 29)Volume 33, Issue 13,42; Eileen McMorrow (1999). "The Office as Change Agent" *Facilities Design & Management* (January)Volume 18, Issue 1, 9.

[23] Ed Kur (1998). "Why Some Successful Change Agents Last and Others Don't" *Employment Relations Today* (Spring) Volume 25, Issue 1, 39-59.

[24] Dave Buchanan, Tim Claydon and Mike Doyle (1999). "Organisation Development and Change: The Legacy of the Nineties" *Human Resource Management Journal* Volume 9, Issue 2, 20-37.

[25] Mike Doyle (2002). "Selecting Managers for Transformational Change" *Human Resource Management Journal* Volume 12, Issue 1, 3-16.

[26] Buchanan, Claydon, and Doyle, 1999.

[27] Edward J. Cripe (1993). "How to Get Top-Notch Change Agents" *Training & Development* (December) Volume 47, Issue 12, 52-57.

[28] James L. Eubanks, Julie B. Marshall, and Michael P. O'Driscoll (1990). "A Competency Model for OD Practitioners" *Training and Development Journal* (November) Volume 44, Issue 11, 85-89.

[29] Alan Carey and Glen H. Varney (1983). "Which Skills Spell Success in OD?"
Training and Development Journal (April) Volume 37, Issue 4, 38-40.

[30] Robert O. Metzger (1989). "With So Many Consultants, Why Aren't We Better" *Journal of Management Consulting*, Volume 5, Issue 3, 9-14.

[31] Jerome L. Franklin (1976). "Characteristics of Successful and Unsuccessful Organization Development"
The Journal of Applied Behavioral Science (October-December) Volume 12, Issue 4, 471.

[32] Kevin C. Wooten and Louis P. White (1983). "Ethical Problems in the Practice of Organization Development " *Training and Development Journal* (April) Volume 37, Issue 4, 16-22.

[33] R. Glenn Ray (1997). "Developing Internal Consultants" *Training & Development* (July) Volume 51, Issue 7, 30-4.

[34] Judith A. Chapman (2002). "A Framework for Transformational Change in Organizations" *Leadership & Organization Development Journal* Volume 23, Issue 1/2, 16-25; Doyle, 2002.

[35] Mike Doyle (2002). "From Change Novice to Change Expert: Issues of Learning, Development and Support" *Personnel Review* Volume 31, Issue 4, 465-481.

[36] Buchanan, Claydon, and Doyle, 1999.

[37] A version of this discussion appears in Rowley and Sherman, 2001.

[38] James F. Gavin and S. Morton McPhail (1978). "Intervention and Evaluation: A Proactive Team Approach to OD" *The Journal of Applied Behavioral Science* (April/May/June) Volume 14, Issue 2, 175.

[39] Michael Beer and Russell A. Eisenstat (1996). "Developing an Organization Capable of Implementing Strategy and Learning" *Human Relations* (May) Volume 49, Issue 5, 597-619.

[40] Gail Scott (2002). "Coach, Challenge, Lead: Developing an Indispensable Management Team" *Healthcare Executive* (November/Decemeber) Volume 17, Issue 6, 16-20.

[41] Howard W. Timm (1980). "Selecting Appropriate Organisation Development Interventions" *Work & People* Volume 6, Issue 1, 15.

[42] David Coghlan and Rachel K. McKee (2000). "Aligning Grid Organization Development and Interlevel Dynamics for Systemic Change" *Organization Development Journal* (Fall) Volume 18, Issue 3, 37-48.

[43] Kamalesh Kumar and Mary S. Thidbodeaux (1990). "Organizational Politics and Planned Organization Change: A Pragmatic Approach" *Group & Organization Studies* (December)Volume 15, Issue 4, 357-365; Nicholas S. Rashford and David Coghlan (1988). "Organisational Levels: A Framework for Management Training and Development" *Journal of European Industrial Training* Volume 12, Issue 4, 28-32; David Coughlan (1987). "Consultation on Organisational Levels: An Intervention Framework" *Leadership & Organization Development Journal* Volume 8, Issue 3, 3-7.

[44] Based upon the model presented in Wendell L. French and Cecil H. Bell, Jr. (2000). *Organization Development: Behavioral Science Interventions for Organization Improvement.* 6th Edition. Upper Saddle River, N.J.: Prentice-Hall, Inc. Not meant to be an exhaustive list.

[45] Peter J. Robertson, Darryl R. Roberts, and Jerry I. Porras (1993). "Dynamics of Planned Organizational Change: Assessing Empirical Support for a Theoretical Model" *Academy of Management Journal* (June) Volume 36, Issue 3, 619-634.

[46] http://www.findarticles.com/cf_dls/g2699/0003/2699000309/p1/article.jhtml, February 27, 2003.

[47] Jane W. Gibson and Dana V. Tesone (2001). "Management Fads: Emergence, Evolution, and Implications for Managers" *The Academy of Management Executive* (November) Volume 15, Issue 4, 122-133.

[48] Paul Sachdey (1997). "Cultural Sensitivity Training through Experiential Learning: A Participatory Demonstration Field Education Project" *International Social Work* (January) Volume 40, Issue 1, 7-25; Marianne Wilson (1995). "Diversity in the Workplace" *Chain Store Age Executive with Shopping Center Age* (June) Volume 71, Issue 6, 21-23.

[49] Elliot Aronson (1980). *The Social Animal.* 3rd Edition. San Francisco, Ca.: W.H. Freeman and Company.

[50] Edgar F. Huse and Thomas G. Cummings (1985). *Organization Development and Change.* 3rd Edition. St. Paul, Minn.: West Publishing Company.

[51] Robert T. Golembiewski (1967). "The 'Laboratory Approach' to Organization Change: Schema of a Method" *Public Administration Review* (September) Volume 27, Issue 3, 211-221.

[52] see Gibson and Tesone, 2001; Robert E. Kaplan (1986). "Is Openness Passe?" *Human Relations* (March) Volume 39, Issue 3, 229-243.

[53] Cary L. Cooper (1977). "Taking the Terror Out of T Groups" *Personnel Management* (January) Volume 9, Issue 1, 22.

[54] A version of this discussion appears in Rowley and Sherman, 2001.

[55] David Sims and Sue Jones (1985). " Mapping as an Aid to Creativity" *The Journal of Management Development* Volume 4, Issue 1, 47-60.

[56] Karl E. Weick, (1979). *The Social Psychology of Organizing.* Reading, Mass.: Addison-Wesley Publishing Company.

[57] Pierre Cossette and Michel Audet (1992). "Mapping of an Idiosyncratic Schema" *The Journal of Management Studies* (May) Volume 29, Issue 3, 325-347.

[58] Robert D. Russell (1999). "Developing a Process Model of Intrapreneurial Systems: A Cognitive Mapping Approach" *Entrepreneurship Theory and Practice* (Spring) Volume 23, Issue 3, 65-84.

[59] Marcia Paul (1994). "Mapping Your Organization" *Training & Development* (February) Volume 48, Issue 2, 59-60.

[60] David B.P. Sims and J.R. Doyle (1995). "Cognitive Sculpting as a Means of Working with Managers' Metaphors" *Omega* (April) Volume 23, Issue 2, 117-124.

[61] Eric Berne (1964). *Games People Play.* New York: Grove Press.

[62] L. David Brown (1983). *Managing Conflict at Organizational Interfaces.* Reading, Mass.: Addison-Wesley Publishing Company.

[63] W. Warner Burke (1982). *Organization Development: Principles and Practices.* Boston, Mass.: Little, Brown and Company.

[64] Huner R. Hollar and O.C. Brenner (1983). "TA in the Office" *Supervisory Management* (January) Volume 28, Issue 1, 14-22.

[65] Ron Clements (1977/8). "Transactional Analysis: A Psychological Approach to Problem Solving" *Manchester Business School Review* (Winter) Volume 2, Issue 3, 12.

[66] Julie Hay (1992). "The Uses and Abuses of Transactional Analysis" *Target Management Development Review* Volume 5, Issue 1, pg. 37-40.

[67] Edgar H. Schein (1969). *Process Consultation: Its Role in Organization Development.* Reading, Mass.: Addison-Wesley publishing Company.

[68] Edgar H. Schein (1997). "The Concept of "Client" From a Process Consultation Perspective: A Guide for Change Agents" *Journal of Organizational Change Management* Volume 10, Issue 3, 202-216.

[69] Edgar H. Schein (1995). "Process Consultation, Action Research and Clinical Inquiry: Are They the Same?" *Journal of Managerial Psychology* Volume 10, Issue 6, 14-19.

[70] David Coghlan (1988). "In Defence of Process Consultation" *Leadership & Organization Development Journal* Volume 9, Issue 2, 27-31.

[71] William B. Cash and Robert L. Minter (1979). "Consulting Approaches: Two Basic Styles" *Training and Development Journal* (September) Volume 33, Issue 9, 26.

[72] Jorgen Svava Lind (1990). "Improving Process Consultation in Business and Organizations" *International Journal of Technology Management* Volume 5, Issue 6, 742-745.

[73] Schein, 1995.

[74] Robert E. Kaplan (1979). "The Conspicuous Absence of Evidence that Process Consultation Enhances Task Performance" *The Journal of Applied Behavioral Science* (July/August/September) Volume 15, Issue 3, 346; Raanan Lipshitz, and John J. Sherwood (1978). "The Effectiveness of Third-Party Process Consultation as a Function of the Consultant's Prestige an Style of Intervention" *The Journal of Applied Behavioral Science* (October/November/December) Volume 14, Issue 4, 493; David G. Bowers (1973). "OD Techniques and Their Results In 23 Organizations - The Michigan

ICL Study" *The Journal of Applied Behavioral Science* (January/February) Volume 9, Issue 1, 21.

[75] Jean Gordon (2002). "A Perspective on Team Building" *Journal of American Academy of Business, Cambridge* (September) Volume 2, Issue 1, 185-188.

[76] George S. Neuman, Jack E. Edwards, and Nambury S. Raju (1989). "Organizational Development Interventions: A Meta-Analysis of Their Effects on Satisfaction and Other Attitudes" *Personnel Psychology* (Autumn) Volume 42, Issue 3, 461-489.

[77] Penny L. Ciaburri (1998). "Building the Team or Team Building? There's a Big Difference. *Rough Notes* (January) Volume 141, Issue 1, 84-85.

[78] Jim Temme (1995). "Team Formation: Don't Just Hope for Success, Plan for it Step by Step" *Plant Engineering* (July 10) Volume 49, Issue 9, 126-127.

[79] Donald D. Tippett and James F. Peters (1995). "Team Building and Project Management: How are we Doing?" *Project Management Journal* (December) Volume 26, Issue 4, 29-37.

[80] Ben Tanzer (2002). "Zen and the Art of Team Building" *Nonprofit World* (January/February) Volume 20, Issue 1, 27-8.

[81] Jim Temme (1995). "Building Teams: Becoming an Effective Team Means Listening, Counseling" *Plant Engineering* (October 9) Volume 49, Issue 3, 156-157.

[82] Deborah S. Kezsbom (2002). "A Personal Viewpoint...Team Building Lessons We Still Need to Learn" *Cost Engineering* (April) Volume 44, Issue 4, 42.

[83] Charles Macadam (1994). "Making the Most of Your Team" *Training Tomorrow* (October), pgs. 33-34.

[84] Donna Robbins (1993). "The Dark Side of Team Building" *Training & Development* (December) Volume 47, Issue 12, 17-21.

[85] William G. Dyer (1977). *Team Building: Issues and Alternatives.* Reading, Mass.: Addison-Wesley Publishing Company.

[86] Charles R. Stoner and Richard I. Hartman (1993). "Team building: Answering the Tough Questions" *Business Horizons* (September/October) Volume 36, Issue 5, 70-78.

[87] Jay S. Liebowitz and Kenneth P. DeMeuse (1982). "The Application of Team   Building" *Human Relations* (January) Volume 35, Issue 1, 1-17.

[88] The description of the team building process is summarized from Dyer, 1977.

[89] Neil Oliver and John Langford (1987). "Safety in Team Building -- The Contracting Process" *Industrial and Commercial Training* (September/October) Volume 19, Issue 5, 3-5.

[90] French and Bell, 1999.

[91] The description of lateral relations is summarized from Jay Galbraith (1973). *Designing Complex Organizations.* Reading, Mass.: Addison-Wesley Publishing Company.

[92] Developed from Jay Galbraith (1977). *Organization Design.* Reading, Mass.: Addison-Wesley Publishing Company.

[93] Richard Beckhard (1969). *Organization Development: Strategies and Models.* Reading, Mass.: Addison-Wesley Publishing Company.

[94] George S. Odiorne (1981). "Management by Objectives" in Stephen R. Michael et al. (1981). *Techniques of Organizational Change.* New York: McGraw-Hill Book Company, 89-136.

[95] James R. Evans and James W. Dean, Jr. (2003). *Total Quality: Management, Organization and Strategy.* 3rd Edition. Mason, Oh.: South-Western.

[96] Rosabeth M. Kanter (1983). *The Change Masters: Innovation for Productivity in the American Corporation.* New York: Simon and Schuster.

[97] A version of this discussion appears in Rowley and Sherman, 2001.

[98] Jay R. Galbraith (2002). *Designing Organizations: An Executive Guide to Strategy, Structure, and Process.* New and Revised. San Francisco, Ca.: Jossey- Bass.

[99] Seth Silver (2001). "Power to the People" *Training* (October) Volume 38, Issue 10, 88.

[100] Robert H. Waterman, Jr. (1987). *The Renewal Factor: How the Best Get and Keep The Competitive Edge.* New York: Bantam Books.

[101] Gary Yukl (1990). *Skills for Managers and Leaders: Text, Cases and Exercises.* Englewood Cliffs, N.J.: Prentice-Hall.

[102] Jennifer S. Macleod (1986). "Self-Empowerment Training Programs for Employees" *Employment Relations Today* Volume 13, Issue 1, 33-36.

[103] Micahel Gering (2003). "The Ten Commandments of Empowerment" *Accountancy SA* (January), p. 9.

[104] Karen Lawson (2001). "Build Your Business From the Inside Out: Four Keys to Employee Empowerment that Will Help Your Business Grow " *Business Credit* (March) Volume 103, Issue 3, 8-10.

[105] French and Bell, 1999.

[106] Carolina Gomez and Benson Rosen (2001) "The Leader-Member Exchange as a Link Between Managerial Trust and Employee Empowerment" *Group & Organization Management* (March) Volume 26, Issue 1, 53-69.

[107]David A. Whetten and Kim S. Cameron (1993). *Developing Management Skills: Gaining Influence and Power.* New York: Harper-Collins College Publishers.

[108] Dafna Evlon and Susan Herman (1999). "Exploring Empowerment: One Method for the Classroom" *Journal of Management Education* (February) Volume 32, Issue 1, 80-94.

[109] Lisa A. Mainiero and Cheryl L. Tromley (1994). *Developing Managerial Skills in Organizational Behavior.* 2nd Edition. Upper Saddle River, N.J.: Prentice-Hall, Inc.

[110] Thomas G. Cummings, Judith F. Blumenthal, and Larry E. Greiner "Managing Organizational Decline: The Case for Transorganizational Systems" *Human Resource Management* (Winter) Volume 22, Issue 4, 377-390.

[111] Russell L. Ackoff (1994). *The Democratic Corporation: A Radical Prescription for Recreating Corporate America and Rediscovering Success.* New York: Oxford University Press.

[112] Joanne C. Preston and Louw DuToit (1992). "Large Systems Change: Issues Related to the Strategy" *Journal of Organizational Change Management* Volume 5, Issue 3, 7-17.

[113] Thomas G. Cummings (1989). "Transorganizational Development" *Academy of Management OD Newsletter* (Summer), p.9.

[114] Alexis A. Halley (1994). "Applications of Transorganizational Development to Congressional-Executive Relations" *Public Administration Quarterly* (Summer) Volume 18, Issue 2, 177-203.

[115] James D. Thompson (1967). *Organizations in Action: Social Science Bases of Administrative Theory.* New York: McGraw-Hill Book Company.

[116] Stephen P. Robbins (1990). *Organization Theory: Structure, Design, and Applications.* Englewood Cliffs, N.J.: Prentice-Hall, Inc.

[117] Jeffrey Pfeffer and Gerald R. Salancik (1978). *The External Control of Organizations: A Resource Dependence Perspective.* New York: Harper & Row, Publishers.

[118] C. Wright Mills (1956). *The Power Elite.* New York: Oxford University Press; Harold Seidman and Robert Gilmour (1986). *Politics, Position, and Power: From the Positive to the Regulatory State.* 4th Edition. New York: Oxford University Press.

[119] Aaron Wildavsky (1984). *The Politics of the Budgetary Process.* Boston, Mass.: Little, Brown and Company.

[120] A modified version. From Don Hellriegel and John W. Slocum, Jr. (2004). *Organizational Behavior.* 10th Edition. Mason, Oh.: South-Western, p. 418.

[121] Jerry Kanter (2003). "Planning and Managing Your Career" *Information Strategy* (Winter) Volume 19, Issue 2, 43-48.

[122] Edwin L. Herr (2002). "Career Development and its Practice: A Historical Perspective" in Fred H. Maidment (ed.) *Annual Editions: Human Resources 02/03.* 12th Edition. Guilford, Conn.: McGraw-Hill/Duskin.

[123] Julia Hordle (2002). "Managing Your Own Career: Lifestyles, Economic Cycles and Counter-Cyclicals" *Business Information Review* (December)Volume 19, Issue 4, 40-45.

[124] Andrew Mayo (1992). "A Framework for Career Management" *Personnel Management* (February)Volume 24, Issue 2, 36-39.

[125] Richard N. Bolles (1993). *What Color is Your Parachute: A Practical Manual for Job Hunters & Career-Changers.* 21st Edition. Berkeley, Ca.: Ten Speed Press.

[126] Angelo S. DeNisi and Ricky W. Griffin (2001). *Human Resource Management.* Boston: Houghton Mifflin Company.

[127] Susan C. Whiston and Briana K. Brecheisen (2002). "Practice and Research in Career Counseling and Development—2001" *The Career Development Quarterly* (December) Volume 51, Issue 2, 98-154.

[128] Susan Cramm (2001). "Go Team, Go" *CIO* (May) Volume 14, Issue 14, 52-54.

[129] Kenneth N. Wexley and Gary P. Latham (1981). *Developing and Training Human Resources in Organizations.* Glenview, Ill.: Scott, Foresman and Company.

[130] Jim Niemes (2002). "Discovering the Value of Executive Coaching as a Business Transformation Tool" *Journal of Organizational Excellence* (Autumn) Volume 21, Issue 4, 61-69.

[131] Terri L. Norvell (1998). "From Goal-Setting to Goal-Getting: With a Little Help from your Coach" *Journal of Property Management* (January/February) Volume 63, Issue 1, 14-16.

[132] Roy Johnson (1998). "Get Ahead, Get a Coach" *The British Journal of Administrative Management* (January/February), pgs. 8-9.

[133] R. Richard Ritti (1994). *Ropes to Skip and the Ropes to Know.* 4th Edition. New York: John Wiley & Sons, Inc.

[134] Baron Goldsmith (2003). "Creating a Company Mentoring Program" *Office Solutions* (January/February) Volume 20, Issue 1, 42-43.

[135] Chao, Georgia T., Pat M. Walz, and Philip D. Gardner (1992). "Formal and Informal Mentorships: A Comparison on Mentoring Functions and Contrast with Nonmentored Counterparts" *Personnel Psychology* (Autumn) Volume 45, Issue 3, 619-636.

[136] Charles R. McConnell (1997). "Effective Employee Counseling for the First-Line Supervisor" *The Health Care Supervisor* (September) Volume 16, Issue 1, 77-86.

[137] Robert L. Minter and Edward G. Thomas (2000). "Employee Development Through Coaching, Mentoring and Counseling: A Multidimensional Approach" *Review of Business* (Spring) Volume 21, Issue 1/2, 43-47.

[138] McConnell, 1997.

[139] Carolyn Petersen (1997). "Employee-Assistance Programs Shaping 'Lean and Mean' Firms" *Managed Healthcare* (August) Volume 7, Issue 8, pgs. 6, 10-11.

[140] Mark S. Teachout and Carig R. Hall (2003). "Implementing Training: Some Practical Guidelines" in Jerry W. Hedge and Elaine D. Pulakos (eds.) *Implementing Organizational Interventions: Steps, Processes, and Best Practices.* San Francisco, Ca.: Jossey-Bass.

[141] Wexley and Latham, 1981.

[142] Stan Camarius (1981). "A New Approach to Designing Training Programs" *Training and Development Journal* (February) Volume 35, Issue 2, 40.

[143] William R. Tracey (1992). *Designing Training and Development Systems.* 3rd Edition. New York: AMACOM.

[144] Raynold A. Svenson and Monica J. Rinderer (1992). *The Training and Development Strategic Plan Workbook.* Englewood Cliffs, N.J.: Prentice-Hall, Inc.

[145] see Daniel J. Rowley, Herman D. Lujan, and Michael G. Dolence (1998). *Strategic Choices for the Academy: How Demand for Lifelong Learning Will Re-Create Higher Education.* San Francisco, Ca.: Jossey-Bass Publishers, 158-163 for a description and examples of Corporate Universities.

[146] Lyman W. Porter and Lawrence E. McKibbin (1988). *Management Education and Development: Drift or Thrust into the 21st Century?* New York: McGraw-Hill Book Company.

[147] Svenson and Rinderer, 1992.

[148] Wexley and Latham, 1981.

[149] Peter Gorb (1978). "Management Development for the Small Firm" *Personnel Management* (January) Volume 10, Issue 1, 24.

[150] Lester A. Digman (1980). "Management Development: Needs and Practices" *Personnel* (July/August) Volume 57, Issue 4, 45.

[151] Ricky W. Griffin (1982). *Task Design: An Integrative Approach.* Glenview, Ill: Scott, Foresman and Company.

[152] J. Richard Hackman and Greg R. Oldham (1976). "Motivation Through the Design of Work : Test of a Theory" *Organizational Behavior and Human Performance* (August) Volume 16, Issue 2, 250-256.

[153] Francis Ulschak (1983). Human Resource Development: The Theory and Practice of Need Assessment. Reston, VA.: Reston Publishing Company.

[154] Lisa A. Mainiero and Cheryl L. Tromley (1994). *Developing Managerial Skills in Organizational Behavior: Exercises, Cases, and Readings.* 2nd Edition. Upper Saddle River, N.J.: Prentice- Hall, Inc.

[155] Ingo Von Ruckteschell (1991). "Building a Theory of Employee Participation" *The Journal for Quality and Participation* (July/August) Volume 14, Issue 4, 42-51.

[156] Carol Reineck (2002). "Leadership's Guiding Light, Part 2: Create a Learning Organization" *Nursing Management* (October) Volume 33, Issue 10, 42-43.

[157] Gail L. Ingersoll, Lois Wagner, Sonna Ehrlich-Merck, Janet C. Kirsch (2002). "Patient-Focused Redesign and Employee Perception of Work Environment" *Nursing Economics* (July/August) Volume 20, Issue 4, 163-171.

[158] Frank Heckman (1996). "The Participative Design Approach" *The Journal for Quality and Participation* (March) Volume 19, Issue 2, 48-51; Kym Fraser and Joseph Novak (1998). "Managing the Empowerment of Employees to Address Issues of Inter-Employee Co-operation, Communication and Work Redesign" *The Learning Organization* Volume 5, Issue 3, 109-120; Aneil K. Mishra and Gretchen M. Spreitzer (1998). "Explaining How Survivors Respond to Downsizing: The Role of Trust, Empowerment, Justice, and Work Redesign" *The Academy of Management Review* (July) Volume 23, Issue 3, 567-578.

[159] Kenneth E. Hultman (1986). "Behavior Modeling for Results" *Training and Development Journal* (December) Volume 40, Issue 12, 60-63.

[160] Gary L. May and William M. Kahnweiler (2000). "The Effect of a Mastery Practice Design on Learning and Transfer in Behavior Modeling Training" *Personnel Psychology* (Summer) Volume 53, Issue 2, 353-373.

[161] Alice Pescuric and William C. Byham (1996). "The New Look of Behavior Modeling" *Training & Development* (July) Volume 50, Issue 7, 24-30.

[162] Ron Zemke (1982). "Building Behavior Models That Work-the Way You Want Them to/More Hints on Successful Modeling" *Training* (January) Volume 19, Issue 1, 22-26.

[163] William R. Daniels (1981). "How to Make and Evaluate Video Models" *Training and Development Journal* (December) Volume 35, Issue 12; 31-33.

[164] William M. Fox (1988). "Getting The Most From Behavior Modeling Training" *National Productivity Review* (Summer) Volume 7, Issue 3, 238-245.

[165] James S. Russell, Kenneth N. Wexley, and John E. Hunter (1984). "Questioning the Effectiveness of Behavior Modeling Training in an Industrial

Setting" *Personnel Psychology* (Autumn) Volume 37, Issue 3, 465-481; Scott B. Parry (1984). "An Uneasy Look at Behavior Modeling" *Training and Development Journal* (March) Volume 38, Issue 3, 57-62.

[166] James C. Robinson and Dana L. Gaines (1980). "Seven Questions to Ask Yourself Before Using Behavior Modeling" *Training* (December) Volume 17, Issue 12, 60.

[167] William C. Byham and Alice Pescuric (1996). "Behavior Modeling at the Teachable Moment " *Training* (December) Volume 33, Issue 12, 50-56.

☙ Chapter Nine ❧
Strategy Evaluation and Control

Chapter Objectives

1. To identify the important processes of monitoring and control as integral parts of the overall strategic management systems of a firm.
2. To develop an understanding of what areas of a firm's performance its managers should concentrate on in conducting its evaluation.
3. To describe methods of control and correction that help the firm maintain an acceptable strategic direction or to move to a

new direction that will help the firm achieve a competitive advantage.
4. To create an understanding of what key success factors are and how they can help guide a firm's strategic planning, evaluation, and control processes.
5. To describe both strategic level and functional level control systems and understand how they work together to create overall control for the firm.

Introductory Case: Hewlett Packard

The story of Hewlett Packard (HP) is both the story of what the American entrepreneurial business climate is able to produce, as well as that of a company that has changed many times over the years to become one of the world's premier companies[1]. It all began in a garage and with $538 in initial capital. In 1938, Stanford engineering graduates, Bill Hewlett and Dave Packard created an audio oscillator which could be used to test sound equipment. They sold their invention to the Walt Disney Studios, who purchased 8 of them for use in their production of Fantasia. They formalized their partnership in 1939 and decided on the name Hewlett Packard through a coin toss.

In the 1940s the company became involved in the war effort and was soon flooded for orders for electronic equipment to support the U.S. armed forces. The company grew slowly from 2 employees to 166 by the end of the decade and recorded revenues of $2.2 million in 1949. Also, the company was starting to build a solid reputation with scientists and engineers and HP responded by not only producing products these communities wanted, but also at the highest level of quality. As managers, both Bill and Dave were fascinated by emerging management techniques and practices, and encouraged other managers in the firm to practice: open-door policies, something called "Management by Walking Around"[2] (a form of management that requires upper management to visit and listen to the lowest employee levels), calling employees (including themselves) by their first names, offering extensive benefits packages, and throwing parties and picnics for employees and their families. This management style was formalized in the 1950s and is called the HP Way. All this was done in an era when more bureaucratic management styles tended to be the norm.

The 1950s and 1960s saw rapid expansion, though HP tried to control expansion so that it could finance most of it through profitability and not rely so much on selling stock or going into debt. The company dramatically expanded its engineering and scientific lines, built its main headquarters in Palo Alto, California, and in 1958 expanded into Europe to become an international company. In 1960 it opened its second manufacturing facility in Loveland, Colorado and in 1961 was listed on the New York Stock Exchange as HWP. It formed a joint venture with Yokogawa Electric Works in 1963 and 18% of its business was then conducted outside the U.S. Two major business expansions also occurred in the 1960s with the purchase of the Sanborn Company of Waltham, Massachusetts in 1961 that pushed HP into the medical equipment field, and then the introduction of its first computer, the HP 2116A in 1966.

The 1970s saw rapid expansion with sales reaching $2 billion in 1978. Innovations in hand-held calculators and its computer lines help lead its growth in both the U.S. and abroad. Dave and Bill decided to begin the process of stepping down and in 1978, John Young took over as CEO. The 1980s were marked with major growth in desk-top as well as larger computer systems. By the mid 1980's HP was strongly competing with IBM for the desk top market and was now also producing high quality peripherals such as printers, and scanners. Compaq Computers was formed in 1982 and by the end of the decade was generating sales of $1 billion in its own right. Compaq was later acquired by HP.

HP grew at the rate of 20% a year through the 1990s but began to face serious challenges to its lines from the PC clones that began to proliferate. It went through a series of retractions and redefinitions seeking to concentrate its resources to help achieve a competitive advantage in the exploding office and business computing markets. As part of this effort

HP isolated its measurement and components businesses into a new company called Agilent Technologies. It ultimately spun Agilent off to become fully independent in 2000.

In the meantime, Compaq continued to grow rapidly as well and at the end of the decade was one of the top three computer manufacturers in the world. To consolidate this position, Compaq purchased Tandem Computers and Digital Equipment Corporation. However, the very rapid growth it experienced, along with the heavy debt it had acquired to purchase competitors weakened its financial position and by 2000 was starting to look for a merger partner. Under CEO Carly Foirina, merger talks went forward and despite negative stockholder and employee actions, the merger was completed on May 3, 2002. HP changed its NYSE ticker symbol to HCP.

Fortune listed HP as #13 in 2001 in its list of the top 500 businesses, and by the end of 2001 was producing sales of $45.2 Billion and had an employee base of 88,000. The merger has been costly for HP and in 2002 went through additional reorganization and consolidation, but the company has been able to continue to grow (through more slowly since the events of 2001) and show a strong profit. From its birth in a garage in 1938, HP has been able to see trends in the electronics business that have allowed it to become a major player on the world stage in engineering, scientific, medical equipment, office technology, and home computing. It has changed when needed to better fit the markets it services, acquired other companies to solidify its potion in the very volatile technology environment of the late 20th and early 21st centuries, and has even begun to spin off operations that, while viable in and of themselves, kept HP from being as focused as it needed to be. Not all of its decisions have been correct, but overall, HP is a highly successful company that has been a major player in the emergence of the Information Age, and a contributor to our understanding of good management and management practices.

The Nature of Evaluation and Control

In the introductory case, HP had to evaluate and control several aspects of its performance. From a strategic perspective, HP was controlling their growth within the context of its profitability. Early expansion had been tempered by the ability of the firm to fund growth through internal resources (rather than through IPO's or corporate bonds). More recently, under performing units, such as Agilent Technologies, were spun off in order to allow it to purchase Compaq (which had already absorbed Tandem Computers and Digital Equipment Corporation). From a sociological viewpoint, early in its history, HP ingrained a need for innovative management, called the HP Way, and created informal control systems which monitored and reinforced the firm's culture.

One of the most important elements in the strategic planning/strategic management model is that of evaluation and control as represented in Figure 9.1. This is the element that makes strategic planning and strategic management a process and not an event. Though strategic decision makers will have worked very hard to create and implement the firm's strategic plan, for the plan to actually work, it must be continuously tested against its own strategic goals and objectives, as well as against the continuing ability of the firm to establish a strong fit with its most crucial environments.

Yet, like the term "management" itself, the terms "evaluation" and "control" are not as well understood or as universally interpreted as one might think. The processes of evaluation and control can take on many different aspects and focus on a variety of levels, conditions, activity, and interest areas within the operation of a firm that may or may not be helpful in the strategic management process. The strategic managers want to focus evaluation and control only in those areas that will identify whether or not the firm is heading in the direction specified by the strategic plan. Other areas are important, but not as crucial as those strategic areas. This chapter, then, focuses on those areas and issues that the strategic decision-makers must engage in on an on-going basis to help assure that the firm maintains a proper path toward attaining, maintaining, or regaining a competitive advantage in its market.

Figure 9.1
The Strategic Planning Process
Step 7 – Evaluating Results and Taking Corrective Action

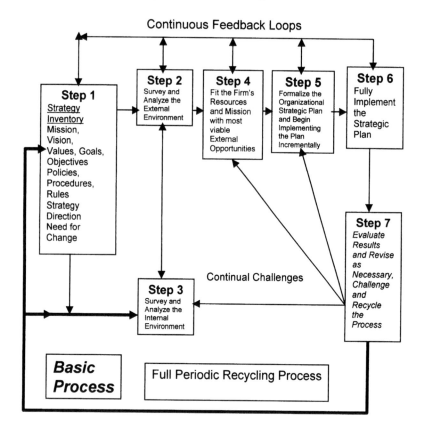

Total Quality Management and Control

W. Edward Deming is given a great amount of credit for fostering an awareness in today's business world of the importance of striving for and maintaining total quality in all of an organization's activities[3]. The four primary objectives of total quality management (TQM) are:

1. Better, less variable quality of the product and service
2. Quicker, less variable response in processes to customer needs
3. Greater flexibility in adjusting to customers' shifting requirements
4. Lower cost through quality improvement and elimination of non-value-adding work.[4]

TQM is now a method of managing organizations that has found its way into for-profit, not-for-profit, and governmental agencies. Its philosophy is simple – do everything at the highest level of quality, and everyone wins. This means that from beginning to end, the value chain must only support those products, services, and practices that assure the highest quality of final output. What Deming also realized was that such outcomes could not exist if the processes themselves were not of the highest quality. Management, line personnel, staff personnel, company policies and practices, and interactions need all conform to the single standard of the highest possible quality. Otherwise, the final outputs will be in someway flawed.

The emergence of TQM and other quality systems has raised management's awareness of the importance and pervasiveness of the control function. Quality products and services cannot be guaranteed if control systems are not in place to ensure that the product of service will meet the highest standards. The Waterford Crystal Company is a TQM company. It hires only those employees who demonstrate the potential of living out the TQM philosophy. Waterford does not count seconds on their production line. After a worker has completed her/his work on a piece of crystal, an inspector will go over that piece looking for even the most minor flaw and if one is found, the crystal object is broken – the worker gets no credit for the piece (regardless of how much time the worker had spent on it), the pieces are recycled to the melting ovens, and the process continues. For Waterford's extensive presentation line (crystal commemorative pieces that customers like the Government of Ireland commission and purchase for presentation to visiting heads of state for example), highly specialized artisans create 3 duplicate objects – one for the customer, one for its personal display gallery, and another one just in case one of the others gets broken or should prove to have a flaw (in which case it is also broken). Artisans can spend weeks or even months in creating just one of these presentation pieces. Yet, that's the philosophy of Waterford, and as a result, customers are always assured of the highest quality crystal, the best possible customer service, and a company that should be there for the long term (See Chapter 10 for a more detailed presentation of the Waterford Crystal Company).

Reengineering and Controlling Change

An additional element of control is controlling change within an organization to keep it viable and responsive to its environment. Reality is that the world is changing constantly and at an increasing level. The option of a no-change strategy has become less and less viable. Because nearly all markets and industries change, it's only logical that the firms within those industries and markets must change or they will lose their fit with their environments. If firms have engaged in substantive strategic planning, have anticipated market and industry change, they should be able to go through change processes on an incremental basis and make operational and strategic changes over time with minimal adverse impact on their firms and their firms' constituents.

For those firms that have not done planning or have miscalculated the actual changes that have come to characterize the industry and its market sets, it may well find that it needs to make major substantive changes, changes that may significantly alter its current operational system and lead to an entirely new organizational form. For changes these dramatic, many firms are undergoing a process referred to as *business process reengineering*. The term business process engineering (BPE) is becoming more and more associated with the restructuring of firms to attain, maintain, or regain a competitive advantage[5].

Firms that become involved with reengineering recognize that unless they make substantive change, they may not be able to withstand environmental changes in its industry and market. They understand they are in trouble. Reengineering is analogous to recreating the firm from the ground up. Most organizations will start reengineering by following the model we have used throughout this book. The strategic planning model provides the same activities and issues that an effective reengineering process will involve. The firm must first evaluate its external environment and test that against its current perceptions. Most likely it will find that the external environmental opportunities and threats are something other than what it had originally thought (especially the presumptions it has held regarding its market and industry). Next, it needs to thoroughly inventory and evaluate its internal resources and then see what areas of fit with its external environments it has made in the past as how accurate those assumptions were. Here is where reengineering can become painful – establishing that matching available resources do not adequately fit current environmental needs, the firm will need to redesign its structure (restructure) and retrench its current operation as it begins to rebuild structures, operations, and philosophies to meet new demands.

Reengineering also involves a substantive evaluation of the current mission and a determination as to whether or not it adequately addresses the optimal future direction of the firm. Tradition may be scrapped, or at least reprioritized, as the firm attempts to refocus its mission to match current resource bases and environmental conditions. The process should then continue on to evaluate vision, values, and major strategic objectives.

Implementation of the reengineered strategic plan is much more difficult than the implementation of the strategic plan as we have described it in the past 2 chapters because the firm is overcoming substantive problems here that add to the challenges of strategic planning implementation. People might be fired, departments may be down-sized or reoriented, and entire divisions might be reorganized or even eliminated as the firm begins to move from one direction into another.

With all the disruption and reorganization that often accompanies reengineering, follow-up, evaluation, and control are essential. It is important to establish how well firm constituents inside and outside the organization are adapting to the changes brought on by reengineering. Strategic managers need real time feedback and should be in a position that allows them to act quickly to support positive results and repair problems. Reengineering is not a process any firm takes on casually, but it may be an important option that moves a firm away from a poor direction toward a new strategic path that hopefully will lead it toward survival.

A Conceptual Overview of the Control Function

Strategic control and evaluation techniques, according to Lorange, Morton and Ghosal, have bee quite misunderstood by both academics and managers alike and note what they call the four fallacies or myths of control:

1. *Control should focus on the internal variables of the firm* – this erroneous belief precludes management from examining key environmental factors (O/T) and assumes the environment has minimal impact on firm operations.

2. *Uncertainly and surprise is to be avoided* – this misleading notion would then eliminate the search for new opportunities (O), resources and competencies (S).

3. *Control is tinkering with a system for most favorable results* – on the contrary, strategy is created and implemented through learning and knowledge formation and may require numerous types of intervention strategies which need to be monitored and evaluated (see Chapters 7 and 8).

4. *Control systems are static and bureaucratic* – quite the opposite, if a control system that can induce systemic change is needed in order for the firm to adapt to dynamic markets then control systems themselves must be flexible and adjust to the firm's changing goals and objectives.[6]

In Chapter 7 we defined successful strategy implementation as those actions by the firm that aligned their strategy with their internal structures, and with their external environment (where learning and organizational knowledge act as the alignment tools). From a strategic and organizational change perspective, organizational control systems then refer to "a system that supports managers in assessing the relevance of the organization's strategy to its progress in the accomplishment of its goals, and when discrepancies exist, to support areas needing attention."[7] In other words, the firm requires a monitoring system that will allow top management to ensure that the firm is following the right strategy and to make slight and/or radical changes in that strategy, internal structure, or the environment in light of the firm's internal and external environment. An essential element then to any control system is the ability to convey market and organizational information to decision-makers in order that market and organizational changes can be detected and analyzed for possible misalignments.

Control as Changing Poor Performance. The most fundamental attribute of any control system is the ability to alter the firm's operation in order to optimize its performance given changing internal and external conditions. Why have a control system if the system cannot be employed to implement change? We're not being naïve here. We fully understand that not everyone in a firm is motivated or properly skilled to perform at an optimal level or that firms always implement best practices. Even so, the evaluation and control systems are essential for allowing strategic managers to understand that if there is a problem with the deployment of human and physical resources that they have an approach that allows them to engage in corrective activities that will appropriately address performance and better control that performance in the future. This definition of control is clearly allied with the objectives and methods of organizational development in helping to formulate a change culture that will provide immediate feedback and assistance to employees as part of the overall strategic management process.

Regardless of whether or not under performance is the result of an individual, a work group, a department, a division, or the entire organization, strategic decision-makers and strategic managers need to be fully aware of what has caused anticipated performance to be missed, and seek to understand the root causes. Then, after determining the exact problems from an objective investigation, they can then recommend actions that will help the firm reengineer faulty operational and strategic activities and move on toward better conformance with the overall plan. This is quite similar to the organizational development/action research model we described previously where the firm intervenes in its own operation due to data that indicates problems in its processes.

Formal and Informal Control Systems. We have noted throughout this text that strategies can be both deliberate (purposive) or emergent (unintended). Since control systems are a product of the strategy formulation process, they also can be either planned or accidental. According to James J. Carroll, control systems can be both formal and informal in nature[8], see Table 9.1 below.

Table 9.1
Formal and Informal Control Systems

Formal	Informal
Cybernetic	Psychological
Management Principles	Sociological
Agency Relationship	
Organizational Structure	

Formal control systems are those sanctioned by the organization and have been developed specifically for the purpose of ensuring that the firm gauges its performance and takes action when the firm varies from accepted standards of performance. *Cybernetic control* systems examine the business operations from a managerial accounting perspective, that is, traditional accounting variables. The control approach is one of management by exception where the accounting variables employed are standardized and not tied to the strategy of the firm. The system works very much like that of a thermostat over room weather conditions, it corrects deviations outside of the standards for performance once detected but is not proactive in changing the conditions of the firm so as to avoid deviations in the first place.

Control as a management principle treats control as an extension of the firm's planning process within a rational systems perspective (see the Appendix in Chapter 1). There are three different types of management evaluations and controls: inputs (resources), employee work behavior, and systems' outputs.[9] Input issues are those of resource acquisition. Evaluation of inputs involves the determination as whether or not the organization has been successful in acquiring the capital, human, and intellectual resources it needs to conduct its operations at an optimal level to meet market and immediate stakeholder needs and expectations. Too many resources can be just as bad as too few resources in that, as an example, a firm may have more highly qualified employees than it has work for them to do – in such an event, the extra number of employees most likely costs the firm excess wages which directly decreases profits. Balancing resources to operational capacity and market demand is one of the important reasons that managers monitor, evaluate, and try to control inputs. Input control is also concerned with the elements of work (equipment, machinery, supplies, and even job descriptions and job specifications) in that the existence of defined work elements is necessary before operations can proceed.

Control of behaviors is the second major management control system. By behaviors, we are referring to the behavioral activities that occur at all levels of the operation: managerial decisions and actions, direct line-employee work activities, and support departmental personnel work activities. Efficiency, effective management relations, productivity, and support of quality are all behavioral considerations that should be evaluated on an on-going basis and then corrected if they are found to be faulty.

Finally, evaluation and control of outputs is essential in any firm. We have described much of these issues throughout this book. Measuring the precise levels of sales growth, both year-to-year as well as over time; calculating profit margins (for the firm as a whole as for divisions as well); determining whether or not the firm has been able to achieve its stated strategic goals and objectives; and monitoring internal and external stakeholders to determine whether or not the firm has been successful in meeting their needs are all examples of organizational outputs that are important data bases to strategic decision-makers.

Control as an agency relationship is the third formal control system and is embedded in the concept of bureaucracy and administrative service.[10] Managers in this system act as agents of the owners, that is, they manage the organization at the behest of the stockholders. They represent the owners' interests yet are not the owners and the authority to direct the firm's operation is entrenched not in the person but in the *position* that the person occupies. The owners control the authority they have delegated to their managers through a checks and balance system by empowering specific departments (and therein positions within those departments) to oversee the administrators. "This approach to control forms the basis for control as described within the auditing and financial accounting fields (see Statement of Auditing Standard No.1)."[11]

Control as organizational structure relates to issues of environmental interface, uncertainty, and organizational design. The organization's structure is used as a buffer or filter to direct external influences that may disrupt the firm's operation away from employees who need to concentrate on task performance rather than processing external data – to maintain the firm's equilibrium even in turbulent environments.[12] The firm can either create structures that increase the flow of information (i.e. network organizations, cross-functional teams, matrix structures, and liaison roles; see Chapters 7 & 8) or structures that reduce the need for environmental communication (self-managed work groups or strategic business units; any self-contained unit such as GM's Saturn Division).

Informal control systems refer to psychological and social control systems that operate in conjunction wit the more formal control techniques. These techniques are not sanctioned by the firm but are utilized by managers and workers alike in order to ensure that their personal goals, and not necessarily the goals of the organization, are achieved.

Psychological control systems refer to the use of informal rewards (both positive and negative) and punishments, personal power, that are outside the normal management system to control employee behavior. These powers may include coercion (the ability to inflict a negative consequence), connection (the ability to influence those who can inflict a negative consequence), referent (the desire of the person to be associated with a specific group), charismatic, information (access to desired data), and expert (access to knowledge).[13] Managers use these control systems in order to overcome worker resistance (coercion, connection), obtain employee compliance (referent, charismatic), or receive commitment (information, expert). Hersey and Blanchard note that employee readiness (their willingness to follow) is critical for determining which control techniques to employ.[14]

Last, *sociological controls* are used in order to obtain employee conformance to the values and attitudes of the organization – what constitutes the organization's culture. As described in Chapter 7, the firm uses ceremonies, symbols, stories, sayings, and icons to informally reinforce the uniqueness of the organization and to provide employees informal guidance on the do's and don'ts in the organization. Culture acts as a very powerful controlling mechanism in determining what is considered right and wrong behavior and acts in conjunction with psychological control systems in rewarding and punishing proper behavior.

Levels of Organizational Control. Throughout this text we have also examined the issue of organizational levels and its impact on strategy formulation and implementation; certainly control is no different. As Figure 9.2 indicates, as one moves from corporate level, to business unit level, to functional, and even individual level, the type of control system shifts from strategic, to tactical, to operational, to individual (whether they are formal or informal in nature). Later in the chapter we will see how these control techniques differ based upon focus, time, and ability to measure and gather control data.

Interestingly enough, much of performance evaluation is on the personal level, and even though strategic management is mostly concerned with overall long-term performance, there is little hope of explaining that performance if evaluators do not incorporate short-term micro performance data as part of their longer-term macro perspective. On the micro level, then, and in presuming that everyone who is involved with the operation of the organization is honest and forthright, evaluation should lead to understanding the precise activities that lead to a particular outcome. In the case of poor performance, the evaluator needs to know all the contributions, not simply those of the employee. With this information, the evaluator can recommend corrective actions, harmonious with the overall strategic plan, to those who control the process that may have to do more with events and circumstances outside the control of the employee and which, unless corrected, will not allow the employee to function at an optimal level of efficiency and productivity. In the case of anticipated or exceptional performance, the

Figure 9.2
Levels of Organizational Control

Strategic Controls	Corporate Level
Tactical Controls	Business Unit Level
Operational Controls	Functional Level
Individual Controls	Individual Level

evaluator will want to do the same level of evaluation to help the firm to know what works well, and also to give backing to the workability of the strategic plan.

Goal Displacement and the Learning Curve. Another topic in the evaluation and control process is that of goal displacement -- the problem that often occurs when a firm is more concerned with the means involved in achieving an objective than in the objective itself, or conversely is more concerned with the goal than the means it took to achieve it. This has clear implications for the control component as well in that if an evaluator needs to take both means and ends into an account in determining whether or not either should be changed (controlled). For example, in 1971 and 1972, the Committee to Reelect President Nixon was obsessed with the goal of winning the election and apparently didn't care how they did it. As a result, they engaged in a dirty tricks campaign and also were involved with the break in of the Democrats' headquarters in the Watergate Office building that led to the national scandal that eventually brought down Nixon's second presidency. The Committee reached its goal, but because of the means they engaged in, their goal was eventually destroyed.[15] The same is true in many other organizations. In Chapter 2, we briefly described the case of Enron, and how it engaged in deceptive, misguided, arrogant, and illegal behaviors to achieve high growth and profitability numbers. When discovered, Enron was forced into bankruptcy and millions of stakeholders were hurt.

It's important to tie organizational evaluations to the on-going development of its learning curve and knowledge databases as it continuously creates itself as a learning organization. It is incorrect to assume that firms engage in evaluation processes and exercise control in a negative perspective. On the contrary, the major goal of all evaluation should be to learn from what has happened that is positive as well as learn from what it has done that hasn't worked out per expectation.

The Control Process: Measuring Performance and Correcting Deviations

The basic underpinning of any control system is the ability to accurately measure organizational performance and the ability to take corrective action when performance does not meet adopted standards. What and how to measure performance is therefore vital to the success of a control system since measures of evaluation and control can prove problematic.[16] In Chapter 4, we identified the issues of measuring organizational criteria based on quantitative as well as qualitative characteristics. While quantitative criteria are more straight forward in allowing measurement for evaluation, qualitative criteria present real difficulties at times. Issues such as customer service; quality of products or services; quality of personnel; quality of planning; quality use of time; efficiencies; and even quality of evaluation instruments are all examples of concerns related to measuring quality in any organization.

It is important that strategic decision-makers also need to consider is the appropriateness of the measures they use. On the surface, this may not sound like much of an issue, but once again consider the issue of measuring qualitative performance. For example, since something like "good management," is important, but cannot be directly measured, as we suggested above, one needs to measure a surrogate. The question becomes, then, what is a good surrogate for good management? There is a wide variety of choices here, and depending on which one (or which ones) the evaluator chooses could or could not adequately measure good management. If one chooses to measure number of complaints from subordinates, this *could* be a measure of good management or it could also indicate that subordinates are so intimidated by their manager that they are afraid to complain. Choosing another measure, say overall productivity of the department compared with the same measure from the previous year, might prove to be a better measure. Overall, many firms have come to develop a wide variety of measures to try to accurately identify the true nature of performance for the organization as a whole, for divisions, for managers at all levels, and for employees. These multi-measures are time-consuming and cumbersome, but if the point is to gain an accurate measure of what is and then determine what should be, they become willing to find valid and reliable measures to give them the true information they need to measure performance against strategic goals.

Timing and Measurement. Another significant issue is the difference in measuring short-term vs. long-term results. For most organizational constituents, short-term work orientation leads to short-term work evaluation criteria and standards. Since most reward systems are based on yearly reviews, and even salaries are referred to in annual numbers (Mary Clark makes $65,000 a year), most performance outcomes have a one-year orientation. These are important measures, and we do not suggest here that they shouldn't be used or should be subordinated to long-term measurements. The problem is that the *strategic outcomes of a firm are long-term in nature*, and since it is these strategic issues that determine survival, they should not be ignored.[17] Further, it is often very difficult for a firm to point to one year's performance and conclude many strategic objectives. For example, Southwest Airlines aspires to be the largest airline business in the United States (it currently has no international aspirations). At the end of 2001, however, it only had 3.2% of the domestic market, compared to American Airlines who had 10.9%.[18] The growth rate of Southwest is, however, approximately twice that of American[19] and one might be tempted to suggest that the higher growth rate will allow Southwest to achieve its goal sometime in the future. Therein lies the problem of time-measurement: one year's data is clearly insufficient to conclude long-term trends and it is only over a more reasonable time frame (perhaps five years in this example) can a more accurate evaluation be made.

Measurement and Performance. Tom Peters has coined a phrase that is an excellent axiom for businesses, "what gets measured, gets done."[20]   There are three typical areas that firms evaluate to establish an understanding of performance: financial measures, stakeholder measures, and measures of management quality.[21]   As we discussed in Chapter 4, financial measures have both operational and strategic implications.   Certainly the two measures that would be of major interest to both control systems are profitability and growth of sales.   Since both have survival implications, as we have discussed throughout, they are highly strategic in nature and major stakeholders will watch these figures to see if they go up or down and conclude some measure of the health of the firm as a result.   Operational personnel will also watch these figures, but from the viewpoint of their contribution to them.   If profits are down and a department can determine that it has not been as efficient as it could have been, then the evaluation will indicate that something needs to be done.   By then better controlling efficiencies, this department should be able to reduce its particular drag on profits and perhaps be part of the overall process of improving performance efficiencies and thereby improving company profits.

Stakeholder measures are both straight forward and nebulous. Stockholders may well want to watch profits and sales growth, but are also normally concerned about the returns measures (ROI, ROA, and ROE).   Suppliers will look for on-time payments and the level of return.   Distributors will look for on-time deliveries, quality of provided goods and services, and the return rates it experiences on the focal firm's product or service base.   More nebulous, the community will look for solid and on-going contributions to helping it solve community needs and governments will look for good corporate citizenship (few to no lawsuits, few to no regulatory problems, paying one's fair share of taxes, and positive contribution to the overall economy).

Management quality is also a concern. Looking back at the Enron case study in Chapter 2, it is obvious that one cannot simply take top management's word that they are doing a good job. (Enron managers were so arrogant at stockholder meetings, for example, that when stockholders asked for balance sheets, income statements, and explanations about financial practices, Jeffrey Skilling is reported to have called them highly degrading names.[22]) Even taking Enron's accountants' word for the worthiness of the company and its management proved to be a mistake. [23] Since the Enron and World Com scandals in particular, stakeholders both inside and outside the organization are becoming more and more skeptical about the quality of corporate management and more and more firms are finding that they need to measure management performance and accurately report it in trying to maintain a higher level of stakeholder confidence.

Once evaluation has been completed, then it is important to make judgments about what the data suggest. Continuing our example of creating effective evaluation and control measures for good management, once an evaluator has been able to obtain a variety of measures that are meant to indicate some level of good management, the obvious question becomes, "good, according to what standard?" The existence of standards is, then, the next major factor in evaluating and controlling a firm's outcomes, which we expand upon in the next sections.

Establishing Measurement Performance Criteria and Standards

As is true for choosing surrogates to represent behavioral and qualitative phenomena outcomes of an organization, there is also a variety of choices of performance criteria and standards from which the strategic decision-maker can choose.[24] Previous performance is an obvious candidate. Comparing current results from historical results provides specific information as to improvement in performance as well as a decline in performance. Wall Street expectations are another set of criteria. Here, expert industry analysts examine industry trends and individual company performance patterns and make predictions as to how well they believe the company or industry will perform on a quarterly or yearly basis. They do this for current and potential stockholders to try to assist them in buy, hold, or sell decisions. If a firm beats Wall Street expectations, this is usually seen as a very good sign. If, however, a firm falls below Wall Street expectation, it can mean loss of market confidence, lower stock pricing, and more activity in selling a firm's stock than in purchasing it. Stockholder expectations are yet another set of performance criteria. Though not as formalized and not as obvious as the other types of criteria, many firms seek to better understand what its stockholders want as a result of their ownership of stock in a given corporation. Sometimes this is more apparent when a retirement fund, mutual fund, or a wealthy investor holds large blocs of stock – these entities are likely to be very vocal at shareholder meetings and usually seek representation on the Board of Directors. In these capacities, they can not only make their expectation known, but then put themselves in a position to do something about it.

Perhaps one of the better sets of determining performance standards is through *benchmarking*. Particularly for the strategic decision-maker, benchmarking is useful because it directly compares a focal company's performance to the standards of the industry.[25] Two measures are appropriate for doing this: one is to establish average performance in the industry (on any measurable level); and a second is to establish the performance of the best performer in the industry. Measuring a given firm's performance against the industry standard tells the firm whether or not it is performing below, at, or ahead of the industry. This is important because if a firm's performance is behind the industry average, it is falling behind.

Industry average, however, is not the entire story. It is also important to benchmark a given firm's performance to that of the strongest competitor in the industry. For example, Coors is presently growing at a rate that is faster than the average of the industry, but its growth in market share compared to Anheuser-Busch is slower.[26] If Coors ever hopes to be the largest brewer in the United States (or in the world) it must be growing fast enough to accumulate market share at a greater rate than its archrival Anheuser-Busch. As long as Anheuser-Busch has growth and market share above that of Coors, Coors will be in a secondary position and, therefore, not a strong as its rival.

Another concern for establishing good performance criteria and standards is to look past the industry and competitors to other business standards. In the Appendix to Chapter 4, we included a variety of finance ratios and their measures, and also indicated how firms use them to gauge operations. Several of these involve basic accounting principles that also should be a consideration in establishing standards. For example, the accounting standard for a current ratio is 2:1 (twice as many current assets as current liabilities); and the accounting standard for a quick ratio is 1:1 (current assets less inventory should equal current liabilities). There are solid reasons for these standards, and they apply to all organizations. In terms of setting standards, these merit additional consideration. For example, in the airline industry for 2001, United had a current ratio of 0.63, the industry ratio was 1.13 as was the case for Southwest Airlines (arguably the current performance leader in the industry). [27]   In recalling that the accounting stand is 2:1, or 2.00, not only is United well below industry and industry leader standards, they are also well below accounting standards, and as we indicated in our introductory case in Chapter 1.   United is in serious financial difficulties – certainly this particular measure against standards indicates at least one area that has contributed to the company's financial troubles.

Internal versus External Measurement Criteria/Standards. We have examined several different issues relative to establishing effective evaluation and control measures here, some of which are internal and some of which are external. One could ask at this point, are one set of criteria better than the other? Should the firm be more sensitive to its own capabilities of setting performance standards and then go about the activities of measuring them, or should the firm be more sensitive to externally devised standards? The firm is choosing between self-regulation (internal standards) and market-driven regulation (external standards).[28] This is neither a straight forward question nor is it an easy issue to resolve and therefore many firms employed mixed standards.

In Chapter 3 we described many of the forces that exist externally that control organizations as an important consideration in the process of strategic management.   External forces are *forces* precisely because they not only have some level of power to influence and try to control the activities and outputs of a firm, but because they cause the organization to be responsive to them. This means that external forces can impose control standards and then expect the focal firm to conform through regulatory and social control mechanisms. The government expects firms to act as good corporate citizens and can punish those who do not reach governmental expectations and meet government product and safety standards. Customers expect the firm to provide the goods or services they want at a price they are willing to pay, and if the firm doesn't do this, they will not buy. The legal and financial systems have rules and regulations that apply to everyone, and for firms that chose not to comply, they can find themselves deeply embroiled in lawsuits and potentially foreclosures that can shut the business down. These, and other examples of imperative external forces, together provide a listing of those external standards every firm should meet.

However, there are many, many more areas of operation that are better handled by internal management and the strategic planning process. Setting a strategic course is one of the major internal decisions that will set standards for the firm over the long-term. The strategic plan itself will define many areas of operational and strategic areas that are critical to the overall survival of the firm, and as such, need to set forth clear standards for performance (and even the methods of acceptable operational activity) that will provide strategic managers with precise guidelines for how the firm should proceed and what it should accomplish.

External Standards of Excellence. Tom Peters and Robert H. Waterman, Jr. in 1982 started "the search for excellence"[29] by asking the question, what are the attributes of a superior corporation and how can we certify their excellence? This search for excellence has lead to the development of quality awards and international standards associations who have developed their own quality criteria and business standards. They are as follows:

1. The Deming Prize – instituted by the Union for Japanese Scientists and Engineers in 1951, the prize is awarded to all companies that have instituted company-wide quality controls and standards (CWQC) in the areas of: corporate policies, organization and operation, education and dissemination, information gathering and

communication, analysis, standardization, control, quality assurance, effects, and future plans.

2. The Malcolm Baldridge National Quality Award – signed into law in 1987, the purpose of the award was to help American companies improve their quality and productivity, recognize the achievements of these companies, and establish guidelines and criteria in evaluating businesses. The criteria consist of a hierarchical set of categories including leadership, strategic planning, customer and market focus, information and analysis, human resource focus, process management, and business results. Businesses applying for the award are evaluated as to their approach (methods used to achievement requirements in each category), deployment (the extent of the use of the approach), and results (outcomes achieved).

3. Other awards programs – the Presidential Award of Quality (www.opm.gov/quality), the European Quality Award, the Canadian Award for Business Excellence, and the Australian Business Excellence Award all use similar but not the exact same standards. Their criteria include leadership, customer focus, improvement planning, people focus, process optimization and supplier focus.

4. ISO 9000:2000 (www.iso.ch) – developed by the International Organization for Standardization (ISO), the purpose of these standards is to homogenize measures of quality across businesses in the European Community (EU), seek to continuously improve product and process quality, and provide confidence to suppliers and customers that quality could be verified. ISO 9000 standards include: quality management systems, management responsibility, resource management, product realization, and measurement analysis and improvement.

5. Six Sigma- developed at Motorola in the mid-1980's, this measure applied one standard to every criteria, that of near zero defects (to be exact, one defect per million). General Electric implemented this concept through a problem-solving approach: one first *defines* the problem, determines key processes to *measure, analyze* the problem for most likely causes, *improve* the process through modification, and *control* the process (DMAIC).[30]

These external standards provide one method for ascertaining which measures to employ yet may not work well for some firms given the nuances associated with their particular industry and company.

Key Success Factors. Key Success Factors (KSFs) designate those particular activities in the organization that are most crucial to firm's overall success and health in their given industry and/or operating domain. Elsewhere, these are also referred to as Key Performance Indicators (KPIs). For our purposes, we define KSFs as: measurable activities, the condition of crucial components of the work process, and strategic output criteria that indicate the operational and strategic health of an organization. It is important that KSFs are both measurable and related to outcomes, and that they be related to crucial functions of the firm. [31] A good key performance indicator has a number of common characteristics, which include: often known to the organization, impact of movement in a day/week can be significant, responsibility can be tied down to teams/individuals, and positive movement affects many other indicators and all in a positive direction.[32]

KSFs tend to be true industry-wide and often reflect crucial areas of operations that are true of all firms in an industry. For example, throughout this book, we have talked about profitability and sales growth. Both of these outcomes meet all the criteria – they are measurable, they are outcomes of performance, they are true for all members in an industry, and they are crucial to overall survival. In another example for the airline industry, additional KSFs include revenue per passenger mile, load factors, fuel costs, average age of aircraft, and average fuel consumption per passenger mile. All of these KSFs reflect crucial areas of airline performance that dramatically impact profitability. When fuel costs go up 2% or 3% they can impact a drop in overall profitability of ½ % to 1%, since fuel is one of the most expensive elements of flying a plane.

Where can one find KSFs? One good place to look is in a corporation's annual filing of a 10-K with the Securities and Exchange Commission. These are accessible by the public through the EDGAR data base[33], Internet financial services such as Yahoo! Finance[34] or Quicken Quotes and Research Center[35], or even through many companies' own websites.

KSF's as performance criteria. KSFs are directly useful as performance criteria. Since they are measurable, and related to specific criteria that are important to the strategic management process, they create an important area of the on-going strategic plan. Can qualitative factors be KSFs? Yes, as long as there are accurate surrogate measures that properly identify outcome performance, no firm should shy away from qualitative KSFs. High quality customer service is a great candidate for KSF status. The issue, though, is how does one measure it? Survey feedback is one way of measuring high quality customer service by sending customers survey forms using standard statistical methods (random selection, adequate sample size, and proper validity and reliability of the measures themselves).[36] While data results may be skewed due to a number of controllable as well as non-controllable factors, this method of developing a strong surrogate measure for the phenomenon. A less expensive method might be to employ focus groups or to measure number of customer complaints from one year to another.

This last example, however, also has issues relative to standards. Would a reduction of customer complaints, as a percentage of the number of sales a firm has recorded over the year, be a good thing or a bad thing? Once again, the real discriminator would be that of comparing performance to a standard. For example, does 1 complaint per every 40 sales this year versus 1 complaint per every 30 sales in the previous year indicate that the firm should conclude that it is problem-free? Most likely not, even common sense would tell an evaluator that this is still a large number of complaints in and of itself, and this company probably has a problem. Establishing a standard is a much better way of evaluating KSP performance criteria. Again, since KSFs are generally industry-related and industry-specific it is reasonable to assume that qualitative KSFs will be replicated across the industry, giving an individual firm a ready standard. Here, then, if we could determine that the industry standard for consumer complaints was 1 per every 1,000 individual sales, we could conclude that not only is our firm in trouble, it is in serious trouble and needs to introduce systems to address the situation, but help it eventually meet the industry standard.

Balanced Scorecard Approach (BSA). Many organizations use an inappropriate mix of financial, stakeholder, and quality KPI's (measurements). The BSA is a fairly new and radical approach to evaluation in that it provides a structured hierarchical framework of KPI's that management can use to link or connect its strategic activities to the ultimate goal of financial value creation. At the top of the framework is financial performance, which is driven by a unique customer value proposition. This is in turn delivered by the right set of business processes (the value chain). At the base of the hierarchy is innovation and growth, which provide the capabilities and infrastructure for a continually evolving value proposition and processes. The cause-and-effect linkages within the balanced scorecard hierarchy can be a powerful tool for strategy evaluation.[37]

The logic of this approach underlies the reason why some managers have adopted a balanced scorecard approach to measuring firm performance, yet balance implies that all measures are equally important in all settings. As we stated earlier, we endorse a multi-measure approach to understanding company performance, but challenge the idea that all measures are equally important irrespective to the firm's strategy.[38] When implementing the balanced scorecard, companies should use the balanced scorecard to empower the organization, delegate accountability to the lowest profit center, use the scorecard as a strategic tool, choose measures that optimize the firm, and dictate learning and growth. On the other hand, companies should not use the scorecard to centralize control, balance the scorecard and thereby distort the strategy, and base incentives purely on the scorecard.[39]

As stated earlier, using the BSA as a control instrument is not without its problems. Research by the Institute of Management Accountants in 2002 on the BSA indicated that financial performance measures were still given high ratings by survey respondents. In contrast, non-financial measures, including metrics in customer performance, internal processes, innovation, and employee capabilities, were rated as being much less effective and useful. These non-financial categories represent areas for improvement in many performance measurement systems.[40] Analysts are also beginning to question what difference BSA's actually make to the overall running of a business.

While some studies show a link between the use of the Scorecard and an improvement in share price, many businesses still feel under-whelmed. The main criticisms of the Scorecard focus on its absence of a people perspective, that it does not take into account the fact that businesses are subject to regulation and the lack of any environmental or community issues in its makeup.[41]

Correcting Deviations from Standards

Once the firm has established its performance measures and measurement instruments, it then must develop methodologies for comparing actual performance to standards and then correcting strategies and operations if there are negative deviations from those standards. Assuming that the measure of a KSF results in performance evaluation that is below the standard, decision decision-makers need to find methods and activities that will correct performance. These activities go beyond the basic strategic plan, but are clearly part of the strategic planning process. As Figure 9.1 indicates, Step 7 not only involves evaluation and control, but can also lead to a reexamination and testing of the entire strategic planning process. Hopefully, the root cause of the lack of higher performance outcomes is relatively simple to address, but the model speaks to the importance and willingness of strategic managers to question every part of the strategic plan in effect and then rewrite any part that has proven to be faulty.

For example, if sales are lower than expectations, and it isn't obvious as to why, strategic managers may not only want to go back and reexamine its external environments to see if they have missed something important, they may also want to reexamine its strategic choices and question whether or not the strategic path it had chosen to follow should be modified or changed altogether. The problem could also be functional, and perhaps a different sales campaign or even a different sales force mix is necessary. Regardless of where the problem lies, the firm needs to be objective in finding the roots of the problem, correct the problem, do damage control for the rest of the operation that was impacted by the problem, rewrite that portion of the strategic plan to reflect different strategic processes, and then begin to monitor the operations around that particular process to help assure that the changes are leading to intended results.

Once the various evaluations are made, then the actual process of control begins. The term control is associated with two types of activity: *maintenance activity* to confirm, support, and perpetuate acceptable performance; and *corrective activity* to change unacceptable performance into more acceptable performance.

Maintenance control involves developing support systems that reward current performance activities and seek to assure that they do not change. In any organizational setting, it is always a mistake to take desired performance for granted. Many employees are used to only hearing from superiors when something is wrong – they seldom hear from superiors when things are going right. While it may be the norm, it is still a mistake not to recognize and support activities of individuals, departments, and divisions that are performing at an expected level of activity. Strategic activities fall into the same category. Those responsible for attaining strategic objectives need to know that what they are doing is successful, just as they need to know when they are not meeting objectives. Through strategic thinking, an objective feedback system can be very helpful in maintaining current performance.

Corrective control is designed to change current performance from what it is currently to what the firm's strategic managers feel it should be. There are a variety of choices strategic managers can choose from in effectively managing and controlling the change process, but which ever method they choose, they will want to use the most effective control method to meet the strategic issue they are addressing. There are several qualities that distinguish effective controls from other options. Effective controls should be:
1. Timely
2. Both long-term and short term in nature
3. Directed and efficient
4. Aimed at important result areas
5. Objective, tied to the roots of issues and problems
6. Tied to the general reward system.

Feedback, Feedback/Real Time, Feed-Forward Systems

Figure 9.1 suggests that a firm develop continual feedback and feed-forward systems that can detect deviations to standards early as possible in the strategic and operational process and allow immediate corrective action. In order for this to work, employees and managers at all levels need to not only be able to know the level of their own performance, but the standards for all of the processes involved as well. With computer technology advances, much of this feedback can occur in real time, with information that is accessible to both the employee and the management of an area. When either one begins to sense that a problem exists, both can immediately investigate to determine if a problem does in fact exist and then proceed to correcting the problem.

It is important that no one view these systems as punitive, they are corrective and focused on discovering flaws in the process and correcting them. This is why an organizational-wide control mentality is important. This is the job of management. When firms decide to engage in organizational control, it is a mistake to keep the process strictly at the top. Top-down control tends to be the norm because the traditional mode of doing business is top-down. The result tends to be a feeling of alienation in lower levels of the organization and little buy-in to top-level decisions.

While top-level managers and members of the Board of Directors will have the greatest stake in creating and implementing an effective control system, employees and managers throughout the organization also have a stake in its success and should be included at some point in its development. Here, the result should then also be lower alienation throughout the firm, greater buy-in, and most importantly, an organizational-wide sense of control. Also, by tying the reward and evaluation systems to organizational controls, people throughout the firm will begin to associate the two and seek to engage in performance that increase efficiency and attain objectives. Organizational-wide control systems hence need to allow for the development and support of real time performance feedback in order to reinforce the linkages between performance and reward systems. [42]

Performance feed-forward is another type of control system. In performance feed-forward systems, communication patterns exist that allow one department to inform other departments in the organization of activities that are about to occur in one area that will affect other areas over time. This allows better planning and control of activities since the department can monitor the resources it receives from another unit (or supplier) and either request alterations to the resources (i.e. raw materials that do not meet standards) or make changes to its operational processes to accommodate the incoming resources.

For example, many companies find that, although they hire individuals who are recent college graduates, in many cases they must train these graduates in what they would consider either basic or simple technical skills (i.e. use of certain standardized computer software packages, memo writing, office etiquette, etc.). These firms are modifying their resources prior to job placement in order to ensure that work processes can occur with minimal problems. See Figure 9.3 below.

Just-in-time inventory systems depend on feed-forward systems to be able to not only anticipate distributor needs, but also allow those distributors to know of scheduling deviances that could create problems. This mutual feed-forward, feedback system allows both partners to make adjustments and allow a smooth operational flow.

Strategic Control Systems[43]

Environmental Scanning. As we have mentioned earlier, corporate level strategies must be evaluated on a continuous basis in light of changes in the environment as well as changes within the firm. The first strategic control, *environmental scanning*, identifies opportunities and threats in the environment and is considered part of any SWOT analysis. Environmental scanning is generally viewed as a prerequisite for formulating effective business strategies but may also act as a control technique to assess the formulation and implementation of strategy. Moreover, effective scanning of the environment is seen as necessary to the successful alignment of competitive strategies with environmental requirements and the achievement of outstanding performance. Research results confirm the moderating role played by

Figure 9.3
Feedforward and Feedback Control Systems

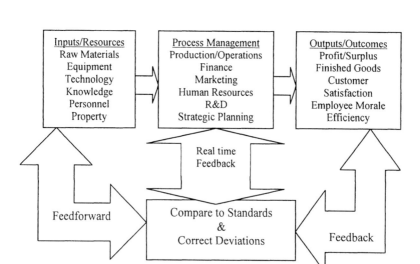

environmental scanning activities in the strategy/performing relationship, thus providing further evidence for the contingency relationship among the environment, the organization's internal processes, and performance.[44]

An environmental scan will always include continual and predictable events that require constant surveillance, such as competitors in the industry, products and product development, regulations, new technologies, and economic and social conditions nationally and globally.[45]

Effective scanning requires answers to two questions. First, what is the best way to generate and make sense of information about the environment? Second, how can the results of a scan be used to build consensus during the feedback process for the environmental factors impacting the strategic plan?[46] Surveys of effective scanning practices in organizations appear to converge on a set of common best-practice principles: 1. Plan and manage scanning as a strategic activity. 2.

Implement scanning as a formal system. 3. Partner with domain experts and IT specialists in designing the scanning system. 4. Manage information as the core of the scanning function.[47] Environmental scanning employs techniques such as data mining (computer programs that look for patterns in industry and competitive data), scenario construction and testing (creating a model of the industry and/or market and evaluating/modifying those models given scanned information), and computer simulations (testing "what if?" situations given scenario construction) in order to create a business intelligence system.[48]

    Premise Control.   Underlying any strategic formulation process is the development of assumptions about the organization and its environment; what are called *planning premises*. These premises are projections about the future of the marketplace and form the underpinnings of any strategic plan. For example, many firms in determining whether to move forward with a project or not factor in the cost of future capital and assume a specific lending rate over a 3-5 year period. If those projected rates turn out to be wrong (either too high or too low) then the strategic planners must reconsider their plans in light of those changes. Lower rates may lead to accelerated plans for growth and expansion while higher rates may completely derail a new product or service. This unmistakably occurred in the periods from 1998 to 2003. The prime lending rate during most of 1998 was 8.5% yet was halved to 4.25% by January of 2003.[49]   Ironically, although the change in the prime lending rate boded well for business growth and new business ventures, other economic factors such as unemployment (a lagging indicator), the Dow Industrials, the NASDAQ, and the consumer spending moved in the opposite direction and therefore hindered business expansion.[50]

    Implementation Control.   As we described in Chapter 7, many strategic plans fail due to poor implementation. The purpose of implementation control systems is to determine whether or not the strategic plan is being implemented properly and whether the plan should be terminated due to the inability of the firm to meet their projected goals and objectives. This requires the development of strategic milestones, benchmarks that the firm must meet or exceed at certain points in time in order to ensure successful strategy implementation.[51]

There are several different techniques that can be employed as implementation control systems and originate from the area of project management. These implementation control systems all require that the strategic plan already have clearly defined and measurable objectives, that the overall plan be subdivided into pieces (called work packages) that are assigned to teams and/or individuals, that a specific set of activities be developed that will lead to the attainment of those objectives, and that time and cost estimates be made for each work activity. These activities, with their associated cost and time estimates, and then graphically portrayed in the form of a network diagram or flow chart which denotes the interdependency and sequence of tasks, cash flow, and time requirements.[52]

The most fundamental implementation control technique is a *Gantt Chart*. Gantt charts are bar graphs that help plan and monitor project development or resource allocation on a horizontal time scale.

Typically, Gantt charts indicate the exact duration of specific tasks, but they can also be used to indicate the relationship between tasks, planned and actual completion dates, cost of each task, the person or persons responsible for each task, and the milestones in a project's development. See Figure 9.4 below as an example.

Other, most sophisticated techniques like Program Evaluation Review Technique (PERT), Critical Path Method (CPM), Precedence Diagramming Method (PDM) and Graphic Evaluation Review Technique (GERT) all employ a network framework and show sequential flow and interrelationships of activities.[53] These techniques, however, have been criticized as truncating important front-end thought processes, such as exploring alternative solutions or forecasting risks, since they force planners into a scheduling mode and operational mode before having defined and fully thought through the firm's strategy.[54] They have also been criticized for assuming that some activities are independent, and that project activities occur in a linear sequence.[55]

Special Alert Control. These controls refer to the need to monitor the external environment for immediate threats to the firm. As the attack on the Twin Towers on September 11, 2001, indicated, there was a need for the United States to establish special alert controls for terrorist activities and to consolidate responsibilities for

Figure 9.4
Gantt Chart: Planned versus Actual Performance[56]

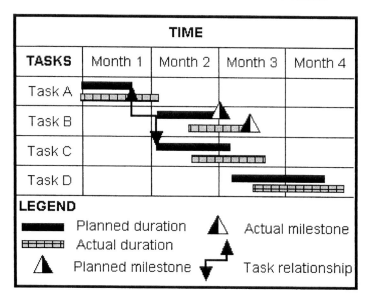

those controls in one government entity responsible for homeland defense.[57] Firms need to take equal care in terms of their own strategic planning and development.

For example, the owners of Riverhead Supply and Lumber (RSL), a regional Eastern Long Island (New York) supplier of home building and construction material were quite worried about the prospect of a superstore like Home Depot walking into their market unannounced. The owners of the firm therefore monitored the numerous local town planning boards for proposals for the development of a "mega-store" home supply company as well as hired a not-for-profit survey organization to determine the community's response to such a proposal. The survey indicated that local consumers would strongly welcome a hardware superstore but that the store could only be located in the Town of Riverhead (legislation was actually passed in two of the local communities prohibiting the building of any store more than 15,000 square feet – superstores tend to be 100,000 square feet[58]). This allowed RSL to focus its attention on one Town's planning board and allowed them to develop a series of temporary barriers that slowed down the opening of a Home Depot and provided them additional time in which to develop a competitive strategy.

Tactical and Organizational Controls

   Tactical control systems are those systems developed at the business unit level that ensure that a particular strategic business unit (SBU) is implementing its own unit strategy and include a more highly defined set of strategic controls (environmental scanning, premise control, implementation control, and special alert control) than control systems for the organization as a whole. Tactical controls are also tied to the specifics of the SBU's strategy: low cost leaders focus on cost management[59] while differentiators focus on measures of quality and customer satisfaction. Cost management and quality control systems are quantitative in nature while customer satisfaction systems are more qualitative.

   Organization-wide control systems focus on the organization development aspects of strategy implementation and try to determine whether: 1) the change agents were able to assist members of the organization in developing the new competencies needed to facilitate change (translation and transference) and 2) the desired changes to the organization were institutionalized (transformation). In terms of translation, competency-based evaluation and assessment can be further broken down into single-loop and double loop learning. Did the employees obtain an understanding of the content of the material they needed to learn (single loop – i.e. managers learning the process of delegating work to employees) and did the employees learn how to teach themselves about similar issues in the future (double loop – i.e. managers research the best methods for developing work assignments)?[60] As you may deduce from the above description, it is desirable to analyze employee competencies before and after training in order to measure the effectiveness of the training sessions.

More importantly, by instituting change only after an evaluation of this training has occurred, a feedforward control system is developed that treats employee competencies as the resources needed in order to implement change processes. The other part of the employee assessment is transference, that is, could the employee use the knowledge or skill he or she gained at his or her specific job? (i.e. Now that I have learned the process of delegation, can I fit this process into the demands of my job and the organization's environment?)[61] From a control perspective this is "real-time" feedback since the firm will receive information as to the employee's ability to bring about the desired change given his or her new skills. Once the change has occurred (whether the change is system-wide, affects a few subsystems or a few groups) then actual outcomes can be compared to expected outcomes (feedback) to determine the overall success of the change strategy.

Operational Controls: Budgets, Schedules, Financial Hurdles

For many organizations, prior to the beginning of a fiscal year, it will engage in operational planning that will define a number of operational activities and goals for the ensuing period. Based on the firm's strategic plan, these operational plans define specific operational areas, boundaries for activity, and anticipated goals for each functional area.

Budgets are perhaps most recognizable of organizational and operational control systems and operate through feedback mechanisms. Highly detailed budgets attempt to outline the level of resources that should be available to the firm over the next year and top-level decision-makers determine how those resources should be distributed throughout the organization to maximize its strategic performance objectives. The Chief Financial Office (CFO) of the firm, along with the CEO and COO will develop the budget based on the best available data they have from current and past data bases or may opt to employ zero-based budget systems (where every item in the budget must be justified).[62] They will tie these performance patterns to desired long-term strategic plans and then translate them down into short-term expectations. Overall corporate budgets are then normally reviewed by the Board of Directors who compare the overall budget against its expectations for organizational performance over the coming year.[63]

Upon top-level approval, budgets are divided down through the firm through the office of the COO and ultimately get down to individual employees in the form of salary, benefits, and use of organizational resources they need to do their jobs as effectively as possible. This is a very stringent form of control, and deviation from the budget often requires major negotiation.

While generally very effective, budgets are not foolproof. Budgets are estimates, they are projections of future events, and never result in exactly predictable outcomes. For example, a budget may estimate cost of supplies at $750,000, but due to price changes, which the planners did not anticipate, the actual cost of supplies may come in at $800,000. When analysts compare budget estimates to actual costs, the differences are referred to as variances - where positive variances indicate cost savings and negative variances indicating additional expenses.

Economic trends, individual supplier increases or decreases in pricing are next to impossible to predict and the budget needs to be sensitive to this. One way to address this lack of specific predictability is to create contingency funds. Another way is to have a predetermined fail-safe system whereby unexpected increases in one area can be compensated by reductions in other areas. This is the phenomenon of organizational slack and is something most top strategic managers are fully cognizant of as they manage through the years operations.

Scheduling is another effective method of instituting control. Like budgeting, scheduling is part of the planning function. Beyond day-to-day operational activities, scheduling involves the identification of specific time frames in which various important firm activities must occur. For example, when a firm decides to introduce a new product, it will do so on a highly regulated and scheduled basis. It will determine when a product will emerge from research and development activities and then the time frame it will go through field-testing. The results of field-testing should be available at a certain point in time, which will then lead to a decision to go, or no go. If the decision is to go forward, the company will then need a schedule to determine how and when the product can go into production, when the marketing department should begin introductory advertising, and when the product will be available in retail outlets for sale to the public. The complexities of all of these various processes, from a variety of departments, are not only necessary, it must be coordinated, and planners engage in developing these schedules as part of their overall planning activities.

Financial realities create an additional set of control activities. Most simply, if a firm can't afford to do something, it can't do it. Or can it? As we explained in Chapter 4, there are three sources of financial resources: profits, capital from borrowing, and capital from selling stock. Borrowing and selling stock have serious drawbacks (increase in interest costs and dilution of ownership control respectively), but are acceptable given the need to increase capital spending and the condition of the bond and/or stock markets. Profit continues to be the preferred method of increasing available capital for new projects and expansion and is beyond the proceeds of sales activities (which is fed into the firm through the budget). All this is to suggest that every organization is constrained in its activities by its own ability to create funding. The control of financial capability is one of the most important considerations for strategic decision-makers in deciding a realistic strategic course for the organization.

Ties to Corporate Strategic Objectives. Operational evaluation and control measures should conform exactly to overall corporate objectives. Deciding to adapt a TQM management system throughout, for example, will only be effective if a dedication to total quality is part of the overall corporate strategic objectives. In today's world, where terms such as world-class imply the highest quality available, there need to be guiding standards in the firm's strategic plan that identify what these terms mean to strategic mangers throughout the firm, and what expectations the firm holds for performance over time

Individual Control Systems

As we mentioned in the discussion on levels of organizational control, formal and informal mechanisms exist for monitoring and providing feedback to employees on a team and individual basis. Formal evaluation techniques may include comparative systems (rank-order, paired comparison and forced distribution) where employees and/or groups are weighed against one another, graphic rating systems where employee and/or groups traits are evaluated on a simple scale, behaviorally anchored rating scales (BARS) where employees and/or groups are evaluated based upon scaled job specific behaviors for each job dimension, and behavioral operation scales (BOS) where employees and/or groups are evaluated based upon a list of desired job behaviors.[64] Feedback is provided individuals and team through formal debriefing sessions with part of the employee's/group's compensation impacted by the evaluation.

Informal control systems include psychological, sociological, and cultural clues as to how the employee and/or group is performing his or her function or task. These informal control systems, as demonstrated by the Hawthorne studies, and the works of Stanley Schachter and Irving Janis, may reinforce unproductive or even counterproductive behavior.[65] Steven Kerr also noted that many personnel evaluation and feedback systems send mixed messages. For example, although colleges and universities uphold teaching as one of the most important functions of a faculty member, little formal and informal recognition is associated with that function. Ironically, faculty members receive funding (grants), tenure, promotion and recognition in their field through research and rarely, if ever, obtain equal status through their instructional expertise.[66] These sentiments are reiterated by Charles J. Sykes who noted that there is a "crucifixion of teaching" in major universities, that excellent teachers are "endangered species", and that the "stars" in postsecondary education do not educate at all, they perform research.[67] Businesses consequently need to understand their own informal control systems and determine its alignment with their formal evaluation structures.

Summary

The final step of the strategic planning process is that of evaluation and control. This is the step that makes strategic planning a process and not simply an event. The movements towards total quality management and reengineering have emphasized the need to develop and utilize control systems that provide the firm information on its ability to change in conjunction with its market. Control systems are both formal and informal in nature and need to be flexible in order to assist firms change where needed. In evaluation and control, the firm must be willing to test and challenge every portion of the strategic planning and strategic management processes and change those areas that do not adequately support the accomplishments of strategic objectives. Evaluation and control should be done at all levels, from the performance of strategic managers all the way down to the performance of line an support personnel.

The control process starts with the development of performance standards, and then compares the firm's performance to those standards. Deciding what to monitor, how to monitor, and how to institute control all suggest a variety of options and issues. Key Success Factors represent the most crucial areas of performance in a firm and are normally linked to industry standards. This helps the focal firm understand how its performance measures up to that of the industry as a whole, but also, through benchmarking, up to that of the industry leader. Once measures and standards are in place, interpretation and control systems should be in place that identify and support positive performance areas and correct those areas that do not meet expectations.

Finally, we discussed strategic control systems, business unit controls, operational controls and personal controls. Important internal controls are those related to annual budgeting and scheduling practices that are common in most organizations, but which we argue must be married to the strategic management process. Another important internal control is the financial position of the firm and the organization's ability to move in certain directions as it is constrained by its ability to accumulate capital. At the individual level, we noted that informal control systems may inhibit the traditional performance evaluation systems and yield undesirable results.

Key Terms and Concepts

After reading this chapter, you should be familiar with the following terms and concepts:

Evaluation; total quality management; business process reengineering; cybernetic, agency, structure, social and psychological control; performance appraisal; performance criteria; performance standards; Key Success Factors; deviations from standards; feedback systems; balanced score card approach; Gantt Chart; feed-forward systems; real time feedback; budgets; schedules; and levels of control.

Web sites

http://www.criticaltools.com/pertmain.htm - a commercial website for Critical Tools™, the site offers examples of *PERT Chart EXPERT*, a Windows-based project management software application that is used to create PERT charts (also known as Network Charts, Precedence Diagrams and Logic Diagrams). Students may download this and other project management software for free on a limited usage basis.

http://www.balancedscorecard.org/ - the home site of The Balanced Scorecard Institute. They are an independent educational institute that provides training and guidance to assist government agencies and companies in applying balanced scorecard concepts to strategic management. Site includes resources, forums, seminars, links and applications.

http://www.isixsigma.com/ca/baldridge/ - isixsigma™'s website includes tons of information on the Malcolm Baldrige National Quality Award, ISO 9000, Six Sigma, best practices, and State Awards for Excellence. Users on the site have access to news, jobs, a newsletter, event calendar, dictionary, sigma calculator, tools and templates, ... (numerous other features).

http://www.baldrigeplus.com/ - another site that deals with excellence and quality management. Includes a newsletter, on-line applications, free subscriptions, and provides a thorough understanding of what it takes to win the MBNQA. Does an excellent job of breaking down the categories within the award and describing criteria and requirements.

http://www.bcentral.com/articles/finance/default.asp - from MSN business central, provides several excellent articles on business budgeting. Site also provides information for numerous other business functions including planning, human resource management, technology, taxes, and marketing.

Discussion Questions

1. Describe the strategic control process. What are the key steps in that process?
2. What are the primary differences between quantitative and qualitative measures?
3. Why are KSFs important to any organization? Where do they fit in a control system?
4. Explain the connection between prevailing corporate strategic objectives and the evaluation and control methods a firm might choose.
5. Describe the differing formal and informal control systems. How do they impact the strategic management process?

Exercises

1. Identify five KSFs for the company you have chosen to study. Be prepared to explain why you choose these particular KSFs and why they qualify as KSFs.
2. Choose one major qualitative KSF for the company you are studying and develop three surrogate measures that the company itself would feel appropriate.
3. How do you think the instructor of this course controls its operations? Give 5 examples.
4. How does your company control its operations? Be prepared to report on your findings.
5. From your company's annual report, 10-K, or other financial data, can you determine what elements are most crucial in its budgeting process? Be prepared to report on your findings.

6. Examining data you have generated from your company, and then describe a project it has been involved with that would have required it to schedule how it carried out that project.

Experiential Exercise

Creating a Control System Around Key Success Factors

Learning Objectives:
1. For students to research the fast food industry and the particular company in question.
2. For students to take generic key success factors, define them. and to develop quantitative and qualitative performance indicators for a particular company within the fast food industry.
3. For students to integrate their performance indicators with strategic control systems.

Procedure:
1. Go back to the experiential exercises in Chapters 1 and 6 and review your work in terms of the fast food industry.
2. Define each of the strategic factors listed.   For example, advertising might be defined as the ability to increase the awareness of the company's target audience. See Table 1.

Table 1
Defining the Strategic Factors in the Fast Food Industry

Strategic Factor	Definition
Advertising	
Product Line	
Brand Image	
Average Meal Price	
Distribution Channel	
Customer Value	
Competitive Advantage	

3.   Using Table 1's definitions, develop one quantitative and one qualitative measure for each strategic factor.   Enter your information into Table 2.

Table 2
Strategic Factors in the Fast Food Industry

Strategic Factor	Qualitative Measure	Quantitative Measure
Advertising		
Product Line		
Brand Image		
Average Meal Price		
Distribution Channel		
Customer Value		
Competitive Advantage		

4.   Select one of the company's websites (http://www.mcdonalds.com/; http://www.burgerking.com/; http://www.wendys.com/index.html) and determine if the company has used these strategic factors.
5.   Complete Table 3.   Indicate whether one of your quantitative and/or qualitative measures would be useful as part of the four strategic control systems listed; place an L (qualitative) or an N (quantitative) in the appropriate box(es).

Table 3
Strategic Factors and Strategic Control Systems

Strategic Controls	Environmental Scanning	Premise Control	Implementation Control	Special Alert Control
Advertising				
Product Line				
Brand Image				
Average				

Meal Price				
Distribution Channel				
Customer Value				
Competitive Advantage				

Questions
1. In step 4, you were asked to review one company's strategic factors relative to those listed in Tables 1-3. What were those strategic factors? How are they measuring these factors? Are you measures similar to theirs?
2. In step 5 you were asked to categorize each qualitative and quantitative measure you developed by four strategic control systems. Explain how your measures can be used for environmental scanning, premise control, implementation control, and special alert control?
3. Which of your control measures use feed-forward, feedback, or feedback in real-time approaches?
4. Given your research, what other control measures would you recommend? Why?

Endnotes

[1] More information of Hewlett Packard's history may be found at http://www.hp.com/hpinfo/abouthp/histnfacts/index.html
[2] Anonymous (1994). "How to Successfully Practice MBWA" *Supervisory Management* (January) Volume 39, Issue 1, 12.
[3] See Deming, W. E. 1986. *Out of the Crisis.* Cambridge, Mass.: MIT Center for Advanced Engineering Studies.
[4] Schonberger, R. J. 1992. "Total Quality Management Cuts a Broad Swath Through Manufacturing and Beyond," *Organization Dynamics.* Spring, 1992, pg.s 16-28.
[5] See Hammer, M. & Champty, J. 1993. *Reengineering the Corporation.* New York: Harper Business.
[6] Peter Lorange, Michael F. Scott Morton, and Sumantra Ghoshal (1986). *Strategic Control.* St. Paul, Mn.: West Publishing Company.

[8] James J. Carroll (1991). "The Effect of Strategy on Managers' Preference for Control Systems" in Herbert Sherman (Ed.) *The Strategic Management Process: Readings, Cases and Exercises.* 2nd Edition. Needham, Mass.: Ginn Press.

[9] David I. Cleland and William R. King (1972). *Management: A Systems Approach.* New York: McGraw-Hill Book Company.

[10] Peter M. Blau and Marshall W. Meyer (1987). *Bureaucracy in Modern Society.* 3rd Edition. New York: Random House, Inc.

[11] James J. Carroll, 1991, p. 95.

[12] Jay Galbraith (1977). *Organization Design.* Reading, Mass.: Addison-Wesley Publishing Company.

[13] Paul Hersey and Kenneth H. Blanchard (1993). *Management of Organizational Behavior: Utilizing Human Resources.* 6th Edition. Englewood Cliffs, N.J.: Prentice-Hall, Inc.

[14] Ibid.

[15] Arthur M. Schlesinger, Jr. (1974). *The Imperial Presidency.* New York: Houghton Mifflin Company.

[16] Uma Sekaran (2003). *Research Methods for Business: A Skill Building Approach.* 4th Edition. New York: John Wiley & Sons.

[17] Robert G. Murdick (1969). *Business Research: Concept and Practice.* New York: International Textbook Company.

[18] Research Insight proprietary data base – Standard & Poor's Company, December, 2002.

[19] Ibid.

[20] Tom Peters (2002). "Tom Peters Revisited: What Gets Measured Gets Done" *Office Solutions* (November/December) Volume 19, Issue 9, 32-33.

[21] Eric M. Olson and Stanley F. Slater (2002). "The Balanced Scorecard, Competitive Strategy, and Performance" *Business Horizons* (May/June) Volume 45, Issue 3, 11-16.

[22] Found in Cruver, B. 2002. *Anatomy of Greed: The Unshredded Truth from an Enron Insider.* New York: Carroll & Graf Publishers.

[23] Ibid.

[24] Brad D. Miller (2001). "Making Managers More Effective Agents of Change" *Quality Progress* (May) Volume 34, Issue 5, 53-57.

[25] Mark E. Ruquet (2002). "Benchmarking is a Tool but not a 'Bible' for Agents" *National Underwriter* (November 18; Property & Casualty/Risk & Benefits Management Edition) Volume 106, Issue 46, 10-11.

[26] Research Insight proprietary data base – Standard & Poor's Company, December, 2002.

[27] Ibid.

[28] Trevor Gambling, Rowan Jones, and Rifaat Ahmed Adbel Karim (1993). "Credible Organizations: Self-Regulation v. External Standard-Setting in Islamic Banks and British Charities" *Financial Accountability & Management* (August) Volume 9, Issue 3, 195-208.

[29] Thomas J. Peters and Robert H. Waterman, Jr. (1982). *In Search of Excellence: Lessons from America's Best-Run Companies.* New York: Harper & Row, Publishers.

[30] James R. Evans and William M. Lindsay (2002). *The Management and Control of Quality.* 5th Edition. Cincinnati, Oh.: South-Western.

[31] Michael G. Dolence, Daniel J. Rowley, and Herman D. Lujan (1997). *Working Toward Strategic Change: A Step-by-Step Guide to the Planning Process.* San Francisco, Ca.: Jossey-Bass Publishers.

[32] David Parmenter (2002). "Winning KPI's" *CA Charter* (November) Volume 73, Issue 10, 66.

[33] Visit the SEC website at http://www.sec.gov/

[34] Visit the Yahoo! Finance website at http://finance.yahoo.com/?

[35] Visit Quicken at http://www.quicken.com/investments/quotesresearch/

[36] William G. Zikmund (2003). *Exploring Marketing Research.* 8th Edition. Mason, Oh.: South-Western.

[37] Mark L. Frigo (2002). "Strategy and the Balanced Scorecard" *Strategic Finance* (November) Volume 84, Issue 5, 6-9.

[38] Eric M. Olson and Stanley F. Slater (2002). "The Balanced Scorecard, Competitive Strategy, and Performance" *Business Horizons* (May/June) Volume 45, Issue 3, 11-16.

[39] Michael Gering and Keith Rosmarin (2002). "The Do's and Don'ts of the Balanced Scorecard" *Accountancy SA* (October) p. 18-19.

[40] Mark L. Frigo (2002). "Nonfinancial Performance Measures and Strategy Execution" *Strategic Finance* (August) Volume 84, Issue 2, 6-9.

[41] Mike Bourne (2002). "The Emperor's New Scorecard" *Financial World* (August), p. 48-50.

[42] Wayne F. Castro (2000). *Costing Human Resources: The Financial Impact of Behavior in Organizations.* 4th Edition. Cincinnati, Oh.: South-Western College Publishing.

[43] Georg Schreyogg and Horst Steinman (1987). "Strategic Control: A New Perspective" *The Academy of Management Review* (January) Volume 12, Issue 1, 91-104.

[44] Kamalesh Kumar, Ram Subramanian, and Karen Strandholm (2001). "Competitive Strategy, Environmental Scanning and Performance: A Context Specific Analysis of Their Relationship" *International Journal of Commerce & Management* Volume 11, Issue 1, 1-33; Reginald M. Beal (2000).

"Competing Effectively: Environmental Scanning, Competitive Strategy, and Organizational Performance in Small Manufacturing Firms" *Journal of Small Business Management* (January) Volume 38, Issue 1, 27-47.

[45] Eileen Abels (2002). "Hot Topics: Environmental Scanning" *American Society for Information Science. Bulletin of the American Society for Information Science* (February/March)Volume 28, Issue 3, 16-17.

[46] Don Clare and Ron Nyham (2001). "A Grand Scan Plan" *Association Management* (January) Volume 53, Issue 1, 73-77.

[47] Chun Wei Choo (1999). "The Art of Scanning the Environment" *American Society for Information Science. Bulletin of the American Society for Information Science* (February/March) Volume 25, Issue 3, 21-24.

[48] Bala Subramanian (2002). "Business Intelligence Using Smart Techniques: Environmental Scanning Using Data Mining and Competitor Analysis Using Scenarios and Manual Simulation" *Competitiveness Review* Volume 12, Issue 1, 115.

[49] http://forecasts.org/interest-rate/prime-interest-rate-yield.htm, February 1, 2003.

[50] http://stats.bls.gov/eag/eag.us.htm, February 1, 2003.

[51] Elliot Jaques, Charlotte Bygrave, and Nancy Lee (2001). "Aligning Multiple Time Horizons and Multiple Functions in Strategic Planning and Budgeting" *International Journal of Organizational Analysis* Volume 9, Issue 3, 257-271.

[52] Jack Gido and James P. Clements (1999). *Successful Project Management.* Cincinnati, Oh.: South-Western College Publishing.

[53] Gido and Clements, 1999.

[54] Karen A. Brown and Nancy L. Hyer (2002). "Whole-Brain Thinking for Project Management" *Business Horizons* (May/June) Volume 45, Issue 3, 47-57.

[55] Neil Hardie (2001). "The Prediction and Control of Project Duration: A Recursive Model" *International Journal of Project Management* (October) Volume 19, Issue 7, 401-409.

[56] From http://www.smartdraw.com/resources/centers/gantt/tutorial1.htm, February 1, 2003.

[57] Howard Fineman (2001). "A President Finds His True Voice" *Newsweek* (September 24; International Edition), p.50.

[58] http://www.homedepot.com/prel80/HDUS/EN_US/diy_main/pg_diy.jsp? CNTTYPE=NAVIGATION&CNTKEY=compinfo%2foverview.jsp&BV_Sess ionID=@@@@1941670718.1044134887@@@@&BV_EngineID=ccdgadchg memijjcgelceffdfgidgki.0, February 1, 2003.

[59] Tom Freeman (1998). "Transforming Cost Management into a Strategic Weapon" *Journal of Cost Management* (November/December) Volume 12, Issue 6, 13-26.

[60] Chris Argyris (1983). *Reasoning, Learning, and Action: Individual and Organizational.* San Francisco, Ca.: Jossey-Bass Publishers.

[61] Richard E. Boyatzis (1982). *The Competent Manager: A Model for Effective Performance.* New York: John Wiley & Sons.

[62] Garry D. Brewer (1978). "Termination: Hard Choices-Harder Questions" *Public Administration Review* (July/August) Volume 38, Issue 4, 338).

[63] Leslie Chadwick (1997). *The Essence of Management Accounting.* 2nd Edition. New York: Prentice-Hall.

[64] Lawrence S. Kleiman (2000). *Human Resource Management: A Managerial Tool for Competitive Advantage.* 2nd Edition. Cincinnati, Oh.: South-Western College Publishing.

[65] See Walter E. Natemeyer and J. Timothy McMahon (Eds.) (2001). *Classics of Organizational Behavior.* 3rd Edition. Prospect Heights, Ill.: Waveland Press, Inc. for specific readings.

[66] Steven Kerr (1975) "On the Folly of Rewarding A, While Hoping for B" *Academy of Management Journal* Volume 18, 769-783.

[67] Charles J. Sykes (1988). *ProfScam: Professors and the Demise of Higher Education.* New York: St. Martin's Press.

ଓ Chapter Ten ଞ
International Strategy and Multinational Corporations

Chapter Objectives

1. To develop an understanding of the growing importance of international business in both domestic and worldwide commerce.
2. To develop an appreciation for the pros and cons associated with doing business in an international environment.
3. To understand the additional considerations that firms must take into account in choosing appropriate international strategies and tactics.
4. To examine the issues that contribute to international competitiveness and what it takes to achieve a competitive advantage in an international setting.

Introductory Case: Waterford Crystal

Waterford Crystal prides itself on producing the world's finest crystal and crystal products. From its hand-cut stemware to the giant ball in Times Square in New York that descends just before the stroke of midnight December 31st of each year to herald the beginning of a new year, Waterford is recognized around the world as one of the world's premier companies.

Waterford is an Irish company that sells its products all over the world. Its biggest manufacturing center is in the City of Waterford on the southern coast of Ireland[1]. It also manufactures its products in Germany, Romania, and Moldova. Well over half of everything that Waterford manufactures is sold in the U.S., yet it does not manufacture any of its products in the United States.

Glass making in Ireland has been done since the Iron Age and has always been honored as a profession. There is documentary evidence that there were glass making firms active during the 13th Century in Ireland, continuing a proud tradition. Waterford can trace its beginnings to 1783, when two brothers, George and William Penrose decided to open a crystal manufacturing operation in the busy port of Waterford in Ireland. It cost them approximately £10,000 which was a tremendous amount of money at the time. Through experimentation, they were able to produce a formula for lead crystal that produced a purity and sparkle unmatched by other manufacturers in either Ireland or England. Over the years, the Waterford Crystal company became to be known throughout Europe and North America for its exceptional high quality and design, and quickly became known as the world's best crystal.

Due to heavy taxation by Ireland's English overlords and a serious lack of capital, the company failed just 100 years after it had been established. However, 70 years later in 1947, after Ireland had won its independence from England and had survived both World War I and World War II, the enterprise was revived on a site very near to its original site. In its rebirth, Waterford Crystal was determined to regain its reputation as the world's finest crystal and painstakingly recreated its original lead crystal formula and set about to master the art of hand finishing that has become a hallmark of its product lines. In 2000,

Total Research Corporation of Princeton, New Jersey conducted a survey of 30,000 American consumers and named Waterford Crystal as the top world class brand in the United States. The survey named Waterford first out of 19 world-class organizations and equated the brand to those of Rolls-Royce Bentley, Bose, Harley-Davidson, and the National Geographic magazine. This is quite a come-back.

While the crystal division is the flagship of Waterford Crystal, the company has also expanded through product development and horizontal integration. It has created the Waterford Table and Bed Linens division, Waterford Stainless Flatware and Silver Gifts division, Waterford Writing Instruments, Waterford Holiday Heirlooms, and Waterford Crystal Jewelry. Waterford has purchased the Wedgewood China Company in England. Again, none of these manufacturing concerns can be found in the United States. Why not?

Waterford structures itself strategically and functionally in a manner that is more suitable in European settings than in American settings. For example, in its core business, Waterford Crystal, all employees who are part of the production process must complete seven years of apprenticeship and often complete another seven years to be eligible to work in the custom design department. Employees work on a piece-work basis and there is quality inspection at each stage of production where, if an inspector finds even the slightest flaw, the piece is smashed and the worker at that stage gets no credit for work performed. Waterford Crystal does not have seconds – it's either first quality or it is smashed and the shards are returned to the furnace to be melted again. Irish and other European workers are culturally conditioned to work in this environment, American workers are not.[2]

Strategically, while heavy taxation and lack of capital might have forced the company to close in the late 1800's, the Ireland of today and the European Union (EU), have provided many financial and trade incentives for companies, such as Waterford Crystal, to concentrate its manufacturing in Ireland. The strategies appear to be working, and customers in the U.S., as well as those from around the world, continue to view Waterford Crystal as a treasure to own and a pleasure to use. Waterford Crystal is a prime example of a true world-class company.

The Emergence of a Worldwide Market

Walt Disney has been right about many things (as we have detailed throughout this text), including that fact that it is a small, small world. Over the past six decades since the end of World War II, the economy of the world has changed dramatically. Immediately following the war, much of the world's economy was associated with rebuilding the decimated societies and businesses of both Europe and Asia. This was also an era that was characterized by intense political rivalries between the capitalistic west and the communistic east. On the brink of war at times, and at the risk of nuclear annihilation, there was little encouragement for the global expansion of business and, instead, isolationism and mistrust tended to rule most international activities between both governments and businesses.   The U.S. economic and military face-off with the forces associated with the now-defunct USSR created a feeling of isolationism and distrust of foreign countries and their companies particularly Japanese businesses who were openly protected by their government and allowed to engage in collusion and product dumping, while American companies were excluded from Japanese markets.

Two factors in the external environment have changed dramatically, particularly in the last two decades.   One is the proliferation of technology and its impact on business, which we will discuss at length in Chapter 11; and two, is the dissolution of the European communist empire and the introduction of capitalist methods in not only former communist governments in Europe, but also in China (which maintains a communist ideology but has introduced capitalistic methods as it has attempted to modernize and become a part of the overall world economy).

Technology, particularly the Internet and the World Wide Web, has opened up international commerce to anyone who has a computer and who is connected to an Internet service. The Internet has no national borders and competition is only constrained by the firm's ability to develop effective websites. As the Information Age continues to grow and define itself, it is clear that we as a worldwide society will embrace electronic businesses (e-businesses) and engage in electronic commerce (e-commerce) to transform, perhaps, the basic shopping habits and preferences of consumers around the world.[3]

The fall of communism has proven to be the other major change agent that is transforming how business is done around the world. The Cold War resulted in tremendous tensions among nations and among philosophies, but in the end, capitalism has won out. Totalitarian economic control proved to bankrupt national economies that had embraced communist ideologies and efforts to control national economies from centralized planning agencies did nothing to inspire innovation, productivity, or motivation. While in the post-communist era, some negative forces have emerged (for example, in Russia, the primary successor state to the USSR, post-communist economy is seriously marred by mafia dominance and corruption)[4], other countries such as Hungary, the Czech Republic, and Poland are emerging as serious capitalistic economies and are anxious to become part of the world-wide capitalist economy by opening themselves up to foreign investment and by working to reverse decades of repression by burgeoning innovative and creative home-grown industries and companies.[5]

All of these changes have broken down suspicions, regulations, and social barriers and has encouraged cross-border development of business. For the United States, these changes have opened up major opportunities for growth and development, just as it has had the similar effect of opening up U.S. markets more directly to growing foreign investment and business development.

Together, the growth of e-business and e-commerce, along with reduction in the restriction of trade among nations, has led to a new reality, especially for U.S. businesses as a whole. Today, a domestic firm (whether that firm be a U.S. firm or a company located in another country) competes internationally, whether it chooses to or not. With the development of trade organizations, especially the EU in Europe, the North American Free Trade Act (NAFTA), and the World Trade Organization (WTO), barriers to trade among nations have been significantly reduced so that American firms can grow through international expansion *and* firms from other countries can grow through expansion into U.S. market. Certainly many companies have been internationally involved for decades (General Motors became an international firm within 5 years of its initial founding and remains an international giant today), while many more companies are finding that they must expand their scope when their original intent was not to grow in this manner.   In the global shift to supporting free trade and encouraging competitive practices, these trends will continue to grow – so it is ridiculous for almost any company to believe it is not part of an international market. It is, whether it chooses to or not.

Becoming a World-Class Organization

How do companies successfully compete on a global basis? One of the key terms that defines those firms that are able to achieve a competitive advantage in the international market is that of being *world-class*. A world-class organization is one that has been able to achieve a level of quality in its products and services that it is recognized as one of the top organizations in the world and can do business successfully anywhere in the world. In our introductory case, we identified that Waterford Crystal has achieved world-class status. Its crystal products are not only recognized around the world, they are valued as the best quality available and the market for its products is strong and continuing to grow. Microsoft, Boeing, Airbus, AT&T, Motorola, Honda, Toyota, Mercedes-Benz, BMW, and IBM are but some of the companies that have achieved world-class status, and each has been able to maintain its competitive advantage world-wide. These are the models that other companies that are beginning to become international aspire to emulate.   They represent a standard of performance and competitiveness that indicates that they have looked at the world-wide business environment and have been able to correctly identify relevant opportunities and threats, and have been able to develop an appropriate strategic plan to help their companies become successful multi-national corporations (MNCs).

Pursuing a Global Competitive Advantage

Strategic management is just as important for firms who engage in international competition as it is for those who concentrate in domestic competition.   However, in adding the parameters of internationalism to the basic strategic planning model, decisions become more complex and the addition of an international perspective causes a firm's decision-makers to add additional considerations to the overall process, as suggested in Figure 10.1, and leads to a more detailed overall corporate strategic plan.

Figure 10.1
The Strategic Planning Process
International Considerations

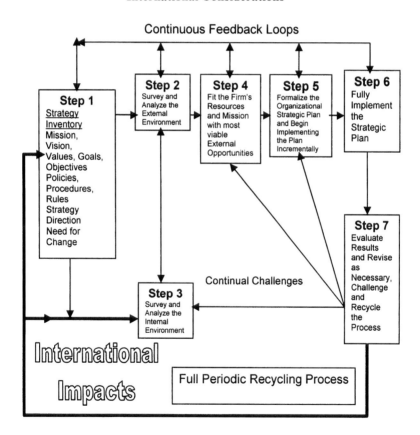

In Chapter 5, we discussed how firms achieve a competitive advantage in their industry through low cost leadership, differentiation, focus, or value for money (blended strategy). International competition, however, adds further nuances to the challenge of achieving competitive advantage since the national economic, social, political, and technological conditions of the focus firm's country impacts the firm's ability to obtain those advantages.

Michael Porter in 1989 extended his concept of competitive advantage to nations. For Porter, international competition occurs at the industry cluster level (supplier industries, industry rivalry, customer industries) where a culmination of forces (what he called the diamond), combined with both chance and government intervention, may impact the competitive factors. These forces are synergistic in nature and are highly interdependent.[6]

Factor Conditions. These factors refer to the nation's position in functions contributing to production, such as skilled labor or infrastructure, necessary to compete in a given industry. Factors are broken down into two types: general and specialized. General factors are the overall infrastructure of the nation including education, transportation, telecommunications, and the environment. These factors are impacted by public policy and government investments and act as the foundation to general economic progress of a nation, yet they alone cannot produce a competitive advantage. Specialized factors are any factors that might lead to a competitive advantage for a nation and are based upon the abundance of certain basic features within a nation. For example, the U.S.'s investments in colleges of agriculture (based upon the U.S.'s general factor of abundant and viable land) has allowed the U.S. to become the breadbasket of the world; while Germany consistently engineers technologically superior vehicles due to the establishment of four specialized university automotive research institutes in southern Germany.[7]

Factor conditions are impacted by the home country's demand for factor-creating investments (i.e. increased demand for post-secondary education by businesses may lead to government investment and student tax incentives), rivalry within a domestic industry cluster (i.e. due to increased competition, businesses will invest in employee education and training to increase their distinctive competencies), perceived international challenges (the USSR's launch of Sputnik stimulated the U.S. government's investment in aerospace engineering and computer technology), and the synergy derived from related and supportive industries (the U.S. computer industry greatly benefited from investments in the space race since it lead to the development of microchip technology).

Demand Conditions. This refers to the nature of a home country's demand for the industry's product or service and is reflective of the socio/psycho demographics and consumption patterns of the nation (i.e. population, social values) as well as the nation's total industry mix. For example, the U.S. is a highly consumer-driven society compared to other capitalist nations such as Japan and has built-in demand for products and service. Demand conditions are influenced by the presence of rivalry in the industry, where rivalry lowers prices (and thereby stimulates demand) and builds a national reputation for the home industry. For example, Japan has been quite successful in building up the reputation of its three major automobile manufacturers (Honda, Nissan, and Toyota) so that Japanese consumers prefer home products over imports. Second, demand is also affected by factors conditions (such as the presence of excellent colleges and universities in the U.S. has attracted foreign students and businesspersons who purchase local goods and services), and internationally successful related and supportive industries.

Related and Supporting Industries. In the supplier country, the presence or absence of related industries that are internationally competitive add or detract from the nation's competitive advantage. For example, the absence of a successful mass-production steel industry in the U.S. in the 1970's and 1980's hindered U.S. car manufacturer's ability to compete with European and Asian car manufacturers who had access to cheaper steel. Supporting industries are positively affected by a large or growing home demand for related products and services, increased domestic rivalry which promotes specialization, and specialized factors that can be used by the related industry (such as the use of just-in-time inventory systems benefits suppliers and buyers as well as the focus firm).

Firms Strategy, Structure, and Rivalry. This refers to the conditions in the nation governing how companies are created, organized, and managed, and the nature of domestic rivalry – see the five forces model described in Chapter 3. Besides buyer power, supplier, power, substitutes and entrance barriers, the firm's strategy, structure and rivalry is influenced by an abundance of general factors (at low cost) or specialized factors (that support differentiation) and early product penetration (fast growth market). [8]

Sustaining an International Competitive Advantage. Some Americans have lamented the loss of the U.S. manufacturing base and the high paying blue-collar jobs that went with these industries and wonder why firms like Bethlehem Steel could not sustain their early market entry advantage. They fear free market trade agreements such as the North American Free Trade Agreement (NAFTA) and would like the U.S. to impose tariffs and other trade barriers in order to protect cottage (home grown) industries which have fled to emerging nations where labor is cheap, and taxes and government regulation are low.

Unfortunately, what these protectionists fail to realize is that in a world market, where goods and services from all nations compete simultaneously, there are no true protections from national competitive advantage except to expand and upgrade one's own nation's advantages – the best defense in the international marketplace is a good offense. An excellent case in point would be Japan's investments in basic and applied research as a tool to combat US consumerism. Japan historically tried to compensate for the larger demand for goods and services in the U.S. by concurrently dumping cheap goods and services on US consumers and embargoing US imports. Ironically, this strategy has had the opposite desired effect – after World War II, Japanese goods were often seen as inferior and Japanese consumers increased their demand for US goods. Japan then realized that by making a better product than the U.S., and allowing their own consumers to know it, they would make better inroads into both markets; R&D was the key.

Unlike the U.S., where R&D spending for consumer goods is decentralized (determined by individual corporations) Japan's Ministry of International Trade and Industry (MITI) has historically guided R&D investments. Japan created an infrastructure for guiding private R&D investments allowing their government to target certain industries.[9] Science and technology continue to be seen by Japanese government and Japanese corporate leaders as vital to ensuring Japan's economic strength in the 21st century. It is increasingly seen and treated as an essential component of Japan's economic infrastructure. Japan's actions, both in terms of institutional reforms and investment, reflect this belief.[10] Yet investment in R&D in the U.S. has just kept pace with inflation, with the total R&D investment by the top 100 firms in the U.S. going from $104.9 billion in 1999 to $109.6 billion in 2000.[11]

The Decision to Enter the International Arena

In fully defining a firm's external environment, international components are becoming more and more important considerations, as we indicated in Chapter 3. From the last section, firms also must understand that they are going to be involved in international competition – either by deciding to enter foreign markets, or by foreign competitors entering the domestic market. This introduces two different sets of circumstances and decision-making formats.

Defending Home Turf Advantage.[12] The strategic posture needed to successfully defend a domestic market once it has been expanded by foreign companies is an issue that came to the fore for the American automobile industry in the late 1970s. As a result of 2 major energy shocks to the economy, in which foreign oil producers decided to punish the United States for its support of Israel during the 7-Day war in the 1973. At the time, the Big Three American automobile manufacturers were coming off a tradition building big, fuel-guzzling cars that were more flash than performance and seemed little concerned for either product quality or gas consumption. Gas prices were as low as 25¢ a gallon and in a strong economy, there was little concern about having to replace a car every 5 years due to planned obsolescence (building products made to breakdown over time). In short, Americans had developed a love affair with their cars and didn't really care what the cost of those cars was.

The two energy crises changed all of that, and introduced the American car consumer to foreign carmakers. Suddenly, gas had tripled in cost, and it was no longer acceptable that a car buyer was expected to pay thousands of dollars for a car that lasted only a few years. From oversees, foreign car producers from Japan and Europe (countries where the level of discretionary income had been significantly lower than that of Americans and had led consumers their demanding higher quality and higher fuel-efficient automobiles) tried to sell their cars in the U.S. market. It worked. Foreign automobile companies, especially Japanese car manufacturers, found a ready market in the U.S., and the Big Three began to experience major sales declines and a major loss of confidence from its traditionally loyal U.S. customer base. The weakest of the three, Chrysler Corporation almost collapsed. As we discussed in Chapter 6, Chrysler didn't know how to respond to the shift of consumer preference and was far too slow to respond. It came perilously close to declaring bankruptcy and, unlike more modern bankruptcy filings that seek the opportunity to reorganize and continue in business, Chrysler was looking at liquidation. Under Lee Iacocca, Chrysler was able to reorganize, reinvent its product line to meet the changed expectations of the American consumer, and eventually reached profitability once again. General Motors and Ford also had hard times, but were able to adjust and begin to produce foreign-style cars before things got too bad. None of the three, however, have been able to return to pre-1970 market dominance and, more recently, Chrysler merged with Mercedes-Benz Motors Company of Germany as a strategic option to improve its market and competitive position.

What all this shows is that foreign competitors do have the ability to enter the U.S. market and can do so in a dominating fashion. Domestic American companies need to not only recognize the potential for this event, but must also understand that these new competitors may well have products or services that are superior to their own. Unless domestic companies are ready to face these threats head on and turn them into opportunities, the experience of the Big Three could well be repeated; again, the best defense is a good offense.

When one considers our opening case of Waterford Crystal of Ireland, it is easy to see how domestic companies can easily be overshadowed by foreign competitors. While Waterford does not manufacture in the U.S. as we described earlier, there are hundreds of glass and crystal manufacturers in the United States – none of whom compete well with Waterford.

Attacking the International Marketplace.[13] The decision to move into international markets is the second major strategic decision companies may make. Unlike bracing to deal with foreign competition on one's home turf, making the decision to be the invader in a foreign industry requires a different set of decisions. First, this is an aggressive activity versus a self-protective activity. Companies who make the decision to go into an international market need to make a determination as to the level of probability that the foreign market will desire its goods or services and at what level. When McDonalds began its international expansion, it did so based on its market research that indicated that foreign consumers had already heard of its products, liked the fact that it was an American product and wanted it in their own areas. In some place there were clear disincentives for McDonalds to move in, but buoyed by strong marketing data, the company decided to go ahead anyway.

For example, in France, marketing surveys indicated that there were a significant number of French consumers who would support the growth of McDonalds franchises in their area. On the other side, there were (and still are) several members of the French legislative bodies who saw McDonalds as an unwelcome intrusion of American life styles and values on traditional French life. For the French, dining is a pleasurable experience. In many French cafes, once a person sits down to a table and places an order, that person can stay at that table for the remainder of the day, reading, conducting business, visiting with friends, or just enjoying life. Fast food is an affront to this life style, and those members of the French government that opposed the introduction or proliferation of McDonalds were attempting to preserve that way of life. However, McDonalds was right, and a substantive market for its products not only existed, but continues to expand, making the decision to enter the French market a wise decision overall. The key was McDonald's marketing research and the data that it generated that allowed decision-makers for the company to make informed decisions based on a variety of facts.[14]

The case of Disney in France presents an interesting counterpoint. While the earlier development of Disneyland-Tokyo had been a major success (though a franchise, due to Japanese trade laws, rather than a wholly-owned subsidiary which Disney would have preferred), it set about to open its first European theme park. There had been serious competition between France and Spain to land the facility, and France ultimately won. Unlike McDonalds, this time the French government actively pursued this major American icon. Unfortunately, despite its location just a few kilometers northeast of Paris, the Disney folks decided that their theme park should appeal to all Europeans and be essentially a clone of the Anaheim and Orlando facilities in the United States. This time the consumers responded negatively. Euro-Disney did not attract the hundreds of thousands of European visitors it had anticipated, and its decidedly American theme was unappealing to the host French. The company floundered and hard decisions needed to be made. Finally, Disney redesigned its approach, seeing that its primary customers were likely to be the French, and that for an entertainment facility to succeed in France, it needed to reflect French values. So, Disney changed. It introduced the open sale of wine in the park (a serious Walt Disney no-no), changed the menus to reflect French taste, and made other amenity changes that began to win over the French consumer. Today, Disneyland-Paris is a success, but only because it adapted to it foreign location.[15]

Sometimes, a country pursues American business. The Disney example above, the clear opportunities for Disney to expand in Japan (Disneyland-Tokyo) and the up-coming Hong Kong Disneyland, are all examples of countries actively courting American businesses. McDonalds was also actively recruited for the emerging market in Russia, and China opened its first Kentucky Fried Chicken on Tiananmen Square in Beijing. Though hard to get, American made cars are still popular items in Japan though the Japanese Government's protection of its own automobile industry precludes American manufacturers from producing their product in Japan, thus reducing substantial market penetration.

Internationalization of business has occurred. All businesses need to not only develop a realization of these significant changes in their external environments, but also be willing to change their operations to more effectively manage emergent opportunities and threats.

Moving from Domestic to International to Global Competition

The strategic decision to move into the international market place is really a decision with several options. As suggested in Figure 10-2 below, most firms begin by doing business in one other country (international management), but over time move to a position in which they do business in a wide number and variety of other countries (global management) so that their basic operational strategies must change.

As complex as running a company can be, the decision to enter the international market brings even higher levels of complexity, thereby increasing risk. As the figure suggests, it is least risky to extend a firm's business to one additional country. The complexity comes because the company must decentralize even further to allow local area management to adapt company practices to local cultures, markets, laws, and regulatory bodies. Issues such as language, local preferences, and local customs also will increase complexity.

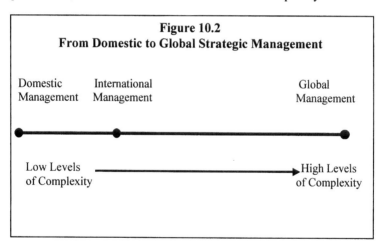

Figure 10.2
From Domestic to Global Strategic Management

Domestic   International   Global
Management   Management   Management

Low Levels   High Levels
of Complexity   of Complexity

The Risks and Rewards/Opportunities and Threats. There are major risks in going international and there are also major rewards to be gained if the firm is capable of taking advantage of them. Each country represents new environments that have their own particular opportunities and threats that the firm faces when it decides to move into those new markets. The better prepared the firm is to directly deal with those new environments the greater its chance for success.

Location.[16] Location presents several important opportunities for businesses looking to grow internationally. Manufacturing firms who find the U.S. labor market too expensive to allow them to produce their products at a price that allows them to be competitive have found other locations around the world where the price of labor is much less and, even with the added expense of shipping and transportation, they can still produce components in one oversees nation, assemble in another, ship finished products back to the U.S. and still significantly undercut the costs of what they would have paid to produce at home.

Off shoring, as the practice is called, was initially viewed as a major threat to the American work force and potentially the American economy. As things have worked out, however, more new jobs have been created within the economy (as a result of the growth of the service and the technology industries) during the 1990s, with the United States having enjoyed one of the longest economic growth expansions with one of the lowest unemployment rates in decades.[17]

This is not to suggest that off shoring is a panacea. There are problems. The use of child or prison labor by profiteers in foreign countries has proven to be an embarrassment to American manufacturers and spokespersons (such as Kathy Lee Gifford when journalists discovered that her line of children's clothing was being produced in factories that employed child labor).[18] The potential for patent theft and copyright theft also exists, especially in Asian countries such as China, where Chinese laws do not create the same levels of penalties for infringement as do U.S. laws.[19] U.S. companies need to be particularly aware of these threats, especially if they intend to off shore any of their core competencies and technologies to be used in questionable foreign settings.

Other advantages include the potential for doing business in environments where tax laws favor foreign development; the possibility of a lesser saturated market for a firm's goods or services; and greater diversity of all product lines and services that could improve domestic offerings. Other disadvantages include different taxing structures and motives (for example, with Europe's high support of its welfare programs, all businesses are taxed much more heavily than in the U.S.); different legal systems and different court structures; and the potential for political change that could damage a foreign business.[20]

Culture, demographics, and market conditions. Doing business in another country is much more than an opportunity to increase sales. It is the opportunity to expand a firm's learning through interacting with a diverse international marketing set and international competitors. One of the greatest issues is that of understanding local culture and then adapting business practices appropriately so avoid offending local consumers, while taking advantage of new business opportunities.

Geert Hofstede has suggested that international cultures have four distinct dimensions, individualism vs. collectivism, masculinity vs. femininity, power distance, and uncertainty avoidance.[21] These different dimensions help a firm's strategic planner better describe the human elements of the environments the firm proposes to enter that will help determine the composition and nature of the work force, the general expectations of the market, and the differing work conditions that will be in place in one location versus another. More specifically, Hofstede suggested that the four different dimensions are particularly important in creating and working with the employee base in a foreign operation.

The dimension of individualism vs. collectivism describes whether the typical worker is more comfortable working alone or in a group. While Americans tend to be more individualistic in nature, their Japanese counterparts are highly communal. Designing a work force in Japan that matched an American model might be a difficult task to complete. The second dimension, masculinity vs. femininity, describes the pursuit of achievement, money, and power as masculine in nature, while seeking satisfying relationships and a higher quality of life are feminine in nature. Americans are considered masculine in their drives while the French and Italians are more feminine in their drives. Power distance, the third dimension, refers to the tolerance of people to respond to concentrated power. What this means is that in some cultures, such as China and Japan, a high power distance exists in that workers accept their position of low power and do not seek to influence top-level managers who make all the major decisions. Low power distance represents a low tolerance of lower level employees for having others make decisions that impact them – here, decentralized decision-making systems and programs such as codetermination (common in countries like Germany and the Scandinavian countries). Finally, the dimension of uncertainty avoidance describes how well people in a particular culture deal with ambiguity. Low uncertainty avoidance refers to those groups who more easily accept that life is uncertain and there may not be clear answers to complicated questions (Hofstede suggests that Ireland and the U.S. tend to support this side of the dimension). High uncertainty avoidance occurs in those cultural groups that go to great lengths to create stable and predictable work environments (Hofstede suggests that countries such as Portugal, Spain, and France mirror these values).

Fons Trompenaars built on Hofstede's work and suggested five different cultural dimensions as shown in Table 10.1, below. [22] While there are clear similarities between Trompenaars and Hofstede, Trompenaars tends to look at the different dimensions from a point of view that provides valuable additional information which aid strategic decision-makers in better describing foreign environments. The dimension of universalism-particularism describes the extent to which a cultural group looks to a single set of rules that apply to everyone (universalism) compared to the extent to which another cultural group believes that rules should vary depending upon the group or the situation involved.

Western countries (the U.S., Germany, the UK, and France) tend to be more universalistic with high levels of unionism and legal contracting in the employment process whereas Eastern countries (China, Korea, and Japan) often times change the rules to fit the demands of the situation. This has proven to be a major cause for concern when American firms try to write binding contracts in China or Japan.

The dimension of neutral-emotional describes the acceptability of showing emotion in public situations. The Japanese are known for their stoicism and can be classified as highly neutral, while business interactions in Latin countries in Europe and South America tend to very emotional at times. Americans, somewhere in the middle,

Table 10.1
Trompenaar's 5 Cultural Dimensions

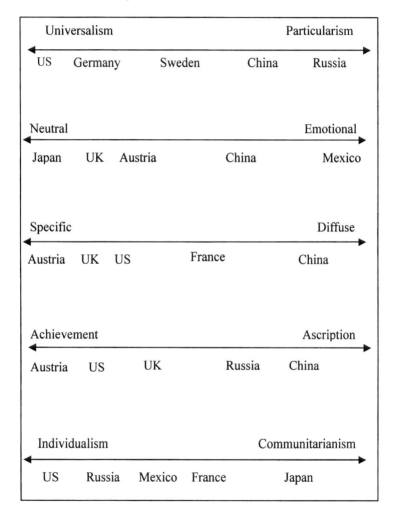

often find both dimensions difficult to deal with in negotiation sessions. The third dimension is specific-diffuse. Here, Trompenaars suggests that some cultures tend to treat individuals differently in different situation (specific), and countries like the U.S. tend to view people as existing in a variety of roles and don't confuse roles (a person can be a college professor, a father, a neighbor, and a member of a weekend golfing group of old college chums – all seen as separate roles and treatment of the individual is a function of what role that person is in at the time). Diffuse cultural tendencies are those that blur roles. In China and Japan, a university president is treated as a person who commands high respect and gets it not only in the office, but at home as a father and husband, as the neighbor that other neighbors defer to, and a person who would only play golf with other men of his same wealth and status. The dimension of achievement-ascription describes the cultural standards that relate to how valuable a person's personal work is in the larger scheme of life. In high achievement cultures, such as Austria and the U.S., the individual seeks high levels of personal achievement and believes these will lead to higher salaries, promotions, and greater respect. In high ascription cultures, such as in China or the post-USSR Russia, status comes with age, class, wealth, who-you-know, and a person's gender (men are considered of higher status than women). Finally, the dimension of individualism-communitarianism, very similar to Hofstede, refers to the cultural acceptability of working independently (as in the U.S.) versus the societal preference of working with groups and working to achieve group goals.

All of these cultural dimensions demonstrate very substantive differences between societies. The impact of these cultural environments can easily create both opportunities and threats for the company that moves into a new cultural setting. These are strategic issues, and cultural pressures are normally much stronger than company preferences and unless strategic planners understand the importance of creating unique fits between their companies' operations and societal cultures, they are headed for trouble.

Language. Strongly linked to cultural differences is language dissimilarities. These differences have historically acted as trade barriers while similarities have created trading partners. The US and England, once subject and master, have become strong allies (both militarily and economically) a century after the American Revolution due to a shared language and culture. The same can be said for other former English-speaking colonies (Canada and Australia) but not for non-English speaking countries such as India and Pakistan.

The U.S. is known as a melting pot, a place where people from around the world have come to pursue economic, political, and religious freedoms. It is not uncommon to walk the streets of our major urban centers (New York City, San Francisco, San Antonio, and Miami, etc.) and hear Spanish, Mandarin, Japanese or even Russian. However, it is clear that the main language of the U.S. is English and that the U.S. tends to accommodate only Spanish as a second language. For most in the U.S., English is the sole standard language spoken.

This is not the case for our European counterparts where English is nearly everyone's second language. Anyone who has traveled in Europe has experienced multilingualism; natives of a particular country speaking several languages besides their native tongue. This is most apparent in Switzerland where, based upon your location, you might hear locals speaking Italian, French, or German and switching languages as necessary. Multilingual countries (and businesses in those countries) have a competitive advantage over mono-linguistic countries since they do not incur the expense and difficulties associated with employing translators or translation technology. For example, research suggests that the discrepancy between U.S. imports and exports arises because of the dominance of English as a world business language. In this situation, foreigners need no help when they export to the United States, however, native-born, monolingual Americans need the help of bicultural immigrants when they export to non-English speaking countries.[23] The California-Pacific Year 2000 Task Force report, by Rep. Mel Levine (D-Los Angeles) and Lt. Gov. Leo T. McCarthy, noted that eliminating all foreign trade barriers would reduce the federal trade deficit by only 10%, and it urged Americans to tackle their own general shortcomings of short-term thinking and lack of foreign-language literacy.[24]

As the US becomes increasingly involved in foreign trade, tourism, and international cooperative ventures, the number of jobs open to fluent speakers of a foreign language increases. Generally, two types of jobs use foreign language skills. The first type is often referred to as language-centered jobs. In these positions, people use their foreign language ability as the primary skill. The second type, language-related jobs, comprises positions in which knowledge of a foreign language complements other skills. Teaching, translating, and interpreting are the main language-centered careers. Many of these jobs require near-native speaking and writing ability. Non-language-centered jobs that use foreign language skills include marketing and finance, clerical, and government positions.[25]

Local economic conditions and currency exchange rates. As we have seen over the past several years, there is a lot of connection between world economies so when one country or region suffers an economic downturn, other countries can be affected as well. However, this relationship is not one-to-one. For example, while the United States has suffered three years of economic downturn between 2000 and 2003, European countries generally did not suffer the same downturns. Ireland, in particular, saw its economy grow substantially over the period. The CIA reports that, "although exports remain the primary engine for Ireland's robust growth, the economy is also benefiting from a rise in consumer spending and recovery in both construction and business investment."[26] The EU has come to feel that economic conditions are good enough that it announced it added 10 more counties to its growing list of members on May 1, 2004. Joining the bloc were Poland, the Czech Republic, Hungary, Slovakia, Slovenia, Lithuania, Latvia, Estonia, Cyprus and Malta[27]. Several of these new partners won't contribute significantly to EU economic output, but they will bring the EU to 450 million consumers, a major economic force.

Currency rates also provide interesting opportunities and threats. Especially for companies that have a presence in a variety of different countries, fluctuating interest rates provide another source of opportunities and threats and constitute another consideration for strategic decision makers.

For example, a U.S. company that is exporting to a foreign country benefits from a decline in the value of the dollar; the same company loses money if the value of the dollar becomes stronger. The way this works is represented in Table 10.2 below.

Table 10.2
Opportunities and Threats of Currency Exchange Rates

	Scenario One: Dollar Declines Against Foreign Currencies	Scenario Two: Dollar Gains Against Foreign Currencies
US Company Exports to Foreign Country 1/1	$10,000,000 Export Value (€1.00 = $1.00)	$10,000,000 Export Value (€1.00 = $1.00)
6 Month Change in Currency Rate	$1.00 = €.95	$1.00 = €1.05
Sale in Foreign Currency (Euros)	€20,000,000	€20,000,000
Conversion Rate	105.26% (€1.00 = $1.0526)	94.25% (€1.00 = $.9425)
Return to Company in U.S. Dollars	$21,052,000	$18,850,000

As the table indicates, if a company can determine that the value of foreign currency against the dollar is going up, this presents an opportunity to sell its goods and services in that foreign country and as the currency does indeed rise against the dollar, the company can experience a greater profit. However, if a company feels that the dollar is gaining in value against a foreign currency, it will most likely lose money over time in the exchange rate. All sorts of other opportunities exist – a domestic firm should import foreign goods when the value of the dollar is going up and resist imports.[28]

Political risks and opportunities. Another aspect of international business is that comes with changes in various company political climates. While business opportunities are currently outweighing political issues in most countries (most notably in China where a communist regime remains in power, but is adopting more and more capitalistic practices to welcome foreign investment and improve its basic economy), instability in middle eastern countries, African countries, and South American countries makes doing business in these countries far more problematic. Also, worldwide terrorism, especially against American targets, makes all U.S. firms think twice about moving into certain markets.[29]

On the other side, political fortunes can change in favor of foreign investment and expansion. China is the most obvious example, but recent changes in Japanese laws are additional incentives to improving the conditions that welcome in foreign investment. Even the growth of the EU is proving to be a positive event in encouraging greater levels of trade, not simply between EU member nations, but between the EU and international trading partners, especially the United States. By evening out various ambiguous and protectionist trade laws that have been in effect in many European countries, and by setting standards of trade performance, the EU has successfully stimulated the growth of trade, and all member nations have benefited greatly.[30] Particularly nations such as Spain, Greece, Italy, and Ireland have seen major benefits from membership in the EU (perhaps Ireland is the biggest winner of all in these activities). Coming from almost poverty status, many current members of the EU can directly attribute their improved fortunes to the development of the EU. Of the 10 countries that joined the EU in 2004, there is general optimism in both the present EU bloc, as well as in the 10 new countries that the era of prosperity will continue once the union grows.[31] The benefits of these major political changes will be easier and more uniform, making it much easier for U.S. companies to enter those markets as well as compete better at home against the increase of foreign firms seeking to enter the American market.

Longer-term, the World Trade Organization (WTO) promises to even out the playing field even more. "The World Trade Organization (WTO) is the only global international organization dealing with the rules of trade between nations. At its heart are the WTO agreements, negotiated and signed by the bulk of the world's trading nations and ratified in their parliaments. The goal is to help producers of goods and services, exporters, and importers conduct their business."[32]   There is little even the WTO will be able to do about countries that continue to experience political instability, but for those countries that achieve membership, the potential for a larger and more stable global market continues to be an emerging promise.

Level of competition. So far, we have dealt with cultural and political realities of doing business in an international environment. Yet, there are other considerations that firms need to take into account as they either decide to move into a new foreign environment or see foreign competition entering the domestic market. What is it that makes the difference as the level of competition increases and the stakes of competition change? What are the opportunities and threats that result?

One of the biggest is that of the firms already in the industry that will be there as the firm moves into a foreign setting, or as foreign competitors more into domestic markets. Certainly one of the reasons that a firm should enter a new foreign market is that it has done an extensive market analysis of the environment of the new country and knows the strengths and weaknesses of competitive firms in the new environment. This analysis needs to show significant opportunities and reasonable threats that suggest to the entering firm that it can compete well, perhaps even on a higher level than is presently the nature of the market in the new country. For example, when Wal-Mart decided to expand into Germany, it saw that there were volume discount stores already in the economy, but that they weren't performing at the level they could and could be rather easily dominated by Wal-Mart should it enter the German market. It decided to do so, and entered the German market by opening up traditional Wal-Mart stores, but also by buying out its competition. The results for Wal-Mart have been mixed (one of the major problems has been mixing the American-style Wal-Mart culture with a retail culture that was quite different – Germans are not particularly friendly either as consumers or as sellers in German consumer sales, and the Wal-Mart, "how can I help you?" culture was initially a turn-off for Germans) but a mutual adjustment between Wal-Mart and German consumers has helped turn things around for both, and Wal-Mart's commitment to a future in Germany is relatively secure.

Being able to maintain or achieve a competitive advantage is still the goal of firms entering foreign markets or having foreign firms enter the domestic market. As movement toward oligopoly or monopoly continue to be unacceptable in the American market, the same is true (or is becoming true) around the world. Clearly, this is one of the central drivers of the WTO; and for those countries that gain WTO membership, each has an implicit understanding that it will encourage competition, not reduce it.

Transferring core competencies across borders. As we suggested earlier, domestic companies have serious questions to consider as they create their strategic plans for international expansion. Whether it be in off-shoring, or in franchising, capital investment in foreign countries, or joint ventures and strategic alliances, a major question is how much of the firm's intellectual property should be share with foreign operations. The problem, of course, is whether or not a company can enjoy the same security in a foreign country that it can enjoy in the United States (or vice versa)? In other countries where the potential of industrial espionage is not as closely monitored or punished as it is in the U.S., a firm is well advised to think twice before sharing its core competencies with those who might use them for unethical purposes.[33]

The other side of the issue is that if a firm wants to expand into a promising market and in order to effectively do so must transfer core competencies across boards, it will do so, but take additional measures to protect them. Fortunately, advances in security technology continually promise that companies are less and less at risk when sending proprietary, patented properties, and market-sensitive properties outside of the home country. This is not a foolproof system, but it is at least comforting to know that security is not only a concern, but also an area of firm management that is improving to allow greater development in foreign markets.[34]

International companies versus global companies. By deciding to move into a single additional country (from the domestic state) the company hopes to keep basic operations the same in both countries. It hopes to produce essentially the same goods or services in the new market area as it does in its home market. One reason for choosing this new country to expand into is to try to achieve this purpose. For example, many American companies that decide to move into Canada will do so without having to change much of their products, services, and operations. General Motors has manufacturing and assembly plants in Windsor, Ontario, just across the river from its headquarters in Detroit. So, little has to change for GM in expanding into Canada. Differences are present, however, so some accommodation must be made. Canadian currency is not indexed to the U.S. dollar and can fluctuate, presenting both opportunities and threats (as we will discuss later in this chapter). While English is the primary language used in Canada, agreements with French-speaking Quebec have led to dual language signage, government documents, and many other areas where the public is involved with business. Canadian government is parliamentary in nature, opposed to our congressional system, and the ministries of the government have their own sets of rules, regulations, and bureaucracies that may pose challenges to the new U.S. firm opening up its business in Canada.[35] These add complexities – true, not great levels of complexity as one might face in attempting to open up a business branch in Japan or China, but its additional complexity none-the-less and it requires that companies expand their management activities to effectively deal with the differences that mark business life across the border.

While a firm may become international and seek to maintain the same products and services in both the domestic and foreign setting, as that firm begins to do business in more and more countries, it begins to find that the uniformity of products and services begins to become a problem. This can be true of simple internationalization as well, if the firm does not specifically look for a country where uniformity is not a problem. For example, McDonalds opened its first restaurants in India in 1996 and has quickly grown to 34 stores.[36] While they use their highly recognizable golden arch design and feature Ronald McDonald, the food they sell is quite different from what one would find in the United States. Because most Indians are vegetarian, many of the McDonalds products have names like, "McAloo Tikki Burger," McVeggie Burger," "Veg Pizza McPuff," and "Veg Surprise." In 2000, McDonalds needed to issue an apology to Indian customers for using a fat to fry their French Fries that contained a beef product that has added to the distinctive taste of the fries from the beginning of the operation itself. This is a major level of complexity, but also recognizes that for McDonalds to be successful in India, it had to prepare and serve food according to Indian habits and customs that happen to be significantly different than what one would find in the U.S. Imagine, then, the amount of local customization that McDonalds faced when it expanded its business into 121 different countries, some of which enjoy the original American cuisine, while others will demanded localized foods and services.

Most global corporations are forced to substitute local customization for uniformity, but they become willing to do so in order to support growth, meet local market needs, and produce a higher-than average profit. They are far more complex the further they develop and their risk rates are higher. Many companies develop management systems that support this form of growth and they succeed, while companies that don't match their growth patterns to local conditions are quickly shut out.

Multinational Corporate Strategic Options

In Figure 10.2, we suggested that as companies move into a global environment, their level of complexity increases (as does their risk factors). Also in that discussion, we suggested that companies tend to move from attempting to provide uniform products and services in increasing international operations to having to create tailored products and services for localized consumption. However, this eventuality is not an absolute – organizations do have a choice about the uniformity or diversity of its products and services. The important point here is that while there may be a drive toward product and service diversity as firms become more mobile, those same firms have choices that allow them to grow in a directed pattern of uniformity as well. Figure 10.3 shows how these choices also fall along a continuum. These choices are important, and should be part of the strategic planning process.

Multinational Strategy (MS). Executives in multinationals have wrestled for years with the issue of whether international strategy is best standardized (globalized), regionalized, or localized. The multinational strategy, the formal statement of the international development we described earlier, is the conscious decision to provide products or services on a worldwide basis in a uniform mode. For multinational strategies to be successful they must use standardization

Figure 10.3
International Strategic Choices

for cost-based competition, localization for firms seeking differentiation, and product leadership in global markets.[37]

MS is a preferable strategy for the firm because it can do the same thing for foreign markets that it does in its domestic markets. This significantly reduces complexity and, therefore, risk. However, it is not always possible to do this (recall the example of McDonalds in India). Amazon.com, for example, conducts its business in a variety of countries around the world. The service may be conducted in languages other than English, but the basic services are exactly the same. We can't be overly concerned that the use of different languages somehow signifies that a firm is doing something different – even for domestic firms, use of a variety of languages is becoming more and more common place. Rather, when one looks at the specific activities of the firm, such as Amazon.com, one can see that the business practices in one country are exactly the same as those in another.

Many computer manufacturing companies as well as most software manufacturers use a multinational strategy. Even though computers must adapt to local electricity use (110 vs. 220), most have now developed their products to include a switch on the back that allows users in 110 wattage countries to switch to 110, and those in 220 wattage countries to switch to 110. Software manufacturers will change language on their products to meet local demand, but don't change the basic programming (as we stated earlier, different spoken languages do not mean a firm cannot pursue a multinational strategy).

Recent research suggests that MS may be a myth. Only in a few sectors, such as consumer electronics, is a MS of economic integration viable. For most other manufacturing, such as automobiles, and for all services, strategies of national and regional responsiveness are required, often coupled with some integration strategies. Successful multinationals now design strategies on a regional basis; unsuccessful ones pursue multinational strategies.[38]

Global Strategy (GS). The GS, the formal statement of the global development we described earlier, is the conscious decision to provide a diversity of products based on local demand on a worldwide basis. For many companies, a fundamental challenge is to create a global strategy which will allow for maximum use of existing product offerings and marketing activities through standardization while simultaneously acting local in order to effectively adjust to unique aspects of any given market. While this is far more complex and risky than a multinational strategy, it is also the only strategy that may work for some firms. In developing a GS, it is important to begin product positioning, differentiation and promotion activities with the fundamental product attributes of quality, price, appearance and availability.[39]

International banking must be responsive to local country laws and regulatory agencies, which means that when CitiBank decides to open offices in Japan, it must conform to Japanese law and regulation. Anytime local conditions, customs, traditions, laws, or other market factors demand that firms doing business in those entities conform to their settings, the firm needs to adopt a global strategy. Why would firms do this? They do this because they see that by entering the market, they have a realistic possibility of being a formidable competitor, can adapt its core competencies to match local demand, and may be able to achieve a competitive advantage. The form of these firms will become more complex, and their risk rates will increase, but the benefits overshadow the risks, so the company decides to more ahead.

Transnational Strategy. A transnational strategy is a synthesis of the multinational and the global strategies.[40] Here, companies try to blend as much uniformity of their product line or service (multinational) with a minimal amount of modifications to meet local demand (global) to provide itself with the benefits of both and avoid the negatives of both. This is the most common corporate strategy that MNCs adopt.

In the earlier McDonalds example, while the company did create several products specifically for the Indian market, other products (French Fries, shakes, even chicken products) remained the same, as did the display of the golden arches. Wal-Mart in Germany has had to change it sales approach and does carry products that Germans want that Americans don't care for, but maintain most of the American approach to retailing. Starbucks has found a ready market in Austria, but has altered its stores by expanding seating areas to accommodate the Austrian (and European) desire to sit for long periods in café settings to read or visit with friends. In all of these examples, companies attempt to provide uniform services and products as much as possible, but have also found a happy medium that also allows them to cater to local preferences.

A recent study by Nikolai Wasilewski investigated whether firms that employed strategies closer to the transnational model perceived their performance to be higher than those of firms that employed other international marketing types. Data were obtained from a survey of SBUs in large US-based MNEs and then analyzed to evaluate the performance of the SBU's under the alternate international strategies. Results indicated a significant, positive relationship between the extent to which the SBU international strategy approached that of the transnational type, and the perceived performance of the SBU. The findings suggested that greater improvements in MNE SBU performance are obtained as the efficiencies from global integration and the flexibilities from national responsiveness are pursued without a tradeoff of one for the other. However, the findings also suggest that there may be limitations to the desirability and attainment of transnational strategies from increasing national responsiveness and/or global integration.[41]

Multinational Corporate Tactical Options

Firms also have choices as to how they move into international settings. In concert with the three strategies we identify above, firms also can choose as to how much risk they want to engage in as they enter the international market. These range from exporting (least risky) to green field development (most risky) and provide strategic decision-makers with additional decision points that will allow their tolerance for risk to help determine which method of international expansion. Table 10.4 demonstrates the relative level of risk of the tactical choices for entering international markets.

Table 10.4
Risk Levels of International Entry Tactics

Exporting and Importing.   The least risky methods of moving into the international market place is to import or export. While this is much more true of product-related firms than services, it is a method that does not import or export a firm's core competencies, does not put the company at political or cultural risk, and does not require additional levels of managerial decentralization.

Importing goods and services seems to be a long-standing tradition in the US since we have experienced a trade deficit (importing more than exporting) for over twenty years.[42] An organization looking to import foreign goods and services will look for unmet market needs (inherent demand) based upon the desire for lower cost products, higher quality and/or support services, or substitutes. Imports are governed by the Uniform Commercial Code (UCC) and the United Nations Convention on Contracts for the International Sale of Goods (CISG). The development of an import relationship with a foreign supplier requires an offer (and perhaps counteroffers) which includes terms for acceptance, warranties, price and delivery, limitations of liability, governing laws, and force majure (acts of God or government which relieves the exporter of liability).[43] Firms may be assisted in their import endeavors by customs brokers, licensed agents (by U.S. Customs) who arrange for the payment of duties, make sure the goods are released from Customs, and represent the firm in any dealing with Customs.

In deciding to export products, a firm must find appropriate freight services, distributors in foreign countries, and retail outlets that would want to actively advertise and sell the focal firm's goods. Some risk exists here, but by and large, the exposure is minimal and this form of sales growth is relatively simple. Firms may either use sales agents, distributors, or have a subsidiary office in the foreign country.[44] According to J. Marc Chittman, there are five basic steps to begin exporting: 1. Assess the export potential of the firm. 2. Obtain expert counseling. 3. Select the best markets. 4. Formulate an export strategy. 5. Select a selling technique. The US Department of Commerce can help US firms in many ways. The Trade Promotion Coordinating Committee (TPCC) is made up of the 19 federal agencies that serve US exporting businesses. The TPCC established the Trade Information Center, which is a one-stop source for information regarding exporter-assistance programs. Other resources include the US and Foreign Commercial Service office of the International Trade Administration, and the National Trade Data Bank.[45]

Licensing. A second choice for becoming involved internationally is to engage in licensing agreements. Here, a domestic firm will engage in a contractual agreement with a company in a foreign country that is engaged in the same industry (or who wants to expand into the same industry) as the focal firm to produce its goods or services for it and to pay it a license fee for the privilege to do so. Foreign licensing covers all sorts of contractual arrangements whereby the business (licensor) provides its patents, trademarks, manufacturing expertise, or technical services to a foreign business (licensee). The risks involved in licensing include limited returns and getting the licensee to meet contractual expectations. This is an opportunity for the licensee to expand its goods or services without having to develop them. The domestic firm benefits because it can expand its brand names without much capital investment. The benefits include: 1. Minimal capital outlay; 2. Savings in tariff and transportation costs; and 3. Support for production, marketing, and post-sale servicing.[46]

On the downside, the licensee must pay a license fee, which decreases the profitability of the product or service (though it does add to increased sales volume). For the domestic company, it only receives the license fee and could increase its profits if it were actually producing in the foreign country.[47] This is the issue for Disneyland-Tokyo – the Disney Company has licensed its Disneyland operation to Japanese concerns and only receives license fees for the operation of the theme park in Japan. Would it prefer to own Disneyland-Tokyo outright? Without a doubt, it would prefer to own the theme park outright, but because of repressive and restrictive Japanese laws, it had little choice but to enter into a licensing agreement. The agreement itself is quite lucrative and the Disney Company benefits from the arrangement, but would still like to the full owner of the operation.

Franchising. Franchising is a risk-sharing method that partners a company with an individual investor (or investor group) that puts up a significant capital investment to open up a business under the banner of a primary firm.[48] Many companies do this to grow, and most chain operations are a combination of both company-owned and franchiser-owned business locations. This is a tactic that also works in international expansion. Some companies who wish to expand into new foreign markets can offer franchise opportunities for local investors who then become partners with the focal firm in establishing its business in the new market. This is more risky than the first two options because the focal firm is beginning to specifically invest in foreign locations, thereby tying themselves more directly in the international economies and markets of which they are becoming a part. Here, however, they are sharing risk, which isn't the case in the next few strategic opportunities.

One source for support for companies looking for possible franchises oversees is the International Franchise Association (IFA). The IFA delivers international programs to its members and creates opportunities in markets where they might not exist at the moment. IFA international programs include Matchmaker Trade Missions, International Financing Programs, Virtual Matchmaker Program, IFA/BFA International Symposium.[49]

Horizontal Integration. The next level of international development that involves greater investment on the part of the focal firm is to begin to purchase its competitors in foreign markets. However, unlike horizontal integration within a domestic setting, governmental regulators may limit or prevent a foreign company from buying out a domestic firm. For example, in the airline industry, U.S. law currently prevents a foreign air carrier from purchasing a domestic air carrier. This is an interesting law, because while takeover is prevented, investment is not. So while a foreign carrier might be allowed to invest in a U.S. airline up to 49%, it could not ultimately increase its stake to over 50% and then assume control[50]. There are national security issues at play here as well as some national pride issues, but the result is that at least for the airlines, horizontal integration is limited. However, Mercedes-Benz was able to take over the Chrysler Corporation in 1998 with relatively little trouble or governmental interference[51]. Coors Brewery has chosen to engage in horizontal integration as its primary method of international expansion and has purchased the England and Wales business of Bass Brewers Ltd from Interbrew on February 4, 2002.[52]

Green Field Development (Country-Centered Strategy). Opposite of a global strategy, the most risky level of international development is that of growing a business from the ground up in an international setting, known as *green field development*. Here, a company builds its own facilities, begins to conduct business completely on its own, and has total responsibility for investment, management, and for the operation's outcome. This is similar to what the firm would have done domestically when it first went into business. In the foreign setting, much of those initial growing pains reoccur and, while the firm can export its core competencies and operational expertise, much of the growth of the new division will be from the ground up. Certain companies will want to do this to maintain complete control over their operations in the foreign setting. However, in doing so, they also do not share the risk of developing the operation and in the case of negative governmental action, would bear the full loss of that action.

Porter recommends what he calls a country-centered strategy when the need for coordination of activities is low (the entire value-chain exists in each and every country the firm is operating in) and the firm is operating a small number of domestic businesses in only one country.[53] Anheuser-Busch (AB) has chosen to follow this path in opening new breweries in the United Kingdom and in China (though in both instances, AB initially entered the market through licensing and still uses licensing in seven other countries: Argentina, Canada, Ireland, Italy, Japan, South Korea, and Spain)[54]. AB, unlike Coors, has chosen to provide its basic American beer product line in the international setting, and in controlling its own operations, can maintain the same formulation and quality standards that has made it the top selling beer company in the United States.

International Joint Ventures and Strategic Alliances. In Table 10.4, we listed joint ventures and strategic alliances as slightly less risky than horizontal integration. Generally, this is true. Not only does a domestic firm share the costs of investment, management, and maintenance of a new venture (joint venture) or of a new joint operation (strategic alliance), it can limit the amount of its core competencies it wishes to have exposed to a foreign partner (and potential competitor). However, these tactics could also be extremely risky due to the financial strength and integrity of the foreign partner, the volatility of the political environment, and the potential loss of control due to remoteness of the venture. These are risks that a domestic firm can attempt to mitigate through well-defined contracting, but because of the volatility of international economics and political change, there may be little a foreign partner can do to protect its interests when things start to go bad.

What are the attributes of a good international joint-venture partner? The answer seems to be culturally based. Yadong Luo found that what Chinese firms are looking for from foreign partners are technological capability, foreign market power, and international marketing expertise, and its organizational attributes, including managerial skills and organizational reputation. By contrast, the financial attributes of a firm (what many western firms would examine) are not important to Chinese partners.[55] However, the assumption that companies from similar national cultures (i.e. Canada and the U.S.) make better partners is not necessarily true. Based on data from a survey of executives from joint ventures between Indian partners and partners from other countries, it was found that the presumed negative effect from culture distance on international joint venture performance originates more from differences in organizational culture than from differences in national culture.[56]

Today, strategic alliances are routine aspects of international business when allies share costs, establish a pool of joint resources, and create a synergistic effect in the problem-solving process. With the increases in strategic alliances, the way in which businesses view themselves and their competition is being drastically altered.[57] Firms with low levels of internationalization may feel the need to speed up their international development in order to be able to complete with multinational enterprises of bigger size and wider scope. Global alliances are a means to achieve such an accelerated process, not only because they allow firms to gain access to several markets at the same time, but also because they make it possible to enhance their own international competitiveness through the use of their partners' resources.[58]

A strategic alliance is also a strategy that allows firms to refresh their competitive strengths in response to globalization. One method in which to find appropriate members for a strategic alliance is through the use of the MTM-space matrix. MTM stands for Manufacturing ability, Technological level, and Market potentiality. In an MTM-space, a firm's high and low levels for each dimension of manufacturing ability, technological level, and market potentiality for each of its product markets can be mapped. Once the mapping is complete, the firm can then look for partners that possess complementary backgrounds and skills (i.e. a low technology firm looks for a high technology partner).[59]

Waterford Crystal Revisited

In examining the practices and outcomes for Waterford Crystal based on the discussion of this chapter, several strong strategic factors are evident. First, Waterford understood, even in its first life, that Ireland was too small a market for its products (particularly given the high-end nature of its products) and became an international company almost immediately. In its second life, Waterford understood its strong position in its market given its ability to produce and distribute. Third, it chose to locate its manufacturing facilities in locations where it could acquire, train, and control its manufacturing process to assure the highest level of quality of a hand-made product possible. Fourth, it saw a way of entering the most valuable market in the world, that of the United States, and has carefully nurtured that market to the point where it dominates it. Finally, the company provides extremely high customer service to its direct customers, through the Internet, and to its distributors and retail outlets. Through all of this, Waterford Crystal has become a world-class operation.

Summary

In this chapter, we have looked at the issues involved when a firm becomes involved in international commerce. International business is becoming more important as the world emerges from an era of political suspicion and challenge to a post-cold-war environment that has embraced capitalistic economies. Becoming an international company may be either a function of expanding a firm's business into a foreign setting (and eventually into a large number of foreign settings) or by foreign competition moving into a focal firm's domestic market place. Internationalization is a phenomenon that faces most firms. To counter, most firms will take advantage of new opportunities evident in new markets. In the chapter we identified a variety of strategies and tactics that firms must consider in developing their strategic plans. Involved in the decision-making process is the issue of additional risk, not only in simply moving into an international environment, but in the method of entry a firm might choose to move into international markets.

Key Terms and Concepts

After reading this chapter, you should be familiar with the following terms and concepts:

Multi-National Corporations; Global organizations; factor conditions, demand conditions, national culture; international political risk; international cultural risk; international competition; international markets; multinational strategies; global strategies; transnational strategies; exporting; importing; licensing; franchising; green field development; international joint ventures; international alliances; world-class organizations.

Web sites

The following websites (besides those in the endnotes) should be of interest:

http://www.odci.gov/cia/publications/factbook/index.html is the website of the Central Intelligence Agency of the United States and provides many detailed facts about foreign country history, government, economy, and vital statistics.

http://www.ita.doc.gov/ - the international trade administration's (U.S. Department of Congress) home site. Includes trade statistics, export data, press releases, hot links, a trade information center, and Export America magazine. Page includes key links by topic and an internal search engine.

Discussion Questions

1. Why is it important for Waterford Crystal to be a world-class organization?

2. Why does it make sense for Anheuser-Bush to build a brewery in China?
3. Would you recommend a U.S. firm, IBM for example, to open a new plant in Columbia; Viet Nam; North Korea? Why or why not?

Exercises

1. Is the company you have chosen to study more aggressive or is it more defensive relative to international competition? Give two substantive examples.
2. Assuming your company is an MNC, how has it chosen to become an international company? What strategies has it used? What tactics has it used? Have these been effective? Be ready to explain your answers.
3. Is your company a world-class company? How do you know this is true?

Endnotes

---

[1] A broader history of Waterford Crystal can be found on their website, http://www.waterford.com/about/aboutus.asp
[2] Tito Conti (2002). "Human and Social Implications of Excellence Models: Are They Really Accepted by the Business Community?" *Managing Service Quality* Volume 12, Issue 3, 151-158
[3] Gary A. Knight and Peter W. Liesch (2002). "Information Internalisation in Internationalising the Firm" *Journal of Business Research* (December) Volume 55, Issue 12, 981-995.
[4] Viktor Myasnikov (2002). "Mafia Runs Amok" *Moscow News* (October 23-29) Issue 41, 1.
[5] Minton F. Goldman (2002). "The Fall: A Comparative Study of the End of Communism in Czechoslovakia, East Germany, Hungary and Poland" *Slavic Review* (Fall) Volume 61, Issue 3, 586-7.
[6] Michael E. Porter (1989). *The Competitive Advantage of Nations.* New York: The Free Press.
[7] Ibid.
[8] Ibid, 132-143.
[9] http://www.staffs.ac.uk/schools/business/bscourse/jbe/jbea2.htm, January 11, 2003.
[10] Phyllis G. Yoshida (2002). "Japan's R&D Remains Strong as Economy Struggles to Turn Corner" *Research Technology Management* (November/December) Volume 45, Issue 6, 2-3.

[11] F.M. Ross Armbrecht, Jr. (2002). "Industrial Research Institute's 3rd Annual R&D Leaderboard" *Research Technology Management* (January/February) Volume 45, Issue 1, 21-23.

[12] Sandra L. Leitch and Murray A. Wood (1994). "Go Global for Growth" *Canadian Insurance* (February) Volume 99, Issue 2, 8-12.

[13] Kerry Capell, Heidi Dawley, Wendy Zellner, and Karen N. Anhalt (2000). "Wal-Mart's Not-So-Secret British Weapon" *Business Week* (January 24) Issue 3665, 132.

[14] Shirley Leung (2002). "McHaute Cuisine: Armchairs, TVs And Espresso -- Is It McDonald's? --- Burger Giant's Makeover In France Boosts Sales; Big Change for Fast Food --- Some Franchisees Have a Beef" *Wall Street Journal* (August 30) Eastern Edition, A1.

[15] Robert F. Hartley (2001). *Marketing Mistakes and Successes.* 8th Edition. New York: John Wiley & Sons.

[16] Michael E. Porter (1986). "Changing Patterns of International Competition" *California Management Review* (Winter) Volume 28, Number 2, 9-40.

[17] Henry R. Nau (1992). *The Myth of Americas Decline: Leading the World Economy into the 1990's.* Oxford, England: Oxford University Press.

[18] http://www7.national-academies.org/internationallabor/project_summary.html, January 11, 2003.

[19] http://hongkong.usconsulate.gov/uscn/trade/ipr/2002/042301.htm, January 11, 2003.

[20] Carl Rodrigues (2001). *International Management: A Cultural Approach.* 2nd Edition. Cincinnati, Oh.: South-Western College Publishing.

[21] a full description can be found in Hofstede, G. 2001. *Culture's Consequences* (2nd edition). Newbury Park, CA: Sage Publications.

[22] Adapted from Trompenaars, F., & Hampden-Turner, C. (1998). *Riding the Waves of Culture: Understanding Cultural Diversity in Global Business* (2nd Edition). New York: McGraw-Hill.

[23] Ivan Light, Min Zhou, and Rebecca Kim (2002). "Transnationalism and American Exports in an English-Speaking World" *The International Migration Review* (Fall) Volume 36, Issue 3, 702-725.

[24] Teresa Watanabe (1990). "Report Blames U.S. for Own Trade Ills" *The Los Angeles Times* (Home Edition; August 21), p. 1.

[25] Verada Bluford (1994). "Working with Foreign Languages" *Occupational Outlook Quarterly* (Winter) Volume 38, Issue 4, 25-32.

[26] More information on Ireland and its economy are available at the CIA website: http://www.odci.gov/cia/publications/factbook/geos/ei.html#Econ

[27] Holley, D. "European Union Agrees on Major Expansion," *the Los Angeles Times.December 14, 2002.* http://www.detnews.com/2002/nation/0212/15/nation-35438.htm

[28] Jeff Madura (2003). *International Financial Management.* 7th Edition. Mason, Oh.: South-Western.

[29] Robert J. Carbaugh (2002). *International Economics.* Cincinnati, Oh.: South-Western.

[30] Leo Cendrowicz (2002). "EU Reforms Antitrust Rules" *Billboard* (December 14) Volume, 114, Issue 50, 7.

[31] Philip Whyman (2002). "Living with the Euro: The Consequences for World Business" *Journal of World Business* (Autumn) Volume 37, Issue 3, 208-215.

[32] http://www.wto.org/english/thewto_e/whatis_e/whatis_e.htm, January 13, 2003.

[33] Daniel J. Morris, Lawrence P. Ettkin, and Marilyn M. Helms (2000). "Issues in the Illegal Transference of US Information Technologies" *Information Management & Computer Security* Volume 8, Issue 4, 164-172.

[34] Elizabeth R. Parker (2002). "Fourth Annual Grotius Lecture" *American Society of International Law*. Proceedings of the Annual Meeting (Washington), 1-8.

[35] Jack Bernstein (2002). "US Distributorships in Canada" (October 29) *Canadian Tax Highlights* Volume 10, Issue 10, 79-80.

[36] more information is available on McDonald's operations in India at http://www.mcdonalds.com/countries/india/index.html

[37] William L. Shanklin and David A. Griffith (1996). "Crafting Strategies for Global Marketing in the New Millennium" *Business Horizons* (September/October) Volume 39, Issue 5, 11-16.

[38] Alan Rugman and Richard Hodgetts (2001). "The End of Global Strategy" *European Management Journal* (August) Volume 19, Issue 4, 333-343.

[39] Bruce D. Keilor, Douglas R. Hawsknecjt, and R. Stephen Parker (2001). "Thinking Global, Acting Local: An Attribute Approach to Product Strategy" *Journal of Euro – Marketing* Volume 10,Issue 2, 24-48.

[40] Marc Jones (2002). "Globalization and Organizational Restructuring: A Strategic Perspective" *Thunderbird International Business Review* (May/June) Volume 44, Issue 3, 325-351.

[41] Nikolai Wasilewski (2002). "An Empirical Study of the Desirability and Challenges of Implementing Transnational Marketing Strategies" *Advances in Competitiveness Research* Volume 10, Issue 1, 123-149.

[42] Roger L. Miller (1997). *Economics Today*. 9th Edition. Reading, Mass.: Addison-Wesley Longman, Inc.

[43] Jeremiah J. Sullivan (1999). *Exploring International Business Environments*. Needham Heights, Mass.: Pearson Custom Publishing.

[44] Ibid.

[45] J. Marc Chittum (1998). "How Do I Go Global?" *Business America* (April) Volume 119, Issue 4, 17-18.

[46] Donald Weinrauch and Arthur Langlois (1983). "Guidelines for Starting and Operating an International Licensing Program for Small Business" *Journal of Small Business Management* (October) Volume 21, Issue 4, 24-31.

[47] Sandra Mottner and James P. Johnson (2000). "Motivations and Risks in International Licensing: A Review and Implications for Licensing to Transitional and Emerging Economies" *Journal of World Business* (Summer) Volume 35, Issue 2, 175-188.

[48] Franklin R. Root (1987). *Entry Level Strategies for International Markets*. Lexington, Mass.: Lexington Books.

[49] Marcel Portmann (2002). "Going International? Lots of Help is Available" *Franchising World* (April) Volume 34, Issue 3, 13-14.

[50] See a full discussion on foreign ownership of American airlines at the Department of Transportation website: http://www.api.faa.gov/conference/procdoc2000/shane.pdf

[51] More on the history of Chrysler can be found at
http://www.daimlerchrysler.com/index_e.htm
[52] Jenny Watts (2002). "The Leith Drops Interbrew for Coors" *Campaign* (August 23), p. 1.
[53] Porter, 1986.
[54] More on Anheuser-Bush's international operations can be found at
http://www.anheuser-busch.com/overview/international.html
[55] Yadong Luo (2002). "Partnering with Foreign Businesses: Perspectives from Chinese Firms" *Journal of Business Research* (June) Volume 55, Issue 6, 481-493.
[56] Vijay Pothukuch, Fariborz Damanpour, Jaepil Choi, Chao C. Chen, and Seung Ho Park (2002). "National and Organizational Culture Differences and International Joint Venture Performance" *Journal of International Business Studies* (Second Quarter) Volume 33, Issue 2, 243-265.
[57] J. Ben Reeves, Deanna S. Stepp, Lewis E. Wertz, Jr., and Dale A. Henderson (2002). "The Paper Industry: Strategic Alliances, Joint Ventures, and Electronic Commerce are Reshaping our Business Models" *Southern Business Review* (Spring) Volume 27, Issue 2, 9-17.
[58] Esteban Garcia-Canal, Cristina L. Duarte, Josep R. Criado, and Ana V. Llaneza (2002). "Accelerating International Expansion Through Global Alliances: A Typology of Cooperative Strategies" *Journal of World Business* (Summer) Volume 37, Issue 2, 91-107.
[59] Magid Kasmai and Junichi Iijima (2002). "MTM Matrix: A New Analytical Framework for Strategic Alliances" *International Journal of Business Performance Management* Volume 4, Issue 1, 45-56.

❧ Chapter Eleven ❧
Strategy Changes: Ethical and Technological Causes

Chapter Objectives

1. To understand the importance of organizational ethics and the impact it has on organizational performance, growth, and profitability.
2. To explore the role of e-business in the emerging Information Age.

Introductory Case: Nokia and Ericsson[1]

Caused by a lightning bolt, the blaze in an Albuquerque, N.M., semiconductor plant burned for just 10 minutes last March. But far away in Scandinavia, the fire touched off a corporate crisis that shifted the balance of power between two of Europe's biggest electronics companies, both major players in the global electronics industry.

Nokia Corp. of Finland and Telefon AB L.M. Ericsson of neighboring Sweden both bought computer chips from the factory, which is owned and operated by Philips Electronics NV of the Netherlands. The flow of those chips, crucial components in the mobile phones Nokia and Ericsson sell around the world, suddenly stopped.

Philips needed weeks to get the plant back up to capacity. With mobile-phone sales booming around the world, neither Nokia nor Ericsson could afford to wait.

But how the two companies responded to the crisis couldn't have been more different. Nokia, which was Europe's largest corporation by market capitalization at the time, met the challenge with a textbook crisis-management effort -- the kind companies of all stripes are finding essential as the pace of global commerce quickens.

Nokia officials outside Helsinki noticed a glitch in the flow of chips even before Philips told the company there was a problem. Nokia's chief supply troubleshooter, an intense 39-year-old Finn who runs marathons and plays rock guitar in his spare time, was on the case within days. Within two weeks, a team of 30 Nokia officials fanned out over Europe, Asia and the U.S. to patch together a solution. They redesigned chips on the fly, sped up a project to boost production, and flexed the company's muscle to squeeze more out of other suppliers in a hurry. "A crisis is the moment when you improvise," says Pertti Korhonen, Nokia's top troubleshooter, a man whose electric-guitar collection includes two classic Fender Stratocasters.

Ericsson, Sweden's largest company, with annual revenue of more than $29 billion, moved far more slowly. And it was less prepared for the problem in the first place. Unlike Nokia, the company didn't have other suppliers of the same chips, known as RFCs, for radio frequency chips. In the end, Ericsson came up millions of chips short of what it needed for a key new product. Company officials say they lost at least $400 million in potential revenue, although an insurance claim against the fire may make up some of it.

"We did not have a Plan B," concedes Jan Ahrenbring, Ericsson's marketing director for consumer goods.

On Friday, the fallout from the New Mexico fire and other component, marketing and design problems reached a climax, as Ericsson announced plans to retreat from the phone handset production market. It said it plans to outsource all its handset manufacturing to Flextronics International Ltd.

When the company revealed the damage from the fire for the first time publicly last July, its shares tumbled 14% in just hours. Since then, the shares have continued to fall along with the declining fortunes of many global telecommunications stocks. Ericsson shares are trading around 50% below where they were before the fire. The company has also overhauled the way it procures parts, including an effort to ensure that key components come from more than a single source. "We will never be exposed like this again," says Jan Wareby, who oversees the mobile-phone division as head of the company's consumer-goods unit.

At Nokia, the main cost has been frayed nerves on the crisis team. Production stayed on target, despite the fire. And although the company's shares have fallen recently amid concern that demand for the mobile phones that make up its core business could decline, Friday's close of 40.25 euros ($37.21) was only about 18% below where the shares were trading the day before the fire.

Score another victory for the upstart Finns, who have wrangled for centuries with their larger Swedish neighbors. In part, the companies' contrasting responses to the fire reflect the national character of the countries that spawned the two companies. Cautious and comfortable in groups, Swedes often move together. Finns, on the other hand, have a reputation for individualistic derring-do. During the short Nordic summer, for example, both Finns and Swedes entertain themselves with boating expeditions across a 400-mile gulf of water that separates the two countries. Swedes often sail in convoys, while Finns tend to strike out solo.

So it was with Nokia and Ericsson. "Ericsson is more passive. Friendlier, too. But not as fast," said one official who dealt with both companies in the fire's aftermath.

Founded 11 years after Nokia, Ericsson has evolved into a more engineering-heavy company. Aside from making mobile phones, which account for about 30% of its revenues, the company is a leader in commercializing complex technologies such as WAP, the software system that most European mobile phones use, and the so-called third-generation, or 3G, networks that may eventually put applications such as video on mobile phones.

Competition between these two national standard-bearers can be intense. Nokia floats hot-air balloons stamped with its name over Stockholm, while Ericsson splashes its name on billboards all over Helsinki. But both companies went global decades ago -- which is why a thunderstorm 4,000 miles away mattered so much.

At about 8 p.m. on March 17, the lightning bolt hit an electric line in New Mexico, causing power fluctuations throughout the state. It was either a sudden drop or surge in power -- authorities don't know which -- that started the blaze in Fabricator No. 22. Philips workers quickly smothered the flames, but the damage was done.

Plastic ceiling lattices were strewn about the floor. Eight trays of silicon wafers, enough to produce chips for thousands of mobile phones, were stuck in the furnace where the fire was concentrated. All were ruined. Water damage, from sprinklers that went off throughout the plant, was extensive. Smoke particles had spread into the sterile room in the heart of the factory, contaminating the entire stock of millions of chips stored there. These tiny squares of etched silicon, smaller than the nail on a baby's pinkie, allow a mobile phone to do anything from sound amplification to finding radio frequencies, depending on how they're coded.

It was immediately clear that repairing the damage would take at least a week, possibly longer. "It's as if the devil was playing with us," said one senior Philips manager who was involved in the clean-up. "Between the sprinklers and the smoke, everything that could go wrong did."

Speeding the clean-up was crucial. Desperate executives in Amsterdam joked about showing up in Albuquerque with toothbrushes to help scrub the fabricator themselves. Instead, they assigned customers priority levels. Nokia and Ericsson, which together bought about 40% of the plant's radio-frequency-chip production, would get preferred treatment, the Philips executives decided. About 30 other smaller customers -- including such telecommunications heavyweights as Lucent Technology Inc., which buys chips from Philips for cards used to link computers into wireless networks -- would have to wait.

Within days, Nokia officials in Finland already had their first inkling that something was amiss. Order numbers weren't adding up, company officials say. On Monday, March 20, Tapio Markki, Nokia's chief component-purchasing manager, found out why. In a phone call to his office at Nokia headquarters in the city of Espoo, a Philips account representative informed him of the fire, saying the company had lost "some wafers" but the plant would be back to normal in a week, according to Mr. Markki. Philips officials say they were passing along the best information they had at the time, as quickly as possible. "We thought we would be back up after a week," said Ralph Tuckwell, a spokesman for Philips semiconductors.

Mr. Markki wasn't terribly alarmed, but he relayed the news up Nokia's chain of command to Mr. Korhonen, anyway. "We encourage bad news to travel fast," says Mr. Korhonen, who has worked at Nokia for 15 years. "We don't want to hide problems."

Mr. Korhonen didn't anticipate a major problem, either. Still, he offered to send two Nokia engineers based in Dallas to the Philips plant to help. Philips, concerned that visitors might add to the confusion, declined. Mr. Korhonen then placed the five components made at the Philips plant on a "special monitor" list, something the company does dozens of times a year when demand for parts is running red-hot, as it was in March. Nokia officials began checking in with Philips officials daily, and sometimes more often, instead of the weekly monitoring the plant usually received.

Nokia officials took advantage of other opportunities to drive their concerns home to Philips officials. At a meeting with Philips officials in Helsinki, Matti Alahuhta, president of Nokia's mobile-phone division, broke from the scheduled meeting agenda to bring up the fire. "We need strong and determined action right now," he says he told the Philips executives in a conference room overlooking choppy waves in the Baltic Sea.

Mr. Alahuhta and his colleagues didn't bang on the table or yell. But Philips executives immediately recognized a characteristic Finnish curtness under pressure -- the Finns call it sisu -- that signaled they meant business. There weren't many pleasantries exchanged, according to one Philips executive who was in the room. "It was clear they were angry," he says. "You got the idea this was a matter of life or death for these guys. We respected that."

As the number of chips coming from Albuquerque plummeted, Mr. Korhonen started to worry that Nokia had a major problem. On March 31, two weeks after the fire, his fears were confirmed when Mr. Markki interrupted a meeting in Helsinki to report that Philips was now saying weeks more would be needed to repair the plant, and months' worth of chip supplies would be disrupted.

Mr. Korhonen grabbed a calculator: Nokia could find itself unable to produce just under four million handsets, the equivalent of more than 5% of the company's total sales at that time. And demand for handsets was booming like never before. "We don't need this," he cried, throwing his hands in the air.

The two men started calling other executives they thought could help, and they scrambled to figure out who else made the parts produced in Albuquerque. Of the five components, two were indispensable. One of those was made by various suppliers around the globe. But the other, semiconductors known as ASIC chips (for application specific integrated circuits), which regulate the radio frequency mobile phones use, were made only by Philips and one of its subcontractors. "This was a big, big problem," Mr. Korhonen remembers realizing.

Nokia officials had learned the hard way that supply disruptions are more the rule than the exception in their business. A few years ago, the company lost out on millions of dollars in potential sales when snags slowed down production. Jorma Ollila, then president and chief executive, vowed it wouldn't happen again. He instituted the practice of aiming executive hit squads at bottlenecks and giving them authority to make on-the-ground decisions. Mr. Korhonen himself once spent months persuading jittery Japanese suppliers to ramp up production to meet Nokia's aggressive forecasts. "I can't even recall how many karaoke songs I have sung," he says.

Within hours of getting the bad news, Messrs. Korhonen and Markki assembled their team of supply engineers, chip designers and top managers in China, Finland and the U.S. to attack the problem.

Meanwhile, across the Gulf of Bothnia in Stockholm, top Ericsson officials still hadn't realized what they were up against. Like Nokia, Ericsson officials first heard of the fire three days after it occurred. But that communication was "one technician talking to another," according to Roland Klein, head of investor relations for the company. "There were a few bits and pieces [of information before that], but nothing formal."

"The fire was not perceived as a major catastrophe," says Pia Gideon, a spokeswoman for the company. When word came from Philips about how serious the problem really was, more time passed before middle managers at Ericsson fully briefed their bosses. Mr. Wareby, who directly oversees the mobile-phone division as head of consumer products for the company, didn't find out about the snag until early April. "It was hard to assess what was going on," he says. "We found out only slowly."

By that time, Messrs. Korhonen and Markki of Nokia were on a plane heading for Philips headquarters in Amsterdam to meet with the company's chief executive. They were joined by Mr. Ollila, currently Nokia's chairman and chief executive, who rerouted a return trip from the U.S. to attend.

Mr. Korhonen says Nokia was "incredibly demanding" with Philips. He says he told Philips' CEO, Cor Boonstra, and the head of the company's semiconductor division, Arthur van der Poel, "We can't accept the current status. It's absolutely essential we turn over every stone looking for a solution."

Messrs. Van der Poel and Boonstra declined to be interviewed. Philips spokesman Mr. Tuckwell, who confirmed the meeting took place, said "it was exactly what we expect from a customer."

Mr. Korhonen and his team were now racing to restore the chip supply line. To replace more than two million power amplifier chips, they asked one Japanese and one U.S. supplier of the same chip to make millions more each. Largely because Nokia is such an important customer, both took the additional orders with only five days lead time, Mr. Korhonen says. Nokia also demanded details about capacity at other Philips plants.

"This was one of the key things we insisted on," says Mr. Korhonen. "We dug into the capacity of all Philips factories and insisted on rerouting the capacity. We asked them, told them, to redo the plan."

And he got results. "They didn't go into denial," he says. "The goal was simple: For a little period of time, Philips and Nokia would operate as one company regarding these components."

Soon more than 10 million of the ASIC chips were replaced by a Philips factory in Eindhoven, the Netherlands. Another Philips plant was freed up for Nokia in Shanghai.

The hit team was drumming up solutions within Nokia, as well. The company quickly redesigned some of its chips so they could be produced elsewhere. A project at Nokia to develop new ways of boosting chip production was also fast-tracked. Once Philips got the New Mexico plant operating again, this allowed the plant to make up for two million of the lost chips.

At Ericsson, on the other hand, officials were finding themselves increasingly behind the curve. Philips officials told them they couldn't produce enough chips to meet their needs, at least not on time. "We were capacity-bound," said Mr. Tuckwell, the Philips spokesman, who noted that too much time was needed to get production going again to meet all orders from all customers. "We found the best solutions we could."

They had nowhere else to turn for several key parts, including ASIC chips. In the mid-1990s, the company had tried to save money by simplifying its supply lines, basically by weeding out backup suppliers for many parts. By the time of the fire, many executives were new to their jobs and unaware that the company was vulnerable. Since the fire, Ericsson has reversed course and signed on second suppliers for key parts, including the chips made in Albuquerque. On Friday it left the handset production business only completely.

Nokia says it was able to meet its production targets despite the fire. The company projects continued strong growth of handset sales for the next year. Mr. Korhonen even had time recently to pull out one of his guitars, leading a band of colleagues in a version of "Twist and Shout" during an employee outing.

Business Ethics and the Social Responsibility of the Firm

As noted in our earlier discussion on corporate objectives, one of the most important qualitative objectives is social responsibility. According to a survey by Rosabeth Moss Kanter, approximately 92% of all American managers believed that U.S. firms should be actively involved in solving many societal ills, including ecological issues such as pollution, while more than 80% said that American businesses should address issues of quality education.[2] Secondly, more than 75% of consumers claim that they would switch brands and retailers to companies that support worthy causes.[3] These studies would tend to indicate that most businesses recognize their role as a member of a communal society and accept their responsibility for contributing to the betterment of society. A contrasting view of social responsibility has been put forth by economist Milton Friedman, who has stated that the most important social responsibility of chief executives is to make as much money for stockholders as they can.[4] Both statements serve to demonstrate the complexity and the potential for misunderstanding what managing to achieve social responsibility entails.

Many writers in the field tend to follow the path of Kanter and suggest that every firm must understand that it exists to serve the community of which it is a part (market and society).[5] Some firms, such as Ben and Jerry's Ice Cream, hold this view of social responsibility and both publicly and in practice do what they say they should do – contribute to the general well-being of their community and make top quality ice cream products.[6] Other writers opinions are most typified by the comments of Samuel Gompers (father of the American labor movement) who said that the worst crime against the working people a company can commit is failure to make a profit[7] – a firm must first secure its own home base before it can begin to provide resources to outside groups, no matter how worthy they are.[8]

Defining Business Ethics and Business Responsibility

Ethics and social responsibility speak to the manner in which firms and their employees (from top managers all the way down to the lower employee ranks) conduct their business within their internal and external environments. This includes the behaviors, the attitudes, the convictions, and the involvement of employees as well as the policies and actions of the firm as instituted by the governing board and the chief executive officer. These are clearly important aspects of organizational life. As we described in the opening case in Chapter 2, Enron's inability to develop a strong code of ethics, let alone live by one, was the primary reason for its collapse.

All organizations live in a competitive world and the potential for unethical behavior exists. However, as firms define, state publicly, and then enforce a strict code of ethical behavior, they find that competition does not necessarily suffer. By stating that the firm will not engage in any illegal or unethical practices, such as bribery, collusion, insider trading, industrial espionage, illegal influencing, and anti-competitive practices, organizations set a pattern of acceptable and unacceptable activity for their managers and employees. Ethical firms define what it means to 'do the right thing' and how they are going to enact these values.

Firms interpret their role in the community, their social responsibility, differently. Many companies take very seriously their role as a citizen of the community and have dedicated major resources to fulfilling their role as community neighbor and friend.[9] Many major companies have formed foundations to carry out their community involvement and have endowed these agencies with resources that will allow them to continue giving to and supporting the community over the long term. This level of community involvement is important, not in that it provides good publicity for the company, but because in many cases, highly important and valuable social and environmental programs could not exist without the support of these firms. For example, almost all of the world's 100 largest multinational enterprises (MNEs) have issued environmental codes or EHS (Environment, Health and Safety) policy statements.[10]

Ethics are the value structure of a firm; its how management and employees interpret right and wrong and how they meet and resolve on-going issues and problems.[11] High ethical standards are associated with people who always seek to do the right thing, even if those actions may hurt themselves and their firm. On the other hand, low ethical standards tend to be reflected in those decisions where the greater good is sacrificed for the enrichment of a single individual or group of individuals.

Ethics and Performance. Most organizations behave ethically because to do otherwise is business suicide. Unethical behavior inevitably spurs customers to flee, other firms to refuse partnerships and employees to leave for companies that live on higher ethical ground. Unethical behavior can expose a company to potential property loss, liability torts and other risks.[12] Ethical organizations, on the other hand, attract and retain customers and employees with integrity and are generally more successful. In a Harvard Business School study, professors John P. Kotter and James L. Heskett found that over an eleven-year period, companies that care about their customers, shareholders and employees (all ways to measure ethics), increased revenues by an average of 682 percent, compared with 166 percent for all others.[13]

Referring back to Table 2.1 and the mission statement of Enron, it is interesting to note that while Enron was very public with its mission statement and values (respect, integrity, communication, and excellence), as our opening case suggested, these public statements had little to do with their actual, unethical behavior. In examining all of the carnage that has resulted from the Enron debacle, one can only speculate if these very ruinous ends would not have been the case had Enron enforced ethical standards for top executives at the same level as their public mission statement.

Code of Ethics.   One way a firm will demonstrate its appreciation of the value of high ethical standards is through the publication of a formal *Code of Ethics*.[14] Like mission statements, a written code of ethics tells the public that the company has at least thought about the importance of ethics and has dedicated resources to produce a statement that makes public acceptable behaviors for its employees and managers. A code of ethics is more than just a formal document outlining related policies. It is about integrating positive values throughout an organization. Some key components to an effective code include: leaders setting the example, applying ethical standards as a core value, everyone participating in rule making, discussing ethics openly, applying rules consistently, and establishing a work environment where workers feel safe to share concerns.[15]

Verschoor, in analyzing the 1996 annual reports of the top 500 companies listed in *Business Week's* top 1000 firms, found that although 75% discussed in detail the adequacy of their control systems, only 33% mentioned codes of ethical conduct. A statistical comparative analysis between companies with and without codes over a three year period indicated that companies with codes of conduct consistently outperformed those that did not. In fact, of the 10 highest ranked firms (by performance) in *Fortune* (1997), 5 had explicit codes of conduct while only 1 firm from *Fortune's* list of the 10 least admired companies had a code of conduct (ranked 428).[16]

While the existence of a code of ethics is encouraging, like the very public Enron values statements, one cannot always believe what she/he is told. The true test of ethical behavior comes from the day-to-day pattern of individual activity and the way in which individuals and organizations act when they are confronted by unusually good opportunities or serious problems. Again, in the case of Enron, top executives took advantage of opportunities in an unethical manner. Some of the things that firms can do to ensure that ethical behavior is:

1. developing a corporate culture where ethical behavior is expected,
2. having officers be vigilant in their policing of corporate ethics,
3. training new employees and regularly reminding current employees of the need to be ethical in all of their corporate actions, and
4. hiring good people that are expected to follow ethical standards. It is important to provide the right infrastructure for the company's code of ethics.

This infrastructure should include a written code of behavior, executive commitment, employee-training and ethics enforcement.[17]

Values and Business Ethics. If doing the right thing (ethics) is more important than doing things right (getting the job done effectively), then how does an employee know what is ethically right or wrong? Right and wrong in terms of the corporation (and employee behavior) has been defined in several different ways.

The firm as an economic enterprise. One value system in the marketplace is best represented by the economist Milton Friedman is that *the purpose of any firm is to increase stockholder wealth – proper actions are those that enhance that wealth.*[18] A firms exist because of its stockholders who provide equity capital to found and grow the business. They do this not because they are interested in the business per se or being socially responsible, but because they trust the business to provide them with better returns (either in the form of regular dividend payments or in the increasing value of their stock) than from other investments. Stockholders select Boards of Directors, who select the firm's top manager (or in some cases, managers), who then are responsible for all other managers, employees, and their collective actions. This is the *agency theory* of management – a firm's Board of Directors and set of managers act on behalf of owners and need to be fully responsible to them for their actions.[19] Further, all of these people have a *fiduciary responsibility* to shareholders, and must act in such a way that the investment of shareholders is protected and grown.[20]

Using this understanding of responsible behavior, managers who maximize stockholder wealth are meeting their obligations to the firm and society by providing needed goods and services, paying taxes, and providing employment. A successful firm serves society by staying within the law and becoming an economic generator of resources for its creditors, suppliers, employees, government, and consumers while increasing the wealth and spending power of its stockholders. In fact, managers that use company resources in a manner that does not yield the highest possible returns (i.e. donate their at work time and the firm's resources to charity) under this scenario are considered irresponsible because: 1) they are reducing shareholder wealth, 2) they are using shareholder wealth in a manner not directly prescribed by the shareholders, and 3) stockholders act on their own behalf when contributing to society.

Friedman's position on ethics has been both greatly referenced and highly criticized.[21] Mulligan, and later Grant, claimed that an examination of Friedman's premises and main lines of deduction showed that his argument was based on a questionable paradigm, a key premise was false, and logical coherence is sometimes missing. Mulligan believed that a commitment to social responsibility can be an integral element in strategic and operational business management without producing the objectionable results envisioned by Friedman: the usurpation of governmental functions, the violation of stockholder trusts, and the possibility of losing other stakeholders' support.[22] Grant, on the other hand, thought that casting managers into purely economic roles discounted the political and social nature of human behavior hence producing a false image of the business enterprise.[23] Nunan argued that it was the nature of the contract between the stockholders and the executives that determined whether managers could or could not pursue corporate altruism.[24] Liechty believed that de-emphasizing business's role in shaping society elevated the role of the state, making the state the only entity standing between the community as a whole and business policies – a type of "creeping socialism" (as law by law and regulation by regulation lead to state control of the economy).[25] Certainly Friedman's position on social responsibility also has its proponents,[26] yet it is important to note that his dissenters equal if not outweigh his supporters.

The firm as a citizen of the community. An alternative viewpoint as to the proper behavior of an employee, and perhaps one of the hardest for managers and employees to grasp, is that managers and employees are part of a community and must take actions that benefit the community.[27] The pressures of doing business often obscure the realities that companies are part of a community – *correction*, they are part of a variety of communities.

First, a firm is part of a community of similar firms within a common industry. There are opportunities and threats that exist in the competitive market that challenge a given firm's ethical standards on an on-going basis. What to do when a competitor falters? Should the firm engage in industrial espionage? Should the firm try to hire away a competitor's better employees? Should the firm try to undermine its competitor(s)?

Second, a firm is also part of its physical community. There are opportunities and issues that involve how a firm acts as a citizen of its community, and its ethical standards will dictate how it takes advantage of them or how it uses these occasions to improve its home base. Should it seek tax advantages to stay in its current location? Should it hire locally or should it move its operations offshore? What should it pay its local employees? How shall it deal with unions? Does the company pollute, and if so, what is it doing about it? Is there a social need in the community that the firm could help address?

As a citizen of the local community, the firm also must address questions of a philanthropic nature. Businesses in the United States have a very rich history of corporate philanthropy which, interestingly enough, has dramatically changed over time. Philanthropic acts were considered illegal in the U.S. as late as the 1880's, yet firms like Macy's contributed to schools, orphanages, and the YMCA.

Increasing industrialization of the workplace in the early 20th century added to the public's acceptance of corporate charity while government legislation legitimized corporate giving in 1932 by making donations to charity a tax-deductible contribution. Philanthropy has become not only a legitimized activity of the private sector but has been accepted by most firms as part of their normal operation.[28] What, if any, not-for-profit organizations and/or causes should the firm support? Business-related and unrelated? Religious based or unaffiliated? Donation of money, personnel, or supplies? If money, what percentage of pre-tax profit?

Third, a firm is also part of a nation and a citizen of the world. There are many more opportunities and issues that face organizations as our economy becomes more international in nature. Should the firm support protectionist legislation? Should the firm conspire with domestic competitors to keep foreign competition out (which is an issue that is legal in other cultures such as Japan), or scheme with foreign partners to keep domestic competition from entering the new market? Should the firm engage in bribery in foreign countries (which may be either tacitly legal or expected in those countries), regardless of U.S. law?

Fourth, a firm that is community-minded will not only take into account the needs of its shareholders (and indirectly the customers, suppliers and creditors) but will include other stakeholders needs (such as the local, regional, national and international communities and the physical environment) as well. These firms will apply a moral standard rather than an economic or legal standard when making corporate decisions and must try to balance the need to maximize wealth of the firm with the need to serve the common good.[29] The moral standard of the firm is based upon the values of the corporate officers as influenced by their family, friends, local community, and society they are a part of.

Fifth, a recent study found a strong link between superior corporate citizenship and better financial performance. The study compared the financial performance of 100 companies, selected in 2001 by Business Ethics magazine as "Best Corporate Citizens" with the performance of the rest of the S&P 500; the best corporate citizens outperformed the remainder of the S&P 500 firms. This may be the most concrete evidence now available that good citizenship really does pay off and add to the bottom line.[30]

Corporate citizenship as a model of ethical behavior is not without its detractors. Few managers have formal training in the areas of social work, community activism, reform and economic development and are not in the best position to make decisions about which community needs should be addressed and dealt with. Their skills are in running a business, not a local United Way agency, and they should leave not-for-profit management to those who understand the service motive and how to work with volunteers.[31] Second, social programming and economic development fall under the auspices of federal, state, regional and local officials who have been elected by the community to deal with these issues, yet businesses are given huge tax incentives (through the formation of foundations) to also provide social services – under what authority does a business perform community service and allocate public resources?

The middle ground – a social capitalist view. In this context, we define social capitalism as an economic system that creates networks of social relationships between businesses and its stakeholders.[32] In the overall study of social responsibility and ethics, it is this third view that should prevail. Every effective organization exists because it has been able to achieve a good fit between its products, services, and business activities and the markets, regulators, and general societal environments of which it is a part. At the same time, strategically planned organizations can be socially responsible and still provide a better than average profit, thus fulfilling its agency relationship with its shareholders. The key is to be both an agent of the stockholders and a corporate citizen, and to do both well.

Business Ethics Issues Inherent in Strategy

A firm's ethical stance and activities are clearly a part of its strategic planning and strategic management activities. In seeking to create an effective fit between the firm's capabilities and resources with the firm's opportunities, management within the firm must address its ethical standards at the very beginning of the planning process. Ethical standards may on the one hand delimit strategic options while simultaneously provide unforeseen prospects. Understanding the importance of community and the benefits that accrue from achieving a good fit within its environment means that the firm can enjoy the best results of strategic planning (possible growth and above average profitability) and be a good neighbor and contributor within its community.

The Need to Win (While Everyone else Loses).[33] The underlying assumption in a competitive market is that there must be winners and losers. This assumption has been reinforced through America's deep fascination with sports activities since one of the major tenets of most sports is that someone must win. Winning is good. Winning brings with it happiness and a sense of achievement. For example, in sporting events, we generally don't like ties – we tend to want one person or one team to clearly win because we feel their win vicariously and often celebrate at a level above that of the winner or the members of the winning team. But being a winner also means that someone else must lose. This is a basic model. It tells us what is acceptable and what isn't when competition is involved. In sports, having winners and losers may be OK, but in business, it can become dysfunctional.

When one firm wins at the expense of another, it's a more substantive issue than is true for sports teams. First, winning and losing may not just be applied to the competition. Firms may become negatively competitive with their other stakeholders as well. Customers, suppliers, creditors, and government agencies may become the 'enemy' to the firm in that the firm enters into any arrangements or agreements with these stakeholders with the outlook of creating inequity – getting more and giving less.[34] Zero sum games will in the long run result in a poor firm reputation and negatively impact future dealings with these stakeholders.

In terms of the competition, the winner may gain an advantage, but the loser may lose not only market share and profits, but stock value as well. This may cause a protracted competitive encounter which could lead to: 1) reduced profits for both firms due to price wars; 2) inappropriate valuing of company worth leading to take-over attempts; 3) escalation of rivalry activities that result in massive marketing and human resource disruption through corporate raiding of competitor personnel; and 4) one company going out of business with a variety of other negative outcomes.

What can counteract these potential negative outcomes? Instead of competitors engaging in win/lose scenarios, they can engage in win/win strategies.[35] This isn't easy. In the United States, companies are precluded from colluding, especially if those activities result in a reduction in competition (unfortunately, activities in which one company may essentially kill another competitor is not necessarily considered illegal except if it creates monopolistic conditions). However, the pattern of competitive behavior can be win/win when a strong member of an industry decides to engage in only ethical behavior, regardless of the ethical stance of competitors. For example, in the beer industry, there are few major competitors left (the result of decades of consolidation in the industry) and competition is fierce. Yet, the three major competitors, Anheuser-Busch, Miller Brewing, and Coors Brewing do not compete on a negative manner – rather, each touts its own products based on their unique characteristics or attractiveness - mostly marketing appeal. Though high competition (advertising costs) has reduced profitability for all three firms, the three companies exercise respect for each other and do not seek to attain a competitive advantage at the expense of each other.

The Need to Cooperate (to Reduce Competition). Cooperation among competitors, as we just discussed, is problematic. In the United States, collusion[36] is expressly illegal and the Securities and Exchange Commission as well as the attorneys general of the 50 U.S. states, as well as the U.S. Attorney General, all enforce any anti-competitive laws and sue companies that cross the line in the U.S.. In many foreign countries, however, collusion is not illegal. The most notorious of colluding industries is the international oil industry, in the form of OPEC, headquartered in Vienna, Austria. For member companies, OPEC sets international pricing for oil as well as oil production. These are clearly anti-competitive activities that American companies may not engage in – they also create an uneven playing field for American companies doing business in foreign settings. The temptation to engage in collusion, in foreign settings if not at home, is great. Even with the Corrupt Foreign Practices Act in place (a U.S. law that says that all U.S. companies are subject to U.S. law even in foreign

countries) the temptation exists for U.S. companies in foreign settings
to act like their foreign counterparts.[37] Simply, U.S. law enforcement
isn't large enough to police what all U.S. companies do in the U.S., let
alone in foreign companies, so the likelihood of getting caught is
proportionately reduced. What will firms do in these circumstances?
The answer lies in whether or not these companies engage in a high or
a low level of ethical standards and practices.

**The Importance of Developing Employees to their
Maximum Potential.** Another choice that has an ethical dimension is
how a firm chooses to deal with its own employees. The two different
approaches tend to be: 1) treat employees as units of labor – each
employee is expected to produce a certain amount of output (product or
service) and will be compensated just for that output; and 2) treat
employees as resources – each employee is a human resource that can
be grown to produce higher levels of output (both in terms of quantity
and quality) both for herself/himself and for the firm.[38] It would make
sense that most firms would choose to adopt the second approach, but
in practice, not all firms do. This is particularly true for firms utilizing
lower-level employees in the services industries. A fast food chain
store might attempt to hire lower-skilled employees, teach them low-
level skills pay minimum wage, and then keep the working conditions
at a minimal so that most employees will leave before they get into a
position where they should be considered for raises. Many might find
this practice unethical, but it is a condition that does exist in many of
the services industries in the United States and overseas.[39]

For firms that view their employee as resources, there is a
different ethic in place. These firms seek to enrich their resources (just
as one would do with a commodity) so that the resource will be more
and more valuable to the firm over time. For example, AT&T has
traditionally hired people that it believes are good resources to begin
with, acclimated them to the company, and then provided them with
assessment centers which tells both the company and the employees
how the employee might avail themselves of training and educational
opportunities that will continually improve them (for themselves and
for AT&T).[40]

**Greening and Socially Responsible Businesses – are they
Competitive?** There is a perception that when a company expends

resources to improve the ecosphere, it does so at the expense of profitability and damages its competitive advantage. This discussion has reached political proportions in the United States, and has become a part of the general political debate. For example, in early 2003, President George W. Bush announced new pollution control guidelines that do not require most manufacturers to install additional pollution control devises when they expand operations. Immediately, many ecologists expressed great concern for the decision and feared that firms in polluting industries in the U.S. would take this opportunity to expand and increase pollution. Whether or not this happens is yet to be seen. How it would happen is a question of ethics and social responsibility.

Whether or not a manufacturing firm continues to manufacture in the United States or has moved offshore much of its manufacturing operations to foreign companies, polluting the environment is still immoral. Domestic firms, such as utilities, that burn fossil fuels or utilize radioactive fuels, engage in operations that can, or could, pollute the air, water, and ground around them. Certainly there are costs involved in installing devices in manufacturing facilities or in electricity generating facilities that drive up the costs of the products they produce. For the manufacturing facilities this is problematic because these additional costs reduce their competitive position (for utilities, they can generally pass along these costs to the consumers, but usually need regulatory agencies to approve price changes).

There are costs to the corporation in installing devices to control the pollution they generate, but there are severe costs to their communities and the world in general, if they do not. Whether one believes in global warming or not, there is demonstrable environmental damage that have been caused by American industry to the U.S. great lakes, several major cities, our forest resources, strip-mined lands, and our nation's rivers and streams. The reality is that industries and the use of motor vehicles in the United States are the greatest contributors to worldwide pollution.[41] For this damage to be reversed, companies must all adopt a level of high ethical standards and social awareness that will sacrifice certain levels of profitability to better the environment. Strategic planning can be a factor here in allowing the firm to add social action and social programs to the overall direction of the firm. Over time, these attitudes could well have a market impact that will allow high desired levels of growth and still support above average returns. This is a difficult issue, but one that everyone will need to face relatively soon.

Defining the e-Business Environment

As we suggested back in Chapter 3, the environments in which companies do business today have changed dramatically over the last half a century. In this chapter, we have examined the role of ethics and its impact on strategy. Another major development over the past decade has been the explosive growth of the Internet and the World Wide Web as a new force in conducting business and in increasing sales. International companies, among others, have seen the advances and opportunities of this mode of modern communication and have used it to expand into new markets, new countries, and new regions it might not have otherwise considered.[42] Using connected-electronic media to improve business practices (e-business) is becoming more and more common. Even for improving communications within single firms, many companies use the Internet as a primary method of doing business within its own four walls. Of course, the ease with which firms can take advantage of e-business methods means that doing business anywhere in the world is becoming just as easy as conducting business within one's own four walls.

This is a substantive and paradigm-shifting event. In a relatively short period of time, use of networked computer systems, both within as well as outside the business, has raised the bar on what it takes to support core competencies and achieve a strategic advantage. Perhaps most importantly, e-business has erased the effects of national borders more so than any other political or economic activities and has proven to be a powerful tool for growth and control.[43] What is even more exciting, however, is that the next several years will bring with them even greater capabilities and new opportunities to use this emerging technology. This will be an exciting world to live in, to do business in, and in which to thrive.

The Impacts of the Internet and the Growth of Technology on e-Business

It wasn't so long ago that a typical office setting was characterized by rows of desks, populated by people working on typewriters, or writing reports, or filling out forms, or talking on the telephone. Along the walls of many of these offices were banks of filing cabinets, filled with paper records. There could well be a conference room in the area where various groups of employees would get together on a weekly basis to report on the progress they were making on whatever work project they were overseeing. Most offices opened at 8:00 a.m. in the morning and closed promptly at 5:00 p.m. and operated from Monday through Friday. If someone went out on a business trip, they were essentially out of touch except for the occasion high-cost long-distance phone call. By and large, this world is now gone.

A typical office today may still have rows of desks (though modern versions tend to support different furniture groupings to better accommodate group interaction and comfort), but the typewriters are gone. Instead, nearly everyone in the office has a computer that still has document writing capabilities, yet connects the employee to other computers that may house spreadsheets and databases that one might want to access in performing her/his own job. The phone is still there, but is normally not the primary source of communication – the new source is e-mail, which not only has voice-capability, but can transfer visuals and documents at the touch of a button. With the cost of this type of communication only a fraction of the traditional telephone bill or letter, it is not only more effective; it is also more efficient. The filing cabinets are fading away as file management systems on the computer not only eliminate the need for paper documentation, but also provide an ease of access that was never possible with the old paper filing methods. A conference room may still be available, but it will be used on a much more active schedule as changing events in one group's work area create the need for instantaneous planning and action sessions. Because everyone is connected, there is little need to report progress, which is information that is easily available to anyone in the work group over the firm's computer system and its databases.[44]

The term "24-7" has come to refer to those firms who operate 24 hours a day, 7 days a week, and are always open on at least a virtual basis. With the expansion of firms into the international setting, this virtual presence is a requirement so that the firm can conduct the same high-level quality of business regardless of the differences between time zones. Finally, in terms of connectivity, not only does the Internet allow universal access to a person's e-mail, company data base systems, and world-wide information centers, the continual development and use of cell phones makes a person who works in the office today, but is in Beijing tomorrow, seem not out of the office at all.

There are positives and negatives to the all-inclusive world of e-business. Positive consequences of information technology have included improved productivity and teamwork, increased competitive advantage (see value chain discussion below), improved customer service and supplier relations, enhanced communication and coordination (see virtual organization discussion below), superior analysis of data, and employee empowerment through self-service.[45]

For Americans, especially, the e-business work environment has allowed many to become workaholics. For example, with the rapid proliferation of Internet kiosks and Web-enabled offices at airports, employees have more chances than ever to catch up on work or personal e-mail correspondence when they're on the road. According to the market research firm Frost & Sullivan, there will be more than 535,000 Internet kiosks in the world by the end of 2001.[46] The ability to work from anywhere at any time has produced a generation of high achievers who work even longer hours than their Japanese counterparts.[47] E-business has also produced the opposite effect, "computer goof-offs."[48] These individuals are time thieves – they surf the net, e-mail or do other computer-related activities (i.e. playing games) that steal time from the company and therein lower corporate productivity.[49] Another disadvantage is derived from security issues related to e-business - the potential for intrusive control by others has been made easier with the development of technology.[50] Securing web services is no easy task. The same virtues that make Web services so promising for e-business - they're platform- independent, text-based, and self-describing - create major security concerns, giving pause to businesses considering a move to the hot new interoperability technology.[51] However, the advantages do outweigh the negatives, and the effective use of technology is becoming more and more the factor that separates those firms who are able to use it to achieve a competitive advantage from those who cannot.

e-Business and Improving the Value Chain

The value chain, as we described it in Chapter 4, traces the route of a product from its most basic state to the final customer. The value chain may be short (which is more the case of the value chain for services, but can also be true for the value chain for a company that controls more than one segment of the process), but still involves a variety of steps from beginning to end. Two concerns that the value chain process is susceptible are: 1) efficiency (cutting down on the potential for loss or waste), and 2) time to market.

Efficiency. Electronic commerce (EC) on the Internet is an attractive technology for business organizations to be more efficient since web-based transactions are more efficient than alternative methods. EC also provides cost-effective marketing and a disintermediation of costly distribution channels. There has been some anecdotal evidence about such benefits, however Khan and Motiwalla conducted a cross-sectional study that measured the impact of EC on financial performance of companies. They analyzed the financial statements of 45 publicly held corporations that have implemented EC initiatives. The results indicated that the majority of the sample companies have experienced improved financial performance in the post e-commerce era.[52]

Time to Market. Internet-enabled washers and dryers are just one example of the soaring popularity of embedded microprocessors with Internet connectivity in industrial applications, either within factories or installed as part of commercial equipment. Impressive reductions in cost and other financial benefits achieved by manufacturers and industrial equipment operators are responsible in large part for the dramatic increase in the use of Internet-enabled micro-controllers. The technology's benefits largely result from a collection of standards-based technologies such as the Internet,

Ethernet and the Web browser, instead of the proprietary interfaces and manufacturing operating systems typically found in industrial equipment. The key advantage is that it is no longer necessary to invent the entire system, due to the underlying interoperability, which naturally provides a faster time to market.[53]

For example, in the more traditional approach we described earlier in the furniture industry, each step from tree to finished table was fraught with the opportunities to either be very efficient or very wasteful. For example, in the initial cutting of the tree, there are issues of how easily recoverable is the fallen tree? Is it easy to recover, or will it take an excessive amount of time and effort to do so? At the sawmill, will the miller cut the log to gain maximum yield or cut it without concern for the amount of waste the process can produce? At the manufacturer, are the tools kept up to reduce downtime and drag (the phenomenon that occurs when, for example, tools are not kept sharp so that it takes longer to cut through wood or in doing so causes scaring that will force the operation to spend more time in finishing)? Once the table is made and finished, how is it stored; how long is it stored; how is it shipped; what is the cost of shipping; and what is the damage potential resulting from shipping? For the distributor, the questions become: what facilities are needed for storage; how will inventory be accounted for; how long will inventory remain in the warehouse; how much shrinkage will occur; and how much damage might occur due to vermin or human accident? Finally, for the retailer, how much storage space must there be for the inventory of tables; what is the typical time to turn an inventory; how much shrinkage will occur; and what is the potential for sold merchandise to be returned? As one can see, the potentials for great savings as well as for great expense is found throughout this process. Also, the potential for getting to market sooner rather than later exists in a very real way.

Now, we introduce e-business techniques. From the beginning to the end, use of electronic business methods can help move more dramatically toward helping the firms in the process reduce waste, maximize output, cut costs, and expedite the process. Satellite views from space can tell loggers not only where healthy timber stands are located, but the easiest ways to remove cut timber. They can also indicate on a moment-to-moment basis, the fastest and most expedient route to the lumber mill. At the mill, laser-guided sawing operations can locate the grain structures and density characteristics and then guide the sawing activity itself to cut the best grades of lumber in a manner that also produces the greatest yield. The mill will then season the lumber using state-of-the-art moisture-content measuring devises that will tell it precisely when the wood will be ready to be shipped. Then, based on the just-in-time inventory system (JIT) of the manufacturer, it will ship the wood to the manufacturer who will temporarily store it in a holding area, but have it in process within 24 hours of receipt. As for the manufacturer, electronic controls not only allow supervisors to know instantaneously where products are within the furniture-making process, but will also detect process problems and enforce maintenance schedules so that the amount of time between receiving lumber on one end and finishing it and putting it on a truck on the other is a precisely controlled and efficient process. By the time the table is on its way to the distributor, the JIT system there will be programmed to know when the table will arrive and where it needs to be taken within the distribution center to be immediate loaded and sent to the retailer. Finally, because the retailer is connected to the JIT systems of the manufacturer and the distributor and has a JIT system in house, once the table arrives, it goes to the floor or to temporary storage (for an larger order of several tables might be held) and is available for sale. Finally, because the retailer has done simulations and modeling on sales patterns, it will know the proper time to advertise, the probability of substantive consumer interest, and can most likely predict when the table will actually be sold. As a bonus, because the process has been so efficient and well controlled throughout, the probability that the customer will find flaws with the table and return it have been reduced as well.

This example demonstrates how e-business solutions can be used in every portion of the value chain process to both increase efficiencies and reduce time to market considerations. More importantly, these methods are far superior to the best techniques and abilities of value chain partners of just a few years ago, and has provided another important way that firms can improve their core competencies and improve their competitive advantage.

Growth of Virtual Organizations and e-Commerce

We've already identified how e-business has improved operations, and have suggested that most firms today need to employee e-business solutions in order to attain or maintain a competitive advantage. Two additional considerations merit a brief discussion here – the growth of network, or virtual organization, and the explosion of e-commerce.

Network, or virtual organizations could not exist easily without e-business technologies and methods. When a firm decides to purchase services it would normally supply itself, it needs to have a strong linkage to the vendor in order to maintain the normal flow of activity. For example, if a given firm has outsourced its Human Resource Management (HRM) division to a firm that handles all level of personnel activities from recruiting to dismissal, and from payroll to benefits negotiations, it must have instantaneous connections between itself and the vendor so that when a personnel issue arises in the firm, the vendor knows it and can begin to formulate a solution. Likewise, when the company management wants to know the exact payroll accrued at the end of business yesterday, it can immediately gain that information from a connected database. In virtual organizations, the need for real-time control is perhaps even a more critical issue than it is for traditional businesses. Without an e-business system in place, it could find itself out of control very rapidly and in a seriously perilous position.

e-Commerce, as the term implies, is marketing and financial activity over the Internet and World Wide Web. Many companies have discovered that Internet users like the comfort and convenience of shopping on-line. Amazon.com has exploited this shift in consumer activity perhaps better than any other Information Age company, but everyday sees more and more retailers developing websites, getting listed on search engines, and finding ways of getting to their potential customers easily through the World Wide Web. For their part, Internet users continue to develop a strong interest in Internet buying. They can directly access a retailer inventory base and choose styles, colors, and sizes directly, and then by simply clicking buttons on the computer keyboard, pay for the item and have it sent directly to their home (or to another location if they wish). The items can be gift-wrapped with a personal message from the purchaser. Further, the sales warranties are just as strong for the Internet user as they are for the in-store shopper.

e-Commerce is also a tool for firms in any area of commerce. Firms can also purchase on-line, determine payments and shipping methods, and track shipments in real time. In financial issues, funds can be easily transferred from one account to another, or from on institution to another without the need for the person to ever leave their office computer. As new ideas come to fruition, more and more commercial activities will be available through computerized technology, promising an exciting world of the future.[54]

Traditional Business and e-Commerce

One concern is whether or not e-commerce is going to displace traditional business. Two thoughts: 1) current market data suggests that while e-commerce is growing, many consumers still want to shop in the traditional method; and 2) many traditional businesses do not view e-commerce so much as a threat as they do view it as an opportunity.

Not everyone in the modern commercial environment is comfortable with e-commerce. Older shoppers don't trust the new technology and want to be more in control of their purchasing activities. Also, many shoppers don't get a full sense of the product or service that a firm may be offering through the Internet and may prefer to physically view the product or talk face-to-face with a service provider before deciding to buy. There are times, and there are particular products where Internet sales are clearly inferior to direct sales, and as a result, there should be little concern for the longer-term viability of traditional commercial businesses. Business to business (B2B) internet commerce has not met growth expectations. Many of the heady forecasts in 1999 and 2000 estimated B2B would reach 30 percent to 50 percent of trade business by 2003, and many of the Net-oriented companies that delivered those prophecies are no longer in business. Forrester Research Inc., despite its earlier predictions of skyrocketing growth, has tracked a very slow upward trend with the overall procurement of a firm over the internet averaging under 10 percent and only a small fraction of companies are buying over 30 percent of their supplies online.[55]

The second perspective is that many traditional businesses are using e-commerce techniques to expand their businesses – click and mortars. The high failure rate of dot.com companies suggests that click-and-mortar strategies may have an edge over pure-plays in the Market, especially in retail.[56] In the field of real estate, many real estate companies not only put their own properties up on the net for view by potential customers, but may also be parts of larger real estate consortiums where they can advertise their own products to a statewide or even national audience. For example, anyone in the world can go to a website located at http://www.coloproperty.com/ and get a real time set of listings for all properties available for sale through real estate brokerages in the State of Colorado. Similar sites can be found in nearly all 50 U.S. states. Likewise, many traditional retailers including Wal-Mart, Target, Marshall-Field, the May Company, Macy's, Sears, and K-Mart have on-line presence that extend shopping opportunities for their customers. One can even order pizza or the week's groceries on line and none of these activities have hurt their core businesses in any way.

From an international perspective, at the root of many of international e-commerce failures is the fact that dot-coms and click and mortars often have flawed or non-existent strategies for tapping into Europe's diverse market. It is a huge business mistake to simply take what worked in the US and transfer it to Europe. Companies have to consider the unique challenges that Europe presents: different cultures, different languages and customer-fulfillment needs, still-undefined regulatory environments, varied payment methods and currencies, and markets in which internet penetration rates are often not as high as in the US. This requires a plan of attack, and, most important, a presence in Europe to act as the strategic core specifically responsible for that market.[57]

Risks and Rewards of E-solutions

The two major risks of e-business and e-commerce are security and SPAM. Beyond the illegal activities of computer hackers who have been able to gain unauthorized access to personal and private information of individuals, companies, and even governments, the lack of adequate fire walls tend to allow criminals to invade private records and highly sensitive information available somewhere on the Internet. SSL capabilities are allowing greater security for the use of credit cards on the Internet and the passage of private information between one party and another using the Internet, but 100% security is not now possible.   Unfortunately, anytime anyone is on the Internet, the possibility exists that some computer hacker somewhere in the world is potentially able to access the information stored on that person's computer.   Heightened security measures are being developed and, perhaps, within the foreseeable future, technology will exist that can assure privacy in personal record keeping via computer, and in business transactions conducted over network systems.[58]

SPAM is the second problem that businesses in e-commerce must overcome.   The amount of unsolicited commercial e-mail consumers forward to spam trackers at the Federal Trade Commission's uce@FTC.gov address has more than tripled in the past year, from 15,000 to 70,000 pieces a day. A lot of spam is for scams. More than 9,000 consumers reported losing $35 million in the first six months of 2002 from one e-mail scam alone -- a purported Nigerian businessman who claims to need help with extracting money from his country. More than half of the Internet e-mail sent to America Online's 35 million members is spam, but much of it is blocked before ever getting to anyone's inbox. And like other companies, AOL is constantly seeking new ways to block spam.[59]

On the one hand, free mass mailing is a boon for firms and the potential of contacting millions upon millions of potential consumers is a serious consideration in the decision to use the capabilities of the Internet. This is another of the ethical considerations that firms face when they decide to use Internet tactics to expand their business. Should they focus their e-mail advertising? Should they ask permission of potential e-mail customers? Should they become SPAMMERS? All of these are issues that firms in most industries that have an Internet capability need to reconcile through their own codes of ethics as they also seek to achieve a demonstrable strategic advantage.

Rewards of doing e-commerce are incalculable. We are still on the beginning side of the curve, and developments are being introduced nearly every day. It is already clear that adapting operations to emerging e-business and e-commerce solutions is becoming more and more important in a firm's ability to support distinctive core competencies and using them to create strategic advantages. One thing for certain, the old way of doing business is no longer adequate to help a firm achieve its strategic objectives and as advances continue to become evident, it will be important for a firm to develop a strategic plan that incorporates major change that involves new and emerging technologies.

Summary

We ended the chapter with a discussion of the emerging world of e-business and e-commerce. The explosion of computer-related opportunities that are proliferating the environments of traditional business practices and marketing patterns are changing the landscape of how firms now approach both aspects of their businesses. There are an unlimited number of opportunities that the Information Age is bringing with it, but there are also new threats. This is a new world for firms that they need to fully examine and attempt to understand as they create their strategic plans to help them achieve both growth and profitability.

Key Terms and Concepts

Ethics; code of ethics; social responsibility; agency theory; e-business; e-commerce; SPAM; SPAMMERS; and e-solutions.

Web sites

http://management.about.com/library/howto/ht_stmt.htm   -   The Business Directory's library. "How to Draft a Mission Statement" provides steps for writing the statement plus helpful tips that will make the job easier. This site also provides access to other management topics including business ethics, corporate governance, strategic planning, and organization development.

http://ecommerce.internet.com/ - Jupiter Media Corporation's e-commerce guide web site. Includes a free newsletter, online access to topical articles, news and trends, research, an internal search engine, conference announcements, and on-line polls.

http://www.internetindicators.com/ - a site with numerous facts and figures on about the internet. Includes mini-case studies, internet economic indicators, archival data, video webcasts, links to government, media, and internet organizations and resources.

Discussion Questions

1. Should a firm concentrate on social responsibility activities or stockholder enriching measures? Why?
2. Describe what is meant by a code of ethics. Does having this code make a firm more ethical?
3. What do you see as the greatest opportunities for firms engaging in e-commerce?
4. What do you see at the greatest threats for firms engaging in e-commerce?

Exercises

1. Does your firm have a written code of ethics? If so, comment on its appropriateness and value. If not, is there any other evidence that this firm acts in an ethical manner, if so give examples, if not, why not?
2. Describe the social responsibility your company exhibits. What are the positive outcomes of these activities for the firm? For the community? Where is your company in terms of its adaptation of e-business and e-commerce? What are the specific impacts you can detect?
3. Is your company a technological leader in its industry? (Yes or No) What difference does this make in terms of it achieving a competitive advantage?

Experiential Exercise[60]

Instructions: Form groups of 4-5 students. Individually, think of an organization that you currently work for or used to work for. If you never worked for an organization (even as a volunteer), please indicate that on your work sheet and answer the questions. On your own, indicate how you feel about each behavior that someone in the organization might have exhibited. Use the following scale and place one number after each behavior to indicate how you feel about the behavior. There are no right or wrong answers.

Scale: 1 = very acceptable, 2 = acceptable, 3 = somewhat acceptable, 4 = uncertain, 5 = somewhat unacceptable, 6 = unacceptable, 7 = very unacceptable.

1. _____ Taking home a few office supplies for personal use (e.g. paper clips, pencils, pens).

2. _____ Calling in sick when some personal time (e.g. playing golf, seeing a movie, etc…) is needed.

3. _____ Using company equipment (e.g. phone, FAX, computer, etc…) for personal business.

4. _____ Making personal copies on a company copy machine.

5. _____ Using a company car to make a personal trip.

6. _____ Eating at a very expensive restaurant on a company business trip and charging the meal to the company expense account.

7. _____ Charging wine and cocktails as well as food on a company business trip at the company's expense.

8. _____ Taking a significant other along on a company business trip at the company's expense.

9. _____ Staying at an expensive hotel on a company business trip.

10. _____ Charging a $7 cab ride to your expense account when you actually walked.

Total Score _____   Questions with a score of '3' or lower? _____

When each member of your group is done, compare scores and determine your group's average score per question. Compare your scores to the data below and discuss your results. When completed, answer the questions at the end of this exercise.

Survey Results: More than 200 managers responded to this survey.
1. 50% thought that taking home a few office supplies was acceptable.
2. 70% reported that calling in sick to take personal time was unacceptable.
3. 75% reported that using office equipment for personal use was unacceptable.
4. 55% indicated that making personal copies on a copy machine was acceptable
5. 71% thought that using a company car for personal trips was unacceptable
6. 59% reported eating at a very expensive restaurant as acceptable.
7. 50% believed that charging wine and cocktails was acceptable.
8. 85% thought that taking a significant other along on a business trip was unacceptable.
9. 55% indicated that staying at an expensive hotel on a company business trip was acceptable.
10. 41% indicated that charging $7 for a cab ride when they walked was very unacceptable.

Questions
1. Examine the managers' answers. Describe any inconsistencies or contradictions you believe exist. Then do the same for you answers and your group's answers.

2. Compare your answers, and your group's answers, to those of the managers. Where are the similarities and differences?

Endnotes

[1] The following was excerted from the Wall Street Journal. *Copyright Dow Jones & Company Inc Jan 29, 2001.*

[2] Kanter, R. M. 1991. "Transcending Business Boundaries: 12,000 World Mangers' Views Change." *Harvard Business Review* 69(3), pg.s 151-164.

[3] Curtis C. Verschoor (1997). "Principles Build Profits" *Management Accounting* (October) Volume 79, Issue 4, 42-46.

[4] Friedman, M. and Friedman, R. D. 2002. *Capitalism and Freedom.* Chicago: University of Chicago Press.

[5] Dalton E. McFarland (1986). *The Managerial Imperative: The Age of Macromanagement.* Cambridge, Mass.: Ballinger Publishing Company.

[6] Ben and Jerry's social programs can be found at http://www.benjerry.com/mission.html

[7] http://www.staffingtoday.net/memberserv/0700ss/story10.htm, January 8, 2003.

[8] Michael E. Porter and Mark R. Kramer (2002). "The Competitive Advantage of Corporate Philanthropy" *Harvard Business Review* (December) Volume 80, Issue 12, 56-68.

[9] Jane Simms (2002). "Business: Corporate Social Responsibility - You Know it Makes Sense" *Accountancy* (November) Volume 129, Issue 1311, 1-5.

[10] Barbara Fliess (2001). "Better Business Behaviour" *Organisation for Economic Cooperation and Development. The OECD Observer* (November) Issue 229, 53-55.

[11] Steve Zalewski (2002). "A Closer Look at Business Ethics" *The Interpreter* (Fall), 3-4.

[12] Richard Carris and Ronald Duska (2003). "Ethics and the Risk Manager" *Risk Management* (April) Volume 50, Issue 4, 28-31.

[13] John P. Kotter and James L. Heskett (1992). *Corporate Culture and Performance.* New York: Simon & Schuster Adult Publishing Group.

[14] Curtis C. Verschoor (2002) "It Isn't Enough to Just Have a Code of Ethics" *Strategic Finance* (December) Volume 86, Issue 4, 22-23.

[15] Max Messmer (2003). "Does Your Company Have a Code of Ethics?" *Strategic Finance* (April) Volume 84, Issue 10, 13-14.

[16] Verschoor, 2002.

[17] Steve Zalewski, 2002.

[18] Thomas Carson (1993). "Friedman's Theory of Corporate Social Responsibility" *Business & Professional Ethics Journal* (Spring) Volume 12, Issue 1, 3-5.

[19] James R. Booth, Marcia Cornett and Hassan Tehranian (2002). "Boards of Directors, Ownership, and Regulation" *Journal of Banking & Finance* (October) Volume 26, Issue 10, 1973-1996.

[20] Rhonda Prussack (2002). "Fiduciary Liability: It's Not Just a Big-Company Concern" (November) Volume 145, Issue 11, 32-37.

[21] John E. Fleming (1987). "Authorities in Business Ethics" *Journal of Business Ethics* (April) Volume 6, Issue 3, 213-217.

[22] Thomas Mulligan (1986). "Critique of Milton Friedman's Essay 'The Social Responsibility of Business Is to Increase Its Profits'" *Journal of Business Ethics* (August) Volume 5, Issue 4, 265-270.

[23] Colin Grant (1991). "Friedman Fallacies" *Journal of Business Ethics* (December) Volume 10, Issue 12, 907-914.

[24] Richard Nunan (1988). "The Libertarian Conception Of Corporate Property: A Critique of Milton Friedman's Views on the Social Responsibility of Business" *Journal of Business Ethics* (December)Volume 7, Issue 12, 891-906.

[25] Daniel Liechty (1985). "On the Social Responsibilities of Business: Contra Milton Friedman" *Management Decision* Volume 23, Issue 4, 54-62.

[26] Bill Shaw (1988). "A Reply To Thomas Mulligan's 'Critique Of Milton Friedman's Essay 'The Social Responsibility of Business to Increase its Profits'" *Journal of Business Ethics* (July) Volume 7, Issue 7, 537-543; Thomas Carson (1993). "Friedman's Theory of Corporate Social Responsibility" *Business & Professional Ethics Journal* (Spring) Volume 12, Issue 1, 3; Geoffrey P. Lantos (2001). "The Boundaries of Strategic Corporate Social Responsibility" *The Journal of Consumer Marketing* Volume 18, Issue 7, 595-630: Philip R.. P. Coelho; James E. McClure; John A. Spry (2003). "The Social Responsibility of Corporate Management: A Classical Critique" *Mid - American Journal of Business* (Spring) Volume 18, Issue 1, 15-24.

[27] Anonymous (2002). "Special Report: Lots of it About - Corporate Social Responsibility" *The Economist* (December 14) Volume 365, Issue 8303, 62-3.

[28] Mark Sharfman (1994). "Changing Institutional Roles: The Evolution of Corporate Philanthropy, 1883-1953" *Business and Society* (December) Volume 33, Issue 3, 236-269.

[29] Robert Hinkley (2002). "28 Words to Redefine Corporate Duties: The Proposal for a Code for Corporate Citizenship" *Multinational Monitor* (July/August) Volume 23, Issue 7/8, 18-20.

[30] Elizabeth Murphy (2002). "Best Corporate Citizens Have Better Financial Performance" *Strategic Finance* (January) Volume 83, Issue 7, 20.

[31] Paul C. Nutt and Robert W. Backoff (1992). *Strategic Management of Public and Third Sector Organizations: A Handbook for Leaders.* San Francisco, Ca.: Jossey-Bass, Inc.

[32] Michael Thomas (2002). "Thoughts on Building a Just Market Society" *Journal of Public Affairs* (May) Volume 2, Issue 2, 9-15.

[33] William Collison (1988). *Conflict Reduction: Turning Conflict into Cooperation.* Dubuque, Iowa: Kendall/Hunt Publishing Company.

[34] Lawrence Barton (1995). *Ethics: The Enemy in the Workplace.* Cincinnati, Oh.: South-Western College Publishing.

[35] Collision, 1988.

[36] Luca Lambertini and Marco Trombetta (2002). "Delegation and Firms' Ability to Collude" *Journal of Economic Behavior & Organization* (April) Volume 47, Issue 4, 359-373.

[37] Wesley Cragg and William Woof (2002). "The U.S. Foreign Corrupt Practices Act: A Study of its Effectiveness" *Business and Society Review* (Spring) Volume 107, Issue 1, 98-144

[38] Douglas McGregor (1960). *The Human Side of Enterprise.* New York: McGraw-Hill Book Company, Inc.

[39] Ray Mosely (1997). "McVictory may be Hollow Critics will Appeal; Judge Slams some of Firm's Practices" *Chicago Tribune* (June 20) North Sports Final Edition, 3.

[40] Jenny C. McCune (1994). "Measuring the Value of Employee Education" *Management Review* (April) Volume 83, Issue 4, 10-15.

[41] Anne Gulland (2002). "Air Pollution Responsible for 600 000 Premature Deaths Worldwide" *British Medical Journal* International Edition (December 14) Volume 325, Issue 7377, 1380.

[42] Peng S. Chan and Dennis Pollard (2002). "Global Challenges in E-Commerce" *International Journal of Management* (September) Journal 19, Issue 3, 445-454.

[43] Rhiannon Lewis and Antie Cockrill (2002). "Going Global - Remaining Local: The Impact of E-commerce on Small Retail Firms in Wales" *International Journal of Information Management* (June) Volume 22, Issue 3, 199-209.

[44] Annelise Berendt (1998). "The Virtual Enterprise Gets Real" *Telecommunications* (April) Volume 23, Issue 4, 32-36.

[45] Andrew J. DuBrin (2003). *Essentials of Management.* 6th Edition. Mason, Oh.: South-Western.

[46] Bob Tedeschi (2001). "Staying Connected on the Road" *New York Times* (March 11), 13.

[47] James Lardner and Trena Johnson (1999). "World-class Workaholics: Are Crazy Hours and Takeout Dinners the Elixir of America's Success?" *U.S. News & World Report* (December 20) Volume 127, Issue 24, 42-53.

[48] DuBrin, 2003.

[49] Neil H. Snyder, Karen E. Blair, and Tina Arndt (1990). "Breaking the Bad Habits Behind Time Theft" *Business* (October-December) Volume 40, Issue 4, 31-34.

[50] Bill Brykczynski and Robert A. Small (2003). "Reducing Internet-Based Intrusions: Effective Security Patch Management" *IEEE Software* (January/February) Volume 20, Issue 1, 50-57.

[51] Anonymous (2002). "Protocols; Securing Web Services is No Easy Task." *PC Magazine* (December 24) Volume 21, Issue 22, 93.

[52] M. Riaz Khan and Luvai Motiwalla (2002). "The Influence of E-Commerce Initiatives on Corporate Performance: An Empirical Investigation in the United States" *International Journal of Management* (September) Volume 19, Issue 3, 503-510.

[53] Karen D. Schwartz (2002). "Industrial Automation Enters the Internet Era" *Electronic Business* (October) Volume 28, Issue 10, S3-S7.

[54] Gary P. Schneider (2002). *Electronic Commerce*. 3rd Edition. Boston, Mass.: Thompson Course Technology.

[55] Rob Spiegel (2002). "Talk is Cheap; Web Sales Weak" *Electronic News* (September 30) Volume 48, Issue 40, 2-3.

[56] Sam Nataraj and Jim Lee (2002). "Dot-Com Companies: Are They All Hype?" *S.A.M. Advanced Management Journal* (Summer) Volume 67, Issue 3, 10-14.

[57] Yvonne Herkemij (2001). "Don't Fall Into the Dot.com Trap" *World Trade* (August) Volume 14, Issue 8, 42-3.

[58] Gail Honda and Kipp Martin (2002). *The Essential Guide to Internet Business Technology*. Upper Saddle River, N.J.: Prentice Hall, Inc.

[59] Janet Kornblum (2003). "Spam? No Thanks, We're Full ; As Junk E-mail Chokes Inboxes, a Fed-up Public Wants it Off the Menu" *USA Today* (Final Edition; January 13), D.06.

[60] adopted from Don Hellriegel and John W. Slocum, Jr. (2004). *Organizational Behavior*. 10th Edition. Mason, Oh.: South-Western, 401-402.

❧ Appendix A ❧

Case Analysis

The use of case analysis in the study of strategic management is the primary method of learning how the various tenets of the subject matter we have described throughout this book work in practice. Case study itself, however, has changed over the past several years, and today's learners have a choice in terms of what kind of cases they study and how they study them. In this appendix, we will describe two different methods of approaching case analysis: 1) the more traditional study of prepared cases[1]; and 2) the newer approach of preparing and studying live cases.[2]

The value of case analysis is in being able to see how strategic planning and strategic management techniques actually work in the real world. This does a number of important things that aid the learner in mastering the subject matter. One, through the study of actual business practices, learners are able to see how many of the theoretical underpinnings of the discipline work in affecting the course of organizational growth, prosperity, and survival.

Two, it takes theory and tests it in practice. The result is often the basis for further introspection and analysis. Often, theory and practice coincide and it is easy to see how a determined strategic approach resulted in an intended result. However, periodically, the theory does not lead to the expected result, or fails completely. Here, it is important to examine why, what went wrong, what was overlooked, or what happened beyond the control of the strategic planners and managers that results in the unanticipated outcomes. Also, results can be mixed with such outcomes providing a rich opportunity for further analysis and discussion that help to more deeply identify and capture the nuances and variables that impact the strategic management process.

Three, case study provides the learner with the opportunity to answer the question, "What would I do in these circumstances? What kinds of decisions would I make that, hopefully, would make a positive difference? How would I know if I was doing the right thing or not?"

Second-guessing real-world decision makers is not only an interesting process; it is also an important educational process. Certainly, the real-world business decision-makers are second-guessed all the time, rightly and wrongly. However, in the classroom, this second-guessing is conducted in an open discussion atmosphere where learners and instructors can examine the pros and cons of what actual decision-makers have done (or are doing) and use this as a forum to more deeply examine the processes and come up with creative alternatives.

Four, case study brings the subject matter to life. While there are some fictitious case studies around (non-factual cases are not considered as legitimate cases by most case journals and case writers), most case studies are real, and the study of what actually happened (or happens) brings the material to life and makes it more meaningful for the learner. This active learning approach has many benefits over other methods of learning the subject matter (such as pure lecturing), and gives learners the opportunity to engage the studies on a first-person basis.[3]

All in all, case study is an important part of the study of strategic management. It cements the learning process, and makes the tenets of the discipline more real. In order to conduct a meaningful analysis, however, there are several areas that learners should analyze in order to develop an objective picture of what is going on. The two methods we describe below are designed to do just that.

The Prepared Case Approach

The use of prepared cases is very common in the study of strategic management. In this approach, the course instructor will choose cases (or have learners select their own cases) from a pre-prepared data bank or case book. Many textbooks come with a series of cases attached, either as part of the basic textbook, or as a stand-alone text. This text is a stand-alone text in that it does not come with what man instructors would call comprehensive cases; instead, each chapter starts with a short introductory case which specifically focuses on the chapter's topic. The stand-alone texts, of course, allow instructors to select a stand-along concepts book from one publisher, and a stand-alone case book from another publisher. Still another method that is commonly used is for the instructor to choose cases (or again have learners choose their own cases) from a data bank on the Internet. Here, with accommodations by the publisher of the course's concepts text, the class can be exposed to a wide variety of prepared cases. These cases may be categorized to emphasize a particular topic area that the instructor or class wants to investigate further, such as small business, cases dealing with ethical issues, international companies, and so on.

There are pros and cons to working with prepared cases. The pros include the fact that these cases have been carefully prepared by case writers who have been able to get in-depth information about the companies they are chronicling, and, in many cases, reviewed by other case writers and instructors. Often, case writers are able to access information that is very difficult for people outside the company to investigate. Another major pro is that instructors can select specific prepared cases to demonstrate specific points. This is particularly helpful if the class is having difficulties grasping the particulars of a given strategic concept or see directly how the concept works in practice. There are several classic prepared cases that demonstrate strategic lessons very well, and studying them adds great value to the course. Last, studying what are commonly called canned cases usually delimits the amount of outside research a student needs in order to make sound recommendations; the case itself includes hints as to the possible alternatives the firm should follow.

One of the cons of using prepared cases includes the fact that they are necessarily dated. Just the process of preparing a case makes it potentially out-dated the moment it is published. A case writer will decide to write up a particular case and then do the research required to develop enough data to develop an interesting and instructive case. Once the case is complete, the writer must then write up a teaching note and then find a suitable method of making other academics aware of it. This might be done through submitting the case to an academic case journal; through submitting it to an academic conference in hopes of having it accepted for presentation as a regional, national, or international conference; or through submitting it directly to a publisher or a textbook author. All of these are time consuming, and assuming that the case was written in year one, it might not have adequate exposure until well into year two. Then, if a publisher (or text book author) decides to include the case in an upcoming publication, it could take an additional 1 to 3 years before the case will finally be published. At this point, the case could be anywhere from 3 to 6 years old. The obvious problem here is that a case that is that old may well not reflect the current condition of the company. For example, one of the authors of this text used a prepared case on United Airlines about 4 years ago, a case that examined the success of its international strategy. Use of that case today would be meaningless, as we've described in this text.

Another con in the use of prepared cases is that they are normally skewed to reflect a particular aspect of a business (or industry) or direction that the case writer wanted to examine. In such cases, it is often difficult to get a full picture of what is going on in the company as a whole, and as a result, the strategic lessons learned are incomplete.

One way to overcome some of these drawbacks to the prepared case is to update them. Fortunately, the Internet and World Wide Web have advanced significantly over the years and provide a wealth of information about many businesses and organizations. Throughout this book we have provided a variety of Internet resources that can not only help demonstrate the points we wanted to make in this book, but also allow instructors and learners the opportunity to obtain deeper and more current information. For example, the author of this text who chose the United Airlines international case a few years ago has found that there are several good Internet sites (especially www.UAL.com) that provide up-to-the-minute news releases, financial statements, and other resources that easily allow the updating of the United case. Campus libraries are another excellent source for finding updated materials on companies and organizations. Through computerized search engines and data bases, most college and university libraries (as well as many public libraries) allow a quick and accurate access to updated materials and data.

All-in-all, prepared cases are a valuable resource in aiding the study of strategic management. Besides all of the pros and cons related to this method, learners can still learn much from the application of theory to practice, and this method of case analysis works well in accomplishing this goal.

The Live Case Approach

An alternative to the prepared case method is the use of live cases. A live case is one that learners create on their own using both library resources and the Internet. This is a much less directed or canned approach, but is also much less structured. Live cases are current, and can be kept up-to-date on a daily basis.

The way a live case works is that at the very beginning of a course, the Instructor directs learners to go out onto the Internet and find a company that they are interested in, perhaps a company they might be interested in working for or one that they might be interested in investing in. Learners should form into study groups and determine what company interests all members of the group – groups can be of any size, but are generally best when there are 2 to 4 learners working together. Then, as a group, the learners should begin to search the World Wide Web for company websites, company-related websites, and general data base websites to make certain that there is a good amount of information available for the chosen company. We also recommend strongly that the company website provide the ability for learners to make an e-mail contact with someone in the company. Some companies are very good at providing such a contact, while others don't want to be bothered. It is best to find this out up front and not choose uncooperative companies, because some of the areas of investigation might require an inside contact to obtain good information, rather than rely on information available on the Internet. With these two tasks completed, the groups should also do a library search to find news articles and descriptions, as well as financial data that go beyond what is available on the Internet.

With this information, the group should begin to write the case, at least the introduction so that it can report on what the company does, a bit of its history, where the company is currently (in trouble, a huge success, or whatever is appropriate), and why the group is interested in this particular company. In class, the first chapter of the textbook provides the basis for this discussion, and each group in the class can add to that discussion based on what they have found in their own research. This is the general pattern, then for the first major segment of the course. Each chapter provides additional material. For example, in this text, Chapter Two identified the various elements of the external environment in four different sets – each group should do research on their own company that identifies the external forces in each set that impacts it and begin to organize these results in such a way as to develop a Opportunities-Threat scores. By the end of the coverage of the text chapters, each group should have developed an objective, up-to-date, and self-written case ready for presentation as a written assignment or as an oral assignment. Though the course instructor will have helped provide some structure and help the groups in developing their cases, each group will have created its own unique case through original research and analysis.

Pros for this approach include the obvious high level of learner-involvement. Not only will learners choose their own case, they will develop it. They will focus on those areas that are most interesting to them, and be responsible for applying the course content directly to their cases and be in a position to explain and discuss their conclusions. This research may also lead to a submission of this work to academic conferences[4] or journals[5] with or without the assistance of the instructor. Another pro is that these cases are not canned; they are as authentic as the group is able to make them. They involve real time events and often force groups to back-track as on-going activities provide new light on earlier conclusions and groups must regroup in order to have a more accurate view of what is going on. This spontaneity makes the live case much more realistic and puts learners in the shoes of concurrent business decision-makers in analyzing the environment, making decisions, and then discovering the consequences.

Cons for this approach include the issue that live cases are completely unpredictable and may or may not follow the script of the course syllabus. For an instructor who is trying to make certain points regarding strategic planning or strategic management, the live case approach can prove to be a clear challenge. Some instructors can hedge this by inserting prepared case examples from time to time to demonstrate the points they feel are important, and augment the live case approach with smaller versions of prepared cases (much in the same manner in which we have introduced case examples in each of the chapters in this text). Another con is that writing one's own case is harder than having a case that someone else has prepared. This is more time-consuming and, as we explained above, unstructured. Live cases are harder to do, but we believe that their positive qualities make them a better learning tool than might be true of prepared cases.

How to Prepare a Case

Regardless of which approach the instructor of the course decides to use, there is a common set of areas that all learners should master in completing their case analyses. This section identifies a common set of analyses areas, along with a brief explanation of each, that allows learners to organize their case data for class discussion and/or presentation.

Introduction:

The introduction to a case should include several elements:
1) Who the company is and what it does?
2) Who founded the company and why?
3) How the company has grown through the years?
4) What is happening as of the case preparation?
5) Why this is interesting?

An Examination of the External Environment:

Based on the material we presented in Chapter Two, the external analysis of the case is one of the most important areas that learners will study. It should include the following:
1) An analysis of the remote environment looking for opportunities and threats in the six areas:
   a) Economic
   b) Sociological
   c) Political and Legal
   d) Ecological
   e) Technological and
   f) International

    g)   Each area should then be rates as to its importance to the company

2) An analysis of the industry, or task, environment looking for opportunities and threats with special attention given to Porter's 5 Forces model.

3) An analysis of the competitive environment looking for opportunities and threats that an examination of major competitors might suggest.

4) An analysis of the company's immediate, community environment, again looking for opportunities and threats.

5) Based on the data generated in the first 4 areas, the group should now summarize all four environmental sets, listing the most crucial strategic opportunities and threats, along with their relevant scores and create an Opportunity-Threat index score.

An Examination of the Internal Environment:

Based on the material we presented in Chapter Three, the internal analysis is another crucial part of the examination of a case. In a way, this analysis is easier to conduct compared to the external analysis because it is often difficult to find external environmental elements that actually impact the company based on what you can see in the prepared case or derive from an investigation in the live case. The internal data is fairly well available, either in the prepared case or from the company's website or data base websites. The objective, here, is to determine the strengths and weaknesses of the company, and fortunately, much of this is readily available from financial data easily accessed. More specifically, the internal analysis should be broken down into four major data areas and then summarized as suggested below:

1) Analysis of the financial data to determine whether or not the firm is profitable and an examination of the financial indicators that might tell the learner why. A solid financial analysis should include the following:

    a)   Statement of profitability for the company and how it compares to the average of the industry.

b) Analysis of the income statement, comparing it with industry averages as well as against standard accounting standards with an explanation of what comparisons tell us.

c) Analysis of the balance sheet, comparing it with industry averages as well as against standard accounting standards with an explanation of what comparisons tell us.

d) Examination of the cash flow statement for the previous 5 years – determine how the company has generated its cash and how it has used it.

e) Look at the company's operating and balance sheet accounting ratios to determine how they stack up against industry averages as well as accounting standards.

f) Calculate the Z-Score and g* as appropriate.

g) Draw a conclusion about the financial strengths/weaknesses of the company:

   i) If profit is above the average of the industry and shows good returns, you might conclude that the company is a clear success (assuming there are no glaring problems with the other financial indices the group has examined).

   ii) If profit is positive, but below the average of the industry, you might conclude that the company is marginally successful and needs to do something to improve profitability and other financial practices to at least match industry performance, and hopefully, top competitor performance after needed turnaround activities.

   iii) If the company is running at a loss, you can conclude the company has a serious problem and needs to do something quickly to turn things around.

2) Analysis of marketing data to determine whether or not the firm is growing as well as an analysis of marketing activities that support or hurt company growth activities:

a) Determine sales growth both on a trend line as well as year-to-year for the past 2 years:

   i) Use regression analysis to establish a trend line – it is important to use up to 10 years of data to establish a reliable trend, even though one can usually get a regression equation with as little as 3 years data (but this is much less reliable). Determine the trend growth rate by taking the 6th regression number and divide it by the 5th regression number, and then subtract 1. For example, if the sales figure for year 6 in your study from the regression trend line is $19,472 Million and the sales figure for year 5 is $17,269, divide the first number by the 2nd, yielding a result in the example of 1.13. Subtract 1, and the result of .13 suggests that the average growth rate for the 10 year period was 13%.

ii) Similarly, when one divides the most year's actual sales by the previous year and subtracts 1, you get an actual sales growth for one year, which is important, but not quite as important as the statistic which comes from the regression line (one year's growth can be impacted by many things that are unusual and not indicative of the longer term experience). Groups can also calculate the actual growth rate for the previous year.

iii) Draw a conclusion.

b) Determine current year market share by dividing company sales for the most recent year in your analysis by total sales in the industry. For example, if industry sales were $258 Billion and your company's sales were $17 Billion, your company would have had a 6.6% market share. Determine the market share of your company's most important competitor as well. Finally, do the same things for the previous 4 years as well. The resulting data will show you how well your company is doing in gaining market share and provide a direct comparison between your company and its nearest competitor.

c) List what marketing tactics your company is using to support sales.

i)   How does it advertise?

ii)   What is its use of the Internet?

iii) Can you determine the state of its sales organization?

iv) What is the company commitment to marketing research?

v)   What audiences does it target, and how successful has it been?

d) Draw a conclusion about the marketing strengths/weaknesses of the company.
   i) If growth is above the average of the industry and shows good returns, you might conclude that the company is a clear success.
   ii) If growth is positive, but below the average of the industry, you might conclude that the company is marginally successful and needs to do something to improve its growth rate and other marketing practices to at least match industry performance, and hopefully, top competitor performance after needed turnaround activities.
   iii) If the company is experiencing declining sales, you can conclude the company has a serious problem and needs to do something quickly to turn things around.

3) Analyze the management and the organizational structure of the business to determine the strengths and weaknesses of this essential part of the case analysis. Examine the following:
   a) Current management:
      i) Who are the top officers, where do the come from, and how much are they paid? This last issue is important in terms of being able to conclude that managers are acting ethically relative to their ability to provide value for stockholders and other stakeholders.
      ii) What is the structure of the company and is it appropriate to the type of business or businesses it is conducting? This is usually discernable in looking at the titles of top level managers. For example, if the company lists vice presidents that are in charge of North America, Europe, South America, Asia, and Australia, this would indicate that the company is set up as a multidivisional international company. If titles for vice president state that they are in charge of Marketing, Production, Customer Relations, Human Resources, and Legal Issues, this would indicate that the company is set up as more of a functional company or product multidivisional company. Is this appropriate?

b) What is the stated direction of top management? This is normally found in documents such as an Annual Report, the most recent 10-K filing with the Securities and Exchange Commission (SEC) and attainable through many company websites, Yahoo and Quicken financial websites, or thought the EDGAR program on the SEC website (www.sec.gov), as well as from news releases and stories. Is the stated direction appropriate and is management doing a good job in following it?

c) Describe and analyze the stock performance of the company. This is usually very easy information to obtain. Most of the Internet data based services (such as Yahoo Finance and Quicken Finance) provide daily, monthly, quarterly, and yearly data – most with down-loadable charts with comparative studies the group can add such as competitor stock prices, S&P, NASDAQ, and Dow Jones comparisons. We suggest that you do a regression analysis on the stock prices (monthly closing prices) for a 4 to 5 year period to again establish a trend line. One can determine the yearly growth rate by dividing the most recent monthly price from the regression line with the sales number from the regression number of 12 months earlier, then subtract 1 to get the annual growth rate. BE CAREFUL WITH THE RESULTS – While stockholders and many financial analysts blame management for stock pricing, events like 9-1-1 tend to impact prices as well and management has had nothing to do with the market downturn that resulted from such a catastrophic event. Take this into account as you do your analysis and decide on your conclusion regarding stock price performance.

d) Evaluate the mission (including mission statement if the company has one), vision, values, and goals of the company. Are they appropriate? How do you know? Is the company following them or using them for public consumption only? Can you follow how strategic management flows from these organizational elements and how well they help provide strategic direction? In suggesting earlier that learners obtain an e-mail connection with the company clearly comes into place in this part of the analysis. Often, the best way of obtaining the information groups will want is by interviewing an insider.

e) What is the quality of management? The group might use an instrument such as found in Table A-1 that looks at 10 different quantitative and 10 qualitative measures and established a grade, very much like standard school grading systems, and allows the group to assign and "A," "B," or whatever else might be appropriate. The key, however, is to look at the assigned grade and ask the question, "Does that make sense?" If not, redo the evaluation. For example, one of the authors used this tool with a class a couple of years ago with a group that examining Microsoft. The group doing the analysis gave Microsoft a "D." The instructor questioned this (noting that Microsoft is one of the major strategic successes of the modern age, and it is unlikely that an "A" company could result from "D" management) and learned that the group had focused on some social faux pas of Bill Gates that had been widely publicized. The group had overlooked the fact that Bill Gates has had the foresight to hire excellent managers to surround him and fill in where he himself might have weaknesses. ....The group was asked to rethink their assessment and ended up finally grading Microsoft management with the "A" it deserves.

f) Overall, determine whether or not current management is a clear success, marginal success or problem.

4) Analyze the technology usage of your company and draw a conclusion, particularly in light of how the company's major competition is using technology to gain a competitive advantage. This analysis should include the following:

a) Currency of the company's MIS systems.

b) How the company uses technology to maintain control.

c) How the company uses technology to improve operations.

d) How the company uses technology to increase sales.

e) Overall, determine how the company is using technology to improve its competitive advantage.

5) Summarize the strengths and weaknesses that the group has identified for the company from the financial, marketing, management, and technological analyses it has conducted, determine the most important, and then establish a Strengths-Weaknesses Index Score.

Establish the Company's Current Strategic Activities

With the external and internal analyses now complete, it is important to examine the firm's current strategic practices. Whether intended or unintended, every company engages in managerial activity that determines its general pattern of activities. The next part of the case analysis looks at whether or not these practices are 1) successful, and 2) strategic in nature.

1) Identify the firm's currently successful core competencies.
   a) What does the company do better than any of its competitors?
   b) Do these competencies lead to a competitive advantage?
2) Identify specifically what competitive advantages the company has and how it uses them. If the company has now particular core competencies and, therefore, no competitive advantages, what are the demonstrable consequences?
3) Identify the current long-term, or grand strategies that the pattern of organizational activities suggest the company is following. Are they working as intended?
4) Identify the current short-term strategies (strategic corrective actions) the company may be engaged in and how well they are working.
5) Identify the current major business level strategies the company's major strategic business units are engaged in, and draw a conclusions as to how well these SBU level strategies are working out for the SBUs and the company overall.
6) Identify 5 or more major key performance indicators (KPIs), or key success factors (KSFs) that help demonstrate important company performance outcomes. As we stated in the text, KPIs or KSFs can normally be found in reports such as the company's 10-K report, where management typically discusses the important

performance outcomes that are essential to it to attain superior performance standards.

Describe the Company's Overall Condition

At this point, the group should restate the most important opportunities and threats of the company's external environment as well as the most important strengths and weaknesses of the company's internal environment. List their O-T Index Score and S-W Index Score and then place the results in the appropriate sector found in Figure 6.3.

Finally, based on the analyses up to this point, draw an overall Problem/Success statement.

a) If overall conditions are above the what you can determine is the average of the industry, you might conclude that the company is a clear success.

b) If overall conditions are positive, but below standards one can see in the industry, your group might conclude that the company is marginally successful and needs to do something to improve its profitability, growth rate, management practices, or use of technology to better match industry performance, after needed turnaround activities.

c) If the company is experiencing serious problems in one or more areas (particularly in profitability and growth), you can conclude the company has a serious problem and needs to do something quickly to turn things around.

Conclusions, Identification of Relevant Options, and Discussion

The most important part of case analysis is to take all of the data and conclusions that have flowed from the first several parts of the analysis and draw conclusions as to the best course of action for the company in the future. Based on all that has come from the analysis, and the strategic management tenets described in the textbook, learners must now draw conclusions and identify options that can help the company be successful in the future. This is the central point of the study of strategic management. We recommend that groups organize their final discussion of their case analyses based on the following areas:

1) Identify the most relevant long-term prospects and options for the company.

   a) What long-term strategies make sense and fit the company profile you have already determined?

   b) Which of these options are most likely to work, and why?

2) If necessary, what short-term strategic strategies should the company consider and why?

   a) If the company is overall a clear success, then there is no need for any short-term strategies because you can generally conclude that the current strategies of the company are working according to plan. It's important here to separate strategic issues from operational issues. Every company has day-to-day problems and must deal with them. However, these are most likely not strategic in nature – they are operational – so it is not appropriate to class these problems in with strategic issues.

   b) If the company is experiencing problems related to poor profitability, poor growth, or poor management, a strategic short-term strategy may well be appropriate, and your group should identify relevant options at this point and discuss which are most likely to achieve the correction that will allow the company to get on with its long-term strategic direction.

3) In summary, embark on a free-wheeling discussion as to how you feel your identified long-term and short-term options will best aid the company in achieving a successful long-term future. This should be a fairly detailed discussion that answers the questions: "How will these strategies support improved profitability?" "How will these strategies support growth?" "How will these strategies assure top-quality strategic management practices?"

4) Again in summary, discuss how your strategic long-term and short-term options will help the company better match the conditions of the external environment. Using your summary list of overall opportunities and threats, identify how your strategic options will help the company take advantage of its most important opportunities and mitigate its most crucial strategic threats.

5) Both these discussions should be open and comprehensive. In both discussions, your group has the opportunity to demonstrate its mastery of the tenets of strategic management. You shouldn't sacrifice levity for demonstrating your understanding. Each discussion should last at least 5 minutes in an oral presentation or 2 to 3 pages in a written presentation. Remember, here you get the chance to demonstrate your mastery of the material.

6) Finally, it is important to give credit where credit is due, and this means that you need to reference the sources of the information you present in your analyses and presentation. Your course instructor may well have a preference for what form she/he prefers, so be sure to ask what that preference might be. In terms of what you should reference, it is a good rule of thumb to reference anything you have required from another source. Many colleges and universities are purchasing services that allow an instructor to submit an entire paper to a centralized data base, and that data base will compare paragraphs, sentences, and phrases to a huge data bank of previously submitted term papers, journal articles, and news articles. If the computer finds a match between your paper and another source, as long as you have properly referenced that source, your group is in the clear. In an age where plagiary and other methods of cheating are, unfortunately, becoming more common, it is always a good idea to play the game straight – be sure to properly reference your work.

Final Comments

Case preparation, as we have described it above, is applicable for both prepared cases (with obvious concessions given the material available to include in the analysis) and live cases where all of the processes we have described above are applicable. Further, these analysis techniques are appropriate for both written and oral case presentations. Altogether, these case analysis techniques provide a comprehensive method of looking at business strategy cases and deriving coherent and relevant evaluations that can lead to the successful selection of appropriate strategic options that should help real-world companies achieve long-term success.

Endnotes

[1] William Naumes and Margaret J. Naumes (1999). *The Art & Craft of Case Writing.* Thousand Oaks, Ca.: Sage Publications.

[2] Lisa K. Gundry and Aaron A. Buchko (1996). *Field Casework: Methods for Consulting to Small and Startup Businesses.* Thousand Oaks, Ca.: Sage Publications.

[3] Thomas G. Cummings and Christopher G. Worley (2001). *Organization Development and Change.* 7th Edition. Mason, Oh.: South-Western College Publishing.

[4] see the Institute of Behavioral and Applied Management at www.ibam.com.

[5] see Journal of Behavioral and Applied Management at www.jbam.org.

❧ Subject Index ❧

✂ Source Index ✂